Windows Server 2025 Administration Fundamentals

A beginner's guide to managing and administering
Windows Server environments

Bekim Dauti

Windows Server 2025 Administration Fundamentals

Group Product Manager: Dhruv Jagdish Kataria

Publishing Product Manager: Neha Sharma

Book Project Manager: Uma Devi Lakshmikanth, Ashwin Dinesh Kharwa

Senior Editor: Sarada Biswas

Technical Editor: Irfa Ansari

Copy Editor: Safis Editing

Proofreader: Sarada Biswas

Indexer: Hemangini Bari

Production Designer: Gokul Raj S.T.

DevRel Marketing Coordinator: Marylou De Mello

First published: December 2017

Second edition: October 2019

Third edition: September 2022

Fourth edition: January 2025

Production reference: 2110725

Published by Packt Publishing Ltd.

Grosvenor House

11 St Paul's Square

Birmingham

B3 1RB, UK

ISBN 978-1-83620-501-2

www.packtpub.com

Just as a great ship sails the ocean, the Earth floats through the universe. And as the crew tends to the ship to keep it from sinking, humanity must care for the planet, safeguarding the environment to ensure our shared future. Save the Earth, and in doing so, you save yourself.

– Bekim Dauti

Foreword

The ever-evolving landscape of technology continues to shape the way we work and communicate. As we embark on a new era of digital transformation, **Windows Server 2025** stands as a cornerstone, empowering organizations to harness the full potential of their IT infrastructure.

This book is a comprehensive guide designed to equip you with the essential knowledge and skills to effectively administer Windows Server 2025. Whether you're a seasoned IT professional or a budding administrator, this book will provide you with a solid foundation to navigate the complexities of this powerful operating system.

Within these pages, you will discover a wealth of information, from fundamental concepts to advanced techniques. You'll learn how to install, configure, and manage Windows Server 2025, including its core services, such as Active Directory, Hyper-V, and Remote Desktop Services. You'll also delve into security best practices, troubleshooting tips, and automation strategies to optimize your server environment.

As technology advances at an unprecedented pace, it's crucial to stay up to date with the latest trends and best practices. This book serves as your trusted companion, providing you with the knowledge and tools you need to succeed in the dynamic world of Windows Server administration.

I fondly recall contributing to the inaugural edition of this book back in 2016. It is truly inspiring to witness Bekim's unwavering commitment to enhancing each subsequent edition, making it an invaluable resource for anyone aspiring to master Windows Server.

This latest edition, dedicated to Windows Server 2025, carries forward this legacy of excellence. It provides a comprehensive and practical guide, empowering you to navigate the complexities of this powerful operating system with confidence. Whether you are a seasoned IT professional or a budding administrator, this book offers the essential knowledge and skills to effectively administer Windows Server 2025.

I encourage you to embark on this learning journey and unlock the full potential of Windows Server 2025.

Dr. Erdal Ozkaya

CISO Xcitium

Contributors

About the author

Bekim Dauti, a distinguished computer technology expert, holds a bachelor's degree in informatics from the University of Tirana, a master's in information technology from UMGC Europe, and a doctorate in computer science from Aspen University. His areas of specialization include server administration, computer networking, and training, with a focus on Cisco, CompTIA, and Microsoft technologies.

With a career spanning over two decades, Bekim has honed his skills as a **Cisco Certified Academy Instructor** (**CCAI**) and a **Microsoft Certified Trainer** (**MCT**). He has also authored numerous books and articles, sharing his expertise in reputable publications such as PC World Albanian and CIO Albanian. His practical knowledge is further validated by his IT certifications from renowned vendors, including ECDL, Certiport, CompTIA, Cisco, Microsoft, and Sun Microsystems.

Currently, Bekim is a Microsoft Certified Trainer at TeKnowledge, where he continues to share his knowledge and expertise. He is also the founder of InfoTech (Academy) and Dautti, further demonstrating his commitment to the field. As a prolific writer, Bekim has contributed to nearly 20 books and published dozens of articles in renowned publications such as PC World Albanian and CIO Albanian.

Bekim's passion for technology extends to maintaining a blog called **Bekim Dauti's Blog**.

I am deeply grateful to God for the gift of life, health, and the opportunity to share knowledge through this work. My heartfelt thanks go to my parents, family, friends, the incredible team at Packt Publishing, my colleagues at TeKnowledge, and everyone who supported and encouraged me throughout the writing of this book. Finally, I extend my sincere blessings to each reader—may peace and prosperity follow you always.

About the reviewer

William M. Wheeler has over 25 years of experience in the industry. During that time, he has honed his experience in IT operations and security, working across both the private and public sectors. His career has been marked by a commitment to enhancing and securing IT environments, ensuring robust and reliable systems. More recently, he has shifted his focus towards cloud migrations and digital transformations, helping organizations modernize their operations and embrace new technologies.

I am deeply grateful to my friends and family for their unwavering support and encouragement in all things I pursue. To my wife, Amy, and my son, Billy, thank you for your endless support.

Table of Contents

Part 1: Introducing Windows Server and Installing Windows Server 2025

1

2

Installing Windows Server 2025   33

3

What to Do After Installing Windows Server 2025   77

Part 2: Setting Up Windows Server 2025

4

Directory Services in Windows Server 2025   127

5

Part 3: Configuring Windows Server 2025

6

Group Policy in Windows Server 2025   235

7

Virtualization with Windows Server 2025   261

8

Storing Data in Windows Server 2025   299

Part 4: New and Enhanced Features in Windows Server 2025

9

Active Directory Domain Services (AD DS) Enhancements   345

10

Configuring SMB over QUIC in Windows Server 2025   373

11

Implementing New Security Enhancements in Windows Server 2025

407

12

Managing Updates with Hotpatching, Azure Arc, and More in Windows Server 2025 449

Part 5: Managing and Maintaining Windows Server 2025

13

Tuning and Maintaining Windows Server 2025 481

14

Updating and Troubleshooting Windows Server 2025   513

Part 6: Studying and Preparing for the AZ-800 Certification Exam

15

Understanding Microsoft Certifications and Preparing for the AZ-800 Exam   549

Preface

Windows Server 2025 is Microsoft's latest server operating system, continuing the legacy of the Windows NT family of operating systems built upon the Windows 11 platform. This version enhances the server operating system with robust performance, increased security features, and seamless cloud integration, empowering organizations to harness the full potential of modern IT solutions. The objective is clear: to democratize cloud capabilities and provide users with the tools necessary for success in an increasingly competitive digital landscape.

This book begins by introducing network fundamentals and Windows Server 2025, establishing a solid foundation in networking essentials before diving deep into the functionalities of Windows Server 2025. The journey unfolds systematically, moving from the installation process in *Chapter 2* to post-installation tasks in *Chapter 3*. You will learn how to efficiently configure directory services and add essential roles in *Chapters 4* and *5*.

Later chapters will guide you through the intricacies of managing user and computer settings and introduce you to the world of server virtualization. You will then explore data storage solutions, followed by insights into **Active Directory Domain Services (AD DS)** enhancements.

Next, you will discover the configuration of SMB over QUIC and learn about the implementation of new security enhancements in Windows Server 2025. The book then delves into hotpatching with Azure Arc, followed by performance tuning and maintenance strategies.

Finally, the book equips you with the skills needed to manage updates and resolve issues effectively. The book concludes with a chapter that will guide you through the essentials of Microsoft certifications and provides valuable tips for exam success.

Through hands-on exercises, practical scenarios, and expert insights, this book aims to provide you with a comprehensive understanding of Windows Server 2025, empowering you to manage complex tasks efficiently. Each chapter includes a concept summary and questionnaire to reinforce your learning, ensuring that you have the knowledge and skills necessary to excel as a system administrator.

By the end of this book, you will be well prepared to administer and manage Windows Server 2025 confidently, with the added opportunity to pursue Microsoft certifications, such as preparing for the AZ-800 exam, should you choose to challenge yourself further.

Who this book is for

This book is designed for IT professionals, such as system administrators, network engineers, and IT managers, who are starting their journey in Windows Server 2025 administration. It is also suitable for those who wish to update their knowledge with the latest tools and features in Windows Server 2025. Whether you are responsible for managing server infrastructure, ensuring network security, or optimizing server performance, this book will provide you with the essential skills and knowledge to excel in your role. If you want to learn from this updated version of Windows Server, then this book is for you.

What this book covers

Chapter 1, Network Fundamentals and Introduction to Windows Server 2025, introduces essential network concepts, including hosts, nodes, IP addressing, and subnetting. It covers **Network Operating Systems** (**NOS**) and provides an overview of Windows Server 2025, its editions, system requirements, and key improvements over Windows Server 2022. Practical exercises on downloading the installation media and Windows Admin Center are included.

Chapter 2, Installing Windows Server 2025, guides you through various installation methods for Windows Server 2025, such as clean installations, network installations using WDS, and unattended installations with Windows ADK and MDT. It also covers in-place upgrades, network service migration, and testing in Azure, with practical exercises on setting up WDS and deploying Windows Server 2025.

Chapter 3, What to Do After Installing Windows Server 2025, covers critical post-installation tasks, including managing device drivers, working with the Windows Server registry, and performing initial server configurations. Topics include setting up the computer name, network, firewall, and system updates, with practical exercises to reinforce your understanding.

Chapter 4, Directory Services in Windows Server 2025, explores AD DS and **Domain Name System** (**DNS**), covering domains, forests, domain controllers, and DNS functionalities. It includes managing user and computer accounts using **Organizational Units** (**OUs**) and groups, with a hands-on exercise on installing AD DS and DNS roles and promoting a server to a domain controller.

Chapter 5, Adding Roles to Windows Server 2025, focuses on configuring server roles and features, including application server roles, web services, remote access, and file and print services. It covers best practices for selecting server hardware and monitoring performance, concluding with a practical exercise on installing web server (IIS) and print server roles.

Chapter 6, Group Policy in Windows Server 2025, introduces **Group Policy** (**GP**) essentials, covering the configuration and management of **Group Policy Objects** (**GPOs**) on local servers and domain controllers. It includes GP processing, order of precedence, and using the **Group Policy Management Console** (**GPMC**), with practical exercises on implementing GPOs.

Chapter 7, Virtualization with Windows Server 2025, explores virtualization technology, focusing on Microsoft Hyper-V. It guides you through installing the Hyper-V role on Windows Server 2025, managing virtual environments with Hyper-V Manager, and creating and configuring **virtual machines (VMs)**, with a hands-on exercise on the installation process.

Chapter 8, Storing Data in Windows Server 2025, covers storage technologies and their roles in server operations, including physical interfaces, disk controllers, and data storage methods. It explores network-based storage systems and protocols such as S2D, SDS, and iSCSI, with a practical exercise on enabling data deduplication in Windows Server 2025.

Chapter 9, Active Directory Domain Services (AD DS) Enhancements, highlights advancements in AD DS for Windows Server 2025, focusing on scalability, security, and cloud integration. It covers robust authentication mechanisms, enhanced security protocols, and the 32k database page size. Practical instructions on implementing these updates and a hands-on exercise on the 32k page size are included.

Chapter 10, Configuring SMB over QUIC in Windows Server 2025, provides an understanding of the SMB over QUIC protocol, its evolution, and its benefits. It covers security considerations, performance optimization, and troubleshooting techniques, with a step-by-step exercise on configuring and enabling SMB over QUIC in Windows Server 2025.

Chapter 11, Implementing New Security Enhancements in Windows Server 2025, delves into advanced security and authentication features, including improved access controls, threat detection, and automated response systems. It covers biometric authentication, conditional access policies, and securing communication channels with TLS, HTTPS, IPSec, and SSH. A hands-on exercise on configuring firewall rules and enabling TLS encryption is included.

Chapter 12, Managing Updates with Hotpatching, Azure Arc, and More in Windows Server 2025, guides you through implementing hotpatching techniques to ensure seamless server updates with minimal disruption. It covers server hotpatching, using Azure Arc to manage on-premises servers, and highlights benefits such as reduced downtime and enhanced availability. You'll learn to prepare servers for hotpatching, apply updates in real time without reboots, and validate patches. This chapter also discusses automating update management tasks, monitoring server health, and troubleshooting techniques. A hands-on exercise on configuring Azure Arc on an on-premises Windows Server 2025 instance is included.

Chapter 13, Tuning and Maintaining Windows Server 2025, provides essential knowledge about server hardware selection and performance evaluation. It covers techniques for monitoring server performance, establishing performance baselines, and generating comprehensive reports. You will learn to identify and address potential performance issues proactively. The chapter concludes with a practical exercise on analyzing performance logs and setting up alerts.

Chapter 14, Updating and Troubleshooting Windows Server 2025, delves into updating and troubleshooting within the Windows Server 2025 environment. It discusses the importance of a well-defined plan for managing updates, monitoring, and maintaining servers to ensure business continuity. You'll learn how to implement a backup and restore disaster recovery plan and perform updates to the operating system, server hardware, and third-party software. This chapter introduces the Event Viewer for examining logs and troubleshooting, concluding with a hands-on exercise on using the Event Viewer to monitor and manage logs.

Chapter 15, Understanding Microsoft Certifications and Preparing for the AZ-800 Exam, serves as a comprehensive guide for candidates aspiring to attain Microsoft certifications related to Windows Server 2025. It covers the significance of Microsoft certifications, detailing the skills assessed in exams and the importance of role-specific certifications. Practical advice for passing certification exams, including study strategies and the exam registration process, is provided. The chapter also explores the AZ-800 certification exam objectives and includes valuable resources such as study materials and practice exams.

Appendix, Assessments, provides answers to the chapter questions. Each chapter includes questions to help reinforce the concepts and definitions. With this appendix, you can check your answers to those questions.

To get the most out of this book

You must have solid experience working with the Windows 10/11 operating system and have a solid knowledge of computer networks and NOSs.

Make sure you have a computer with a processor that supports virtualization technology and has a minimum of 8 GB or a recommended 16 GB of RAM.

Conventions used

There are several text conventions used throughout this book.

`Code in text`: Indicates code words in the text, database table names, folder names, filenames, file extensions, pathnames, dummy URLs, user input, and Twitter handles. Here is an example: "You also learned how to use the `regedit` tool."

A block of code is set as follows:

```
# Example to check the status of Windows Defender Antivirus
$baselineStatus = $false
$currentStatus = (Get-MpPreference).DisableRealtimeMonitoring
if ($currentStatus -eq $baselineStatus) {
    Write-Host "Security baseline is intact."
} else {
    Write-Host "Security baseline drift detected. Review settings."
}
```

Bold: Indicates a new term, an important word, or words you see onscreen. For instance, words in menus or dialog boxes appear in **bold**. Here is an example: "In the **Enter Product Key** window, type the product key and click **OK**."

Any command-line input or output is written as follows:

```
Get-VMNetworkAdapter -VMName <YourVMName> | Set-VMNetworkAdapter
-MacAddressSpoofing On
```

> **Tips or important notes**
> Appears like this.

Get in touch

Feedback from our readers is always welcome.

General feedback: If you have questions about any aspect of this book, email us at customercare@packtpub.com and mention the book title in the subject of your message.

Errata: Although we have taken every care to ensure our content's accuracy, mistakes happen. If you have found an error in this book, we would be grateful if you would report this to us. Please visit www.packtpub.com/support/errata and fill in the form.

Piracy: If you come across any illegal copies of our works on the internet, we would be grateful if you would provide us with the location address or website name. Please contact us at copyright@packt.com with a link to the material.

If you are interested in becoming an author: If there is a topic that you have expertise in and are interested in either writing or contributing to a book, please visit authors.packtpub.com.

Share Your Thoughts

Once you've read *Windows Server 2025 Administration Fundamentals*, we'd love to hear your thoughts! Scan the QR code below to go straight to the Amazon review page for this book and share your feedback.

https://packt.link/r/1-836-20501-5

Your review is important to us and the tech community and will help us make sure we're delivering excellent quality content.

Making the Most Out of This Book –
Get to Know Your Free Benefits

Unlock exclusive free benefits that come with your purchase, thoughtfully crafted to supercharge your learning journey and help you learn without limits.

UNLOCK NOW

Note: Have your purchase invoice ready before you begin.

```
https://www.packtpub.com/
unlock/9781836205012
```

Figure 1.1: Next-Gen Reader, AI Assistant (Beta), and Free PDF access

Enhanced reading experience with our Next-gen Reader:

- Multi-device progress sync: Learn from any device with seamless progress sync.
- Highlighting and Notetaking: Turn your reading into lasting knowledge.
- Bookmarking: Revisit your most important learnings anytime.
- Dark mode: Focus with minimal eye strain by switching to dark or sepia modes.

Learn smarter using our AI assistant (Beta):

- Summarize it: Summarize key sections or an entire chapter.
- AI code explainers: In Packt Reader, click the "Explain" button above each code block for AI-powered code explanations.

Note: AI Assistant is part of next-gen Packt Reader and is still in beta.

Learn anytime, anywhere:

- Access your content offline with DRM-free PDF and ePub versions—compatible with your favorite e-readers.

Unlock Your Book's Exclusive Benefits

Your copy of this book comes with the following exclusive benefits:

- Next-gen Packt Reader
- AI assistant (beta)
- DRM-free PDF/ePub downloads

Use the following guide to unlock them if you haven't already. The process takes just a few minutes and needs to be done only once.

How to unlock these benefits in three easy steps

Step 1

Have your purchase invoice for this book ready, as you'll need it in *Step 3*. If you received a physical invoice, scan it on your phone and have it ready as either a PDF, JPG, or PNG.

For more help on finding your invoice, visit `https://www.packtpub.com/unlock-benefits/help`.

> **Note**
>
> Bought this book directly from Packt? You don't need an invoice. After completing Step 2, you can jump straight to your exclusive content.

> **Step 2**
>
> Scan the following QR code or visit `https://www.packtpub.com/unlock/9781836205012`
>
>

Step 3

Sign in to your Packt account or create a new one for free. Once you're logged in, upload your invoice. It can be in PDF, PNG, or JPG format and must be no larger than 10 MB. Follow the rest of the instructions on the screen to complete the process.

> **Need help?**
>
> If you get stuck and need help, visit `https://www.packtpub.com/unlock-benefits/help` for a detailed FAQ on how to find your invoices and more. The following QR code will take you to the help page directly:
>
>

> **Note**
>
> If you are still facing issues, reach out to `customercare@packt.com`.

Part 1: Introducing Windows Server and Installing Windows Server 2025

This part provides a comprehensive overview of Windows Server 2025, highlighting its distinctive features and installation methods. You will build a foundational understanding of core concepts and acquire practical skills to perform installations, upgrades, migrations, network-based deployments, and unattended installations.

This part contains the following chapters:

- *Chapter 1, Network Fundamentals and Introduction to Windows Server 2025*
- *Chapter 2, Installing Windows Server 2025*
- *Chapter 3, What to Do After Installing Windows Server 2025*

1

Network Fundamentals and Introduction to Windows Server 2025

In this chapter, we establish the foundation for your journey into **Windows Server 2025**. Understanding the fundamentals is crucial, so let us get started!

We begin by exploring the essentials of computer networks. Imagine a bustling city of interconnected roads—devices (hosts) communicate with each other via these pathways. We will delve into concepts such as **hosts**, **nodes**, **client-server architecture**, and other network components. Additionally, we will demystify IP addressing and subnetting, which function like the postal codes of the digital world.

Next, we shift our focus to the **Network Operating System** (**NOS**). Think of the NOS as the conductor of our network orchestra. We will discuss the hardware and software requirements for running a server. Furthermore, we will take an in-depth look at Windows Server 2025 itself—its editions, improvements over **Windows Server 2022**, and exciting new features. Imagine enhanced security protocols, seamless hybrid cloud integration, and cutting-edge technical support—all part of the Windows Server 2025 symphony.

Ready to roll up your sleeves? We will cover the detailed system requirements for Windows Server 2025. Additionally, this chapter will guide you through downloading and preparing the installation media. Consider it your backstage pass to server greatness.

Finally, we will equip you with practical skills. You will download and install Windows Server 2025's trusty sidekick, **Windows Admin Center**. This tool will be your companion as we venture into more advanced topics in the upcoming chapters. By the end of this chapter, you will have a solid grasp of networking principles, NOS essentials, and the specifics of Windows Server 2025. Buckle up—it's a transformative journey that will lead to you mastering server management in today's dynamic IT landscape!

In this chapter, we're going to cover the following main topics:

- Understanding hosts, nodes, and client/server architecture
- Overview of IP addressing and subnetting
- Getting to know the server
- Understanding Network Operating System (NOS)
- Overview and editions of Windows Server 2025
- Key differences between Windows Server 2025 and Windows Server 2022
- Minimum and recommended system requirements for Windows Server 2025
- Downloading Windows Server 2025 and Windows Admin Center

Technical requirements

To complete the exercises in this chapter, ensure you have a PC running **Windows 11 Pro**, equipped with a minimum of **8 GB of RAM**, **500 MB** of available disk space, and an **active internet** connection.

Understanding hosts, nodes, and client/server architecture

As you embark on this section, you might initially question the relevance of learning about computer networking when your primary interest lies in Windows Server. This concern is valid at first glance. However, as you progress deeper into the realm of Windows Server, you will increasingly recognize the importance of a solid understanding of computer networks.

This chapter covers foundational concepts—such as IP addressing, subnetting, and network components—that are integral to effectively managing server environments. By understanding these basics, you'll gain the context needed to approach **Windows Server** tasks with confidence, making it easier to handle real-world configurations and troubleshooting down the line. While the book will focus on Windows Server, these networking principles serve as the backbone of every server environment, giving you the tools to navigate server management with precision.

To grasp the significance of computer networks, let us revisit their origins. The necessity for resource sharing sparked the initial development of networking technologies many years ago, during the 1960s and 1970s. As demand grew, so did the advancement of these technologies, leading to the creation of comprehensive terms and concepts essential for describing computer networks. Thus, terms such as **network types**, **topologies**, **architectures**, and **components** emerged, marking computer networks as one of humanity's monumental communication innovations. The internet exemplifies the profound societal benefits of computer networks, connecting countless computers and bridging geographical distances in communication.

With this background, let us delve into the basics of computer networks.

What is a computer network?

According to the Merriam-Webster dictionary, a network is defined as *a group of people or organizations that are closely linked and work with each other*. Additionally, networking is described as *the exchange of information or services among individuals, groups, or institutions*. These definitions provide a simple, concrete basis for understanding computer networks.

In essence, a computer network is a group of computers connected through networking devices and media to share resources. These resources typically include data, network services, and peripheral devices. For instance, sharing files, applications, printers, and other peripherals is straightforward in a networked environment. It is essential to distinguish between what a computer network is and what it does. The former explains the structure and components, while the latter highlights the benefits and functionalities. *Figure 1.1* illustrates that a computer network comprises interconnected computers sharing resources.

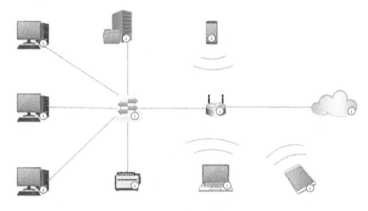

Figure 1.1 – A typical computer network

Computer networks come in various types, each serving different purposes and covering other areas. Let us explore these types individually.

Types of computer networks

Designing and building a computer network is a fascinating process closely tied to its definition. At its core, a computer network requires at least two computers. The number of computers and how they access shared resources determines the categorization of network types, which will be detailed in the following sections. Generally, computer networks are categorized based on the area they cover and their intended purpose. We will discuss some of the most common types of computer networks here.

Personal area network

A **Personal Area Network** (**PAN**), depicted in *Figure 1.2*, connects and transmits data among devices within a private area, typically belonging to an individual. For example, in your home office, your laptop, smartphone, printer, and headphones might all be connected via Bluetooth or Wi-Fi. Often referred to as a **Home Area Network** (**HAN**), a PAN uses technologies such as Bluetooth and Wi-Fi to interconnect devices.

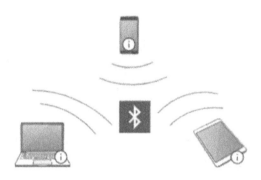

Figure 1.2 – A PAN

Another type of network is the **Local Area Network** (**LAN**), which has a much more extensive coverage area compared to a PAN. Let us explore this in the next section.

Local area network

A LAN connects two or more computers within a local area, such as a single room, a floor, several floors, a building, or multiple adjacent buildings. LANs typically use a central device and networking media such as twisted-pair, coaxial, or fiber optic cables to interconnect computers. *Figure 1.3* illustrates an extended LAN that utilizes two switches to connect multiple devices. This configuration enhances network capacity and allows for greater scalability by enabling communication across different segments of the network. The use of multiple switches in the extended LAN ensures efficient data transfer between devices, improving overall network performance and reliability. This setup is commonly used in larger environments to accommodate growing network demands while maintaining optimal performance and minimal latency.

Furthermore, comparing PANs and LANs, a PAN is primarily dominated by portable devices such as smartphones, while a LAN mainly consists of fixed devices. Both cover local areas, but a LAN has a broader range, potentially spanning an entire building or multiple buildings. A PAN is organized around an individual, whereas a LAN is organized around a specific site.

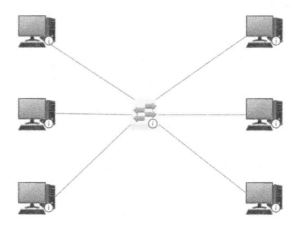

Figure 1.3 – A LAN

The next type of network we will examine is the **Metropolitan Area Network** (**MAN**), which has even more excellent coverage than a LAN.

Metropolitan area network

A MAN, illustrated in *Figure 1.4*, connects multiple LANs within a town or city. MANs exist to facilitate resource sharing and access within a metropolitan area. They offer more excellent coverage than LANs but less than **Wide Area Networks** (**WANs**). MANs are faster than both LANs and WANs, often using fiber optics and gigabit layer 3 switches for high-speed interconnection.

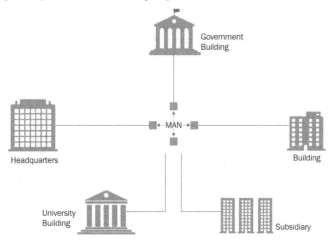

Figure 1.4 – A MAN

Finally, we will understand WANs, which have the most significant coverage.

Wide area network

A WAN, depicted in *Figure 1.5*, covers extensive geographic areas beyond the reach of LANs and MANs. WANs use dedicated telecommunication lines, such as telephone lines, leased lines, or satellites, making them accessible from geographic limitations. The internet is a quintessential example of a WAN.

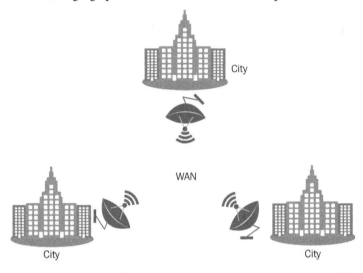

Figure 1.5 – A WAN

> **Note**
>
> You can learn more about the types of computer networks at https://www.lifewire.com/lans-wans-and-other-area-networks-817376.

After exploring the various types of computer networks, we will examine their underlying components.

Understanding computer network components

Just as **Personal Computers** (**PCs**) have their components, computer networks also consist of essential elements. While PCs and peripheral devices are familiar to most people, IT professionals focus on components such as networking devices, networking media, and NOSs.

First, let us clarify the roles of clients and servers within a computer network.

Understanding clients and servers

In the context of a computer network, **clients** and **servers** revolve around accessing and providing network resources. Clients typically initiate requests for resources, while servers are responsible for delivering and managing access to these resources. Both play vital roles in network operations. For instance, as depicted in *Figure 1.6*, a server connected directly to a printer offers printing services to PCs acting as print requesters.

Figure 1.6 – Client and server in a computer network

> **Note**
>
> The term *server* originates from *serve*, indicating its role in providing beneficial services, as per the Merriam-Webster dictionary. In a computer network, servers fulfill this role by serving clients.

Although clients and servers are fundamental network components, their roles are defined differently in network terminology. Let us explore how they fit into the broader network structure.

Understanding hosts and nodes

Have you ever come across terms such as **hosts** and **nodes** and wondered about their distinctions? While they may initially seem similar, hosts and nodes serve distinct purposes in network communication. All hosts can be considered nodes, but not every node functions as a host. A host refers to any device with an assigned IP address on its network interface actively requesting or providing networking services. Typically, clients, servers, and routers operate as hosts.

> **Note**
>
> An **Internet Protocol (IP)** address is a logical sequence of decimal numbers separated by dots that uniquely identifies a host within a computer network.

On the other hand, a node is any device capable of receiving and transmitting network services but lacks an IP address assignment on its interface. Nodes typically have network interfaces used for management purposes. For example, in *Figure 1.7*, PCs and the file server act as hosts, while switches function as nodes.

In a Windows Server environment, understanding the distinction between hosts and nodes is essential, as Windows Server frequently operates in a client-server model. In this model, the server provides resources, and client devices connect to access these services. This setup supports effective resource distribution across networks and is fundamental to IT administration.

As you may know, switches operate by forwarding frames within a local network, ensuring data is efficiently transmitted between devices on the same network segment. In contrast, routers are responsible for forwarding packets across different networks, enabling communication between separate network segments or even across the internet. Both switches and routers play critical roles in network infrastructure, with switches focusing on local traffic management and routers handling more complex inter-network routing to ensure seamless connectivity. Understanding the distinction between these two devices is fundamental for effective network design and troubleshooting.

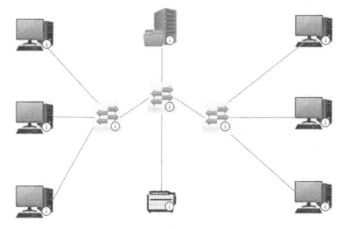

Figure 1.7 – Hosts and nodes in a computer network

Now that we understand a network and its essential components, we can explore network architectures.

Understanding Computer Network Architectures

Discussions about computer networks often involve exploring fundamental and overarching concepts, such as the components that comprise them. That includes considerations of network types based on coverage areas and physical and logical topologies governing their physical layout and structural organization. Computer network architecture encompasses a comprehensive framework that integrates elements such as physical and logical topologies, network components, communication protocols, and operational principles.

Moreover, computer network architecture serves as a design framework enabling computers to communicate using a request and response paradigm. The most prevalent network architectures include **Peer-to-Peer** (**P2P**) and client/server models.

Let us begin by exploring the P2P network architecture.

Peer-to-Peer (P2P) network architecture

In a **P2P network**, illustrated in *Figure 1.8*, hosts operate without predefined roles. Instead, they dynamically switch roles between the client and server based on their current network activities. For instance, if PC1 requests services from PC2, PC1 acts as the client while PC2 serves as the server. Conversely, if PC2 initiates a request to PC1, PC2 becomes the client and PC1 the server. PANs often exemplify P2P network setups.

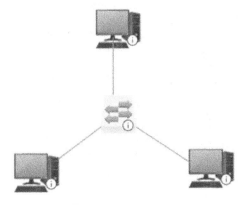

Figure 1.8 – A P2P computer network

> **Note**
> In the P2P network architecture, all hosts participate equally. This equality is a fundamental aspect of the model, where each host may assume the role of client or server as needed, making everyone feel included in the network.

The subsequent network architecture type is the client/server architecture.

Client/Server network architecture

In contrast, a **client/server network architecture**, presented earlier in *Figure 1.7*, designates specific roles to hosts. Clients are devices that request services, while servers are devices that provide services within the network. This structured approach to networking ensures efficient operations by clearly defining the roles of each device. Typically, client and server responsibilities are designated to specific machines, allowing for streamlined communication and resource management across the network. This architecture is foundational in many enterprise environments where scalability and reliability are crucial.

Each component of networking, from hosts and nodes to client-server architecture, directly supports your work within Windows Server 2025. Whether configuring access permissions, setting up resource sharing, or monitoring network traffic, these concepts will recur throughout your server management tasks.

With a clearer understanding of network operations, the next section will delve into the fundamental requirement for computers to communicate within a network: the IP address.

Overview of IP addressing and subnetting

In order for a computer to effectively communicate within a network, an IP address is required, serving as its unique identifier on that network. Think of an IP address as a device's unique identifier, similar to a postal address. In server management, IP addressing enables you to define the network structure and configure devices to communicate efficiently within and across networks.

In more complex networks, subnetting is used to define specific segments within the larger network structure, dividing it into smaller, more manageable parts. This segmentation enhances both security and performance—two key factors when managing Windows Server environments, where maintaining streamlined communication and data flow is essential.

Currently, two leading IP addressing technologies are recognized globally: IPv4 and IPv6. Despite the increasing prominence of IPv6, IPv4 remains the predominant addressing standard in internet traffic.

Let us begin by examining IPv4 network addresses.

IPv4 network addresses

IPv4, or **Internet Protocol version 4**, assigns addresses consisting of 32 bits organized into four octets, separated with dots for readability (e.g., 192.168.1.1). The designation "v4" denotes the fourth iteration of IP addressing, specified in IETF publication **RFC 791**. IPv4 addresses are categorized into classes—A, B, C, D, and E—based on their initial octet ranges, as shown in *Table 1.1*.

IPv4 classes	The IPv4 range of the first octet
A	1–127
B	128–191
C	192–223
D	224–239
E	240–255

Table 1.1 – IPv4 classes and their corresponding ranges

As you progress through this chapter, you may encounter areas that require further clarification, especially if you are new to IT. To address these challenges, it is crucial to focus on practical applications of the concepts discussed. Understanding how these foundational networking principles directly apply to Windows Server management will enhance your learning experience.

Now, let us explore the IPv6 addressing technology that was introduced to address the exhaustion of IPv4 network addresses.

IPv6 network addresses

IPv6, or **Internet Protocol version 6**, was designed to overcome the limitations posed by the exhaustion of IPv4 addresses, which are only 32 bits in length and provide around 4.3 billion unique addresses. In contrast, IPv6 employs a 128-bit address format, allowing for an astronomical total of approximately 340 undecillion unique addresses, as specified in IETF RFC 2460. This vast address space is represented in hexadecimal notation and segmented by colons, exemplified by addresses such as 2001:0DB8:85A3:0000:0000:8A2E:0370:7334.

The implementation of IPv6 not only provides an expansive range of addresses but also includes several features that enhance network efficiency and security. For instance, IPv6 supports auto-configuration, enabling devices to generate their IP addresses without the need for a DHCP server. That is particularly beneficial in dynamic environments where devices frequently connect and disconnect, such as in **Internet of Things** (**IoT**) applications. Additionally, IPv6 incorporates built-in security features such as IPsec, which provides end-to-end encryption and authentication, further safeguarding data transmission across networks.

To illustrate the practical benefits of IPv6, consider a smart home setup that includes various connected devices such as smart thermostats, lights, and security cameras. With the extensive address space of IPv6, each device can have a unique IP address, allowing for seamless communication and management without the complexities of address translation or the risk of address conflicts inherent in IPv4 networks. Furthermore, the ability to use multicast addressing in IPv6 facilitates efficient data distribution, such as streaming video to multiple devices simultaneously without requiring multiple unicast streams.

IPv6 not only resolves IPv4's address scarcity but also introduces significant advancements that improve network management, security, and scalability, making it a vital evolution in internet architecture as the number of connected devices continues to soar.

Next, we will delve into IPv4 subnetting, which plays a crucial role in identifying network addresses.

IPv4 subnetting

Subnetting involves logically partitioning a more extensive network into smaller subnetworks. A subnet mask is crucial for defining these subnetworks and identifying the network, host addresses, and broadcast addresses within each subnet. Default subnet masks, also known as classful networks, vary depending on the class of IPv4 addresses, as detailed in *Table 1.2*.

IPv4 class	Default subnet mask
A	255.0.0.0
B	255.255.0.0
C	255.255.255.0

Table 1.2 – IPv4 classful networks

> **Note**
>
> For further exploration of IPv4 addressing and related topics, visit this page on IPv4 exhaustion and classful networks: `https://blogs.igalia.com/dpino/ 2017/05/25/ipv4-exhaustion/`.

The networking fundamentals covered in this section provide a critical framework for the tasks you will perform in Windows Server 2025. However, as we transition into Windows Server topics, we will focus more specifically on its functionalities and practical applications, ensuring that your understanding of these foundational concepts directly supports your server management skills. For additional support, consider leveraging resources such as online forums and targeted literature that can provide deeper insights into Windows Server administration.

Having covered fundamental networking concepts, including types, components, architectures, and addressing, it's important to note that tools such as PowerShell and scripting are valuable for managing Windows Server environments. While this chapter doesn't delve into these topics in detail, they will be explored further in later chapters, providing you with essential skills for automating and streamlining server management tasks. The following section will introduce Windows Server and its core concepts.

Getting to know the server

Since we have already defined the server concept earlier, let us now focus on Windows Server in this section. Over its history, Windows Server has evolved from a primary file server to a sophisticated operating system capable of managing complex network environments such as corporate networks. It serves various network functions, such as domain controllers, web servers, print servers, and file servers, and it also acts as a platform for running enterprise applications such as **Exchange Server**, **SQL Server**, and **SharePoint Server**. With its robust performance and advanced security features, Windows Server now plays a pivotal role in shaping the landscape of cloud computing.

Understanding server hardware and software

As previously mentioned, computer hardware and software encompass both physical and logical components. Because servers are tasked with providing network services to clients, they require robust hardware. This hardware is designed to support advanced network services efficiently. Therefore, servers need high-quality components to ensure continuous service delivery and support for network operations. Servers differ from standard computers not only in their hardware but also in the specific types of services they provide. For instance, a database server necessitates significant memory capacity and storage space.

Key hardware components of servers include the **CPU**, **memory**, **disk subsystem**, and **network interfaces**, all of which significantly impact overall server performance. Monitoring the performance of these components is crucial to maintaining optimal server functionality under both regular and heavy workloads.

You will likely be familiar with these concepts already. However, the following list will jog your memory about the basics:

- **Central Processing Unit (CPU)**: Often referred to as the **processor**, this is a chip located on the server's motherboard that handles all processing and calculations. Modern CPUs are based on 64-bit architecture, which allows for more efficient data exchange between the CPU and RAM compared to older 32-bit architecture.

- **Random Access Memory (RAM)**: This serves as the server's working memory, utilized by Windows Server 2025 and its applications. The amount of RAM directly affects multitasking capabilities, enabling more applications to run simultaneously. Further details on RAM can be found in the *Understanding Memory* section of *Chapter 13, Tuning and Maintaining Windows Server 2025*.

- **Disks**: Data storage in servers typically relies on disks, often organized into a disk subsystem. Disk performance, specifically read/write speeds, is critical as faster throughput enhances overall disk subsystem performance. Servers commonly employ **Solid State Drives (SSDs)** and **Hard Disk Drives (HDDs)**. SSDs offer faster read and write speeds due to their lack of moving parts, while HDDs are known for durability and high-capacity storage.

- **Network interface**: This facilitates a server's connection to both LANs and the internet within an organization. Servers often feature multiple network interfaces, with higher network connection speeds enabling greater data throughput to and from the network.

Now that we have covered what constitutes a server, let us explore various server sizes, form factors, and configurations.

Understanding server sizes, form factors, and shapes

If we consider a server as essentially a computer, then similar principles governing the form factor of laptops also apply to servers. That raises the question: what exactly is a form factor? In hardware design, the form factor defines the size, shape, and technical specifications of an electronic device. Today, servers are available in three primary form factors, each tailored to specific operational needs:

- **Rack-mountable servers**: As the name suggests, these servers are designed to be mounted on racks. These servers function as general-purpose computers capable of supporting a wide range of applications and network services. Typically housed in on-premises server rooms or data centers, rack-mountable servers are secured to racks due to their weight and are depicted in *Figure 1.9*.

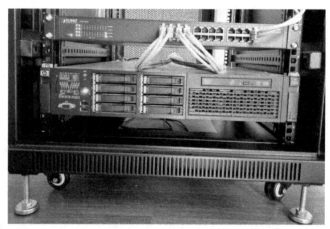

Figure 1.9 – An HP server in a rack

- **Blade servers**: These are modular units that enable multiple servers to be deployed within a compact space. Characterized by their slim design, blade servers typically include CPU, memory, network interfaces, and storage disks. They are commonly found in data centers or facilities requiring high processing power, owing to their ability to house multiple servers on a single shelf.

- **Tower servers**: These resemble vertical-case PCs but are equipped with advanced hardware that provides significantly higher processing power compared to standard PCs. These servers are commonly utilized for testing purposes or to support local services in **Small Office–Home Office** (**SOHO**) environments.

> **Note**
> A 64-bit Windows Server installed on 64-bit hardware can handle twice the data compared to a 32-bit Windows Server running on 32-bit hardware.

In this section, we have explored server hardware components, such as CPU, memory, disk, and network interface, and discussed server sizes, form factors, and configurations. Furthermore, servers are equipped with an operating system that enables them to provide network services similar to conventional computers. Let us explore this aspect further.

Understanding Network Operating System

A **NOS** is specialized software designed to manage, maintain, and provide various services within a network environment. These services include file and application sharing, web services, authentication and authorization, access control, user and computer administration, configuration tools, resource management, and other network-related functions. Consequently, a NOS plays a crucial role in effectively managing network resources.

A NOS forms the foundation of server functionality, enabling centralized control of network resources and client-server interactions. Windows Server 2025 functions as a NOS, offering tools and features tailored for seamless device management, application hosting, and data handling. Understanding the role of a NOS is essential for fully leveraging Windows Server's capabilities.

Prominent examples of NOSs today are **Windows Server**, **Linux Server**, and **macOS Server**, each capable of delivering comprehensive network services. Let us delve into each of these systems individually.

Windows Server overview

Windows Server, a cornerstone of Microsoft's server product line, is renowned for its robust **Graphical User Interface (GUI)** and extensive capabilities in managing network resources. Since its inception in 1993, Windows Server has evolved to meet the demands of modern computing environments. The lineage began with Windows NT 3.5 in the early 1990s and formally started with Windows 2000 Server. Key milestones include the introduction of Windows Server 2008, which brought features such as Server Core and Hyper-V, and the release of Windows Server 2016, which enhanced support for cloud integration, illustrating its adaptability.

Initially available for both 32-bit and 64-bit architectures, Windows Server transitioned exclusively to 64-bit architecture with the release of Windows Server 2012. The server's native filesystem remains the **New Technology File System (NTFS)**. However, Windows Server 2012 introduced the **Resilient File System (ReFS)**, primarily used in database applications due to its resilience and efficiency.

As organizations increasingly transition to cloud services, Windows Server remains relevant by providing hybrid solutions that seamlessly connect on-premises resources with cloud infrastructure. *Figure 1.10* illustrates the properties of the Windows `C:` drive, showcasing key attributes that support the management of file storage and system resources. With features such as Windows Admin Center and PowerShell, Windows Server empowers IT professionals to automate and streamline server management tasks, ensuring its continued relevance in an increasingly digital and cloud-centric world.

Figure 1.10 – NTFS continues to be used by Windows Server 2022

Note

For more details on ReFS, visit `https://docs.microsoft.com/en-us/windows-server/storage/refs/refs-overview`.

Linux Server overview

Linux is distinguished in the operating system landscape by its open source nature and extensive community support. Developed by Linus Torvalds in the early 1990s as a Unix-like system, Linux quickly gained popularity due to its robustness and flexibility. Licensed under the GNU **General Public License (GPL)**, Linux has evolved into numerous distributions tailored to various user needs. Linux servers, such as Ubuntu Server (illustrated in *Figure 1.11*), are prevalent in hosting web servers and powering supercomputers due to their security and scalability, both on-premises and in cloud environments.

Figure 1.11 – Downloading Ubuntu Server from ubuntu.com

> **Note**
>
> Learn about running the Linux subsystem on Windows Server 2025 at `https://docs.microsoft.com/en-us/windows/wsl/install-on-server`.

macOS Server overview

Although **macOS Server** has a smaller market share than Windows Server and Linux Server, it is renowned for its reliability and seamless integration with Apple's ecosystem. As a Unix-based operating system, macOS Server adheres to Apple's intuitive GUI design philosophy. Initially supporting both 32-bit and 64-bit platforms, macOS Server now exclusively operates on 64-bit platforms following Apple's transition to Intel processors. Apple continues to release updates and provide support for macOS Server, maintaining its relevance in specialized environments.

> **Note**
>
> Explore more about macOS Server at `https://www.apple.com/macos/server/`.

In this section, we have gained insights into Windows Server, Linux Server, and macOS Server. In the next section, our focus will expand further into Windows Server, enhancing our understanding of its capabilities and administration.

Overview and editions of Windows Server 2025

If someone were to ask, "What is Windows Server?" you might respond with the following: Windows Server is a server operating system developed by Microsoft, part of the Windows NT family. In server environments—whether using Windows Server, Linux Server, or macOS Server—the primary objective is to ensure the system provides the necessary services to support an organization's network. However, there are significant differences among these systems in terms of deployment processes, user interfaces, resource management, and server maintenance. These distinctions can significantly influence the overall efficiency and effectiveness of the server's operation within an enterprise environment.

To understand its development, let's explore the different eras of Windows Server and how it has evolved over the years.

Windows Server eras overview

For nearly 30 years, beginning with the masses era, that of Windows NT, Microsoft has consistently anticipated and integrated emerging needs within the server landscape. This foresight has driven a fascinating evolution of Windows Server, which I am eager to share with you. Pay close attention to the technological progressions and transitions over the years—they are truly impressive. The eras of Windows Server's development are presented in the following table:

Server for the masses era (1996–2000)	Enterprise era (2000–2008)	Data center era (2009–2013)	Cloud era (2016–present)
Windows NT Server 3.5		Windows Server 2008	Windows Server 2016
	Windows 2000 Server		Windows Server 2019
Windows NT Server 4.0	Windows Server 2003	Windows Server 2012	Windows Server 2022
			Windows Server 2025

Table 1.3 – Windows Server eras overview

In this section, you have gained an overview of Windows Server and its eras. In the next section, we will explore the steps to download Windows Server 2025.

Windows Server 2025 overview

Windows Server 2025, illustrated in *Figure 1.12*, is the latest release in Microsoft's Windows NT family of server operating systems, generally available as of **November 2024**. Announced on 26 January 2024, Windows Server 2025 marks a shift from its predecessors—such as Windows Server 2016, 2019, and 2022—which were built on Windows 10. This new version is based on **Windows 11**, specifically **version 23H2** from the October 2023 update. Unlike Windows 11, Windows Server 2025 does not mandate TPM 2.0 for deployment, thus providing increased flexibility for varied deployment needs.

Figure 1.12 – Windows Server's 2025 Desktop and Start menu

In today's cloud-centric era, server operating systems must be designed with cloud capabilities in mind. This trend began with Windows Server 2016, which Microsoft aptly named **Windows Server for the cloud**. This focus has only intensified with subsequent releases, such as Windows Server 2022, which further enhanced its capabilities with improved security, flexibility, and robust support for hybrid deployments, mainly through innovations in the Windows Server 2022 Datacenter Azure edition. Each iteration, including Windows Server 2019, introduced significant features, such as System Insights, hybrid cloud tools, and enhanced security measures such as Storage Migration Service and Kubernetes support.

Microsoft has consistently evolved Windows Server to enhance security, connectivity, Azure integration, application platform capabilities, storage management, and other essential features. In today's cloud-driven landscape, Windows Server continues to play a crucial role. Its integration with Microsoft Azure allows for the seamless management of hybrid environments, enabling organizations to leverage both on-premises and cloud resources. Features such as Windows Admin Center and PowerShell facilitate efficient cloud management, underscoring Windows Server's ongoing relevance in a hybrid cloud world.

Building on this foundation, Windows Server 2025 introduces several new features designed to meet the evolving demands of modern cloud environments. Notably, **Active Directory Domain Services (AD DS)** has been enhanced with support for a larger 32k database page size, enhancing scalability and improving data handling for multi-valued attributes. New schema updates expand AD functionality, allowing administrators to repair objects with missing core attributes efficiently. Additionally, Windows Server 2025 introduces **Server Message Block over Quick UDP Internet Connections (SMB over QUIC)**, which allows the SMB protocol to run over QUIC, enhancing file-sharing performance and security across all editions. Security enhancements within AD DS further bolster network defenses, ensuring robust protection against contemporary threats.

Moreover, Windows Server 2025 pioneers **hot-patching** capabilities, enabling the seamless application of security patches without requiring server restarts. This feature minimizes downtime and enhances system uptime, which is critical for maintaining operational continuity. Specific requirements must be met to utilize hot-patching, including the use of **Virtualization-Based Security (VBS)** enclaves. VBS enclaves provide an isolated environment that enhances security by protecting critical processes from potential threats, ensuring that hot-patching can be performed securely and effectively.

Leveraging **AI-driven management optimizations**, Windows Server 2025 offers enhanced management capabilities that provide administrators with proactive insights and operational efficiencies. These advancements underscore Microsoft's commitment to delivering a server OS that sets new standards for performance, security, and manageability in today's IT landscapes, solidifying its position at the forefront of cloud computing innovation.

> **Note**
>
> Unlike **Remote Server Administration Tools (RSATs)**, which rely on traditional methods, Windows Admin Center is a modern server management platform built on web technologies. It offers a more streamlined and user-friendly experience, with an interface closely resembling that of Azure, enabling seamless navigation for administrators familiar with cloud environments. Windows Admin Center provides a comprehensive set of tools for managing servers and infrastructure efficiently. After installing Windows Server 2025, a dialog box for Windows Admin Center automatically appears, granting users free access to this powerful management interface, further simplifying server administration tasks. It can be downloaded from `https://www.microsoft.com/en-us/evalcenter/download-windows-admin-center`.

Next, let us explore the various editions available in Windows Server 2025.

Windows Server 2025 editions

Windows Server 2025 is available in various editions, each designed to meet specific organizational requirements. The primary editions include the following:

- **Datacenter Edition**: Ideal for extensive virtualization and cloud environments, this edition offers unlimited virtual instances and a range of advanced features. Enhancing security and performance requires VBS enclaves.

- **Standard Edition**: This edition is tailored for smaller organizations with fewer virtual instances. It includes all essential server features needed for efficient operation. VBS enclaves are also recommended for this edition to ensure robust security.

- **Azure Edition (for VM evaluation only)**: Specifically designed for evaluating Windows Server within Azure VMs, this edition allows organizations to test and assess its capabilities in the cloud. VBS enclaves are utilized to provide a secure evaluation environment.

- **Annual Channel for Container Host**: Focused on container workloads, this edition ensures efficient deployment and management of containerized applications. VBS enclaves support secure and isolated container environments.

These editions clearly outline the options available within Windows Server 2025, each catering to different needs and use cases. Next, we will explore how Windows Server 2025 compares to its predecessors.

Key differences between Windows Server 2025 and Windows Server 2022

In today's rapidly evolving technological landscape, new products are often initially perceived as mere incremental updates to their predecessors. This sentiment might also apply to Windows Server 2025 at first glance, suggesting only superficial enhancements over Windows Server 2022. However, a closer examination of Windows Server 2025 reveals substantial improvements and new features. The following subsections aim to highlight some of the most significant differences and advancements between these two operating systems.

When comparing Windows Server 2025 with its predecessor, Windows Server 2022, several notable advancements and enhancements become apparent:

- **AD DS enhancements**:
  - **Windows Server 2025**: Introduces a larger 32k database page size for AD, enhancing scalability. New schema updates extend AD functionality, and enterprise administrators can repair objects with missing core attributes.
  - **Windows Server 2022**: Focused on improving AD management and schema flexibility.

- **SMB over QUIC**:

  - **Windows Server 2025**: SMB can now be configured across all editions using QUIC, enhancing file-sharing performance and security

  - **Windows Server 2022**: Introduced initial support for SMB over QUIC

- **Security enhancements**:

  - **Windows Server 2025**: Includes hypervisor-based code integrity, enhanced Secured-core server, and hardware-enforced stack protection. Default support for TLS 1.3 improves network security.

  - **Windows Server 2022**: Featured improvements in security protocols, including Secured-core Server and enhanced TLS support.

- **Hot-patching support**:

  - **Windows Server 2025**: Implements hot-patching capabilities, allowing for seamless updates without downtime

  - **Windows Server 2022**: Continued support for robust update management tools

- **AI-based management**:

  - **Windows Server 2025**: Offers enhanced management capabilities with AI-driven optimizations

  - **Windows Server 2022**: Introduced initial AI-driven management tools

- **Platform flexibility**:

  - **Windows Server 2025**: Focuses on dynamic routing and improved service account management

  - **Windows Server 2022**: Introduced **Dynamic Source Routing** (**DSR**) and improvements in virtualized time zones

- **Windows Admin Center enhancements**:

  - **Windows Server 2025**: Features advanced management capabilities, including automated extension life cycle management and customizable VM information views

  - **Windows Server 2022**: Supported enhanced Windows Admin Center tools

- **Kubernetes support**:

  - **Windows Server 2025**: Enhances support for Kubernetes environments with advancements in container management

  - **Windows Server 2022**: Provided initial support for Kubernetes and improvements in container orchestration

> **Note**
>
> Hotpatching requires Azure Arc connectivity, which enables the integration of on-premises servers with Azure services. Other dependencies include Azure Update Management to ensure that updates are managed and deployed efficiently, compatibility with specific server roles and features (not all roles may support hot-patching initially, so it's important to verify compatibility), and sufficient system resources to ensure that hardware and network resources are adequate to handle hot-patching processes.

Understanding these differences between Windows Server 2025 and Windows Server 2022 will help you determine which version best suits your needs. Now, let us examine the minimum and recommended system requirements.

Minimum and recommended system requirements for Windows Server 2025

Before discussing the specific system requirements, it's important to distinguish between the minimum and recommended hardware specifications. The minimum requirements allow for the basic installation and operation of the OS, while the recommended specifications ensure optimal performance and user experience. Understanding these requirements is crucial for selecting the appropriate hardware to match the intended usage and workloads. According to Microsoft's publications, Windows Server 2025 maintains hardware requirements similar to those of its predecessors.

The following are the minimum system requirements:

- **Processor**: 1.4 GHz 64-bit processor
- **RAM**: 512 MB (2 GB for the Desktop Experience installation option)
- **Disk space**: 32 GB
- **Network**: Ethernet adapter capable of at least 1 gigabit throughput
- **Graphics device and monitor**: Capable of Super VGA (1024 x 768) or higher resolution
- **Other hardware**: DVD drive (for installations from DVD media), keyboard, mouse (or compatible pointing device), TPM, and internet access

The following are the recommended hardware requirements:

- **Processor**: 2.0 GHz 64-bit processor or higher
- **RAM**: 32 GB or more
- **Disk space**: 256 GB SSD and 1 TB HDD
- **Network**: At least 1 gigabit Ethernet NIC

- **Graphics device and monitor**: Capable of super VGA (1024 x 768) or higher resolution

- **Other hardware**: DVD drive, keyboard, mouse (or compatible pointing device), TPM, and internet access

This section provides insights into the minimum and recommended hardware requirements for Windows Server 2025, reflecting its alignment with previous versions while ensuring robust performance for modern server environments. Understanding these requirements is crucial for making informed decisions about hardware investments to meet your server deployment needs. In the following sections, we will explore the new features and enhancements introduced in Windows Server 2025.

Chapter exercise 1.1 – downloading Windows Server 2025

In this chapter's exercise, you will be guided through the process of downloading Windows Server 2025. This version introduces several advanced features and improvements designed to enhance server performance, security, and management. By carefully following the outlined steps, you will learn how to access and download the installation files, ensuring that you are prepared to work with the latest version of Microsoft's server operating system. This exercise is essential for IT professionals looking to stay up to date with industry standards and leverage the new capabilities of Windows Server 2025 in their environments.

Downloading Windows Server 2025

To download Windows Server 2025 on your Windows 11 computer, follow these steps:

1. Press the Windows key + *R* to open the **Run** dialog.

2. Type `Microsoft-edge:` and press *Enter*.

3. In Microsoft Edge, click on the address bar and type `https://www.microsoft.com/en-us/evalcenter`, then press *Enter*.

4. On the **Evaluation Center** page, click **Windows Server** on the horizontal menu at the top. Then, select the **Windows Server** option. From the list of available versions, choose **Windows Server 2025**, as shown in *Figure 1.13*.

Microsoft
Evaluation Center
Windows
Windows Server
SQL Server
System Center
Microsoft Security
Windows Server
Windows Server 2025
Windows Server Essentials
Windows Server 2022
Hyper-V Server
Windows Server 2019
Windows Admin Center
Windows Server 2016
Windows Virtual Hardware Lab Kit (VHLK)
Center has the tools you need to evaluate Microsoft pro

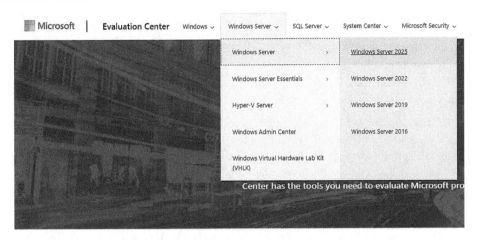

Figure 1.13 – Selecting Windows Server 2025 from the list

5. In the **Get started for free** section of the **Windows Server 2025** page, select **Download the ISO** as your product experience.
6. Complete the form as shown in *Figure 1.14*, then click **Download now**.

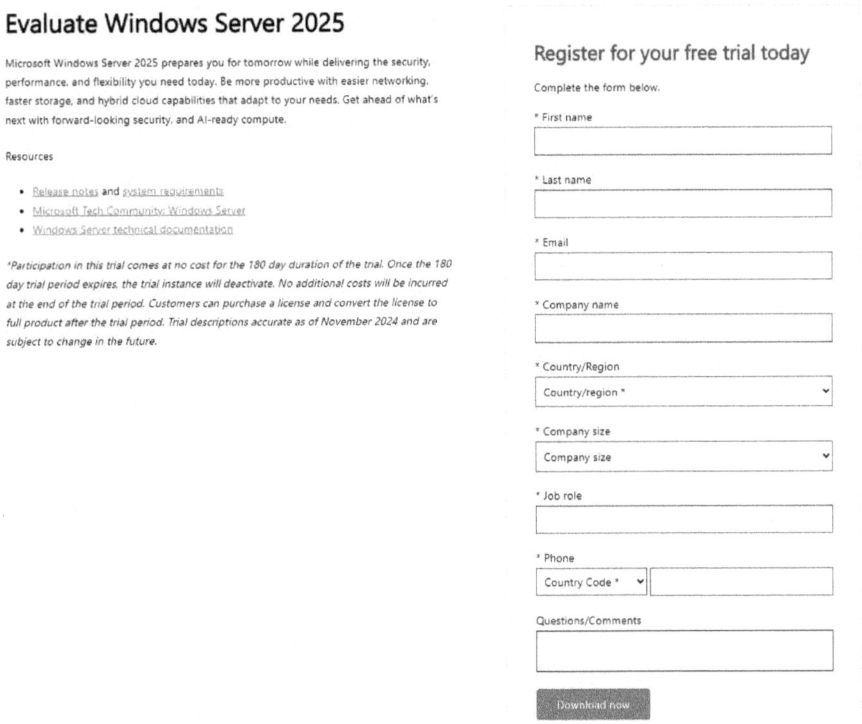

Evaluate Windows Server 2025
Microsoft Windows Server 2025 prepares you for tomorrow while delivering the security, performance, and flexibility you need today. Be more productive with easier networking, faster storage, and hybrid cloud capabilities that adapt to your needs. Get ahead of what's next with forward-looking security, and AI-ready compute.
Resources
Release notes and system requirements
Microsoft Tech Community: Windows Server
Windows Server technical documentation
*Participation in this trial comes at no cost for the 180 day duration of the trial. Once the 180 day trial period expires, the trial instance will deactivate. No additional costs will be incurred at the end of the trial period. Customers can purchase a license and convert the license to full product after the trial period. Trial descriptions accurate as of November 2024 and are subject to change in the future.
Register for your free trial today
Complete the form below.
* First name
* Last name
* Email
* Company name
* Country/Region
Country/region *
* Company size
Company size
* Job role
* Phone
Country Code *
Questions/Comments
Download now

Figure 1.14 – Registering for the free trial to evaluate Windows Server 2025

7. Next, please select your Windows Server 2025 download by choosing the language.

8. Shortly after, the Windows Server 2025 download will begin. If not, you may want to click the **Download** button.

> **Note**
>
> After downloading Windows Server 2025, you will need to burn the ISO file to a USB flash drive to create a bootable USB. You can follow this guide on how to burn an ISO file to a USB drive: `https://www.lifewire.com/how-to-burn-an-iso-file-to-a-USB-drive-2619270`. Once this process is complete, you will be ready to proceed with installing the Windows Server 2025 evaluation version.

Chapter exercise 1.2 – downloading Windows Admin Center

In this chapter's exercise, you will be guided through the steps required to download and set up Windows Admin Center. This tool serves as a centralized management interface for Windows Server environments, providing a streamlined approach to administering multiple servers and devices. By following the detailed instructions, you'll learn how to obtain and install Windows Admin Center, setting the foundation for efficient server management and configuration through its intuitive, web-based interface. This exercise is crucial for IT professionals seeking to enhance their ability to manage Windows Server resources with greater ease and control.

Downloading Windows Admin Center

To download Windows Admin Center on your Windows 11 computer, follow these steps:

1. Open Microsoft Edge and navigate to `https://www.microsoft.com/en-us/cloud-platform/windows-admin-center`.

2. Click the **Download Windows Admin Center** button on the Windows Admin Center site, as shown in *Figure 1.15*.

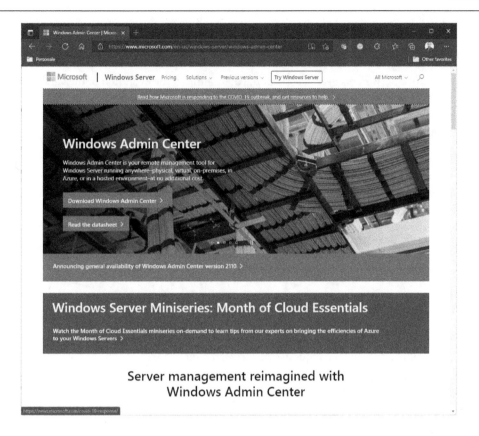

Figure 1.15 – Windows Admin Center download site

3. When prompted, choose either **Open** or **Save As** to download the file.

4. After the download is complete, proceed with the installation by following the steps in the **Windows Admin Center Setup** wizard.

These exercises were designed to reinforce the chapter's key concepts by providing practical experience. By completing them, you gained firsthand knowledge of how to install and manage server software and tools, which are crucial skills for successfully administering a modern server environment. This practical application not only solidified your understanding of the theoretical content but also prepared you for real-world scenarios in server management.

Summary

In this chapter, you have explored the foundational concepts of computer networks and gained insights into Windows Server. Specifically, you have been introduced to various types, components, and architectures of computer networks, as well as IP addressing and subnetting. Additionally, you have learned about server hardware and software, different server sizes, form factors, and NOSs. This chapter also provided a comprehensive overview of the Windows Server timeline.

In the *Windows Server eras overview* section, you examined the evolution of the various versions of Windows Server 2025. You also compared the differences between Windows Server 2022 and Windows Server 2025, including their minimum and recommended system requirements. Furthermore, you delved into Windows Server 2025, Linux Server, and the macOS Server NOS.

The chapter also included practical exercises that guided you through downloading Windows Server 2025 from the Technet Evaluation Center portal and Windows Admin Center from the WAC portal, thus enhancing the lab-oriented learning experience. With the knowledge gained in this chapter, you should now understand what a computer network is, be able to identify different network architectures, and comprehend IP addressing and subnetting. Additionally, you will be able to recognize key hardware components, understand NOSs, and appreciate the historical evolution of Windows Server.

In the following chapter, you will learn about installing Windows Server 2025.

Questions

1. **True or false**: The computer network architecture is a design that enables computers to communicate using the request-response paradigm.

2. **Fill in the blanks**: _____ usually requests access to resources, and _____ is responsible for providing and managing access to the resources.

3. **Multiple choice**: Which of the following are considered to be types of computer networks? (Choose all that apply)

   - PAN

   - LAN

   - MAN

   - WAN

   - All of the above

4. **True or false**: Windows Server is Microsoft's operating system and is part of the Windows NT family.

5. **Fill in the blank**: _____ can provide network services such as domain controllers, web servers, print servers, and file servers.

6. **True or false**: The subnet helps to identify a specific network within the overall network.

7. **Multiple choice**: Which of the following are considered to be network architectures? (Choose two)

    - Peer-to-Peer (P2P)

    - Client/server

    - Network Operating System (NOS)

    - Network topology

8. **True or false**: The CPU, memory, disk, and network are the critical system components that affect the overall performance of your servers.

9. **Fill in the blanks**: The _____ represents the physical component of a server, while the _____ represents the logical component.

10. **Multiple choice**: Which of the following are considered to be IP-addressing technologies? (Choose two)

    - IPv2

    - IPv4

    - IPv6

    - IPv8

11. **True or false**: Windows Admin Center is a new server management app introduced with Windows Server 2022.

12. **Fill in the blank**: _____ technology has enabled easy-to-build, deploy, and run application images.

13. **Single choice**: What is the new server management app introduced with Windows Server 2025?

    - Windows administrative tools

    - Windows PowerShell

    - Windows Admin Center

    - Active Directory Administrative Center

14. **Short answer**: Discuss the importance of a well-designed network architecture in supporting modern business operations.

15. **Short answer**: Explain the role of each critical system component (CPU, memory, disk, and network) in optimizing server performance.

Further reading

- *What is computer networking?*: https://www.ibm.com/topics/networking
- *What's new in Windows Server 2025*: https://learn.microsoft.com/en-us/windows-server/get-started/whats-new-windows-server-2025
- *Linux vs. Windows Server: The Ultimate Comparison*: https://phoenixnap.com/blog/Linux-vs-Microsoft-windows-servers
- *Windows Admin Center overview*: https://docs.microsoft.com/en-us/windows-server/manage/windows-admin-center/understand/windows-admin-center

Unlock this book's exclusive benefits now

This book comes with additional benefits designed to elevate your learning experience.

Note: Have your purchase invoice ready before you begin.

https://www.packtpub.com/unlock/9781836205012

2

Installing Windows Server 2025

This chapter will guide you through the installation of **Windows Server 2025**, a powerful and versatile operating system for servers. You will learn how to perform different types of installation, such as **clean installation**, **network installation** using **Windows Deployment Service (WDS)**, **unattended installation** using the **Windows Assessment and Deployment Kit (Windows ADK)**, **Microsoft Deployment Toolkit (MDT)**, in-place upgrades, migration of network services to a new server, and testing Windows Server 2025 in **Azure**.

You will follow precise and detailed instructions, supported by helpful graphics, to complete the installation process with ease and efficiency. This chapter will help you master the skills and knowledge needed to install Windows Server 2025 on your servers quickly and effectively.

At the end of the chapter, you will practice setting up WDS, a valuable tool for deploying Windows operating systems over the network. That will give you practical experience with one of the installation methods covered in the chapter.

In this chapter, we're going to cover the following main topics:

- Understanding disk partitioning and storage options

- Exploring boot configurations and startup options

- Installation options for Windows Server 2025

- Various methods for deploying Windows Server 2025

- Perform clean installation, network deployment, in-place upgrade, migration, and Azure-based deployment

Technical requirements

To practice the skills learned in this chapter, you will need the following resources:

- A computer with **Windows 11 Pro**, a minimum of 16 GB of RAM, 1 TB of **disk space**, and an internet connection

- A virtual machine running **Windows Server 2012 R2 Standard** (Desktop Experience), with at least 2 GB of RAM, 100 GB of disk space, and an internet connection

- A virtual machine running **Windows Server 2022 Standard** (Desktop Experience), with at least 4 GB of RAM, 100 GB of disk space, and an internet connection

Understanding disk partitioning and storage options

Installing new operating systems is a routine task for a system administrator. This task involves several critical steps, such as preparing the installation media, executing the OS installation, checking the installation results, and setting up the initial server configuration. These steps are essential for laying the groundwork for further operations. While some servers may come with preinstalled operating systems, the system administrator's expertise is often required to ensure the server has the most suitable OS to meet specific needs.

Before we start the installation process, let us review the importance of partition schemes in organizing disk partitions.

Understanding partition schemes

Disk partitioning is the process of dividing a physical disk into logical sections called partitions. Each partition can have a different filesystem, such as **New Technology File System (NTFS)** or **Resilient File System (ReFS)**, and store various types of data. Partitions can also be used to create separate volumes, which are logical units of storage that can span multiple disks. The partition scheme is the technique that determines how these partitions are created and managed on the disks. There are two main partition schemes:

- **Master Boot Record (MBR)**: This is an older partitioning scheme that is now considered outdated and no longer recommended for modern systems. MBR operates on a 512-byte disk sector and supports only 4 primary partitions or 1 extended partition containing up to 26 logical partitions. It uses **Logical Block Addressing (LBA)** to manage disks with a maximum size of 2 TB. While MBR was once useful for multiboot systems, it has several limitations that make it incompatible with today's technology. Its 2 TB size restriction is insufficient for many modern storage devices, and the limited number of partitions can be a bottleneck for more complex setups. Additionally, MBR lacks the advanced redundancy and recovery features found in newer partitioning schemes. These shortcomings led to the development of the GUID Partition Table, which offers better scalability, support for larger drives, and improved reliability.

- **GUID Partition Table** (**GPT**): This is a modern partition scheme that overcomes MBR's drawbacks. GPT uses a 128-bit **Global Unique Identifier** (**GUID**) to identify resources. It supports block sizes from 512 bytes and above, with a common default of 4,096 bytes. Each partition entry is 128 bytes. GPT is part of the **Unified Extensible Firmware Interface** (**UEFI**) standard, which replaces the older BIOS to work with modern hardware. GPT is resilient and can handle up to 9.4 **zettabytes** (**ZB**) of disk storage and 128 partitions per disk. GPT also provides better reliability and security features, such as a protective **MBR** and a **CRC32 checksum**. With MBR already explained, it's important to understand CRC32, a checksum algorithm used to detect errors in data transmission or storage. CRC32 generates a unique value, known as a checksum, derived from the data's contents. This value is then compared to the original checksum to verify the integrity of the data. If the two values do not match, it suggests possible data corruption, meaning the data may have been altered or compromised during transmission or storage, highlighting a failure in maintaining data accuracy.

To install Windows Server 2025, utilizing a GPT partition scheme is essential. This necessity arises from the requirement for UEFI, which supersedes the traditional BIOS and exclusively boots from GPT disks. UEFI not only enables quicker and more secure boot processes but also supports advanced functionalities such as **Secure Boot** and **BitLocker**, enhancing the overall system security and efficiency. Moreover, Secure Boot and BitLocker are key security features that work together to protect a system. Secure Boot safeguards the boot process by allowing only authorized and verified software to run, blocking untrusted or malicious code, such as rootkits, from compromising the system. BitLocker complements this by providing full-disk encryption, ensuring that data remains secure even if the storage device is physically removed or accessed without authorization. Together, these features enhance system security, protect sensitive information, and prevent unauthorized access, ensuring both the integrity and confidentiality of data.

In Windows Server 2025, you can create and manage disk partitions using the **Disk Management tool** or the **Diskpart command-line utility**. Alternatively, the **Windows Setup wizard** can be employed during the installation process to create and format partitions. If you need to convert an existing MBR disk to GPT, it is essential to first delete all partitions on the disk, which will result in data loss. Therefore, it is strongly advised that all data be backed up before proceeding with the conversion.

In addition to choosing a partition scheme, you can also customize the boot settings to facilitate the installation process. **Boot settings** are options that tell your computer how to start the operating system from different sources. For example, you can boot from a DVD, a USB flash drive, or a network server. To change the boot settings, you need to access the **Basic Input/Output System** (**BIOS**) or UEFI interface and modify the boot order or enable the boot menu. We will discuss the boot settings in more detail in the *Exploring boot configurations and startup options* section.

Note

To create a bootable USB flash drive, consider using the **Windows 7 USB/DVD Download Tool**, which you can download from Microsoft's official page at `https://www.microsoft.com/en-us/download/windows-usb-dvd-download-tool`.

One of the key aspects of setting up your server is choosing the right storage options that can deliver high performance, availability, and scalability. Windows Server 2025 provides various storage features that can help you achieve different goals and requirements. In the following section, we will discuss these storage features and how they can benefit the server environment.

Overview of storage options

Beyond disk partitioning, Windows Server 2025 offers various storage options to enhance your server's performance, availability, and scalability. Key storage features include the following:

- **Storage Spaces**: This feature allows the creation of virtual disks from a pool of physical disks, offering different resiliency levels such as *simple*, *mirror*, or *parity* to safeguard data against disk failures. It also supports tiered storage, automatically moving frequently accessed data to faster **Solid State Drives (SSDs)** and less accessed data to **slower HDDs**.

- **Storage Spaces Direct**: This feature enables the formation of a shared storage pool from local disks across a server cluster, facilitating highly available and scalable storage solutions such as **hyper-converged infrastructure (HCI)** or **software-defined storage (SDS)**. HCI represents a contemporary IT framework that merges computing, storage, and networking into a cohesive system managed through software. This integration streamlines management and scalability by consolidating hardware resources and virtualization into a single, unified platform, leading to enhanced efficiency and cost reductions. Conversely, SDS is a storage management strategy that decouples storage hardware from the controlling software. By leveraging virtualization, SDS enables dynamic management and allocation of storage resources, offering increased flexibility, scalability, and cost-effectiveness while facilitating more efficient and automated storage operations across various hardware setups.

- **Storage Replica**: This feature provides data replication between servers or clusters using synchronous or asynchronous replication, enabling robust disaster recovery solutions such as **stretch clusters** or **site-to-site replication**. Stretch clusters offer a high-availability solution by distributing a single cluster across multiple physical locations or data centers. This arrangement ensures uninterrupted operation and data redundancy, even if one site fails, as the cluster continues to function across the other locations. Site-to-site replication, meanwhile, synchronizes data between two geographically distant sites, ensuring that essential data is continuously updated and accessible at both locations. This approach bolsters disaster recovery and data resilience by maintaining an up-to-date backup, facilitating continuous data availability, and safeguarding against disruptions at any single site.

After completing the installation process, understanding advanced startup options becomes crucial. These options provide valuable functionality beyond the initial setup. Let us delve into them.

Accessing the advanced startup options

Windows Server 2025 does not have the *F8* option for restoring the server OS. Instead, you need to access the **Advanced startup** options from the **Settings** menu. To do this, you need to perform the following steps:

1. Click the **Start** button on the desktop.

2. From the **Start** menu, select the **Settings** icon.

3. On the **Settings** screen, find and click the **System** option.

4. From the list of options, select the **Recovery** option.

5. On the right-hand side of the screen, click the **Restart now** button under the **Recovery options** section, as shown in *Figure 2.1*.

Figure 2.1 – Navigating to Advanced startup in Windows Server 2025

6. We will restart your device to save your work dialog box. Click again on the **Restart Now** button to confirm. Choose the reason and click **Continue**.

7. After the system restarts, select **Troubleshoot** from the *Choose an option* screen.

8. On the **Advanced options** screen, as shown in *Figure 2.2*, you can select various options to recover or repair your server OS.

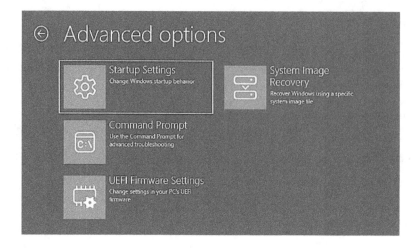

Figure 2.2 – Advanced Options in Windows Server 2025

This section provided an overview of the partition schemes, boot options, and advanced startup options in Windows Server 2025. The following section will explain the different server installation options in more detail.

Exploring boot configurations and startup options

Before a computer can load the operating system, it must go through a booting process that involves initializing hardware components and loading system software. This process is managed by firmware, either BIOS or UEFI, depending on the motherboard and hardware. Both BIOS and UEFI are responsible for configuring boot options, including boot order, boot mode, and boot device selection.

Boot options significantly impact the server's performance and its interaction with other devices and networks. Understanding the differences between BIOS and UEFI, along with their respective advantages and disadvantages, is crucial. In this section, we will delve into the boot options available in BIOS and UEFI and how they can be configured and customized in Windows Server 2025.

Understanding boot options in UEFI

To boot your system correctly, it is essential to understand the boot options available in the UEFI (Unified Extensible Firmware Interface), which has largely replaced the legacy BIOS in modern systems. UEFI is a firmware interface that initializes hardware and loads the operating system efficiently. You can access UEFI settings during startup by pressing specific keys, which may vary based on the manufacturer. Common keys include *F2*, *F10*, *Delete*, or *Esc*.

Unlike older systems, UEFI offers advanced features such as Secure Boot, faster boot times, and support for larger hard drives using GPT. To ensure a smooth installation process, configuring the boot order and verifying UEFI settings are vital for a successful installation of Windows Server 2025.

Within the UEFI settings, set the primary boot device to your installation media (USB or DVD) to initiate the Windows Server setup correctly.

Additionally, enabling Secure Boot is highly recommended to enhance security. This feature allows only trusted software to load during the boot process, helping prevent malware from altering it. Secure Boot is often required to comply with modern security standards, so ensure that you're using a GPT-partitioned drive, as Secure Boot does not support MBR partitions.

By confirming these configurations before installation, you can significantly reduce the likelihood of installation failures caused by mismatched boot settings or security incompatibilities, resulting in a more secure and seamless setup for Windows Server 2025.

When you enter the BIOS, you will see various boot options. Let us look at them:

- **Installation Media (DVD)**: A common type of installation media is a bootable DVD. To use this media, you need to prepare your computer to boot from the DVD drive. That requires you to access the BIOS settings and change the boot order. First, insert the bootable DVD into the drive that can read it. Then, enter the BIOS settings and select the DVD drive as the primary boot device. After saving the changes and exiting the BIOS, your computer will boot from the DVD and launch the installation process.

- **USB Flash Drive**: Another way to install an operating system is by using a bootable USB flash drive. This device must have at least 8 GB of storage space and be compatible with your computer. Before you start the installation, you need to plug in the USB flash drive and access your computer's BIOS settings. There, you need to choose the USB flash drive as the first option in the boot sequence. Then, you need to save your settings and exit the BIOS. Your computer will then boot from the USB flash drive and start the installation process.

- **Network Boot (PXE Boot)**: Another method of installing an operating system is network booting, which allows you to load the installation files from a remote server over the LAN. To use this method, you need to configure your computer to boot from the network. That involves accessing the BIOS settings and enabling the *network boot* option. You also need to set the network boot as the priority in the boot order. After saving your changes and exiting the BIOS, your computer will reboot and connect to the network server to start the installation process.

You can choose any of these methods to install an operating system, depending on your preferences and availability of resources. The installation process will vary depending on the source of the installation files.

Getting to know the startup process in BIOS

For any server technician, knowing how the hardware components and the startup process work is a valuable skill. It enables them to resolve issues related to hardware quickly and reduce downtime. To effectively diagnose and fix a server startup problem, they need to be familiar with the steps involved in starting up a server. Therefore, let us first examine the BIOS, which plays a crucial role in booting up a server.

When you power on a server, the initial activity involves a chip on the motherboard, known as ROM, which activates the BIOS program. The BIOS plays a crucial role in managing the server's hardware functionality. It detects and configures hardware components such as the CPU, memory, and disks. Additionally, the BIOS identifies bootable devices such as CD-ROMs, USB drives, and network interfaces, determining the sources from which the server can initiate the boot process. This process is illustrated in *Figure 2.3*.

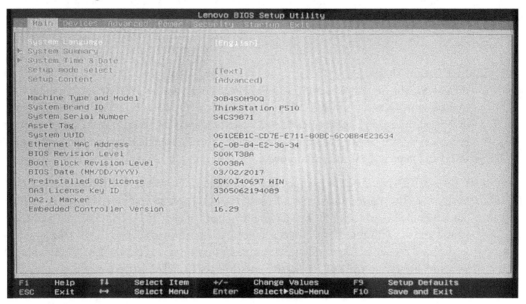

Figure 2.3 – The BIOS configuration screen

🔍 Quick tip: Need to see a high-resolution version of this image? Open this book in the next-gen Packt Reader or view it in the PDF/ePub copy.

🔖 **The next-gen Packt Reader** and a **free PDF/ePub copy** of this book are included with your purchase. Unlock them by scanning the QR code below or visiting https://www.packtpub.com/unlock/9781836205012.

However, BIOS has limitations and drawbacks that render it inadequate for modern servers. To address these issues, UEFI was developed as a replacement. UEFI provides numerous advantages over BIOS, including faster and more secure booting, support for larger disks and partitions, and an enhanced graphical interface. In the following section, we will explore UEFI in greater detail and examine its functionality in Windows Server 2025.

A different firmware program for booting modern computers

Modern computers no longer rely on the outdated BIOS system; instead, they utilize the UEFI, as depicted in *Figure 2.4*. Developed by the UEFI Consortium, UEFI addresses the limitations of BIOS in supporting contemporary hardware during startup. It can operate in both 32-bit and 64-bit processor modes and access the entire memory available in the system. UEFI employs the GPT partition scheme, which supports disks larger than 2 TB. Additionally, UEFI can be easily updated by downloading firmware updates from the manufacturer's website, offering a significant advantage over BIOS.

To access UEFI, begin by restarting your computer from the **Start** menu or by powering it off and on again. During the initial boot sequence, press the designated key or key combination to enter the UEFI settings; commonly used keys include *F2, F10, F12, Delete*, or *Esc*, though the specific key may vary depending on your computer's manufacturer and is often briefly shown on the screen. Once in the UEFI menu, use the arrow keys or mouse (if available) to navigate and configure various firmware settings, such as boot order, security options, and hardware configurations. Be sure to save any modifications before exiting to ensure that your changes are implemented.

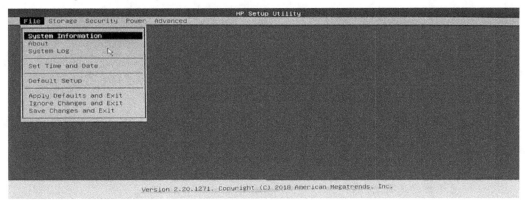

Figure 2.4 – The UEFI setup utility

Next, we will discuss the **Trusted Platform Module** (TPM).

Understanding TPM

The TPM is a security chip embedded in the server motherboard designed to store encryption keys, certificates, passwords, and other sensitive data securely. TPM plays a crucial role in measuring the integrity of the boot process, ensuring that no unauthorized changes have been made to the server's firmware, bootloader, or operating system. It works in conjunction with **BitLocker**, a feature that encrypts the server's disks to prevent unauthorized data access. BitLocker leverages TPM to store the encryption key, unlocking it only if the server successfully passes the integrity check. This collaboration between TPM and BitLocker provides robust security for the server's data, protecting against tampering and theft. *Figure 2.5* shows the TPM Management console in Windows Server 2025, accessible by typing tpm.msc in the **Run** dialog box.

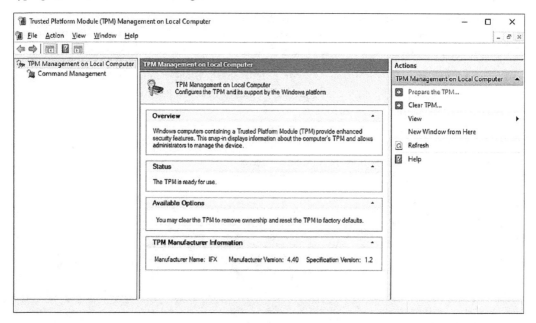

Figure 2.5 – The TPM Management console

Next, we will discuss the **Power-On Self-Test** (**POST**).

A crucial test for server hardware

For a server to start up correctly, its hardware must be in good condition. That is ensured by the POST (Power-On Self-Test), a diagnostic test that runs automatically when the server is powered on. POST checks the CPU, memory, disks, and other devices for errors or faults and communicates any issues through beep codes or error messages displayed on the screen or via the speaker. The POST process can be customized to run more or fewer tests to optimize boot time. As a vital tool for diagnosing and fixing hardware issues, POST is performed by the BIOS/UEFI, which manages server hardware operations.

Since different BIOS/UEFI manufacturers use varying beep codes, it is helpful to familiarize yourself with them. Beep codes are audio signals a computer's motherboard generates during startup to indicate hardware issues or errors. These codes contain short and long beep sequences that help diagnose problems when the system cannot provide visual error messages. Each beep pattern indicates a specific type of hardware malfunction, such as issues with memory, the graphics card, or the motherboard itself. To effectively troubleshoot and resolve these issues, users can consult the motherboard's manual or the manufacturer's documentation to decode the beep patterns and identify the underlying problems.

Particular attention should be paid to components like processors, memory, and graphics cards, as they are among the first to be tested by POST. If any of these components are defective, the server will not boot.

> **Note**
>
> For more information on the various beep codes used by different BIOS manufacturers, visit `https://www.computerhope.com/beep.htm`.

Next, we will discuss the GUID Partition Table (GPT) and the boot programs.

GPT and the boot programs

Once the server's hardware passes the POST, the BIOS/UEFI transfers control to the first boot device. The BIOS/UEFI then scans the boot device for the partition table, which indicates where the operating system is located. The partition table can be either MBR or GPT. GPT is a modern standard that supports larger disks and more features than MBR. It enhances reliability and recoverability by storing multiple copies of the partition table on the disk. Each partition in GPT is assigned a GUID, preventing conflicts and errors. GPT works with UEFI, a firmware program that replaces the traditional BIOS, providing a more secure and faster boot process. UEFI employs a boot loader capable of reading GPT partitions and loading the operating system from them. Depending on the Windows OS installed on the server's disk, the boot loader can be **NT Loader (NTLDR)**, **Boot Manager (BOOTMGR)**, or both. These programs are responsible for loading the OS into RAM. *Table 2.1* provides details on the NTLDR and BOOTMGR boot programs.

NTLDR (Windows NT to Windows Server 2003)	BOOTMGR (Windows Vista to Windows Server 2025)
BOOT.INI	Boot configuration data
NTDETECT.COM	WinLoad.exe
NTOSKRNL.EXE	NTOSKRNL.EXE
HAL.DLL	Boot-class device drivers

Table 2.1 – The boot programs NTLDR and BOOTMGR

Having covered the fundamentals of GPT, it's time to explore **Boot Configuration Data (BCD)**.

A database for booting Windows OS

BCD is a crucial database that stores settings and options for booting the Windows operating system. BCD can be managed and modified using the bcdedit.exe command-line tool or the graphical tool **BCDEdit**, which is part of the **Windows Recovery Environment**. It contains entries for each boot loader and operating system the server can load, such as NTLDR or BOOTMGR. It includes parameters for configuring the boot environment, such as display mode, memory limits, debugging options, and recovery settings. BCD is essential for managing the boot process and troubleshooting boot issues. It provides a standardized boot option interface for modern Windows OS versions, from Windows Vista to Windows Server 2025, regardless of the firmware, enhancing security compared to the previous boot.ini system. Administrators can set permissions to manage boot options, and BCD is accessible during all stages of system configuration. For example, bcdedit.exe (see *Figure 2.6*) is a file used to access the BCD data store located inside the disk partitions, unlike boot.ini.

Figure 2.6 – Running bcdedit.exe in Windows Server 2025

In a multiboot scenario, both NTLDR and BOOTMGR may be present, with boot.ini and bcdedit.exe displaying the respective OS lists. In such cases, bootsect.exe (discussed later in the *Understanding boot sector* section) can be used to update the MBR for hard disk partitions requiring a switch between NTLDR and BOOTMGR.

When installing Windows Server 2025, disk partitioning and driver compatibility challenges are common. Disk partitioning issues often arise with mismatched partition styles (MBR for legacy BIOS or GPT for UEFI) or insufficient space on a partition, which can be resolved by verifying the boot mode, using compatible partition styles, and ensuring NTFS formatting. Driver compatibility challenges may occur when the installation doesn't recognize certain hardware components, such as storage controllers. To address this, download the latest drivers from the manufacturer, load them during setup, and consider switching the boot mode if necessary to resolve conflicts. Addressing these issues before installation can streamline the setup and reduce errors.

With an established understanding of GPT and BCD, let us now explore the bootloader.

What is the bootloader?

A **bootloader**, also known as a **bootstrap loader** or **boot manager**, is a critical program responsible for initiating a computer's startup process. Once the POST confirms that the hardware is functioning correctly, the bootloader takes control. It resides in the MBR/GPT and is tasked with loading the Windows OS kernel into memory or onto disk. Windows operating systems utilize two main bootloaders, shown earlier in *Table 2.1*:

- **NTLDR**: The older bootloader used from Windows NT through Windows Server 2003
- **BOOTMGR**: The newer bootloader employed from Windows Vista to Windows Server 2025

Next, we will explore the boot sector, which contains the essential information needed to load the bootloader and start the server.

What is the boot sector?

The **boot sector** is a critical region on a disk that contains the essential information required to start the computer. Located in the first sector of the initial track on the disk, it typically includes either the MBR or the GPT. These are small programs responsible for initiating the bootloader. The bootloader, in turn, loads the Windows OS kernel into memory or onto disk. Depending on the Windows OS version, the bootloader could be NTLDR or BOOTMGR. The boot sector is fundamental to the boot process and must be compatible with the system's firmware (BIOS or UEFI) and partition scheme (MBR or GPT). Therefore, in systems using BIOS with MBR, the boot sector is made up of the MBR, which incorporates both the **Master Boot Code** (**MBC**) and the **Partition Table** (**PT**), a common setup in older computers or those running Windows 7 and earlier. Conversely, BIOS systems using GPT rely on a **Protective MBR** (**PMBR**) to ensure compatibility by simulating an MBR layout, thus avoiding problems with software that does not recognize GPT. UEFI systems that utilize MBR do so with a **Compatibility Support Module** (**CSM**) to mimic traditional BIOS boot processes, enabling UEFI firmware to interact with the MBR as if it were a BIOS system, typically seen in configurations running Windows 7 or older Linux versions. On the other hand, UEFI systems with GPT include the **EFI System Partition** (**ESP**), which stores the boot loaders and essential files needed to start the operating system, a standard setup for modern systems running Windows 10 or recent Linux distributions. These scenarios illustrate how various firmware and partition schemes interact with boot sectors to manage system startup and ensure compatibility.

Next, we will examine the boot menu, which facilitates the selection of different operating systems when multiple OSes are installed on the computer.

How to use the boot menu?

The **boot menu** is a valuable feature for selecting from multiple Windows operating systems installed on your computer, a process known as **multi-booting**. This capability is particularly beneficial for testing or troubleshooting different OS configurations. When you start your computer, the boot menu appears, allowing you to choose the OS to boot into. For older Windows versions, such as Windows NT through Windows Server 2003, this menu is managed by a text file called `boot.ini`, located in the root partition of the disk, typically `C:\boot.ini`. This file contains essential boot options, including the bootloader and available operating systems. In contrast, newer Windows versions, from Windows Vista to Windows Server 2025, utilize the BCD database to control boot settings.

The `boot.ini` file, which represents a critical configuration component, was used in earlier Windows operating systems such as Windows XP and Windows Server 2003. This file plays a key role in handling multiple operating systems on a single computer by listing all installed OSes and their corresponding boot options. It enables users to choose which operating system to boot into during system startup. Each entry within the `boot.ini` file details the path to the OS kernel files and includes parameters such as boot timeout settings and default options. Showcasing this configuration demonstrates how `boot.ini` facilitates the management and selection of different operating systems, simplifying the boot process and user experience.

The boot menu also provides access to Safe Mode, a diagnostic mode that loads only essential drivers and services. Safe Mode is valuable for identifying and resolving system issues.

How does Safe Mode operate?

When you encounter issues with booting your Windows operating system, such as improper loading or system crashes, **Safe Mode** can be a valuable diagnostic tool. Safe Mode is a troubleshooting feature that starts Windows with only the essential drivers and services necessary for basic functionality. This minimal setup can help you identify and resolve issues affecting your system. The method to access Safe Mode varies based on the Windows version you are using. For older versions such as Windows NT through Windows Server 2003, you can press the *F8* key during the boot process and select **Safe Mode** from **Windows Advanced Options Menu**, as depicted in *Figure 2.7*.

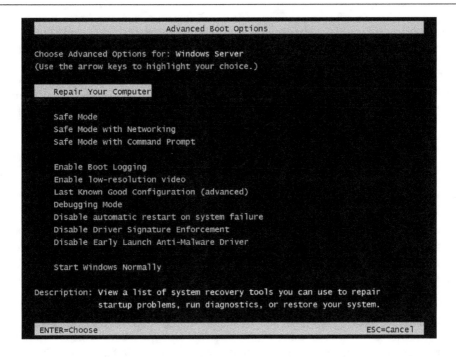

Figure 2.7 – Advanced Boot Options in Windows Server 2025

For newer versions, including Windows Vista through Windows Server 2025, you need to utilize the **Advanced startup** options. That involves holding down the *Shift* key while selecting **Restart** from the **Power** menu. Follow these steps to enter Safe Mode:

1. On the **Choose an option** screen, select **Troubleshoot**.
2. On the **Advanced options** screen, click **Startup Settings**.
3. Press the **Restart** button on the **Startup Settings** screen.
4. Once the system restarts, the **Advanced Boot Options** screen will appear, as shown in *Figure 2.8*. From there, select the **Safe Mode** option.

Windows setup and disk configuration errors

When preparing for the installation of Windows Server 2025, it's crucial to address common disk configuration errors to ensure a smooth setup process. One of the first considerations is the filesystem format requirements. Windows Server 2025 primarily utilizes the NTFS for system drives, which supports larger files and volumes compared to FAT32. If your drives are formatted in an incompatible filesystem, such as FAT32 or exFAT, you will need to reformat them to NTFS.

To format a drive or change its partition size, you can use Disk Management, a built-in Windows utility that provides a graphical interface for managing disk partitions. Here's how you can use Disk Management to resolve formatting issues:

- **Access Disk Management**: Right-click on the **Start** menu and select **Disk Management**. This will open the **Disk Management** console, where you can view all connected drives and their partitions.

- **Format a drive**: If a drive is not formatted or needs to be changed to NTFS, right-click on the partition and select **Format**. Choose **NTFS** as the filesystem and follow the prompts to complete the formatting process. Ensure that you back up any important data before formatting, as this will erase all data on the drive.

- **Resize partitions**: If you encounter errors due to insufficient space on a partition, you can resize partitions using Disk Management. Right-click on the partition you wish to resize and select **Shrink Volume** or **Extend Volume**. Shrinking a volume allows you to free up space for other partitions while extending a volume can help you add space to a partition that is running low.

- **Confirm compatibility**: After making changes, confirm that the drives are now in the NTFS format and that the sizes meet the installation requirements for Windows Server 2025.

By proactively managing your disk configuration and ensuring compatibility with NTFS, you can minimize the likelihood of encountering errors during the installation process, leading to a smoother and more efficient setup of Windows Server 2025.

In this section, we have explored various elements of the Windows boot process, including BIOS, UEFI, TPM, POST, MBR, BCD, bootloaders, boot sectors, boot menus, Safe Mode, and disk configuration errors. The following section will focus on business continuity and the strategy for maintaining it.

Installation options for Windows Server 2025

When deploying Windows Server, selecting the appropriate installation option is crucial to meet your specific needs. Windows Server provides various installation options, each catering to different requirements in terms of disk space, memory usage, features, and graphical interfaces. These options also influence security, performance, management, and compatibility. This section will explore and compare the three primary installation options for Windows Server: **Desktop Experience**, **Server Core**, and **Nano Server**. We will discuss the benefits and considerations of each, along with guidance on how to switch between them based on your operational needs. By the end of this section, you will be equipped to choose the most suitable installation option for your Windows Server deployment.

Understanding the role of your server

When installing Windows Server 2025, it's crucial to consider the specific roles and responsibilities your server will fulfill. This foresight can significantly influence the configuration choices you make during installation, including hardware specifications and service selection.

- **Assessing workloads**: Determine whether your server will primarily handle read operations, write operations, or a balanced mix of both. For example, a file server that primarily serves files to multiple clients may benefit from faster disk speeds and larger RAM to accommodate high read demands. In contrast, a database server that handles extensive write operations may require optimized storage solutions and potentially more robust processing power.

- **Memory requirements**: Different server roles may have varied memory requirements. For instance, virtualization servers typically need more RAM to manage multiple virtual machines effectively. Ensuring your server has adequate memory will help maintain performance and responsiveness under load.

- **Selecting components and services**: Choosing the right components is critical. For a web server, you might prioritize **network interface cards** (**NICs**) for high-speed connectivity. In contrast, for a database server, you might focus on fast, high-capacity disks to handle data transactions efficiently.

- **Planning for future growth**: When planning your installation, consider future scalability. Will the server need to accommodate more users or handle increased data? Factor this into your hardware choices to avoid potential bottlenecks as demands grow.

By integrating these considerations into your installation planning, you can ensure that your Windows Server 2025 environment is tailored to effectively meet your organizational needs.

Pre-installation checks – resource compatibility checks

Before diving into the installation of Windows Server 2025, it is essential to perform thorough resource compatibility checks to ensure that your hardware meets the necessary requirements for optimal performance. This step can save time and prevent frustration during and after the installation process. Here are key points to consider:

- **System requirements**: Verify that your hardware meets or exceeds the minimum system requirements for Windows Server 2025. Key specifications include the following:

  - **CPU**: Ensure that the processor is compatible with Windows Server 2025, typically requiring a minimum of a 1.4 GHz 64-bit processor. Consider opting for a multi-core processor for better performance, especially in environments with multiple users or applications.

  - **RAM**: Confirm that the server has adequate RAM. The minimum requirement is generally 2 GB, but for better performance and to handle heavier workloads, it's advisable to have 4 GB or more, depending on the intended use and applications.

- **Resource availability**: In addition to meeting the minimum specifications, check the availability of resources on the server. This includes the following:

  - **Disk space**: Ensure that there is enough disk space for the installation, as well as for future updates and applications. A minimum of 32 GB of free space is often recommended, though more may be needed based on your configuration and usage scenarios.

  - **Network resources**: Assess network bandwidth and connectivity, particularly if you are deploying in a cloud or hybrid environment. Sufficient bandwidth is necessary for downloading updates, accessing network resources, and ensuring a smooth installation process.

- **Performance considerations**: Installing Windows Server on underpowered hardware can lead to performance issues that affect not only the server's operation but also any applications or services running on it. By ensuring compatibility and availability of resources upfront, you can avoid potential performance bottlenecks post-installation.

- **Compatibility with existing applications**: If you plan to run specific applications on Windows Server 2025, double-check their compatibility with the new operating system version. Some applications may have specific resource requirements that need to be accounted for.

By conducting these resource compatibility checks before installation, you set the foundation for a successful deployment of Windows Server 2025, minimizing the likelihood of performance-related problems down the line. This proactive approach not only enhances system reliability but also optimizes the overall user experience.

Which installation option for Windows Server 2025 should I choose?

When installing Windows Server 2025, you have three distinct options to choose from, each offering unique advantages and limitations based on your server needs, hardware specifications, and management preferences. The following is an overview of each option:

- **Desktop Experience**: This option provides a complete **graphical user interface** (**GUI**) along with all associated tools and functionalities of Windows Server 2025. While it offers a comprehensive user experience, it requires more hardware resources and might present a higher security risk compared to the other options.

- **Server Core**: Recommended by Microsoft for its efficiency, Server Core is a minimal installation option that omits the GUI, focusing instead on core server functionalities. It consumes fewer resources and has a reduced attack surface. Management can be performed locally via **Windows PowerShell** or remotely using **Server Manager**.

- **Nano Server**: An advanced version of Server Core, Nano Server is designed to be even more lightweight and efficient. It supports only 64-bit applications and lacks local login capabilities, requiring management through remote tools such as **Windows Admin Center** or **Windows PowerShell**. Nano Server is particularly suited for cloud environments or containerized applications that demand minimal maintenance and updates.

Before proceeding with the installation of Windows Server 2025, evaluate these options to determine which best aligns with your operational requirements. In the next section, I will guide you through comparing Nano Server with Server Core.

Comparing Nano Server and Server Core

This section compares and discusses the Nano server and the server core.

Here is an overview of the Nano Server:

- **Lightweight deployment**: Nano Server is a headless (no GUI) installation option for Windows Server that is optimized for cloud environments and containers. It has a minimal footprint, making it ideal for running specific workloads efficiently.
- **Use cases**: Nano Server is particularly suited for microservices, cloud applications, and containerized environments. It's often used for hosting web services, application servers, and specialized workloads such as Hyper-V.

Here is an overview of the Server Core:

- **Reduced installation**: Server Core is a minimal installation option for Windows Server that offers a reduced GUI (no traditional desktop interface) but retains the command-line tools and Windows Management Framework. It provides a balance between functionality and resource consumption.
- **Use cases**: Server Core is suitable for traditional server roles such as **Active Directory Domain Services** (**AD DS**), DNS, and file services. It's commonly deployed in environments where administrators require more features than Nano Server but still want to limit the server's attack surface.

Comparison and scenarios

These are the considerations for choosing Nano Server:

- **Containerization**: If an organization is moving toward microservices and containerization, Nano Server is an excellent choice due to its lightweight nature and compatibility with Docker
- **Cloud-first deployments**: For enterprises focused on cloud-native applications, using Nano Server in Azure or hybrid environments can optimize resource usage and speed up deployment times
- **Web applications**: Nano Server is ideal for hosting **Internet Information Services** (IIS) and web applications that require a small footprint and high performance

These are the considerations for choosing Server Core:

- **Traditional roles**: If the server needs to support traditional roles such as AD DS or file services, Server Core is the better option. It provides the necessary functionalities without the overhead of a full GUI.

- **Compatibility requirements**: For applications that require compatibility with more traditional Windows server features or management tools, Server Core offers a more robust environment while still limiting the surface area for potential attacks.

- **Management needs**: Server Core allows for remote management via PowerShell, which is essential in larger enterprises where centralized management is critical.

By providing specific use cases for both Nano Server and Server Core, you can better understand how to select the appropriate installation option based on your organizational needs and workload requirements. This approach not only clarifies the differences but also illustrates how these technologies fit into modern IT strategies. Next, we will examine using logs to diagnose installation failures.

Using logs to diagnose installation failures

When facing installation issues with Windows Server 2025, log analysis can be an invaluable tool for diagnosing and resolving problems. Windows Setup generates several logs that contain detailed information about the installation process, helping administrators identify where the failure occurred. Two key logs to focus on are `setupact.log` and `setuperr.log`.

Key installation logs

Following are the key installation logs:

- `setupact.log`: This log records the entire installation process and contains timestamps, component states, and detailed information about actions taken during the setup. It is generally located in the `C:\Windows\Panther` directory. This log is useful for identifying the overall flow of the installation and determining which stage may have encountered issues.

- `setuperr.log`: In contrast, this log captures errors encountered during installation. It provides information about any failures that prevented components from installing successfully. This log is also found in the `C:\Windows\Panther` directory and is critical for troubleshooting specific error messages that may appear during the installation.

Locating installation logs

Here is how you locate installation logs:

- After a failed installation, access the logs by booting into the recovery environment or using a bootable USB drive to access the `C:\Windows\Panther` folder

- Copy the log files to a USB drive or a secondary drive for analysis, as these logs are essential for diagnosing issues

Interpreting the logs

The following details how you interpret the logs:

- Open `setupact.log` in a text editor and scroll through the entries to find any abnormal entries or timestamps that correspond to the installation failure. Look for keywords such as `error`, `failed`, or `warning` to identify problematic areas.

- In `setuperr.log`, review the entries for error codes or specific messages indicating what went wrong. Microsoft's documentation can provide insights into specific error codes, aiding in finding resolutions.

Action steps

The following details the steps you take as action after interpreting the logs:

- Once you identify the errors, cross-reference the error messages with Microsoft's knowledge base or community forums for potential solutions. Common issues may involve driver compatibility, disk partitioning problems, or network configuration errors.

By understanding and utilizing these logs effectively, administrators can streamline the troubleshooting process and enhance their ability to resolve installation issues with Windows Server 2025, ensuring a smoother setup experience. Next, we will look at network connectivity and domain joining, emphasizing how vital network connectivity is for domain-joining tasks.

Network connectivity and domain joining

When deploying Windows Server 2025, mainly through network installations, ensuring reliable network connectivity is crucial for successful domain joining and overall deployment. Network-related issues can prevent the server from accessing essential resources or joining the domain properly. Here are some troubleshooting steps to address these common challenges:

1. **Verify IP configuration**: Ensure that the server has a valid IP address by checking the network settings. For static IP configurations, confirm that the IP address is correctly assigned and falls within the appropriate range for your network. If using DHCP, ensure that the server successfully receives an IP address from the DHCP server.

2. **Check DNS settings**: The **Domain Name System** (**DNS**) is vital for locating domain controllers and other network resources. Confirm that the server is pointing to the correct DNS servers, typically the IP addresses of your domain controllers. You can test DNS resolution by using the `nslookup` command to ensure the server can resolve domain names.

3. **Examine firewall configurations**: Firewalls can block necessary communication between the server and the domain controller. Review the firewall settings to ensure that the appropriate ports are open. For domain joining, ensure that ports such as 53 (DNS), 88 (Kerberos), and 389 (LDAP) are allowed through the firewall. You may need to temporarily disable the firewall for testing purposes to see whether it's causing the issue.

4. **Ping the domain controller**: Use the `ping` command to check connectivity to the domain controller. This simple test can help identify whether the server can reach the DC. If `ping` fails, investigate network routing, cabling, or switch issues that may be affecting connectivity.

5. **Review network adapter settings**: Confirm that the network adapter settings are correctly configured. Check for issues such as network adapter being disabled, improper VLAN settings, or connectivity issues with physical network hardware.

6. **Logs and error messages**: Pay attention to any error messages during the installation or domain joining process. Windows Server logs can provide insights into what went wrong. Check the Event Viewer for any relevant logs that might indicate network-related problems.

By following these troubleshooting steps, administrators can effectively diagnose and resolve network connectivity issues that may arise during the deployment of Windows Server 2025, ensuring a smooth domain joining process and reliable network performance. Next, activation and licenses are considered important elements of smooth operations on a Windows Server 2025.

Activation and licensing issues

When installing Windows Server 2025, it is crucial to address activation and licensing, particularly when deploying in Azure or hybrid environments. Proper activation ensures that the operating system is genuine and can receive essential updates and features. However, users may encounter common activation problems during or after the installation process. Understanding how to troubleshoot these issues can save time and ensure compliance with licensing agreements.

One common issue is activation failure due to connectivity problems. In cloud or hybrid setups, ensure that your server has a stable internet connection to reach Microsoft's activation servers. For Azure deployments, confirm that the correct Azure resource group and virtual network settings are in place. If activation fails despite proper connectivity, it may be necessary to use the `slmgr` command-line tool to troubleshoot. Running commands such as `slmgr /ato` attempts to activate the product key manually, providing feedback on any specific issues encountered.

Licensing issues can also arise when using volume licensing keys in multiple environments. Each instance of Windows Server must be properly licensed, and organizations using volume activation should verify that they are following the required licensing model. For hybrid deployments, consider using Azure Hybrid Benefit, which allows existing Windows Server licenses to be applied to Azure virtual machines, reducing costs. Ensure that the necessary licenses are linked to your Azure subscription and that you understand the implications of your licensing choice on compliance and support.

Addressing activation and licensing issues early in the installation process is vital for the smooth deployment of Windows Server 2025. By ensuring proper connectivity, utilizing command-line tools for troubleshooting, and understanding licensing models, organizations can avoid potential disruptions and maintain compliance in their cloud and hybrid environments. Next, let us examine the various deployment methods of Windows Server 2025.

Various methods for deploying Windows Server 2025

Several installation methods are available for Windows Server 2025, each suited to a different scenario. Here are some common approaches.

Clean install

This method involves setting up a fresh instance of Windows Server 2025 on a server and erasing any previous data or configurations. It is ideal for new deployments or when starting with a clean slate.

Chapter exercise 2.1 – performing a clean installation of Windows Server 2025

When installing Windows Server 2025 on a new or existing hard drive, a clean installation is an effective option. This process will remove the current operating system from the disk and replace it with a fresh installation of Windows Server 2025. Although you will need to interact with the setup, it is less intensive than performing an upgrade. Follow these steps for a clean installation:

Insert the bootable media, plug in a USB flash drive, or connect a network cable to the server.

1. Power on your computer and select your preferred boot option, such as DVD, USB flash drive, or network boot. A confirmation message will appear on the screen.
2. The installation files will load into memory (RAM).

3.   Choose your language and other preferences for the installation, then click **Next**, as shown in *Figure 2.8*.

Figure 2.8 – Selecting language settings

4.   Choose the keyboard or other input method and then click Next.

5.   Select the **Install Windows Server** option and ensure that I agree that everything will be deleted, including files, apps, and settings box, and that it is checked, as shown in Figure 2.9. Click **Next**.

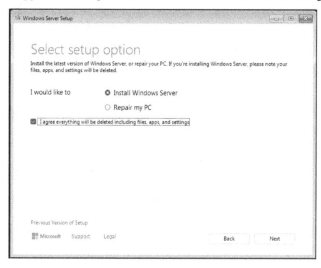

Figure 2.9 – Selecting setup option

6. Select **Windows Server 2025 Datacenter (Desktop Experience)** and click **Next**, as illustrated in *Figure 2.10*.

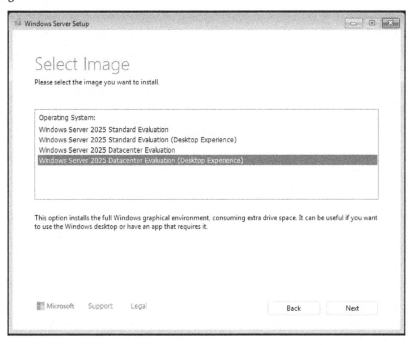

Figure 2.10 – Selecting the image to install

7. Take the time to read the Applicable notices and license terms. Click Accept.

8.   Select a location to install Windows Server 2025, as shown in *Figure 2.11*.Click Next.

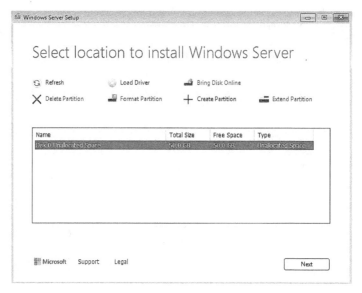

Figure 2.11 – Selecting disk or partition to install Windows Server 2025

9.   On the **Ready to install** page of Windows Server Setup, click the **Install** button, as illustrated in *Figure 2.12*.

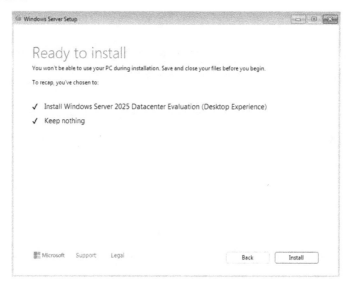

Figure 2.12 – Starting the installation of Windows Server 2025

10. Windows Server Setup will now begin installing Windows Server 2025. You can sit back and relax during this process.

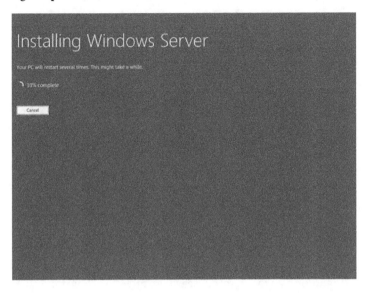

Figure 2.13 – Starting the installation of Windows Server 2025

11. After the installation is complete and the system restarts several times, set up the administrator password and click **Finish**, as shown in *Figure 2.14*.

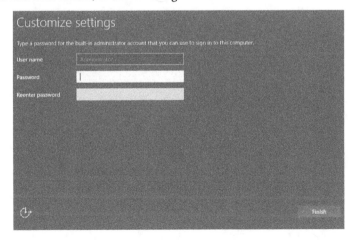

Figure 2.14 – Setting up an administrator's password

12. Press **Ctrl + Alt + Delete** to unlock the system, as depicted in Figure 2.15. Enter the administrator password and press **Enter** to log in for your first login.

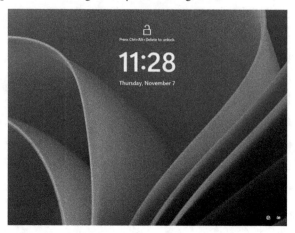

Figure 2.15 - Press Ctrl+Alt+Del to unlock the system

13. In Send diagnostic data to Microsoft, select the preferred choice and click Accept.

14. Congratulations! You have successfully installed Windows Server 2025, as in Figure 2.16.

Figure 2.16 Start menu and desktop in Windows Server 2025

> **Note**
>
> One of Microsoft's standout features is the **Windows Installer**, an **application programming interface (API)** for software installation, maintenance, and uninstallation.

With the clean installation process mastered, you are now ready to explore other installation methods. Next, we will delve into deploying Windows Server 2025 using the MDT.

Deploying with the MDT

By using the MDT, you can streamline and automate the installation process. This method is particularly useful for deploying multiple servers efficiently and consistently.

Chapter exercise 2.2 – performing an installation of Windows Server 2025 using the MDT

An unattended installation automates the deployment process, requiring minimal interaction. This method is ideal for deploying multiple servers in enterprise environments. Although Microsoft has deprecated WDS in Windows 11 and Windows Server 2025, the Windows ADK and MDT offer robust alternatives for automating installations. These tools, available for download, simplify the deployment process.

The key to an unattended installation is the **answer file**, an XML file that provides the necessary responses to installation prompts. You can create an answer file manually using Notepad or download sample files from the internet. Microsoft also offers several tools to aid in this process, such as the **Windows System Image Manager (Windows SIM)** included in the Windows Assessment and Deployment Kit (ADK) and the Microsoft Deployment Toolkit (MDT).

> **Note**
>
> Microsoft's official documentation offers a range of examples and in-depth explanations via the **Windows System Image Manager (WSIM)** answer file. For example, although the **TechNet Gallery** has been archived, it still provides valuable community-contributed samples for various scenarios. **GitHub** repositories often host user-shared answer files that cater to different deployment requirements. **Deployment Research** offers a collection of practical templates and samples with detailed explanations for Windows deployment. Additionally, **Microsoft Learn** provides extensive guides and examples on creating and utilizing answer files, complete with downloadable samples. These resources are essential for finding and comprehending answer file samples and facilitating efficient Windows deployment and configuration.

To install Windows Server 2025 using the MDT, follow these steps:

1. Download and install the Windows ADK on a Windows 11 computer (see *Figure 2.17*).

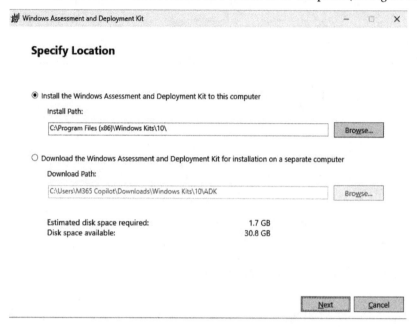

Figure 2.17 – Installing Windows ADK

2. Download and install **Windows Preinstallation Environment** (**Windows PE**) by running `adkwinpesetup.exe` (refer to *Figure 2.18*).

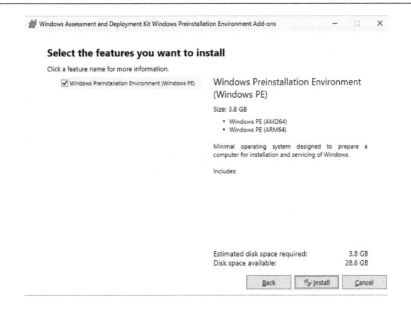

Figure 2.18 – Installing Windows PE

3. Install MDT on a Windows 11 computer, as illustrated in *Figure 2.19*.

Figure 2.19 – Installing the MDT

4. After installing the Windows ADK, PE, and MDT, run **Deployment Workbench** and select **New Deployment Share Wizard** (*Figure 2.20*).

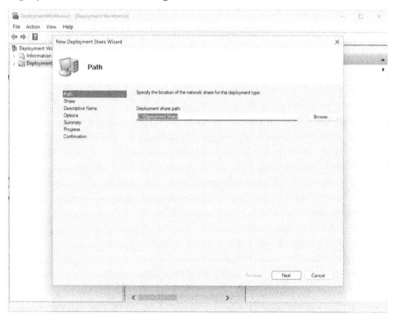

Figure 2.20 – New Deployment Share Wizard

5. Share the DeploymentShare folder through File Explorer, allowing **Everyone to read** permissions.

6. Run **Import Operating System Wizard** to import the Windows Server 2025 files.

7. Use **New Task Sequence Wizard** to create the answer file for the unattended installation.

8. On **MDT Deployment Share Properties**, within the **Platforms Supported** section, uncheck **x86**, as depicted in *Figure 2.21*, and click **OK**.

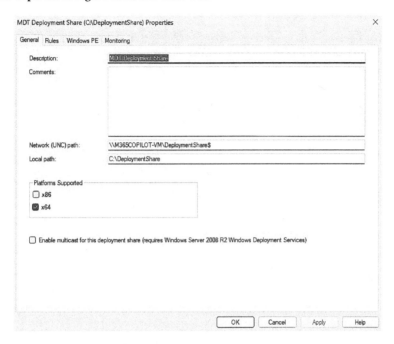

Figure 2.21 – Disabling the x86 platform on the MDT

9. Update the deployment share to create a bootable PE image.

10. Boot the new server with the **LiteTouchPE_x64 image**, located in the `Boot` subfolder of the `DeploymentShare` folder. After a successful boot, select **Run the Deployment Wizard to install a new Operating System** (*Figure 2.22*).

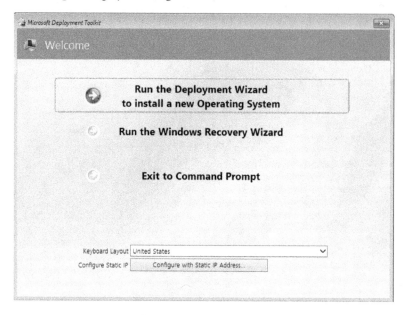

Figure 2.22 – Deploying Windows Server 2025 over the MDT

11. Provide credentials to access the `DeploymentShare` folder, ensuring the user has complete control.

12. Select the task sequence and the answer file created earlier with **Deployment Workbench**, then click **Next**.

13. Enter the computer details, locale, and time settings, and specify whether to capture the image or configure BitLocker.

14. Begin the deployment of Windows Server 2025 (see *Figure 2.23*).

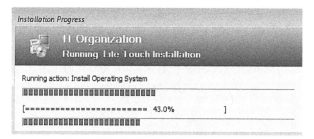

Figure 2.23 – Installing the operating system over the MDT

15. The MDT will then handle the deployment of Windows Server 2025. Once the installation process is completed, the system will configure the devices, and **Windows Server 2025 Standard** (Desktop Experience) will be successfully deployed.

> **Note**
>
> You can obtain the Windows ADK by visiting this link: `https://learn.microsoft.com/en-us/windows-hardware/get-started/adk-install#download-the-adk-101261001-may-2024`. For the MDT, download it from this page: `https://www.microsoft.com/en-us/download/details.aspx?id=54259`.

Now, let us explore how to perform an in-place upgrade, which allows you to update the existing OS to a newer version while retaining user settings, applications, and data.

In-place upgrade

This approach upgrades an existing Windows Server installation to Windows Server 2025, preserving existing settings and data. It is suitable for updating from previous versions while maintaining the current configuration.

Chapter exercise 2.3 – performing an in-place upgrade of Windows Server 2022 to Windows Server 2025

To change your current operating system to a newer one, you can do an upgrade. This way, you can keep your files and settings as they are. That is also known as an **in-place upgrade** because it takes place on a machine that already has an operating system installed. Before doing an upgrade, it is advisable to back up the Windows state, files, and folders. Microsoft says that Windows Server 2025 can be upgraded directly from Windows Server 2012 R2, 2016, 2019, or 2022.

To do an in-place upgrade from Windows Server 2022 to Windows Server 2025, follow these steps:

1. Insert the Windows Server 2025 installation disk or connect the bootable USB flash drive and run the setup file.

2. The **Install Windows Server** window will show up. Click **Next** to continue, as shown in *Figure 2.24*.

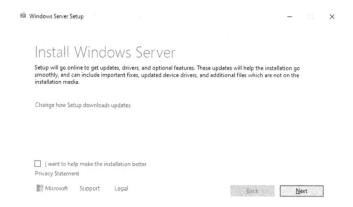

Figure 2.24 – Beginning the in-place upgrade in Windows Server 2022

3. As shown in *Figure 2.25*, select the Windows Server 2025 edition you want to install and click **Next**.

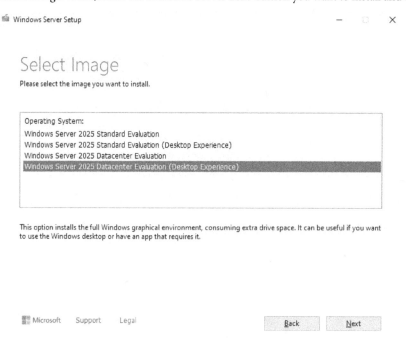

Figure 2.25 – Pick the Windows Server 2025 edition to install

4. Click the **Accept** button in **Applicable notices and license terms** to agree to the license terms.

5. Select what to keep, and then click **Next** to continue.

6. Once the updates are downloaded and the Windows Server 2022 setup ensures there is enough disk space on the server, you are ready to install. Click the **Install** button to continue with the upgrade, as shown in *Figure 2.26*

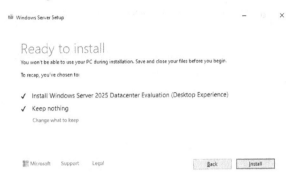

Figure 2.26 – Ready to run the in-place upgrade

7. The in-place upgrade will begin. Either relax or do other work until the upgrade is completed.

8. After several restarts, the upgrade from Windows Server 2022 to Windows Server 2025 will be completed successfully, as shown in *Figure 2.27*.

Figure 2.27 – The system properties confirm the in-place upgrade

Next, let us learn how to perform the migration using the **Windows Server Migration Tool (WSMT)**. This will help migrate the services from an old server to a new one.

Migration

Migration involves moving from an older server or environment to Windows Server 2025, often using tools or services to transfer applications, data, and settings to the new server.

Chapter exercise 2.4 – migrating network services from Windows Server 2012 R2 to Windows Server 2025

When upgrading to a new server, whether physical or virtual, you must transfer roles, features, applications, settings, and network services from the old server to the new one. This process is known as migration. Start by installing the operating system on the new server and then initiate the migration. Ensure that Windows Server 2025 is compatible with your existing applications. The WSMT feature can assist with migration, and **PowerShell cmdlets** can be used to migrate specific services.

For example, to migrate the **DHCP server** from an old server (Windows Server 2012 R2) to a new server (Windows Server 2025), follow these steps:

1. On the old server (Windows Server 2012 R2), open **Windows PowerShell** as an administrator and run the following cmdlet :

```
Export-DhcpServer -File C:\DHCPdata.xml -Leases -Force
-ComputerName <OldServerName> -Verbose
```

💡 **Quick tip**: Enhance your coding experience with the **AI Code Explainer** and **Quick Copy** features. Open this book in the next-gen Packt Reader. Click the **Copy** button (**1**) to quickly copy code into your coding environment, or click the **Explain** button (**2**) to get the AI assistant to explain a block of code to you.

```
                                              Copy      Explain
function calculate(a, b) {
  return {sum: a + b};                          1          2
};
```

🔒 **The next-gen Packt Reader** is included for free with the purchase of this book. Unlock it by scanning the QR code below or visiting https://www.packtpub.com/unlock/9781836205012.

2. Stop the DHCP service and move the DHCPdata.xml file to a shared folder that is accessible to everyone.

3. On the new server (Windows Server 2025), use **Server Manager** to add the **DHCP Server** role, as shown in *Figure 2.28*.

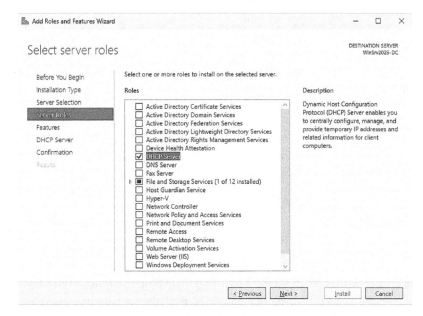

Figure 2.28 – Adding DHCP Server to a new server

4. Access the shared folder on the old server and copy the `DHCPdata.xml` file to the root directory on the new server.

5. Open Windows PowerShell as an administrator on the new server and run the following cmdlet (see *Figure 2.29*):

```
Import-DhcpServer -File C:\DHCPdata.xml -BackupPath C:\
DHCP\ -Leases -ScopeOverwrite -Force -ComputerName
<NewServerName> -Verbose
```

```
Windows PowerShell
Copyright (C) Microsoft Corporation. All rights reserved.

Install the latest PowerShell for new features and improvements! https://aka.ms/PSWindows

PS C:\Users\Administrator> Import-DhcpServer -File C:\DHCPdata.xml -BackupPath C:\DHCP\ -Leases -ScopeOverwrite -Force -
ComputerName WinSrv2025-DC -Verbose
VERBOSE: The configuration (and leases) from the file C:\DHCPdata.xml will be imported to server WinSrv2025-DC.
VERBOSE: Dhcp Server database has been backed up at C:\DHCP\ on WinSrv2025-DC.
VERBOSE: Importing configuration on server WinSrv2025-DC from file C:\DHCPdata.xml.
VERBOSE: Importing classes on server...
VERBOSE: Class 'Default Routing and Remote Access Class' of type User already exists on server WinSrv2025-DC and will
not be changed.
VERBOSE: Class 'Default BOOTP Class' of type User already exists on server WinSrv2025-DC and will not be changed.
VERBOSE: Class 'Microsoft Windows 2000 Options' of type Vendor already exists on server WinSrv2025-DC and will not be
changed.
VERBOSE: Class 'Microsoft Windows 98 Options' of type Vendor already exists on server WinSrv2025-DC and will not be
changed.
VERBOSE: Class 'Microsoft Options' of type Vendor already exists on server WinSrv2025-DC and will not be changed.
VERBOSE: Importing option definitions on server...
VERBOSE: Option definition Classless Static Routes already exists on server WinSrv2025-DC and will not be changed.
VERBOSE: Option definition Subnet Mask already exists on server WinSrv2025-DC and will not be changed.
VERBOSE: Option definition Time Offset already exists on server WinSrv2025-DC and will not be changed.
VERBOSE: Option definition Router already exists on server WinSrv2025-DC and will not be changed.
VERBOSE: Option definition Time Server already exists on server WinSrv2025-DC and will not be changed.
VERBOSE: Option definition Name Servers already exists on server WinSrv2025-DC and will not be changed.
VERBOSE: Option definition DNS Servers already exists on server WinSrv2025-DC and will not be changed.
VERBOSE: Option definition Log Servers already exists on server WinSrv2025-DC and will not be changed.
VERBOSE: Option definition Cookie Servers already exists on server WinSrv2025-DC and will not be changed.
VERBOSE: Option definition LPR Servers already exists on server WinSrv2025-DC and will not be changed.
```

Figure 2.29 – Importing the DHCP Server to the new server

6. Restart the DHCP service. Once the restart is complete, the DHCP server will be successfully migrated to the new server.

Next, we will explore how to install Windows Server 2025 in the cloud, such as on Microsoft Azure, to facilitate running services in a cloud environment.

Deploying in Azure

Nowadays, where businesses rely heavily on cloud services, an operating system optimized for cloud environments is essential. Multiple services from the cloud undoubtedly need an operating system optimized for the cloud environment. For about 25 years, Microsoft has offered Windows Server for midrange servers for businesses that want to entrust their network services to a cloud-based solution, ensuring scalability, reliability, and optimized performance for cloud operations.

Chapter exercise 2.5 – installing Windows Server 2025 on Azure

To explore Windows Server 2025 without impacting your existing machines, consider using **Microsoft Azure**, a cloud platform. First, you need an Azure account and subscription, which you can obtain for free on the Azure website. Once signed in to the **Azure portal**, follow these steps to create a **virtual machine (VM)** with Windows Server 2025:

1. Navigate to **Virtual machines** and click **Create a virtual machine** to open the configuration wizard.

2. Select your subscription and choose either an existing resource group or create a new one.

> **Note**
>
> In Azure resource management, you have the option to either utilize an existing resource group or establish a new one. An existing resource group serves as a predefined container that organizes and manages related resources, streamlining administration and coordination. If there is no suitable resource group already in place, you can create a new one tailored to your specific requirements, such as by project, department, or environment. This flexibility ensures that resources are systematically grouped and managed, maintaining an orderly structure within your Azure environment.

3. Name your VM and select the region where you want it to run.

4.   For the OS image, select **Windows Server 2025 Datacenter – Gen2** (see *Figure 2.30*).

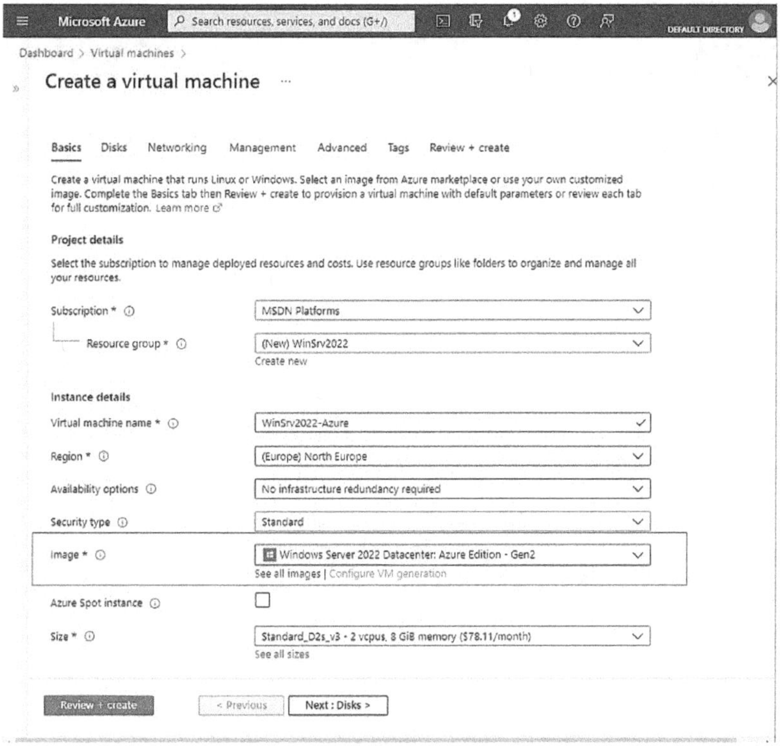

Figure 2.30 – Setting up the VM with Windows Server 2022 in Azure

5.   Complete the fields in the **Basics** tab, then proceed to configure the settings in the **Disks**,
     Networking, **Management**, **Advanced**, and **Tags** tabs.

6.   After entering all the details, click **Review + create** to verify them (see *Figure 2.31*).

Figure 2.31 – Validating the VM's entries

7. If everything is correct, click **Create** to start the deployment of the VM with Windows Server 2025 Azure edition (see *Figure 2.32*).

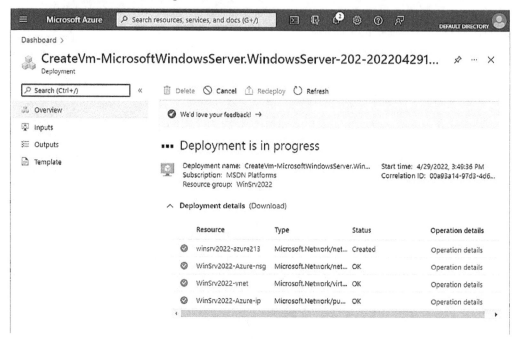

Figure 2.32 – Deploying a VM in Azure

8. Once the deployment is complete, go to the resource and access the VM using the **Connect | RDP** option from the Azure portal or **Remote Desktop Connections** by entering the public IP address.

In this section, we've covered various methods for installing and deploying Windows Server 2025, including clean installation, network installation, unattended installation, in-place upgrades, migrations, and using Azure. These methods offer flexibility for both on-premises and cloud-based deployments.

Additionally, while **System Center Configuration Manager** (**SCCM**) is another option for deploying Windows Server 2025, it is more complex and requires an enterprise-level IT infrastructure. As this method involves advanced configuration, it is not covered in this book.

Summary

In this chapter, you learned about the various methods for installing and deploying Windows Server 2025. You explored how to choose the appropriate installation method based on specific scenarios and requirements, such as clean installations, network installations, in-place upgrades, migrations, and Azure-based installations. You also delved into different partition schemes, boot options, and advanced startup settings that influence the installation process. Through detailed steps and screenshots, you practiced executing each installation method. By the end of the chapter, you have gained the skills needed to install Windows Server 2025 on any physical or virtual machine, whether on-premises or in the cloud. To gain insights into its development, next, we will examine the timeline of Windows Server and explore how it has progressed over the years.

Questions

1. **Fill in the blank:**_____ is a new partition scheme that overcomes the limitations of the MBR partition scheme.

2. **True or false?** A clean installation enables automated installation over a network.

3. **Fill in the blank:**_____is a replacement for Server Core that takes up far fewer hardware resources than the two other installation options, has more periodic updates, and supports only 64-bit applications.

4. Which of the following tools is provided by Microsoft to automate the installation of Windows Server 2025? **Choose two:**

   - Windows ADK

   - MDT

   - SharePoint Server 2022

   - SQL Server 2022

5. **True or false?** An unattended installation requires interactivity during the installation of an operating system.

6. **Fill in the blank:**_____ takes place when you bring in a new machine (physical or virtual) and you want to move the roles, features, apps, and settings into it.

7. Which of these are installation options in Windows Server 2025? **Choose three:**

   - Desktop Experience

   - Server Core

   - Nano Server

   - KDE and GNOME

   - Windows PowerShell

8. Discuss the pros and cons of the three boot options: installation media (DVD), USB flash drive, and network boot.

9. Discuss the installation types: clean installation, network installation, unattended or automated installation, in-place upgrade, and migration.

Further reading

- *Boot to UEFI Mode or legacy BIOS mode*: https://docs.microsoft.com/en-us/ windows-hardware/manufacture/desktop/boot-to-uefi-mode-or- legacy-bios-mode

- *Feature update, clean install, or migrate to Windows Server*: https://learn.microsoft. com/en-us/windows-server/get-started/install-upgrade-migrate

- *How to Setup Windows Server 2025? Step by Step Guide*: https://medium.com/@ theusapdf/how-to-setup-windows-server-2025-step-by-step-guide- 0867cf024d36

3

What to Do After Installing Windows Server 2025

This chapter provides a comprehensive guide on the essential tasks to undertake after installing Windows Server 2025. It is divided into three main sections for ease of understanding.

The first section focuses on device drivers, the crucial software components that facilitate communication between the operating system and hardware devices. You will learn how to perform various operations on device drivers, including **installation**, **removal**, **disabling**, **updating**, **upgrading**, and **rollback**.

The second section delves into the **Windows Server OS** registry, a structured database that holds configuration settings and options for both the operating system and installed applications. This section also covers how to manage programs running in the background, ensuring optimal performance and stability.

The third section emphasizes the initial configuration of Windows Server 2025, a vital step post-installation. You will learn how to set up basic settings such as the **computer name, network configurations, firewall settings**, and **system updates**. Each topic is thoroughly explained with step-by-step instructions and illustrative graphics.

At the end of the chapter, you will find an exercise designed to reinforce your understanding of the initial Windows Server configuration process.

In this chapter, we're going to cover the following main topics:

- Understanding and managing devices and drivers, including Plug and Play, IRQs, and driver signing
- Managing and optimizing registry entries and service accounts
- Performing initial server setup for better performance and security
- Performing an initial Windows Server configuration

Technical requirements

To effectively apply the concepts covered in this chapter, you will need the following resources:

- A computer running **Windows 11 Pro**, equipped with at least 16 GB of RAM, 1 TB of HDD, and an active internet connection

- A virtual machine with **Windows Server 2025 Standard** (Desktop Experience), equipped with at least 4 GB of RAM, 100 GB of HDD, and an internet connection

Understanding and managing devices and drivers, including Plug and Play, IRQs, and driver signing

An operating system is more than just a collection of code; it also plays a crucial role in managing the physical components of a computer. The interaction between hardware and software is integral to the system's functionality. To fully grasp this relationship, it's essential to understand how the operating system identifies and interacts with various hardware components. What mechanisms enable the OS to detect and manage these hardware elements?

Understanding computer devices and device drivers

Computers come in various shapes and sizes, but they all share standard physical components essential for their operation. These components can be categorized into four main types:

- **Internal devices**: These are located inside the computer case and include crucial hardware such as the power supply, motherboard, processor, memory, storage drives, and expansion cards. These elements form the computer's core structure.

- **External devices**: These are peripherals connected to the outside of the computer case, enhancing user interaction with the system. Examples include keyboards, monitors, mice, speakers, headphones, webcams, and microphones.

- **Peripheral devices**: Positioned near the computer but not essential for its basic operation, peripheral devices include printers, scanners, projectors, and plotters, which perform specific functions and tasks.

- **Network devices**: These are peripherals that connect to the computer via network cables, facilitating communication and shared resources. Examples include network printers, scanners, backup libraries, **network-attached storage (NAS)**, and **storage area networks (SAN)**.

Additionally, devices can be classified as input or output devices. Input devices, such as keyboards, send data to the computer, while output devices, such as monitors, display information from the computer. Some devices, such as touch-enabled screens, function as both input and output devices by receiving user input and displaying visual output.

> **Note**
>
> It is important to note that external devices are sometimes referred to as peripheral devices, as they are added to the computer system to extend its capabilities. Essentially, any device outside the core computer structure can be considered a peripheral.

A **device driver** is a software program that acts as an intermediary between the computer hardware and the operating system. It enables the OS to manage and control hardware components. Device drivers are typically included with the device on a DVD or can be downloaded from the manufacturer's website. However, many modern operating systems, such as Windows 10 and 11, support **Plug and Play** (**PnP**) technology, which allows for the automatic detection and configuration of new devices without the need for separate drivers. This chapter will further explore PnP, IRQ, DMA, and driver signing in the subsection titled *Understanding PnP, IRQ, DMA, and driver signing*.

Next, we will delve into how to manage devices and device drivers to enhance server functionality.

Managing devices and device drivers

As an IT professional, you can manage devices and their drivers in Windows using two primary tools: **Windows Settings** and **Device Manager**. Windows Settings provides a contemporary interface for configuring and customizing various system aspects, including device management. On the other hand, Device Manager, a traditional utility, allows you to view and adjust the properties of device drivers that control hardware components.

In **Device Manager**, device drivers are represented by different icons indicating their status (see *Figure 3.1*):

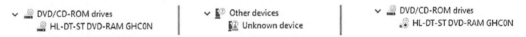

Figure 3.1 – Device drivers' representation in Device Manager

These icons are of the following types:

- **Generic icon**: This indicates that the device is using a default or generic driver, which may not optimize the device's performance or functionality.

- **Black exclamation point in a yellow triangle**: This signifies that the device driver is either missing or incompatible. To resolve this issue, you need to install the appropriate driver for the device to function correctly.

- **Downward black arrow**: This indicates that the device is currently disabled. Although the driver is installed, the device is not active. To enable it, right-click on the device driver and select **Enable** from the menu.

By gaining a comprehensive understanding of these tools and their icons, you are now equipped with the knowledge to manage your devices and device drivers effectively. This knowledge empowers you to make informed decisions and take appropriate actions.

Customizing the Start menu for efficient navigation

Before diving into the various configurations of Windows Server 2025, know that personalizing the **Start** menu is a helpful way to streamline your workflow on Windows Server 2025, allowing quick access to frequently used applications and tools. By organizing and pinning essential apps, administrators can optimize server navigation, reducing time spent searching for core management utilities.

Pinning applications to the Start menu

The following steps will pin applications to the Start menu:

1. **Locate the application**: Find the application you want to pin, either in the **Start** menu itself or via the search bar.

2. **Right-click to pin**: Right-click the application and select **Pin to Start**. This action places the app as a tile in the **Start** menu.

3. **Organize your pinned apps**: Drag and arrange the pinned applications to organize them by function or frequency of use. You can also resize tiles to highlight priority apps.

Grouping and organizing tiles

For a more structured layout, group related applications together by dragging tiles to create named groups. This organization enables quick access to tools based on task type, such as networking tools, monitoring utilities, or common administrative applications.

By customizing the **Start** menu, you enhance accessibility to critical tools, facilitating a more efficient and responsive server management experience.

Working with devices and Device Manager

You can use Windows Settings and Device Manager to manage the devices and device drivers on your system. Windows Settings allows you to add, remove, and update devices and device drivers, as well as change their settings and preferences. Device Manager allows you to view the details of the device drivers, disable or enable them, uninstall or reinstall them, and troubleshoot any problems. Here are the steps to access these tools.

Windows Settings

To open Windows Settings, click the **Start** button and then click the **Settings** icon. Alternatively, you can press the **Windows key** + **I** shortcut. In Windows Settings, click **Devices** to see the list of devices connected to your system.

Device Manager

To open Device Manager, right-click the **Start** button and then select **Device Manager**. Alternatively, you can press the *Windows* key + *X* shortcut and then choose **Device Manager**. You can also type devmgmt.msc in the **Run** dialog box and press **Enter**. In Device Manager, you will see the device drivers organized by categories, such as display adapters, network adapters, sound, video, and game controllers. You can expand each category to see the specific device drivers under it, as shown in *Figure 3.2*.

Figure 3.2 – The Device Manager

Note

The secret Start menu, also known as the Power User menu, is a hidden menu that provides quick access to various system tools and settings, such as Device Manager, Disk Management, Command Prompt, and Task Manager. You can open it by right-clicking the **Start** button or pressing the *Windows* key + *X* shortcut.

Adding devices and installing device drivers

To connect a new device to your system using **Windows Settings**, follow these steps:

1. Open the Start menu by clicking the **Start** button.

2. Select the **Settings** icon to open Windows Settings.

3. Click on **Devices**.

4. Navigate to **Bluetooth & other devices** in the **Devices** section.

5. Click **Add Bluetooth or other devices** to begin the connection process.

If you need to install a device driver from a file, whether it is on a DVD or downloaded from the internet, proceed with these steps:

1. Insert the DVD into the DVD drive or locate the driver file on your computer.

2. Open **File Explorer** and execute the `setup` or `install` file.

Once the device drivers are installed, you will learn how to update them in the next section.

> **Note**
>
> Windows Server offers multiple methods to access various settings and management windows. One efficient way is through **Microsoft Saved Console (MSC)** files, such as `Services.msc` for managing services. Many familiar MSC files are still supported in Windows Server 2025, including `virtmgmt.msc` for virtual machine management, `devmgmt.msc` for device management, and `services.msc` for service control. These shortcuts provide quick access to essential management consoles, streamlining server administration.

Updating device drivers

To update the device driver using **Device Manager**, take the following steps:

1. Right-click the **Start** button to open the secret Start menu.

2. In the secret **Start** menu, select **Device Manager**.

3. In the **Device Manager** window, expand the device's category.

4. Right-click the device and choose **Update driver** from the context menu.

5. Select **Browse my computer for drivers** (see *Figure 3.3*). If you lack a device driver, let the **Update Drivers** wizard do the work for you by clicking on **Search automatically for drivers**.

Figure 3.3 – Updating a device driver

> **Important note**
>
> To install or update a driver using Device Manager, select the **Update driver** option from the context menu. Additionally, it's important to prioritize security when installing drivers, especially those downloaded from the internet. Choose digitally signed drivers whenever possible, as these have been validated for authenticity and integrity, minimizing the risk of malware or corrupted files. Digitally signed drivers offer extra assurance against tampering, which is essential for keeping your server environment secure.

Now, let us learn how to remove and uninstall device drivers.

Removing devices and uninstalling device drivers

You can use **Windows Settings** to disconnect a device from your system. Here are the steps to do so:

1. Open the **Start** menu by clicking the **Start** button.

2. Click the **Settings** icon on the **Start** menu.

3. Click **Devices** in **Windows Settings**.

4. Click **Bluetooth & other devices** in the **Devices** navigation menu and choose the device you want to disconnect.

5.   Click the **Remove device** button, as shown in *Figure 3.4.*

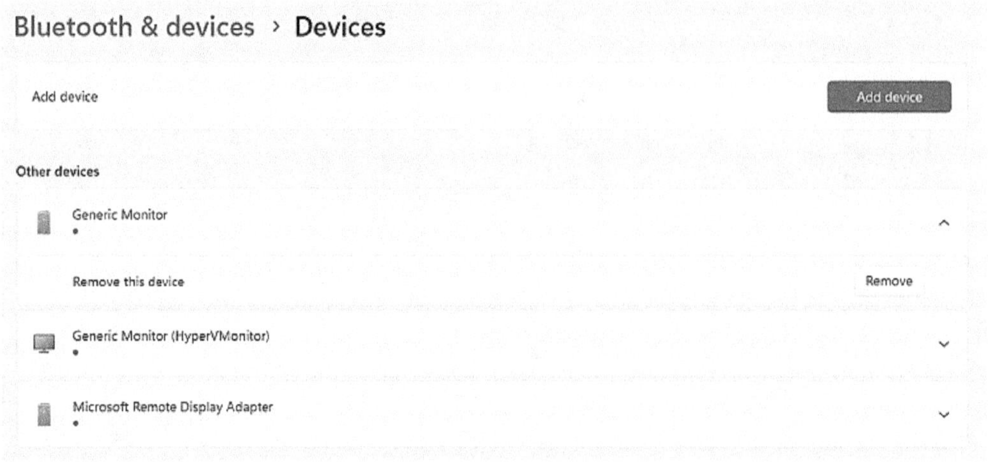

Figure 3.4 – Disconnecting a device

You can use **Device Manager** to delete a device driver from your system. Here are the steps to do so:

1.   Right-click the **Start** button to open the secret **Start** menu.

2.   In the secret **Start** menu, select **Device Manager**.

3.   In the **Device Manager** window, expand the device's category.

4.   Right-click the device and choose **Uninstall device** from the menu that appears.

5.   Click the **Uninstall** button.

Next, let us learn how to manage and disable device drivers.

Managing devices and disabling device drivers

You can manage devices through **Windows Settings** by following these steps:

1.   Click the **Start** button to open the **Start** menu.

2.   Select the **Settings** icon.

3.   Navigate to **Devices**.

4.   In the **Devices** section, choose **Printers & scanners** and select the device you wish to manage.

5.   Click on the **Manage** button.

Alternatively, to disable a device driver using **Device Manager**, proceed with these steps:

1. Right-click the **Start** button to open the secret **Start** menu.

2. Select **Device Manager** from the menu.

3. In the **Device Manager** window, locate the device category and click it to expand the list.

4. Right-click the specific device and select **Disable device** from the context menu.

5. Confirm your action by clicking **Yes** in the confirmation dialog, as illustrated in *Figure 3.5*.

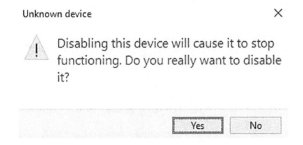

Figure 3.5 – Disabling the device driver

In the next section, we will cover how to roll back device drivers.

Rolling back device drivers

One of the ways to restore a device driver to its previous version is by using **Device Manager**. Here are the steps you need to follow for this method:

1. Right-click the **Start** button to access the secret Start menu.

2. From the secret **Start** menu, choose **Device Manager**.

3. In the **Device Manager** window, locate the device's category and click it to show the devices under it.

4. Right-click the device and select **Properties**.

5.   Click the **Driver** tab and then click the **Roll Back Driver** button, as shown in *Figure 3.6*. Click **OK**.

Figure 3.6 – Restoring a device driver to its previous version

> **Note**
>
> If you encounter issues after updating a device driver, rolling it back to a previous version may resolve the problem. Note, however, that if the driver you installed is the first one for that device, rollback won't be available. Also, be cautious with driver dependencies and always back up the server before rolling back to prevent potential disruptions.

Next, let us learn about some solutions when troubleshooting device drivers.

Troubleshooting a device driver

One of the challenges you may face with device drivers is that they may not work correctly or cause errors. In such cases, you have several alternatives (see *Figure 3.7*) to fix them:

- **Update Driver**: This allows you to install the latest driver automatically or manually select the driver software from the server

- **Roll Back Driver**: This allows you to restore the previous version of the driver if the current one is problematic

- **Disable Device**: This allows you to turn off the driver if it is causing significant issues, such as system instability

- **Uninstall Device**: This allows you to remove the existing driver if you have obtained the correct driver from the device manufacturer

Figure 3.7 – Troubleshooting options for the device driver

In this section, you have learned about the different methods to manage devices. Next, let us explore various system resources, such as PnP, IRQ, DMA, and driver signing.

Understanding PnP, IRQ, DMA, and driver signing

The operating system relies on system resources to manage hardware components such as the CPU, memory, disks, **Input/Output (I/O)** devices, and network connections. Key system resources include **I/O ports**, **memory addresses**, **interrupt request (IRQ) lines**, and **direct memory access (DMA) channels**, all of which are crucial for the OS to communicate with hardware effectively.

PnP

Developed through a partnership between Intel and Microsoft, PnP significantly streamlined the process of installing devices and their drivers. With PnP, you can connect a device to your computer, and the Windows OS will automatically detect and configure it. The system uses its **Driver Store** to install the necessary drivers for the device. For instance, in Windows Server 2025, the Driver Store is located at `C:\Windows\System32\DriverStore`.

Interrupt Request (IRQ) and Direct Memory Access (DMA)

In contemporary computing, IRQs are numbers ranging from 0 to 31 that signify signals sent by devices to request processor attention when they require processing. Conversely, DMA channels, numbered from 0 to 8, allow devices to access RAM directly without involving the processor.

To view IRQ and DMA resource settings using **Device Manager**, follow these steps:

1. Right-click the **Start** button to open the context menu.
2. Select **Device Manager**.
3. In the **Device Manager** window, expand the relevant device category.
4. Right-click the device and choose **Properties** from the context menu.
5. Click the **Resources** tab to review the resource settings, as depicted in *Figure 3.8*.

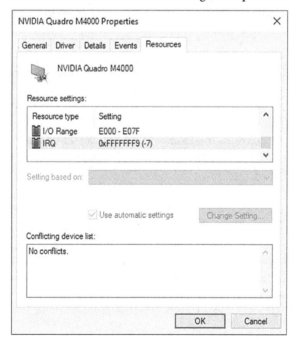

Figure 3.8 – Driver's Resources settings

Next, look at the driver's signature, which helps verify both the driver's integrity and identity.

Digital signature of the driver

A driver's **digital signature** serves as an electronic mark that verifies both the source and integrity of the driver's package. That indicates that Microsoft has validated and certified the driver as being both compatible with and secure for installation. This digital signature is essential for confirming that the driver remains unaltered and authentic. To verify a driver's digital signature in Windows Server 2025, follow these steps:

1. Right-click the **Start** button to open the context menu.

2. Select **Device Manager** from the menu.

3. In the **Device Manager** window, expand the category of the relevant device.

4. Right-click the device and choose **Properties** from the context menu.

5. Go to the **Driver** tab and click the **Driver Details** button to access the **Driver File Details** window, as illustrated in *Figure 3.9*.

Figure 3.9 – Digital signature information of the driver

This section has covered the essentials of computer devices and drivers, including various management techniques and the system resources used for device communication. The upcoming section will delve into the Windows Server registry and services, focusing on configuration and management practices for Windows registries and services.

Managing and optimizing registry entries and service accounts

The **Windows registry** and **Windows services** are critical components for managing and configuring the Windows operating system. The Windows registry is a structured database that keeps track of system settings, application configurations, and hardware options. Meanwhile, Windows services are background processes that handle essential functions such as networking, security, and printing. This section will guide you through the management and optimization of both the Windows registry and Windows services, utilizing various tools and techniques to ensure efficient system performance and stability.

Windows Server registry

The Windows registry is a fundamental component that tracks changes to the server's hardware and software. It functions as a hierarchical database, maintaining configuration and security settings for the operating system, applications, and hardware devices. The registry's interface displays a console tree on the left side, organized into five primary **registry keys** known as **hives (HKEYs)**. These keys follow a syntax similar to file paths, separated by backslashes. In Windows Server 2025, the five HKEYs are as follows:

- **HKEY_CLASSES_ROOT**: Contains information about installed applications and their associated file extensions
- **HKEY_CURRENT_USER**: Stores settings and data related to the currently logged-in user
- **HKEY_LOCAL_MACHINE**: Holds configuration data specific to the local computer, including details about hardware and software
- **HKEY_USERS**: Maintains data on all user profiles that have accessed the server
- **HKEY_CURRENT_CONFIG**: Records data collected during the system boot process, such as display settings

Services Control Manager and Windows Server services

The **Services Control Manager** is a crucial utility for overseeing the services operating on your Windows Server. **Services** are background processes that offer various functionalities essential for the operating system, applications, and network operations. Through the Services Control Manager, you can start, stop, restart, or pause these services as needed. Additionally, this tool allows you to configure service properties, including startup types, dependencies, and recovery options, to ensure optimal performance and reliability of your server.

Understanding service startup types

In the Services Control Manager, each service is assigned a startup type that determines how and when it is activated (see *Figure 3.10*). The available startup types are as follows:

- **Automatic:** The service is initiated automatically by the operating system during the boot process.
- **Automatic (Delayed Start):** The service begins approximately two minutes after all other automatic services have started.
- **Manual:** The service must be manually started by a user or another service that relies on it.
- **Disabled:** The service is not initiated by the operating system, users, or dependent services.

Figure 3.10 illustrates these different service startup types in Windows Server.

Figure 3.10 – Windows Server service startup types

Next, we will explore how to access and manage both services and registry settings.

Accessing and managing the Windows registry and services

To effectively manage the Windows registry and Windows services, you can utilize two essential tools: the **Registry Editor** and the **Services Control Manager**. The Windows registry serves as a comprehensive database that holds important configuration and security settings for the operating system, applications, and hardware devices. Windows services, on the other hand, are background processes that perform various functions that are crucial to the operating system, applications, and network operations. This section will guide you through the process of accessing and managing these components using the Registry Editor to handle registry settings and the Services Control Manager to oversee service operations.

Working with registry keys and values in the Registry Editor

To manage and modify the Windows registry, which stores critical settings for the operating system, applications, and hardware, you can use the Registry Editor. Here is how you can access it:

1. Type `regedit` into the search bar on the taskbar and press *Enter*.

2. The **Registry Editor** will open, as illustrated in *Figure 3.11*.

Figure 3.11 – Windows Server Registry Editor

In the following subsection, you will learn the procedures for altering registry values.

Modifying a registry value

To alter the data of a registry value, which controls the behavior of the operating system, applications, or hardware devices, you can use the Registry Editor. Follow these steps:

1. Type `regedit` into the search box on the taskbar and press *Enter*.

2. In the Registry Editor, navigate to the appropriate registry key and sub-key(s) on the left pane that includes the value you wish to modify.

3. On the right pane, locate the value you want to change, right-click it, select **Modify**, and then adjust the **Value data** field, as shown in *Figure 3.12*.

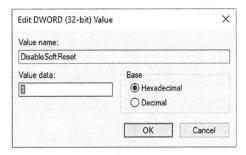

Figure 3.12 – Changing a registry value

Next, you will learn how to rename a registry value.

Renaming a registry value

To rename a registry value that impacts the settings of the operating system, applications, or hardware devices, you can use the Registry Editor. Here is how:

1. Search for regedit on the taskbar and press *Enter*.

2. In the Registry Editor, navigate to the relevant registry key and sub-key(s) on the left pane.

3. On the right pane, locate the value you wish to rename, right-click on it, select **Rename**, and then enter the new name, as illustrated in *Figure 3.13*.

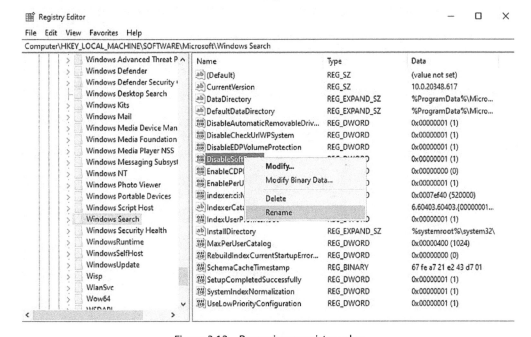

Figure 3.13 – Renaming a registry value

Following this, you will learn how to delete a registry value.

Removing a registry value

To delete a registry value that affects the operation of the operating system, applications, or hardware devices, you can utilize the Registry Editor. Here is how to do it:

1. Search for `regedit` in the taskbar and press *Enter*.

2. In the Registry Editor, navigate to the registry key and sub-key(s) on the left pane where the value you want to delete is located.

3. On the right pane, find the value you wish to remove, right-click it, select **Delete**, and confirm your action, as depicted in *Figure 3.14*.

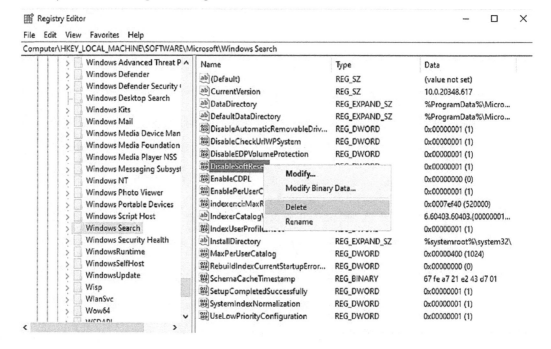

Figure 3.14 – Deleting a registry value

> **Note**
> The procedures for managing registry values, such as deleting, renaming, and exporting, can also be applied to registry keys. That allows for consistent and efficient management of both values and keys within the Windows Registry.

Managing and accessing Windows services

To manage and access Windows services—background programs that handle various tasks for the operating system and applications—follow these steps:

1. Click the **Start** button.

2. Select the **Windows Tools** option from the **Start** menu.

3. Locate and click on **Services** from the available list.

4. That will open the **Windows Services Control Manager**, as illustrated in *Figure 3.15*.

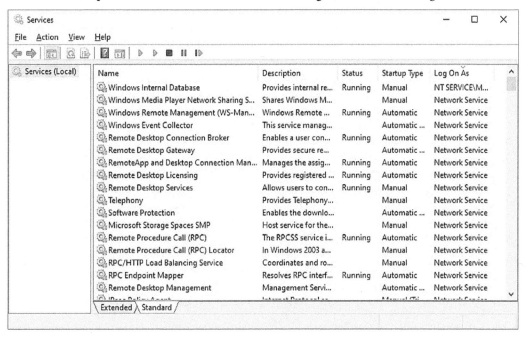

Figure 3.15 – Windows Services Control Manager

The following subsection will guide you through configuring service recovery options using the Control Manager.

Configuring how to recover from service failures

To configure how your computer responds to service failures, such as restarting the service or rebooting the system, follow these steps using the **Control Manager**:

1. Click the **Start** button.

2. Select **Windows Tools** from the **Start** menu.

3. Find and click on **Services** from the list.

4. In the **Services** window, locate the service you want to configure and right-click on it.

5. From the context menu, select **Properties**.

6. In the **Properties** window, navigate to the **Recovery** tab. Note that while many services allow you to configure recovery options, some critical system services do not provide these settings, as they are essential for stable operation.

7. Define the actions for the first, second, and subsequent failures of the service, as depicted in *Figure 3.16*. In Windows OSs, specific actions can be defined for managing service failures at different stages to maintain stability and minimize disruption. For the first failure, the system can be set to restart the service to reduce downtime automatically. Upon a second failure, the service can be restarted again, or alternate actions, such as running a custom script or sending a notification to the administrator, can be triggered. For any subsequent failures, options include restarting the system, taking no action, or continuing to attempt restarts after a specified delay. These configurable actions provide a flexible approach to maintaining service reliability and system performance.

> **Note**
>
> In Windows operating systems, specific actions can be defined to manage service failures at different stages, ensuring stability and minimizing disruption. For the first failure, the system can be configured to restart the service, reducing downtime automatically. If a second failure occurs, the service can be restarted again, or alternative actions, such as running a custom script or sending a notification to the administrator, can be triggered. For any subsequent failures, options include restarting the system, taking no action, or continuing to attempt restarts after a specified delay. These configurable actions offer a flexible approach to maintaining service reliability and system performance.

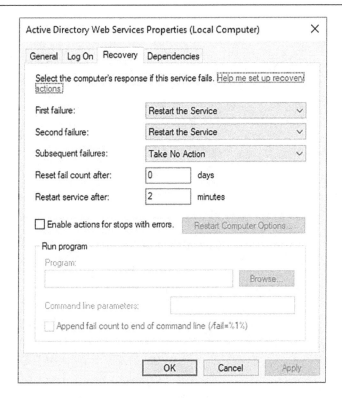

Figure 3.16 – Configuring recovery options for service failures in Windows Server 2025

8. Click **OK** to apply your changes and close the dialog box.

In the following subsection, we will explore how to set a delay for the start of a service.

Delaying the start of a service

To delay the start of a service using Control Manager, which can enhance system performance and stability by initiating the service after other automatic services, follow these steps:

1. Click the **Start** button.

2. From the **Start** menu, select **Windows Tools**.

3. Locate and click on **Services**.

4. In the **Services** window, right-click on the service you wish to delay.

5. Choose **Properties** from the context menu.

6. In the **Properties** window, navigate to the **General** tab and click the **Startup type** drop-down list.

7.   Select **Automatic (Delayed Start)** from the options, as depicted in *Figure 3.17*.

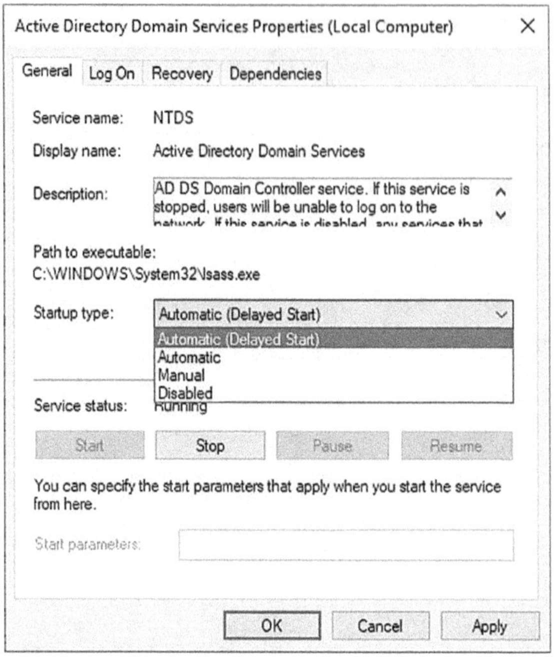

Figure 3.17 – Configuring the delayed startup of a service in Windows Server 2025

8.   Click **OK** to apply the changes and close the dialog box.

In the following subsection, we will discuss how to configure the logon settings for a service.

Logon settings for a service

To configure the user account under which a service operates using Control Manager, follow these steps to enhance security and manageability:

1.   Click the **Start** button.

2.   From the **Start** menu, select **Windows Tools**.

3.   Find and click on **Services**.

4.   In the **Services** window, right-click the service you wish to configure.

5.   Choose **Properties** from the context menu.

6.   In the **Properties** window, navigate to the **Log On** tab.

7.   Select the **This account** option under the **Log on as** section.

8. Enter the user account name, including the domain name followed by a backslash, and input the password and confirm it, as illustrated in *Figure 3.18*.

Figure 3.18 – Configuring the log-on settings for a service in Windows Server 2025

9. Click **OK** to apply the changes and close the dialog box.

In the following subsection, we will explore how to start the configured service.

Starting the service

To start a service on your computer using Control Manager, follow these steps:

1. Click the **Start** button.
2. From the **Start** menu, select **Windows Tools**.
3. Locate and click on **Services** from the list.
4. In the **Services** window, right-click the service you wish to start.

5. From the context menu, select **Start**, as depicted in *Figure 3.19*.

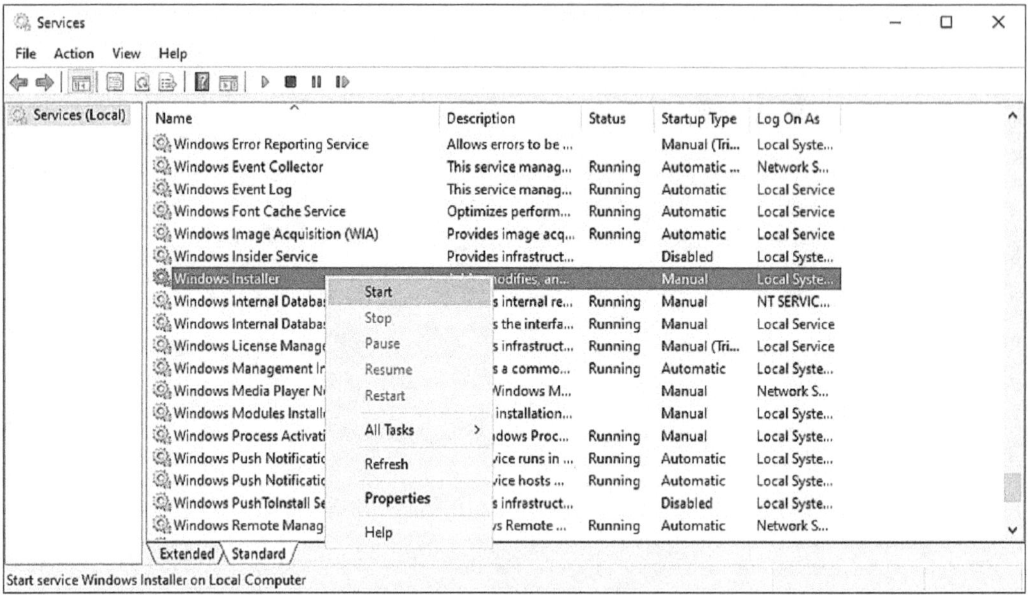

Figure 3.19 – Starting the service

In the upcoming subsection, we will cover how to stop a service.

Stopping a service

To stop a service on your computer using Control Manager, follow these steps:

1. Click the **Start** button.
2. Select **Windows Tools** from the **Start** menu.
3. Choose **Services** from the available options.
4. In the **Services** window, right-click the service you wish to stop.

5.   Select **Stop** from the context menu, as depicted in *Figure 3.20*.

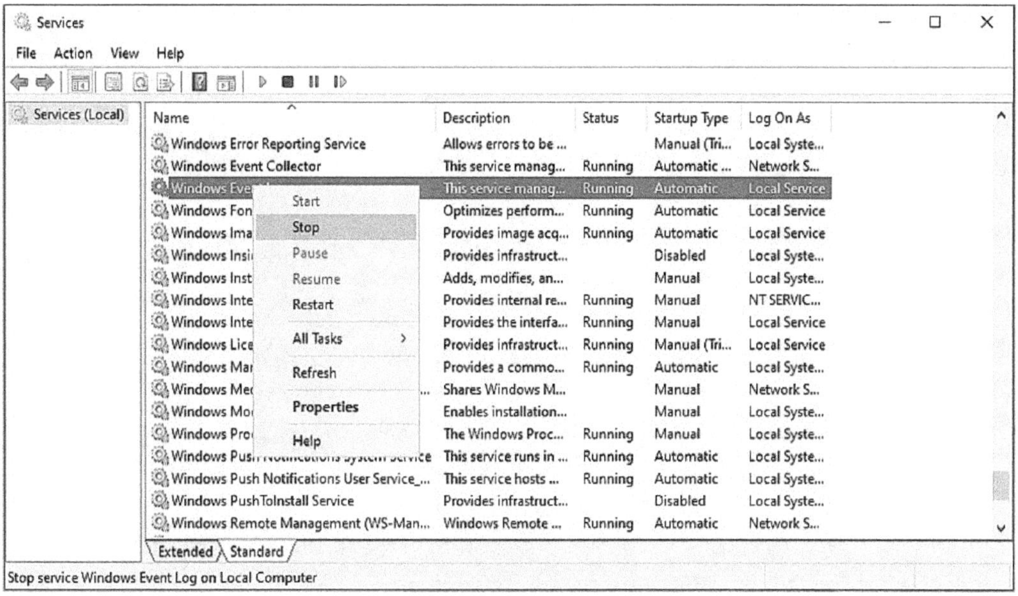

Figure 3.20 – Stopping the service

In the next section, we will cover how to restart a service.

Restarting the service

To restart a service on your computer using Control Manager, follow these steps:

1.   Click the **Start** button.

2.   Select **Windows Tools** from the **Start** menu.

3.   Locate and choose **Services** from the list.

4.   In the **Services** window, right-click the service you wish to restart.

5.   From the context menu, select **Restart**, as illustrated in *Figure 3.21*.

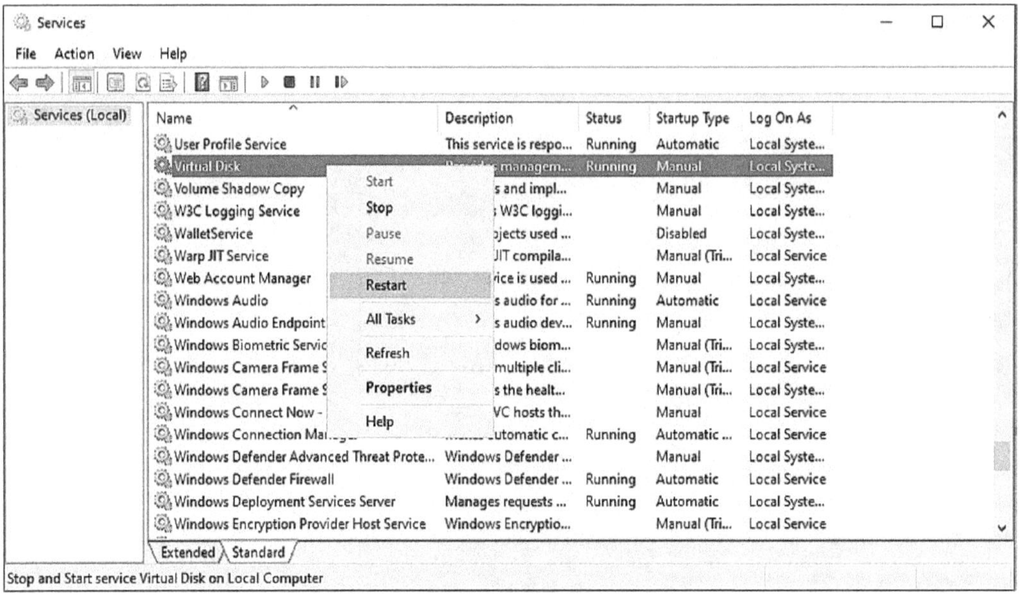

Figure 3.21 – Restarting the service

In the upcoming section, we will explore registry entries, service accounts, and dependencies.

Understanding registry entries, service accounts, and dependencies

In managing Windows Server, you may find the need to create or modify registry keys and values to address issues or introduce new features. Given the critical nature of the Windows registry, it is essential to exercise caution during any modifications. Windows Server also relies on various services, which operate under different service accounts. These accounts can be native to Windows Server or custom ones created for managing services. The choice of service account impacts the level of access that services have to local and network resources, affecting security. Windows Server 2025 includes several native service accounts, as illustrated in *Figure 3.22*:

- **Local System**: This built-in account possesses the highest level of privileges on a Windows OS, often referred to as a superuser, and surpasses even administrator accounts in terms of power

- **NT Authority\Local Service**: This built-in account has the same privileges as members of the user group, providing a minimal level of access

- **NT Authority\Network Service**: This built-in account has more privileges than user group members, offering greater access

Furthermore, services often have dependencies on other services to operate effectively. Stopping a service with dependencies will require halting the dependent services, while starting such a service necessitates starting its dependencies as well.

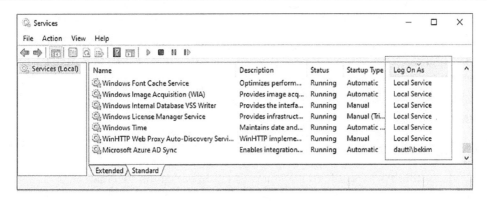

Figure 3.22 – Native service accounts in Windows Server 2025

In the following section, we will cover how to create a new registry key.

Creating a New Registry Key

The Registry Editor allows you to create new registry keys or sub-keys within the Windows registry, a crucial component for storing system configuration settings and options. To add a new registry key, follow these steps:

1. Open the Registry Editor by typing `regedit` into the search box on the taskbar and pressing *Enter*.

2. In the Registry Editor, navigate to the desired location in the left pane where you want to create the new key. Right-click on the chosen registry key or sub-key.

3. Select **New** and then **Key** from the context menu, as illustrated in *Figure 3.23*.

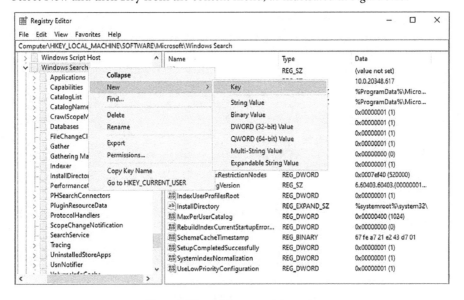

Figure 3.23 – Adding a registry entry

> **Note**
>
> To add a new registry value, right-click in the empty area on the right pane of the Registry Editor after selecting the relevant registry key or sub-key. Then, choose **New** from the context menu and enter the desired value.

In the upcoming section, we will explore how to create a service account.

Creating a service account

A **service account** is a specialized account used to run background services on Windows Server, performing tasks such as managing network access, enhancing security, and monitoring performance. These accounts can be targets for malicious activity, so using **managed service accounts (MSAs)** in a domain environment is beneficial; MSAs automatically rotate passwords and support audit trails for added security. In cloud environments, managed identities offer similar security benefits by handling identity and access management. To assign a service account to a service, follow these steps:

1. Click the **Start** button and select **Windows Tools** from the **Start** menu.
2. Locate and choose **Services** from the list of tools.
3. In the **Services** window, right-click on the service you wish to assign a service account to.
4. From the context menu, select **Properties**.
5. In the **Properties** window, navigate to the **Log On** tab, as illustrated in *Figure 3.24*.

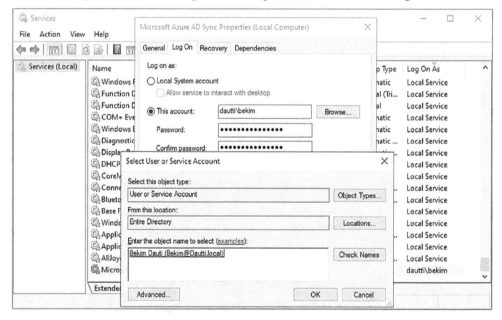

Figure 3.24 – Creating a service account

6. Choose the **This account** option and click the **Browse** button to locate the desired service account. Ensure the account is a valid user in your organization's **Active Directory** with administrator privileges, as only administrators can be set as the **Log On** account.

7. Enter and confirm the password for the selected service account.

8. Click **OK** to apply the changes and close the **Properties** window.

In the next section, we will cover how to set up service dependencies.

Adding a service dependency

To establish a service dependency, you'll need to use the Registry Editor and follow these steps:

1. Open the Registry Editor by typing `regedit` into the taskbar search box and pressing *Enter*.

2. Navigate to the service in question located under `HKEY_LOCAL_MACHINE\SYSTEM\CurrentControlSet\Services\`.

3. Locate the `DependOnService` value or create a new multi-string value with this name if it doesn't already exist.

4. Enter the precise name of the service on which the current service will depend.

5. Restart the server to apply the changes.

6. After the server restarts, open the **Services** window, locate the service you configured, right-click it, and select **Properties**.

7. Go to the **Dependencies** tab to confirm that the newly added service appears as a dependency.

This process demonstrates how to use the Registry Editor and services to manage service dependencies in Windows Server. Next, we will explore configuring initial settings for both the Desktop Experience and Server Core installation options.

Performing initial server setup for better performance and security

One of the essential tasks after installing Windows Server 2025 is to configure the initial settings for the server. That involves customizing the server name and domain membership according to the role that the server will play in the network. Furthermore, it includes enabling **Remote Desktop** for remote management, setting up a static IP address for network identification, changing the time zone to match the local time, activating Windows Server 2025 with a valid license key, turning off **Internet Explorer (IE)** enhanced security for easier browsing, and checking for updates to keep the server secure and updated. These steps will prepare the server for its intended function in the IT environment.

Initial settings for Windows Server

Before assigning roles to your server, it's crucial to configure several fundamental settings that impact both performance and security. Begin by setting a static IP address to ensure the server's network identity. Adjust the time zone to reflect the local time accurately, activate your Windows Server 2025 license, and apply the latest updates and patches. Rename the server to something meaningful, join it to your domain to facilitate resource access, enable Remote Desktop to allow for remote management, and turn off IE enhanced security to simplify web access. This section will guide you through these initial setup steps for both **Desktop Experience** and **Server Core** installation options.

Configuring the server with Server Manager

Server Manager is a graphical tool that you can use to customize the basic settings of your server in Desktop Experience. It opens automatically when you log in to Windows Server 2025 for the first time, and you can change this behavior if you want. To access the server configuration options using Server Manager, click on **Configure this local server** in the **WELCOME TO SERVER MANAGER** section, as shown in *Figure 3.25*.

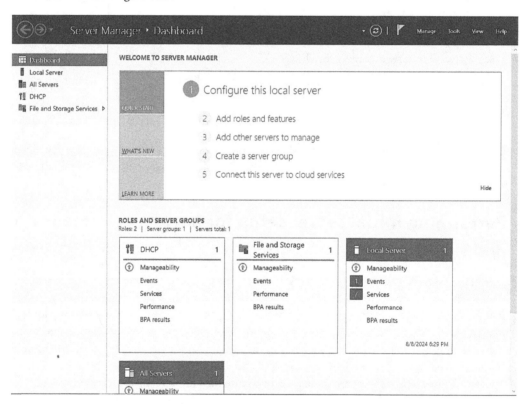

Figure 3.25 – Server Manager in Windows Server 2025

Alternatively, you can use the **Server Configuration tool**, which is a command-line tool that allows you to configure the server in CLI mode. We will discuss this tool in the next section.

Initial server settings in CLI mode

When setting up a Windows Server 2025 installation in **Server Core** mode, you can use the Server Configuration tool to manage essential settings. Access this command-line interface by entering SConfig.cmd at the Command Prompt, as illustrated in *Figure 3.26*.

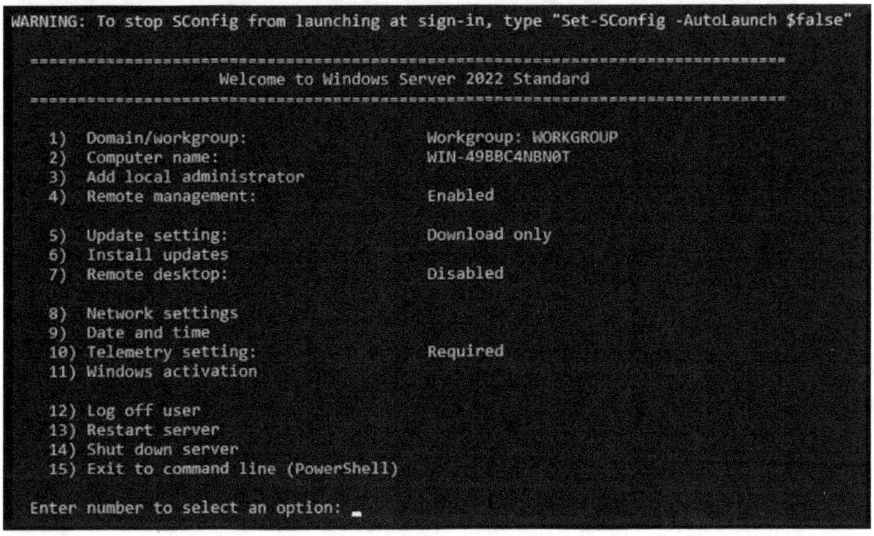

```
WARNING: To stop SConfig from launching at sign-in, type "Set-SConfig -AutoLaunch $false"

==============================================================================
                    Welcome to Windows Server 2022 Standard
==============================================================================

    1) Domain/workgroup:                 Workgroup: WORKGROUP
    2) Computer name:                    WIN-49BBC4NBN0T
    3) Add local administrator
    4) Remote management:                Enabled

    5) Update setting:                   Download only
    6) Install updates
    7) Remote desktop:                   Disabled

    8) Network settings
    9) Date and time
    10) Telemetry setting:               Required
    11) Windows activation

    12) Log off user
    13) Restart server
    14) Shut down server
    15) Exit to command line (PowerShell)

Enter number to select an option: _
```

Figure 3.26 – Server Configuration tool in CLI mode

The Server Configuration tool provides options to modify various server settings, including the server name, domain membership, IP address, time zone, remote management settings, product activation, and updates.

Managing configuration drift with PowerShell Desired State Configuration

After setting up Windows Server 2025, maintaining consistent configurations across multiple servers is crucial to avoid configuration drift—a common issue where servers gradually deviate from their intended settings over time. Configuration drift can impact security, performance, and compliance, and tracking down inconsistencies can become challenging without proper tools.

PowerShell **Desired State Configuration** (**DSC**) provides a powerful solution to manage and automate configuration settings. DSC enables administrators to define the desired state of a server configuration through PowerShell scripts, which specify the exact setup requirements for each server. Once defined, DSC continuously monitors server configurations to ensure they align with the desired state and can automatically correct any deviations. This feature is valuable in environments with multiple servers where consistent configurations are necessary for compliance and stability.

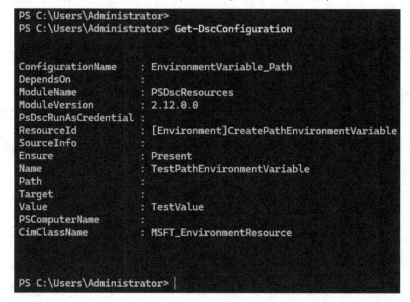

Figure 3.27 – Querying the current state of the configuration

PowerShell DSC can be leveraged to set up configurations such as network settings, firewall rules, and installed features. Additionally, DSC can be used to enforce these configurations across various servers, making it easier to maintain alignment with organizational standards and preventing issues associated with configuration drift.

Validating hardware stability with memory testers and burn-in applications

Before deploying a new server, it's essential to ensure that the hardware can withstand the demands of a production environment. Conducting hardware validation tests—particularly on newly installed memory and other critical components—can help detect potential faults early. Memory testers and burn-in applications rigorously evaluate hardware under simulated workloads, allowing IT teams to identify weak points that may otherwise cause issues later on.

Most server manufacturers, including Dell, HP, and Cisco, provide built-in utilities designed explicitly for hardware testing. These tools are tailored to each manufacturer's systems, offering diagnostic features that run comprehensive checks on components such as memory, storage, and processors. Leveraging these utilities before deployment not only boosts confidence in the server's stability but also helps minimize unplanned downtime by catching failures that may occur shortly after initial setup.

In the following section, we will guide you through the process of configuring your server using this tool. Let us get started.

Chapter exercise – performing an initial Windows Server configuration

This exercise aims to demonstrate how to configure the fundamental settings of Windows Server using two distinct tools: Server Manager and Server Configuration. Server Manager, a graphical interface available in Desktop Experience mode, allows you to adjust various server settings, including the server name, IP address, domain, remote access, time zone, activation, and updates. Conversely, Server Configuration is a command-line utility used in Server Core mode to perform similar tasks. This chapter will guide you through the process of using both tools to customize your server's initial setup to meet your specific requirements.

Using Server Manager to configure the initial settings for Windows Server

In this section, you will learn how to use **Server Manager**, a user-friendly graphical interface, to adjust the basic settings for Windows Server 2025 Standard (Desktop Experience), such as the server name, domain, IP address, and more.

Renaming the server

To rename your server, follow these steps, as illustrated in *Figure 3.28*:

1. Begin by selecting the highlighted default computer name in the **Properties** section.
2. In the **System Properties** window, click the **Change** button to access the **Computer Name/ Domain Changes** dialog.

3. Enter the desired new name for your server in the **Computer name** field and click **OK**.

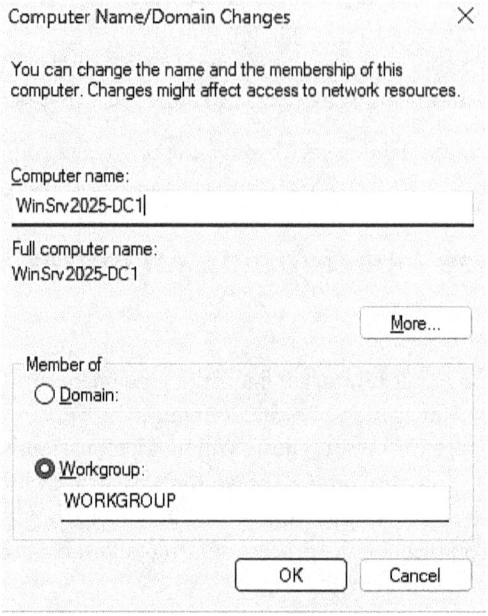

Figure 3.28 – Renaming the server

4. A prompt will appear, notifying you that a restart is required for the changes to take effect. Click **OK** to proceed.

5. Close the **System Properties** window by clicking the **Close** button.

6. In the **Microsoft Windows** dialog box, choose **Restart Now** to reboot the server and apply the changes.

Following this, we will guide you through the process of joining the server to a domain.

Connecting the server to a domain

Connecting your server to an organizational domain is essential based on its intended role. For instance, if the server is to act as a **domain controller** (**DC**), it will automatically join the domain upon the installation of the **Active Directory Domain Services** (**AD DS**) role, and no additional steps are necessary. However, if the server will fulfill any other role, it needs to be joined to the domain manually. To connect the server to a domain, follow these steps, as illustrated in *Figure 3.29*:

1. In the **Properties** section, click on the highlighted workgroup name.

2. In the **System Properties** window, select the **Change** button.

3. In the **Computer Name/Domain Changes** dialog, opt for the **Domain** selection, enter your organization's domain name, and click **OK**.

Figure 3.29 – Connecting the server to a domain

4. In the **Windows Security** prompt, provide the credentials for an account with domain joining permissions, then click **OK**.

5. A confirmation message will appear welcoming the server to the domain; click **OK** to close this message.

6. Confirm that you want to restart the server by clicking **OK**.

7. Close the **System Properties** window by clicking **Close**.

8. When prompted by the **Microsoft Windows** dialog box, click **Restart Now** to apply the changes.

Following these steps will successfully join the server to your domain. The next topic will cover enabling Remote Desktop to allow remote access to the server.

Enabling Remote Desktop

To enable **Remote Desktop** on your server, follow these steps, as depicted in *Figure 3.30*:

1. Open the **System Properties** dialog box and navigate to the **Remote** tab.

2. Select the **Allow remote connections to this computer** option in the **System Properties** window.

3. A notification will appear indicating that the Remote Desktop firewall exception will be enabled. Click **OK** to acknowledge this and close the dialog.

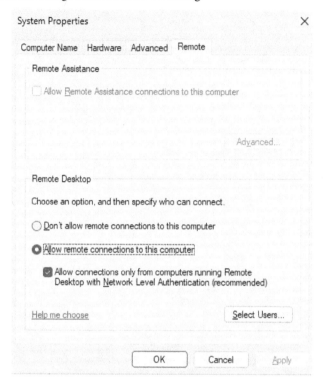

Figure 3.30 – Enabling Remote Desktop

4. To designate users who can access the server via Remote Desktop, click the **Select Users…** button.

5. In the **Remote Desktop Users** window, click **Add** to choose users or groups from your AD DS. After selecting the appropriate users or groups, click **OK** to finalize your selections and close the window.

6. Click **OK** again to exit the **System Properties** window.

After enabling Remote Desktop, the next topic will cover configuring a fixed IP address for your server, which is essential for stable network operations.

Configuring the IP address

Configuring a **static IP address** for your server is essential to ensure that its address remains consistent. To set this up, follow these steps, as illustrated in *Figure 3.31*:

1. Access the Ethernet settings highlighted in the **Properties** section.

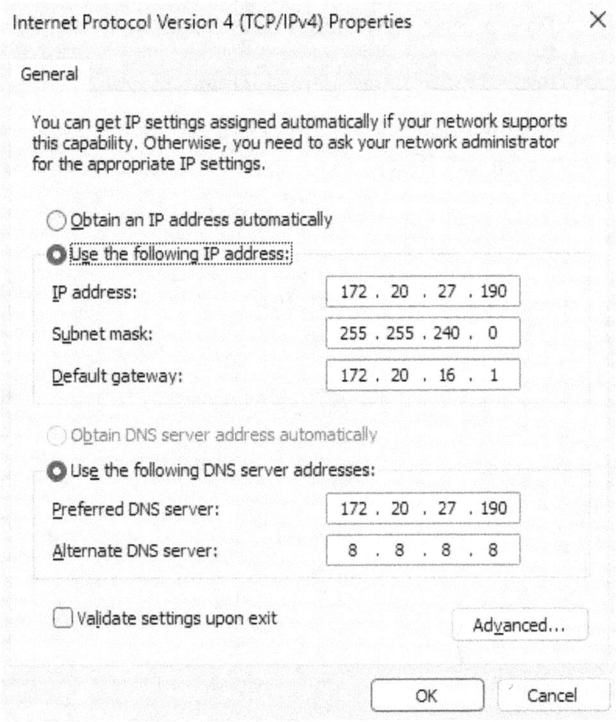

Figure 3.31 – Configuring the IP address

2. In the **Network Connections** window, right-click on your server's Ethernet connection and select **Properties** from the context menu.

3. Within the **Ethernet Properties** window, locate **Internet Protocol Version 4 (TCP/IPv4)** and click the **Properties** button.

4. In the **Internet Protocol Version 4 (TCP/IPv4) Properties** window, choose **Use the following IP address** and input the desired values for **IP Address**, **Subnet Mask**, and **Default Gateway**. Additionally, select **Use the following DNS server addresses** and enter the **Preferred DNS server** and **Alternate DNS server** details. Click **OK** to apply these settings.

5. Close the **Ethernet Properties** window by clicking **Close**.

6. Exit the **Network Connections** window by clicking the red **X** button in the top-right corner.

In the following section, we will cover how to check for updates, an important task to complete after installing Windows Server 2025.

Verifying the updates

To verify and apply updates on your server, follow these steps, as illustrated in *Figure 3.32*:

1. Select the **Last checked for updates** setting highlighted in the **Properties** section.

2. In the **Settings** window, under the **Windows Update** section on the right side, review the list of available updates, if any. If updates are available, click the **Install now** button to proceed with the installation.

Figure 3.32 – Verifying the updates

Please note that the update process may take some time, and a server restart is often required for the updates to take full effect.

> **Note**
>
> For administrators who prefer command-line tools, Windows Server 2025 supports using WinGet and PowerShell to streamline update management. Running `winget upgrade --all` provides a straightforward way to download and install available updates. Alternatively, the `PSWindowsUpdate` module in PowerShell offers comprehensive options for managing updates, including scheduling and automation, which can enhance efficiency in server maintenance tasks.

In the next section, we will guide you on how to disable IE Enhanced Security Configuration in Windows Server 2025, despite Microsoft officially discontinuing IE.

Turning off IE Enhanced Security Configuration

To disable **IE Enhanced Security Configuration**, follow these steps, as depicted in *Figure 3.33*:

1. Access the **IE Enhanced Security Configuration** setting highlighted in the **Properties** section.

2. In the **Internet Explorer Enhanced Security Configuration** window, select the **Off** option under the **Administrators** section.

3. Click **OK** to apply the changes and close the window.

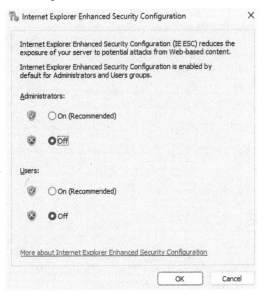

Figure 3.33 – Disabling IE Enhanced Security Configuration

Note

Internet Explorer Enhanced Security Configuration (IE ESC) is designed to minimize the exposure of servers to potential security risks by adjusting security settings. While IE ESC primarily affects Internet Explorer, it can also impact Microsoft Edge when using IE mode for compatibility with legacy applications. Disabling IE ESC can help resolve access issues but may increase the server's vulnerability to security threats. It is essential to balance security needs with accessibility requirements when managing IE ESC settings. With this setting adjusted, the next topic will guide you through changing the time zone, which is crucial for maintaining accurate timestamps and ensuring proper operation of network services.

Adjusting the time zone

To adjust the time zone, follow these steps, as illustrated in *Figure 3.34*:

1. Click on the highlighted time zone setting in the **Properties** section.

2. In the **Date and Time** window that appears, select the **Change time zone** button.

3. In the **Time Zone Settings** window, choose your desired time zone from the drop-down menu.

4. Click **OK** to close the **Time Zone Settings** window.

5. Click **OK** again to close the **Date and Time** window.

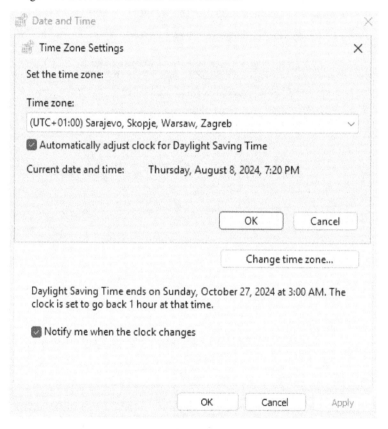

Figure 3.34 – Adjusting the time zone

Once you've adjusted the time zone, the next section will guide you through the process of activating Windows Server, a necessary step for all Windows operating systems, including Windows Server 2025.

Windows Server activation

To fully utilize the features of your Windows Server 2025 (Desktop Experience), activation is required. Follow these steps to complete the activation process, as depicted in *Figure 3.35*:

1. Click on the **Not activated** link under the product ID highlighted in the **Properties** section.

Figure 3.35 – Activating Windows Server 2025

2. In the window that appears, enter your **Windows Server 2025 product key** and click **Next**.

3. Microsoft's **Activation Server** will validate your product key. If the key is valid, click **Next** in the **Activate Windows** window.

4. Once activation is successful, click **Close** to exit the confirmation window.

This section has covered how to configure Windows Server using Server Manager initially. The following section will guide you through performing this configuration using Server Configuration.

How to use Server Configuration for Windows Server initial setup

This section will walk you through the process of configuring Windows Server 2025 Standard (Server Core) using the **Server Configuration tool**. You will learn the essential steps for performing the initial setup of the server in this command-line interface environment.

Renaming the server

You can follow these steps to rename the server, as shown in *Figure 3.36*:

1. At the **Server Configuration** menu prompt, type 2 as the option you want and press *Enter*.

2. Type the new name for the server and press *Enter*.

3. When the **Restart** dialog box appears, click **Yes** to reboot the server.

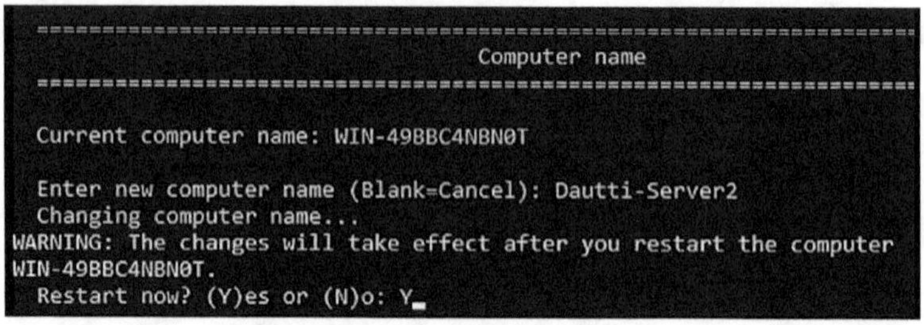

```
==============================================================================
                              Computer name
==============================================================================

Current computer name: WIN-49BBC4NBN0T

Enter new computer name (Blank=Cancel): Dautti-Server2
Changing computer name...
WARNING: The changes will take effect after you restart the computer
WIN-49BBC4NBN0T.
Restart now? (Y)es or (N)o: Y_
```

Figure 3.36 – Renaming the server

4. The server will restart to apply the new name.

In the next section, we will show you how to add the server to a domain.

Connecting to the domain

To connect your server to the domain, ensure you have completed the initial configuration using Server Manager, as outlined earlier. Then, follow these steps to establish the domain connection, as depicted in *Figure 3.37*:

1. At the **Server Configuration** prompt, select option **1** and press *Enter*.
2. To link the server to your organization's domain, type D and press *Enter*.
3. Input your organization's domain name and press *Enter*.
4. Provide the credentials of an authorized domain user and press *Enter*.
5. Enter the associated password and press *Enter*.
6. When prompted by the **Change Computer Name** dialog box, choose **No** if you do not wish to alter the server's name.

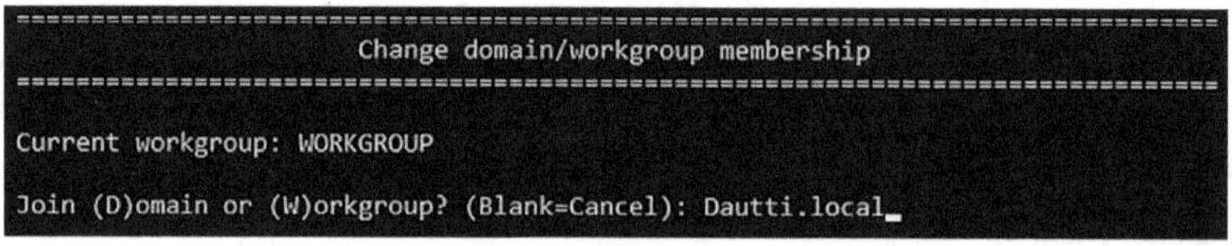

```
==============================================================================
                     Change domain/workgroup membership
==============================================================================

Current workgroup: WORKGROUP

Join (D)omain or (W)orkgroup? (Blank=Cancel): Dautti.local_
```

Figure 3.37 – Connecting to the domain

Next, we will guide you through enabling Remote Desktop, which is essential for remote access to the Windows Server 2025 Server Core edition.

Configuring Remote Desktop

To configure Remote Desktop, follow these steps, as outlined in *Figure 3.38*:

1. At the **Server Configuration** menu prompt, enter 7 and press *Enter* to select the **Remote Desktop configuration** option.

2. Type E and press *Enter* to enable Remote Desktop.

3. Choose option **1** and press *Enter* to select a more **secure access mode**.

4. In the **Remote Desktop** dialog box that appears, click **OK** to confirm that Remote Desktop has been successfully activated.

Next, we will guide you through the process of setting up the IP address, which is essential for the Windows Server 2025 Server Core edition.

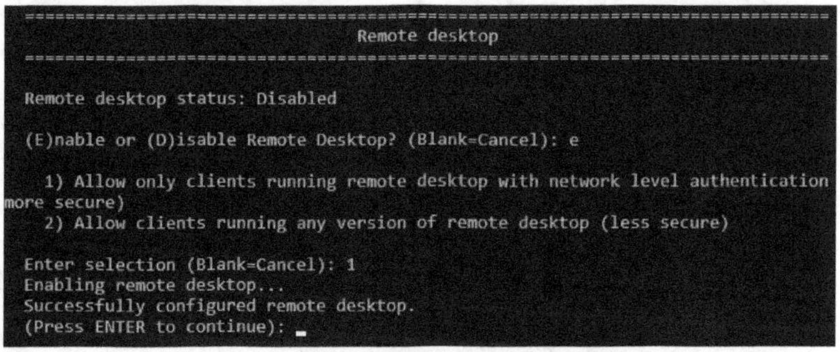

Figure 3.38 – Enabling Remote Desktop

Next, let us learn how to set up the IP address because even Windows Server 2025 Server Core edition requires a static IP address.

Setting up the IP address

To configure the IP address, as depicted in *Figure 3.39*, follow these instructions:

1. From the **Server Configuration** menu, choose option **8** and press *Enter*.

2. Enter the number associated with the network adapter you want to configure and press *Enter*.

3. In the next sub-menu, select option **1** to configure the network adapter's address and press *Enter*.

4. Choose **S** to set a static IP address and press *Enter*.

5. Enter the static IP address you wish to assign and press *Enter*.

6. Provide the subnet mask and press *Enter*.

7.   Enter the default gateway and press *Enter*.

8.   In the sub-menu, select option **2** to configure the DNS servers and press *Enter*.

9.   Input the primary DNS server address and press *Enter*.

10. Confirm the settings by clicking **OK** in the **Network Settings** dialog box.

11. Enter the secondary DNS server address and press *Enter*.

12. Finally, choose option **4** to exit the sub-menu and return to the main menu.

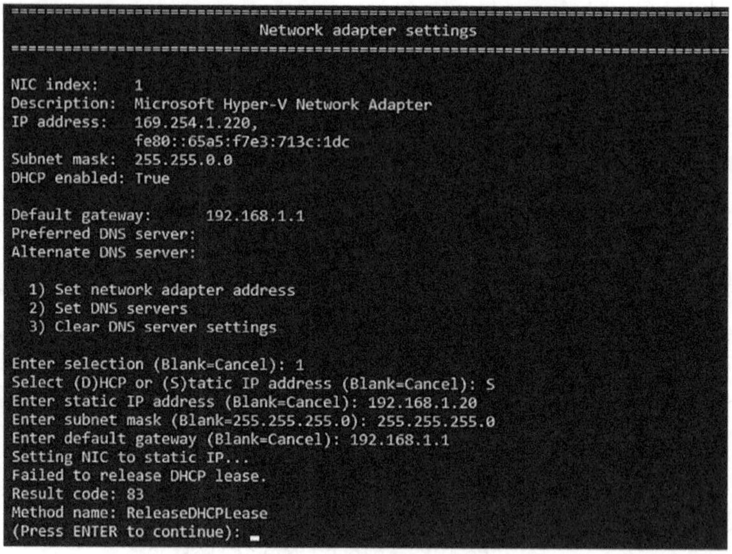

Figure 3.39 – Setting up the IP address

Next, let us learn how to check for updates to the Windows Server 2025 Server Core edition.

Updating Windows Server 2025 Server Core edition

To check for updates and update your Windows Server 2025 Server Core edition, follow these steps, as illustrated in *Figure 3.40*:

1.   At the **Server Configuration** menu prompt, enter 5 and press *Enter* to access the update options.

2.   In the **Update options** window, type A to install all updates or R to install only recommended updates, then press *Enter*.

3.   **Windows Update** will proceed to search for available updates.

4.   If updates are found, you can choose to install all updates by typing A, none by typing N, or select individual updates by typing S, then press *Enter*.

5. The selected updates will be downloaded and installed. If prompted, click **Yes** to restart the server and apply the updates.

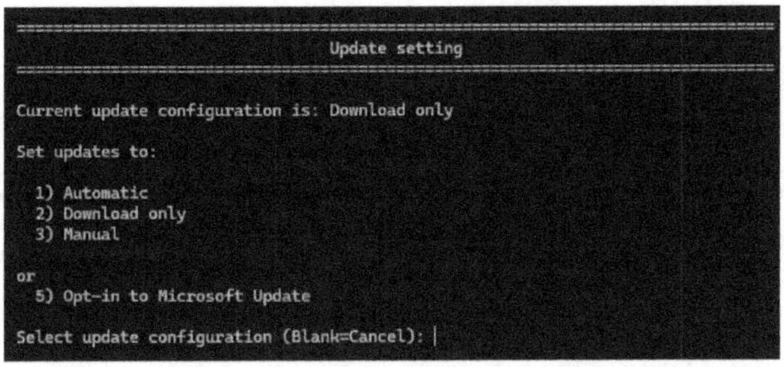

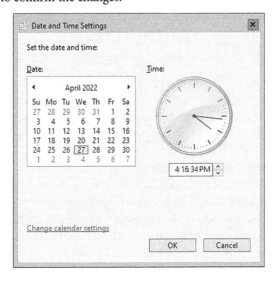

Figure 3.40 – Updating Windows Server 2025 Server Core edition

Next, we will guide you through the process of changing the time zone on your server.

Adjusting the date and time

To adjust the date and time, follow the steps shown in *Figure 3.41*:

1. Type 9 and press *Enter* at the **Server Configuration** menu prompt to choose the option.

2. In the **Date and Time** window, click the **Change date and time** button.

3. Set up the date and time by clicking on the **Date** or **Time** section.

4. Click **OK** to exit the **Date and Time** window.

5. Click **OK** again to confirm the changes.

Figure 3.41 – Adjusting the date and time

Next, we will explain how to activate the Windows Server 2025 Server Core edition.

How to activate Windows Server

You need to activate Windows Server 2025 Server Core after installing it. You can do this by following the steps shown in *Figure 3.42*:

1. Type 11 and press *Enter* at the **Server Configuration** menu prompt to select the option.

2. Type 3 and press *Enter* in the sub-menu to enter the product key for Windows Server 2025.

3. In the **Enter Product Key** window, type the product key and click **OK**.

4. Type 2 and press *Enter* in the sub-menu to start the activation process.

5. Wait for a few moments until Windows Server 2025 is activated—type Exit to close the activation window.

6. Type 4 and press *Enter* in the sub-menu to go back to the main menu.

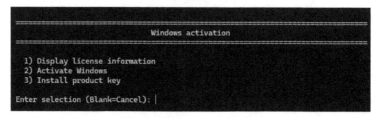

Figure 3.42 – How to activate Windows Server 2025?

This chapter exercise has taught you how to perform the initial configuration of Windows Server 2025 using Server Manager and Server Configuration.

Summary

This chapter provided a comprehensive overview of post-installation tasks in Windows Server 2025, covering key aspects such as device drivers, registry management, and service configurations. You explored how devices are organized within a computer system and the crucial role that device drivers play. Additionally, you gained insights into managing system resources, including how to handle the Windows Server registry and services effectively. Topics included the various registry keys, service startup types, and practical tasks such as installing, uninstalling, and updating drivers, as well as starting, stopping, and restarting Windows services. You also learned how to use the regedit tool for basic operations such as adding, modifying, and deleting registry keys. Furthermore, you were introduced to the concept of Windows Server's initial configuration, which facilitated the completion of post-installation tasks covered in this chapter. The upcoming chapter will delve into **Directory Services** within Windows Server 2025.

Questions

1. **True or false?** A device driver is a program that acts as the translator between computer hardware and an operating system.

2. **Fill in the blank:**_____works on the principle that when a device is plugged into a computer, the device is immediately recognized by the operating system.

3. Which of the following are known as computer system resources? **Choose two:**

   A. IRQ

   B. DMA

   C. SAN

   D. NAS

4. **True or false?** A driver's digital signature identifies its publisher.

5. **Fill in the blank:**_____ is a hierarchical database that stores hardware and software configurations and system security information.

6. Which Windows Server tools are used to operate devices and device drivers? **Choose two:**

   A. Devices

   B. Device Manager

   C. Registry Editor

   D. Control Manager

7. Which Windows Server tools are used to operate the registry and services? **Choose two:**

   A. Services Control Manager

   B. Registry Editor

   C. Device Manager

   D. Devices

8. **Fill in the blank:**_____is the Windows Server native account or an account you created to manage running services.

9. Discuss Windows registry keys.

10. Discuss Windows service startup types.

Further reading

- *How to Use the Windows Device Manager for Troubleshooting*: `https://www.howtogeek.com/167094/how-to-use-the-windows-device-manager-for-troubleshooting`

- *Structure of the Registry*: `https://learn.microsoft.com/en-us/windows/win32/sysinfo/structure-of-the-registry`

- *21 Windows Tools Explained*: `https://www.howtogeek.com/193922/21-windows-administrative-tools-explained/`

- *Introduction to Windows Service Applications*: `https://learn.microsoft.com/en-us/dotnet/framework/windows-services/introduction-to-windows-service-applications`

- *Using Device Manager*: `https://learn.microsoft.com/en-us/windows-hardware/drivers/install/using-device-manager`

Unlock this book's exclusive benefits now

This book comes with additional benefits designed to elevate your learning experience.

Note: Have your purchase invoice ready before you begin.

`https://www.packtpub.com/unlock/9781836205012`

Part 2:
Setting Up
Windows Server 2025

This part will explain how to configure essential roles and services in Windows Server 2025. Upon completion, you will be able to establish a domain environment and deploy critical network services, such as DNS, DHCP, Print Server, Web Server, WDS, and WSUS.

This part contains the following chapters:

- *Chapter 4, Directory Services in Windows Server 2025*
- *Chapter 5, Adding Roles to Windows Server 2025*

4

Directory Services in Windows Server 2025

In this chapter, you will progress in establishing your organization's IT infrastructure by thoroughly exploring domain services, which are pivotal for managing a Windows-based domain network. You will gain insight into **Active Directory Domain Services (AD DS)** and **Domain Name System (DNS)**, understanding their integral roles in network management. Key concepts such as **domains**, **forests**, **tree domains**, **child domains**, and **Domain Controllers (DCs)** will be covered, along with functional levels and trust relationships that facilitate network integration and resource sharing. Additionally, the chapter will delve into DNS functionalities, including forward and reverse lookup zones and DNS records, which are crucial for resolving domain names and ensuring reliable network communication.

Furthermore, you will explore how **Organizational Units (OUs)**, **default containers**, **user accounts**, and different group scopes and types are utilized to effectively manage user and **computer accounts** within a domain-based network. By understanding these components, you'll be able to streamline account management and enhance organizational structure within your network. The chapter culminates with a hands-on exercise where you will install the AD DS and DNS roles and promote a server to a DC. This practical experience will equip you with the skills needed to implement and manage a Windows Server domain, setting the stage for more advanced network configurations and administration.

In this chapter, we're going to cover the following main topics:

- Understanding the **Active Directory (AD)** infrastructure in Windows Server 2025
- Adding and configuring the AD DS role
- Exploring DNS fundamentals and configurations in Windows Server 2025
- Managing OUs and default containers
- User and group management within AD
- Installing the AD DS and DNS roles and promoting the server to a DC

Technical requirements

To complete the exercises in this chapter, you will require the following hardware:

- A **Windows 11 Pro PC** equipped with a minimum of 16 GB of RAM, a 1 TB **hard disk drive (HDD)**, and a stable internet connection

- A **Windows Server 2025 Standard** (Desktop Experience) virtual machine, designated as Virtual Machine 1, configured with a tree domain (`Dautti.local`), featuring at least 4 GB of RAM, 100 GB of HDD space, and internet access

- Another Windows Server 2025 Standard (Desktop Experience) virtual machine, designated as Virtual Machine 2, set up with a tree domain (`ITTrainings.local`), also with a minimum of 4 GB of RAM, 100 GB of HDD space, and internet connectivity

- A third Windows Server 2025 Standard (Desktop Experience) virtual machine, designated as Virtual Machine 3, configured with a child domain (`Programming.Dautti.local`), including at least 4 GB of RAM, 100 GB of HDD space, and internet access

This setup ensures that you have the necessary resources and configurations to perform all tasks effectively.

Understanding the AD infrastructure in Windows Server 2025

AD is a foundational technology from Microsoft that serves as a distributed directory service. It's essential for organizing and managing network resources in a hierarchical and secure manner. It acts as a centralized repository where critical objects—such as user accounts, computers, printers, and network services—are stored, each with its own distinct security settings.

The unique attributes of each object within AD enable granular control over resource management, allowing for precise administration across the network. For instance, each object, whether a user account, computer, printer, or network service, possesses specific attributes, including **Security Identifiers (SIDs)**, group memberships, and Access Control Lists (ACLs). These attributes empower administrators to define individual permissions, roles, and access policies, ensuring that security measures and functionalities are tailored to the requirements of each object.

The architecture of AD, as illustrated in *Figure 4.1*, is structured around three fundamental tiers:

- **Domain:** The basic unit of administration, providing a boundary for policies and security settings

- **Tree:** A collection of domains linked by a contiguous namespace, reflecting a hierarchical relationship among them

- **Forest:** The highest level of organization, which can encompass multiple trees and serves as the topmost layer that integrates the entire directory service

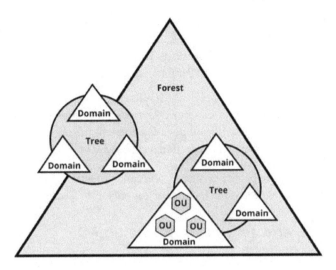

Figure 4.1 – AD architecture (source – Websentra)

This layered approach facilitates efficient resource management and scalability while supporting complex organizational structures. It allows businesses to customize their network infrastructure to align with specific operational needs while maintaining robust security and administrative oversight.

In the sections that follow, we will explore the specific features and configurations of AD, equipping you with the necessary knowledge and skills to effectively implement and manage directory services within your organization.

Addressing the importance of AD

AD is not just a directory service; it is the backbone of modern IT infrastructures, playing a critical role in the management of Windows environments. For those new to IT, understanding the significance of AD is essential for grasping its functionalities and benefits:

- **Centralized management**: One of the primary advantages of AD is its ability to centralize management. IT administrators can manage users, computers, and resources from a single location, significantly reducing complexity and administrative overhead. This centralized approach streamlines the process of user provisioning and deprovisioning, making it easier to maintain an organized and efficient network.

- **Enhanced security**: AD enhances security through its use of SIDs and ACLs. By ensuring that only authorized users can access specific resources, AD protects sensitive information and reduces the risk of unauthorized access. This security model is crucial for safeguarding organizational data and maintaining compliance with regulatory standards.

- **Scalability**: The hierarchical structure of AD supports the scalability of organizations. As businesses grow, AD allows for the seamless integration of new users and resources without compromising performance or security. This flexibility enables organizations to adapt to changing needs and expand their IT infrastructure effectively.

- **Policy enforcement**: AD facilitates the application of Group Policies across the network, allowing organizations to enforce security settings and compliance standards uniformly. This capability ensures that all users and devices adhere to the organization's policies, enhancing the overall security posture and operational efficiency.

By understanding these core principles of AD, one can appreciate its pivotal role in managing and securing network resources, laying the foundation for effective IT administration.

Core protocols and services supporting AD

AD relies on several critical protocols and services to ensure its seamless operation, each contributing to different aspects of network management and security:

- **Lightweight Directory Access Protocol (LDAP)**: This is a foundational protocol that plays a crucial role in enabling users and applications to query and interact with the directory's data. LDAP provides a standardized method for accessing and managing the information stored within AD, making it a key element in directory service operations.

- **Kerberos**: This is a sophisticated authentication mechanism that underpins AD's security framework. Kerberos uses a ticketing system to securely verify the identities of users and servers on the network, preventing unauthorized access and ensuring that all entities communicating within the network are properly authenticated. This protocol is vital for maintaining the integrity and confidentiality of the network environment.

- **DNS**: This protocol is also integral to AD's functionality. DNS serves as a directory for the internet and internal networks, translating user-friendly domain names into numerical IP addresses. This translation process is essential for locating and accessing network resources efficiently. Within an AD environment, DNS not only resolves domain names but also supports AD-specific functions, such as locating DCs and ensuring that services are reachable across the network.

Together, these protocols and services form the backbone of AD, enabling it to deliver a secure, scalable, and efficient directory service that supports complex organizational needs.

Tools and roles for administering AD

AD is a robust framework that provides comprehensive services to enable centralized management of network resources, streamlining the work of system administrators in complex IT environments. To effectively manage various aspects of AD services, Microsoft offers a suite of administrative consoles within the **Microsoft Management Console** (**MMC**) (mmc.exe), each tailored to specific tasks within the directory service:

- **Active Directory Administrative Center** (dsac.exe): A key tool depicted in *Figure 4.2*, this is instrumental in managing Windows Server's directory services. This modern interface integrates several management functions, enabling administrators to oversee these services efficiently. It includes the **Active Directory Users and Computers** (dsa.msc) snap-in, which is essential for managing user accounts, computer objects, OUs, and their associated properties. This tool is foundational for daily administrative tasks, such as creating and managing users, groups, and devices and organizing them within the AD structure.

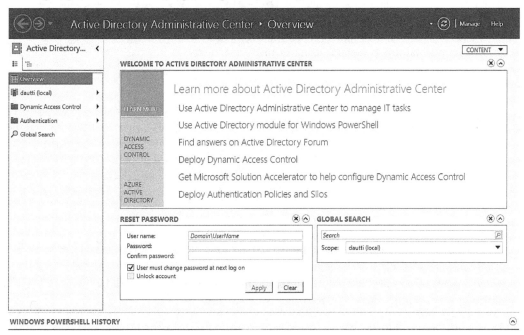

Figure 4.2 – The Active Directory Administrative Center in Windows Server 2025

- **Active Directory Domains and Trusts console** (domain.msc): This console is employed for tasks related to domain management. This tool allows administrators to configure and manage domain trusts, which are crucial for enabling secure communications and resource sharing between different domains within the same or different forests. It also handles the setup and management of **Domain Functional Levels** (**DFLs**), which determine the features available within a domain based on the version of Windows Server being used.

- **Active Directory Sites and Services console** (dssite.msc): This is a critical tool in managing replication between different AD sites. Sites in AD represent the physical structure of a network, and this tool allows administrators to optimize and control how directory information is replicated across various geographic locations, ensuring consistency and availability of data across the entire organization. It also manages services such as global catalog servers and ensures that authentication requests are routed efficiently.

- **AD module for Windows PowerShell**: Not a graphical tool, this offers a command-line interface for more advanced and automated management tasks. PowerShell cmdlets allow administrators to script complex operations, automate repetitive tasks, and manage AD objects at scale, making them invaluable for large or highly customized environments.

To deploy directory services in an organization, the AD DS role must be installed and configured on a Windows Server. AD DS is the backbone of the AD environment, enabling the storage, organization, and management of information about network resources such as users, groups, computers, and policies. It also supports advanced security features, such as centralized authentication and authorization, which are vital for maintaining the integrity and security of the network.

> **Note**
>
> You can access a wealth of free PowerShell scripts at Microsoft's Script Center (`https://technet.microsoft.com/en-us/scriptcenter/bb410849.aspx`) and PowerShell Gallery (`https://www.powershellgallery.com/`). These platforms serve as renowned repositories where IT professionals can find and share scripts for various administrative tasks. Both resources include extensive collections of scripts specifically related to AD and DNS, making them invaluable for automating and simplifying complex network management activities.

For a detailed walkthrough on setting up AD DS, including the installation of the DNS role and the promotion of a server to a DC, see *Chapter 5, Adding Roles to Windows Server 2025*. This chapter includes practical exercises to guide you through the process, ensuring a solid understanding of the necessary steps to integrate AD DS into your infrastructure.

As we move forward, the following section will delve into the critical components of an AD infrastructure, starting with an in-depth look at DCs, which are the cornerstone of any AD environment.

Adding and configuring the AD DS role

In Windows Server environments, the role of the AD DS is crucial for providing centralized directory services, which facilitate network management and authentication. This section delves into the process of adding and configuring the AD DS role, covering key tasks such as deploying DCs, setting up and managing domains, and creating hierarchical structures such as tree and child domains. Additionally, we will explore the concept of namespaces to streamline directory organization and examine how sites enhance network **performance** and replication efficiency. By mastering these aspects, you will be equipped to implement and manage a robust and scalable AD DS infrastructure, optimizing both functionality and performance for your organization.

Understanding DCs

A DC, as depicted in *Figure 4.3*, is a server that plays a critical role in managing and verifying user identities within an organization's network. Its primary function is to authenticate users and authorize access to network resources based on the security policies defined within the domain. In earlier Windows environments, specifically Windows NT, domain management relied on a **Primary Domain Controller** (**PDC**) to handle main domain functions, with **Backup Domain Controllers** (**BDCs**) providing redundancy. However, this model was replaced with the multi-master replication model introduced in Windows 2000, allowing multiple DCs to share the responsibility of managing domain functions. This approach enhances reliability and availability, as all DCs can perform read and write operations, ensuring that authentication and directory services remain robust and accessible across the network.

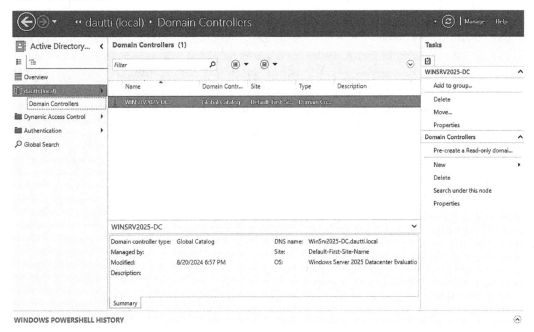

Figure 4.3 – Accessing DCs through the Active Directory Administrative Center

Windows Server 2025 has revolutionized the approach to DCs by eliminating the traditional primary and backup roles. Instead, DCs are now identified by sequential numbers, such as **DC1** and **DC2**, which denote their sequence rather than their function. This modern approach paves the way for a more flexible and scalable domain management environment, where all DCs are considered equal partners in the domain, sharing the responsibility for authentication and directory services. This evolution keeps you, as an IT professional, informed and up to date in your field.

> **Note**
>
> When a server joins a domain but does not take on the role of a DC, it is classified as a **member server**. Member servers operate under the domain's policies and access control but do not handle authentication requests or domain management tasks.

Given that DCs are central to domain access and authentication, understanding the concept of domains is not just important. It's essential to grasp the full scope of AD infrastructure. As an IT professional, your role is significant in understanding the intricacies of domain structures and their role within the network. Therefore, we will next explore these intricacies in detail.

Understanding domains

Domains are fundamental components in network management that organize and group users, computers, devices, and network services under a unified administrative framework. This logical grouping allows for centralized management of resources and security policies. A DC is crucial in this setup, with the AD DS playing a pivotal part in establishing and maintaining domain functionality. *Figure 4.4* demonstrates the domain configuration process within the **Active Directory Domain Services Configuration Wizard** window, showcasing how domains are created and managed.

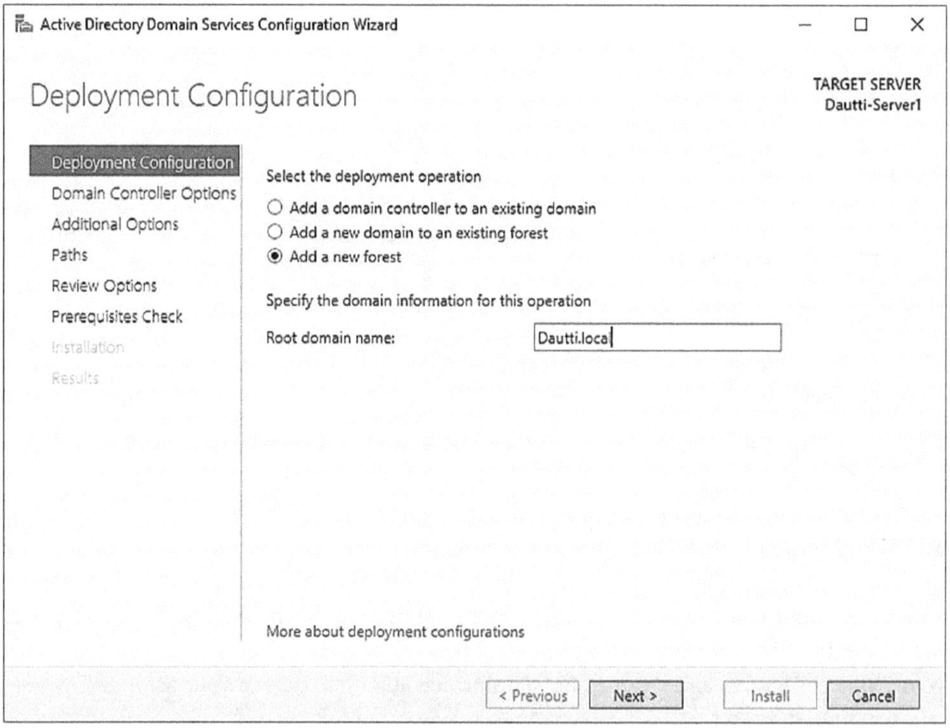

Figure 4.4 – Setting up a root domain in Windows Server 2025

> **Note**
>
> It is crucial to differentiate between a directory domain and a domain name. In the context of directory services, a domain refers to a structured database of network resources, including users, servers, and devices, that are managed collectively under specific administrative policies. This domain facilitates effective management and security within an organization's IT infrastructure. On the other hand, a domain name is part of the DNS, which is a hierarchical naming system used to identify and locate resources on the internet, such as websites and email servers.

Furthermore, domains can be organized into a **domain tree**, which represents a hierarchical structure of multiple domains. This structure allows for the organization of domains into a parent-child relationship, where each domain within the tree can inherit policies and settings from its parent domain while maintaining its distinct configuration. The following section will explore the concept of domain trees in detail, explaining how they extend the domain structure and facilitate more complex organizational setups.

Understanding the Domain Tree

To fully understand the AD architecture, it's important to delve into the concept of a domain tree. A domain tree represents a logical structure within AD, consisting of one or more domains that share a common namespace and are arranged hierarchically. This hierarchical setup not only organizes the domains but also ensures that they inherently trust one another due to the transitive trust relationship. In AD, a trust relationship (as shown in *Figure 4.5*) allows users in one domain to authenticate and access resources in another domain without needing separate credentials. Transitive trust means that if domain A trusts domain B and domain B trusts domain C, then domain A will automatically trust domain C. This built-in trust simplifies resource sharing and authentication across domains within the same tree domain. When introducing a new domain into an existing tree, it is necessary to provide the parent domain's name during the server promotion process to establish the appropriate hierarchy.

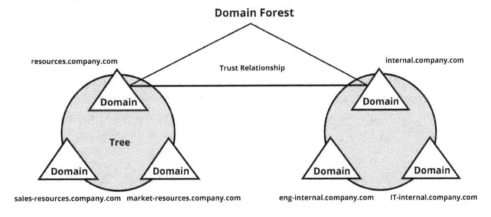

Figure 4.5 – Hierarchical architecture of Domain Forest (source – Websentra)

The process involves specifying the parent domain during the server promotion phase to integrate a new domain into an existing domain tree. This addition allows the new domain to inherit policies and settings from its parent while establishing its own unique identity within the tree. *Figure 4.6* provides a visual representation of creating a child domain in Windows Server 2025. It illustrates how a new domain is incorporated into the existing tree structure and how it aligns with the overall namespace.

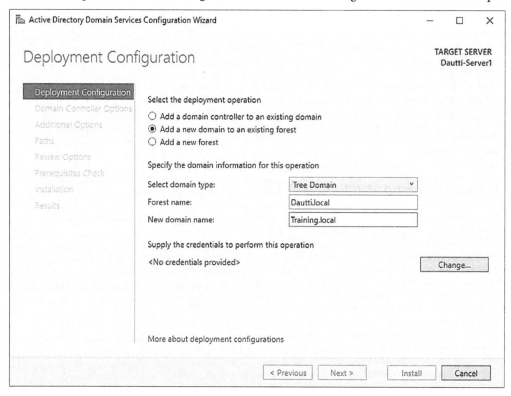

Figure 4.6 – Setting up a tree domain in Windows Server 2025

The domain tree concept becomes more expansive when multiple domain trees are combined to form a forest. A forest represents a broader organizational structure that groups all the domain trees within an enterprise, allowing for a unified directory environment. The forest serves as the highest level of the AD hierarchy, providing a framework for managing multiple trees and their interconnected domains. The detailed structure and functions of a forest will be discussed in the subsequent section.

Understanding the Forest

In AD, the concept of a **forest** is analogous to a natural forest, which is composed of multiple trees. An AD forest can consist of a single domain tree or a collection of interconnected domain trees. Each domain tree within a forest shares a common schema and global catalog, but the trees themselves do not have to share the same namespace. A root domain is the first domain created within a domain tree and serves as the foundation for the entire domain structure. It often holds critical roles such as the schema master and domain naming master. A domain tree that operates as a root domain can exist independently within a forest, but when multiple trees are present, the forest acts as an overarching framework that integrates and manages these trees, creating a cohesive and scalable directory environment.

The forest acts as the highest level of AD structure, providing a unified directory system that enables resource sharing and administrative management across all domains within it. Although this might initially seem like circular logic, the concept of a forest as both a domain and an encompassing structure reflects its dual role in organizing and linking various domains.

To create and configure a forest in Windows Server 2025, you use the AD DS configuration wizard, which is also employed for setting up tree domains. This wizard facilitates the forest creation process, guiding you through the necessary steps and configurations, as depicted in *Figure 5.3*.

Within the framework of a domain tree, additional subdomains, referred to as child domains, can be established. These child domains function as subdivisions of the parent tree domain, allowing for a more granular organization and management of resources. The upcoming section will explore the role of child domains in detail, including their setup and functionality, as well as how they contribute to the overall structure of AD.

Understanding the Child Domain

A **child domain** is a subordinate domain within a tree domain structure in AD. For example, as shown in *Figure 4.6*, there are two tree domains: `Dautti.local` and `Training.local`. `Dautti.local` serves as the root domain of the forest, establishing the foundational namespace. In this setup, `Training.local` includes a child domain called `Administration.Dautti.local`. This child domain is an extension of the parent domain's namespace, ensuring a cohesive and organized directory hierarchy.

Creating a child domain in Windows Server 2025 is accomplished using the AD DS configuration wizard, which is also used for setting up other types of domains. The wizard guides you through the necessary steps, as illustrated in *Figure 4.7*, making the process straightforward and consistent.

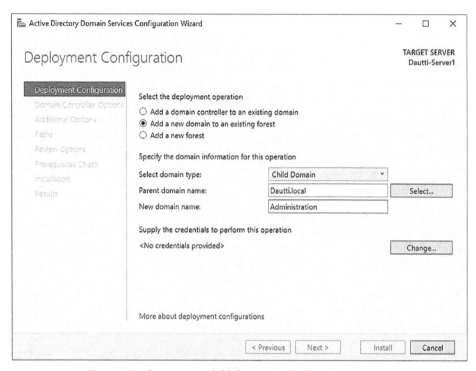

Figure 4.7 – Setting up a child domain in Windows Server 2025

The structure of tree and child domains resembles a tree data structure, where each domain functions as a node with a parent-child relationship. This hierarchical arrangement facilitates efficient resource management and delegation of administrative tasks. The parent domain oversees the child domains, while child domains inherit certain attributes and policies from their parent yet retain their own unique identity.

Understanding this hierarchical organization is fundamental for managing an AD environment effectively. The next topic will delve into the operations master roles, which are critical for maintaining the stability and functionality of the AD infrastructure.

Understanding Operations Master Roles

AD DS is a robust and intricate system that necessitates thorough planning and execution to optimize its capabilities. Once deployed, its operational benefits become increasingly evident. A key component of AD DS is the **operations master roles**, which are essential for maintaining and managing the directory services effectively.

In our previous discussion, we created the root domain, Dautti.local, which serves as the primary domain for the forest. This domain is hosted on a server that also functions as a DC, overseeing the network's directory services.

When the AD DS role is installed and the server is promoted to a DC, AD DS automatically assigns five critical operations master roles. These roles are split into the following two categories:

- **Forest-wide roles**: The **schema master** and **domain naming master** roles are forest-wide. The schema master oversees the directory schema, which dictates the attributes and classes of objects within the directory, ensuring consistency across the entire forest. The domain naming master, on the other hand, manages the namespace and guarantees that each domain name within the forest is unique, preventing naming conflicts.

- **Domain-wide roles**: The remaining three roles—**RID master**, **PDC emulator**, and **infrastructure master**—are domain-wide. The RID master allocates SIDs to DCs to create new security principals. The PDC emulator handles password changes and manages time synchronization within the domain, serving as a bridge for backward compatibility with older systems. The infrastructure master is responsible for maintaining and updating references to objects in other domains, ensuring that cross-domain object references remain accurate and up-to-date.

In the example provided, illustrated in *Figure 4.8*, the `Dautti.local` root domain holds the schema master and domain naming master roles for the entire Dautti forest. Each tree domain within this forest, such as `Dautti.local` and `Training.local`, possesses its own RID master, PDC emulator, and infrastructure master roles to manage domain-specific tasks and operations.

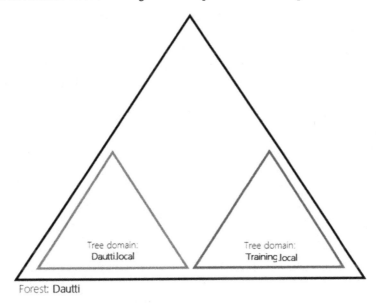

Figure 4.8 – AD DS structure

These five operations master roles are known as **Flexible Single Master Operations** (**FSMO**) roles. The term *flexible* reflects their ability to be transferred to other DCs if necessary. At the same time, *single* indicates that only one DC can hold each role at any given time to prevent conflicts and ensure consistency. Understanding these roles and their functions is crucial for managing and troubleshooting AD environments. The following section will delve into the differences between domains and workgroups, further expanding on network management concepts.

Understanding the difference between domains and workgroups

To effectively differentiate between a domain and a workgroup, it is important to understand the underlying network architectures they represent: **peer-to-peer (P2P) networking** and **client/server networking**, which were briefly mentioned in *Chapter 1, Network Fundamentals and Introduction to Windows Server 2025*.

In a P2P network, commonly known as a **workgroup**, each computer operates independently and manages its resources. This architecture is ideal for smaller networks, such as those found in home or small office environments, where simplicity and direct resource sharing are key. In a workgroup, each device holds its user accounts and permissions, with no centralized management or control. This decentralized approach can be advantageous for straightforward setups but becomes increasingly challenging to manage as the number of computers grows. Without a central administration, there is a heightened risk of inconsistent security policies and user management issues, making workgroups less suitable for larger or more complex environments, particularly where sensitive data is involved.

Conversely, a client/server network, or domain, provides a more structured approach to managing resources and security. In a domain, a central server known as a DC oversees administrative tasks and enforces security policies across the entire network. This centralized management enables efficient user authentication, policy application, and resource allocation, which is crucial for larger organizations and environments such as **Metropolitan Area Networks (MANs)** or **Wide Area Networks (WANs)**. Domains support hierarchical structures and more complex security requirements, allowing for better scalability, control, and consistent policy enforcement across all networked devices. Consequently, domains are more appropriate for large, complex environments where sensitive data is processed, while workgroups may be suitable for smaller entities with less stringent security needs.

The following table, *Table 4.1*, provides a comparative summary of the key differences between domains and workgroups, outlining their respective strengths and limitations based on network scale and management needs. This comparison is instrumental in determining the most suitable network architecture for a given environment.

Domain	Workgroup
A dedicated server is used to provide services	Computers share resources equally without needing a dedicated server
An example is the client/server network	An example is a P2P network

Table 4.1 – Domain vs. Workgroup

Understanding these distinctions will help in making informed decisions about network design and management. The subsequent section will explore the concept of trust relationships between a computer and a DC, further enhancing our grasp of network security and administration.

Understanding trust relationships

A key concept in AD is the trust relationship, mentioned briefly in the *Understanding the Domain Tree* subsection, which plays a crucial role in how computers, DCs, and domains interact within a networked environment. When a computer is integrated into a domain, it shifts from relying on its local **Security Account Manager** (**SAM**) for authentication to depending on the DC's authentication system, typically **Kerberos**. This transition is significant because it centralizes user authentication, ensuring that credentials are verified by the DC rather than the local machine. That not only streamlines the authentication process but also enhances security by enforcing consistent policies across the network.

Trust relationships extend beyond individual computers to encompass entire domains within a forest—a logical grouping of multiple tree domains. Within a forest, each domain automatically trusts the authentication methods of the others, establishing a cohesive security framework. For instance, as illustrated in *Figure 5.6*, if the `Dautti.local` domain authenticates a user, this authentication is implicitly recognized and trusted by another domain in the same forest, such as `Training.local`. This trust is rooted in the shared infrastructure of the forest, where domains such as `Dautti.local` serve as the foundation for this interconnected network.

Understanding trust relationships is essential for grasping the broader administrative and communication structures that facilitate secure and efficient operations within an AD environment. These relationships ensure that users can access resources across different domains without the need for redundant authentication processes, thereby promoting seamless collaboration and resource sharing.

In the next section, we will delve into the functional levels of domains and forests, which define the capabilities and compatibility of the AD environment. We will also explore how to check and configure these functional levels to optimize the performance and security of your network.

Understanding functional levels

Functional levels in AD are critical elements that shape the functionality, compatibility, and overall behavior of the AD environment. They help define the specific features that can be utilized and ensure that all DCs within the environment are running compatible versions of Windows Server. There are two primary functional levels to understand, as illustrated in *Figure 4.9*:

- **Forest Functional Level (FFL)**: This is pivotal in determining which versions of Windows Server can operate on the DCs across the entire forest, which is the topmost structure within AD that can consist of one or more domains. By setting the FFL, you not only define the minimum server version allowed but also unlock specific forest-wide features that enhance security, replication, and management capabilities across all the domains within that forest.

For instance, certain advanced features such as the AD Recycle Bin or fine-grained password policies are only available at higher functional levels.

- **Domain Functional Level (DFL):** This applies to individual domains within the forest. It specifies which Windows Server versions are supported on the DCs within that domain and enables domain-specific features. Raising the DFL can unlock enhancements in domain-specific functionalities, such as improvements in authentication protocols, group policy management, and replication methods. This level of control allows administrators to gradually upgrade parts of the AD infrastructure without immediately affecting the entire forest, providing a flexible approach to modernization.

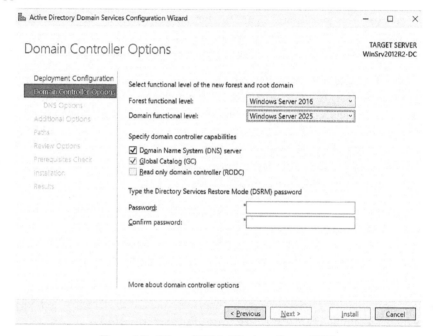

Figure 4.9 – FFL and DFL in Windows Server 2025

In the context of Windows Server 2025, the minimum FFL and DFL can be set to Windows Server 2016. This requirement ensures that the forest remains compatible with modern features while still allowing for some backward compatibility with older systems. Both the FFL and DFL can be elevated to Windows Server 2025, which enables the most current features and optimizations offered by the latest server technology. It's important to note that once a functional level is raised, it cannot be lowered. So, careful planning is essential to avoid compatibility issues with older systems that may still be in use.

Verifying and managing DFLs and FFLs

To verify and manage the forest and DFLs in Windows Server 2025, you can follow these steps:

1. Click the **Start** button, and from the **Start** menu, select **Server Manager**.

2. In the **Server Manager** window, click on **Tools** in the menu bar and choose **Active Directory Domains and Trusts**.

3. In the **Active Directory Domains and Trusts** window, right-click the root domain and select **Properties** from the context menu.

4. Within the **Properties** dialog box, under the **General** tab, the current **Domain functional level** and **Forest functional level** are displayed, as shown in *Figure 4.10*.

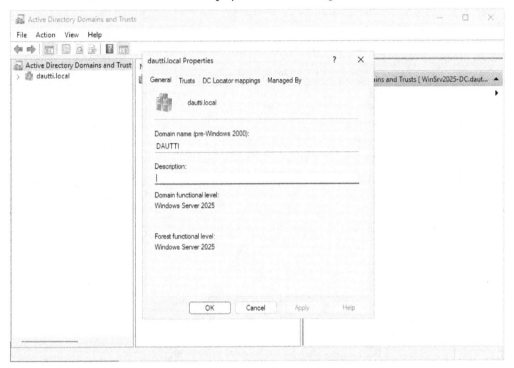

Figure 4.10 – Verifying the FFL and DFL

Understanding and managing FFL and DFL is essential for ensuring that your AD environment operates smoothly and securely, with all the necessary features available to support your organizational needs. These levels also play a crucial role in the overall architecture and strategy of your AD deployment, allowing for both flexibility and control as you scale and adapt your infrastructure.

With a solid grasp of how functional levels impact your AD environment, you can explore the concept of a contiguous namespace. This concept is integral to maintaining a logical and seamless connection between child domains and their parent domains within the same tree structure, ensuring efficient and organized management of your AD hierarchy.

Exploring the concept of namespaces

In AD DS, the concept of a namespace is fundamental to the organization and management of domains and forests within a network. A namespace serves as a logical identifier that uniquely names a domain or a forest, providing structure and clarity to the AD DS environment. For example, in *Figure 4.9*, the `Training.local` domain functions as both the root domain and the overarching forest. Within this forest, `Training.local` and `ITTrainings.local` are distinct domain trees, each representing a separate branch within the same hierarchical structure. Additionally, within the `Training.local` tree domain, a child domain named `Programming` exists. The `Training.local` component, which is shared across these domains, signifies a contiguous namespace, meaning that all domains within this forest are connected through a common naming convention.

In AD DS, the concept of a namespace is fundamental to the organization and management of domains and forests within a network. A namespace serves as a logical identifier that uniquely names a domain or a forest, providing structure and clarity to the AD DS environment. For example, in *Figure 4.11*, the `Dautti.local` domain functions as both the root domain and the overarching forest. Within this forest, ITTrainings.local and Administration.local are distinct domain trees, each representing a separate branch within the same hierarchical structure. Additionally, within the `Dautti.local` tree domain, a child domain named `Programming.Dautti.local` exists. The `Dautti.local` component is shared across these domains and signifies a contiguous namespace, meaning that all domains within this forest are connected through a common naming convention.

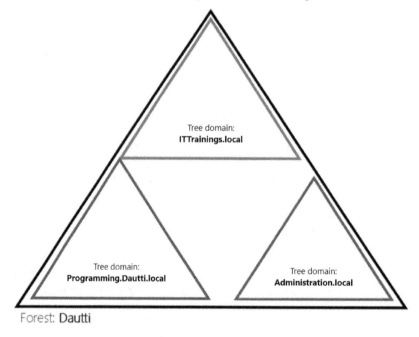

Figure 4.11 – The namespace concept in AD DS

A contiguous namespace is crucial for maintaining a consistent and organized AD DS structure. It ensures that all domains within the forest are logically linked, facilitating easier management and navigation within the network. That shared naming structure not only simplifies the identification and management of domains but also reflects the hierarchical nature of the AD DS environment, where each domain is part of a larger, interconnected system.

To better understand namespaces, it can be helpful to draw an analogy to the **Uniform Resource Locator** (**URL**) system used on the internet. Just as a URL uniquely identifies and locates a specific website on a web server, a namespace in AD DS uniquely identifies and organizes domains within a forest. This logical structure allows administrators to manage resources, apply policies, and maintain security across the network efficiently.

Understanding the role of namespaces is essential for effective AD DS management, as it directly influences how domains are structured, named, and related to one another within a forest. With a clear grasp of namespaces, administrators can ensure a well-organized and navigable AD DS environment. Moving forward, the next topic to explore is the concept of a site within a domain, which represents a physical or logical location in a network. This concept is key to optimizing network traffic and replication within the AD DS infrastructure.

Sites explained

In addition to its logical structure, AD incorporates a physical structure that reflects the network's geographical or organizational layout, known as a *site*. A site represents a specific physical location within an organization's network infrastructure and can encompass one or more domains connected by high-speed links. The purpose of defining sites in AD is to optimize network traffic and enhance overall performance, particularly by managing the replication and authentication traffic between different locations more effectively.

Sites play a crucial role in reducing unnecessary network traffic, especially across **wide-area networks** (**WANs**) where bandwidth might be limited or expensive. By ensuring that replication traffic—used to synchronize directory data across DCs—is confined to fast, local network links whenever possible, AD helps maintain data consistency without overwhelming slower network connections. That is particularly important in large, distributed environments where DCs might be spread across multiple cities, regions, or even countries.

Moreover, sites in AD aren't just about replication efficiency; they also play a key role in authentication processes. When a user logs in, AD directs the authentication request to a DC within the same site as the user, thus speeding up the authentication process and reducing the load on remote servers. This localization of authentication and replication activities significantly improves the user experience and the reliability of network services.

Understanding how sites function, as well as their impact on replication, is essential for IT professionals tasked with managing or designing an AD infrastructure. Proper site design ensures that network resources are used efficiently, users experience minimal delays, and the network remains resilient even as it scales. Before exploring the details of how AD replication works to keep data consistent across domains, it's important to grasp how sites contribute to the robustness and efficiency of an AD environment, particularly in large or complex networks.

Exploring replication

Replication in AD is a foundational feature that ensures data consistency and integrity across all DCs within a forest. This process is essential for maintaining an up-to-date and synchronized directory service, where any modifications—whether they involve user account details, security policies, or configuration settings—are promptly reflected across the entire network of DCs. The replication mechanism operates continuously to propagate these changes, preventing any potential conflicts or inconsistencies that could arise if different parts of the network hold divergent versions of the directory data.

The efficiency of replication is managed by the replication topology, which refers to the network of routes that replication data travels between DCs. This topology isn't random; it is meticulously generated and optimized by the **Knowledge Consistency Checker** (**KCC**). The KCC assesses the network's structure and dynamics, creating a replication path that balances speed and load distribution, thus ensuring that data updates are disseminated quickly without overwhelming the network's resources. This automated process is crucial for large and complex AD environments, where manual configuration would be impractical and prone to error.

Additionally, AD supports both intra- and inter-site replication. Intra-site replication occurs within the same site, typically using high-speed connections, and is more frequent, ensuring near-real-time data synchronization. Inter-site replication, on the other hand, occurs between different sites and is less frequent. It's optimized to reduce the impact on bandwidth, particularly over slower or more expensive WAN links. Administrators can configure inter-site replication schedules and compression settings to manage this process effectively, balancing the need for up-to-date information with the constraints of network resources.

Understanding replication is not just about grasping the mechanics of how data is synchronized; it also involves recognizing its critical role in maintaining the overall health and performance of the AD environment. If replication fails or is misconfigured, it can lead to outdated or conflicting data across DCs, which can cause a host of issues, from authentication failures to incorrect policy applications.

After mastering replication, the next step in managing AD is to understand the schema—a comprehensive blueprint that defines the structure of all objects and attributes within the directory. The schema is central to how AD organizes and stores data, dictating what types of objects (such as users, groups, or computers) can exist in the directory and what attributes those objects can have. Familiarity with the schema enables administrators to extend or modify the directory to meet specific organizational needs while ensuring compatibility and stability within the AD infrastructure.

Understanding the schema

The **schema** in AD is a critical component that underpins the organization and management of all data within the directory service. It functions as a structured blueprint, dictating how data is stored, organized, and accessed across the entire AD infrastructure. The schema is composed of three core elements:

- **Objects**: These are distinct entities within the directory, such as users, computers, printers, or security groups, each representing a real-world resource or function.

- **Classes**: Objects are categorized into classes, which define the type of the object and set the framework for what it can represent within the directory. For instance, a user object might belong to a `User` class, which outlines specific attributes such as username, password, email address, and department.

- **Attributes**: These are the properties or characteristics assigned to objects, providing detailed information about them. For example, the attributes of a `user` object might include a user's full name, job title, phone number, and login credentials.

The schema not only defines what objects and attributes exist but also sets the rules for how these elements can be created, modified, and managed within the AD environment. That ensures that data integrity and consistency are maintained across the entire network. Changes to the schema are carefully controlled and replicated across the network. This controlled approach ensures that all DCs within the forest remain synchronized, maintaining a uniform structure and enabling seamless management and querying of directory data across different domains and sites. Your understanding of this process is key to ensuring the stability and reliability of the network.

In the following section, we will delve into Microsoft Passport, a modern authentication method that enhances security by allowing users to sign in without traditional passwords, relying instead on more secure alternatives such as biometrics or PINs. This approach not only strengthens security but also improves the overall user experience by simplifying the login process.

Microsoft Passport explained

In today's digital environment, managing an ever-increasing number of passwords for various applications, websites, and services presents a significant challenge. Traditional password-based authentication is not only inconvenient but also fraught with security vulnerabilities, as passwords can easily be forgotten, guessed, stolen, or compromised through phishing attacks. Recognizing these issues, Microsoft introduced *Microsoft Passport*, which is now part of Windows Hello for Business. This cutting-edge, password-less authentication system is designed to enhance both security and user convenience.

Microsoft Passport leverages the **Fast ID Online (FIDO) Alliance** standard, a widely recognized framework for secure, password-free authentication. The system operates using a two-factor authentication model that combines a single sign-in service with a wallet service. This means that instead of relying on a password, users authenticate their identity using something they possess, such as a trusted device (for example, a smartphone or a security key), along with something unique to them, such as biometric data (fingerprint or facial recognition) or a secure PIN. The combination of these factors ensures that even if one factor is compromised, the other remains secure, significantly reducing the risk of unauthorized access.

By adopting passwordless as part of Windows Hello for Business, organizations can enhance their security posture while simplifying the user experience. Moving away from traditional passwords reduces the risk of security incidents, as passwords are often easily forgotten, guessed, or stolen, especially when not paired with **multi-factor authentication** (**MFA**). Users no longer need to remember complex passwords or manage multiple credentials, which leads to fewer password-related security incidents and a decrease in support requests. This approach aligns with the broader industry shift toward more secure and user-friendly authentication methods. By embracing passwordless solutions, organizations can mitigate the vulnerabilities associated with password management and foster a more robust security framework that incorporates multi-factor and biometric-based solutions.

In this section, we have delved into the core components of the AD infrastructure, including domains, forests, trees, sites, schemas, and namespaces. We have also covered how to configure and verify the domain and FFLs in Windows Server 2025. Understanding these elements is crucial for anyone tasked with managing an AD environment. In the next section, we will explore the DNS and its pivotal role in the functioning and management of AD, ensuring seamless name resolution and directory services across the network.

Exploring DNS fundamentals and configurations in Windows Server 2025

The DNS emerged from the ARPANET project in the 1960s, addressing the need for a user-friendly way to identify network devices beyond numerical IP addresses. This concept evolved into the DNS as we know it in the early 1980s, with the release of foundational specifications documented in **Request for Comments** (**RFCs**). DNS is organized into a hierarchical structure akin to a tree, where the root zone branches into various domains and sub-domains, each containing resource records that provide essential information about network resources. A domain name is constructed from multiple segments, known as labels, separated by dots—such as `packtpub.com`. This system is underpinned by a distributed database that utilizes a client-server architecture, where network hosts act as name servers. These servers are responsible for resolving domain names to their corresponding IP addresses, ensuring seamless navigation and connectivity across the internet. This hierarchical and distributed approach enhances scalability, efficiency, and reliability in managing domain names and network resources.

Understanding how DNS works

To fully understand how the DNS operates, it's helpful to follow the sequence of steps that occur when you attempt to access a website. DNS is essential for translating human-readable domain names into machine-readable IP addresses, facilitating communication between users and websites. The following describes the DNS resolution process, explaining how your browser finds the correct IP address to connect to when you enter a web address such as `www.packtpub.com`:

1. **Entering the URL**: When you enter `www.packtpub.com` into your browser's address bar and press *Enter*, your browser sends a request to connect to this domain.

2. **Recursive resolver**: This request first reaches a crucial component of the DNS infrastructure known as the **recursive resolver**. Typically managed by your **Internet Service Provider (ISP)**, this resolver is responsible for handling queries on your behalf.

3. **Root servers**: The recursive resolver then communicates with **global root servers**, which hold information about **top-level domains (TLDs)** such as **.com**. These servers do not have complete DNS information, but they direct the resolver to the appropriate TLD servers.

4. **TLD servers**: The TLD servers, in turn, respond by providing information that directs the resolver to the authoritative name servers for the specific domain, such as `packtpub.com`.

5. **Authoritative name servers**: The resolver queries these **authoritative name servers** to find the exact IP address associated with `packtpub.com`. The authoritative servers contain the actual DNS records that map domain names to IP addresses.

6. **Returning the IP address**: Once the resolver obtains the IP address of the web server hosting `packtpub.com`, it relays this information back to your browser.

7. **Connecting to the web server**: With the IP address, your browser can establish a connection to the web server and retrieve the website's content for you to view.

This step-by-step process illustrates the intricate workings of DNS, highlighting its role in converting domain names into IP addresses that enable seamless communication across the internet. Understanding this process underscores the importance of correctly configuring the DNS role within your network. By doing so, you ensure efficient domain name resolution, which is critical for both internal network operations and external internet access.

Installing the DNS role

In Windows Server 2025, the DNS role is crucial for enabling the server to translate domain names into IP addresses, facilitating seamless network communication and access to resources. This role can be configured using the **Server Manager tool**, which provides a straightforward interface for managing server roles and features. As depicted in *Figure 4.12*, the process begins by accessing the Server Manager and selecting the option to add roles and features.

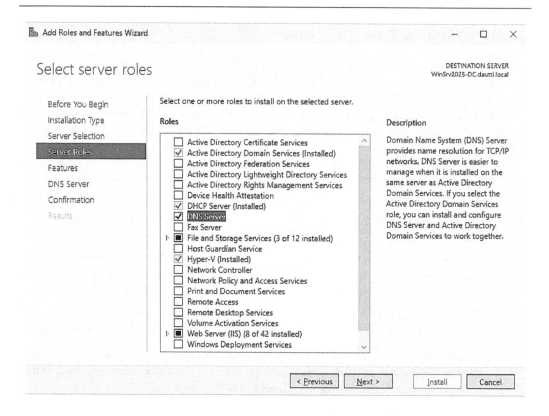

Figure 4.12 – Installing the DNS role

You can either install the DNS role as an independent service or in conjunction with AD DS. When installed separately, the DNS role functions autonomously to handle domain name resolution. However, integrating the DNS with AD DS, as shown in *Figure 4.13*, enhances the overall functionality of the network by allowing the DNS server to support AD operations, such as DC location and service record lookups. This integration is particularly beneficial for managing large-scale networks where AD and the DNS work together to streamline operations.

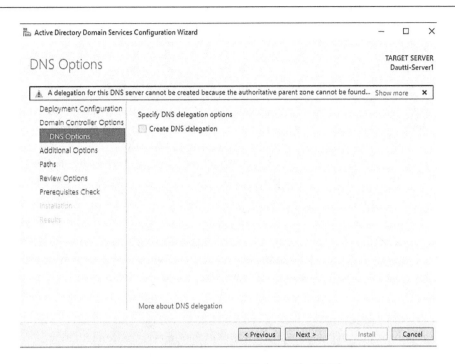

Figure 4.13 – Adding the DNS alongside AD DS

Furthermore, the DNS role is often included as part of the AD DS installation process, providing a cohesive setup that supports the resolution of domain names within the AD environment. This streamlined approach ensures that DNS services are properly configured to support AD's needs, including the automatic creation of necessary DNS records.

With the DNS role successfully installed and configured, you will be well-equipped to manage domain name resolution and enhance network functionality. The next step involves understanding how **hosts** and **LAN Manager hosts (lmhosts)** files contribute to local name resolution, which complements the role of DNS in your network setup.

Understanding the role of hosts and lmhosts files

In any network environment, effective name resolution is fundamental to ensuring seamless communication between devices, and the hosts and lmhosts files are pivotal in facilitating this process. These files are typically located in the `C:\Windows\system32\drivers\etc` directory and provide a straightforward yet powerful mechanism for resolving network names, even in the absence of dedicated name resolution services:

- **Hosts**: This file acts as a static and customizable mapping tool, linking specific IP addresses to **hostnames**. That allows for local DNS name resolution, ensuring that devices on the network can be identified by easily recognizable names rather than numerical IP addresses. That is particularly beneficial in environments where DNS services may be unavailable or unreliable, or where it could require manual overrides for testing and administrative purposes. By editing the hosts file, administrators can control and dictate how names are resolved within the local network, ensuring that critical systems are always reachable by their designated names.

- **LMHOSTS**: The LMHOSTS file maps IP addresses to **NetBIOS** computer names. While its relevance has diminished in modern networks, it may still hold value in specific scenarios, particularly in legacy environments that rely on the NetBIOS protocol for name resolution. This file provides a mechanism for resolving NetBIOS names even when a **Windows Internet Name Service (WINS) server** is not available. However, with the growing emphasis on DNS as the primary name resolution method in Windows Server 2025 and the phasing out of WINS, the practical use of LMHOSTS may be limited for most contemporary applications.

Both the hosts and lmhosts files require manual entries, with each mapping recorded on a separate line to maintain clarity and organization. This manual configuration allows network administrators to have granular control over name resolution, ensuring that network traffic is directed correctly and efficiently.

Figure 4.14 visually represents the location and structure of the hosts and lmhosts files within a Windows Server 2025 environment, highlighting their importance in network configuration.

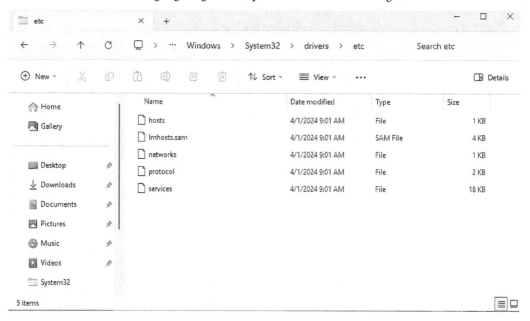

Figure 4.14 – The hosts and lmhosts files in Windows Server 2025

Moreover, the concept of a hostname, which serves as the domain identifier for the local computer within a network, is essential for local network identification. This concept, previously discussed in this chapter, is integral to understanding how devices are recognized and communicated within a networked environment. By effectively managing the hosts and lmhosts files, administrators can ensure consistent and reliable name resolution, which is vital for the smooth operation of network services and applications.

Understanding hostnames

As an IT professional, your familiarity with hostnames is a fundamental aspect of effective network management. Hostnames serve as the backbone for device identification and communication within a network, as shown in *Figure 4.15*. A hostname is a logical label assigned to a device, ensuring its unique recognition across a network and enabling seamless interaction, particularly within a **Local Area Network** (**LAN**). This identifier is not only crucial for local network operations but also plays a significant role in broader network interactions, as it is often synonymous with a domain name. By assigning clear and meaningful hostnames, you can easily manage and troubleshoot devices, ensuring that each system is readily identifiable and can be efficiently accessed.

The assignment of hostnames is a key step in configuring devices, particularly in environments such as Windows Server 2025, where the correct identification of servers and other networked devices is critical for maintaining order and functionality. A well-chosen hostname simplifies network management by allowing administrators to locate and manage devices quickly within the network infrastructure.

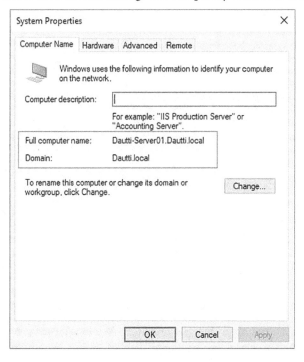

Figure 4.15 – Example of assigning a hostname in Windows Server 2025

In addition to understanding hostnames, it is vital to grasp the concept of DNS zones, which act as administrative segments within a DNS. These are covered in the following subsection.

Understanding DNS zones

A deep understanding of **DNS zones** is not just theoretical but also practical. This level of understanding is crucial for mastering network management. These zones form the backbone of the hierarchical DNS structure that governs how domain names are resolved across a network. DNS zones are integral to the AD namespace, which is closely aligned with the broader DNS namespace, providing a structured and scalable approach to managing domain-related data. By segmenting DNS zones, administrators can store and manage information about specific domains more effectively, ensuring that domain name resolution is both accurate and efficient.

There are three primary types of DNS zones, each serving a distinct purpose:

- **Primary zone**: The primary zone is the authoritative source of DNS information for a domain. It holds the definitive, editable copy of the DNS database and is responsible for maintaining all DNS records within its scope. This zone is the central authority for domain name resolution, ensuring that DNS queries are answered correctly and consistently.

- **Secondary zone**: The secondary zone acts as a backup to the primary zone, containing a read-only copy of the DNS records. This zone is crucial for redundancy, as it allows DNS resolution to continue uninterrupted even if the primary zone becomes inaccessible. The secondary zone is synchronized with the primary zone, ensuring that it reflects the most current DNS information.

- **Stub zone**: A stub zone is a specialized variant of the secondary zone. Unlike the secondary zone, which contains a complete copy of the DNS database, the stub zone only holds enough information—specifically, the IP addresses of the **authoritative DNS servers** for the zone—to direct queries to the correct authoritative server. That makes stub zones useful for simplifying DNS administration and optimizing network traffic by reducing the need for full DNS data replication.

The role of DNS servers in managing these zones is crucial. An authoritative DNS server, which operates the DNS records for a specific domain, plays a critical role in this structure. This server can be configured manually by a system administrator, allowing for precise control over DNS entries or dynamically by other DNS servers through zone transfers and updates. The authoritative server is the final arbiter of DNS queries for its domain, ensuring that responses are accurate and up-to-date. In contrast, a **non-authoritative DNS server** relies on cached data from previous DNS lookups and does not hold the original DNS records. While non-authoritative servers can provide quick responses based on cached information, they are not the definitive source for DNS resolution. That can sometimes lead to outdated or inaccurate responses if the cache is not properly maintained.

Beyond DNS zones, it is also important to understand WINS, a legacy service that resolves NetBIOS names. Although DNS has largely superseded WINS in modern networks, it remains relevant in environments where older systems and applications still rely on NetBIOS for name resolution.

Familiarity with WINS can be particularly important in networks that maintain legacy infrastructure, as it ensures that all systems, both old and new, can communicate effectively.

Getting to know WINS

Understanding WINS is crucial for automating the resolution of NetBIOS names to IP addresses, a task that is essential for maintaining smooth network operations. Your role in this is particularly valuable in environments where NetBIOS names are used. WINS helps resolve these names into IP addresses, enabling seamless access to shared resources such as folders and printers across a network. By managing this name resolution process, WINS ensures that network resources are consistently and efficiently available to users.

In Windows Server 2025, WINS is available as a feature that can be installed through the Server Manager, utilizing the **Add Roles and Features Wizard**, as depicted in *Figure 4.16*. This integration into the server management tools facilitates the setup and administration of WINS, allowing network administrators to configure and maintain the service effectively. The WINS server database is not just updated but updated dynamically as NetBIOS name registrations occur, providing up-to-date resolution information in real time.

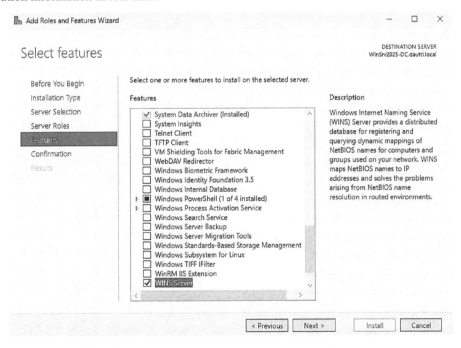

Figure 4.16 – Installing the WINS feature in Windows Server 2025

In addition to understanding WINS, it is beneficial to become familiar with the **Universal Naming Convention** (**UNC**), which is covered in the following subsection.

The UNC explained

Understanding the **UNC** is crucial for effectively managing and navigating network resources. The UNC offers a consistent way to identify shared network assets across different operating systems, including Unix, by following a standardized format. This format begins with double backslashes, followed by the server name and the specific shared folder, such as \servername\folder (illustrated in *Figure 4.17*). By providing a clear and uniform structure, the UNC simplifies network navigation and resource access.

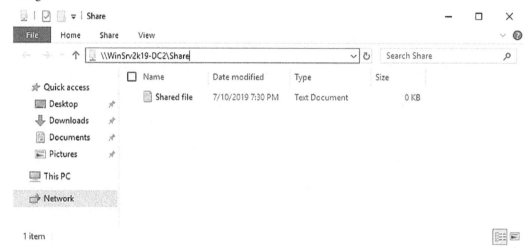

Figure 4.17 – A UNC path

Previously, we explored the DNS, examining its essential components and operations. Now, we will transition to discussing OUs and containers. OUs are critical in structuring and managing AD environments, as they can contain other containers and link to **Group Policy Objects** (**GPOs**). In contrast, containers can hold AD objects but do not support GPO links. This distinction is key to ensuring effective AD management and establishing a well-organized directory hierarchy.

Managing OUs and default containers

Understanding the roles of OUs and containers is a cornerstone of effective AD management. These elements, accessible via the **AD Users and Computers** console, are integral to organizing and administering directory objects. OUs provide a flexible structure, allowing administrators to create a hierarchical organization within the AD environment, making it easier to apply GPOs and manage permissions across different departments or user groups. In contrast, default containers serve as predefined locations for certain types of objects, such as users and computers. Still, they lack the same level of customization and policy control that OUs offer. The following sections will delve deeper into these concepts, examining how OUs can be leveraged to create an organized and secure AD infrastructure while also understanding the limitations and uses of default containers. By mastering these components, administrators can enhance their ability to efficiently manage and secure their AD environments, ensuring a well-structured and easily navigable directory.

Understanding OUs

OUs are critical components within the AD that enable a structured and efficient approach to managing users, groups, computers, and other directory entities. Functioning similarly to folders in a file system, OUs allow administrators to logically group and manage AD objects based on organizational needs. This logical grouping is pivotal in simplifying administrative tasks, such as applying GPOs and managing permissions across different departments, teams, or geographical locations within an organization.

Typically, organizations design their OU structures to reflect their internal business hierarchies, allowing for a tailored management approach that aligns with their operational framework. Each domain within an AD forest can establish its own unique OU configuration, creating a flexible and scalable system that adapts to the evolving needs of the business. This flexibility is particularly valuable in complex environments where different domains may require distinct policies and management practices, as shown in *Figure 4.18*.

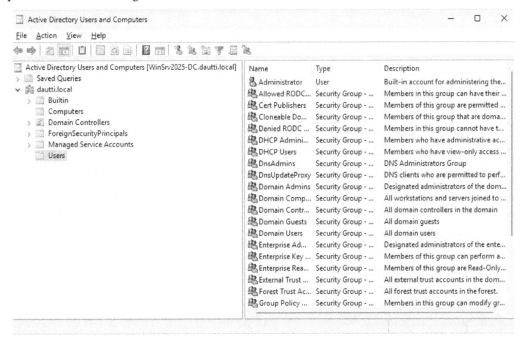

Figure 4.18 – An example of OU hierarchy in Windows Server 2025

In addition to OUs, it is essential to understand the role of default containers in AD. These containers are predefined locations where users, computers, and other objects are automatically placed during their creation. Containers are discussed in the following subsection.

Default containers explained

Gaining a thorough understanding of **predefined containers** is essential when a server is promoted to a DC. This promotion automatically triggers the creation of several default containers, which are visually represented in *Figure 4.17*. These containers play a critical role in AD and are distinguished by their immutable nature—they cannot be renamed, deleted, or recreated, and they are not eligible for linkage to any GPO. This immutability, by design, ensures that the foundational elements of AD remain consistent and secure, thereby preserving the directory's structural integrity.

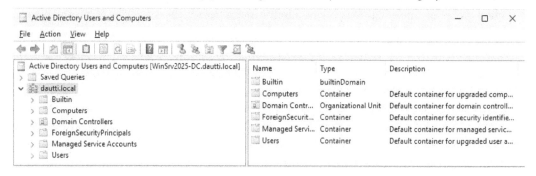

Figure 4.19 – Default containers in Windows Server 2025

These default containers serve specific purposes, such as organizing users, computers, and other directory objects in a standardized manner. They provide a stable environment for core AD operations, ensuring that certain critical objects are always stored in a predictable location. Although they are not as flexible as OUs, which can be customized to fit the needs of the organization, default containers are still vital for maintaining the AD's foundational structure.

In the following subsections, we will explore the concept of hidden default containers in greater detail. These hidden containers, though not visible in the standard AD interface, play significant roles in the background processes and overall functioning of AD. Understanding both **visible and hidden default containers** will provide a comprehensive view of how AD maintains its integrity and supports the management of directory objects.

Understanding hidden default containers

Understanding the concept of hidden default containers in AD is crucial for system administrators, even though these containers might not be immediately relevant to everyday tasks. These hidden containers serve a significant purpose in maintaining a streamlined and organized view within the **AD Users and Computers** console, preventing unnecessary clutter that could complicate the management of AD objects. By keeping certain containers out of sight, AD ensures that the interface remains user-friendly and manageable, particularly in large and complex environments.

Security considerations also drive the concealment of these containers. Hidden containers protect sensitive system objects, ensuring that only users with the appropriate permissions and knowledge can access them. This layer of security helps safeguard the integrity of the directory and reduces the risk of accidental modifications or unauthorized access to critical system components.

To reveal these hidden default containers, administrators must enable the **Advanced Features** option from the **View** menu, as depicted in *Figure 4.20*. Activating this feature uncovers the hidden containers, allowing for a more comprehensive view and enhanced control over the directory's resources. This capability is particularly valuable for advanced administrative tasks, such as detailed auditing, fine-tuning security settings, or managing objects that are not typically exposed in the standard view.

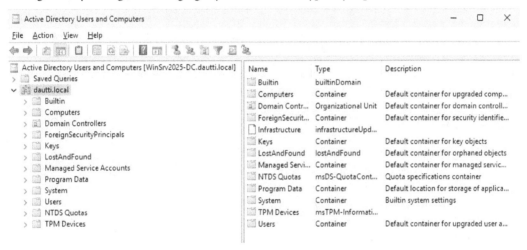

Figure 4.20 – Default hidden containers in Windows Server 2025

Having gained an understanding of these hidden default containers, it's essential to delve into their practical applications and roles within the AD environment. These containers often house crucial system information, such as infrastructure objects, security principals, and replication data, which are vital for the smooth operation of AD. By understanding how to access and manage these hidden containers, administrators can ensure that they are fully equipped to maintain a secure, efficient, and well-organized directory infrastructure.

The purpose of default container types

The default containers in Windows Server 2025 are integral to the organization and management of AD objects, each serving a distinct purpose:

- **Computers**: This container is the default repository for newly created computer accounts, providing a centralized location for these objects

- **DCs:** This container is specifically designed to house all DC accounts, ensuring they are organized and easily accessible

- **ForeignSecurityPrincipals**: This container is reserved for SIDs from external domains, facilitating cross-domain security and permissions

- **Keys**: This container stores cryptographic key objects, which are essential for secure communications and encryption within the network

- **LostandFound:** This container plays a critical role in maintaining directory integrity by holding orphaned objects that have become detached from their original containers, preventing potential issues with object references

- **Managed Service Accounts**: This container is dedicated to managed service accounts, which are used to provide enhanced security and management for services running on servers

- **Users:** This container is the default location for upgraded or newly created user accounts, making it easier to manage and access user-related objects

Having established an understanding of these default containers, the next step is to delve into the concept of delegating control to an OU. Delegating control involves assigning specific administrative permissions to users or groups for particular OUs, allowing them to manage objects within that OU without granting them full administrative rights across the entire AD environment. This delegation process is crucial for maintaining a secure and organized directory, as it enables administrators to assign responsibilities to non-administrative users while limiting those users' access to only the objects and functions necessary for their roles. This approach helps in balancing administrative control with security, ensuring that users have the appropriate level of access to perform their tasks effectively without compromising the integrity of the overall AD infrastructure.

Delegating authority within an OU

Understanding the function of OUs in AD is essential for effective directory management. OUs serve as a means to organize and manage AD objects systematically. To enhance administrative efficiency, control can be delegated to specific users or groups within an OU. This process allows for the distribution of administrative responsibilities without granting users **full administrative rights** across the entire AD environment. To delegate control, users or groups must first be moved into the designated OU, as shown in *Figure 4.21*.

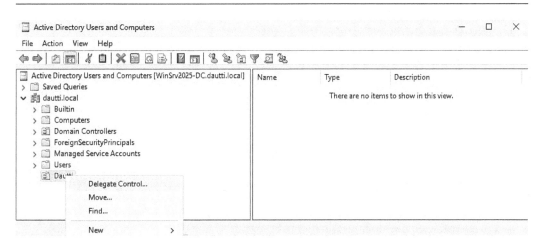

Figure 4.21 – Delegating control to an OU in Windows Server 2025

Delegating control involves assigning specific administrative permissions, such as managing user accounts, resetting passwords, or modifying group memberships within that OU. This focused delegation helps ensure that appropriate personnel perform administrative tasks while maintaining security and organization. By confining permissions to particular OUs, administrators can manage resources more effectively and reduce the risk of unauthorized access or unintended changes.

The delegation of control also enables the implementation of role-based administration, which can improve operational efficiency and accountability. Each delegated administrator can be assigned tasks that are relevant to their role, making it easier to track changes and manage directory objects according to organizational policies.

In the following section, we will further explore the management of user accounts, computer accounts, and groups within AD, delving into how these elements interact with OUs and contribute to a well-structured and secure directory environment.

User and group management within AD

Understanding user and computer accounts, along with groups, is fundamental for managing network access within a Windows-based domain environment. These accounts are crucial elements of AD, enabling both user and device authentication throughout the network. In this centralized system, groups are particularly significant as they simplify the process of assigning and managing rights and permissions. Groups aggregate multiple accounts, allowing administrators to apply policies and permissions collectively rather than individually. This streamlined approach enhances both security and efficiency. The following sections offer an in-depth exploration of the various types of accounts and groups, detailing their functions and how they are utilized within AD. By examining these components, we will gain a comprehensive understanding of their roles and applications in managing network resources effectively.

Domain accounts explained

Understanding **domain accounts** is essential for managing network access effectively within an AD environment. Domain accounts are authenticated by AD, which enables users to access both local and network resources according to the permissions assigned to the account itself or inherited from group memberships. This centralized authentication framework ensures a streamlined and secure approach to managing access across various services and applications within the network.

To create a domain account in Windows Server 2025, follow these steps:

1. Open the **Active Directory Users and Computers** console by navigating to **Windows Tools**.
2. Right-click on the **Users** container, then select **New** and choose the user.
3. Enter the required user information, as shown in *Figure 4.22*, then click **Next**.

Figure 4.22 – Creating a domain account in Windows Server 2025

4. Set a temporary password, confirm it, and proceed by clicking **Next**.
5. Click **Finish** to complete the creation of the domain account.
6. This process establishes the domain account and integrates it into the AD structure, providing users with access to network resources based on the assigned permissions.

In the following subsection, we will explore the creation and management of **local accounts**, which are also critical for managing user access and security on individual machines and within specific local environments.

Understanding the Local Accounts

Understanding local accounts is crucial for effective access management on individual computers. Unlike domain accounts, which are authenticated through AD and provide network-wide access, local accounts are specific to the computer where they are created and are managed by the Windows **Security Accounts Manager** (**SAM**). These accounts offer access to resources on the local machine and can interact with shared resources in a P2P network without requiring additional domain-level permissions.

Local accounts are particularly useful in scenarios where a computer operates independently of a domain, or when domain connectivity is not available. They are created and managed locally, allowing for granular control over permissions and user access on a per-machine basis. That can be advantageous for managing small workgroups or standalone computers where centralized domain management is not feasible.

To create a local account in Windows Server 2025, follow these steps:

1. Access the **Computer Management** console through **Windows Tools**. This console provides a centralized interface for managing various system components, including user accounts.

2. Navigate to **System Tools**, expand the **Local Users and Groups** section, right-click on the **Users** container, and select **New**, followed by the user.

3. Enter the necessary user details, such as the user's name and password, as illustrated in *Figure 4.23*. Then click **Create** to complete the process.

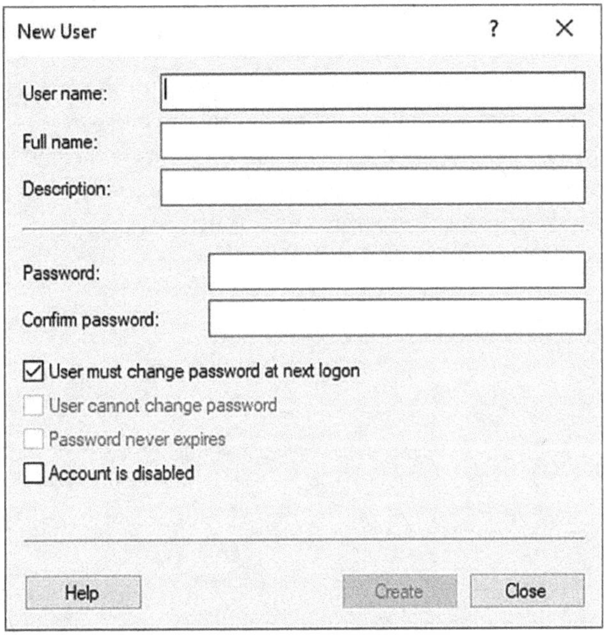

Figure 4.23 – Creating a local account in Windows Server 2025

> **Important note**
>
> An important consideration when creating a local account in Windows Server 2025 is that the server should not be operating as a DC. If the server is designated as a DC, it will handle domain-related functions and manage AD DS, which complicates local account management. By ensuring that the server is not a DC, you avoid the complexities of domain management, allowing for the straightforward setup and management of local accounts without the additional overhead of domain services.

Local accounts are stored and authenticated by SAM on the local machine, which ensures that access control and permissions are enforced independently of the network domain. These accounts are ideal for scenarios where local administration and access control are required.

In the following subsections, we will delve into **user profiles**, which are essential for storing and managing information about individual users. User profiles contain critical data that helps personalize and manage the user experience on both local and networked systems.

The User Profiles Explained

Understanding the different types of **user profiles** in Windows Server environments is fundamental for effective user management and customization. The following sections provide a brief explanation of the three types of user profiles in AD: local user profiles, which are tied to a specific machine; roaming user profiles, which offer flexibility across multiple devices; and mandatory user profiles, which maintain a fixed configuration without user modifications. Let's take a closer look:

- **Local user profile**: When a user logs into a computer for the first time, a local user profile is created and stored on that specific machine, as depicted in *Figure 4.24*. This profile includes the user's settings and documents, as well as application data tailored to that particular computer. The local profile is ideal for individual use on a single machine but lacks flexibility when users need to access their environment from multiple devices.

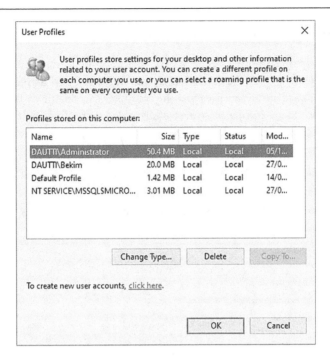

Figure 4.24 – User profiles in Windows Server 2025

- **Roaming user profile**: This kind of profile enhances this flexibility by allowing users to access their personalized settings and files from any computer within the network. This profile is essentially a copy of the local profile stored on a network share. When a user logs in from a different computer, their roaming profile is retrieved from the network, providing a consistent experience across different machines. This type of profile is especially useful in environments where users frequently switch between computers.

- **Mandatory user profile**: This type of profile enforces a fixed profile configuration. These profiles, which are also stored on a network share, are based on a pre-configured template. Any changes made by the user during their session are not saved when they log off. That ensures that every time the user logs in, they start with the same baseline configuration, which is useful in environments where uniformity is required and user customizations are not desired.

In summary, local user profiles are tied to individual computers, roaming profiles provide flexibility by being accessible from any networked machine, and mandatory profiles maintain consistency by discarding user changes and relying on a fixed template. Each type of profile serves distinct purposes, helping administrators manage user environments effectively based on organizational needs.

Next, we will delve into computer accounts, which play a critical role in identifying and managing computers within both local and centralized domain environments. These accounts are essential for maintaining network security and ensuring proper access control across the network.

Understanding Computer Accounts

In an AD environment, **computer accounts** are critical for identifying and managing computers within a domain. Before joining the domain, each computer must have a unique hostname to prevent conflicts. This unique identifier ensures that the computer can accurately be tracked and managed within the network. Once a computer is successfully added to the domain, it retains its hostname for continuous interaction with other domain resources, including files, applications, and services. This setup allows for seamless communication and integration with the domain.

The **Active Directory Users and Computers** console efficiently handles computer account administration, as illustrated in *Figure 4.25*. This console enables administrators to view and manage computer accounts, configure properties, and apply policies. Tasks such as resetting passwords, enabling or disabling accounts, and modifying account settings are performed here.

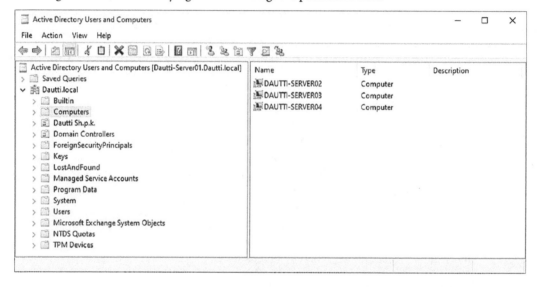

Figure 4.25 – Computer accounts in Windows Server 2025

Understanding computer accounts is essential for maintaining network integrity and ensuring proper resource access. These accounts play a vital role in authenticating and authorizing computers within the domain, thus supporting effective network management and security.

As we move forward, we will shift our focus to groups within the AD framework. Groups are integral to managing permissions and access rights, simplifying the assignment of roles and privileges, and streamlining administrative tasks. They help organize users and computers, apply consistent policies, and enhance overall network security.

Understanding Group Types

Understanding **group types** within AD is fundamental for optimizing network management and ensuring security. AD groups simplify the administration of permissions and rights by allowing administrators to manage multiple AD objects collectively rather than configuring each object individually. This approach not only enhances efficiency but also helps maintain consistent security policies across the network. Groups themselves are also AD objects and can be moved or reorganized within different OUs to align with organizational changes or administrative needs.

As presented in *Figure 4.26*, groups are administered using the **Active Directory Users and Computers** console. In AD, groups are classified into two primary categories:

- **Security groups**: These groups are essential for managing access to shared network resources such as files, folders, and printers. They apply permissions and enforce security policies across the network. Security groups can be nested within other security groups to create a hierarchical permission structure, allowing for more granular control over resource access.

- **Distribution groups**: These groups are designed to facilitate the distribution of email messages within an organization. They simplify the process of sending communications to large groups of users by acting as mailing lists. While distribution groups do not have permissions assigned to them and cannot be used to control access to resources, they play a crucial role in streamlining internal communication.

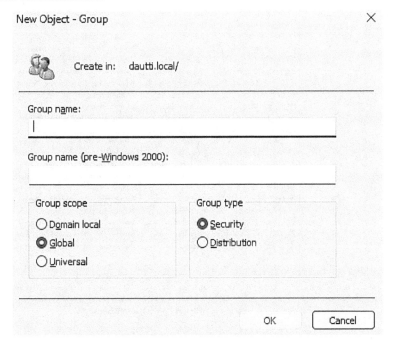

Figure 4.26 – Group types in Windows Server 2025

Understanding these group types and their functions enables administrators to manage network resources and communication effectively. In the subsequent sections, we will delve into default groups—predefined groups that come with AD—and the process of creating new groups. This knowledge is essential for organizing user roles, managing access to resources, and delegating administrative tasks efficiently within an AD environment.

Getting to know default groups

Understanding default groups in AD is fundamental for effective network administration. When a server is promoted to a DC, it automatically generates a variety of default groups, as shown in *Figure 4.27*, which illustrates the default groups in Windows Server 2025. These default groups are designed to simplify administrative tasks by grouping related AD objects, thereby easing the process of assigning permissions and access rights.

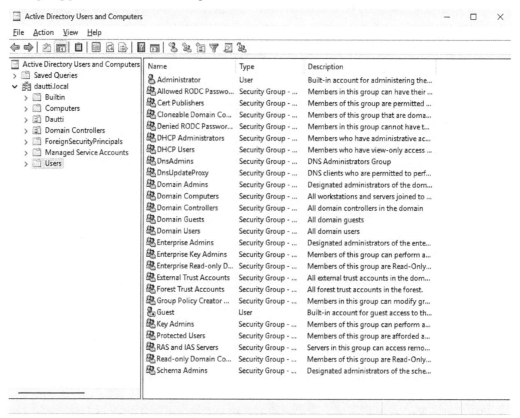

Figure 4.27 – Default groups in Windows Server 2025

Default groups are pre-configured with specific roles and permissions, which can significantly streamline network management. For example, default groups such as **Domain Admins**, **Enterprise Admins**, and **Schema Admins** have predefined levels of administrative privileges that are crucial for managing different aspects of the AD environment. By leveraging these groups, administrators can efficiently manage user access and enforce security policies without the need to configure permissions for each user or object manually.

Furthermore, default groups help ensure consistent application of policies and permissions across the network, which enhances both security and operational efficiency. They also facilitate the delegation of administrative tasks by providing predefined roles that can be assigned to users based on their responsibilities. In the next section, we will delve into the concept of group scopes and explore the various types that are available. Understanding group scopes is essential for optimizing group management within an AD environment, as they determine how groups interact with AD objects and influence the scope of permissions and policies applied across the network.

Understanding group scopes

Understanding **group scopes** is a foundational aspect of managing AD environments effectively, as they directly influence how permissions and policies are applied across an organization's network. Group scopes define the reach and applicability of group memberships within the AD structure, which is crucial for maintaining security and efficiency in resource management.

In AD, there are three primary group scopes, each serving distinct purposes and contexts, as illustrated in *Figure 4.28*:

- **Domain local group scope**: This scope is designed to manage access to resources within the local domain. It allows the inclusion of accounts, domain local groups, global groups, and universal groups, enabling administrators to assign permissions to local resources efficiently. Domain local groups are particularly useful when managing access to resources such as file shares, printers, and other domain-specific resources where you want to limit access to users and groups within that domain.

- **Global group scope**: The global group scope is used to organize users and groups within the same domain that share common access requirements. This scope includes accounts and global groups specific to the parent domain's global group. Global groups are typically employed for assigning permissions to resources across different domains within the same forest, making them ideal for scenarios where users from multiple domains need access to shared resources.

- **Universal group scope**: The universal group scope is the most expansive, allowing the inclusion of accounts, global groups, and universal groups from any domain within the forest. This scope is essential for managing permissions across multiple domains, making it highly effective in large, multi-domain environments. Universal groups are particularly useful when you need to assign permissions consistently across an entire forest, ensuring that users in different domains have appropriate access to resources regardless of their domain membership.

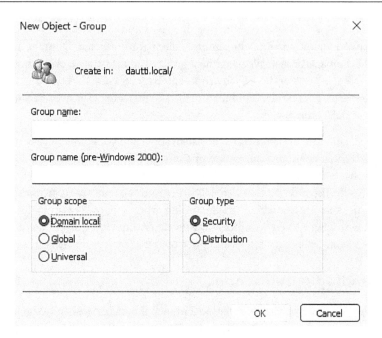

Figure 4.28 – Group scopes in Windows Server 2025

Each of these group scopes plays a critical role in ensuring that permissions and policies are applied appropriately and consistently within the AD environment. By understanding and utilizing these scopes correctly, administrators can enhance both the efficiency and security of their network management practices.

Moreover, the proper use of group scopes can prevent common issues such as over-permission, where users have more access than necessary, or under-permission, where legitimate access is denied. This balance is crucial for maintaining a secure and well-functioning AD environment.

In the following subsection, we will delve into the concept of group nesting. This concept builds upon the principles of group scopes by allowing administrators to create more complex and flexible group structures. Group nesting further refines the ability to manage permissions and access rights, offering a powerful tool for large-scale AD environments.

Group nesting explained

Understanding group nesting within AD is a fundamental aspect of efficient and secure permission management in complex IT environments. Group nesting allows for the hierarchical organization of groups, enabling administrators to assign permissions more effectively by leveraging a structured, tiered approach. This method not only simplifies the administration of access controls but also reduces redundancy and potential errors that could arise from individually assigning permissions to numerous user accounts.

In practice, group nesting is guided by best practices such as Microsoft's **Accounts, Global, Domain Local, Permissions (AGDLP)** and **Accounts, Global, Universal, Domain Local, Permissions (AGUDLP)** methodologies. These models offer a systematic approach to managing group memberships and permissions across a network:

- In the AGDLP model, user accounts are first assigned to a global group, which typically represents a specific role or department within the organization. This global group is then nested within a domain local group, which is responsible for managing access to specific resources within the local domain. Permissions are assigned to the domain local group, thereby granting access to all members of the global group in one step. This method is particularly effective in environments where users need consistent access to resources within a single domain.

- The AGUDLP methodology extends the AGDLP model by incorporating a universal group into the nesting structure. Here, the global group is first added to a universal group, which can span multiple domains within a forest. The universal group is then included in a domain local group, which controls access to resources. This approach is ideal for larger multi-domain environments, where users require access to resources across different domains. By utilizing universal groups, administrators can maintain a consistent permission structure across the entire forest, ensuring that users have the necessary access regardless of the domain they are operating within.

These structured methodologies not only streamline the management of permissions but also enhance the security and scalability of the AD environment. By reducing the number of individual permissions assignments and centralizing control within well-defined group structures, administrators can more easily enforce security policies, audit access controls, and respond to organizational changes.

After gaining a solid understanding of the foundational elements of AD, such as DNS, OUs, and containers, as well as the classification of computer accounts and groups, the next step is to proceed with the installation of the AD DS and DNS roles. This phase is crucial as it lays the groundwork for configuring and managing the AD environment, ensuring that it meets the security, scalability, and administrative needs of the organization.

Chapter exercise – installing the AD DS and DNS roles and promoting the server to a DC

In this chapter's exercise, you will be guided through the essential steps to install the AD DS and DNS roles, culminating in the promotion of your server to a fully functional DC. This process is a critical aspect of establishing a secure and efficient network infrastructure within an organization.

The exercise begins with the installation of AD DS, which is the backbone of identity and access management in Windows Server environments. It's followed by the configuration of DNS, which is crucial for name resolution within the domain. You will then proceed to promote the server to a DC, a key role that manages network security, user authentication, and policy enforcement across the domain.

By following the detailed instructions provided, you will gain a comprehensive understanding of how to implement and configure these roles, ensuring that your network is both robust and well-organized. This exercise not only enhances your practical skills but also deepens your theoretical knowledge, preparing you for more advanced network administration tasks.

To begin the installation process for AD DS and DNS roles and to promote the server to a DC, complete the following steps:

1. Start by accessing **Server Manager**. Click the **Start** button and select the **Server Manager** tile from the **Start** menu.

2. In the **Server Manager** window, find the **WELCOME TO SERVER MANAGER** section and click on **Add Roles and Features**, as illustrated in *Figure 4.27*. That will launch the **Add Roles and Features Wizard**; click **Next** to proceed.

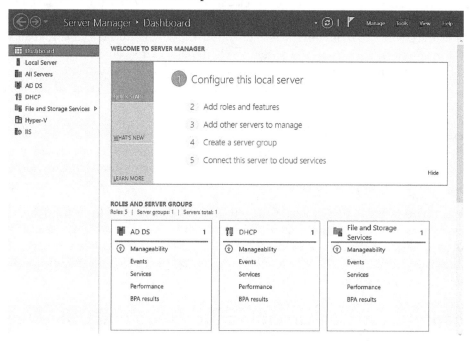

Figure 4.29 – Adding roles and features to the server using Server Manager

3. Select the **Role-based or feature-based installation** option and click **Next**.
4. Ensure that the **Select a server from the server pool** option is checked, then click **Next** again.

5. You will now choose the **Active Directory Domain Services** role from the list, as shown in *Figure 4.29*, and click **Next**.

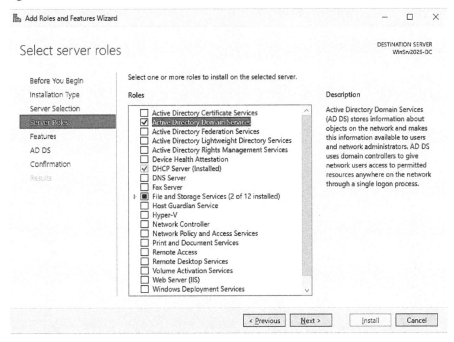

Figure 4.30 – Installing AD DS in Windows Server 2025

6. When prompted with the **Add features that are required for Active Directory Domain Services** window, click **Add Features** and then click **Next**.

7. Leave the default settings in the **Select Features** step unchanged, and click **Next** once more.

8. Carefully read through the description and key points about AD DS installation, and then click **Next**.

9. Next, confirm the installation selections for the AD DS role and click **Install**. You can either close the wizard or wait for the installation to complete.

10. Once finished, click **Close** to exit the **Add Roles and Features Wizard**.

11. In the **Notifications** area, you will see a **Promote this server to a domain controller** option. Click on it to start the AD DS configuration wizard.

12. Choose the **Add a new forest** option, as depicted in *Figure 4.31*, and enter the desired **Root domain name** value. Click **Next** to continue.

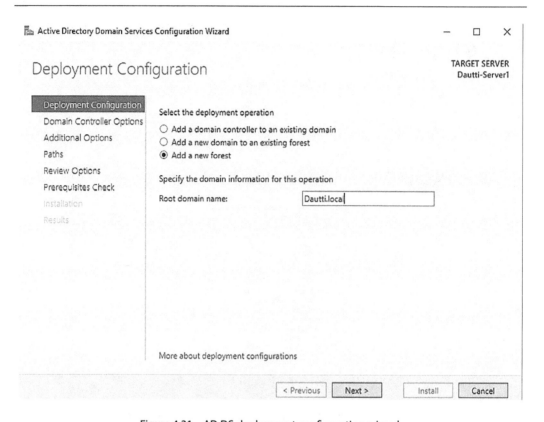

Figure 4.31 – AD DS deployment configuration wizard

13. Accept the default settings for the forest and DFLs, and then set a **Directory Services Restore Mode (DSRM)** password. Click **Next**.

14. If your network already has a DNS server, you may need to manually create a delegation for that DNS server to ensure proper name resolution from outside your domain; otherwise, no action is needed. Click **Next**.

15. You can either accept the default **NetBIOS** name or modify it as necessary. Click **Next**.

16. Similarly, you can accept the default paths for the AD DS database, log files, and SYSVOL or change them according to your requirements. Click **Next**.

17. Review your configuration options, then click **Next**.

18. Once the wizard confirms that all prerequisites have been met, click **Install**. The server will then restart to complete its promotion to a DC.

This exercise has provided you with step-by-step instructions on installing AD DS and DNS roles and promoting your server to a DC. Completing these steps equips you with the foundational skills needed to manage and secure your network infrastructure effectively.

Summary

In this chapter, you developed a comprehensive understanding of directory services and the key principles of naming resolution, which are fundamental to managing and securing a network environment. We started by delving into the AD DS role, which serves as the backbone of identity management within a network, enabling the authentication of users and devices. Alongside this, we examined the DNS role, which plays a crucial part in translating human-friendly domain names into IP addresses, ensuring seamless communication across the network. We also explored the structure and functionality of OUs in AD, which are vital for logically organizing resources and delegating administrative control. By learning how to delegate controls within OUs, you gained the ability to distribute administrative tasks effectively, thereby enhancing the efficiency and security of your AD environment. The chapter further covered the setup and management of user accounts and groups, which are essential for maintaining an organized and secure user base by appropriately assigning users to relevant organizational groups based on their roles and responsibilities.

Moreover, we walked through a detailed chapter exercise that provided hands-on experience in installing the AD DS role and promoting a server to a DC. This practical component not only reinforced your theoretical knowledge but also equipped you with the skills necessary to implement these services in a real-world setting. As we move forward, the next chapter will focus on expanding your server's capabilities by adding and configuring additional roles in Windows Server 2025. That will further enhance your ability to manage and optimize your network infrastructure.

Questions

1. **True or False?** An AD is a distributed database that stores objects in a hierarchical, structured, and secure format.

2. **Fill in the blank:**_____ minimizes the number of individually assigned permissions to users or groups.

3. Which of the following user profiles are used mainly in Windows-based domain networks?

    A. Domain user profile

    B. Security user profile

    C. Roaming user profile

    D. Mandatory user profile

4. **True or False?** The WINS server maps the IP addresses to BIOS names.

5. **Fill in the blank:**_____ is a set of communication paths through which the DC's replication data travels.

6. Which of the following are AD's group scopes?

   A. OU

   B. Security group

   C. Global group

   D. Universal group

7. **True or False?** UNC is a standard to identify a share in a computer network.

8. **Fill in the blank:**_____ is a server responsible for securely authenticating requests to access your organization's domain resources.

9. Which snap-ins for MMC are used to manage AD?

   A. Active Directory Administrative Center

   B. Active Directory Users and Computers

   C. UNC

   D. OU

10. **True or False?** The best example of a domain is a client/server network where a dedicated server on the network is used to provide services.

11. **Fill in the blank:**_____ stores the primary copy of the DNS database and maintains all DNS zone records.

12. Which of the following are forest-wide operations master roles?

   • Master schema

   • Domain naming master

   • LAN manager hosts

   • Default containers

13. Discuss AD DS and DNS roles and their implementations.

14. Discuss Microsoft's recommendations, AGDLP and AGUDLP, for assigning permissions.

Further reading

- *AD DS Deployment*: `https://docs.microsoft.com/en-us/windows-server/identity/ad-ds/deploy/ad-ds-deployment`

- *Domain Name System (DNS)*: `https://learn.microsoft.com/en-us/windows-server/networking/dns/dns-top`

- *Creating an Organizational Unit Design*: `https://docs.microsoft.com/en-us/windows-server/identity/ad-ds/plan/creating-an-organizational-unit-design`

- *Managing Groups*: `https://docs.microsoft.com/en-us/windows/win32/ad/managing-groups`

Unlock this book's exclusive benefits now

This book comes with additional benefits designed to elevate your learning experience.

Note: Have your purchase invoice ready before you begin.

`https://www.packtpub.com/unlock/9781836205012`

5

Adding Roles to Windows Server 2025

This chapter aims to equip you with knowledge about the factors influencing server hardware selection and the best practices for evaluating server performance. Understanding the server's role within a network and its hardware components will enable you to choose the most suitable server hardware for your requirements and troubleshoot hardware-related issues effectively. Moreover, the chapter will cover the techniques and strategies for monitoring server performance. Effective performance monitoring involves not only identifying and mitigating potential performance issues before they escalate but also actively engaging in prompt responses to prevent further performance degradation. Establishing a performance baseline—documenting the server's performance under typical workloads—is crucial for generating comprehensive reports on overall performance and playing a vital role in the monitoring process. The chapter concludes with a practical exercise focused on analyzing performance logs and setting up alerts.

In this chapter, we're going to cover the following main topics:

- Understanding server roles and features in Windows Server 2025
- Exploring application server roles and their implementations
- Configuring web services and their roles in Windows Server 2025
- Setting up remote access roles and their functionalities
- Deploying file and print services for network environments
- Installing web server (**Internet Information Services (IIS)**) and **Print and Document Services (PDS)** roles

Technical requirements

To complete the tasks outlined in this chapter on various servers using Windows Server 2025, you will need specific hardware and software configurations:

- It would be best if you had a PC running **Windows 11 Pro**, equipped with at least 16 GB of RAM and a 1 TB hard drive, with internet connectivity.

- Additionally, you will need three **virtual machines** (**VMs**) running **Windows Server 2025 Standard** (Desktop Experience). Each VM should have a minimum of 4 GB of RAM and 100 GB of hard drive space and have internet access.

These VMs will serve different roles: one as a file server, another as a web server, and the third as a print server.

Understanding server roles and features in Windows Server 2025

Before assigning roles to a server, it's essential to clearly define its intended function within your organization's IT infrastructure. This chapter provides a comprehensive overview of the various roles, role services, and features available in Windows Server 2025, helping you make informed decisions about server configuration.

Roles and features overview

A **server role** defines the core function that a server performs within a network. For example, if a server's primary purpose is to store and manage shared files, then the File and Storage Services role is installed to fulfill that responsibility. Similarly, a server designated to host web applications will have the Web Server (IIS) role to handle HTTP requests securely, providing an essential platform for internet and intranet services. Servers that enable secure remote access will implement the Remote Access role, which facilitates connectivity solutions such as **virtual private networks** (**VPNs**) and DirectAccess, allowing users to access network resources securely from remote locations.

In most cases, assigning a single role to each server is optimal, as this ensures streamlined performance and simplifies server management. However, there are scenarios where multiple roles may be deployed on a single server. In such cases, careful planning is essential to balance hardware resources against role-specific requirements, ensuring compatibility and preventing potential conflicts or performance bottlenecks. This modular approach allows Windows Server 2025 to serve a range of purposes within an organization, with each role contributing to a reliable, responsive, and secure network infrastructure.

Role services explained

Beyond the basic roles, Windows Server 2025 offers **role services**—optional components that enhance or extend the functionality of a server role. These services allow administrators to tailor the server's capabilities to specific needs. For instance, enabling remote printing over the internet requires not only the installation of the PDS role but also the addition of the Internet Printing role service. This layered approach enables you to customize the server's functionality to meet precise operational requirements, providing flexibility in how the server supports your organization's needs.

Core native roles and features

Windows Server 2025 includes a range of built-in roles and features designed to support critical infrastructure needs without relying on additional applications. The choice to highlight three specific roles—**Active Directory Certificate Services** (**AD CS**), **Rights Management Services** (**RMS**), and **Network Policy Server** (**NPS**)—is based on their relevance to foundational aspects of Windows Server management: security, access control, and data protection. These roles provide essential infrastructure capabilities that many organizations rely on, regardless of additional applications, such as Exchange or SQL Server:

- **AD CS**: This role provides a scalable, secure method to issue and manage digital certificates within an organization. It is fundamental for supporting secure communication, data integrity, and user authentication. It plays a crucial role in environments that prioritize security by enabling tasks such as **Secure Sockets Layer** (**SSL**) / **Transport Layer Security** (**TLS**) for websites and authenticating users and devices.

- **RMS**: RMS is vital for protecting information and safeguarding sensitive documents and communications by enforcing access and usage restrictions. This ensures that only authorized users can interact with protected content, which is especially critical in industries handling sensitive or regulated data.

- **NPS**: NPS functions as a RADIUS server, supporting centralized network access authentication, authorization, and accounting. This capability is invaluable for managing secure network access, particularly in environments where multi-site and cloud integration is essential, facilitating secure connections for VPNs, wireless networks, and other remote access solutions.

While these roles are critical, Windows Server 2025 also includes several other valuable native features that warrant exploration:

- **File and Storage Services**: Integral for centralized file sharing, storage management, and data deduplication, addressing core needs in networked environments

- **Hyper-V:** Essential for organizations leveraging virtualization, optimizing server utilization, and providing isolated virtual environments for various applications

- **DNS and DHCP**: These fundamental roles underpin network infrastructure, providing domain name resolution and **IP address management (IPAM)**

- **Windows Server Update Services (WSUS)**: Critical for patch management, ensuring that servers and connected devices receive timely updates to maintain security and compliance

Expanding in a broader selection of these roles provides a more comprehensive view of Windows Server's native capabilities, equipping administrators with a solid foundation for managing network security, compliance, and accessibility. This understanding lays the groundwork for extending server functionalities through additional applications, aligning with the technical reviewer's feedback to emphasize the importance of native features in Windows Server environments.

Understanding server features

In addition to roles and role services, **server features** are supplementary components that support or enhance specific functions within the server environment. For example, installing the .NET Framework 3.5 feature might be necessary to run particular applications or services. In contrast, the IPAM feature provides advanced management capabilities for DHCP and DNS roles. Features such as WINS can be crucial in environments where resolving NetBIOS names across multiple subnets is necessary. By carefully selecting and installing the appropriate features, you can ensure that your server is fully equipped to handle its designated tasks efficiently and effectively, thus contributing to the overall stability and performance of your IT infrastructure.

In summary, understanding and strategically configuring roles, role services, and features in Windows Server 2025 is key to optimizing server performance and meeting the unique needs of your organization's IT environment. This chapter equips you with the knowledge to make informed decisions that enhance the functionality and reliability of your server deployments.

An overview of Server Manager

Server Manager is a crucial tool for adding, configuring, and managing server roles in Windows Server 2025. First introduced with Windows Server 2008, this tool has continually improved, offering a streamlined and intuitive interface that simplifies server administration. Whether you are working with a local server or managing remote servers, Server Manager allows you to install and oversee server roles efficiently. The interface is divided into two main sections: the **scope pane**, which displays all installed roles, and the **details pane**, which provides comprehensive information and management options for each selected role. This central console not only helps in monitoring the health and performance of the server but also allows for easy access to role-specific tools and settings. As shown in *Figure 5.1*, Server Manager is indispensable for performing a wide range of administrative tasks, making it an essential component of Windows Server 2025's management suite.

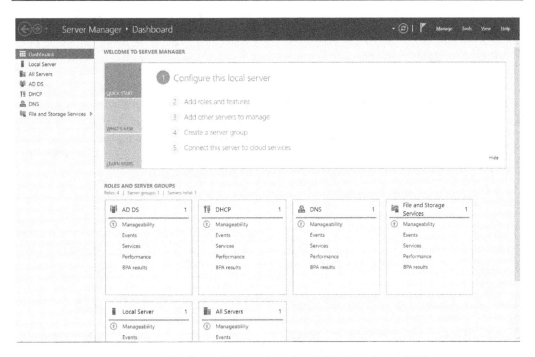

Figure 5.1 – The Server Manager interface in Windows Server 2025

🔍 Quick tip: Need to see a high-resolution version of this image? Open this book in the next-gen Packt Reader or view it in the PDF/ePub copy.

🔒 **The next-gen Packt Reader** and a **free PDF/ePub copy** of this book are included with your purchase. Unlock them by scanning the QR code below or visiting `https://www.packtpub.com/unlock/9781836205012`.

With a solid understanding of server roles and features through Server Manager, the next section will delve into the concept and types of application servers, expanding your knowledge of server infrastructure and management.

Exploring application server roles and their implementations

This section delves into the various types of application servers that are integral to IT operations. Application servers are specialized network-based servers designed to provide specific services to users or other applications within an organization. They play a crucial role in handling diverse tasks, including email communication, web hosting, and database management, among others. The following subsections will explore some of the most widely used and up-to-date application servers, highlighting their importance and functionality.

We begin our exploration with the practical implementation of a mail server, which is a core element of IT infrastructure. A mail server manages the sending and receiving of emails across the internet, making it an essential tool for effective communication within any organization. By learning how to install and configure a mail server on Windows Server 2025, you will gain valuable skills that are directly applicable to real-life IT environments.

Understanding the email server in Windows Server 2025

An **email server**, often referred to as a **mail server**, plays a crucial role in handling the transmission and reception of emails across the internet. To function as an email server, a server must have specialized software installed. **Exchange Server** is commonly used for Windows-based systems. Exchange Server provides a comprehensive platform that allows system administrators to configure and manage email accounts, enabling the server to handle tasks such as sending, receiving, and storing emails.

Several key components and communication protocols underpin the functionality of an email server:

- **Mail Transport Agent (MTA)**: This component is essential for transferring emails between servers. The MTA handles the routing of emails from the sender's server to the recipient's server.

- **Mail Delivery Agent (MDA)**: Once emails reach their destination server, the MDA takes over, ensuring that the messages are correctly delivered to the appropriate user's inbox.

- **Mail User Agent (MUA)**: This component provides the interface for users to compose, send, receive, and read emails. The MUA interacts with both the MTA and MDA to ensure seamless email communication.

- **Simple Mail Transfer Protocol (SMTP)**: SMTP is the protocol used by the MTA to transfer emails between servers. It operates on port 25 and is the backbone of email delivery in most systems.

- **Post Office Protocol (POP)**: POP is a protocol that operates on port 110. It allows users to download emails from the server to their local devices, enabling offline access to their messages. POP is useful in scenarios where emails are stored locally and not synchronized across multiple devices.

- **Internet Message Access Protocol (IMAP)**: IMAP, operating on port 143, is a more flexible protocol compared to POP. It allows users to retrieve emails from the server and synchronizes them across multiple devices. With IMAP, users can access their emails from different locations without the need to download them, as they remain stored on the server.

While Exchange Server provides a robust and advanced solution for managing email communications within an organization, there are situations where a more straightforward setup might be sufficient. For example, if the goal is to establish a basic email service that focuses on sending and forwarding emails, Windows Server 2022 allows you to add the SMTP Server feature. This lightweight option is suitable for environments where full Exchange Server capabilities are not required.

> **Note**
>
> One available option for establishing an email service within your organization's network is the upcoming **Exchange Server Subscription Edition** (**Exchange Server SE**), anticipated for release in 2025. This Microsoft product enables you to set up and manage a mail server tailored to your organization's needs. To leverage its features, you must install and configure Exchange Server SE on your organization's server infrastructure. Exchange Server SE provides a comprehensive range of functionalities designed to enhance email communication and collaboration across your organization's network.

SMTP Server feature removed in Windows Server 2025

In Windows Server 2025, the SMTP Server feature, which allows servers to send and forward emails over the internet, has been discontinued. As a result, organizations need to explore alternative solutions for managing email services. One option is to use Exchange Server, a comprehensive and advanced email platform that provides extensive functionalities for managing email communications within an organization. Exchange Server is capable of handling various email-related tasks, including hosting mailboxes, managing calendars, and ensuring secure communication.

For those looking for a cloud-based solution, Microsoft 365 offers **Exchange Online** (its admin center is illustrated in *Figure 5.2*), a part of the Microsoft 365 suite that delivers email and calendaring services without the need for on-premises infrastructure. Exchange Online operates in the cloud, hosted by Microsoft, which eliminates the need for organizations to manage physical or virtual servers directly. This cloud-based approach provides the advantage of reduced maintenance and simplifies upgrades. However, it also means relinquishing some control over configuration and system changes compared to an on-premises Exchange Server deployment.

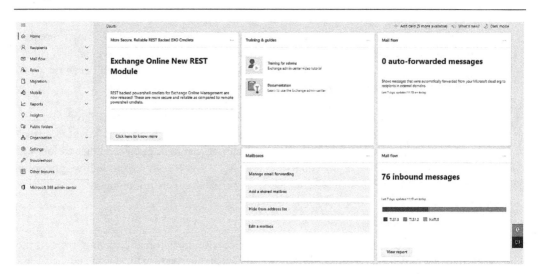

Figure 5.2- Exchange Online admin center

It is crucial to comprehend the distinctions between Exchange Server and Exchange Online to make informed decisions about which solution aligns best with your organization's needs. Exchange Server offers more control and customization options, while Exchange Online provides convenience and scalability by leveraging Microsoft's cloud infrastructure.

With your newfound knowledge of email servers and the available alternatives in Windows Server 2025, you are well prepared to delve into the next section. This section will introduce you to database servers and their access protocols, further enhancing your understanding of server roles and their implementation in Windows Server 2025.

Understanding the database server

A **database server** is a critical component in any IT infrastructure, designed to efficiently manage, store, and retrieve large volumes of data while providing secure access to authorized users. Serving as the backbone of data management, a database server centralizes data, ensuring it can be easily backed up, maintained, and shared across an organization's network. This centralization not only improves data integrity but also enhances collaboration by allowing multiple users to access and interact with the same data in real time.

To configure a Windows-based server as a database server, you can utilize the **SQL Server client/ server application**. SQL Server enables the creation, management, and organization of databases, facilitating complex data operations such as querying, reporting, and analysis. For seamless data access and communication, SQL Server relies on several key protocols. These include the following:

- **Data**: The most critical asset managed by the database server. Data is the core element around which all database operations revolve. Without data, the server's functionality and purpose are nullified.

- **Database Application**: This software acts as the intermediary between users and the database server, enabling interactions such as data entry, queries, and report generation.

- **Users**: The individuals or systems that access the database server. Users range from administrators managing the database to end users retrieving data for specific purposes.

- **Open Database Connectivity (ODBC)**: A widely-used protocol that allows applications to establish a connection with the database server, regardless of the **Database Management System (DBMS)** in use.

- **Java Database Connectivity (JDBC)**: A protocol developed by Sun Microsystems that allows Java applications to connect and interact with the database server, ensuring that Java-based solutions can seamlessly access and manipulate data.

- **Object Linking and Embedding Database (OLEDB)**: A Microsoft protocol that provides a standard method for applications to access data stored in a database, facilitating data manipulation and retrieval across various Microsoft and non-Microsoft systems.

> **Note**
>
> **SQL Server 2022** (`https://www.microsoft.com/en-us/sql-server/sql-server-2022`) is a Microsoft application designed for deploying a database server within an organization's network. To set up a database server using SQL Server 2022, you will need to install and configure the application appropriately.

Understanding these components and protocols is essential for managing and optimizing database server performance, ensuring that data remains accessible, secure, and efficiently handled. With this knowledge, we can now delve into the role and functions of collaboration servers, which play a crucial part in enhancing organizational teamwork and communication.

Understanding the collaboration server

A **collaboration server** facilitates teamwork and information sharing in a digital environment, offering features that support document collaboration, chat, event scheduling, video conferencing, and more. For Windows-based servers, **SharePoint Server** is a robust solution for setting up a collaboration server. SharePoint Server allows you to create, manage, and share websites, libraries, and files within your organization. It leverages networking protocols to provide access to these resources, ensuring seamless collaboration among users.

SharePoint is available in two primary versions: **SharePoint Server** and **SharePoint Online** (see *Figure 5.3*). SharePoint Server, an on-premises solution, is installed on your servers, offering extensive customization and control over your environment. This version allows for deep integration with other on-premises systems and is particularly beneficial for organizations that prioritize complete control over their data and infrastructure.

Figure 5.3 – SharePoint Online admin center

On the other hand, SharePoint Online is a cloud-based service that is included in Microsoft 365. It provides many of the same features as SharePoint Server but is hosted and maintained by Microsoft. That means that Microsoft manages updates, security, and scalability, reducing the need for in-house maintenance. SharePoint Online offers greater flexibility, allowing users to access and collaborate on documents from anywhere with an internet connection.

Understanding the differences between SharePoint Server and SharePoint Online is crucial for selecting the right solution for your organization's needs. SharePoint Server offers more control and customization for on-premises deployments, while SharePoint Online provides a more streamlined, cloud-based approach with easier maintenance and scalability.

> **Note**
>
> To establish an online collaboration platform within your organization's network, **SharePoint Server Subscription Edition** (**SharePoint Server SE**) is a viable option. This Microsoft product enables you to create and manage websites, libraries, files, and various resources on your server infrastructure. SharePoint Server SE offers a range of features designed to enhance teamwork and information sharing, including document collaboration, real-time chat, calendar management, video conferencing, and more. To utilize SharePoint Server SE, you will need to install and configure it on your organization's server infrastructure. The platform relies on networking protocols to grant access to its resources, ensuring smooth collaboration across your organization.

Next, we will delve into the concept of monitoring platforms and how they can be utilized to oversee and manage server performance and operations.

Understanding the monitoring server

The **monitoring server**, a cornerstone in the management of an organization's IT environment, provides a centralized view of network health and performance. This system, whether tracking on-premises, cloud-based, or hybrid infrastructure, is essential for administrators. It empowers them to monitor server performance, client/server applications, network services, IT infrastructure, and websites. The use of configurable alerts ensures that any issues are promptly detected and addressed, keeping system administrators informed and in control.

The **System Center Operations Manager** (**SCOM**) is a robust and comprehensive tool that can transform a server into a powerful monitoring server for Windows-based environments. With its extensive capabilities, SCOM is a reliable choice for managing and monitoring devices and services across an enterprise. However, the System Center suite is not limited to SCOM, and it encompasses several other components that further enhance its functionality:

- **System Center Configuration Manager (SCCM)**: This tool helps manage large groups of Windows-based computers. SCCM is used for software distribution, patch management, and operating system deployment. It streamlines administrative tasks by automating updates and configuration processes.

- **System Center Orchestrator**: Orchestrator focuses on automating and orchestrating IT processes and workflows. It enables the automation of repetitive tasks, integrates various systems, and ensures that complex workflows are executed efficiently.

- **System Center Virtual Machine Manager (SCVMM)**: SCVMM manages virtualized environments, providing a unified approach to deploying and managing VMs. It simplifies virtual infrastructure management and ensures optimal resource utilization.

- **System Center Data Protection Manager (System Center DPM)**: System Center DPM is dedicated to backup and recovery. It ensures that data is consistently backed up and can be quickly restored in case of data loss or system failure.

The System Center components, when used collectively, significantly enhance the monitoring and management of IT infrastructure. They provide comprehensive solutions for network service monitoring, configuration management, automation, VM management, and data protection. By leveraging these tools, organizations can effectively manage their IT environments, maintain system reliability, and improve overall operational efficiency.

> **Note**
>
> **System Center 2022** is a robust software suite from Microsoft designed to assist in establishing a monitoring server for your IT infrastructure. This suite features SCOM, a crucial tool for monitoring and managing the health and performance of network devices and applications. Utilizing System Center 2022 allows you to oversee various network metrics, ensuring optimal system performance and the rapid identification and resolution of potential issues. Additionally, Microsoft has announced that System Center 2025 is slated , released on November 1st, 2024, promising further advancements in monitoring and management capabilities.

In the following section, we will delve into threat management servers and their role in securing IT environments.

Understanding the Data Protection Server

A **data protection server** plays a critical role in ensuring an organization's continuity and resilience by providing robust data backup and recovery solutions. This server is integral to implementing a comprehensive **business continuity and disaster recovery** (**BCDR**) strategy. To establish a data protection server on a Windows-based system, you would utilize the System Center DPM application. DPM offers a suite of features that cater to diverse backup and recovery needs.

With DPM, administrators can perform application-aware backups, which are essential for protecting complex applications, such as Exchange Server, SQL Server, and SharePoint Server. That means backups are not only taken of the files but also the application's metadata and configuration, ensuring that complete and functional restorations are possible. Additionally, DPM facilitates the backup of individual files, folders, and entire volumes, as well as system state data, which is crucial for recovering the operating system and its settings.

Moreover, DPM supports the backup of VMs hosted on **Hyper-V**, encompassing both Windows and Linux environments. This functionality is significant for virtualized environments where the integrity of VMs must be preserved for operational continuity. By leveraging DPM, organizations can ensure that their data is consistently protected against loss or corruption and that recovery processes are streamlined and effective.

> **Note**
>
> To set up a data protection server for your organization's network, one practical approach is to utilize **Microsoft's System Center 2022**. This software suite features the DPM, a client/server application that must be installed and configured on a Windows-based server. DPM provides comprehensive backup and recovery capabilities, allowing you to safeguard and restore data across various applications and systems. It supports backups for Exchange Server, SQL Server, and SharePoint Server, as well as files, folders, volumes, system states, and VMs hosted on Hyper-V for both Windows and Linux environments.

In this section, you have explored several application servers utilized in on-premises environments, providing insights into various client/server applications. This overview has equipped you with knowledge about their key features, components, protocols, and functionalities. Moving forward, the next section will shift focus to the different types of web services, expanding your understanding of their roles and implementations within IT infrastructure.

Configuring web services and their roles in Windows Server 2025

A web service is a standardized framework that enables different software applications, often operating on diverse platforms, to communicate and interact with each other efficiently. This interoperability is achieved through the use of **Extensible Markup Language** (**XML**)-based formats and protocols, such as **Simple Object Access Protocol** (**SOAP**), **Web Services Description Language** (**WSDL**), and **Universal Description, Discovery, and Integration** (**UDDI**). These technologies facilitate the exchange of data and the invocation of functionalities over a network, allowing applications to work together seamlessly, regardless of their underlying systems.

Web services can be broadly classified into two types:

- **RESTful web services**: These are built on the **Representational State Transfer** (**REST**) architecture, which uses **Hypertext Transfer Protocol** (**HTTP**) methods such as GET, POST, PUT, and DELETE, along with **Uniform Resource Identifiers** (**URIs**), to access and manipulate resources. This approach is known for its simplicity and scalability, making it well suited for web-based interactions.

- **SOAP-based web services**: These rely on SOAP, which uses structured XML messages and envelopes to communicate with a service endpoint. SOAP is more rigid and standardized, offering built-in error handling and security features, which makes it ideal for enterprise-level applications where reliability and security are paramount.

Next, we will delve into IIS, a crucial component for hosting web services and applications.

IIS Explained

IIS is Microsoft's robust and versatile web server platform designed to deliver scalable, manageable, and reliable web applications. IIS facilitates communication between the browser and the web server through a variety of protocols, including HTTP, **HTTP Secure** (**HTTPS**), **File Transfer Protocol** (**FTP**), **FTP Secure** (**FTPS**), SMTP, and **Network News Transfer Protocol** (**NNTP**). Additionally, Microsoft has introduced **Active Server Pages** (**ASP**), a server-side scripting technology that enables the creation of dynamic web content.

With the release of **IIS version 10**, Microsoft has significantly enhanced the security and performance of the platform. This version supports longer script execution times and introduces HTTP/2 support. Moreover, in January 2020, Microsoft launched a new Chromium-based browser called **Microsoft Edge**, further complementing the IIS ecosystem. IIS 10 also brought new features in Windows Server 2025, such as improved server-side cipher suite negotiation for HTTP/3, IIS administration through PowerShell cmdlets, support for wildcard host headers, the ability to run IIS on Nano Server and within containers, and a user interface for managing **HTTPS Strict Transport Security** (**HSTS**). These enhancements have collectively elevated the performance and security of IIS.

Adding IIS on Windows Server 2025

To set up a web server on Windows Server 2025, IIS must be added as a server role as follows:

1. Log in to your Windows Server 2025 with an admin account. Open **Server Manager** from the Start menu. In Server Manager, click **Manage** in the upper-right corner, then select **Add Roles and Features**. That starts **Add Roles and Features Wizard**.

2. Click **Next** on the **Before You Begin** page. Choose **Role-based or feature-based installation** and click **Next**. On the **Server Selection** page, select the local server and click **Next**.

3. Check the box for **Web Server (IIS)** on the **Server Roles** page, as shown in *Figure 5.4*. A dialog will pop up—click **Add Features**, then click **Next**.

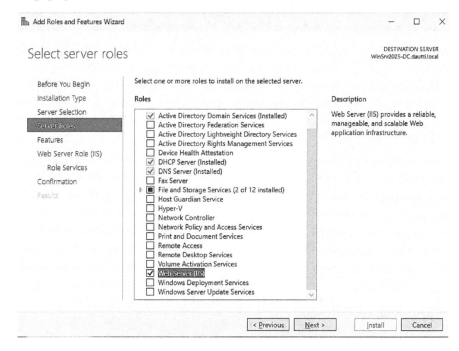

Figure 5.4- Adding Web Server (IIS) on Windows Server 2025

4. On the **Features** page, you can add extra features, but the default options are enough for most setups. Click **Next**. Review the **Web Server (IIS)** role overview and click **Next**.

5. On the **Role Services** page, you can add more IIS features, such as FTP Server or security options, if needed. Click **Next** when done.

6. Review your selections on the **Confirmation** page. You can choose to restart the server if needed automatically. Click **Install** to start the process.

7. The installation will begin, and you can watch its progress. Once it's finished, click **Close** to exit the wizard.

Once installed, IIS Manager serves as the administrative console for managing the web server. Accessible through Server Manager, Windows Administrative Tools, or by running the `inetmgr` command in the **Run** dialog box, IIS Manager allows administrators to efficiently manage their web applications, as depicted in *Figure 5.5*.

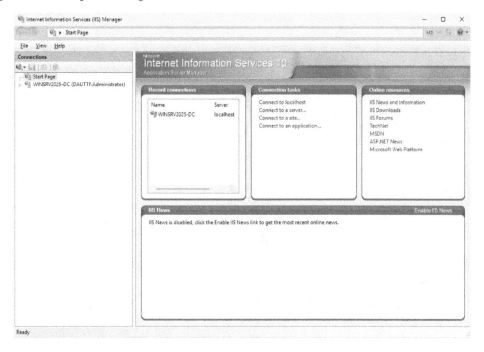

Figure 5.5- IIS Manager in Windows Server 2025

Next, we will explore the fundamentals of the **World Wide Web** (**WWW**).

WWW overview

The **WWW** is a global information system that operates over the internet. It enables users to access and interact with web pages via HTTP. Web pages, typically written in **Hypertext Markup Language** (**HTML**), can include text, images, videos, and other multimedia elements, making the web a rich and dynamic platform for information sharing.

The WWW was first proposed by Tim Berners-Lee in 1989 while working at CERN, and it quickly evolved into the vast network we use today. The core technologies behind the web include HTML for structuring content, HTTP for transmitting data between servers and clients, and **uniform resource locators** (**URLs**) for addressing resources on the web.

Initially, the web was a static medium, but it has since advanced to support interactive applications, real-time communication, and complex web services. As seen in *Figure 5.6*, which illustrates a sample web page and its underlying HTML code, the web has grown from a basic document-sharing platform into a fundamental part of modern IT infrastructure, supporting everything from e-commerce to social networking.

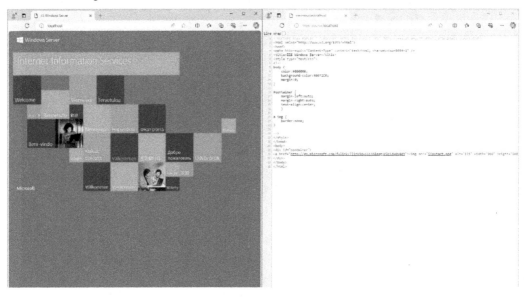

Figure 5.6- A web page and its source code

In the following subsection, we will delve into the FTP, another essential tool for managing files across the internet.

Understanding an FTP

FTP serves as a fundamental method for transferring files across the internet, offering a secure and efficient mechanism for exchanging data between computers. Initially developed in the early 1970s, FTP has remained a vital tool in networked environments due to its simplicity and reliability. It is widely employed for a range of tasks, including transmitting corporate data within internal networks, managing website content, and facilitating the upload and download of files to and from web servers.

FTP operates on a **client/server model**, utilizing two distinct ports to manage its operations. Port 21 is designated for establishing the control connection, allowing commands and responses to be exchanged between the client and server. Once this connection is established, port 20 is used for the actual data transfer, handling the transmission of files between the systems. This **dual-port system**, a testament to the protocol's efficiency, ensures that command and data traffic are kept separate, enhancing the protocol's performance.

Setting up an FTP Server on Windows Server 2025 involves several key steps. First, you must install the Web Server (IIS) role on your server, which lays the foundation for hosting various web and FTP services. After that, you add the FTP Server role service under the Web Server role, as depicted in *Figure 5.7*. This configuration enables the server to handle FTP connections, providing administrators with a robust tool for managing file transfers in a controlled, secure, and scalable manner.

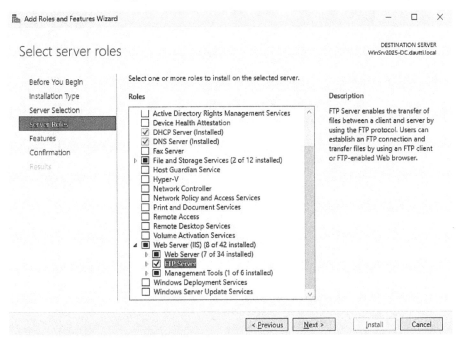

Figure 5.7- Adding an FTP Server as a role service in Windows Server 2025

Following this, we will delve into the concept of worker processes, exploring their pivotal role in managing server resources and ensuring the smooth operation of web and FTP services. Understanding how to access and configure these processes is not just crucial, but it's your key responsibility for maintaining optimal server performance.

Worker processes and how to access them?

In IIS, each application pool is associated with its dedicated worker process. This **worker process** is a crucial component that handles the execution of web applications contained within that pool. By assigning a separate worker process to each application pool, IIS ensures isolation between different pools. This isolation is advantageous because it means that if an issue arises within one web application, it remains contained within that pool and does not interfere with the functioning of web applications in other pools. To manage and configure the worker process settings for an application pool, you can access IIS Manager, select the **Application Pools** node, and then click on **Advanced Settings** in the **Actions** pane on the right side of the interface, as depicted in *Figure 5.8*. That allows you to customize various parameters related to the worker processes, such as process recycling and idle timeout settings, to optimize performance and reliability.

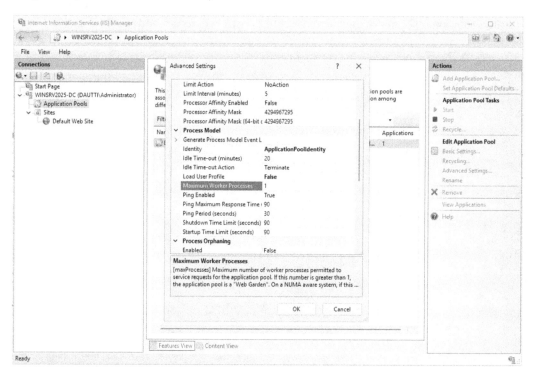

Figure 5.8- An application's pool worker process in IIS

In the subsequent section, we will delve into the procedures for installing additional features for IIS on Windows Server, which will enhance its capabilities and support a broader range of functionalities.

Installing more features for IIS

When configuring IIS on Windows Server, you start by installing the Web Server (IIS) role. During this installation, you can choose from various role services that align with your server's needs. This selection is made during a subsequent step in the installation wizard, as detailed in *Figure 5.7* of the *Understanding an FTP* subsection. These role services encompass a range of functionalities, such as FTP server capabilities, management tools, and additional modules that extend the server's features.

If you need to add or modify these Role Services after the initial installation, you can do so through Server Manager. By launching **Add Roles and Features Wizard**, you can install or adjust additional IIS features and services. This process allows you to customize your IIS environment further, adding components such as URL rewrite modules, security features, or additional management tools as required.

In the next section, we will explore the concepts of sites and websites, providing a detailed explanation of their definitions, roles, and how they function within the IIS framework.

Sites overview

A **site**, also known as a **website**, is a collection of web pages designed to present content over the internet using web services. These web pages are typically built using HTML, which provides the fundamental structure and layout of the content. However, to create more engaging and interactive experiences, additional scripting languages, such as **JavaScript**, or server-side languages, such as **PHP** or **ASP.NET**, are often utilized. This combination of technologies allows for dynamic content and user interactions.

When you install the Web Server (IIS) role on Windows Server 2025, the setup process automatically creates a default website that serves a single introductory web page. This default site serves as a placeholder and a starting point for further configuration, as illustrated in *Figure 5.9*:

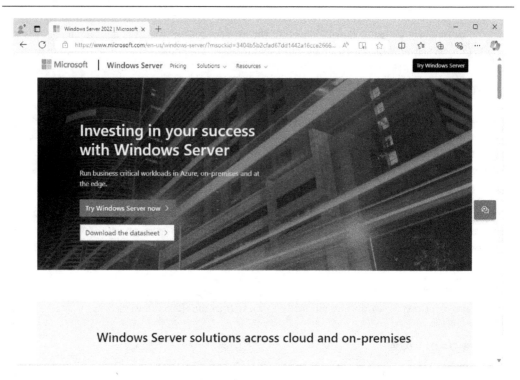

Figure 5.9- Windows Server's website powered by Microsoft

To expand your server's capabilities, you can create additional websites within the same server environment using IIS Manager. That is done by navigating to the **Sites** node, right-clicking it, and selecting **Add Website**, which is shown in *Figure 5.10*:

Figure 5.10 – Adding a website via IIS Manager in Windows Server 2025

This feature allows you to host multiple sites on a single server, each with its unique domain or path, and manage them efficiently through IIS Manager.

In the following subsection, we will explore the concept of software ports, their role in network communications, and how they facilitate the interaction between web services and clients.

Ports overview

Ports are crucial components in computer networking, categorized into hardware ports and software ports. A **hardware port** is a physical interface on a computer or electronic device that enables data transfer and communication. Examples include USB ports for connecting peripherals, Ethernet ports for network connectivity, and HDMI ports for video output, all of which are fundamental for seamless interaction between devices.

In contrast, a **software port**, or **application port**, is a virtual endpoint used by software applications and services to manage network traffic. These logical identifiers help direct data to the appropriate process or application running on a server or network device. Software ports are divided into three main types:

- **Well-Known Ports**: Ranging from 0 to 1023, these ports are assigned to widely used protocols and services by the **Internet Assigned Numbers Authority** (**IANA**). They are standardized for common services to ensure consistency across different systems. For instance, port 80 is used for HTTP traffic, port 443 for HTTPS traffic, port 21 for FTP, and port 25 for SMTP. These ports are essential for fundamental web services, secure communications, file transfers, and email transmissions.

- **Registered Ports**: These ports, spanning from 1024 to 49151, are used by software applications that are not as universally recognized as those using well-known ports. Registered with IANA, these ports avoid conflicts and ensure dedicated access for specific applications. For example, MySQL databases use port 3306, and PostgreSQL databases use port 5432.

- **Dynamic or Private Ports**: Covering the range from 49152 to 65535, these ports are typically used for ephemeral purposes. They are assigned temporarily for short-lived communication sessions and are not permanently associated with any specific service. These ports are commonly used for client-side applications to establish temporary connections with server-side services.

The following table provides a summary of some common application ports, their protocols, and transport methods:

Protocol	Port	Transportation protocol
FTP	21	TCP
SSH	22	TCP
Telnet	23	TCP
SMTP	25	TCP
HTTP	80	TCP and UDP
POP3	110	TCP
NNTP	119	TCP
NTP	123	TCP
IMAP4	143	TCP
HTTPS	443	TCP

Table 5.1- The well-known application ports

Each port and protocol combination plays a specific role in network communications. For instance, FTP uses port 21 for file transfers, **Secure Shell** (**SSH**) on port 22 facilitates secure remote access, and HTTP on port 80 manages standard web traffic.

In the following section, we will delve into SSL technology, which provides an additional layer of security by encrypting data transmitted over networks.

What is SSL?

SSL is a crucial technology for securing data exchanged between a web server and a web browser. By encrypting the data transmitted, SSL ensures that any communication between these two entities remains confidential and integral. When a web browser connects to a website that employs SSL, it uses the HTTPS protocol, which operates over port 443, to initiate a secure connection.

This secure connection is established through the use of digital certificates, which are cryptographic documents issued by trusted **certificate authorities** (**CAs**). These certificates authenticate the identity of the website and facilitate the establishment of a secure, encrypted communication channel. During this process, the browser and the server use the certificate to agree on a shared secret key. This key is then employed to encrypt all data transmitted between them, preventing unauthorized parties from intercepting or deciphering the information, thereby ensuring a secure and protected online experience.

SSL not only ensures the confidentiality of the data but also verifies the legitimacy of the website, protecting users from potential cyber threats, such as phishing attacks. By employing encryption, SSL helps to maintain data integrity, ensuring that the data remains reliable and unchanged during transmission. This secure exchange is visually represented in *Figure 5.11*:

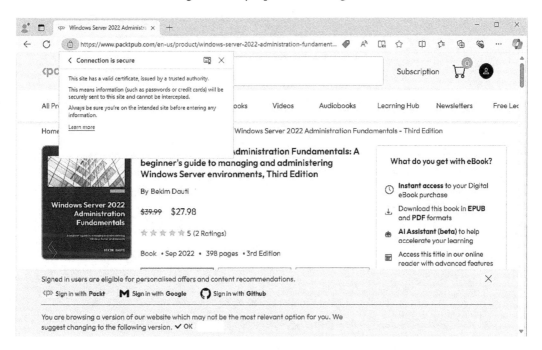

Figure 5.11- Secure communication between browser and website

> **Note**
>
> Transport Layer Security (TLS) improves upon SSL by addressing its limitations with enhanced security features. Unlike SSL, TLS supports more robust encryption algorithms and more secure cryptographic practices, offering better protection against vulnerabilities and attacks. TLS also refines the handshake process and certificate validation methods, ensuring a more secure and resilient connection. These advancements make TLS a superior choice for safeguarding data transmitted over networks, effectively overcoming the shortcomings of its predecessor.

In the following subsection, we will explore the evolution of SSL into TLS and its role in further enhancing data security.

How do certificates work?

Digital certificates are crucial for establishing secure communication over the internet, particularly between a website and a browser. These certificates, issued by a trusted entity known as a CA, authenticate the website's identity and enable encrypted data exchange. As illustrated in *Figure 5.12*, the CA is responsible for validating and issuing certificates, ensuring that they are trustworthy and accurate.

Figure 5.12- Certificate issued by a CA

Digital certificates operate within the framework of **public key infrastructure (PKI)**. PKI is a system designed to manage digital keys and certificates, providing a robust method for verifying the ownership of public keys. Each certificate contains a public key and information about the certificate holder, such as the organization's name and address. The CA's role is to confirm that the public key contained in the certificate indeed belongs to the entity it claims to represent. This validation process helps prevent fraudulent activities and ensures that the data exchanged remains secure.

TLS has evolved from SSL to address its limitations and enhance security. TLS offers more robust encryption algorithms, improved cryptographic practices, and better mechanisms for key negotiation and certificate validation. These advancements resolve SSL's vulnerabilities, providing a more secure and resilient framework for protecting data transmitted over networks.

When a browser connects to a website that uses SSL/TLS, the digital certificate is used to establish a secure connection. The website's server and the browser use the certificate to agree on a shared encryption key. This key is then used to encrypt and decrypt the data exchanged, ensuring that sensitive information remains confidential and protected from unauthorized access.

In addition to encryption, digital certificates also provide data integrity and authentication. They ensure that the data sent between the website and the browser is not tampered with during transmission and that the identity of the website is genuine.

> **Note**
>
> For a more in-depth understanding of PKI, you can refer to the comprehensive resources available at Oracle's PKI documentation: `https://docs.oracle.com/cd/B10501_01/network.920/a96582/pki.html`. This source provides detailed information on the principles, components, and implementation of PKI, offering valuable insights for enhancing your knowledge of secure data management and encryption technologies.

The following section will introduce the role of remote access in Windows Server 2025 and detail how it supports secure remote connectivity and access management.

Setting up remote access roles and their functionalities

Remote Access in Windows Server 2025 is an essential role that provides users with the flexibility to access network resources from virtually any location and at any time while also allowing administrators to manage and secure these remote connections efficiently. This capability is precious in today's increasingly remote work environments, where maintaining secure and reliable access to corporate networks is critical. The Remote Access role integrates several key technologies that support different types of network connections, each tailored to meet specific remote access requirements:

- **DirectAccess**: This is one of the core components of Remote Access, which was initially introduced in Windows Server 2008 R2. It offers a seamless and secure connection to corporate networks without the need for a traditional VPN. By encrypting communications between DirectAccess clients and servers using IPsec, DirectAccess ensures that data remains protected as it travels across the internet. Moreover, it utilizes IPv6 over IPv4 tunneling to facilitate connectivity to the intranet, making it easier for users to access internal resources securely from remote locations.

- **The Routing and Remote Access Service (RRAS)**: This succeeded the **Remote Access Service (RAS)** from the Windows NT era, which was launched in Windows 2000. RRAS is a versatile service that combines the capabilities of VPN and dial-up connections, enabling the creation of secure links between remote sites. Additionally, RRAS supports routing traffic between different sub-networks, making it an essential tool for managing complex network environments and ensuring that remote users can connect to the resources they need.

- **Web Application Proxy**: This is available on Windows Server 2025. Acting as a reverse proxy, the Web Application Proxy enables secure access to web applications hosted on the intranet from external networks. That is achieved through integration with **Active Directory Federation Services (AD FS)**, which authenticates corporate users and ensures that only authorized individuals can access sensitive internal applications via an extranet. This technology is beneficial for organizations that need to provide secure remote access to web-based resources without compromising security.

Setting up a remote access server in Windows Server 2025 involves adding the Remote Access role to the server, as depicted in *Figure 5.13*. This role configuration is the first step in enabling a range of remote access technologies that enhance both the connectivity and security of remote users. By implementing these technologies, organizations can ensure that their employees have the tools they need to work effectively from any location. At the same time, IT administrators can maintain control over the security and management of these connections.

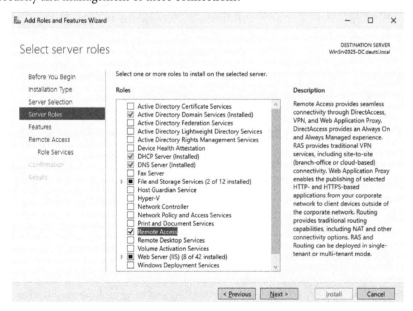

Figure 5.13- Adding the Remote Access role in Windows Server 2025

In the upcoming subsection, we will delve into the **Remote Assistance feature**, providing detailed instructions on how to enable and configure this feature on your server, further enhancing your organization's remote support capabilities.

How to use Remote Assistance

Remote Assistance in Windows Server 2025 is a valuable feature that enables a trusted individual, typically an IT support professional (the initiator), to remotely view and control a user's desktop (the invitee) to assist with diagnosing and resolving technical issues. This capability is particularly beneficial for organizations with remote employees or distributed networks, as it allows support personnel to provide real-time help without being physically present, thereby reducing downtime and increasing efficiency. The process begins when the invitee requests assistance, granting the initiator permission to access their system. That ensures that the invitee remains in control and can oversee the troubleshooting process, enhancing both security and user comfort. To activate the Remote Assistance feature on a server, administrators need to use **Add Roles and Features Wizard**, a straightforward process illustrated in *Figure 5.14*.

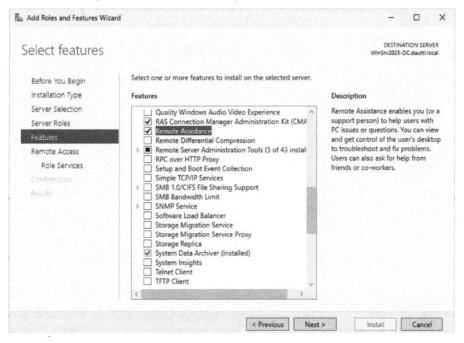

Figure 5.14- Adding the RSAT feature in Windows Server 2025

In the upcoming subsection, we will explore the **Remote Server Administration Tools** (**RSAT**) feature, a robust set of tools that further enhances remote management capabilities by allowing administrators to manage roles and features on other servers from a single workstation, streamlining the management of Windows Server environments.

How does RSAT work?

RSAT in Windows Server 2025 empowers system administrators to remotely manage server roles and features across other servers running Windows Server 2025. RSAT provides both graphical and command-line interfaces, giving administrators flexibility in how they interact with their server environments. Additionally, RSAT is compatible with client computers running Windows 10 or 11, enabling centralized management from a broader range of devices.

Administrators can use **Add Roles and Features Wizard**, depicted in *Figure 5.15*, to enable the RSAT feature. Once activated, RSAT facilitates a wide array of administrative tasks, from configuring Active Directory settings to managing Group Policy and monitoring server performance.

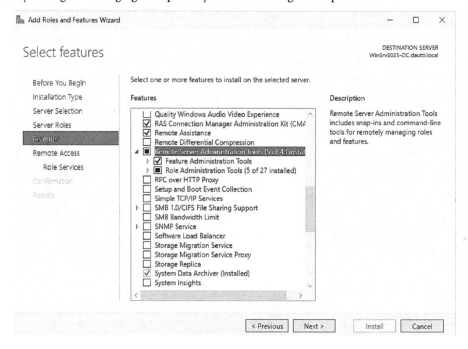

Figure 5.15- Adding the RSAT feature in Windows Server 2025

In comparison, **Windows Admin Center** offers a modern, browser-based alternative to RSAT. While RSAT provides a more traditional approach to remote server management, Windows Admin Center integrates multiple management tools into a single, unified interface, streamlining the management experience. This tool allows administrators to manage servers, clusters, hyper-converged infrastructure, and Windows 10 or 11 devices with ease, all through a web-based interface that can be accessed from anywhere.

In the next section, we will discuss the **Remote Desktop Services** (**RDS**) server and its configuration.

Explaining RDS

RDS plays a key role in Windows Servers, enabling users to access the graphical interfaces of computers and applications from remote locations, whether they are on the same network or connecting over the internet. Previously known as **Terminal Services (TS)** until its rebranding in Windows Server 2008 R2, RDS provides robust functionality, allowing users to run virtualized applications directly on their desktops. This feature is precious in enterprise environments where centralized management of applications and desktops is critical.

By default, Windows Server permits two concurrent Remote Desktop sessions without requiring additional licensing. This limitation is sufficient for basic administrative tasks, but when more than two users need to connect simultaneously, an RDS licensing server must be configured to manage additional licenses. To enable and adequately configure RDS on a Windows Server 2025 environment, the RDS role must be added through the server's management interface, as depicted in *Figure 5.16*.

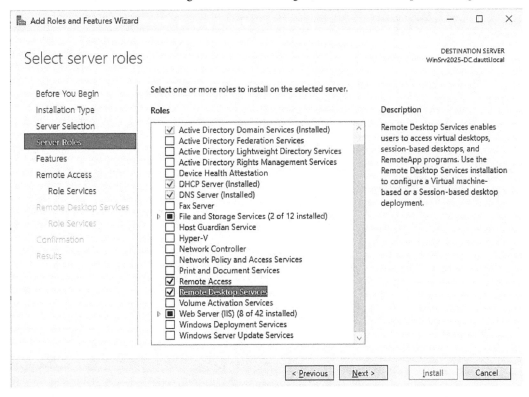

Figure 5.16- Adding the RDS role in Windows Server 2025

In the upcoming section, we'll delve into the installation and configuration of the RDS licensing server, which is essential for expanding beyond the default session limitations.

How to manage RDS CALs

Remote Desktop Services Client Access Licenses (**RDS CALs**) are required for users and devices to access a **Remote Desktop Session Host** (**RDSH**) server, which allows remote connections to desktops and applications. The RDS licensing server is pivotal in managing these licenses and issuing and tracking their usage within the network. By default, the RDS licensing server supports up to two concurrent Remote Desktop sessions without additional licensing. For organizations that need more than these two free connections, purchasing extra RDS CALs is necessary to comply with licensing requirements and support additional users.

To configure an RDS licensing server on Windows Server 2025, you must first install the RDS role on the server. Afterward, select **Remote Desktop Licensing** as a role service, as depicted in *Figure 5.17*. This setup ensures that the server can issue the appropriate number of licenses to accommodate your organization's remote access needs.

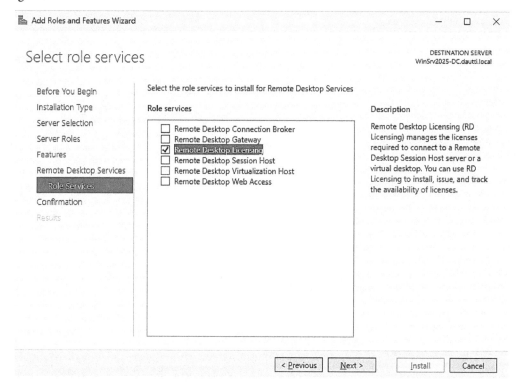

Figure 5.17- Adding Remote Desktop Licensing Role Services in Windows Server 2025

Additionally, it is crucial to regularly review and manage your RDS CALs to ensure compliance with licensing agreements and avoid service interruptions. In the subsequent section, we will delve into the **Remote Desktop Gateway** (**RDG**) server, focusing on how to configure it to provide secure remote access to your network resources.

Setting up RDG

The **RDG** is an essential role service in Windows Server that facilitates secure remote access to computers within a private network from anywhere on the internet. It acts as an intermediary, or proxy, between the Remote Desktop client and the internal target computer, ensuring that all communications are encrypted and secure. By implementing RDG, organizations can provide remote users with access to network resources without exposing internal systems directly to the internet.

To install and configure an RDG server on Windows Server 2025, begin by adding the RDS role to the server. After installing this role, select **Remote Desktop Gateway** as the specific role service, as shown in *Figure 5.18*. This setup allows the RDG server to handle incoming Remote Desktop requests, authenticate users, and establish a secure, encrypted connection between the client and the network resources.

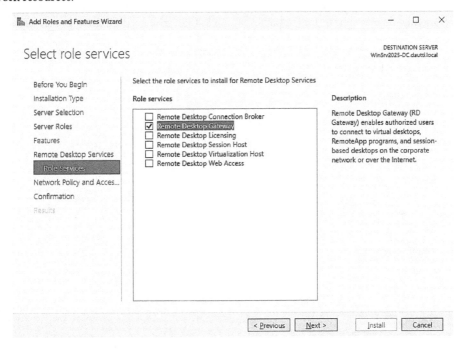

Figure 5.18- Adding RDG role services in Windows Server 2025

Additionally, RDG supports advanced features, such as centralizing user access management and enforcing security policies. For example, RDG can integrate with NPS to enforce conditional access policies, ensuring that only compliant devices and users can connect.

In the following subsection, we will introduce VPNs, explain their role in enhancing remote access security, and detail the steps for implementing a VPN solution.

What is a VPN?

A **VPN** provides a secure way to connect and transmit data over the internet between computers located on different networks. By leveraging tunneling protocols and encryption techniques, a VPN creates a virtual link that simulates a direct connection between the endpoints. This technology is essential for connecting remote users to their corporate networks or for linking different organizational networks over the internet. There are two primary types of VPNs:

- **Remote-Access VPN**: This is designed to grant telecommuters or remote workers access to their company's private network from any location. This type of VPN creates a secure tunnel from the user's device to the corporate network, ensuring data privacy and integrity during transmission.

- **Site-to-Site VPN**: This connects entire networks from different locations, allowing seamless communication between two distinct networks over the internet. This type of VPN is ideal for organizations with multiple branches or offices that need to share resources and data securely.

To set up a VPN server in Windows Server 2025, you need to install the Remote Access role and select the **DirectAccess and VPN (RAS)** role services, as depicted in *Figure 5.19.*

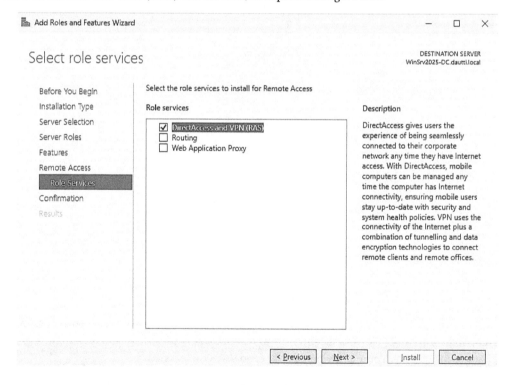

Figure 5.19- Adding the DirectAccess and VPN (RAS) role services in Windows Server 2025

DirectAccess and VPN, while similar in their aim to provide secure remote connectivity, differ significantly in their implementation and use cases. DirectAccess provides a more seamless experience by automatically connecting remote users to the corporate network without requiring a separate VPN client. It integrates directly with the Windows operating system and offers features such as **always-on connectivity** and **automatic access** to internal resources. On the other hand, traditional VPN solutions require users to initiate a connection manually and often involve additional client software. VPNs are generally more versatile and can be used across various operating systems and devices, whereas DirectAccess is tailored explicitly for environments with a homogeneous Windows infrastructure.

In the upcoming subsection, we will delve into the **Application Virtualization** (**App-V**) service. App-V enables the execution of applications without the need for local installation, leveraging virtualization technology to achieve this. By isolating applications from the local environment, App-V helps minimize conflicts and compatibility issues that can arise from varying application requirements and settings. This service proves to be an invaluable tool for IT professionals seeking to streamline application management, deployment, and security, enhancing overall efficiency and reducing potential disruptions.

Explaining App-V

Microsoft App-V enables users to access applications hosted on a server rather than installed locally, offering a seamless experience as though the applications were running directly on their devices. This service simplifies application management by reducing conflicts and compatibility issues that may occur with traditional installations. App-V allows system administrators to manage application access centrally, thereby controlling which applications users can interact with. To implement App-V, you would first need to obtain the **Microsoft Desktop Optimization Pack** (**MDOP**) from Microsoft's website.

In modern environments, App-V is increasingly utilized in cloud-based settings rather than traditional on-premises installations. **Cloud-based App-V** deployment provides several advantages, including scalability, reduced infrastructure costs, and easier updates and maintenance. By leveraging cloud resources, organizations can deploy and manage virtualized applications more flexibly, ensuring that users have access to the latest applications without the need for local installation or extensive hardware. This approach enhances the efficiency and security of application management, particularly in dynamic and distributed work environments.

> **Note**
>
> For detailed guidance on deploying Microsoft App-V on a local server, please visit the official documentation at Microsoft's App-V deployment guide `https://learn.microsoft.com/en-us/microsoft-desktop-optimization-pack/app-v/appv-deploy-the-appv-server`. This resource provides comprehensive instructions and best practices for successfully setting up and configuring the App-V server in your local environment.

Next, we will delve into the topic of managing multiple ports and their applications.

Understanding multiple ports

In this subsection, we will explore the concept of using **multiple ports**, which is essential for managing network communications effectively. A key example is the **App-V** service, which allows applications to run on a server rather than being installed locally on each user's device. This virtualization technology helps prevent software conflicts and compatibility issues by isolating applications from the local operating system. For IT professionals, App-V offers a streamlined approach to application management and deployment, enhancing security and operational efficiency.

Previously, we discussed RDS and the use of port 3389 for establishing Remote Desktop connections. However, RDS, by default, only supports one active remote session per port. To facilitate concurrent access to multiple computers, RDS employs additional port numbers, beginning with 3390 and increasing sequentially. Each port number corresponds to a different remote session, allowing multiple users to connect simultaneously within a **local area network** (**LAN**).

Furthermore, remote access to multiple systems can be managed using IP sockets, which combine an IP address with a port number to specify unique communication channels. An IP socket helps direct data traffic accurately between the client and the server. The format for an IP socket is as follows:

Syntax: `Public_IP_address:Port_number`

Example: `113.79.43.133:3389`

Understanding and managing multiple ports is crucial for optimizing network performance and ensuring efficient remote access. This section covered the fundamentals of port usage with RDS and App-V, setting the stage for our following discussion on file and print services in Windows Server 2025.

Deploying file and print services for network environments

File and print services trace their origins to the early days of computer networking when the primary goal was to enable resource sharing among users. These services have significantly evolved over the years and are now fundamental to both home and business networks. They encompass the management of file storage, allowing users to store, retrieve, and share files efficiently, as well as print services, which enable the sharing of printers across a network, facilitating access to printing resources from multiple devices. Modern **network operating systems** (**NOSs**), including Windows Server 2025, provide advanced file and print services that support enhanced features such as network security, access control, and integration with cloud storage solutions. These services are designed to streamline data management and enhance productivity by ensuring that files and printers are readily accessible, secure, and efficiently managed across various network environments. As networking technologies continue to advance, file and print services adapt to offer improved performance, scalability, and compatibility with emerging technologies.

File Services overview

The **File Services role** in Windows Server 2025 is an integral network component that is automatically included during the installation of the operating system (see *Figure 5.20*). This role provides essential functionalities for data management and accessibility across a network. Key features encompassed within the File Services role include the following:

- **File Sharing**: This feature allows users to share files and folders across the network, making them accessible to authorized users from various devices and locations. It simplifies collaboration and data exchange within organizations.

- **Work Folders**: This functionality enables users to synchronize their work files between their local devices and the server, ensuring that their data is consistently updated and available across multiple endpoints.

- **Distributed File System (DFS) Namespaces**: DFS namespaces offer a unified view of file shares, allowing users to access files and folders from a single namespace, regardless of their physical location on the network. That simplifies file access and enhances user experience.

- **BranchCache**: This feature optimizes network performance by caching frequently accessed files locally at branch offices. It reduces bandwidth consumption and improves access speed, making it particularly useful for remote locations with limited connectivity.

Together, these features provide a comprehensive suite of tools for managing and accessing data efficiently within a networked environment. They support various data access scenarios, from local file sharing to remote synchronization and efficient caching.

In the following subsection, we will explore the role of PDS, including its various components and installation procedures, to further enhance network resource management.

PDS Role overview

The **PDS role** in Windows Server 2025 plays a crucial role in centralizing the management of network printing and scanning functions. By supporting network printers and scanners, the PDS role streamlines the process of sending and receiving print jobs, as well as managing scanned documents within the network. To configure a print server, the PDS role must first be installed on Windows Server 2025, as depicted in *Figure 5.20*. Once installed, various additional role services can be added to extend the PDS capabilities.

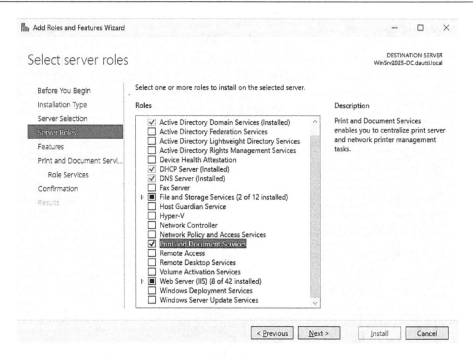

Figure 5.20- Adding PDS role in Windows Server 2025

Key role services available with PDS include the following:

- **Print Server**: This service manages print queues, handles the deployment of printers, and facilitates the migration of print servers, ensuring that print jobs are processed efficiently and that printer resources are utilized optimally.

- **Internet Printing**: This feature allows users to print documents over the web using the **Internet Printing Protocol (IPP)**. It provides a convenient method for remote printing, enabling users to submit print jobs from anywhere with internet access.

- **Line Printer Daemon (LPD) Service**: The LPD service enables printing from Unix-based systems and other non-Windows operating systems using the **Line Printer Remote (LPR)** protocol. This service ensures interoperability across different platforms, making it easier to integrate diverse printing environments.

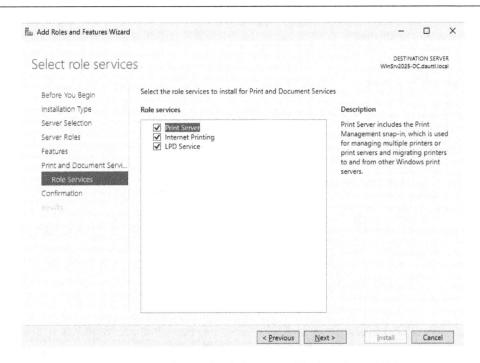

Figure 5.21- Installing PDS Role Services in Windows Server 2025

Additionally, the PDS role supports advanced features, such as print management, auditing, and secure print release, which enhance the control and security of printing tasks. In the following subsection, we will explore various printer-related concepts, starting with the setup and management of local printers, and expand on how these concepts fit into a broader network printing strategy.

What is a local printer?

A **local printer** is directly connected to a single computer via a parallel port or USB port, functioning primarily to print documents for that specific computer. This direct connection limits its accessibility to the host machine unless printer sharing is enabled, allowing other networked computers to use it. Local printers are straightforward to set up and manage but may become a bottleneck in larger environments where multiple users need access.

In contrast, **network printers** are connected to a network and can be accessed by multiple computers simultaneously without requiring a dedicated connection to each one. These printers are often equipped with their **network interface card** (**NIC**) or are connected through a print server, allowing them to handle print jobs from any authorized user on the network. This setup centralizes printing, improves efficiency, and simplifies management by eliminating the need for individual printer connections on each workstation.

Similarly, **internet printers**, which can be a type of network printer, enable printing over the internet. These printers are accessible via **web protocols**, allowing users to print documents from remote locations. Internet printers often utilize specialized software or cloud-based services to facilitate printing from anywhere, providing greater flexibility and accessibility compared to local and network printers.

In summary, while local printers are suitable for individual use or small setups with shared access, network, and internet printers offer scalable solutions for larger organizations by providing centralized, remote, and more flexible printing options.

Network printer explained

A **network printer** differs from a local printer in that it does not rely on a direct connection to a single computer. Instead, it features its network interface, either wired or wireless, allowing it to be accessed by multiple devices on the same network. This capability eliminates the need for individual connections to each workstation, making network printers ideal for shared environments. Additionally, with proper configuration, network printers can be accessed remotely over the internet, extending their functionality beyond the local network. While the concept of network printers was introduced in a previous subsection, this section focuses on the deployment and management of network printers within a Windows Server 2025 environment. Examining the web address displayed in the browser in *Figure 5.22* illustrates how network printer services effectively manage network printers.

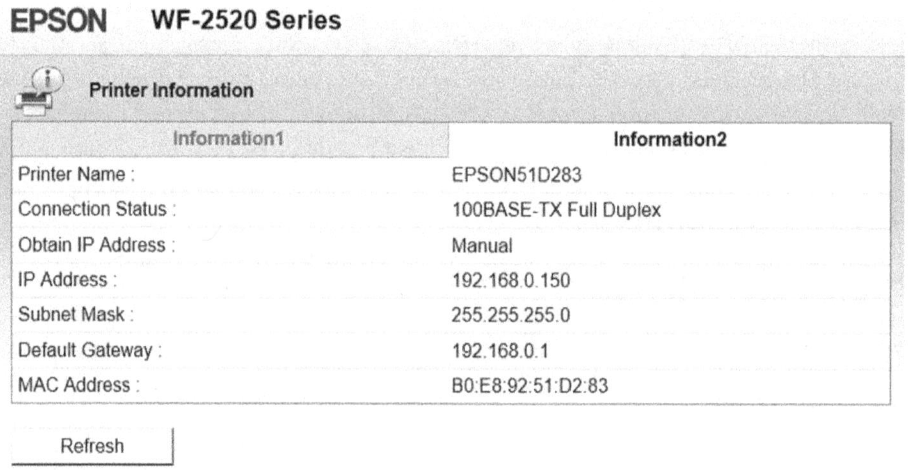

EPSON   WF-2520 Series

Printer Information

Information1	Information2
Printer Name :	EPSON51D283
Connection Status :	100BASE-TX Full Duplex
Obtain IP Address :	Manual
IP Address :	192.168.0.150
Subnet Mask :	255.255.255.0
Default Gateway :	192.168.0.1
MAC Address :	B0:E8:92:51:D2:83

Refresh

Figure 5.22- Adding a network printer

In the subsequent section, we will explore printer pooling, which provides further enhancements for managing multiple printers and optimizing print resources.

Understanding printer pooling

Printer pooling in Windows Server 2025 is a critical feature for optimizing print management within a corporate environment. By combining multiple physical printers into a single virtual printer, printer pooling helps streamline printing operations and increase efficiency. In a large organization, this setup is particularly beneficial as it balances the print load across several devices, minimizing the risk of any single printer becoming a bottleneck or experiencing downtime.

In practical terms, printer pooling allows for more reliable and scalable printing services by handling higher volumes of print requests and reducing the likelihood of printer congestion. When users send print jobs to the virtual printer, these jobs are automatically distributed among the available printers in the pool. This distribution ensures that print tasks are completed more quickly and that no single printer is overwhelmed by excessive demand.

Additionally, printer pooling simplifies printer management by presenting a unified printer interface to end users, even though multiple physical devices are in operation. That means users only need to interact with one printer queue, making the printing process more intuitive and less prone to errors.

To set up printer pooling, you need to install the PDS role along with the Print Server role services on your Windows Server 2025. Once installed, you can add printers to the pool and configure the pooling options via the **Print Management** console, as shown in *Figure 5.23*. This configuration not only enhances print service reliability but also contributes to overall organizational productivity by ensuring efficient and consistent printing capabilities.

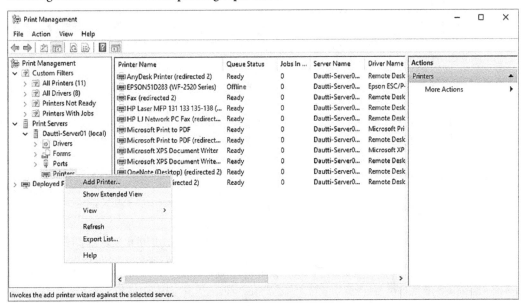

Figure 5.23 – Adding printers in a printer pooling in Windows Server 2025

In the following section, we will delve into how to integrate and manage shared network resources, which further supports effective IT infrastructure management.

Internet printing overview

Internet printing allows users to send print jobs to network printers via a web browser, offering a convenient and remote method to manage printing tasks. Previously, we discussed the concept of internet printing, which enables users to access and utilize network printers through web-based interfaces. This section will focus on a practical example of deploying internet printing within your organization. To set up internet printing on a Windows Server 2025, you must install the PDS role and select the Internet Printing role service. Additionally, configuring the web server role (IIS) is necessary to support this feature.

Once configured, users can access available printers by navigating to `http://servername/printers` in their web browser, as shown in *Figure 5.24*. This setup allows for remote printing, making it easier for users to manage print jobs from various locations within the network, thus enhancing overall efficiency and flexibility. In the next section, we will delve into managing web printing services, focusing on configuration and optimization to better serve organizational needs.

Figure 5.24- Web printing

Next, we will explore the management of web printing services. That involves configuring and optimizing web-based printing solutions to ensure efficient operation and ease of use within an organization. We'll cover key aspects such as setting up and maintaining web print servers, managing user access, and troubleshooting common issues to ensure a smooth and effective printing experience.

Understanding Web Printing Management

Web printing management, often referred to as **internet printing**, offers more than just the ability to print documents over the web; it also provides comprehensive tools for managing print jobs remotely. This functionality enables users to interact with their print tasks from any web browser, offering a similar level of control and convenience as if they were using a local or network printer directly. To utilize this feature, users must enter `http://servername/printers` into their browser's address bar, which will display a management interface (see *Figure 5.25*) where they can view and control their print jobs.

Figure 5.25- Web printing management

This capability is particularly beneficial for environments where users need to manage print tasks from different locations or when centralized control over printing resources is required. However, before you can take advantage of web printing management, ensure that the Internet Printing role service is installed. That involves first adding the PDS role, followed by the Internet Printing role service.

In the following subsection, we will delve into the deployment and management of printer drivers, which are essential for ensuring that printers operate correctly and efficiently within your network.

Understanding Printer Driver Deployment

Understanding **printer driver deployment** is a critical component of effective print management within a networked environment. The Print Management administrative console in Windows Server 2025 facilitates this process by offering a centralized platform for managing printers and their drivers. Deploying printer drivers through this console involves selecting the appropriate driver for a specific printer and then pushing this driver to one or multiple computers on the network. That ensures that the printer operates with the latest driver version, which is crucial for maintaining compatibility, functionality, and performance across different systems.

In addition to installing or upgrading drivers, the console provides tools for managing print queues, monitoring print jobs, and configuring printer settings. This centralized approach simplifies the administration of print resources and helps address any potential issues quickly.

Figure 5.26 demonstrates how to deploy print drivers using the **Print Management** console in Windows Server 2025, highlighting the steps involved in ensuring that all networked printers are equipped with the correct and most up-to-date drivers.

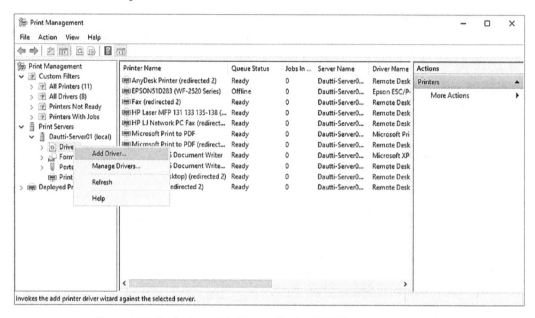

Figure 5.26- Deploying print drivers with the Print Management console

In the subsequent section, we will explore user rights, **New Technology File System** (**NTFS**) permissions, and share permissions. Understanding these concepts is essential for managing access control and ensuring the security of shared resources in a networked environment.

Understanding User Rights and Permissions Management

Effective access management and security are fundamental to maintaining the integrity of any networked environment. To ensure robust protection and proper resource management, administrators must have a comprehensive understanding of **user rights**, **NTFS permissions**, and **share permissions**. User rights specify the capabilities and restrictions of users regarding system operations and resources. NTFS permissions control access to files and directories, whether on a local machine or a network drive. In contrast, share permissions govern access to network-shared resources. Mastering these concepts enables administrators to enforce appropriate access levels, safeguard data, and prevent unauthorized access to sensitive information. In the following sections, we will explore each of these elements in detail, offering practical guidance on configuration and management.

NTFS permissions explained

To effectively manage access and security within a Windows environment, it's essential to grasp the nuances of **NTFS permissions**. When managing a folder's security settings in Windows, you can access a detailed view of permissions by right-clicking the folder, selecting **Properties**, and navigating to the **Security** tab. Here, you'll encounter several types of permissions that control how users interact with files and folders:

- **Full Control**: This permission provides comprehensive access, enabling users to perform all actions, including reading, writing, modifying, executing, changing attributes and permissions, and deleting files and subfolders. It grants complete administrative capabilities over the folder's contents.

- **Modify**: This allows users to view and alter the contents, which includes adding, editing, and deleting files and subfolders, but does not permit changing permissions or attributes.

- **Read & Execute**: Users can run executable files and manage their execution. This permission also allows viewing files and their contents but does not permit modifications.

- **List Folder Contents**: This enables users to see the names and properties of files and subfolders within the folder but does not grant access to open or modify the files.

- **Read**: This provides the ability to view the files and their properties but does not allow any changes to the file contents.

- **Write**: This permits users to add new files and modify the contents of existing ones but does not allow reading or executing files.

- **Special Permissions**: This offers advanced, granular control over specific file or folder operations, such as creating files, deleting subfolders, and more nuanced actions.

Permissions are applied in an *allowed* or *denied* manner (refer to *Figure 5.27*), which directly impacts user access levels. The configuration of these permissions determines how users can interact with system resources, thereby influencing data security and operational efficiency.

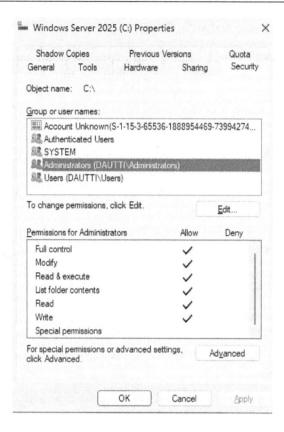

Figure 5.27- NTFS permissions in Windows Server 2025

By understanding and appropriately assigning these permissions, administrators can effectively manage user access and maintain a secure network environment.

Understanding Share Permissions

In addition to NTFS permissions, which manage access to files and folders on a local server, **share permissions** are essential for controlling access to resources shared across a network. Share permissions determine how users can interact with these network-shared resources and are categorized into three distinct levels:

- **Full Control**: This grants users complete authority over the shared resource, enabling them to read, modify, and alter permissions and ownership of files and subfolders

- **Change**: This permission allows users to read, execute, write, and delete files and subfolders but does not grant the ability to modify permissions

- **Read**: This permission limits users to viewing and listing the content of the shared resource without any capability to make changes

These permissions work in tandem with NTFS permissions to provide a layered security model. For instance, if NTFS permissions restrict access to a file, share permissions cannot override this restriction, and vice versa. Proper configuration of share permissions ensures that users have appropriate access based on their roles and needs while maintaining the security of network resources. *Figure 5.28* provides a visual representation of how to set and manage these permissions in Windows Server 2025, illustrating the steps necessary to configure network access and ensure effective resource management.

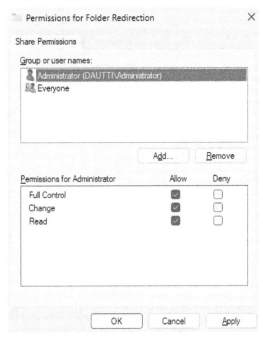

Figure 5.28- Shared permissions in Windows Server 2025

Configuring User Rights

Effective management of user rights is fundamental to ensuring both system security and proper operational efficiency. User rights can be configured using tools such as **Local Group Policy Editor** (gpedit.msc), **Local Security Policy**, or **Default Domain Policy**. To access these settings, navigate to Computer Configuration|Windows Settings|Security Settings| Policies|User Rights Assignment. These policies allow administrators to define specific system privileges for user accounts, including who can log in locally, access the network, or manage system services. In a domain environment, some user rights may already be established according to the organization's default domain policies (see *Figure 5.29*).

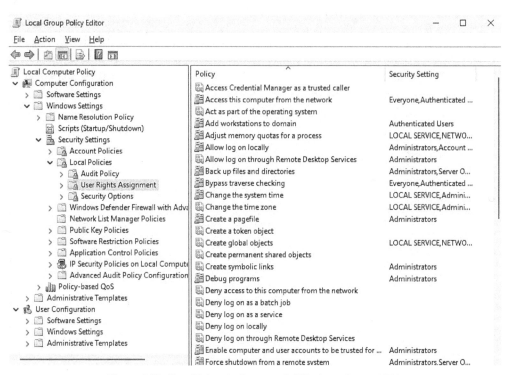

Figure 5.29- User Rights Assignment in Windows Server 2025

Understanding the distinction between user rights and permissions is essential for effective system management. *User rights* dictate what actions a user can perform on the system as a whole, such as shutting down the server or managing system services. In contrast, *permissions* are more granular and control access to specific resources, such as files and folders.

Proper configuration of both user rights and permissions ensures that users have the necessary access to perform their roles while maintaining the security and integrity of the server environment. This comprehensive approach helps prevent unauthorized access and ensures that security policies align with organizational requirements.

Monitoring file server activities

Given the critical role that file servers play in an organization's IT infrastructure, maintaining rigorous oversight through auditing is essential for ensuring data security and compliance. **Auditing** enables administrators to track and document all activities related to file access, modifications, and deletions. That includes capturing detailed records of who accessed specific files, what changes were made, and when these actions occurred. Such comprehensive monitoring is indispensable for detecting unauthorized access, troubleshooting issues, and ensuring adherence to organizational policies and regulatory requirements.

To set up and manage auditing in Windows Server 2025, you should use Local Group Policy Editor (`gpedit.msc`), Local Security Policy, or Default Domain Policy. Navigate to `Computer Configuration|Windows Settings|Security Settings|Local Policies|Audit Policy` to configure the audit settings according to your needs (see *Figure 5.30*). This setup allows you to define which activities are logged and how they are reported, enabling detailed and actionable insights into file server operations.

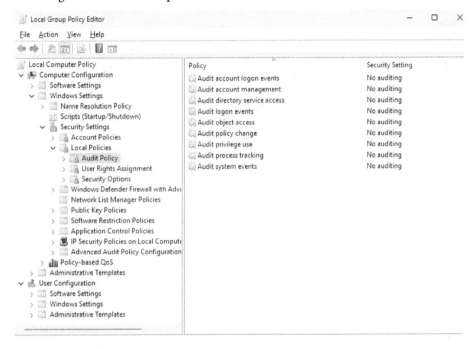

Figure 5.30- Audit policies in Windows Server 2025

Effective auditing not only helps safeguard sensitive data but also plays a pivotal role in maintaining the overall health of the IT infrastructure. It provides transparency, aids in compliance, and supports proactive management. In the next section, we will shift our focus to installing and configuring the Web Server (IIS) and PDS roles, which are essential for expanding and optimizing server functionalities.

Chapter exercise – installing webserver (IIS) and PDS roles

In this chapter's exercise, you will be guided through two critical tasks that are essential for enhancing your server's capabilities:

- First, you'll install the Web Server (IIS) role, which allows your server to host and manage web applications, websites, and a variety of web-based services, making it a central point for internet or intranet activities. This step is crucial for any environment where web services play a key role in business operations.

- Next, you'll install the PDS role, a vital component for any networked environment that relies on centralized management of printers and print jobs. This role enables your server to efficiently oversee printing tasks, ensuring that networked printers are effectively managed, print jobs are handled with priority, and resources are utilized optimally.

Together, these tasks will equip your server with the foundational tools needed to support both web hosting and document services in a networked setting, making it a more versatile and powerful asset in your IT infrastructure.

Setting up a Web Server (IIS) role

Setting up the Web Server (IIS) role in Windows Server 2025 allows you to host and manage web applications and services efficiently. To install this role, follow these steps:

1. Begin by opening **Server Manager** from the Start menu.

2. Click on **Add Roles and Features** to launch **Add Roles and Features Wizard**, as shown in *Figure 5.31*.

3. Choose the **Role-based or feature-based installation** option, and then click **Next**.

4. Ensure the correct server is selected from the server pool by choosing **Select a server from the server pool** and then clicking **Next**.

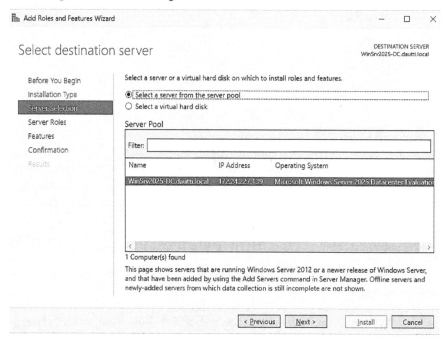

Figure 5.31- Selecting the destination server

5. In the list of available roles, check the box next to **Web Server (IIS)**.

6. When prompted with a message to add features required for Web Server (IIS), click the **Add Features** button.

7. At this point, you do not need to add any additional features, so click **Next**.

8. Please review the description and installation notes for the Web Server (IIS) role before proceeding. Then, click **Next**.

9. You can accept the default role services for Web Server (IIS) or customize them based on your specific needs.

10. Once you have reviewed your selections, click the **Install** button to begin the installation process.

11. After the installation is complete, click **Close** to exit the wizard. At this point, a server restart is not necessary.

By following these steps, you will have successfully installed the Web Server (IIS) role on your server, equipping it to host and manage a wide range of web applications and services. This setup is foundational for any server that will be serving web content or providing web-based services in a networked environment.

Installing a PDS role

Setting up the PDS role in Windows Server 2025 enables your server to manage printers and print jobs effectively across the network. To install this role, follow these steps:

1. Begin by opening **Server Manager** from the Start menu.

2. Click on **Add Roles and Features** to launch **Add Roles and Features Wizard**.

3. Choose the **Role-based or feature-based installation** option, and then click **Next**.

4. Ensure the correct server is selected from the server pool by choosing **Select a server from the server pool** and then clicking **Next**.

5. In the list of available roles, check the box next to **Print and Document Services**.

6. When prompted with a message to add features required for PDS, click the **Add Features** button, as shown in *Figure 5.32*.

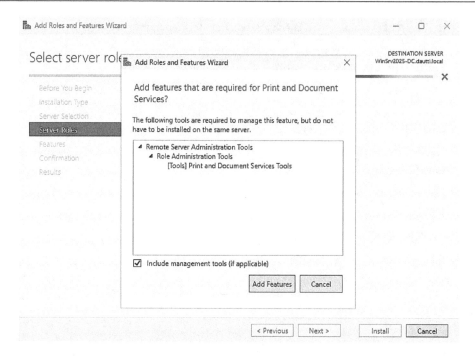

Figure 5.32- Adding features that are required for the PDS role

7. At this point, you do not need to add any additional features, so click **Next**.

8. Please review the description and installation notes for the PDS role before proceeding, then click **Next**.

9. You can accept the default role services for PDS or customize them based on your specific needs.

10. Once you've reviewed your selections, click the **Install** button to begin the installation process.

11. After the installation is complete, click **Close** to exit the wizard. A server restart is not necessary at this point.

The server now has the PDS role installed, enabling efficient management of printing and document services on the network.

By following these steps, you will have successfully installed and configured the Web Server (IIS) role, enabling your server to host and manage web applications and services effectively. In the next section, we will delve into advanced IIS configurations and management practices to optimize your server's web hosting capabilities. Similarly, by completing the steps outlined earlier, you have installed and set up the PDS role, allowing your server to manage network printing tasks efficiently.

Summary

In this chapter, you were introduced to the foundational concepts of roles, role services, and features within Windows Server 2025. We delved into critical aspects of file server management, including user rights, NTFS permissions, share permissions, and the importance of auditing to ensure secure and efficient server operations. Additionally, you gained insights into various common application servers, such as email servers, database servers, collaboration servers, monitoring servers, and data protection servers, along with the installation and configuration of web services, such as IIS, FTP, SSL, and digital certificates. The chapter also covered essential remote access services, including Remote Assistance, RSAT, RDS, RDS licensing, RDG, VPN, App-V, and the management of multiple ports. These topics are crucial for effectively adding and managing roles in Windows Server 2025 and securing your file server through the proper application of user rights, NTFS permissions, and share permissions.

Furthermore, this chapter included practical exercises on installing the Web Server (IIS) and PDS roles, equipping your server to host web applications and manage network printing efficiently. As we move forward, the next chapter will focus on Group Policy in Windows Server 2025, providing you with the knowledge to apply more granular and precise settings to both user and computer accounts.

Questions

1. **True or False:** A server role defines the primary function that a server performs within a network.

2. **Fill in the Blank:** _____ transfers files from computer to computer, computer to server, or vice versa, both on a LAN and WAN.

3. **Multiple Choice:** Which of the following are NTFS permissions in Windows Server 2025? (*Choose three.*)

   - Modify

   - Write

   - Change

   - Read

4. **True or False:** A web service is a communication method between two devices based on the request/response methodology using the FTP protocol.

5. **Fill in the Blank:** _____ is any logical endpoint where applications on your computer communicate with applications on other computers, both on a LAN and WAN.

6. **Multiple Choice:** Which of the following protocols are utilized by mail servers? (*Choose two.*)

   - FTP

   - HTTP

   - SMTP

   - POP

7. **True or False:** Remote Assistance is a feature that enables a helper to access the host's desktop remotely to assist with resolving issues.

8. **Fill in the Blank:** _____ is responsible for securing the communication channel between a website and a browser.

9. **Single Choice:** Which of the following ports is used by RDS?

   - 25

   - 110

   - 443

   - 3389

10. **True or False:** Web printing enables users to print files to network printers through Windows Explorer.

11. **Fill in the Blank:** _____ have to do with user access to shared folders and drives on the network.

12. **Multiple Choice:** Which of the following are share permissions? (*Choose two.*)

    - Read

    - Change

    - Write

    - Modify

13. **Short Answer:** Discuss the Remote Access and RDS roles.

14. **Short Answer:** Explain the differences between user rights, NTFS permissions, and share permissions.

Further reading

- *IIS Web Server Overview*: https://docs.microsoft.com/en-us/iis/get-started/introduction-to-iis/iis-web-server-overview

- *DirectAccess*: https://docs.microsoft.com/en-us/windows-server/remote/remote-access/directaccess/directaccess

- *User Rights Assignment*: https://docs.microsoft.com/en-us/windows/security/threat-protection/security-policy-settings/user-rights-assignment

- *Exchange documentation*: https://learn.microsoft.com/en-us/exchange/

- *Microsoft SQL documentation*: https://learn.microsoft.com/en-us/sql/?view=sql-server-ver16

Unlock this book's exclusive benefits now

This book comes with additional benefits designed to elevate your learning experience.

Note: Have your purchase invoice ready before you begin.

https://www.packtpub.com/unlock/9781836205012

Part 3: Configuring Windows Server 2025

This part focuses on essential configurations in Windows Server 2025, encompassing Group Policy, virtualization, and storage technologies. By the end of this section, you will be proficient in managing Group Policy Objects (GPOs), configuring virtual machines (VMs), and effectively utilizing storage technologies.

This part contains the following chapters:

- *Chapter 6, Group Policy in Windows Server 2025*
- *Chapter 7, Virtualization with Windows Server 2025*
- *Chapter 8, Storing Data in Windows Server 2025*

6

Group Policy in Windows Server 2025

In the previous chapters, you learned how to install, configure, and add roles and features to Windows Server 2025. Building on that foundation, this chapter delves into **Group Policy** (**GP**) in Windows Server 2025, a powerful tool for controlling and restricting user and computer settings across your network. You'll explore how to effectively manage GP on both local servers and domain controllers, gaining a deeper understanding of the various settings and options available within **Group Policy Objects** (**GPOs**) and how they are implemented.

The latter part of this chapter will focus on **Local Group Policy Editor**, where you'll learn to create and modify GPOs on individual servers. Additionally, you'll discover how to refresh and update local GPOs to help you differentiate between computer and user configurations.

To solidify your understanding, the chapter concludes with practical exercises featuring GPOs that are particularly useful for system administrators. These hands-on examples will enhance your proficiency in managing GP within Windows Server 2025.

In this chapter, we're going to cover the following main topics:

- Understanding GP fundamentals in Windows Server 2025
- Exploring GP processing mechanisms and order of precedence
- GP editors overview
- Examples of GPOs for system administrators

Technical requirements

To effectively work through the content in this chapter, it's essential to have the following hardware configuration in place.

- First, you'll need a personal computer running **Windows 11 Pro**, equipped with at least 16 GB of RAM, 1 TB of hard disk space, and a stable internet connection

- Additionally, you'll need a virtual machine configured with **Windows Server 2025 Standard** (Desktop Experience), featuring a minimum of 4 GB of RAM, 100 GB of hard disk space, and internet access

This setup ensures that you have the necessary resources to follow along with the exercises and concepts discussed in the chapter.

Understanding GP fundamentals in Windows Server 2025

System administrators often need to enforce specific configurations across an organization's network to ensure consistency and security. For example, they may set the company's website as the default home page on all browsers across the organization's computers and restrict access to removable media drives. Additionally, they might need to disable the use of Microsoft accounts on Windows 10 and 11 systems. These tasks can be efficiently managed using GP within a Windows Server environment, providing a centralized way to apply and enforce policies without relying on third-party tools or utilities.

GPO's default location

GP is a crucial feature in Windows Server that allows administrators to enforce policies at both the user and computer levels. Through GPOs, administrators can define and enforce settings that control user and computer behavior across the network. GPOs provide administrative templates that specify permissible actions and configurations for users and devices, ensuring that organizational standards and security measures are uniformly applied. Additionally, GPOs can be leveraged as a security mechanism, applying critical security settings to users and computers in a domain-controlled network, thus enhancing the overall security posture of the organization.

> **Note**
>
> It is important to briefly differentiate between **Group Policy Preferences** (**GPP**) and **Group Policy settings** (**GPS**). While GPS enforces specific configurations and settings on users and computers, GPP provides more flexibility by allowing users to modify their settings without administrative intervention. Understanding this distinction can help readers leverage both tools effectively in managing their environments.

By default, GPOs are stored in the `C:\Windows\SYSVOL\sysvol\<domain>\Policies` directory on the domain controller, as depicted in *Figure 6.1*. This default location ensures that all configured policies are systematically managed and replicated across domain controllers.

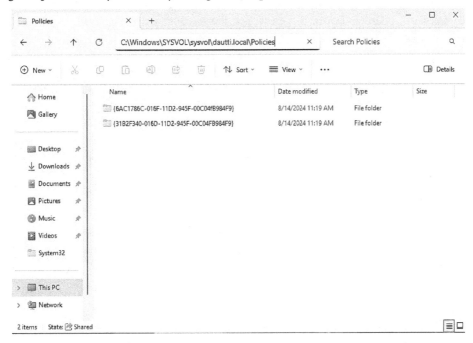

Figure 6.1 – GPOs' default location in Windows Server 2025

With a solid understanding of GP and GPOs, the next phase involves learning how to effectively manage and configure these policies to align with organizational needs and security requirements. That will include practical exercises on creating, modifying, and troubleshooting GPOs to ensure they meet the intended administrative and security objectives.

> **Note**
>
> Effective troubleshooting of GPs is crucial for maintaining a well-functioning Windows Server environment. Utilizing tools such as **Resultant Set of Policy** (**RSoP**), `gpresult`, and Group Policy Log Viewer can significantly enhance your ability to diagnose and resolve issues. These tools provide valuable insights into policy application, allowing administrators to identify conflicts, assess policy precedence, and ensure that configurations are applied as intended. In the upcoming sections, we will delve into these tools, equipping you with practical strategies for effective troubleshooting within your organization.

Managing Group Policy Objects (GPOs)

Efficient management of GPOs is crucial for system administrators to enforce and standardize configurations across a network. The **Group Policy Management Console** (**GPMC**) is an essential tool for this task, offering a centralized interface to create, configure, and apply GPOs within a domain-based network. The GPMC is divided into two main panes: the **Forest** pane and the GPOs pane. The **Forest** pane displays the hierarchical structure of the domain, allowing administrators to navigate through **domains** and **organizational units** (**OUs**) effectively. The GPOs pane provides detailed tabs, including **Status**, **Linked Group Policy Objects**, **Group Policy Inheritance**, and **Delegation**. These tabs enable administrators to view the current state of GPOs, understand how policies are applied and inherited, and manage delegation settings to control who has the authority to modify policies. *Figure 6.2* demonstrates the GPMC interface as it appears on a domain controller, highlighting its key components and layout.

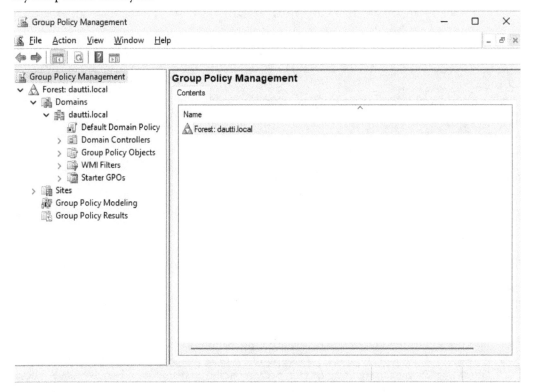

Figure 6.2 – The GPM console in the domain controller

Accessing the GPM console in Windows Server 2025 can be achieved through multiple methods, each offering different ways to launch the tool based on administrative needs. These methods will be explored in the following sections, providing a comprehensive understanding of how to efficiently use the GPMC to manage GP settings and ensure consistent policy enforcement across the network.

> **Note**
>
> Providing clear guidance on how to exclude or filter specific users and devices from the GP application is essential. Many environments require tailored policy configurations to meet organizational needs effectively. Discussing the nuances of GP processing, including filtering and security settings, will empower administrators to navigate complex environments with confidence. For more insights, refer to the comprehensive resources on GP processing on Microsoft Learn: `https://learn.microsoft.com/en-us/windows-server/identity/ad-ds/manage/group-policy/group-policy-processing`.

Managing administrative templates

Administrative templates are a critical component of GP management in Windows Server 2025. They provide a structured way to configure and enforce policies across the environment. Understanding how to install and update these templates is essential for effective policy implementation. Here are key considerations:

Installing administrative templates

Administrative templates for Windows Server come as `.ADMX` files and are typically included in the Windows Server installation. However, to access the latest settings, especially for new features or updates, administrators should periodically download the most recent versions from the Microsoft Download Center. Once obtained, the `.ADMX` files can be placed in the Central Store for GP in the `SYSVOL` folder of the domain controller. This ensures that all GPOs can reference the latest administrative template settings.

Updating administrative templates

Keeping administrative templates up to date is crucial as Microsoft releases new templates with updates and service packs. To update templates, do the following:

1. Download the latest versions from the Microsoft website.
2. Replace the existing `.ADMX` files in the Central Store with the new versions.
3. Update the associated `.ADML` language files, which are also stored in the Central Store, reflect any new or changed settings.
4. After updating, ensure that all GPMC instances are refreshed to recognize the changes.

Best practices for template management

Effective management of administrative templates is essential for optimizing GP performance and ensuring consistent configuration across your organization:

- Regularly check for updates to administrative templates, particularly after significant Windows updates or feature releases

- Test new templates in a non-production environment to assess their impact before widespread deployment

- Maintain documentation of any changes made to the templates, including the rationale and date of updates, to aid in future audits and troubleshooting

By incorporating these practices, administrators can ensure that they are leveraging the full capabilities of GP and staying aligned with the latest configurations available in Windows Server 2025. This will enhance their ability to manage settings effectively while minimizing the risk of configuration errors.

Accessing the GPM Console via Administrative Tools

To open the GPM console, you can use the **Administrative Tools** option available in the Start menu, which provides access to a variety of management tools for configuring Windows Server features and roles:

1. Begin by clicking the Start button, then navigate to **Windows Tools** within the Start menu.

2. In the list of available tools, select **Group Policy Management**, as illustrated in *Figure 6.3.*

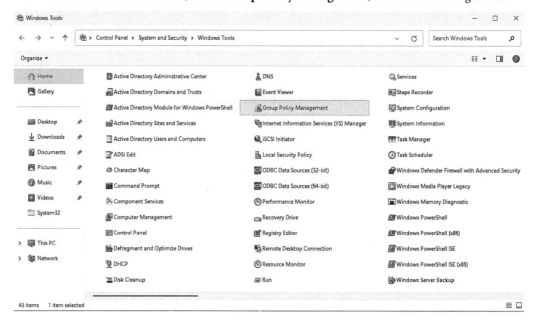

Figure 6.3 – Accessing the GPM console from Windows Tools

Alternatively, you can quickly access the GPMC using the **Run** dialog box. This method provides a convenient shortcut for accessing **Group Policy Management** directly, which is explained in the following subsection.

Launching the GPM Console via the Run Dialog Box

Another efficient method to open the GPM console is through the **Run** dialog box. This approach allows you to access the console quickly using a simple command. Here's how to proceed:

1. Begin by pressing the Windows key + *R* simultaneously to open the **Run** dialog box.

2. In the text field of the **Run** dialog, enter `gpmc.msc` and then click **OK**, as illustrated in *Figure 6.4*. This command will immediately launch the GPMC, providing you with a centralized interface for managing GP settings.

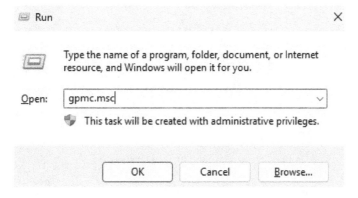

Figure 6.4 – Accessing the GPM console from the Run dialog box

In the upcoming section, we will explore how to access the GPM console through the Server Manager menu, offering you an additional method to manage GP within your Windows Server environment efficiently.

Accessing the GPM Console from the Server Manager

The GPM console can also be launched through the **Server Manager** option found in the Start menu. This method provides access to various Windows Server management tools. Follow these steps to open the GPM console:

1. Begin by clicking the **Start** button. From the Start menu, select **Server Manager**.

2. Once the Server Manager window is open, navigate to the **Tools** menu and select **Group Policy Management**, as depicted in *Figure 6.5*. This action will open the GPMC, enabling you to manage GP settings efficiently.

Figure 6.5 – Accessing the GPM console from the Server Manager

Best practices for Group Policy Management

Effective management of GP is essential for maintaining a secure and efficient Windows Server environment. By adhering to best practices, administrators can optimize GP implementation, ensure compliance, and minimize potential issues. Here are key recommendations:

- **Limit the Use of Default GPs**: Default GPs can be comprehensive and complex. Instead of relying heavily on these out-of-the-box policies, create custom GPOs tailored to your organization's specific needs. This approach reduces the risk of unintended consequences that may arise from default settings and helps streamline policy management.

- **Establish Clear Naming Conventions**: Implement a consistent naming scheme for GPOs that reflects their purpose and scope. For example, you might use a prefix to indicate the department (e.g., `HR-PasswordPolicy`) followed by a brief description of the policy. Clear naming not only simplifies identification but also aids in troubleshooting and auditing.

- **Regularly Review and Clean Up GPOs**: Periodically audit your GPOs to assess their relevance and effectiveness. Remove any obsolete or redundant GPOs to maintain a tidy and manageable policy landscape. This practice can also enhance system performance by reducing processing time during GP updates.

- **Test GPOs Before Deployment**: Always test new or modified GPOs in a controlled environment before applying them to production systems. This testing phase allows you to identify potential conflicts and ensure that the policies behave as expected, safeguarding your network from unintended disruptions.

- **Document GPO Settings and Changes**: Maintain thorough documentation for all GPOs, including their settings, intended purpose, and any modifications made over time. Documentation serves as a reference point for future administrators and aids in understanding the policy landscape, particularly during audits or compliance reviews.

- **Implement Security Filtering and Windows Management Instrumentation (WMI) Filtering**: Utilize security filtering and WMI filtering to target GPOs to specific users, groups, or computers. This approach helps ensure that policies are only applied where necessary, reducing clutter and the risk of unintended policy application.

- **Leverage GP Modeling**: Use the GP modeling feature to simulate how policies will affect users and computers in different scenarios. This tool can help you predict the impact of changes before implementation, allowing for informed decision-making.

By following these best practices, administrators can enhance the effectiveness of GP management, ensuring a more secure, efficient, and compliant Windows Server environment.

Real-life applications of Group Policy

GP is more than just a tool for managing settings in Windows Server; it plays a crucial role in driving organizational efficiency and security. By implementing effective GP strategies, organizations can align their IT practices with business objectives, streamline operations, and enhance data protection. This subsection explores real-life scenarios where GP has been instrumental in helping organizations meet their security and operational goals, demonstrating the tangible benefits of mastering this powerful management tool.

Enhancing security through Group Policy in a financial institution

A mid-sized financial institution faced challenges with ensuring consistent security settings across its diverse network of users. To mitigate risks, the IT team implemented GPOs to enforce strict password policies, requiring all employees to use complex passwords and change them every 90 days. Additionally, they configured GPOs to disable local administrative rights on workstations, significantly reducing the potential attack surface.

The results were profound. The organization experienced a 40% decrease in security incidents within the first year. By monitoring compliance through GP reports, the IT department could demonstrate adherence to regulatory requirements, ultimately fostering a culture of security awareness among employees.

Streamlining user experience in a university

A large university wanted to streamline the user experience for its faculty and students, who often faced challenges with varying desktop configurations across campus. The IT department employed GP to establish standardized desktop settings, including specific applications pinned to the taskbar, default printer configurations, and access to shared network drives.

By implementing these GPOs, the university not only reduced help desk calls related to configuration issues by 30% but also enhanced user satisfaction. Faculty and students reported an improved workflow, as they could rely on consistent settings regardless of which computer they logged into on campus.

Managing software updates in a healthcare organization

In a healthcare organization, timely updates to medical software and systems are critical for maintaining compliance with health regulations. The IT team utilized GP to configure **Windows Server Update Services** (**WSUS**) settings, ensuring that all devices automatically received the latest updates and security patches.

This proactive approach minimized downtime caused by software vulnerabilities, enabling healthcare professionals to access up-to-date tools for patient care. As a result, the organization not only achieved a higher compliance rate with health standards but also gained recognition for its commitment to patient safety and data integrity.

These examples underscore how GP can be leveraged to enhance security, improve user experience, and ensure compliance in various organizational contexts. By providing such scenarios in the chapter, readers can better understand the practical applications of GP in real-life situations.

In the following section, we will delve into the various GPO configuration settings, which will help you understand how to configure and manage GPOs in your Windows Server environment effectively.

Exploring GP processing mechanisms and order of precedence

In Windows Server administration, effectively applying GP to users and computers within a domain is essential for managing various aspects of the system, including security and application settings. To ensure that GP functions smoothly and reliably, it's important to grasp how GP is processed and the order in which policies are applied. Understanding these processes will help you prevent or address any conflicts that may arise when multiple policies are assigned to the same users or devices. In this section, we'll explore the principles behind GP processing, the hierarchy of policy application, and the rules for resolving conflicts. With this knowledge, you will be equipped to design and implement GP strategies that offer robust control over your IT environment.

Configuring GPO settings

Configuring GPO settings is a crucial task for system administrators, as it empowers them to control and manage various user and computer behaviors within a networked environment. GPOs are essentially predefined templates that can be customized to enforce specific policies, with their settings directly corresponding to registry keys in the **Windows Registry Editor**. These settings dictate how policies are applied across the network, giving administrators control over everything from security configurations to application management.

There are three main configurations for GPO settings, as illustrated in *Figure 6.6*:

- **Not Configured**: This is the default state for a GPO. In this setting, no specific registry value is assigned, meaning the policy is inactive and has no effect on the targeted users or computers. It essentially leaves the system in its default state.

- **Enabled**: Activating this setting changes the corresponding registry value to 0x1. That means the GPO is now active, and the policy it represents will be enforced across the network, ensuring that users and computers adhere to the defined rules.

- **Disabled**: When this setting is applied, the registry value is altered to 0x0, deactivating the GPO. In this state, the policy is turned off, and its effects are nullified, allowing the system to operate without the constraints imposed by the policy.

Figure 6.6 – GPO settings configuration values

After configuring the desired GPO settings, the policy is ready for deployment within the network. However, to ensure that GPOs function as intended and to avoid potential conflicts, it's crucial to have a deep understanding of the order in which these policies are processed. This order of precedence plays a significant role in how GPOs interact with each other, mainly when multiple policies are applied to the same users or computers. In the following section, we will delve into the mechanisms behind GPO processing and the hierarchy that governs their application, equipping you with the knowledge needed to implement your GPO strategies effectively.

GPO application

GPOs are powerful tools that system administrators use to enforce specific configurations and behaviors across users and computers within a domain environment. These policies, which are stored within the system registry, serve as authoritative guidelines that cannot be overridden by individual users, ensuring consistency and control across the network. GPOs can be implemented at various levels, either locally on individual machines through **Local Group Policy Editor** or across the entire domain using the GPMC.

The application of GPOs follows a meticulously structured hierarchy, a key element for system administrators in maintaining an orderly and predictable environment:

- **Local GPOs**: These are the first to be applied and are the bedrock of GP enforcement. They affect all users and settings on the local machine, providing specific policies for the individual computer.

- **Site GPOs**: These follow in the order of application. These policies apply to all computers within a specific geographical site. That allows administrators to enforce policies relevant to the physical location of the computers, which can be useful in large organizations with multiple sites.

- **Domain GPOs**: These are applied after site policies. These policies affect all computers that belong to the same domain, providing a centralized way to manage and enforce settings across a broader network. This centralized management ensures that policies are consistently applied, making administrators more efficient in their roles.

- **OU GPOs**: These represent the pinnacle of policy application. These policies target specific OUs within the domain, providing a level of control that is tailored to the unique needs of each unit. This granular control empowers administrators to enforce policies that are most effective for different departments or teams within an organization.

Methods to configure GPOs

Administrators have the flexibility to configure GPOs from two perspectives:

- **Local Computer GPOs**: These are set directly on the individual computer. These policies influence local settings and are particularly useful for standalone machines or those not joined to a domain.

- **Domain Computer GPOs**: These are managed by the domain controller and affect all computers within the domain. This centralized approach ensures that policies are uniformly applied across all devices, making it easier to manage large networks.

The timing of the GPO application is a crucial consideration. GPOs targeting user accounts are applied at user logon, ensuring user-specific settings are in place before the session begins. Conversely, GPOs targeting computer accounts are enforced during system startup, ensuring machine-specific policies are active as soon as the computer boots up. This understanding of GPO timing empowers administrators to apply policies exactly when needed, minimizing disruptions and ensuring a seamless user experience.

> **Note**
>
> Microsoft has introduced a valuable resource for administrators working with Windows Server 2022: a GP settings reference spreadsheet. This comprehensive spreadsheet includes detailed information on administrative templates for both computer and user configurations that can be managed through GP. By using this tool, administrators can easily stay up to date with the latest GP settings, ensuring they apply the most current configurations across their network. The spreadsheet can be accessed directly from the following URL: `https://www.microsoft.com/en-us/download/details.aspx?id=104005`. This resource is indispensable for maintaining effective and consistent policy management in a Windows Server environment.

In this section, we have covered the foundational aspects of GP in Windows Server 2025, including how to manage GPOs using the GPMC, the different types of configuration settings, and the hierarchical order in which GPOs are applied. As we move forward, the next section will focus on Local Group Policy Editor, providing detailed guidance on how to update and manage local GPOs and settings for both users and computers, further enhancing your ability to maintain a well-managed and secure IT environment.

GP editors overview

System administrators managing Windows Server 2025 have several tools at their disposal for configuring GPO settings, depending on whether the policies need to be applied locally or across a domain. Local Group Policy Editor is the **Microsoft Management Console** (**MMC**) snap-in that allows administrators to manage local GPOs for individual users and computers on a single machine. This tool comes pre-installed with Windows Server 2025, making it readily accessible for local policy management. In contrast, the **Group Policy Management Editor**, another MMC snap-in, requires the installation of **Active Directory Domain Services** (**AD DS**) and the setup of a **domain controller**. This tool is essential for administrators who need to create and modify domain-based GPOs, linking them to specific sites, domains, or OUs. Together, these editors provide a comprehensive framework for effective GPO management across both local and domain environments.

Local Group Policy Editor

Local Group Policy Editor is not just a tool but an essential component for system administrators who manage Windows Server 2025, especially when dealing with servers that are not part of a domain. This tool provides a straightforward way to configure and enforce GPO settings on individual servers, ensuring that specific policies are applied consistently across user and computer configurations. Unlike domain-based GPOs, which are managed centrally, local GPOs are edited directly on the server, making Local Group Policy Editor particularly useful for standalone or isolated systems.

Accessing Local Group Policy Editor is a quick and easy process for administrators, adding to the convenience and efficiency of their tasks.

By pressing the Windows key + *R*, they open the **Run** dialog box, where typing gpedit.msc and clicking **OK** will launch the editor.

Once open, Local Group Policy Editor presents a straightforward interface, as depicted in *Figure 6.7*, where administrators can navigate and modify both user and computer policies.

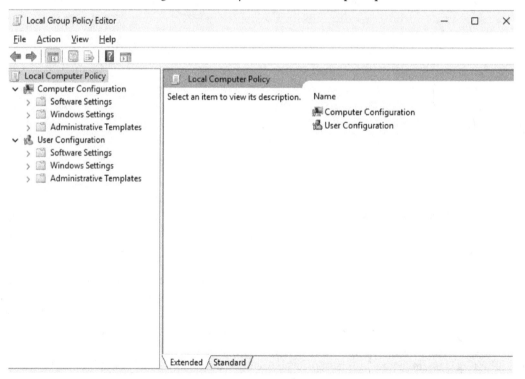

Figure 6.7 – The Local Group Policy Editor in Windows Server 2025

This tool allows for granular control over the server's settings, making it possible to enforce security measures, restrict access to certain features, or configure specific applications, all without requiring a domain controller. Additionally, understanding how to update these local GPOs is crucial for maintaining compliance and ensuring that the latest policies are enforced.

The following subsection will delve into the process of updating GPOs, ensuring that administrators can keep their servers aligned with organizational requirements.

Applying local GPOs

To ensure that your configured local GPOs are applied effectively on your server, you can update them by following these steps:

1. Begin by pressing the Windows key + *R* to open the **Run** dialog box.

2. In the dialog box, type the `gpupdate /force` command and click **OK**. This command, as depicted in *Figure 6.8*, forces an immediate update of the GPOs.

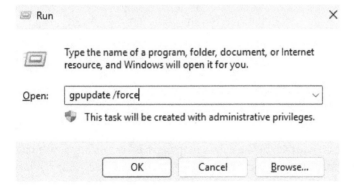

Figure 6.8 – Running the gpupdate /force command via the Run dialog box

3. Once executed, a Command Prompt window will appear, displaying the `Updating policy...` message, as illustrated in *Figure 6.9*. That indicates that the system is processing the updates to apply the new or modified policies.

```
Updating policy...

Computer Policy update has completed successfully.
User Policy update has completed successfully.

The following warnings were encountered during user policy processing:

The Group Policy Client Side Extension Folder Redirection was unable to apply one or
 more settings because the changes must be processed before system startup or user l
ogon. The system will wait for Group Policy processing to finish completely before t
he next startup or logon for this user, and this may result in slow startup and boot
 performance.

For more detailed information, review the event log or run GPRESULT /H GPReport.html
 from the command line to access information about Group Policy results.

Certain user policies are enabled that can only run during logon.

OK to log off? (Y/N)|
```

Figure 6.9 – The process of deploying the policy

The gpupdate /force command is particularly useful because it ensures that all GPOs, including those that have yet to be applied, are enforced without delay. This process includes both computer and user configurations, ensuring that any changes you've made to the local policies are immediately reflected across the system.

During this process, the Command Prompt window remains open to show the progress of the policy update. Once the update is completed and the system has successfully applied the policies, the window will close automatically, signaling that your local GPOs have been fully updated and are now active.

> **Note**
>
> On Windows Server 2025, the Local Group Policy Editor tool can be accessed through various methods, including using the search box on the Start menu or by typing gpedit.msc in Windows PowerShell or the Command Prompt. While these methods are convenient for opening the editor, special consideration should be given when updating GPO settings. Although the gpupdate /force command is commonly used to apply GP updates, it re-applies all policies, which can create unnecessary system load. Instead, it is often more efficient to use the gpupdate command without the /force option, as this will only update the GPOs that have been modified, reducing the strain on system resources.

This procedure is crucial for administrators who need to quickly enforce new policies or troubleshoot existing configurations on a local server, ensuring that all settings are properly applied and effective without the need for a system reboot.

Exploring GPO settings categories

GPOs consist of two primary categories of settings that specifically target users and computers. These settings play a crucial role in shaping the behavior and security of the server environment. In the following sections, we will delve deeper into these categories to understand their impact in greater detail. The settings are not randomly scattered, but they are systematically arranged in a hierarchical structure of folders and subfolders, which can be navigated using Local Group Policy Editor or the Group Policy Management Editor. This structured approach allows administrators to efficiently manage and configure policies that enhance the overall security and performance of the server.

Configuring GPOs for computers

To configure GPOs at the computer level, which apply settings across the entire machine regardless of the user logged in, follow these steps:

1. Open the **Run** dialog by pressing the Windows key + R.

2. Enter `gpedit.msc` in the **Run** dialog box and click **OK** to access the Group Policy Editor.

3. In the GPMC's **Forest** pane, right-click the domain, select **Create a GPO in this domain, and Link it here...**, as illustrated in *Figure 6.10*.

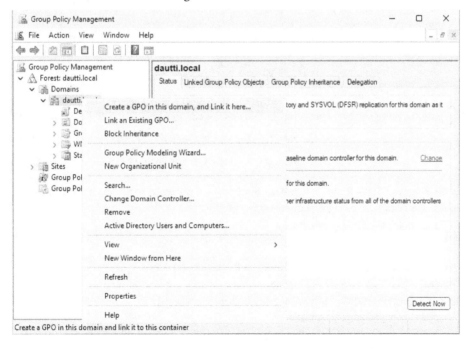

Figure 6.10 – Creating a GPO in the domain controller

4. Assign a name to the new GPO in the **New GPO** window and click **OK** to proceed.

5. Navigate to the GPOs pane, and under the **Linked Group Policy Objects** tab, right-click the newly created GPO and choose **Edit**.

6. In the Group Policy Management Editor, expand **Policies** under **Computer Configuration** and select the administrative template you wish to configure, as shown in *Figure 6.11*.

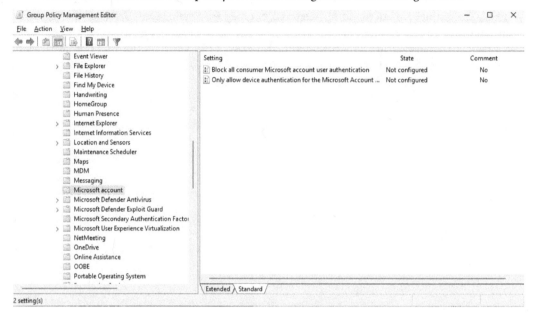

Figure 6.11 – Configuring the GPO for computers

7. After making the necessary changes, click **Close** to exit the Group Policy Management Editor.

8. Return to the GPOs pane, right-click the newly created GPO, and select **Enforced**.

9. Confirm your selection by clicking **OK** in the **Group Policy Management** dialog box.

These steps ensure that computer-level GPOs are applied during the system's boot-up process, affecting both local and domain-based machines as required.

Configuring GPOs for users

User configuration GPOs are settings specifically designed to impact the user level, regardless of the computer the user logs into. These settings are consistently applied to the user account across different devices. To configure GPOs at the user level, follow these steps:

1. Begin by following the initial steps in the *Configuring GPOs for computers* section.

2. In the Group Policy Management Editor, navigate to **Policies** under **User Configuration**, and then select the appropriate user administrative template you wish to configure, as illustrated in *Figure 6.12*.

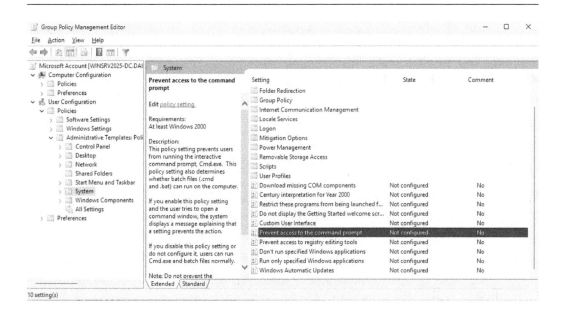

Figure 6.12 – Configuring the GPO for users

3. Once the configuration is complete, click **Close** to exit the Group Policy Management Editor.

4. In the GPOs pane, right-click on the newly created GPO and choose **Enforced**.

5. Confirm by clicking **OK** in the **Group Policy Management** dialog box.

Through these steps, you have learned how to manage user-level GPOs using Local Group Policy Editor. Additionally, you have gained insight into the different types of configuration policies. In the following section, we will explore examples of GPOs that are particularly useful for system administrators.

> **Note**
>
> The Resultant Set of Policy (RSoP) tool, accessed via `rsop.msc`, is invaluable for users looking to understand which GPs are applied or missing on their systems. RSoP allows administrators to simulate and analyze policy settings, providing clarity on how policies interact and the resultant configurations for users and computers. This tool enhances troubleshooting and management by ensuring that the intended policies are effectively enforced in the environment.

Chapter exercise – examples of GPOs for system administrators

In this chapter's exercise, you will be introduced to several key GPOs that are highly beneficial for system administration. You will gain hands-on experience in applying GPOs to perform tasks such as renaming the administrator account, disabling the guest account, blocking the use of Microsoft accounts, restricting access to the Control Panel and PC settings, and preventing the use of removable media drives. These GPOs are crucial for improving the security and manageability of your network. Additionally, you will learn how to use the GPMC to create, link, and enforce these GPOs within your domain, ensuring a more secure and controlled environment.

Renaming the administrator account

Renaming the default administrator account is not just a step but a strategic move in bolstering network security within Windows Server 2025. By changing the name of this account through a GPO, you obscure the default administrator identity, which significantly reduces the risk of unauthorized access and targeted attacks. Default administrative accounts are often a prime target for attackers, as they are widely recognized and expected. By renaming this account, you make it less obvious and, therefore, less vulnerable to brute force or other attack methods aimed at exploiting default credentials:

1. Access the GPO you wish to modify and navigate to `Computer Configuration| Policies|Windows Settings|Security Settings|Local Policies| Security Options`.

2. Locate and double-click on **Accounts: Rename the administrator account**, as illustrated in *Figure 6.13*.

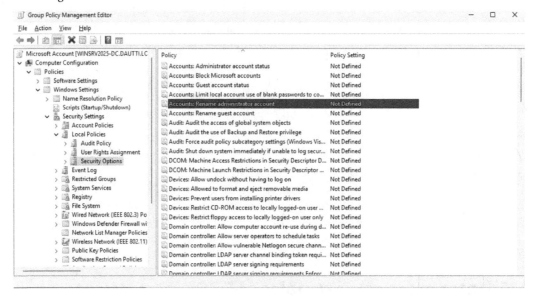

Figure 6.13 – Renaming the administrator account

3. In the **Properties** dialog box, enable the policy setting by selecting **Define this policy setting** and entering the new name for the administrator account.

4. Click **OK** to apply the changes and close the **Properties** dialog box.

Applying this policy ensures that the new name is enforced across all relevant machines, thereby providing a layer of obscurity and defense against potential intruders who may seek to exploit well-known default account names. This practice is part of a broader strategy to protect your network's infrastructure and resources, ensuring they are not easily accessible to unauthorized users or malicious actors. Following this, we will address how to similarly enhance security by renaming the guest account through a GPO, further securing your network environment.

Renaming the guest account

Renaming the default guest account is an important security measure to enhance network protection within Windows Server 2025. By changing the name of the guest account through a GPO, you help mitigate risks associated with unauthorized access and potential misuse of this account. The guest account is often targeted because its default status can be easily identified and exploited. Therefore, modifying its name adds an extra layer of security by making it less recognizable to potential attackers:

1. Access the GPO you wish to modify and navigate to `Computer Configuration | Policies | Windows Settings | Security Settings | Local Policies | Security Options`.

2. Locate and double-click on **Accounts: Rename guest account**, as shown in *Figure 6.14*.

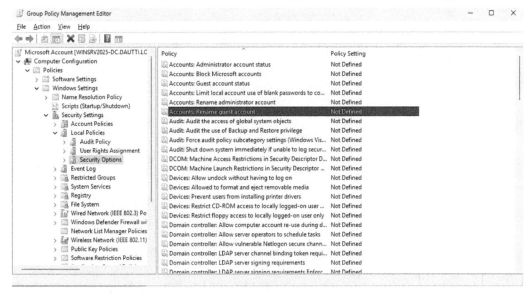

Figure 6.14 – Renaming the guest account

3. In the **Properties** dialog box, enable the policy setting by selecting **Define this policy setting** and entering the new name for the administrator account.

4. Click **OK** to apply the changes and close the **Properties** dialog box.

Implementing this policy helps obscure the guest account's identity, thereby reducing the likelihood of it being targeted for unauthorized access. By effectively managing and renaming such accounts, you strengthen your network's overall security posture. In the next section, we will explore how to block Microsoft accounts using GPOs to secure your system further.

Blocking the Microsoft accounts

You can also use a GPO in Windows Server 2025 to prevent users from using Microsoft accounts to access or add to the network computers. That can enhance the security of your network by restricting the use of personal accounts that the organization does not manage. To implement this policy, you need to do the following:

1. Access the GPO you wish to modify and navigate to Computer Configuration | Policies | Windows Settings | Security Settings | Local Policies | Security Options.

2. Locate and double-click on **Accounts: Block Microsoft accounts** (see *Figure 6.15*).

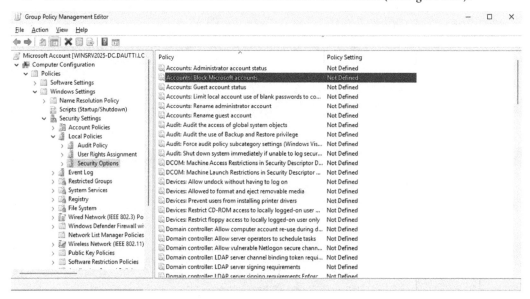

Figure 6.15 – Blocking the Microsoft accounts

3. In the **Properties** dialog box, enable the policy setting by selecting **Define this policy setting** and entering the new name for the administrator account.

4. Click **OK** to apply the changes and close the **Properties** dialog box.

This policy applies to the user configuration settings and blocks the use of Microsoft accounts on the network computers. By doing this, you can prevent users from accessing or adding their accounts, which may compromise the security of your network services and resources. Next, we will see how to use a GPO to deny access to the Control Panel and PC settings.

Prohibiting access to the Control Panel and PC settings

To bolster network security and control system settings, you can use a GPO in Windows Server 2025 to restrict user access to the Control Panel and PC settings. This measure helps prevent unauthorized or unintended alterations to system configurations, thus enhancing overall security and maintainability:

1. Access the GPO you wish to modify and navigate to User Configuration|Policies |Administrative Templates|Control Panel.

2. Locate and double-click on **Prohibit access to the Control Panel and PC settings** (depicted in *Figure 6.16*).

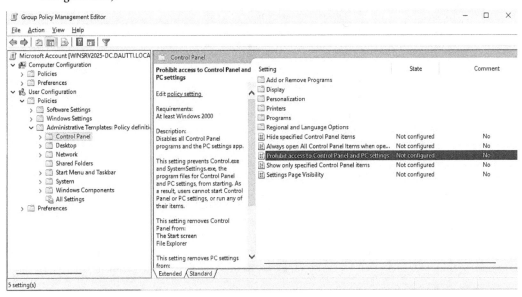

Figure 6.16 – Prohibiting access to the Control Panel and PC settings

3. In the **Properties** dialog box that appears, select the **Enable** option to activate the policy. Confirm your changes by clicking **OK**.

This configuration ensures that only authorized administrators can access or modify critical system settings, thereby protecting the integrity of your network environment. The policy will be applied to all users linked to the GPO, effectively preventing them from accessing or altering the Control Panel and PC settings. In the subsequent section, we will explore how to use a GPO to restrict access to removable media drives, further securing your network against potential threats.

Denying access to all removable storage classes

Another way to improve the security and management of your network is to use a GPO in Windows Server 2025 to disable access to all removable storage devices. That can prevent users from transferring data to or from external drives, which may pose a security risk. To enable this policy, you need to do the following:

1. Access the GPO that you want to modify and navigate to this location: `User Configuration | Policies | Administrative Templates | System | Removable Storage Access`.

2. Select **All the removable storage classes: Deny all access**, as shown in *Figure 6.17*, and double-click it to open it.

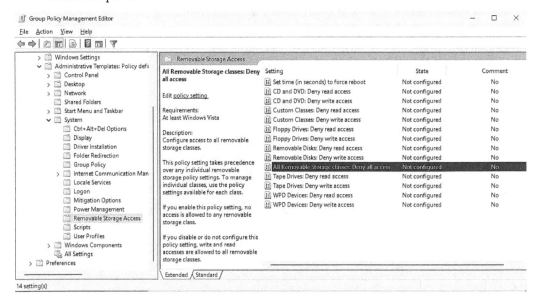

Figure 6.17 – Denying access to all removable storage classes

3. In the **Properties** dialog box, mark the **Enable** option and click **OK** to exit the dialog box.

This policy applies to user configuration settings and blocks the use of removable storage devices on network computers. You can also enhance this policy by enabling the **Prohibit access to the Control Panel and PC settings** policy, which prevents users from changing system settings.

These are just some of the GPO configuration examples that you can use in Windows Server 2025. There are many more GPOs that you can explore and customize according to your needs. These GPOs can help you manage and secure your network services and resources more effectively. That concludes this chapter exercise.

Summary

In this chapter, you were introduced to the fundamental concept of GP in Windows Server 2025, a crucial tool for managing and enforcing user and computer settings across your network. You gained insights into the GPMC, which is essential for creating, editing, and managing GPOs at the domain level. Additionally, you explored Local Group Policy Editor, which provides a method for configuring policies on individual machines that is useful for scenarios where domain-based GPOs are not applicable. The chapter provided an in-depth look at various computer and user configuration settings that can be applied through GPOs, including security policies, account settings, and restrictions. You also learned how to refresh GPOs, ensuring that updates and changes are applied correctly on both local servers and domain controllers. This skill is vital for maintaining up-to-date configurations and policies across your network.

Furthermore, practical examples were provided to illustrate the application of GPOs in real-life scenarios, such as renaming accounts, restricting access to system settings, and managing device usage. These examples are designed to help you understand how to implement and enforce security measures and administrative controls effectively. With these foundational skills, you are now equipped to deploy and manage GPOs on both individual computers and across a domain, enhancing the security and efficiency of your network. The next chapter will build on this knowledge by exploring the topic of virtualization within Windows Server 2025, offering insights into how virtualization technologies can further optimize and streamline your IT infrastructure.

Questions

1. **True or False:** GPOs are processed in the following order: local, site, domain, and OUs.

2. **Fill in the Blank:** The _____ are administrative templates that enable system administrators to configure what users can and cannot do on computers, peripheral devices, and network applications across the organization's network.

3. **Multiple Choice:** Which of the following represent GPO configuration values? (*Choose two.*)

    A. Enabled

    B. Disabled

    C. Allow

    D. Deny

4. **True or False:** The GPM is a console in the domain controller that enables configuring and deploying GPOs across an organization.

5. **Fill in the Blank:** The _____ displays the hierarchical structure of the domain, whereas the _____ contains the Status, Linked Group Policy Objects, Group Policy Inheritance, and Delegation tabs.

6. **Single Choice:** Which of the following commands is used to update GPOs?

   A. `gpupdate /enforce`

   B. `gpupdate /setup`

   C. `gpupdate /run`

   D. `gpupdate /force`

7. **True or False:** Not configured is the default setting for GPOs, meaning that the registry value has not been manipulated.

8. **Fill in the Blank:** The _____ is another MMC snap-in that enables you to manage GPO settings on a local computer.

9. **Single Choice:** GPOs assigned to the computer level are applied when computers are in which of the following states?

   A. Turned on

   B. Turned off

   C. In hibernate mode

   D. In sleep mode

Further reading

- *Group Policy Objects*: https://docs.microsoft.com/en-us/previous-versions/windows/desktop/policy/group-policy-objects

- *Linking GPOs to Active Directory Containers*: https://docs.microsoft.com/en-us/previous-versions/windows/desktop/policy/linking-gpos-to-active-directory-containers

- *Applying Group Policy*: https://docs.microsoft.com/en-us/previous-versions/windows/desktop/policy/applying-group-policy

- *Group Policy Best Practices*: https://www.netwrix.com/group_policy_best_practices.html

7

Virtualization with Windows Server 2025

Cloud computing has become a prominent and rapidly evolving trend in the IT industry. It enables the delivery of services and resources over the internet from a network of interconnected servers. At the heart of cloud computing lies a critical technology known as **virtualization**. This technology allows multiple **virtual machines** (**VMs**) to operate on a single physical server or across a cluster of servers, effectively creating a virtualized infrastructure that underpins cloud services.

In this chapter, you will delve into the concept of virtualization and its role in cloud computing. You will focus on using **Hyper-V**, a Microsoft technology that facilitates virtualization for both Windows clients and servers. The chapter will guide you through the process of installing the Hyper-V role on Windows Server 2025, utilizing the **Hyper-V Manager** for managing virtual environments and creating and configuring VMs. These steps will provide you with a solid understanding of virtualization principles and practical skills for implementing Hyper-V.

By the end of this chapter, you will be equipped with the knowledge to activate the Hyper-V role, set up VMs, and manage virtual environments effectively. The chapter concludes with a hands-on exercise designed to reinforce your learning by walking you through the installation of the Hyper-V role on Windows Server 2025. This practical experience will be crucial in understanding how virtualization enhances cloud computing and IT infrastructure.

In this chapter, we're going to cover the following main topics:

- Understanding virtualization fundamentals in Windows Server 2025
- Adding and configuring the Hyper-V role on Windows Server 2025
- Exploring Hyper-V Manager for VM administration
- Installing the Hyper-V role on Windows Server 2025

Technical requirements

To practice the skills learned in this chapter, you will need the following resources:

- A computer with Windows 11 Pro, a minimum of 16 GB of RAM, 1 TB of disk space, and an Internet connection

Understanding virtualization fundamentals in Windows Server 2025

Virtualization is a transformative technology that allows for the creation and operation of multiple VMs on a single physical server or a network of interconnected servers, known as a cluster. Each VM acts as an independent computer, complete with its own operating system, applications, and allocated resources, operating in isolation from other VMs. This technology also extends to virtualizing storage devices and network resources, which enhances the flexibility and efficiency of the virtualized environment. By consolidating workloads onto fewer physical servers, virtualization can significantly reduce hardware costs, lower power consumption, and minimize the physical space required for data centers.

Windows Server 2025 incorporates Hyper-V, a powerful virtualization feature that enables effective deployment and management of VMs on both Windows client systems and server environments. Hyper-V, a successor to the earlier **Windows Virtual PC**, has evolved from its inception in Windows Server 2008 to become a widely adopted and highly regarded platform among system administrators. Its robust suite of services and tools supports the creation, configuration, and administration of VMs, providing a comprehensive solution for managing virtual environments.

In the sections that follow, you will gain insights into various aspects of server virtualization, starting with an examination of different virtualization modes. That will include an exploration of how Hyper-V integrates into the broader virtualization landscape, the benefits of its features, and practical applications to optimize your IT infrastructure.

Emphasizing the connection between Hyper-V and cloud computing

Hyper-V, Microsoft's robust virtualization technology, serves as a critical building block for cloud computing infrastructure. As organizations increasingly adopt cloud services, understanding Hyper-V equips IT professionals with the foundational skills necessary to design, deploy, and manage virtualized environments efficiently:

- **Foundation of Cloud Infrastructure:** Hyper-V facilitates the creation and management of VMs on a physical server, enabling efficient resource utilization. This virtualization capability is essential for cloud environments, where resources must be dynamically allocated to meet varying workloads. By mastering Hyper-V, IT professionals can leverage this technology to create scalable, flexible cloud infrastructures.

- **Integration with Microsoft Azure:** Microsoft Azure, one of the leading cloud platforms, heavily relies on virtualization principles similar to those employed by Hyper-V. Understanding Hyper-V enables professionals to seamlessly transition their on-premises virtualization skills to Azure, where they can deploy Azure Virtual Machines and utilize features such as Azure Site Recovery for disaster recovery. This familiarity fosters a smoother migration process and enhances overall cloud management capabilities.

- **Cost Efficiency and Resource Management:** The skills learned through Hyper-V, such as VM configuration and resource allocation, directly translate to cost management in cloud computing. Professionals can apply these skills to optimize cloud resource usage, ensuring that organizations only pay for what they need. This financial acumen is invaluable as companies strive to balance performance and costs in their cloud strategies.

- **Enhanced Disaster Recovery Solutions:** Hyper-V offers features such as virtual machine replication, which are integral to establishing disaster recovery plans. Understanding these features not only prepares IT professionals to implement reliable backup and recovery solutions but also enhances their ability to design resilient cloud architectures that can withstand failures, ensuring business continuity.

- **Skills in Hybrid Environments:** As businesses increasingly adopt hybrid cloud models, where on-premises infrastructure coexists with cloud resources, expertise in Hyper-V becomes even more critical. Knowledge of how to manage VMs locally can simplify the integration of cloud services, enabling professionals to create a unified environment that optimally leverages both on-premises and cloud resources.

By developing foundational skills in Hyper-V, IT professionals not only enhance their technical proficiency but also position themselves as valuable assets to organizations navigating the complexities of cloud computing. The knowledge gained from mastering Hyper-V will catalyze exploring advanced cloud technologies and strategies, ultimately leading to more effective IT management in an increasingly cloud-centric world.

Virtualization modes

Virtualization allows for the operation of multiple **operating systems** (**OSes**) on a single physical server or across a cluster of servers by leveraging different modes. Each mode offers distinct features and benefits tailored to various needs in virtualized environments:

- **Fully Virtualized Mode**: In this mode, each OS runs in its own isolated and secure virtual environment, as if it were on a separate physical machine. The **virtualization layer**, or **hypervisor**, manages the resources of the host server and allocates them to each VM. This approach provides robust isolation between VMs, ensuring they can operate independently without altering their configurations. Fully virtualized environments are ideal for scenarios requiring robust security and separation, as the guest OSes remain unaware of the underlying virtualization infrastructure. *Figure 7.1* depicts how Windows Server 2025 operates within such an isolated environment, emphasizing the separation of resources and processes between different VMs.

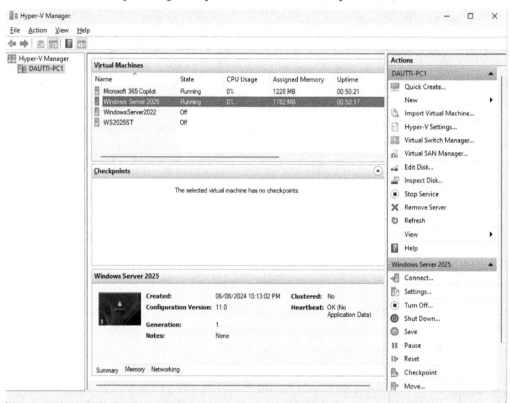

Figure 7.1 – Windows Server 2025 running in an isolated and secure virtual environment

- **Paravirtualized Mode**: Paravirtualization offers a more integrated approach by allowing the guest OS to communicate directly with the hypervisor. Unlike fully virtualized mode, where the guest OS is unaware of the virtualization layer, paravirtualized systems require the guest OS to be modified to interact efficiently with the hypervisor. This mode employs an **Application Program Interface** (**API**) to enable direct communication, which reduces the overhead typically associated with hardware emulation. The result is a significant boost in performance and resource utilization, making it a compelling choice for environments where efficiency and speed are paramount.

- **Containerization Mode**: Containerization focuses on encapsulating applications along with their runtime environments, system tools, and settings into self-contained units known as **containers**. Unlike VMs, which virtualize entire operating systems, containers virtualize at the application layer, providing a lightweight and portable solution. Each container operates independently but shares the host OS kernel, making it an efficient choice for deploying and managing applications across different environments. Containers enhance scalability, streamline application deployment, and ensure consistency by packaging all necessary components together. This approach is particularly useful for developing, testing, and consistently deploying applications across various platforms.

> **Note:**
>
> A physical server operates with an operating system known as the host OS, which manages the server's hardware resources. In contrast, a VM runs an operating system referred to as the guest OS, which operates within a virtual environment created by the host OS or a hypervisor. For example, in my configuration, my laptop is equipped with Windows 11 Pro as the host OS, while a VM on the same machine runs Windows Server 2025 Standard as the guest OS. The host OS plays a critical role in allocating and controlling hardware resources, enabling the guest OS to function seamlessly within the virtualized environment.

Performance considerations in virtualization

In virtualization, performance is a critical factor that can significantly influence the effectiveness of deployed VMs. Understanding the impact of different storage types and infrastructure configurations is essential for optimizing VM performance.

Storage types – SANs vs. Local Disks

When designing a virtualized environment, understanding the differences between **Storage Area Networks (SANs)** and local disks is crucial, as each storage solution presents unique performance characteristics and implications for VM operations:

- **Storage Area Networks (SANs)**: SANs provide a centralized storage solution that allows multiple servers to access a shared pool of storage resources. While SANs offer benefits such as high availability and scalability, they can introduce latency that affects performance. This latency arises from network overhead, as data must travel over the network fabric to reach the storage array. In high-demand environments where rapid data access is crucial, this delay can result in slower VM performance, particularly for I/O-intensive applications.

- **Local Disks**: In contrast, local disks are directly attached to the physical server hosting the VM. This configuration typically yields lower latency, as data does not need to traverse a network. Local storage is ideal for applications requiring fast data access and high throughput, such as databases and transaction processing systems. However, local disks limit redundancy and scalability compared to SANs, making them less suitable for larger virtualized environments.

Hyper-Converged Infrastructure (HCI)

Hyper-converged infrastructure (**HCI**) integrates computing, storage, and networking into a single software-driven solution, offering a unified approach to virtualization. HCI can enhance performance in several ways:

- **Improved Data Locality**: By utilizing local storage within each node of the HCI cluster, data access times are significantly reduced. This locality minimizes latency, providing faster VM performance, especially for applications with high I/O requirements.

- **Scalability and Elasticity**: HCI allows organizations to scale their resources seamlessly. As demand increases, additional nodes can be added to the cluster, effectively distributing workloads and enhancing performance without compromising the integrity of the storage system.

- **Intelligent Resource Management**: Many HCI solutions incorporate advanced analytics and resource management features that optimize workload placement based on performance metrics. This capability ensures that VMs are allocated to the most appropriate resources, further enhancing overall performance.

The choice of storage type—whether SANs or local disks—directly impacts the performance of virtualized environments. Additionally, leveraging HCI can provide significant advantages in managing resources efficiently and ensuring optimal performance for VMs. Understanding these factors enables IT professionals to make informed decisions that align with their organization's performance requirements and business objectives.

Understanding these virtualization modes allows you to select the most appropriate method for your infrastructure, depending on your performance, security, and scalability requirements.

Adding and configuring the Hyper-V role on Windows Server 2025

A significant advantage of server virtualization is its ability to run multiple VMs on a single physical server while maximizing performance and resource efficiency. Hyper-V, a robust and versatile technology, allows you to create, manage, and operate VMs seamlessly on Windows Server 2025. In this section, we will guide you through the process of adding the Hyper-V role to your server and configuring it to meet your organization's specific needs. Whether your goal is to reduce operational costs, enhance system efficiency, or establish a virtualized testing environment, mastering the installation and configuration of Hyper-V on Windows Server 2025 is essential for modern IT infrastructure management.

Hyper-V architecture

To fully comprehend the Hyper-V architecture, it's helpful to picture it as a tree structure, with the hypervisor acting as the root and deeply integrated into the hardware foundation, which serves as the soil. The **hypervisor** is the fundamental component of the Hyper-V virtual platform, with direct access to the physical server's hardware resources, including CPU, memory, storage, and networking. This direct control allows the hypervisor to manage and allocate these resources efficiently among multiple VMs.

From the hypervisor, branches extend to form separate execution environments known as **partitions**. Each partition is isolated, meaning it operates independently without interference from others. This isolation is crucial for security and stability, as it ensures that an issue in one partition does not affect others. The partitions themselves do not have direct access to the physical hardware; instead, they interact with a virtualized layer provided by the hypervisor or the root partition. This virtualized layer abstracts the hardware, presenting the guest operating systems with a consistent and manageable environment in which to operate.

The **root partition** is the first and most privileged partition, running both the host operating system and the Hyper-V role. It acts as the central hub, managing hardware interactions and overseeing the creation and operation of other partitions, known as child partitions. These child partitions host the guest operating systems, which can include various versions of Windows or Linux, allowing for a diverse and flexible computing environment.

Communication between the root and **child partitions** is facilitated by specialized components known as the **Virtualization Service Provider** (**VSP**) and the **Virtualization Service Consumer** (**VSC**), as illustrated in *Figure 7.2*. These components use a logical communication channel called the **Virtual Machine Bus** (**VMBus**) to exchange data and commands efficiently. This setup ensures that the guest operating systems in the child partitions can perform necessary operations, such as accessing storage or network resources, without direct hardware access.

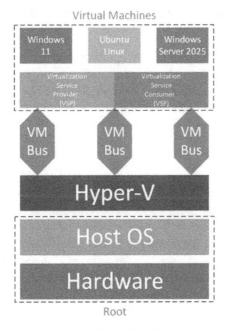

Figure 7.2 – Hyper-V architecture

Understanding this architecture is key to appreciating how Hyper-V supports different types of virtualization, including full virtualization, where the guest operating system operates unchanged within the virtual environment. This capability is critical for scenarios requiring compatibility and minimal modification of existing software. However, before deploying Hyper-V, it's essential to be aware of the specific hardware and software requirements, as well as the prerequisites, to ensure a successful implementation and optimal performance.

Hyper-V installation requirements

Before installing and utilizing Hyper-V, it is crucial to ensure that your server meets the specific prerequisites necessary for enabling the hypervisor. The primary requirement is that your server must support **hardware-level virtualization**, which is the backbone of Hyper-V's functionality. That involves having a processor with virtualization technology enabled, such as **Intel VT-x** or **AMD-V**. These technologies are essential as they allow the processor to efficiently manage multiple VMs by allocating resources dynamically and securely without significant overhead.

In addition to virtualization support, your server must also have other features enabled, such as **Data Execution Prevention** (**DEP**), which provides an additional layer of security by preventing malicious code from executing in protected memory regions. Furthermore, the server's BIOS or UEFI firmware must be configured correctly to support these technologies, with virtualization options such as **Intel VT** or **AMD-V** turned on.

Another important consideration is **nested virtualization**, particularly in environments where you intend to run Hyper-V inside a VM. This advanced feature enables you to create virtual environments within VMs, providing flexibility for testing, development, and training scenarios without needing additional physical hardware.

Beyond these hardware requirements, it's also vital to ensure that your operating system is compatible with Hyper-V. For instance, Hyper-V is only available on specific editions of Windows Server and Windows client operating systems, such as **Windows 11 Pro** or **Enterprise**. Ensuring that your server meets these conditions is key to achieving a smooth and efficient Hyper-V deployment, allowing you to leverage the benefits of virtualization in your IT environment fully.

Nested virtualization

Nested virtualization is an advanced feature that allows you to run a VM inside another VM. Essentially, this means that the hardware of the host machine is capable of running Hyper-V within a guest operating system, enabling the guest OS to create and manage additional VMs, just as if it were running directly on physical hardware. This capability, though it might initially seem theoretical, has been supported by Microsoft since Windows Server 2016 and has become an invaluable tool in various scenarios, such as testing complex configurations, training environments, or running virtual labs where multiple layers of virtualization are required.

To put it simply, nested virtualization allows you to treat a guest operating system as if it were the host operating system, running Hyper-V and creating a virtualized environment within an already virtualized environment. This nested setup can be particularly useful for scenarios that require multiple isolated environments or for developers and IT professionals who need to test deployments and configurations in a safe and controlled manner.

Setting up nested virtualization in Windows Server 2025 is straightforward using **Windows PowerShell**. Begin by right-clicking the **Start** button and selecting **Windows PowerShell (Administrator)** from the admin menu. Once in the PowerShell window, execute the following command:

```
Set-VMProcessor -VMName <YourVMName> -ExposeVirtualizationExtensions
$true
```

💡 **Quick tip**: Enhance your coding experience with the **AI Code Explainer** and **Quick Copy** features. Open this book in the next-gen Packt Reader. Click the **Copy** button (**1**) to quickly copy code into your coding environment, or click the **Explain** button (**2**) to get the AI assistant to explain a block of code to you.

```
                                          Copy      Explain
function calculate(a, b) {
  return {sum: a + b};                     1           2
};
```

🔖 **The next-gen Packt Reader** is included for free with the purchase of this book. Unlock it by scanning the QR code below or visiting `https://www.packtpub.com/unlock/9781836205012`.

This command enables the guest VM to expose the necessary virtualization extensions, allowing it to run Hyper-V.

```
Get-VMNetworkAdapter -VMName <YourVMName> | Set-VMNetworkAdapter
-MacAddressSpoofing On
```

This command enables MAC address spoofing on the VM's network adapter, which is required for networking functionality in a nested virtualization scenario.

After these configurations, you can proceed with installing Hyper-V within the guest VM, following the instructions provided later in the chapter that discuss installing Hyper-V on Windows Server 2025.

In summary, this section has covered various aspects of virtualization, including virtualization modes, the architecture of Hyper-V, installation requirements, and the concept of nested virtualization. With this knowledge, you're now prepared to learn how to use Hyper-V Manager effectively, which will be covered in the next section.

Exploring Hyper-V Manager for VM administration

Hyper-V Manager is a versatile and essential tool for administering VMs within a Windows Server 2025 environment. It provides a centralized interface for managing a variety of VM-related tasks, streamlining the administration of virtualized resources. With Hyper-V Manager, you can efficiently create new VMs, import existing ones, and delete those that are no longer needed, thus offering flexibility in managing your virtual infrastructure. The tool also allows you to set up and manage virtual switches, which are critical for connecting VMs to your network and ensuring they can communicate effectively with other network resources. Additionally, Hyper-V Manager facilitates the creation of a **Storage Area Network (SAN) manager**, enabling VMs to connect to shared storage solutions. This capability is vital for maintaining high availability and performance across your virtual environment.

Furthermore, Hyper-V Manager includes features for inspecting and optimizing virtual disks, allowing you to adjust disk space allocation and improve performance based on your requirements. You can also manage the state of your VMs by stopping them or shutting them down, which is helpful for maintenance and troubleshooting purposes.

The interface of Hyper-V Manager in Windows Server 2025, depicted in *Figure 7.3*, is organized into five main sections: **the server pane**, which displays the list of servers; **the VM pane**, which shows the VMs on the selected server; **the checkpoint pane**, which provides access to VM checkpoints for restoring states; **selected VM details**, which offers information and settings for the currently selected VM; and **the Actions pane**, which provides access to various management actions. Each of these components plays a crucial role in managing and configuring your virtual environment efficiently.

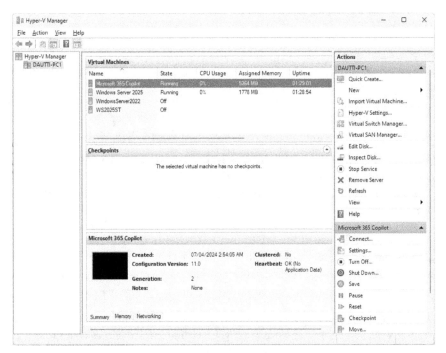

Figure 7.3 – The Hyper-V Manager in Windows Server 2025

Understanding key Hyper-V Manager functions

As users navigate through Hyper-V Manager, it is essential to familiarize themselves with specific **user interface** (**UI**) elements that play a critical role in managing virtual environments. This section focuses on two important features: **Replication Health** and the ability to export VMs.

Replication Health

The **Replication Health** column within the **Virtual Machines** window provides valuable insights into the status of VM replication. This feature is crucial for maintaining data integrity and availability, especially in disaster recovery scenarios:

- **Importance of Replication:** Replication allows for the duplication of VMs to a secondary host, ensuring that a backup is readily available in the event of a failure. The **Replication Health** status can display indicators such as **Normal, Warning,** or **Critical**, each representing the current health of the replication process.

- **Monitoring and Action:** Regularly monitoring **Replication Health** can help identify and address potential issues proactively. A **Normal** status indicates that the replication is functioning correctly, while warnings or critical alerts necessitate immediate investigation to safeguard data availability in failover situations.

Exporting VMs

Another vital function available in Hyper-V Manager is the capability to export a virtual machine to another host. This feature is essential for resource management and operational continuity:

- **Export Process Overview**: Exporting a VM involves creating a complete copy, including its configuration settings, virtual hard disks, and any associated snapshots. This functionality allows for seamless migration of VMs between different Hyper-V hosts.

- **Benefits for Administrators**: Understanding how to export VMs equips IT professionals with the skills necessary to adapt their virtual environments to evolving organizational needs. This flexibility ensures minimal disruption during maintenance or when balancing workloads across hosts.

By grasping the significance of these UI functions—**Replication Health** and VM exporting, IT professionals can enhance their proficiency in using Hyper-V Manager. This knowledge not only improves the ability to manage virtualized environments effectively but also prepares professionals for real-world challenges in cloud computing and IT infrastructure management.

In the following section, we will delve into the process of configuring Hyper-V settings that will influence the VMs you deploy, ensuring that your virtual infrastructure is optimized to meet your specific operational needs and organizational goals.

Configuration settings in Hyper-V

Before you embark on creating and managing virtual machines, it's essential to configure the Hyper-V settings on your server effectively. These settings are accessible through the **Hyper-V Settings...** option found in the **Actions pane** of Hyper-V Manager. As depicted in *Figure 7.4*, several key configuration areas can be tailored to optimize your virtual environment:

- **Virtual Hard Disks:** This setting allows you to specify a default directory for storing virtual complex disk files. Proper configuration here is vital for maintaining organized storage and ensuring that disk space is used efficiently across your VMs.

- **Virtual Machines:** This option enables you to define the default location for VM configuration files. By setting this location, you ensure that all VM settings and metadata are managed in a centralized and easily accessible manner.

- **Physical GPUs:** Here, you can designate which **graphical processing unit** (**GPU**) will be assigned to your VMs. That is particularly important for workloads requiring high graphical performance, such as graphic-intensive applications or virtual desktops.

- **NUMA Spanning:** This setting controls whether VMs can span multiple **Non-Uniform Memory Access** (**NUMA**) nodes. NUMA spanning can enhance virtual machine performance by allowing them to access a broader range of computing resources, which is especially useful for environments running multiple VMs or high-performance applications.

- **Storage Migrations**: This configuration allows you to set the maximum number of concurrent storage migrations that your server can handle. Efficient storage migration management is crucial for maintaining performance and minimizing downtime during data movement operations.

- **Enhanced Session Mode Policy**: This option enables or disables the ability to redirect local devices and resources (such as printers, USB drives, or local disks) from the host machine to **Virtual Machine Connection** (**VMConnect**). This feature enhances the user experience by allowing seamless interaction between the host and the VM.

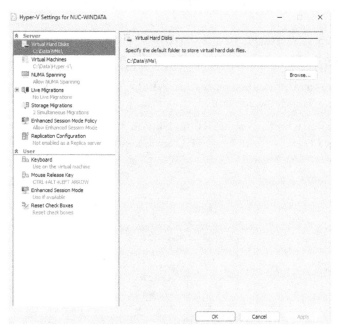

Figure 7.4 – Hyper-V Settings in Windows Server 2025

Note:

In addition to the core functionalities of Hyper-V Manager, it is essential to acknowledge the significance of the **Replication Configuration** feature. This functionality allows administrators to set up Hyper-V Replica, which provides disaster recovery capabilities by enabling the replication of VMs to another host. Additionally, the **Live Migrations** option facilitates the seamless movement of running VMs from one host to another without downtime, enhancing flexibility and resource management in virtualized environments. Understanding and utilizing these features can significantly improve your disaster recovery strategies and optimize resource utilization in Hyper-V.

By thoroughly configuring these settings, you set a solid foundation for effectively managing and optimizing your virtual machines. Once these initial configurations are complete, you will be well-prepared to dive into the creation and management of virtual hard disks, which will be covered in the next section.

How to make and adjust VHDss

To create and manage a **virtual hard disk** (**VHD**) on Windows Server 2025 using Hyper-V Manager, follow these detailed steps:

1. Click the **Start** button, then navigate to **Windows Tools** and select **Hyper-V Manager** from the menu to launch the application.

2. In Hyper-V Manager, open the **Actions** pane on the right side of the interface. Click **New** and select **Hard Disk...** to initiate the VHD creation process, as depicted in *Figure 7.5*.

Figure 7.5 – Creating a virtual hard disk

3. The **New Virtual Hard Disk Wizard** will appear. On the first page, click **Next** to begin the setup.

4. Choose the format for the VHD. You can select **VHDX** for enhanced performance and larger capacity or **VHD** for compatibility with older systems. Click **Next** to proceed.

5. Determine the type of VHD that best fits your needs. Options include **fixed size** (where the disk size is set and remains constant), **dynamically expanding** (where the disk size grows as data is added up to a maximum size), or **differencing** (which tracks changes from a base VHD, useful for snapshots and testing). Click **Next** to continue.

6. Specify the name and location of the VHD file. Ensure that the location has sufficient space for the VHD's intended use. Click **Next** to proceed.

7. Decide whether to create an empty VHD or to import data from an existing physical disk. If you choose to import, you'll need to follow additional steps to select the physical disk and configure the import settings. Click **Next** to move forward.

8. Review your selections, and click **Finish** to complete the wizard and create the VHD. The process will generate a new VHD that you can use on your VMs.

Once your VHD is created, managing the VM's memory allocation is crucial, as it directly impacts performance. Properly configuring virtual RAM ensures efficient operation and stability of your virtual environments.

Adjusting the RAM of a VM

To adjust the RAM allocation for a VM in Windows Server 2025 using Hyper-V Manager, follow these comprehensive steps to ensure optimal performance and resource management. Begin by ensuring that the VM is powered off to prevent any conflicts or issues during the configuration process. Here is a detailed guide:

1. Click the **Start** button, then navigate to **Windows Tools** and select **Hyper-V Manager** to launch the application.

2. In Hyper-V Manager, locate the **VM** you want to configure from the list of available VMs. Right-click on the selected VM (make sure it is turned off) and choose **Settings…** from the context menu, as shown in *Figure 7.6*.

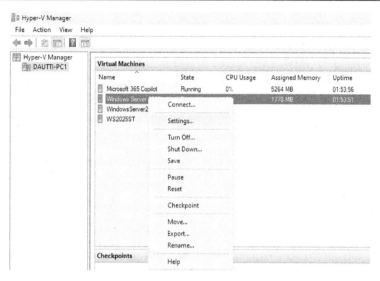

Figure 7.6 – VM settings in Hyper-V

3.   The **Settings** window will open. In the left-hand pane, under the **Hardware** section, select **Memory** to access the memory configuration options.

4.   You now have two options for configuring the VM's memory (refer to *Figure 7.7*):

Figure 7.7 – Managing virtual memory in Hyper-V

5. To allocate a fixed amount of memory, input the desired memory size in **megabytes (MB)** in the **RAM** box. This setting ensures that the VM always has access to this amount of memory, regardless of its current needs.

6. To use dynamic memory, check the **Enable Dynamic Memory** box. This feature allows Hyper-V to allocate memory based on the VM's demand. You can set a **Minimum RAM** value, which is the least amount of memory the VM will always have, and a **Maximum RAM** value, which is the maximum amount of memory the VM can use. Dynamic memory can improve resource utilization by adjusting memory allocation as needed.

7. After configuring the desired memory settings, click **OK** to apply the changes and close the VM settings window.

Adjusting RAM allocation is crucial for optimizing VM performance and ensuring efficient resource management. Once the memory settings are configured, you can proceed to set up a virtual network to enable communication between your VMs, allowing them to interact and share resources effectively. Another interesting perspective is that **overprovisioning** refers to the practice of allocating more virtual resources—such as CPU, memory, and storage—than physical hardware can support, which can enhance flexibility and resource availability in a virtualized environment. While this approach can facilitate the deployment of multiple VMs and improve utilization rates, it also carries risks, such as performance degradation and increased contention for resources, if the physical server reaches its limits. Therefore, it is crucial to balance resource allocation carefully, considering workload requirements and physical capacity, to avoid overprovisioning pitfalls while maximizing the benefits of virtualization. Understanding overprovisioning is essential for anyone venturing into virtualization, as it directly impacts performance, scalability, and the overall efficiency of IT operations.

Virtual networks in Hyper-V Manager

Setting up a virtual network is crucial for ensuring seamless communication between VMs and between VMs and the external physical network. In Hyper-V, this is accomplished by configuring a virtual switch, which acts as a bridge for network traffic. There are three primary types of virtual switches, each serving different networking needs:

- **External Switch:** This type connects VMs directly to the host server's physical network adapter, allowing VMs to communicate with the physical network and other devices on it. This configuration is useful for scenarios where VMs need to interact with external networks or the internet.

- **Internal Switch:** An internal switch connects VMs to the host server but does not provide access to the external network. This setup is ideal for scenarios where VMs need to communicate with the host and with each other but do not require external network access.

- **Private Switch:** A private switch allows communication solely between VMs on the same host. It does not connect to the host server or any external network. This is useful for isolated environments where VMs need to interact without external interference.

Setting up a virtual network

To set up a virtual switch in Windows Server 2025 using Hyper-V Manager, follow these steps to ensure proper network configuration:

1. Click the **Start** button, navigate to **Windows Tools**, and select **Hyper-V Manager** to launch the application.

2. In Hyper-V Manager, access the **Actions** pane and click on **Virtual Switch Manager...** as shown in *Figure 7.8*. That opens the Virtual Switch Manager interface.

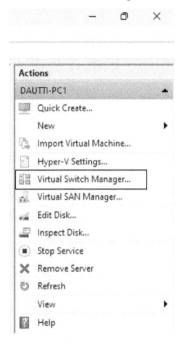

Figure 7.8 – Creating a virtual switch

3. In the Virtual Switch Manager window, select the type of virtual switch you wish to create (**External**, **Internal**, or **Private**), and then click **Create Virtual Switch** as indicated in *Figure 7.9*.

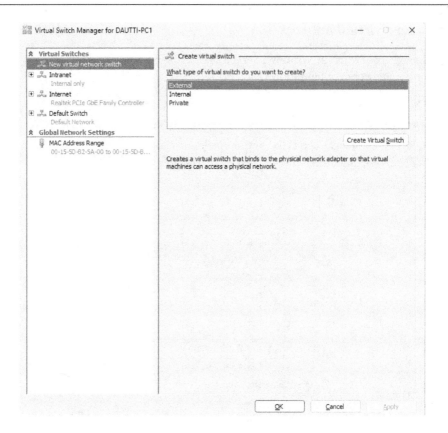

Figure 7.9 – Virtual switch properties

4. Provide a descriptive name and optional description for the virtual switch to identify its purpose and functionality easily.

5. Choose the appropriate connection type that aligns with the switch type selected. For an external switch, select the **physical network adapter**; for internal or private switches, configuration options will vary accordingly.

6. If needed, enable **Virtual LAN (VLAN) Identification** to manage network traffic and enhance security by segregating network traffic within the virtual network.

7. Click **OK** to apply the settings and close the Virtual Switch Manager window.

With the virtual switch set up, you can now manage network traffic and connectivity for your VMs based on the switch type chosen. This configuration is foundational for effective VM management. In the following section, we will discuss checkpoints, a valuable feature that enables you to capture and restore the state of VMs, facilitating recovery from issues that may arise during updates, installations, or configuration changes.

Understanding checkpoints

Checkpoints in Hyper-V are a pivotal feature that allows you to capture and preserve the state of a VM at a specific point in time. This feature is invaluable for maintaining system stability and mitigating risk during critical operations such as updates, installations, or configuration changes. By creating a checkpoint, you can revert a VM to its previous state if something goes awry, ensuring that you can recover from issues without significant downtime or data loss.

To create a checkpoint for a VM, follow these detailed steps:

1. Click the **Start** button, navigate to **Windows Tools**, and select **Hyper-V Manager** to open it.

2. In Hyper-V Manager, locate the **VM** for which you want to create a checkpoint. Right-click on this VM and choose **Checkpoint** from the context menu, as shown in *Figure 7.10*.

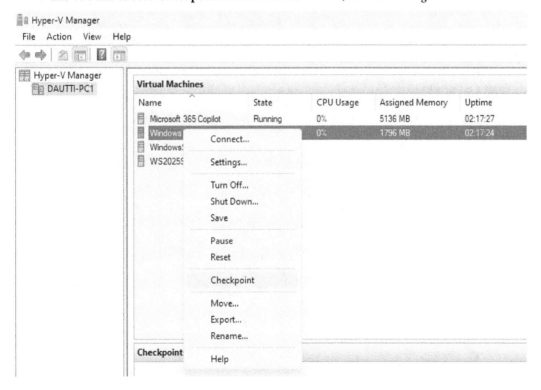

Figure 7.10 – Creating a checkpoint

3. The checkpoint will now appear in the **Checkpoints** section of the **VM details** pane. This section lists all existing checkpoints, allowing you to manage them effectively.

4. If the VM is running when you create the checkpoint, you will receive a notification confirming the successful creation of the checkpoint, as depicted in *Figure 7.11*. This confirmation ensures that the checkpoint has been established correctly and is ready for use.

Figure 7.11 – Checkpoint creation confirmation

Types of checkpoints

Hyper-V offers two types of checkpoints, as illustrated in *Figure 7.12*, each catering to different needs:

- **Production Checkpoint**: This type focuses on capturing the VM's state from the operating system's perspective without including the state of running applications. It is optimized for scenarios where application consistency is not as critical, making it suitable for production environments where minimal disruption is desired.

- **Standard Checkpoint**: This type captures the complete state of the VM, including all running applications and their states. It provides a full snapshot of the VM, which is essential for scenarios where complete restoration is required, including the applications and their configurations.

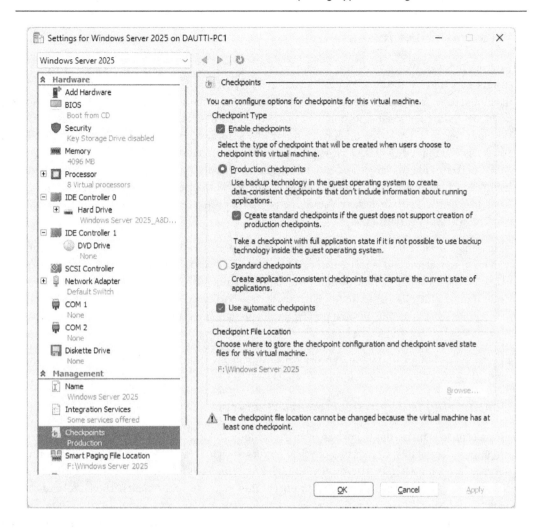

Figure 7.12 – Checkpoint types

Understanding these checkpoints is crucial for maintaining both data and application consistency. Data consistency ensures that all users see a unified view of the data, reflecting all changes and transactions made. Application consistency, on the other hand, ensures that the entire application state is preserved, allowing for coordinated backups and restorations across all components. In Hyper-V, checkpoints play a key role in backing up virtual machines, containers, and cloud services, providing a reliable method for recovery and minimizing potential disruptions.

In the following section, we will explore VHD and VHDX files, which are fundamental to understanding virtual disk management within Hyper-V. These files represent the virtual storage where the operating system, applications, and data are stored and managed, forming the backbone of VM functionality.

VHD and VHDX formats

Since its debut in Windows Server 2008, Hyper-V has significantly evolved in terms of virtual disk storage capabilities. Initially, Hyper-V used the **Virtual Hard Disk** (**VHD**) format, which had a maximum disk size limitation of 2 TB. This format served as the standard for virtual machine storage, providing basic functionality for many virtualized environments. However, with the introduction of Windows Server 2012, Microsoft enhanced Hyper-V's storage capabilities by introducing the **Virtual Hard Disk Extended** (**VHDX**) format. VHDX not only increased the maximum disk size limit to 64 TB, accommodating larger and more data-intensive applications, but also introduced additional features such as improved resilience to power failures, better performance, and support for larger block sizes. VHDX also includes enhancements such as protection against data corruption and more efficient disk space utilization.

Despite these advancements, the VHD format remains supported in Windows Server 2025 for compatibility with existing systems and legacy environments. Both VHD and VHDX formats allow administrators to choose the most appropriate option based on their storage needs and compatibility requirements. Understanding the differences and capabilities of these formats is crucial for effective virtual machine management and ensuring optimal performance and data integrity in virtualized environments.

In the next section, we will explore the process of converting physical machines to virtual machines, an essential technique for migrating workloads from on-premises infrastructure to the cloud, thereby facilitating more flexible and scalable IT operations.

Transitioning from physical to virtual servers

Virtualization is increasingly favored by organizations seeking to optimize resources, reduce costs, and improve scalability. Converting physical servers to virtual machines is a key part of this process, achieved by creating VHDs. **Microsoft's Disk2vhd** tool simplifies this transition by converting physical disk drives into VHD files that can be imported into virtual environments. The Disk2vhd tool, as depicted in *Figure 7.13*, enables the seamless transformation of physical storage into a virtual format. After generating the VHD, you can use Hyper-V Manager to set up a new virtual machine and attach the VHD to it, completing the **physical-to-virtual** (**P2V**) migration. This migration process not only modernizes IT infrastructure but also enhances flexibility and manageability by consolidating multiple physical servers into fewer virtual ones. By adopting this approach, organizations can better allocate resources, improve disaster recovery capabilities, and scale their operations more efficiently.

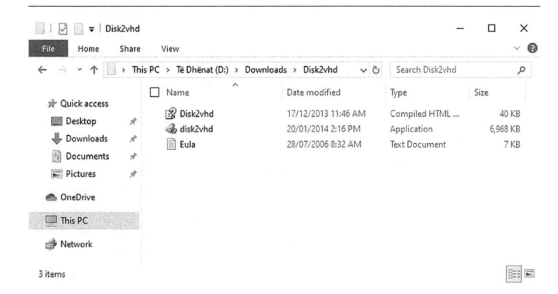

Figure 7.13 – The Disk2vhd app facilitates the conversion of a physical disk drive into a VHD

> **Note:**
>
> The Disk2Vhd tool, essential for converting physical servers to virtual machines, can be downloaded from the official Sysinternals website at `https://docs.microsoft.com/en-us/sysinternals/downloads/disk2vhd`. This tool facilitates the seamless migration of physical disk drives into VHDs, enabling efficient P2V conversions. As we proceed, we will explore the process of converting virtual machines back to physical servers, known as **virtual-to-physical (V2P)** conversions.

Reverting from virtual to physical servers

Although virtualization is increasingly adopted for its benefits, such as cost savings, enhanced resource utilization, and scalability, there are specific scenarios where organizations might need to transition their virtual servers back to physical hardware. This reverse process, known as V2P conversion, is less straightforward and generally not as well-supported as P2V migrations. Many hypervisor vendors, including Microsoft, do not provide dedicated tools for V2P conversions, which makes this task more challenging. As a result, organizations often need to explore third-party solutions that can facilitate this process, though these tools may vary in functionality and reliability.

Another approach to managing this transition involves a manual migration process. That entails setting up a new physical server with Windows Server 2025 and then manually transferring the virtual server's settings, applications, and data to the physical server. This method can be more labor-intensive but offers the advantage of tailored configuration and optimization for the new physical environment.

During this process, it is crucial to carefully plan and execute the migration to ensure that all necessary data and settings are accurately transferred and to minimize downtime or disruption to services.

Note:

To carry out a V2P conversion, you can utilize the **EZ Gig IV** cloning software, which is available for download on Apricorn's website: `https://www.apricorn.com/upgrades/ezgig`. This tool simplifies the process by following three straightforward steps: first, choose the source drive from which the data will be cloned; second, select the destination drive where the data will be transferred; and finally, click the **Start Clone** button to begin the cloning process. This approach helps facilitate the transfer of data from a virtual environment to physical hardware.

Migrating from VMware to Hyper-V

As organizations increasingly recognize the benefits of Hyper-V, transitioning from VMware to Hyper-V has become a strategic move for many. This process involves several critical steps to ensure a smooth migration while minimizing downtime and maintaining data integrity.

Key considerations before migration

Before initiating the migration from VMware to Hyper-V, it is essential to consider several key factors that will influence the success of the transition and ensure a seamless integration into the new environment.

- **Assessment of Current Environment**: Begin by evaluating the existing VMware infrastructure. Identify the number of VMs, their resource allocations, and the applications they host. This assessment will inform the planning and execution of the migration process.

- **Compatibility and Licensing**: Verify that the applications running on VMware are compatible with Hyper-V. Additionally, compliance with licensing agreements for both VMware and Hyper-V should be ensured to avoid legal issues.

- **Data Backup**: Prior to initiating the migration, back up all data associated with the VMs. This backup serves as a safeguard against any potential data loss during the migration process.

Migration tools

Microsoft provides several tools to facilitate the migration from VMware to Hyper-V, including these:

- **Microsoft Virtual Machine Converter (MVMC)**: This tool allows for the conversion of VMware VMs to Hyper-V format. It supports both physical and virtual machine migrations, making it versatile for different environments.

- **Disk2VHD:** A free utility from Sysinternals, Disk2VHD enables the creation of VHD files from physical disks, allowing for easy transfer of workloads into Hyper-V.

Migration process overview

The migration process from VMware to Hyper-V involves a systematic approach that encompasses careful planning, execution, and validation to ensure that virtual machines are transferred effectively while minimizing downtime and maintaining data integrity:

1. **Prepare the Hyper-V Environment**: Set up Hyper-V on the target host, ensuring that the server is configured correctly and updated. This includes enabling virtualization features in the BIOS and installing the Hyper-V role through Server Manager or PowerShell.

2. **Convert VMs**: Utilize the chosen migration tool to convert VMware VMs to Hyper-V. The process may involve exporting the VM from VMware and importing it into Hyper-V. Ensure that the virtual hardware settings are appropriately configured to match the capabilities of Hyper-V.

3. **Testing**: After the migration, thoroughly test the VMs in the Hyper-V environment. Check for application performance, connectivity, and any dependencies that may have been affected during the migration.

4. **Finalization**: Once testing is successful, update DNS records and make necessary changes to network configurations to reflect the new Hyper-V environment. Finally, the VMware infrastructure can be decommissioned if it is no longer needed.

Migrating from VMware to Hyper-V can offer organizations significant advantages, including cost savings and enhanced integration with other Microsoft services. By following a structured approach and leveraging the right tools, IT professionals can ensure a successful transition that aligns with their organization's operational goals. For further details on migration strategies and tools, refer to the resources provided in the *Further reading* section of this chapter.

Next, we will delve into configuring settings specific to individual VMs. Understanding these VM-specific settings is crucial as it highlights the distinctions between general Hyper-V configuration and settings applied directly to each VM.

Adjusting VM settings

To effectively manage a VM in Hyper-V, you can access its settings by right-clicking on the VM's name in Hyper-V Manager and selecting **Settings** from the context menu. This action opens a comprehensive configuration window where you can fine-tune various aspects of the VM, as detailed in *Figure 7.14*. Here is an overview of the settings you can adjust:

*   **Add Hardware**: This option allows you to attach additional devices to the VM, such as network adapters or memory controllers, to expand its capabilities.

*   **Firmware:** Configure the virtual firmware settings for the VM, ensuring compatibility with the underlying hardware and enabling features such as secure boot or boot from virtual devices.

*   **BIOS**: Configure the boot order to determine the sequence in which the VM's virtual devices are used during startup. This setting is crucial for ensuring the VM boots from the correct device.

- **Security**: Enable encryption to secure the VM's state files and data during migration. That ensures that sensitive information remains protected as the VM moves across different environments.

- **Memory**: Adjust the amount of memory allocated to the VM, either by setting a fixed amount or enabling **Dynamic Memory** to allow the VM to use memory more flexibly based on its workload requirements.

- **Processor**: Specify the number of virtual processors assigned to the VM, which can influence its performance and ability to handle multiple tasks simultaneously.

- **IDE Controller 0 and 1**: Manage the hard drives and CD/DVD drives connected to the IDE controllers. That includes adding or removing storage devices and configuring their settings for optimal performance.

- **SCSI Controller**: Configure hard drives connected to the SCSI controller, which can be useful for high-performance storage solutions and attaching multiple drives.

- **Network Adapter**: Set up and customize the network adapter settings to control how the VM connects to the network, including configuring VLANs and network bandwidth.

- **COM 1 and COM 2**: Set up virtual COM ports for serial communication, which can be useful for legacy applications or specialized hardware interactions.

- **Diskette Drive**: Select and configure a virtual floppy disk file, which may be necessary for specific legacy applications or to provide additional storage options.

Figure 7.14 – Establishing VM settings

By carefully adjusting these settings, you can optimize the VM's performance, ensure proper connectivity, and tailor it to meet specific operational requirements.

In the next section, we will delve into techniques for managing multiple VMs simultaneously in Hyper-V, including best practices for resource allocation and automation.

Working with VMs

When managing VMs in Hyper-V, leveraging both the **Actions** pane and the VM's context menu can significantly streamline administrative tasks. The **Actions** pane, depicted in *Figure 7.15*, is an essential component of Hyper-V Manager that facilitates comprehensive VM management. It provides options to create new virtual machines, configure Hyper-V settings, set up virtual switches, and establish virtual **Storage Area Networks (SANs)**. This pane also allows for modifications and examinations of virtual disks, stopping and starting services, deleting VMs, and refreshing the list of available VMs. Its role as a central management tool ensures that administrators can perform a wide range of tasks from a single interface, enhancing efficiency and ease of use.

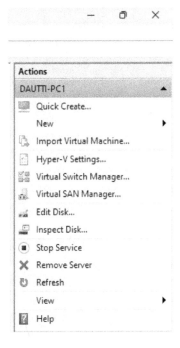

Figure 7.15 – Actions pane in Hyper-V Manager

The VM's context menu, illustrated in *Figure 7.16*, complements the **Actions** pane by offering options specific to the selected VM. This menu includes essential functions such as **Connect...** for accessing the VM's console, **Rename...** for updating the VM's name, and various other management options tailored to the individual VM. For instance, you can manage the VM's settings, checkpoints, and snapshots or even control its power state (e.g., start, stop, pause) directly from this menu. The context menu's specificity allows for precise, focused management of individual VMs, making it a valuable tool for handling VM-specific tasks.

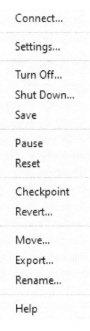

Figure 7.16 – Context menu in Hyper-V Manager

Understanding how to use both the **Actions** pane and the context menu equips you with a robust set of tools for efficient VM management in Hyper-V.

Best practices for VM startup and recovery settings

Configuring VM startup and recovery settings is essential for ensuring smooth operations and system resilience, particularly after a host reboot. These settings allow administrators to control the behavior of VMs in response to host restarts, minimizing potential downtime and optimizing resource allocation:

- **Startup Action:** Configuring VMs based on operational needs is recommended. Options include the following:

  - **Do Nothing:** Ideal for non-critical VMs, which can help preserve host resources upon restart.

  - **Automatically Start if Running:** For essential VMs, this setting ensures they resume their prior state without requiring manual intervention, which is helpful for consistent service continuity.

  - **Always Start:** Suitable for critical systems that must be operational immediately after a host restart, regardless of their prior state.

- **Automatic Start Delay:** Staggering VM startups can prevent performance bottlenecks by reducing the immediate load on CPU and memory. This feature is beneficial in environments with multiple VMs on a single host.

- **Automatic Stop Action:** Configuring VMs to gracefully shut down when the host is shut down or rebooted helps prevent data loss and maintains VM integrity.

Hyper-V provides options in the **Automatic Start Action** and **Automatic Stop Action** settings for each virtual machine, allowing administrators to configure how VMs behave when the Hyper-V host starts or shuts down. These settings are essential in Hyper-V environments for the following:

- Ensuring uptime for critical workloads by automatically restarting essential VMs

- Managing resource allocation during host reboots by setting delays for non-critical VMs, helping prevent performance bottlenecks

- Preserving VM data integrity by configuring the shutdown action to power down VMs before the host shuts down gracefully

These startup and recovery configurations are integral to Hyper-V's management options and play a key role in maintaining reliable, resilient VM operations. Adhering to these practices ensures a well-orchestrated VM environment, with minimized impact from unexpected reboots and optimized performance across workloads.

Real-world applications of Hyper-V for modern IT environments

To enhance understanding and provide practical insights, this section highlights real-world scenarios where Hyper-V plays a crucial role in modern IT operations. These examples not only demonstrate Hyper-V's versatility but also offer actionable steps for common industry practices, such as migration, disaster recovery, automation, and backup.

Migrating from VMware to Hyper-V

For many organizations, migrating from VMware to Hyper-V represents a strategic shift toward consolidating IT resources within Microsoft's ecosystem. This migration requires thoughtful planning, starting with a comprehensive compatibility assessment of existing VMs. Utilizing tools such as **Microsoft Virtual Machine Converter** (MVMC) or **System Center Virtual Machine Manager** (SCVMM) can streamline the migration process by automating certain stages, such as VM disk conversion and network configuration. Testing each VM in a staging environment prior to live deployment ensures optimal functionality and mitigates potential issues. With careful preparation, organizations can transition to Hyper-V while maintaining high performance and minimizing service disruptions.

Disaster recovery with Hyper-V Replica

Hyper-V Replica is a powerful feature for disaster recovery, enabling organizations to replicate VMs to a secondary site, either on-premises or in the cloud. This setup provides a critical safety net, ensuring rapid recovery and minimal data loss in the event of a primary site failure. Configuring Hyper-V Replica involves setting up replication at the VM level, defining the frequency of replication based on **recovery point objectives** (**RPOs**), and configuring the network connections between primary and replica sites. By regularly replicating VMs to a standby site, businesses can safeguard their data and reduce downtime, supporting a resilient infrastructure.

Automating VM checkpoints with PowerShell

Routine maintenance, such as system updates, can introduce changes that impact VM stability. Automating VM checkpoints with PowerShell before each update is a best practice to facilitate rollback if issues arise. The following PowerShell script captures a checkpoint for each running VM, labeling each snapshot with a timestamp for easy identification:

```
Get-VM | Where-Object { $_.State -eq 'Running' } | ForEach-Object
{Checkpoint-VM -VMName $_.Name -SnapshotName "Pre-Update Checkpoint
$(Get-Date -Format yyyyMMdd-HHmm)"}
```

This script helps administrators save time while implementing a safety mechanism across multiple VMs, promoting operational consistency and minimizing the risk associated with updates.

Hyper-V VM backups using Windows Server 2025

Regular backups of Hyper-V VMs are essential for business continuity, regulatory compliance, and data protection. Windows Server 2025 provides tools such as Windows Server Backup and System Center **Data Protection Manager** (**DPM**) to schedule automated backups or create on-demand snapshots. Configuring routine backups ensures that VM state, configuration, and data are securely saved, supporting rapid recovery in case of accidental data loss or cyber incidents. By implementing regular backups, organizations not only protect critical data but also build a resilient and compliant IT infrastructure capable of meeting modern business demands.

These real-world examples emphasize Hyper-V's capabilities in achieving reliable and efficient virtualized environments, helping IT professionals apply these best practices directly in their organizations.

With this foundation, you are prepared to move on to practical exercises, such as installing the Hyper-V role in Windows Server 2025, to enhance your skills further and apply your knowledge in real-world scenarios.

Chapter exercise – installing the Hyper-V role on Windows Server 2025

To install the Hyper-V role on Windows Server 2025, begin by preparing your server environment for the role installation. Hyper-V is a powerful virtualization platform that allows you to create and manage virtual machines on Windows Server. This process ensures that your server is configured to support virtualization, enabling you to optimize resources and run multiple virtualized workloads efficiently.

The installation process involves several straightforward steps, which are outlined in detail next. Once you have completed these steps, you will have successfully installed Hyper-V and can start leveraging its capabilities to deploy and manage virtual machines.

To install the Hyper-V role on Windows Server 2025, follow these detailed steps using Server Manager:

1. Open Server Manager by clicking the **Start** button and selecting **Server Manager** from the **Start** menu.

2. In the **Server Manager** window, click on the **Add Roles and Features** hyperlink to begin the installation process.

3. On the **Before You Begin** screen, click **Next** to proceed.

4. On the **Installation Type** screen, select **Role-based or Feature-based Installation** and click **Next**.

5. On the **Server Selection** screen, choose the appropriate server from the server pool and click **Next**.

6. On the **Server Roles** screen, check the box for the **Hyper-V** role, as illustrated in *Figure 7.17*.

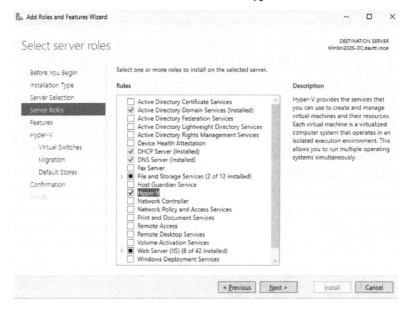

Figure 7.17 – Selecting the Hyper-V role

7.   Click the **Add Features** button to include the necessary features for Hyper-V.

8.   If no additional features are required, click **Next**.

9.   On the Hyper-V screen, review the information and click **Next**.

10. Select the network adapter(s) to be used for Hyper-V and click **Next**.

11. Check the box labeled **Allow this server to send and receive live migrations of virtual machines**. If you want to enable live migration, then click **Next**.

12. Specify the location where virtual machines will be stored and click **Next**.

13. Review the installation selections for the Hyper-V role and click **Install** to begin the installation process.

14. Once the installation is complete, click **Close** (refer to *Figure 7.18*). The server will automatically reboot to apply the changes.

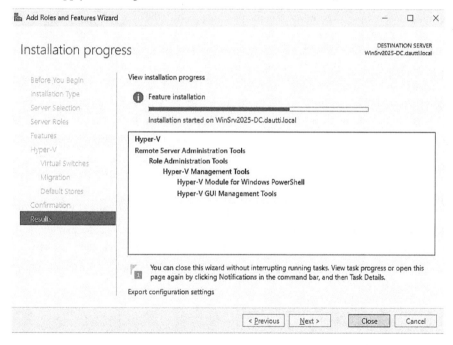

Figure 7.18 – Installing the Hyper-V role on Windows Server 2025

15. After the server reboots, the Hyper-V role will be installed and ready for use.

Ensure that you verify the installation and configure Hyper-V settings to suit your specific requirements. This setup marks the beginning of utilizing virtualization to enhance server management and operational efficiency in your environment.

> **Note:**
>
> For those looking to gain experience with PowerShell and streamline the installation process, Hyper-V can also be installed using the following PowerShell command:
>
> ```
> Install-WindowsFeature -Name Hyper-V -ComputerName <computer_
> name> -IncludeManagementTools -Restart
> ```
>
> This command installs the Hyper-V role and the management tools and automatically restarts the computer to complete the installation.

Summary

In this chapter, you were introduced to Hyper-V, a powerful virtualization platform designed to enhance server efficiency and flexibility by enabling the creation and management of multiple virtual machines on a single physical server. You gained insights into the core concepts, essential components, and various features of Hyper-V, which allow for the simultaneous operation of different operating systems and applications, optimizing resource utilization. The chapter included a hands-on exercise where you learned to install the Hyper-V role on Windows Server 2025, providing you with practical experience in configuring and deploying virtual environments. As you progress, the next chapter will shift focus to data storage solutions in Windows Server 2025. This upcoming section will offer a detailed exploration of the various data storage options available, including their advantages and best practices for managing and safeguarding your data within the server infrastructure.

Questions

1. **True or False**: Hyper-V provides services you can use to create and manage VMs and their resources.

2. **Fill in the Blank**: _____ is based on a hierarchical format where the first level represents the hypervisor as the main element of the Hyper-V virtual platform.

3. **Multiple Choice**: Which of the following are virtualization modes in Hyper-V? *(Choose two)*

    A. Fully virtualized mode

    B. Paravirtualized mode

    C. Production checkpoints

    D. Standard checkpoints

4. **True or False**: Checkpoints enable you to make a backup of the disk image at a specific time so that when unexpected situations arise, you can revert your VM to a previous state.

5. **Fill in the Blank**: Components such as _____ and _____, through a logical channel for communication known as VMBus, enable communication between the root portion and the branch OSes.

6. **Multiple Choice**: Which of the following are checkpoint types in Hyper-V? *(Choose two)*

   A. Production checkpoints

   B. Standard checkpoints

   C. Inspect disk

   D. Edit disk

7. **True or False**: Organizations migrate their physical servers to virtual servers (P2V) for cost, ease of management, and future expansion.

8. **Fill in the Blank**: _____ is an administration tool that you can use to manage VMs.

9. **Multiple Choice**: Which of the following are elements of the Hyper-V architecture? *(Choose two)*

   A. Hypervisor

   B. Root

   C. Branch

   D. Snapshot

10. **Short Answer**: Discuss nested virtualization.

11. **Short Answer**: Discuss P2V conversion.

12. **Short Answer**: Discuss V2P conversion.

Further reading

- *Virtualization:* https://docs.microsoft.com/en-us/windows-server/virtualization/virtualization

- *How to Work with Hyper-V VHD and VHDX Files: Essential Basics:* https://www.nakivo.com/blog/work-hyper-v-vhd-vhdx-files-essential-basics/

- *Disk2vhd v2.01:* https://docs.microsoft.com/en-us/sysinternals/downloads/disk2vhd

- *Set up Hyper-V Replica:* https://learn.microsoft.com/en-us/windows-server/virtualization/hyper-v/manage/set-up-hyper-v-replica

- *Working with Hyper-V and Windows PowerShell:* https://learn.microsoft.com/en-us/virtualization/hyper-v-on-windows/quick-start/try-hyper-v-powershell

8

Storing Data in Windows Server 2025

In this chapter, you will explore the fundamentals of **storage technologies** and their critical roles in server operations. **Disks** are crucial hardware components of servers, responsible for various tasks related to digital data, including storage, retrieval, management, and the provision of files and services. Understanding these technologies is vital for effective computer management and data handling.

The chapter delves into essential topics such as physical interfaces, disk controllers, and data storage methods within various storage media. You will gain insights into network-based storage systems and key storage concepts and protocols, including **Data Deduplication**, **Storage Spaces Direct (S2D)**, **Software-Defined Storage (SDS)**, **Small Computer System Interface (SCSI)**, **Internet Small Computer System Interface (iSCSI)**, **Fiber Channel (FC)**, and **Fiber Channel over Ethernet (FCoE)**. Furthermore, you will learn to manage server storage using both **Server Manager** and **Windows PowerShell**.

Additionally, the chapter introduces the concept of **Redundant Array of Independent Disks (RAID)** and explores different storage technologies based on their volatility. These include RAM, ROM, **hard disk drives (HDDs)**, **solid-state drives (SSDs)**, optical drives, and flash memory drives and cards. To consolidate your learning, you will complete an exercise on enabling Data Deduplication in Windows Server 2025, reinforcing your understanding and practical skills in server storage management.

In this chapter, we're going to cover the following main topics:

- Understanding storage technologies and their evolution in Windows Server 2025
- Exploring storage architectures and their implications for network environments
- Overview of storage protocols and their roles in data transmission and access
- Managing server storage using Server Manager and Windows PowerShell

- Understanding RAID principles and configurations
- Understanding primary storage concepts and optimizing storage solutions in Windows Server 2025
- Enabling Dedup on Windows Server 2025

Technical requirements

To effectively practice and refine the skills discussed in this chapter, it is essential to have the appropriate technical setup:

- Ensure you have access to a PC equipped with **Windows 11 Pro**, featuring a minimum of 16 GB of RAM, 1 TB of hard drive space, and a stable internet connection
- Additionally, you will need a **virtual machine (VM)** running **Windows Server 2025 Standard** (Desktop Experience) edition, configured with at least 4 GB of RAM, 100 GB of hard drive space, and internet connectivity

These resources will enable you to configure and manage the various storage technologies within Windows Server 2025, providing a practical environment to apply your learning.

Understanding storage technologies and their evolution in Windows Server 2025

Storage technologies are foundational to the operation of any computer system, especially servers, which are tasked with storing, managing, and processing extensive volumes of data. These technologies are diverse, each offering unique characteristics, functions, and designs based on their intended application. For ICT professionals and those preparing for certification exams, understanding these differences is crucial. In this section, we will introduce you to the key storage technologies that are vital in the field, such as **Integrated Drive Electronics (IDE)**, **Serial Attached SCSI (SAS)**, **SCSI**, **Direct Attached Storage (DAS)**, **Network Attached Storage (NAS)**, **Storage Area Network (SAN)**, and **RAID**. Each of these technologies serves distinct purposes, ranging from direct data storage solutions to complex networked storage systems, and plays a pivotal role in ensuring data availability, reliability, and performance in enterprise environments.

We will also discuss the significance of each technology in various scenarios, including how they impact system performance, scalability, and data protection strategies. By understanding these technologies, you'll be better equipped to make informed decisions when configuring, managing, or troubleshooting storage solutions. Following this overview, we will explore each storage type in greater detail, examining their specific features, advantages, and use cases to provide a comprehensive understanding of how they contribute to the overall efficiency and reliability of IT infrastructures.

Exploring different storage types

Different storage technologies bring unique features and functionalities to the table, each serving specific roles in the IT landscape. A thorough understanding of these technologies is crucial for IT professionals who need to select the appropriate solutions for different scenarios. Here is how the main categories of storage technologies can be classified:

- **Optical disks**: Often used for archival and backup purposes, optical disks offer substantial storage capacity and reliable read-and-write speeds. Although they were once more prevalent, especially for media distribution and data backup, their role as primary storage solutions has diminished with the rise of more advanced technology.

- **HDDs**: For many years, HDDs were the standard choice for operating systems and general data storage due to their large capacity and robust read-and-write performance. However, as technology has evolved, HDDs have become less favored as primary storage options. However, they remain widely used for storing large volumes of data in client/server applications where cost-effectiveness and capacity are prioritized over speed.

- **SSDs**: SSDs have rapidly become the preferred storage medium in modern computing environments. With their superior read-and-write speeds, enhanced durability, and continuously increasing capacity, SSDs are often chosen for operating systems and applications that require fast access to data. Their lack of moving parts also makes them more reliable and less prone to physical damage than HDDs.

- **Non-Volatile Memory Express (NVMe)**: NVMe is a modern interface designed specifically for SSDs. It allows for faster data transfer speeds by leveraging the PCIe bus. This technology significantly reduces latency and enhances throughput compared to older storage protocols, making it ideal for high-performance computing environments. NVMe has become increasingly popular for applications that demand rapid data access, such as databases, virtualization, and intensive computing tasks.

Understanding these core storage types is essential for making informed decisions about data management and storage strategies. With this foundation, we can now delve into the various interfaces used to connect and manage these storage technologies within computer systems, including **Advanced Technology Attachment (ATA)**, **Parallel ATA (PATA)**, **Serial ATA (SATA)**, and **SCSI**. Each interface has its advantages, compatibility considerations, and use cases, making it important to understand how they influence storage performance and system architecture.

Understanding ATA and SCSI interfaces

Various interfaces are essential for connecting storage devices such as HDDs, optical drives, and even legacy floppy drives to computer systems. These interfaces are often recognized by their acronyms—

ATA, PATA, SATA, and SCSI—which each signify specific characteristics and functions that define their roles in data management and system architecture:

- **ATA**: Also known as **IDE (Integrated Drive Electronics)**, ATA is a foundational interface developed to connect storage devices to computers. Despite its age, ATA laid the groundwork for subsequent storage interfaces. The ATA interface has evolved into two main subtypes, as shown in Figure 8.1:

  - **PATA**: PATA, which uses a **40-pin ribbon cable** for data transfer and a **Molex connector** for power, was widely used in earlier PCs. This interface connects the storage device directly to the motherboard and power supply. A key feature of PATA is that the disk controller is built directly into the drive, simplifying the connection process. However, the parallel nature of data transmission, with multiple bits sent simultaneously, can result in slower data transfer rates compared to more modern interfaces.

  - **SATA**: SATA succeeded PATA and quickly became the standard in modern computing due to its superior speed and efficiency. It uses a **7-pin cable** for data transfer and a **15-pin power connector**, which are both smaller and more flexible than their PATA counterparts. Like PATA, the disk controller is integrated into the drive. Still, SATA's serial data transmission method—sending bits one after another—allows for faster data transfer speeds and better airflow inside the case, which is crucial for maintaining optimal system performance.

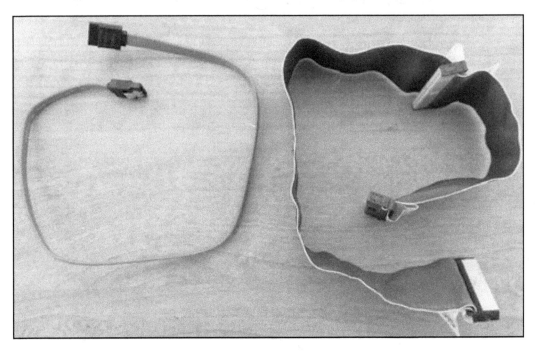

Figure 8.1 – PATA (left) and SATA (right) data cables

- **SCSI**: Pronounced *scuzzy*, SCSI is a more advanced interface designed to connect a variety of peripherals, including storage devices, to computer systems. SCSI has evolved with two prominent variants:

  - **SCSI Parallel Interface** (**SPI**): SPI is the older parallel version of SCSI. It was once widely used in enterprise environments for its ability to connect multiple devices on a single bus. However, due to limitations in speed and scalability, SPI has been largely phased out in favor of newer technologies.

  - **SAS**: SAS represents the modern evolution of SCSI, offering significantly higher data transfer speeds and enhanced reliability. SAS uses point-to-point serial connections, similar to SATA, but it is designed to meet the demanding needs of enterprise environments. It supports a more significant number of devices and offers features like dual-port access for redundancy, making it a preferred choice for servers and high-performance workstations.

Understanding these interfaces is critical for IT professionals tasked with managing storage solutions, as each interface offers unique benefits and is suited to specific use cases. As we move forward, we will delve into the role of **Peripheral Component Interconnect** (**PCI**) and **PCI Express** (**PCIe**) expansion cards, which further enhance system capabilities by providing additional connectivity options and improving overall performance in various computing environments.

PCI and PCIe overview

PCI is an interface standard that emerged in the 1990s, becoming a foundational technology for connecting various hardware components in personal computers. Developed by *Intel*, PCI represented a significant upgrade from the older **Industry Standard Architecture** (**ISA**) interface, which *IBM* initially created. The ISA interface, with its 16-bit internal bus specification, had been the standard for a time. Still, it could not keep pace with the increasing demands for faster data processing and more efficient system performance. PCI addressed these limitations by offering both 32-bit and 64-bit internal bus specifications, allowing more robust and quicker data transfer between the computer's components and its memory (RAM). That made PCI a vital element in the development of more powerful and versatile computing systems throughout the 1990s and early 2000s.

As technology continued to evolve, however, the need for even greater speed and efficiency led to the development of a new interface standard: PCIe. PCIe was designed to replace PCI and surpass its capabilities, offering a significant performance boost. Unlike PCI, which uses a parallel bus architecture, PCIe utilizes a serial communication protocol. This serial bus standard supports various connection types, including **PCIe x1**, **PCIe x4**, **PCIe x8**, and **PCIe x16**, with each kind differing in the number of lanes available for data transfer. These lanes are crucial because they enable full-duplex communication, meaning data can be sent and received simultaneously, thereby maximizing the speed and efficiency of data transmission within the system. PCIe has become the standard interface for high-speed components such as graphics cards, SSDs, and network cards, providing the necessary bandwidth for today's demanding applications.

PCIe slots, depicted in *Figure 8.2*, prominently featured on modern motherboards, accommodate these connections and play a critical role in a computer system's overall performance. PCIe's flexibility and scalability make it ideal for a wide range of applications, from high-performance gaming and professional workstations to enterprise servers and data centers.

Figure 8.2 – The PCIe slot

With this understanding of PCI and PCIe interfaces, we are now equipped to delve into the concept of local storage, explicitly focusing on the internal disks that store data within a computer. This exploration will further enhance our comprehension of how these storage solutions integrate with the interfaces we've discussed, ensuring optimal system performance and reliability.

Explaining local storage

Local storage pertains to the internal disk drives within a server or computer, encompassing both HDDs and SSDs. These drives are directly connected to the system via cables, a configuration known as DAS. DAS refers to any storage device that is physically attached to a computer or server through a direct connection, such as internal drives housed within the system unit or external drives connected via interfaces such as SATA, USB, or PCIe. For instance, the HDD installed in your computer is a classic example of DAS, as is any external hard drive or SSD connected to the system.

DAS systems offer the advantage of high-speed access to data, as the storage devices are directly linked to the system's internal buses. This direct connection typically results in lower latency and faster data transfer rates compared to network-based storage solutions. However, DAS is limited by its lack of scalability and flexibility. Adding more storage or upgrading existing drives often requires physical changes to the system, which can be cumbersome in large-scale environments.

To illustrate, consider a single HDD or a collection of disks connected to a server—each disk in this setup is a part of the DAS system (see *Figure 8.3*), directly interfacing with the server's internal architecture. This setup allows straightforward data storage and retrieval, with all data management occurring within the confines of the individual server or computer.

Figure 8.3 – DAS system

As we have established a clear understanding of local storage and its direct-attachment configuration, the next step is to explore network storage solutions. Network storage contrasts with DAS by offering remote access to storage resources over a network, and we will examine how it differs in terms of connectivity, scalability, and operational efficiency.

Exploring storage architectures and their implications for network environments

Network storage encompasses systems that connect to a network to provide centralized data services to multiple users and devices, distinguishing it from local storage, which is confined to the internal disk of a single computer or a directly attached storage device. Network storage solutions leverage network interfaces and protocols to enable seamless data access and sharing across a networked environment. Two primary types of network storage are NAS and SAN, each offering unique features and benefits.

Network-Attached Storage

Network-Attached Storage (**NAS**) is a specialized storage device that connects to a network via a switch, functioning as a dedicated file server. NAS devices use standard Ethernet connections to provide file-sharing capabilities directly over the network. They offer a simple and scalable solution for file storage, allowing multiple users and devices to access, share, and manage files concurrently. NAS systems are particularly useful for environments that require centralized data management and collaborative file access without the need for additional server infrastructure. Their ease of deployment and cost-effectiveness make them an attractive choice for small to medium-sized businesses and home networks, providing practical solutions for their file storage needs (see *Figure 8.4*).

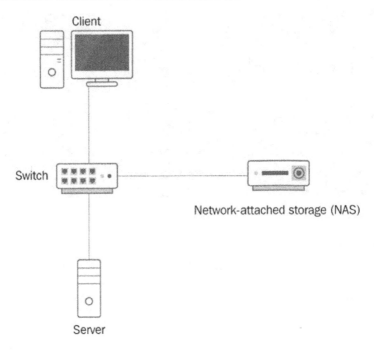

Figure 8.4 – NAS system

Storage Area Network

Storage Area Network (**SAN**), on the other hand, is a more advanced and high-performance storage solution designed for more extensive and more demanding environments. A SAN consists of a dedicated network that interconnects multiple storage devices, creating a shared pool of storage resources accessible to servers and clients. SANs use either Ethernet or FC connections to link storage devices with servers, with FC providing higher data transfer speeds. To facilitate this, servers in a SAN environment are equipped with **Host Bus Adapters** (**HBAs**), which are specialized expansion cards that enable the servers to connect to the SAN. SANs often utilize proprietary protocols or **Simple Network Management Protocol** (**SNMP**) for managing storage resources, offering advanced features such as high availability, redundancy, and efficient data management. They are ideal for high-performance computing environments, data centers, and enterprise applications where speed and reliability are critical, introducing you to cutting-edge storage technology (see *Figure 8.5*).

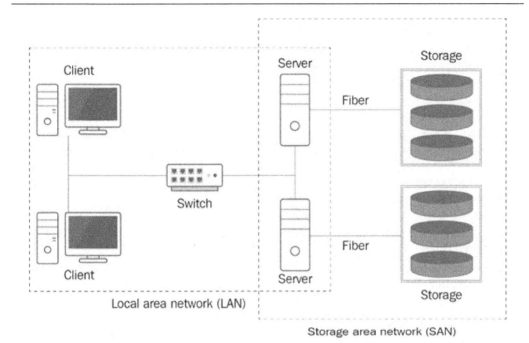

Figure 8.5 – SAN system

With a comprehensive understanding of both NAS and SAN systems, we can now turn our attention to the concepts of block-level and file-level storage. These two approaches represent different methods of organizing and managing data within various storage technologies, each suited to different use cases and performance requirements.

Understanding block-level and file-level storage

When managing data on storage devices, understanding the distinctions between file-level and block-level storage is crucial for optimizing performance and meeting specific storage needs. File-level storage and block-level storage are two fundamental approaches to organizing and accessing data, each with unique characteristics and advantages:

- **File-level storage**: This type organizes data into a hierarchical structure of files and folders, which can be easily accessed and modified by users and applications through file systems. This method presents data in a familiar format, making it straightforward for users to manage and interact with their data. File-level storage is commonly used in NAS systems, which are designed to provide centralized file access and sharing across a network. Its simplicity and ease of use make it well-suited for scenarios where file access and sharing are primary needs, such as in collaborative environments or for general-purpose storage.

- **Block-level storage**: This manages data by dividing it into fixed-size blocks, each with a unique identifier, and storing these blocks within a logical volume. This approach abstracts the data storage process from the file system, allowing for more detailed control over how data is written and retrieved. Block-level storage is ideal for applications requiring high performance and low latency, such as databases, VMs, and high-throughput applications. It is commonly employed in SANs, where it provides a high-speed, low-overhead storage solution that supports complex data operations. The block-level method's granularity and flexibility enable efficient data management, including the ability to perform advanced features such as snapshots, cloning, and replication.

The following table (*Table 8.1*) provides a comparative overview of file-level and block-level storage, summarizing their key differences and similarities. This comparison highlights the strengths and limitations of each method, offering insights into their appropriate use cases.

File-level storage	Block-level storage
Data is stored and accessed in the form of files and folders	Data is stored in blocks representing volumes, which the operating system then manages
Used by NAS	Used by SAN

Table 8.1 – File-level versus block-level storage

Before delving into the next topic, it's essential to understand the role of adapters and controllers in the data transfer process. These hardware components are critical for facilitating communication between storage devices and computer systems, ensuring efficient data exchange and system performance. Adapters and controllers manage the data flow, interface with various storage technologies, and support the connectivity required for effective data management.

Understanding how adapters and controllers operate

Disk controllers are crucial electronic components embedded within storage devices, responsible for managing essential functions such as rotating the platters, positioning the read/write heads, and facilitating data transfer between the disk and system memory. These controllers are located underneath the sealed enclosure of the disk, as depicted in *Figure 8.6*. The controller ensures that the disk operates efficiently by regulating its mechanical movements and handling data read and write requests. That includes converting digital signals into physical operations and vice versa, ensuring accurate data retrieval and storage.

Figure 8.6 – Disk controller in an HDD

To fully comprehend how data is processed and communicated by storage devices, it is also important to explore the underlying technologies of serial bus systems and data transmission protocols. Serial buses, such as those used in modern interfaces such as SATA and USB, transmit data one bit at a time over a single channel, offering streamlined and efficient data transfer. Data transmission technologies dictate the speed and reliability of these transfers, influencing overall system performance. In the upcoming section, we will examine these technologies in detail, providing insights into their role in optimizing data communication and enhancing the functionality of storage systems. This deeper understanding will help in selecting and configuring storage solutions that meet specific performance and reliability requirements.

Data transmission in storage devices

Storage devices utilize two main communication methods for data transfer: parallel and serial:

- **Parallel communication**: This type of communication transmits multiple bits simultaneously, typically handling 8 bits or 1 byte at a time. This method can theoretically offer high-speed data transfer, as multiple bits are sent at once. However, parallel communication can face challenges such as signal degradation and timing issues, known as data skew, especially over long distances.

- **Serial communication**: This type of communication sends data one bit at a time sequentially. Although it transmits data more slowly than parallel communication in raw bit terms, serial communication often proves more efficient and reliable for storage devices. That is because serial communication reduces the complexity associated with managing multiple data paths simultaneously and minimizes issues such as interference and signal degradation. By processing bits in a continuous stream, serial interfaces such as SATA, SAS, FC, and USB allow stable and high-performance data transfer. These interfaces ensure that data transmission is streamlined and less susceptible to the errors that can arise from parallel communication's complexity.

In the upcoming section, we will compare storage protocols and network protocols. This analysis will elucidate how these protocols interact with data transmission, highlighting their respective roles and examining their similarities and differences to provide a comprehensive understanding of data communication in various contexts.

Overview of storage protocols and their roles in data transmission and access

Storage protocols play a pivotal role in IT infrastructure, serving as the foundation for data transfer, access, and management across networks. They are key to determining the efficiency, scalability, and security of storage systems, directly impacting the quality of data transactions. The choice of protocol varies based on the type and scale of storage required, with each protocol offering unique benefits to optimize performance and minimize latency. As enterprise systems continue to evolve, the importance of selecting the appropriate storage protocol to meet growing demands cannot be overstated. In this section, we will delve into the core storage protocols that enable data transmission and access, exploring their functions, applications, and the technical considerations that guide their deployment in diverse IT environments.

Communication protocols in storage devices

Storage devices rely on various protocols to manage data storage and retrieval efficiently. These protocols establish the rules and formats that enable seamless communication between storage devices and other system components. Key protocols used in storage technologies, such as NAS and SAN, are as follows:

- **SCSI**: SCSI is a well-established protocol used for block-level storage systems, allowing devices to exchange data efficiently. It facilitates communication between the operating system and storage devices by utilizing SCSI commands to manage data transfers. SCSI supports a range of devices and offers various command sets, making it versatile for different storage configurations.

> **Note**
>
> For a comprehensive understanding of SCSI, including its history, functionality, and applications, you can refer to detailed resources available at Lifewire's SCSI Guide `https://www.lifewire.com/small-computer-system-interface-scsi-2626002`. This source offers valuable insights into how SCSI operates, its various command sets, and its relevance in modern storage solutions.

- **iSCSI**: iSCSI extends SCSI commands over IP networks by encapsulating them within IP packets. This protocol allows organizations to utilize standard network infrastructure to connect storage devices, providing a cost-effective solution for remote storage access. Its ability to integrate seamlessly with existing IP networks makes iSCSI suitable for both small-scale and large-scale deployments, enhancing flexibility and scalability in modern data centers.

- **FC**: FC is a high-speed network protocol designed for block-level storage, transferring data with low latency and high reliability. Ideal for enterprise environments requiring robust performance, FC networks facilitate the efficient consolidation of storage resources. Its capability to cover long distances makes it essential for large data centers where high availability and speed are critical.

- **FCoE**: FCoE integrates the FC protocol with Ethernet frames, allowing FC traffic to traverse Ethernet networks. This convergence enables organizations to leverage their existing Ethernet infrastructure while still enjoying the performance benefits of FC. FCoE simplifies network management by unifying storage and network traffic onto a single fabric, supporting high-speed data transfers crucial for modern enterprise applications.

Each of these protocols plays a crucial role in optimizing storage systems, offering varying levels of performance, scalability, and integration. By understanding these protocols, IT professionals can select the most appropriate technology for their specific storage needs and ensure efficient data management across their infrastructure.

File-sharing protocols

File-sharing protocols play a crucial role in enabling the efficient transfer and access of data across various networks by defining specific rules and formats for requesting and exchanging files between clients and servers. These protocols not only ensure that data can be shared seamlessly but also address security and compatibility issues across different systems. Here is a more detailed look at some of the most common file-sharing protocols:

- **Server Message Block (SMB)**: This protocol facilitates file sharing over **local area networks (LANs)** and is widely used in Windows environments. SMB allows applications to read and write to files and request services from server programs. An extension of SMB, **Common Internet File System (CIFS)**, developed by Microsoft, provides enhanced functionality and is used for sharing files over the Internet as well.

- **Network File System (NFS)**: NFS supports file sharing over both local and **wide area networks (WANs)**, particularly within Unix and Linux systems. It allows users to mount remote directories on their local systems, allowing them to access files stored on remote servers as if they were on the local machine. NFS is known for its ability to integrate seamlessly with Unix-based file systems.

- **File Transfer Protocol (FTP)**: FTP is designed to transfer files over the Internet between servers and clients. It operates in a client-server model where the client initiates a connection to the server to upload or download files. FTP supports various commands and responses that facilitate efficient file transfer, making it suitable for transferring large files or batches of files.

- **Hypertext Transfer Protocol (HTTP)**: HTTP is the foundation of data communication on the web. It is used to deliver files through web browsers and other web-based applications. HTTP enables the retrieval of web pages, images, and other resources from web servers, facilitating a wide range of online activities.

- **Secure Shell (SSH)**: SSH provides a secure channel for remote file sharing by encrypting the data during transmission. It is commonly used for accessing remote servers securely and transferring files via protocols such as **Secure Copy Protocol (SCP)** or **Secure File Transfer Protocol (SFTP)**. SSH ensures that data integrity and confidentiality are maintained during file exchanges.

> **Note:**
>
> For further information about SSH and its applications, please visit the official SSH website at `https://www.ssh.com/ssh/`. This resource offers comprehensive details on SSH protocols, including their secure communication capabilities, encryption methods, and various use cases in remote server management and file transfer.

Each protocol has distinct features that cater to different networking environments and security requirements, making it integral to managing and sharing files efficiently across diverse platforms and networks.

Next, we will explore how HBAs and FC switches facilitate the connection and operation of network storage technologies, such as SANs. HBAs are specialized hardware components that enable servers to interface with storage networks. At the same time, FC switches manage the data traffic within the SAN, ensuring efficient and reliable data transfer between servers and storage devices. Understanding these components is crucial for optimizing the performance and scalability of networked storage solutions.

HBA and FC switches

In this subsection, we will briefly discuss the essential functions of HBAs and FC switches within network storage infrastructures. Understanding these components is crucial for understanding how data storage and retrieval are efficiently managed in modern IT environments.

- An **HBA switch** is a crucial component that provides fiber connectivity between a server and the storage network, enabling efficient data transfer. It essentially acts as an interface that allows the server to communicate with the storage array over high-speed fiber links.

- An **FC switch** operates at Layer 3 of the OSI model, managing and directing data traffic within the network. The FC switch plays a pivotal role in the SAN by facilitating communication between multiple HBAs and storage devices.

The two components are connected by high-speed FC cables, which form the FC fabric. The FC fabric comprises one or more FC switches interconnected to create a network topology that supports high-performance data transfer. This network fabric is essential for maintaining the efficiency and reliability of data storage and retrieval operations within a SAN.

Understanding the interaction between HBAs and FC switches is fundamental for grasping how SANs are structured and managed. In the following section, we will shift our focus to iSCSI hardware, another technology used for connecting network storage systems, and compare its functionalities with those of FC-based systems.

iSCSI hardware

iSCSI is a protocol that enables block-level storage communication over IP networks, providing a means for transferring data between servers and storage devices over long distances using standard networking infrastructure. iSCSI operates by encapsulating SCSI commands—known as **command descriptor blocks** (**CDBs**)—into IP packets, which are then transmitted over TCP/IP networks. This encapsulation allows the integration of storage devices into IP networks, making it possible to use existing network equipment and infrastructure for storage purposes.

In the iSCSI architecture, storage devices are identified as targets, while clients that initiate communication are referred to as initiators. Each logical disk within a SAN is assigned a unique identifier known as a **Logical Unit Number** (**LUN**), which helps in organizing and accessing storage resources effectively. iSCSI uses two key **TCP ports**: **port 860** for the iSCSI system port, which is used for management and configuration, and **port 3260** for the iSCSI default port, which handles data transfers. This dual-port setup facilitates both control and data paths, ensuring efficient communication between initiators and targets.

iSCSI's ability to leverage existing IP networks and its flexibility in integration make it a cost-effective solution for enterprises looking to expand their storage capabilities without the need for specialized hardware. By using standard Ethernet infrastructure, iSCSI enables scalable and manageable storage solutions, enhancing data availability and accessibility across various network environments.

In the next section, we will explore S2D, a technology that enables the creation and management of storage pools. S2D is designed to optimize storage efficiency and performance, providing a scalable solution for modern data storage needs.

Explaining S2D

S2D is a robust feature introduced in Windows Server 2016 and carried forward into Windows Server 2025, designed to streamline and enhance storage management in data centers. S2D enables the construction of high-availability storage infrastructure by leveraging locally attached disks within a cluster of servers. One of its key capabilities is storage tiering. It improves performance by utilizing faster storage media such as SSDs or NVMe drives as a cache for frequently accessed data, while slower but higher-capacity disks handle less critical data. This tiered approach ensures that data retrieval times are minimized, thereby optimizing the overall performance of the storage system.

Additionally, S2D supports the creation and management of **SDS pools**. By consolidating multiple physical disks into these pools, administrators can create flexible and scalable virtualized storage spaces. These storage pools can be dynamically expanded or reconfigured to meet changing storage needs without the need for physical hardware changes. S2D also incorporates features such as resilience and automated healing, which enhance data protection and ensure continuous availability in case of hardware failures.

Figure 8.7 illustrates the process of creating a new storage pool in Windows Server 2025, highlighting the user-friendly interface and options available for setting up and managing these pools.

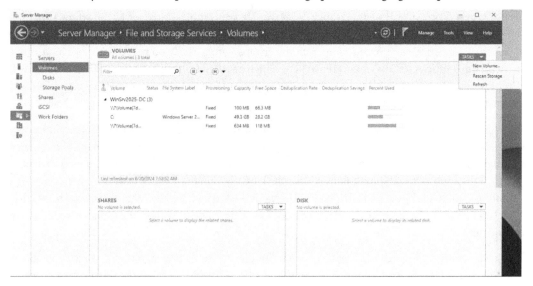

Figure 8.7 – Creating a new storage pool in Windows Server 2025

In the following section, we will explore the deduplication feature, which complements S2D by reducing storage costs and improving efficiency through the elimination of redundant data.

An introduction to dedup

Data Deduplication (**Dedup**) is an essential server role that addresses disk space inefficiency by systematically eliminating redundant data blocks within a dataset. This process begins with a comprehensive scan of the data to identify and catalog identical blocks. Once duplicates are detected, deduplication keeps a single, original copy of each unique block on the disk. In contrast, subsequent duplicate instances are replaced with pointers that direct to this original data block. This technique drastically reduces the amount of storage space required, as only one copy of each piece of data is physically stored, yet all references to it remain intact.

Additionally, deduplication not only conserves disk space but also enhances data management efficiency and reduces storage costs, contributing to improved overall system performance. This functionality is particularly beneficial in environments with large volumes of similar or identical files, such as backup repositories and virtualized environments.

Figure 8.8 provides an installation of the deduplication role within Windows Server 2025, highlighting the steps for enabling and configuring this feature. It demonstrates how administrators can leverage deduplication to maximize storage efficiency while maintaining data integrity and accessibility.

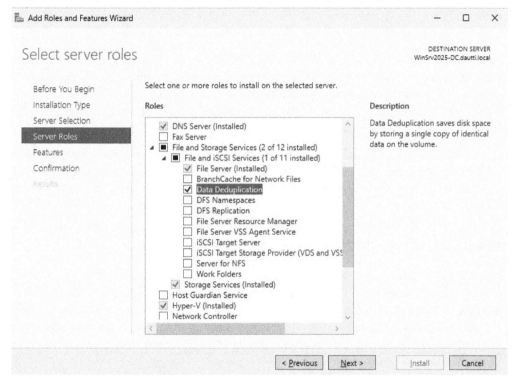

Figure 8.8 – Installing dedup in Windows Server 2025

> **Note**
> **Cluster rolling upgrades** are a way to update the server operating system across cluster nodes while ensuring uninterrupted Hyper-V operations. This process allows you to upgrade each node in a cluster sequentially, minimizing downtime and maintaining continuous availability of VMs throughout the upgrade. By performing the upgrade one node at a time, you ensure that the cluster remains operational and functional during the transition to the new operating system version, avoiding disruptions to critical services and applications.

Following this, we will explore the concept of storage tiering, which enhances data management by strategically placing data on fast storage devices based on access patterns and performance requirements.

Storage tiering

Storage tiering is a sophisticated feature built into Windows Server that enhances storage efficiency by optimizing the placement of data across various types of storage devices. This feature enables the integration of different storage media—such as high-performance SSDs and cost-effective HDDs—into a single storage pool. The primary goal of storage tiering is to balance the need for speed and cost-effectiveness by dynamically managing where data is stored based on its usage patterns.

With storage tiering, Windows Server uses automated processes to analyze data access frequency. Frequently accessed files, which require fast retrieval times, are automatically moved to high-performance storage tiers, such as SSDs. Conversely, data that is rarely accessed is relocated to slower, more economical storage tiers, such as HDDs. This method not only optimizes performance but also reduces overall storage expenses by leveraging the strengths of each storage type.

Furthermore, storage tiering helps maintain system responsiveness and efficiency as the system adapts to changing data access patterns over time. That ensures that high-demand applications and services continue to operate at peak performance without incurring unnecessary costs for high-speed storage.

Overview of Network Automated Tiered Storage Control in Windows Server 2025

Network **Automated Tiered Storage Control** (ATC) is a powerful feature of Windows Server 2025 that automates the management of storage resources, optimizing performance and efficiency in various deployment scenarios, especially within **Hyper-Converged Infrastructure** (HCI) environments. This feature intelligently manages data placement across different storage tiers, ensuring that frequently accessed data resides on high-performance storage devices. In contrast, less critical data is moved to lower-cost storage options.

The key benefits of Network ATC are as follows:

- **Automation of storage management**: Network ATC simplifies storage management by automating data tiering based on access patterns and predefined policies. This automation reduces the need for manual intervention, allowing administrators to focus on more strategic tasks.

- **Optimized performance**: Network ATC enhances overall system performance by automatically moving data to the most appropriate storage tier. High-demand workloads benefit from faster access times, while less frequently accessed data is efficiently stored without impacting performance.

- **Seamless integration with NAS**: Network ATC seamlessly connects to NAS solutions, providing a unified approach to managing both local and remote storage resources. This capability is particularly beneficial in HCI environments, where storage and compute resources are tightly integrated.

- **Scalability and flexibility**: As organizations grow and their storage needs evolve, Network ATC allows easy scaling of storage resources. Administrators can add new storage devices to the network without disrupting existing operations, ensuring that the infrastructure remains agile and responsive to changing requirements.

To implement Network ATC, understanding its configuration and management within Windows Server 2025 is essential. Administrators can leverage Windows PowerShell and Server Manager to set up and monitor tiering policies, making it easier to maintain an optimal balance of performance and cost in their storage architecture.

Real-world applications of storage technologies in managed security service providers

In the realm of **managed security service providers** (**MSSPs**), the efficient management and utilization of storage technologies are paramount. Here are several real-world examples that illustrate how MSSPs leverage storage solutions to enhance their operations and deliver value to their clients.

Data retention and compliance

MSSPs are often required to retain vast amounts of data to meet regulatory compliance standards. For instance, a financial services MSSP implemented a hybrid storage solution that combined on-premises storage with cloud-based resources. This approach allowed them to store sensitive client data securely while ensuring quick access to audits and compliance checks. By using cloud storage, they could easily scale their data retention capabilities in response to changing regulations without significant upfront investment in physical infrastructure.

High-performance storage for threat detection

In a cybersecurity MSSP, the demand for high **Input/Output Operations Per Second** (**IOPS**) is critical when analyzing large volumes of data for potential threats. The MSSP adopted SSDs in their storage architecture to enhance read and write speeds for real-time threat detection. As a result, they could process security logs and alerts more efficiently, reducing response times to potential security incidents and improving overall service quality for their clients.

Disaster recovery and business continuity

An MSSP providing managed services to healthcare organizations recognized the need for robust disaster recovery solutions to protect sensitive patient data. They deployed a storage solution utilizing RAID configurations coupled with cloud backup solutions. This hybrid strategy not only safeguarded against data loss due to hardware failures but also ensured that data could be restored quickly in the event of a ransomware attack, thereby maintaining compliance with healthcare regulations.

Dynamic scaling with SDS

As an MSSP expanded its operations, it faced challenges in managing diverse storage needs across multiple client environments. The organization implemented SDS solutions to abstract storage resources and manage them through a centralized interface. This allowed the MSSP to quickly adapt to varying client requirements, allocate storage dynamically, and optimize costs, thereby improving their service delivery and client satisfaction.

Leveraging iSCSI for virtual environments

Many MSSPs operate in virtualized environments where storage flexibility is crucial. By utilizing iSCSI protocols, an MSSP connects its VMs to remote storage solutions over existing IP networks. This not only simplifies the infrastructure but also reduces costs by using standard network equipment. The MSSP benefits from improved scalability and can serve multiple clients with different storage needs effectively.

These examples highlight how MSSPs apply storage technologies to address real-world challenges, demonstrating the relevance of storage management in a fast-paced, compliance-driven industry. By integrating both traditional and innovative storage solutions, they can optimize performance, enhance security, and ensure the continuity of services, providing valuable insights for those of you who are looking to implement similar strategies in your organizations.

In the subsequent section, we will examine how to effectively manage and configure storage using tools such as Server Manager and Windows PowerShell, focusing on their roles in simplifying and automating storage management tasks.

Managing server storage using Server Manager and Windows PowerShell

Storage management is a critical component of maintaining an efficient and reliable server environment. Effective storage management ensures that data is stored, accessed, and protected in a manner that supports both performance and cost-efficiency. In Windows Server, two key tools for managing storage are Server Manager and Windows PowerShell.

Managing storage using Server Manager

In Windows Server, effective storage management is facilitated through the use of **Server Manager**, a robust tool that offers a graphical interface for configuring and monitoring storage resources. To leverage Server Manager (`servermanager.exe`) for comprehensive storage management, the first step is to install the File and Storage Services role on the server. This installation can be easily completed by selecting the **Add Roles and Features** option within Server Manager. Once this role is in place, it provides a comprehensive suite of tools necessary for the effective management of storage devices and data.

Server Manager serves as a centralized hub for overseeing various facets of server storage, including the setup and administration of storage pools, virtual disks, and shared folders. It supports the configuration of disk properties, the allocation of storage space, and the execution of storage replication and backup strategies. Additionally, Server Manager enables administrators to monitor the health and performance of storage resources, delivering critical insights into storage usage and trends that aid in proactive management and optimization.

With Server Manager, administrators can streamline the management of existing storage configurations and apply best practices for data protection and performance enhancement. This tool ensures that storage environments are efficiently managed and tailored to organizational needs, thereby improving overall system performance. *Figure 8.9* demonstrates how Server Manager can be used to view and manage storage on the local server, highlighting its intuitive interface designed for executing these essential tasks:

Figure 8.9 – Managing storage with Server Manager

Managing storage with Windows PowerShell

Windows PowerShell provides a robust command-line interface for managing storage on Windows Server, offering a range of cmdlets that simplify the configuration, monitoring, and administration of storage resources. By using cmdlets such as `Get-Disk`, `Get-Partition`, and `Get-Volume`, administrators can efficiently query and manage the various aspects of storage, including disk properties, partition configurations, and volume statuses. *Figure 8.10* demonstrates how Windows PowerShell can be effectively utilized to view and manage storage resources, highlighting its role in delivering comprehensive and automated storage management solutions.

- The Get-Disk cmdlet allows users to retrieve information about physical disks, including their health status and capacity

- The Get-Partition provides details on the partitions created on a disk, such as their size and file system type

- The Get-Volume cmdlet further extends these capabilities by showing information about volumes, including their available space and drive letters

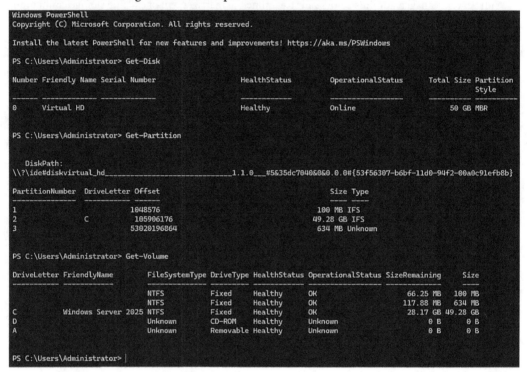

Figure 8.10 – Managing storage with Windows PowerShell

These cmdlets enable administrators to script and automate complex storage management tasks, providing greater flexibility and control.

Moreover, Windows PowerShell supports additional cmdlets for more advanced storage management functions, such as New-Partition, Format-Volume, and Resize-Partition, which facilitate creating new partitions, formatting volumes, and adjusting partition sizes, respectively. By integrating these cmdlets into scripts, administrators can automate routine storage tasks, enhance efficiency, and ensure consistent configuration across multiple servers.

In this section, you have explored a range of critical topics related to storage, including various storage technologies, types of adapters and controllers, and essential storage protocols. Specifically, you have learned about iSCSI and FC, which facilitate communication between servers and storage devices, and how to use SMB and NFS for network file sharing. Additionally, you have gained insights into managing storage using both Server Manager and Windows PowerShell, which offer graphical and command-line tools for efficient storage configuration and monitoring. Moving forward, the next section will delve into RAID, focusing on how this technology can enhance the performance and reliability of your storage systems.

Understanding RAID principles and configurations

RAID, which stands for **Redundant Array of Independent Disks** or sometimes **Redundant Array of Inexpensive Disks**, is a critical technology in modern IT infrastructure for enhancing data protection and system reliability. The term "Independent Disks" emphasizes that the disks can be separate and distinct units. In contrast, "Inexpensive Disks" highlights that RAID can effectively utilize low-cost drives to achieve high availability and fault tolerance. By combining multiple physical disks into a single logical unit, RAID allows data to be distributed, mirrored, or both across these disks, thereby creating redundancy that significantly increases fault tolerance. This redundancy ensures that even if one or more disks fail, the data remains accessible, minimizing the risk of data loss and system downtime. However, while RAID provides robust protection against hardware failures, it is not a comprehensive data protection solution on its own. It does not guard against data corruption, accidental deletion, or catastrophic events that could affect the entire array. Therefore, it is essential to complement RAID with a solid backup strategy to ensure complete data security. In this section, we will explore the various RAID levels, detailing how each configuration offers different benefits in terms of performance, redundancy, and storage efficiency, helping you choose the right RAID setup for your specific needs.

RAID variants

RAID technology offers a range of configurations, each tailored to balance performance, reliability, and storage efficiency according to specific needs. Some of the most commonly implemented RAID variants are as follows:

- **RAID 0 (Striping)**: This configuration splits data evenly across two or more disks without storing any redundant data. By distributing data blocks across multiple disks, RAID 0 significantly enhances read and write speeds, making it ideal for environments where performance is critical, such as video editing or high-speed data processing. However, RAID 0 lacks redundancy; if even one disk fails, all data in the array is irretrievably lost. In Windows Server 2025, creating a striped volume involves converting the disk from basic to dynamic, allowing faster access speeds at the cost of data security.

- **RAID 1 (Mirroring)**: RAID 1 focuses on data redundancy by creating exact copies, or mirrors, of the data on two or more disks. That ensures that if one disk fails, the system can continue operating using the mirrored copy. While RAID 1 offers excellent read performance due to the ability to read from either disk, write performance is similar to that of a single disk because each write operation must be duplicated. The primary drawback is its inefficiency in disk usage, as it requires double the storage capacity. In Windows Server 2025, a mirrored volume is set up by converting the disk from basic to dynamic, providing a straightforward way to enhance data protection.

- **RAID 5 (Striping with Parity)**: RAID 5 combines the performance benefits of striping with added data protection through parity. It distributes both data and parity information across at least three disks, allowing the array to recover from the failure of any single disk. That makes RAID 5 a popular choice for systems that need to balance performance, storage efficiency, and fault tolerance. While it provides better storage utilization than RAID 1, its write performance is slightly lower due to the need to calculate and write parity information. In Windows Server 2025, RAID 5 volumes can be created using the Storage Spaces feature, providing a flexible solution for environments where data availability is crucial.

- **RAID 10 (1+0)**: RAID 10 is a hybrid configuration that combines the mirroring of RAID 1 with the striping of RAID 0. This setup requires a minimum of four disks and provides high striping performance along with redundancy in mirroring. RAID 10 delivers exceptional speed and fault tolerance, making it ideal for high-transaction environments such as databases or virtualized systems. However, it is more expensive and complex to implement, as it requires twice the number of disks to achieve the desired storage capacity. In Windows Server 2025, RAID 10 volumes can be configured using the Storage Spaces feature, enabling high availability and performance for critical applications.

As we continue, we will delve into the differences between hardware RAID and software RAID, exploring how each approach influences performance, flexibility, and system design.

RAID implementation methods

When implementing RAID, organizations have two primary options to consider, each with distinct advantages, cost implications, and performance characteristics:

- **Hardware RAID implementation**: This method utilizes a dedicated RAID controller, which is a specialized circuit board installed directly into a server's motherboard. The RAID controller, often provided by the server's manufacturer or installed by a technician, is configured prior to the operating system installation. Hardware RAID is known for its superior performance and reliability because it offloads RAID processing from the server's main CPU, resulting in faster data access and better overall system efficiency. Additionally, hardware RAID often includes features such as battery-backed cache and advanced error handling, which further enhance data integrity and performance. However, this approach tends to be expensive due to the additional hardware costs. It is typically used in enterprise environments where maximum uptime, high performance, and robust fault tolerance are critical (as illustrated in *Figure 8.11*).

Figure 8.11 – The RAID controller

- **Software RAID implementation**: This is a more cost-effective option that does not require specialized hardware. Instead, it relies on software to manage the RAID configuration, which is set up after the operating system has been installed. Software RAID is generally easier to implement and can be managed through the server's operating system or a third-party application purchased from various vendors. While it is more budget-friendly, software RAID typically provides lower performance than hardware RAID as it relies on the server's CPU to perform RAID calculations, potentially impacting other system operations. This method is suitable for small to medium-sized businesses or environments where cost considerations outweigh the need for maximum performance. Despite its limitations, software RAID provides flexibility and can be a practical solution for less demanding applications or when hardware RAID is not feasible.

Following this, we will delve into SDS, a transformative technology that uses software to create flexible, scalable, and cost-effective storage solutions tailored to modern IT environments.

SDS overview

For organizations that may lack the budget to invest in traditional, high-cost storage solutions such as NAS or SAN, SDS provides a versatile and cost-effective alternative. SDS enables businesses to create a storage infrastructure by leveraging existing local storage resources, particularly through the use of S2D in Windows Server 2025. This approach decouples the storage management software from the physical storage hardware, which not only reduces the reliance on proprietary systems but also increases the flexibility to mix and match various storage technologies, such as SSDs, HDDs, or even cloud-based storage.

By separating the control layer from the physical hardware, SDS allows organizations to dynamically scale their storage capacity, enhance resource utilization, and optimize performance according to their specific needs. This flexibility also simplifies storage management and makes it easier to implement new storage innovations without the need for expensive hardware upgrades. Moreover, SDS supports automation and orchestration, which can lead to more efficient storage operations and a reduction in manual administrative tasks.

In the next section, we will delve into how leveraging redundancy with S2D not only enables fault tolerance but also enhances storage efficiency, ensuring that data remains secure and accessible even in the event of hardware failures.

Fault tolerance with S2D

S2D in Windows Server 2025 is designed to deliver exceptional fault tolerance and data protection. Its advanced resiliency features ensure that data remains safe in the event of disk or server failure. S2D employs sophisticated techniques akin to RAID, such as data mirroring and parity, to safeguard against data loss. However, S2D extends these capabilities with several key advantages.

One of S2D's primary benefits is its dynamic resiliency adjustment. This feature allows S2D to adapt its protection mechanisms based on the current configuration of disks, including their number, type, and capacity. As a result, S2D can scale its resiliency to match the evolving needs of the storage environment. Additionally, S2D enhances the efficiency of data rebuilding processes, enabling faster and more reliable recovery from hardware failure. This efficiency is crucial for maintaining continuous access to data and minimizing downtime.

Moreover, S2D supports various resiliency options, including simple, mirror, and parity layouts, allowing administrators to choose the level of protection that best fits their performance and capacity requirements. This flexibility ensures that organizations can tailor their storage solutions to meet specific needs while maintaining high levels of data protection.

In the next section, we will delve into the concept of High Availability, focusing on how it further enhances the reliability and accessibility of storage systems by ensuring that critical data and services remain available even in the face of component failures.

High Availability

High Availability (**HA**) is a critical characteristic of modern IT systems that ensures that they remain operational and accessible with minimal downtime. A system that achieves HA is designed to provide continuous service and support regardless of potential failures or disruptions. The pursuit of HA involves meeting several key criteria and implementing robust mechanisms to maintain system functionality and data integrity.

To achieve HA, a storage system must integrate multiple components and features. These include the following:

- **Backup solutions**: Regular and reliable backups are essential for safeguarding data from loss or corruption. They enable quick recovery in case of hardware failure or data corruption events.

- **Fault tolerance**: The system must be capable of handling hardware or software failure without impacting overall performance. That is often achieved through redundant components and automatic failover mechanisms.

- **Resilience**: The ability of the system to recover quickly and efficiently from disruptions or failures. Resilience is supported by technologies that can detect, respond to, and rectify issues promptly.

- **Reliability**: Consistent and dependable performance over time, ensuring that the system operates as expected under normal and peak conditions.

The following table outlines the specific criteria necessary for achieving HA:

Availability (%)	Downtime per month	Downtime per year
99%	7.20 hours	3.65 days
99.9%	43.2 minutes	8.76 hours
99.99%	4.32 minutes	52.6 minutes
99.999%	25.9 seconds	5.26 minutes
99.9999%	2.59 seconds	31.5 seconds

Table 8.1 – HA criteria

> **Note**
>
> Downtime refers to periods when a system, service, or application is unavailable or not operational. It can result from maintenance, system failures, upgrades, or unexpected incidents. Understanding the implications of downtime is crucial, as it can lead to lost productivity, reduced revenue, and damage to an organization's reputation. Minimizing downtime is essential for maintaining business continuity, ensuring that operations run smoothly, and delivering reliable services to customers. Effective planning, monitoring, and recovery strategies are vital for reducing downtime and its associated effects.

In this section, we have covered a range of topics related to storage solutions, including various RAID configurations, the distinctions between hardware and software RAID, SDS, the fault tolerance features of S2D, and the principles underlying high availability. Moving forward, we will delve into different types of disk technologies, offering a deeper understanding of the storage options and how they can be effectively utilized for data management.

Understanding primary storage concepts and optimizing storage solutions in Windows Server 2025

A **disk** refers to a physical storage device that is used to save and retrieve data. The term *data storage* encompasses the processes of writing data to and reading data from the disk. Understanding the various types of disks, their classifications, and their technical specifications is crucial for effectively managing storage solutions and optimizing performance. Each disk type has unique features and capabilities that impact factors such as speed, capacity, and reliability.

To fully grasp how disks function and their applications, it is essential to examine their characteristics in detail. This includes learning about different disk technologies, such as HDDs and SSDs, and understanding their respective advantages and limitations. By familiarizing yourself with these details, you will be better equipped to make informed decisions regarding storage solutions that meet specific needs.

We will begin by exploring the HDD, which is a traditional storage technology known for its mechanical components and its role in providing reliable, large-capacity storage solutions. Understanding HDDs will lay the foundation for comparing and contrasting with other disk types as we progress.

Understanding HDDs

As illustrated in *Figure 8.12*, an HDD is a widely used secondary storage device that relies on electromagnetic principles to store data. The core component of an HDD is its spinning disk, or platter, which is coated with a magnetic material. An electromotor inside the drive rotates this platter at high speeds. Data is stored on the platter in a series of concentric circles called tracks, which are further divided into smaller segments known as sectors. The data is written to and read from these tracks and sectors by a read-and-write head that hovers just above the platter's surface, maintaining a precise gap to prevent contact and potential damage.

The capacity of an HDD is quantified in bytes, with modern drives commonly measured in **gigabytes** (**GB**) and **terabytes** (**TB**), reflecting their ability to store large volumes of data. The rotational speed of the platter is measured in **revolutions per minute** (**RPM**), which influences the drive's performance. Standard RPM rates for consumer HDDs typically range from 5,400 RPM to 7,200 RPM, with higher speeds, such as 10,000 RPM to 15,000 RPM, found in enterprise-level and server HDDs. Higher RPMs generally result in faster data access times and improved overall performance.

HDDs are usually installed inside a computer's case and mounted in dedicated drive bays to ensure stability and secure operation. External HDDs, which connect via USB or other interfaces, provide additional storage capacity for backup and data transfer without affecting the internal system. Given their magnetic storage nature, HDDs require careful disposal practices to protect sensitive information. For instance, disk shredding is a recommended method for secure data destruction, particularly in sectors handling confidential information, such as financial institutions and government agencies.

Figure 8.12 – An HDD

In the following subsection, we will explore SSDs, which provide a different set of technical specifications and performance characteristics than HDDs. We'll get some insights into their benefits and applications.

Understanding Solid-State Drives (SSDs)

SSDs, as depicted in *Figure 8.13*, are a modern advancement in secondary storage technology for both personal computers and servers. Unlike HDDs, SSDs are built entirely from semiconductor memory chips and lack moving mechanical components. This absence of moving parts contributes to several key advantages: SSDs typically operate at lower power levels, generally around 5V, compared to the 12V required by HDDs to spin their platters. This efficiency translates into reduced energy consumption and lower heat generation.

Additionally, SSDs operate silently and are more resilient to physical shock and vibration, making them more durable than HDDs. The absence of mechanical parts means that SSDs can provide significantly faster data access and transfer speeds than HDDs, which enhances overall system performance. Over the past few years, SSDs have advanced to offer storage capacities comparable to HDDs, making them increasingly viable as primary storage solutions.

Due to their superior speed and reliability, SSDs have become the preferred choice for installing operating systems and running applications. As a result, many modern systems use SSDs as the primary storage medium for critical operations. At the same time, HDDs are often employed for secondary storage needs, such as archival or less frequently accessed data. Furthermore, SSDs are widely utilized in NAS and SAN solutions, where high-speed data access is essential for networked environments and enterprise applications.

The integration of SSDs into various storage architectures reflects their growing importance in optimizing performance and reliability in both personal and enterprise-level systems.

Figure 8.13 – An SSD

Next, let's learn about **optical disk drives (ODDs)** and **optical disks (ODs)** to become familiar with lands and pits.

Optical disk drives (ODDs) and optical disks (ODs)

ODDs are specialized devices that use lasers to read and write data on ODs, such as **CDs, DVDs**, and **Blu-ray disks**, as depicted in *Figure 8.14*. Unlike HDDs, which employ spinning magnetic platters to access data, ODDs rely on optical technology to manage data stored on the surface of the disks. These disks are organized with spiral tracks that are read by the laser. The process begins from the inner part of the disc and moves outward, in contrast to HDDs, which start from the outer edge.

Optical disks have varying storage capacities measured in bytes. CDs typically offer between 650 MB and 700 MB of storage, whereas DVDs can hold from 4.7 GB to 8.5 GB, depending on whether they are single-layer or dual-layer. Blu-ray disks further extend this range, providing significantly higher capacity: single-layer Blu-ray disks can store 25 GB, dual-layer disks hold 50 GB, triple-layer disks offer 100 GB, and quadruple-layer disks reach up to 128 GB. These capacities make Blu-ray disks suitable for high-definition video and large data backups.

The speed of ODs is measured in **kilobytes per second (KB/s)** and is indicated by an **X** rating. Each **X** represents 150 KB/s of data transfer speed. For instance, a drive rated at 24x translates to a transfer rate of 24 x 150 KB/s, or 3,600 KB/s (3.6 MB/s). This rating helps determine how quickly data can be read from or written to the disk.

ODs come in various formats based on their recording capabilities:

- **CD-ROMs and DVD-RAMs**: These are read-only formats, meaning data can be accessed but not modified.

- **CD-Rs and DVD-R/DVD+Rs**: These are write-once formats that allow data to be recorded a single time, making them suitable for permanent data storage.

- **CD-RWs and DVD-RWs/DVD+RWs**: These are rewritable formats that support multiple cycles of writing and erasing, providing flexibility for data management and reuse.

The choice of OD type and format depends on the specific needs for data storage, retrieval, and long-term preservation. Blu-ray technology, in particular, has gained prominence due to its substantial storage capacity and is commonly used for storing high-definition content and large data volumes.

Figure 8.14 – The ODD

Following this, we will delve into the fundamental concepts of disk partitions, focusing on the **Master Boot Record** (**MBR**) and **GUID Partition Table** (**GPT**) schemes. Understanding these partitioning methods is crucial for effectively managing and organizing data storage in different system environments.

Understanding basic disks

Once the operating system is installed on a server's hard disk, the disk is organized using a **basic configuration**. This configuration divides the disk into partitions, each serving as a distinct volume for managing data. Basic disks use two primary partitioning schemes: MBR and GPT. MBR is an old scheme that supports up to four primary partitions per disk or three primary partitions and one extended partition. In contrast, GPT is a more modern scheme that supports a much larger number of partitions and is required for disks larger than 2 TB.

A key limitation of basic disks is that a partition cannot span across multiple physical disks. That means that if more storage space is needed, the only option is to extend the partition by utilizing unallocated space on the same physical disk. This constraint can limit flexibility, particularly in environments where storage needs frequently change.

Next, we will delve into dynamic disks, which provide a more advanced and flexible solution for managing storage. Dynamic disks offer the capability to create volumes that span multiple disks and provide enhanced options for performance and fault tolerance, which can significantly improve read-write operations and overall system reliability.

Understanding dynamic disks

Dynamic disk configuration offers a sophisticated approach to disk management, addressing the limitations of basic disks by enabling more flexible storage options and improved performance. This configuration allows the creation of volumes that can span multiple physical disks, overcoming the constraints imposed by traditional partitions. Here's a detailed look at the types of volumes available with dynamic disks:

- **Simple volume**: This volume represents a single contiguous segment of a physical disk, functioning as an independent storage unit. It is similar to a basic partition but benefits from the dynamic disk's flexibility. Simple volumes are useful for straightforward storage needs but do not offer performance enhancements or redundancy.

- **Mirrored volume**: Designed for fault tolerance, a mirrored volume replicates the data across two or more physical disks. That means that if one disk fails, the system can still access the data from the remaining disks. This setup provides a high level of data protection but requires double the disk space to store the duplicated data.

- **Striped volume**: Also known as RAID-0, a striped volume distributes data evenly across multiple disks, improving overall read and write performance through disk striping. This setup enhances throughput and efficiency but does not offer any data redundancy. If one disk fails, all data in the striped volume is lost.

- **Spanned volume**: A spanned volume combines unused space from multiple disks into a single logical volume. It enables the aggregation of storage capacity from several disks, creating a larger volume that can accommodate more data. However, like striped volumes, spanned volumes do not provide performance improvements or redundancy and are vulnerable to data loss if one of the disks fails.

- **RAID-5 volume**: RAID-5 volumes use disk striping with parity, spreading data and parity information across three or more disks. This setup provides a balance between performance and redundancy. The parity information allows for data recovery in the event of a single disk failure, making it a popular choice for many applications that require both fault tolerance and efficient storage utilization.

Dynamic disks allow a more versatile and resilient storage architecture compared to basic disks, enabling administrators to optimize performance, capacity, and data protection according to their specific requirements.

Changing a basic disk to a dynamic disk

To convert a basic disk to a dynamic disk in Windows Server 2025, follow these steps:

1. To begin, right-click the **Start** button and select **Disk Management** from the context menu.

2. Locate and right-click the disk you wish to convert, then choose **Convert to Dynamic Disk...** from the menu that appears (refer to *Figure 8.15*):

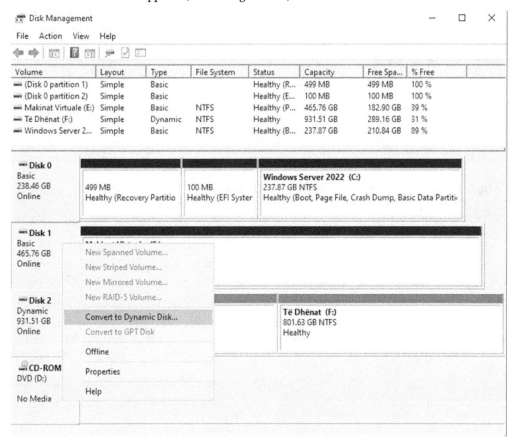

Figure 8.15 – Converting a basic disk into a dynamic disk

3. If multiple disks are available, select the ones you want to convert in the **Convert to Dynamic Disk** window and click **OK**.

4. In the **Disks to Convert** window, click **Convert** to initiate the process.

5. Please review the information provided in the **Disk Management** dialog box and click **Yes** to proceed with the conversion if you agree to the terms.

6. The conversion process will be completed shortly, turning your basic disk into a dynamic disk.

Once you have converted the disk, we will next explore using mount points to expand a folder's storage capacity.

Optimizing disk performance

In the realm of data storage, the speed at which disks operate plays a crucial role in overall system performance. One of the key metrics for evaluating disk performance is IOPS. This measurement reflects the number of read and write operations a storage device can handle within a second, making it essential for determining the suitability of a disk for specific applications and workloads.

Importance of IOPS

High IOPS is particularly important for workloads that involve frequent data access and modification, such as database systems with substantial write operations. For example, transaction-heavy databases, such as those used in e-commerce platforms, require disks capable of handling a large number of I/O requests without introducing latency. When disks fail to meet the necessary IOPS thresholds, a queue can form, leading to delays in data processing and negatively affecting application performance.

Aligning storage with workload requirements

To ensure optimal performance, it is vital to align storage solutions with the demands of workloads. Here are some considerations for different types of applications:

-   **Transactional databases**: These applications typically require high IOPS and low latency. Utilizing SSDs can be advantageous as they provide superior read and write speeds compared to traditional HDDs.

-   **File storage**: For workloads that involve large files with infrequent access, such as media files, traditional HDDs may suffice. In these cases, focusing on capacity rather than IOPS can provide a cost-effective solution.

-   **VMs**: Virtualized environments can benefit from high IOPS due to the concurrent access patterns of multiple VMs. Implementing storage solutions that support IOPS scaling, such as S2D, can enhance performance in these scenarios.

Incorporating an understanding of IOPS and workload alignment into storage planning is critical for maximizing performance in Windows Server 2025 environments. By carefully selecting storage technologies based on the specific needs of applications, administrators can ensure that data retrieval and processing are both efficient and effective, thereby enhancing overall server performance and user experience.

Getting to know the mount points

A **mount point** is a crucial feature in managing disk storage that allows the expansion of a folder's capacity by linking it to an unallocated partition on the same or a different physical disk. This method is advantageous for efficiently utilizing additional disk space without the need to modify or move existing partitions. When a partition's allocated space is exhausted, you can create a mount point to connect it to an available unallocated partition, thereby increasing the folder's storage capacity seamlessly.

In Windows Server 2025, this process is facilitated through the **Disk Management utility** (`diskmgmt.msc`). To set up a mount point, you start by selecting an unallocated partition and linking it to a designated empty folder on an existing volume. This setup allows the folder to utilize the extra space provided by the partition dynamically. The configuration process is visually represented in *Figure 8.16*, which illustrates the steps for setting up a mount point within Disk Management.

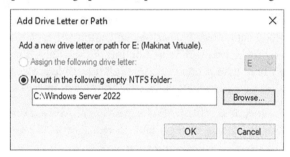

Figure 8.16 – Creating a mount point with Disk Management

By employing mount points, administrators can optimize storage allocation and manage disk space more effectively, ensuring that data storage needs are met without the complexity of traditional partition adjustments. Next, we will explore the role of file systems in managing and organizing data within these storage devices, examining how they impact data accessibility and integrity.

Filesystem overview

A **filesystem** is a critical component of any storage architecture. It is responsible for organizing, managing, and providing access to files and directories on various storage media such as hard drives, ODs, and flash drives. It not only dictates how data is stored and retrieved but also governs the structure and organization of files in the storage medium. The filesystem ensures that data operations, including naming, renaming, copying, moving, and deleting, are executed efficiently and accurately. Without a filesystem, the data would be chaotic and inaccessible, as there would be no systematic way to locate or manage files.

Here are the key filesystems commonly used in Windows operating systems:

- **File Allocation Table** (**FAT**): Developed in the early days of MS-DOS, the FAT filesystem is one of the oldest and simplest filesystems. It utilizes a table to keep track of the clusters on the disk, which are units of logical storage. The most recent version, FAT32, expanded on the original FAT16 by supporting larger volumes and files. FAT32 is widely used for removable storage devices due to its broad compatibility across different operating systems, though it has limitations with very large files and partitions.

- **New Technology File System (NTFS)**: NTFS was introduced with Windows NT 3.1 in the early 1990s and remains the standard filesystem for modern Windows operating systems, including Windows Server 2022 and Windows 11. NTFS offers a range of advanced features, such as support for large files and volumes, file and folder permissions, encryption via the **Encrypting File System (EFS)**, and detailed logging through the journaling feature. It also supports disk quotas and the **Volume Shadow Copy Service (VSS)**, making it suitable for both personal and enterprise environments.

- **Resilient File System (ReFS)**: Introduced with Windows Server 2012, ReFS is designed to provide high resilience, scalability, and data integrity. It aims to address the limitations of NTFS by offering built-in data integrity checking and automatic repair, which enhances reliability, particularly in environments with large amounts of data. ReFS is particularly suited for server environments where data protection and fault tolerance are critical, and it is available in Windows Server 2025 as an option for certain types of storage.

- **Extended File Allocation Table (exFAT)**: exFAT is an evolved version of the FAT filesystem designed for flash drives and other portable storage devices. It provides support for large files and high-capacity storage devices, addressing some of the limitations of FAT32. Notably, exFAT is platform independent, meaning it can be used across various operating systems, including Windows and macOS, which makes it ideal for external drives and flash memory cards that need to be compatible with multiple systems.

> **Note**
>
> **Journaling** is an essential feature of many modern filesystems. It is designed to maintain data integrity by recording changes in a log before they are applied. This approach helps in recovering data in the event of unexpected interruptions, such as power outages or system crashes. However, it is important to note that Microsoft has phased out the journaling feature in Windows Server 2016 and later versions, including Windows Server 2025, by removing `Journal.dll`. This decision reflects a shift in how data integrity and recovery are managed in these environments.

Next, we will explore how to mount a **virtual hard disk (VHD)**, which allows it to operate as if it were a physical disk, providing additional flexibility in managing storage.

Mounting a VHD

As discussed earlier, a VHD is a file format that represents a virtualized storage device. When mounted, a VHD operates as a virtual drive mapped to an empty folder within an NTFS volume, effectively functioning as a physical disk but using a drive path rather than a traditional drive letter. This setup allows flexible storage management and can be particularly useful in virtualized environments or for managing large volumes of data.

To mount a VHD in Windows Server 2025, follow these detailed steps:

1. Press the *Windows key + R* to open the **Run** dialog box.

2. Type `diskmgmt.msc` into the **Run** window and press *Enter*. That will launch the Disk Management utility, where you can manage the physical and virtual disks.

3. In the **Disk Management** window, click on the **Action** menu at the top and select **Attach VHD** from the drop-down menu (see *Figure 8.17* for reference).

Figure 8.17 – Attaching a VHD using Disk Management

4. A dialog box will appear and prompt you to specify the location of the VHD file. Choose the file you wish to attach and confirm your selection.

5. The attached VHD will now be visible in the Disk Management window. It will appear as a new disk, and you can initialize and format it as needed, just like a physical disk.

Mounting a VHD allows it to integrate seamlessly into your system's directory structure, making it accessible for data storage and management without needing additional drive letters. This virtual drive behaves like a physical disk, offering the same file operations and access methods.

In the upcoming subsection, we will explore the **Distributed File System** (**DFS**). DFS is a critical feature for managing files across multiple locations. It provides enhanced data redundancy, availability, and simplified access to distributed data resources. DFS can be particularly beneficial in large-scale environments where data needs to be synchronized and accessible from various locations.

DFS explained

In Windows Server 2025, the **Distributed File System** (**DFS**) is a critical feature that enhances file synchronization, organization, and access across multiple servers within a network. DFS allows administrators to create a unified namespace that aggregates shared folders from various servers into a single logical structure. That means users can access these folders as if they were located on a single server, regardless of their actual physical location. The DFS feature is essential for managing large-scale file storage environments and ensuring high availability and consistency of shared data.

To use DFS, you need to install the **File and Storage Services** role on your server. During the installation, you should select the relevant DFS subfeatures, including **DFS Namespaces**, **DFS Replication**, and **File Server Resource Manager**. DFS Namespaces provides a virtual view of shared folders, while DFS Replication ensures that changes to files are consistently replicated across servers, maintaining data integrity and availability. File Server Resource Manager provides additional tools for managing and monitoring file storage usage.

Figure 8.18 shows how to navigate the installation wizard for the File and Storage Services role, where the DFS components are highlighted. This visual guide will help you configure DFS and integrate it into your server environment.

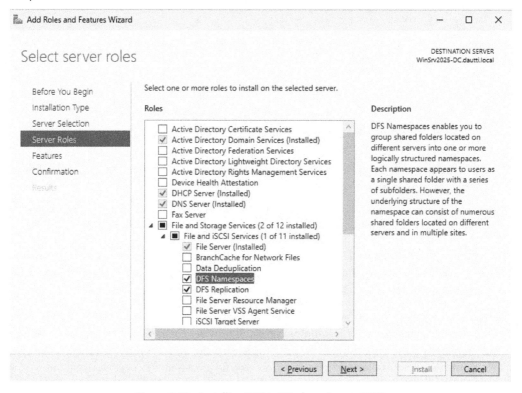

Figure 8.18 – Installing DFS in Windows Server 2025

Following this, we will explore Data Deduplication, a feature that optimizes storage efficiency by eliminating duplicate copies of files, thereby reducing the overall storage footprint on Windows Server 2025.

Chapter exercise – enabling Dedup on Windows Server 2025

In this exercise, you will explore how to activate and configure the **Data Deduplication** feature on Windows Server 2025. Data Deduplication is a powerful storage optimization tool designed to enhance efficiency by eliminating redundant copies of data across your server's storage volumes. It works by scanning data and identifying duplicate blocks, storing only one unique copy of each block while replacing duplicates with pointers to the original.

This process not only conserves valuable disk space but also improves storage performance and reduces backup time by minimizing the amount of data that needs to be handled. Implementing Data Deduplication can lead to significant cost savings on storage resources, make data management more streamlined, and boost overall server efficiency. By enabling this feature, you will ensure that your server operates at peak performance while making the most of your available storage capacity.

To enable the Data Deduplication feature on Windows Server 2025, follow these detailed steps:

1. Open **Server Manager** and navigate to the **WELCOME TO SERVER MANAGER** section, then select **Add Roles and Features**.
2. On the **Before You Begin** screen, click **Next**.
3. Proceed by selecting **Next** on the **Installation Type** screen.
4. Continue by choosing **Next** on the **Server Selection** screen.
5. Expand the File and Storage Services category, then select **File and iSCSI Services**.
6. Check the box labeled **Data Deduplication**, as shown earlier in *Figure 8.7*.
7. Click **Next** on the **Features** screen.
8. Review your selections and click **Install** to begin the installation process.
9. Once the installation is complete, click **Close**, as depicted in *Figure 8.19*.

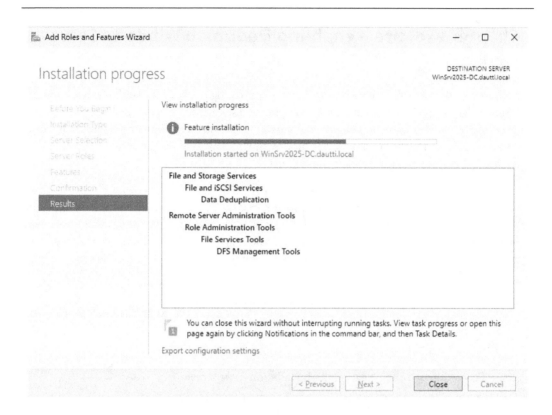

Figure 8.19 – Installing Data Deduplication role on Windows Server 2025

You have now successfully installed the Data Deduplication role on Windows Server 2025. To fully utilize the deduplication capabilities, you will need to enable the feature on specific volumes and configure it according to your storage needs. This additional setup ensures that the Data Deduplication feature operates effectively to optimize your server's storage efficiency.

Summary

In this chapter, you have delved deeply into the various storage options and their management within Windows Server 2025. You began by examining the different types of storage available, such as local storage, NAS, block-level storage, and file-level storage, and how these interact with various adapters, controllers, buses, and protocols. You also explored file-sharing methods that facilitate data access across different systems. The chapter provided detailed instructions on how to utilize both Server Manager and Windows PowerShell for effective storage administration, allowing you to tailor your storage setup according to your specific needs. Additionally, you gained insights into RAID configurations, learning about the advantages and limitations of both hardware and software RAID configurations. This knowledge is crucial for implementing solutions that ensure the high availability and reliability of your services.

Furthermore, you completed a hands-on exercise demonstrating how to activate the Data Deduplication feature in Windows Server 2025. This feature plays a vital role in optimizing storage efficiency by identifying and removing redundant data blocks, which can significantly reduce the amount of storage space required. As you move forward, the next chapter will introduce you to the enhanced features and improvements in **Active Directory Domain Services** (**AD DS**) within Windows Server 2025, further expanding your understanding of server management and configuration.

Questions

1. **True or False**: DFS enables the sharing of data from your server in an authorized and controlled way.

2. **Fill in the Blank**: _____ is a network appliance that connects with computers and servers through a switch and acts as dedicated storage in an organization's network.

3. **Multiple Choice**: Which of the following are network storage technologies? (Choose two)

    A. DAS

    B. NAS

    C. RAM

    D. ROM

4. **True or False**: Block-level storage stores data in files and folders representing volumes managed by the server operating system.

5. **Fill in the Blank**: _____ is an electronic circuit that resides on a hard disk and performs operations such as spinning disks, moving heads for reading and writing, and transferring data to and from RAM.

6. **Multiple Choice**: Which of the following are storage protocols? (Choose two)

    A. SCSI

    B. FC

    C. PATA

    D. SATA

7. **True or False**: The HDD is a computer component that uses the motor to spin the disk, has a magnetic read-and-write head, and has metal platters that permanently store data.

8. **Fill in the Blank**: _____ is a characteristic of a system that never fails, thus is available at all times.

9. **Multiple Choice**: Which of the following are RAID types? (Choose two)

    A. RAID 1

    B. RAID 5

    C. RAID 15

    D. RAID 20

10. **True or False**: SCSI, pronounced scuzzy, is another interface that connects storage and peripheral devices to computers.

11. **Fill in the Blank**: _____ is a legacy interface that connects HDDs, ODDs, floppy disk drives, and related storage technologies to computers.

12. **Multiple Choice**: Which of the following are optical disks? (Choose two)

    A. CD-ROM

    B. DVD-RAM

    C. EPROM

    D. POST

13. **Short Answer**: Discuss Dedup in Windows Server 2025.

14. **Short Answer**: Discuss S2D in Windows Server 2025.

Further reading

For those looking to deepen their knowledge of storage technologies in Windows Server 2025 beyond this chapter's scope, the following resources provide detailed guidance:

- Hard drive: `https://www.computerhope.com/jargon/h/harddriv.htm`

- Overview of Disk Management: `https://learn.microsoft.com/en-us/windows-server/storage/disk-management/overview-of-disk-management`

- Optical Disk types: `https://www.ifixit.com/Wiki/Optical_Disc_Types`

- Difference between basic disk and dynamic disk: `http://www.differencebetween.net/technology/difference-between-basic-disk-and-dynamic-disk`

- What is RAID?: `https://stonefly.com/resources/what-is-raid`

- For a deeper understanding of HDDs, check this out: `https://www.computerhope.com/jargon/h/harddriv.html`

- For additional information about SSDs, check this out: `https://www.lifewire.com/solid-state-drive-833448`

- For further details on various types of ODs, check this out: `https://www.ifixit.com/Wiki/Optical_Disc_Types`

- New storage features in Windows Server 2025: NVMe-OF initiator, update for S2D, deduplication for ReFS: `https://4sysops.com/archives/new-storage-features-in-windows-server-2025-nvme-of-initiator-update-for-s2d-deduplication-for-refs/`

- SMB security hardening in Windows Server 2025 & Windows 11 `https://techcommunity.microsoft.com/blog/filecab/smb-security-hardening-in-windows-server-2025--windows-11/4226591`

Unlock this book's exclusive benefits now

This book comes with additional benefits designed to elevate your learning experience.

Note: Have your purchase invoice ready before you begin.

`https://www.packtpub.com/unlock/9781836205012`

Part 4:
New and Enhanced Features in Windows Server 2025

This part explores the new and enhanced features of Windows Server 2025, exploring advancements in Active Directory, SMB over QUIC, and security improvements. It also introduces innovative server management capabilities, such as hotpatching with Azure Arc, which facilitates seamless updates and better integration with hybrid cloud environments.

This part contains the following chapters:

- *Chapter 9, Active Directory Domain Services (AD DS) Enhancements*
- *Chapter 10, Configuring SMB over QUIC*
- *Chapter 11, Implementing New Security Enhancements*
- *Chapter 12, Managing Updates with Hotpatching, Azure Arc, and More in Windows Server 2025*

Active Directory Domain Services (AD DS) Enhancements

This chapter provides a comprehensive overview of the latest advancements in **Active Directory Domain Services** (**AD DS**) for Windows Server 2025, focusing on key improvements in scalability, security, and cloud integration. It covers notable enhancements, such as more robust authentication mechanisms and enhanced security protocols to safeguard your AD environment from evolving threats, along with seamless integration with cloud services and hybrid environments. A critical update in this release is the introduction of the **32k database page size**, which replaces the traditional 8k size and significantly enhances scalability, optimizing replication, backup, and recovery processes while reducing database fragmentation. Detailed instructions are provided for implementing this update using the `ntdsutil` tool, emphasizing thorough testing in non-production environments.

The chapter also addresses schema updates, focusing on expanding **Active Directory** (**AD**) schema capabilities to support modern applications alongside best practices for managing schema conflicts and maintaining long-term stability. In addition, the new AD object repair features are explored, offering guidance on diagnosing, repairing, and restoring AD objects to improve object management and recovery processes. Finally, the chapter concludes with a practical exercise on implementing a database with a 32k page size, allowing you to apply your knowledge in a hands-on scenario. By the end of this chapter, you will be equipped to optimize and secure your AD DS environment in Windows Server 2025.

In this chapter, we're going to cover the following main topics:

- Overview of AD DS enhancements in Windows Server 2025
- Implementing the 32k database page size for scalability
- Understanding schema updates and extending AD schema capabilities
- Utilizing AD object repair for enhanced object management
- Implementing 32k database page size in Windows Server 2025

Technical requirements

To complete the exercises in this chapter, you will require the following hardware:

- A **Windows 11 Pro** PC equipped with a minimum of 16 GB of RAM, a 1 TB **hard disk drive (HDD)**, and a stable internet connection

- A **Windows Server 2025 Standard** (Desktop Experience) virtual machine, designated as virtual machine 1, configured with an AD DS, featuring at least 8 GB of RAM, 100 GB of HDD space, and internet access

This setup ensures that you have the necessary resources and configurations to perform all tasks effectively.

Overview of AD DS enhancements in Windows Server 2025

Windows Server 2025 introduces significant enhancements to AD DS, focusing on improving scalability, performance, and manageability within AD environments. A notable upgrade is the increase in the default database page size, which enhances the efficiency of managing large directories by minimizing database fragmentation. Additionally, updates to the AD schema support seamless integration with modern technologies and applications, ensuring that AD environments can accommodate evolving enterprise needs. The introduction of advanced object repair features provides IT professionals with powerful tools to maintain the integrity of the AD database, ensuring reliable domain services and robust object management across enterprise settings.

Key enhancements in Active Directory Domain Services for Windows Server 2025

The Windows Server 2025 release introduces a suite of substantial enhancements to AD DS, designed to improve both functionality and security:

- **New Domain and Forest Functional Level:** One of the most significant upgrades is the introduction of a new domain and forest functional level, designated as *Level 10*. This functional level brings with it a range of new features and optimizations that benefit both **AD DS** and **AD Lightweight Directory Services (AD LDS)**.

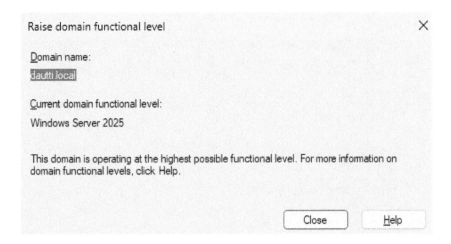

Figure 9.1 – Raising domain functional level in Windows Server 2025

- **Database Engine Page Size Expansion**: A key improvement is the expansion of the database engine's page size from 8k to 32k, a change that allows for the storage of larger directory objects and accommodates up to 3,200 values in multi-valued attributes. This enhancement is particularly beneficial in environments with complex directory structures and extensive attribute usage. Notably, while new domain controllers will default to this 32k page size, they also retain support for the legacy 8k page mode to ensure compatibility within mixed environments. The transition to the 32k page size is managed at the forest level, allowing for a gradual and controlled upgrade process.

- **Scalability and Performance Enhancements**: Scalability and performance have been significantly enhanced with the introduction of **non-uniform memory access (NUMA)** support, enabling AD DS to leverage CPUs across all processor groups efficiently. That is particularly advantageous in large-scale environments where high performance and responsiveness are critical.

- **New Performance Counters**: New performance counters in Performance Monitor, illustrated in *Figure 9.2*, have been integrated into the system to provide detailed monitoring and analysis of AD operations. These counters cover various aspects, including **Local Security Authority (LSA)** lookups, **DC Locator efficiency**, and **LDAP client performance**, offering administrators deeper insights into system performance and potential bottlenecks.

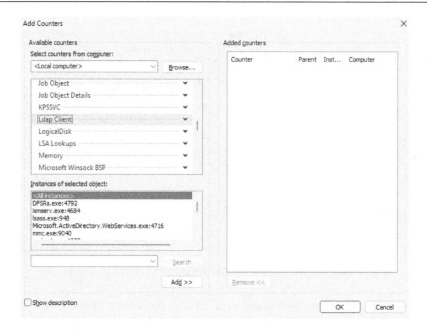

Figure 9.2 – New performance counters in Windows Server 2025

- **Updated Domain Controller Location Algorithm:** Another critical improvement is the updated domain controller location algorithm, which modernizes the discovery process by eliminating the reliance on outdated techniques, such as WINS and Mailslots for NetBIOS name resolution. This update ensures a more reliable and efficient method for locating domain controllers, reducing potential points of failure in the network.

- **Enhanced Security Features:** Windows Server 2025's security enhancements are comprehensive and targeted at addressing both current and emerging threats. Notably, **Kerberos support** has been improved with enhanced handling of the RC4 algorithm, and the introduction of TLS 1.3 support for LDAP over TLS further strengthens the encryption and security of directory communications. These improvements align with best practices in securing directory services against sophisticated attacks.

- **Password Change Methodology:** Additionally, the default password change methodology is shifting away from the SAM-RPC interface, which is being phased out in favor of more secure alternatives. This change also affects members of the **Protected Users** group and local accounts on domain-joined computers, ensuring that only the most secure methods are employed for password changes and authentication processes.

Overall, these enhancements in Windows Server 2025 AD DS represent a significant step forward in both the performance and security of directory services, making it a robust choice for modern enterprises looking to safeguard their network infrastructure while optimizing operational efficiency.

> **Note**
>
> Before implementing the new AD DS enhancements, it is essential to ensure that you have a complete backup of your Active Directory environment. This precaution is crucial because some changes introduced by these updates may be irreversible. Having a full backup will allow you to restore your environment to its previous state if any issues arise during the update process.

Having outlined the key enhancements in AD DS with Windows Server 2025, we now shift focus to the significant strides made in security and authentication. The following subsection will explore the latest security improvements and enhanced authentication mechanisms, which are crucial for fortifying the integrity and protection of your directory services against modern threats.

Significant security improvements and enhanced authentication mechanisms in Windows Server 2025

Windows Server 2025 introduces a comprehensive suite of security enhancements to AD DS, designed to reinforce authentication protocols and safeguard critical infrastructure from increasingly sophisticated cyber threats. At the heart of these improvements is the enhancement of **Kerberos authentication**, which has been a cornerstone of AD DS for many years. In this release:

- Kerberos benefits from more robust encryption algorithms, bolstering defense against common vulnerabilities, such as **Pass-the-Ticket** and **Golden Ticket** attacks. These vulnerabilities are commonly exploited in lateral movement attacks within a network. With these upgrades, Windows Server 2025 enforces higher cryptographic standards, reducing the likelihood of credential theft and unauthorized access.

- Another key advancement is the **improved integration** of **multi-factor authentication** (**MFA**) capabilities, which have become essential in mitigating modern cybersecurity risks. Windows Server 2025 provides more seamless and flexible MFA integration with conditional access policies, allowing organizations to dynamically enforce MFA based on various factors, such as the sensitivity of the resources being accessed, the user's role, or even the location of access. This contextual approach to security ensures that privileged resources receive the highest level of protection while minimizing friction for regular users working on routine tasks. The inclusion of biometrics and token-based MFA further enhances the security framework, aligning with Zero Trust security models that prioritize continuous verification.

- **Group Policy management** also sees significant enhancements in Windows Server 2025. Administrators can now implement and enforce security policies with increased precision, benefiting from a broader range of predefined security templates tailored for different organizational needs. These templates (shown in *Figure 9.3*) help streamline the deployment of security configurations across AD DS environments. Coupled with real-time monitoring and alerting capabilities, these enhancements enable faster detection and remediation of potential security threats. Organizations can fine-tune access control settings and monitor user activity, thereby minimizing attack vectors within the network.

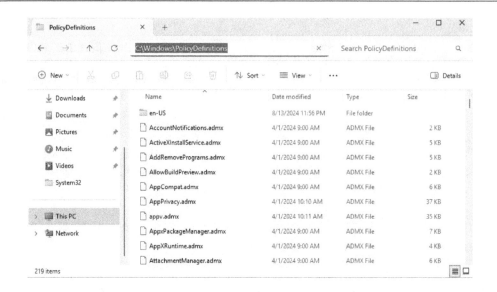

Figure 9.3 – ADMX files in Windows Server 2025

- In addition to these features, Windows Server 2025 enhances **auditing and logging mechanisms** within AD DS. The introduction of more granular auditing capabilities allows security teams to gain deeper insights into authentication patterns and detect anomalies more quickly. With improved event logging, organizations can better track login attempts, access patterns, and potential breaches, which is critical for forensic investigations and compliance with security regulations. That ensures that security teams are equipped to respond swiftly to unauthorized access attempts and maintain continuous vigilance over the network.

Collectively, these security advancements position AD DS as a vital tool for protecting modern IT environments, especially in organizations with hybrid cloud architectures. By strengthening foundational authentication protocols, improving MFA integration, enhancing policy management, and providing deeper visibility into security events, Windows Server 2025 offers a comprehensive defense against the evolving threat landscape. These improvements empower organizations to adopt a proactive security posture, ensuring that their IT infrastructure remains resilient against emerging cybersecurity challenges.

> **Note**
>
> You can access a wealth of free PowerShell scripts at Microsoft's Script Center (`https://devblogs.microsoft.com/powershell-community/`) and PowerShell Gallery (`https://www.powershellgallery.com/`). These platforms serve as renowned repositories where IT professionals can find and share scripts for various administrative tasks. Both resources include extensive collections of scripts specifically related to AD and DNS, making them invaluable for automating and simplifying complex network management activities.

With a solid understanding of the advanced security features and authentication mechanisms in place, it's important to consider how these improvements integrate with broader IT infrastructures. The upcoming subsection will discuss the integration of AD with cloud services and hybrid environments, emphasizing how these advancements facilitate seamless and efficient management across diverse platforms.

Integration with cloud services and hybrid environments

The integration features of Windows Server 2025 have undergone significant enhancements, particularly in the area of AD DS and their connectivity to cloud platforms. These updates are not just essential, but they are a significant step forward in ensuring the efficiency and security of hybrid environments that combine on-premises infrastructure with cloud-based solutions. This trend continues to gain momentum as organizations seek to leverage the scalability and flexibility of the cloud:

- **Seamless Integration with Cloud Services:** With the growing adoption of cloud services, such as Microsoft Azure, the seamless integration between on-premises AD DS and Microsoft Entra ID has become critical. In Windows Server 2025, **synchronization processes** have been optimized for greater efficiency and security, while tools such as the updated Microsoft Entra Connect provide robust support for smooth and secure identity replication. That ensures users have consistent access to both on-premises and cloud resources, with minimal disruption and improved security controls.

- **Enhanced Support for Hybrid Identity Models:** A notable advancement in Windows Server 2025 is the introduction of enhanced support for **hybrid identity models**. That allows organizations to easily extend their on-premises AD DS environment into the cloud, fully utilizing the benefits of Microsoft Entra ID for identity management, including advanced **single sign-on** (**SSO**) functionality. The unified identity framework introduced in this version not only simplifies the process of managing access to cloud applications, such as Microsoft 365, alongside traditional on-premises resources but also significantly improves the user experience. With a single set of credentials, users can seamlessly access services across both environments, a capability particularly advantageous for businesses that operate in hybrid settings and require centralized identity management to ensure efficiency and security. This integration also reduces the need for multiple logins and streamlines access control, making the user experience more convenient and efficient.

- **Simplified Hybrid Resource Management:** Windows Server 2025 makes hybrid resource management more straightforward by incorporating cloud-native features that allow administrators to manage Azure-based services directly through AD DS. By leveraging tools such as **Windows Admin Center**, IT teams can monitor, configure, and troubleshoot both on-premises and cloud resources from a single interface. This integration reduces complexity and provides a holistic view of the organization's IT infrastructure, significantly improving operational efficiency. It also helps IT departments manage the transition to cloud environments, easing the learning curve for administrators who may be more familiar with traditional on-premises tools.

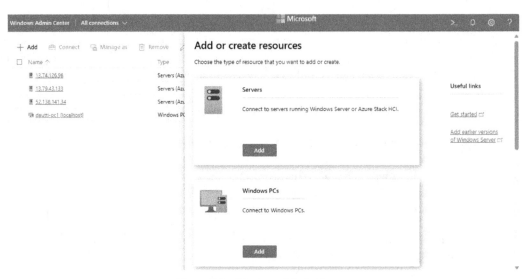

Figure 9.4 – Windows Admin Center

- **Support for Modern Cloud-Based Applications:** Another critical improvement is the **expanded support** for modern, cloud-based applications and services. Windows Server 2025 ensures that AD DS can securely extend an organization's identity infrastructure to encompass cloud-native applications, which are increasingly central to modern business operations. The integration between AD DS and Microsoft Entra ID offers enhanced conditional access policies, allowing businesses to implement detailed security measures based on specific criteria such as user location, device health, and the sensitivity of the data being accessed. These enhancements support the adoption of a **Zero Trust security model**, where all access requests are continuously validated, irrespective of whether the user is operating within a trusted network or from a remote location.

- **Granular Control Over Cloud Identity and Access Management:** Windows Server 2025 provides administrators with more granular control over cloud identity and access management, facilitating the deployment of security protocols that align with both on-premises and cloud operations. That ensures that businesses can maintain consistent governance and security policies across all environments. The improved integration also allows for better monitoring and auditing of hybrid environments, helping organizations identify potential security risks more quickly and take action to mitigate them.

With these advancements, Windows Server 2025 positions AD DS as a crucial component for organizations managing hybrid environments. By enabling deep integration with Microsoft Entra ID and other cloud-native services, the server ensures centralized identity management without sacrificing flexibility or scalability. These improvements enhance organizations' ability to streamline operations, manage resources more effectively, and implement consistent security and identity governance across all platforms—on-premises, cloud, and hybrid. This positions businesses for tremendous success as they increasingly rely on hybrid cloud environments to meet evolving operational needs.

> **Note**
>
> In hybrid environments, it is essential to keep Microsoft Entra Connect updated and correctly configured to prevent synchronization issues between on-premises Active Directory (AD) and Microsoft Entra ID. Regularly monitoring synchronization logs for potential errors is crucial to maintaining seamless integration and ensuring that both directories remain in sync.

This section has detailed the significant advancements in AD DS introduced with Windows Server 2025, covering key enhancements, considerable security improvements, and integration with cloud services. To continue enhancing our understanding of AD infrastructure, the next section will focus on implementing the 32k database page size. This crucial development addresses scalability challenges and optimizes performance, ensuring that AD can manage extensive directory environments efficiently.

Implementing the 32k database page size for scalability

One of the key enhancements introduced in Windows Server 2025 is the increase of the default AD database page size from 8k to 32k, as depicted in *Figure 9.5*). This change significantly improves the **scalability** of AD DS, particularly in environments that manage large volumes of objects or experience frequent modifications. By increasing the page size, the frequency of page splits is significantly reduced, which in turn minimizes database fragmentation and enhances overall performance. That results in lower overhead for database management, making AD DS more efficient, especially in large-scale deployments.

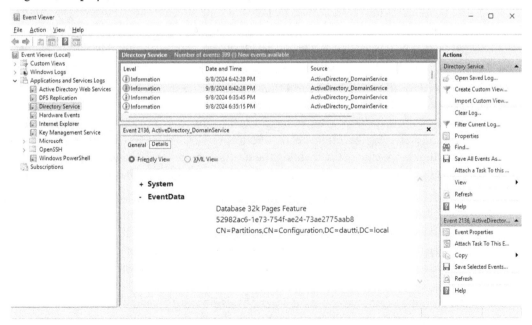

Figure 9.5 – AD Database 32k page size in Windows Server 2025

Implementing the 32k database page size requires a precise and systematic approach. Administrators must first prepare the environment by performing a complete backup of the current AD database to ensure data safety. Next, the `ntdsutil` tool is used to adjust the page size. This process is both critical and irreversible. Given the potential impact of this update, it is essential to conduct thorough testing in a non-production environment prior to full deployment. That ensures the stability of directory services and minimizes the risk of disruption during the transition. Additionally, administrators should be prepared for a complete restart of directory services as part of the process. By following these steps, organizations can smoothly transition to the new 32k page size and fully benefit from the scalability and performance improvements it offers.

Optimized replication for large-scale environments

Windows Server 2025 introduces significant advancements to the replication processes within AD DS, designed to address the needs of extensive and complex environments. These enhancements are specifically aimed at improving the efficiency and effectiveness of managing large networks with multiple domain controllers and global catalogs. The primary focus of these upgrades is to reduce replication latency and optimize bandwidth usage, which is crucial for maintaining high performance and consistency across widely distributed locations:

- **Advanced Replication Algorithms:** A key development is the deployment of advanced replication algorithms that enhance both the speed and reliability of data synchronization between domain controllers. These new algorithms are engineered to reduce the amount of data transferred during replication by utilizing sophisticated compression techniques, thus minimizing network bandwidth usage. This results in faster and more efficient replication processes, which is particularly beneficial for organizations handling substantial volumes of changes and large AD databases.

- **Enhanced Conflict Resolution and Consistency Checks:** Windows Server 2025 introduces enhanced conflict resolution mechanisms and more robust consistency checks. These improvements ensure prompt and effective resolution of data discrepancies, mitigating the risk of replication errors and preserving the integrity of the directory service. The system also supports incremental replication more efficiently, enabling the transfer of only the changes made since the last replication. This approach further optimizes resource utilization and boosts overall performance.

- **Advanced Monitoring and Diagnostic Tools:**In addition to these improvements, Windows Server 2025 features advanced monitoring and diagnostic tools. Administrators now have access to more detailed logging and reporting capabilities, providing deeper insights into replication health and performance. This enhanced visibility facilitates quicker detection and resolution of replication issues, preventing potential disruptions to the broader network.

Overall, the optimized replication features in Windows Server 2025 offer significant advantages for organizations with large-scale AD deployments. By reducing replication latency, improving bandwidth efficiency, and providing advanced monitoring tools, these enhancements contribute to a more resilient and high-performing directory service environment. This is especially critical for organizations that need reliable and robust replication to support their global operations and intricate IT infrastructures.

> **Note**
>
> When deploying the optimized replication features in Windows Server 2025 for large-scale environments, thorough testing in a non-production environment is essential to ensure advanced compression techniques and incremental replication processes do not interfere with critical services. It is important to configure monitoring tools carefully to track replication health while consistently reviewing logs to identify and resolve any inconsistencies. Additionally, verify that your AD Sites and Services settings are optimized for the most efficient replication topology. Lastly, a robust disaster recovery plan is crucial to safeguard against potential issues, especially in complex or geographically dispersed networks.

Having examined how the 32k database page size optimizes replication for large-scale environments, it is essential also to address how robust backup and recovery mechanisms can further enhance scalability. The following subsection will delve into advanced backup and recovery strategies, which are crucial for ensuring data integrity and availability in extensive directory setups.

Enhanced backup and recovery mechanisms

In Windows Server 2025, the backup and recovery mechanisms within AD DS have been significantly enhanced to provide improved reliability and efficiency in safeguarding essential directory data. With modern IT environments becoming increasingly complex and distributed, ensuring timely backups and quick recovery of directory services is critical for maintaining business continuity. The updated Windows Server introduces optimized backup solutions that shorten the time required to back up large AD DS databases while minimizing system performance impact during the process:

- **Efficient Incremental Backups:** A key improvement is the more efficient handling of **incremental backups**, as shown in *Figure 9.6*, which captures only changes made since the last backup. This approach reduces storage requirements and accelerates recovery times. Additionally, Windows Server 2025 strengthens its integration with cloud-based backup services, allowing administrators to leverage cloud storage for offsite backups. That added redundancy is particularly valuable for organizations using hybrid environments, ensuring that critical AD DS data is secure and available from multiple locations.

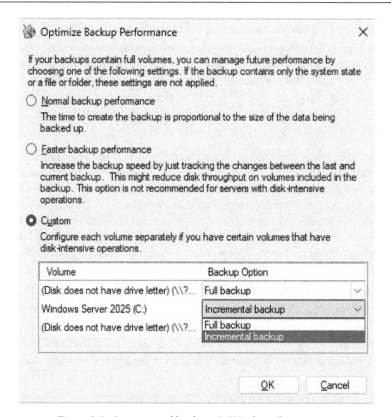

Figure 9.6 – Incremental backups in Windows Server 2025

- **Simplified Recovery Process:** The recovery process has also been simplified with advanced tools that facilitate quicker restoration of AD DS in case of failures or corruption. **Automated recovery validation checks** ensure that backed-up data remains intact and recoverable, reducing the likelihood of failed recoveries during critical moments. Enhanced logging and reporting tools provide deeper insights into backup operations, allowing administrators to monitor backup health and address issues before they become problematic.

These improvements in backup and recovery mechanisms give organizations a more robust approach to managing their AD infrastructure, ensuring faster recovery and enhanced protection for essential directory data across on-premises and cloud environments.

> **Note:**
> After enabling the 32k database page size, make sure to update your backup configurations. Some older backup solutions may not be compatible with the new database size and structure. . Ensuring that your backup systems are up-to-date will help maintain data integrity and prevent potential issues during recovery processes.

Wrapping up this section, we have explored the implementation of the 32k database page size, emphasizing its role in optimizing replication and strengthening backup and recovery mechanisms. Building on these scalability enhancements, the next section will shift focus to understanding schema updates and extending AD schema capabilities. This upcoming discussion will provide insights into managing schema changes, addressing conflicts, and applying best practices further to improve the functionality and flexibility of AD.

Understanding schema updates and extending AD schema capabilities

The schema updates introduced in Windows Server 2025 incorporate new attributes and classes, thereby augmenting AD's capacity to support contemporary applications and emerging technologies. These updates are essential for environments that depend on current software solutions, as they introduce new object types and relationships within the **AD schema** to meet businesses' evolving demands.

Extending the AD schema is not just a task. It's a sophisticated endeavor that requires meticulous planning and precise execution. Before making any modifications, administrators must thoroughly evaluate the potential impacts on existing systems and verify compatibility with all dependent applications. Utilizing tools such as **ADSchemaAnalyzer** to analyze the changes beforehand is highly advisable, and it is imperative to perform a complete backup of the schema to safeguard against any possible issues. Adhering to these best practices ensures a smooth and controlled process for schema extension, minimizing disruptions to critical services.

Managing schema conflicts and versioning

Effectively managing **schema conflicts** and **versioning** in Windows Server 2025 is critical for maintaining the integrity, stability, and scalability of AD. As organizations increasingly rely on a variety of applications and services, the risk of schema conflicts grows, particularly when these systems attempt to define or modify the same attributes or classes within the AD schema. Such conflicts can lead to inconsistencies, service disruptions, or even operational failures across the AD infrastructure. To safeguard against these risks, AD uses **schema versioning**, as depicted in *Figure 9.7*. This built-in mechanism carefully tracks every schema update, ensuring changes are implemented in an orderly fashion and are compatible with the existing directory structure. This process helps prevent conflicts from causing widespread issues in the environment.

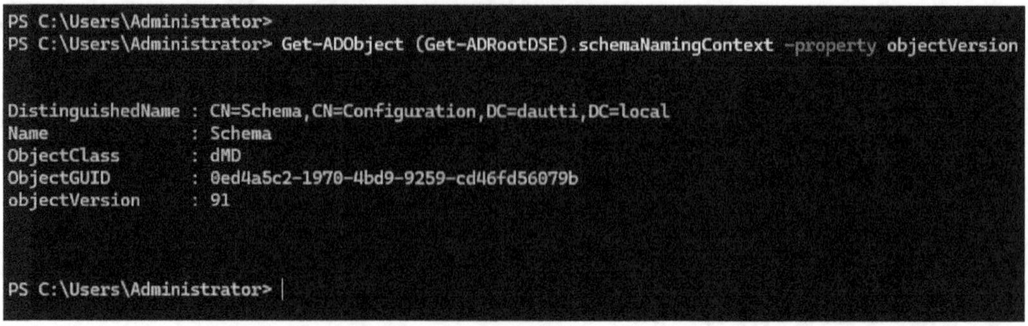

```
PS C:\Users\Administrator>
PS C:\Users\Administrator> Get-ADObject (Get-ADRootDSE).schemaNamingContext -property objectVersion


DistinguishedName : CN=Schema,CN=Configuration,DC=dautti,DC=local
Name              : Schema
ObjectClass       : dMD
ObjectGUID        : 0ed4a5c2-1970-4bd9-9259-cd46fd56079b
objectVersion     : 91



PS C:\Users\Administrator> |
```

Figure 9.7 – New version of AD scheme in Windows Server 2025

Prior to implementing any schema updates or extensions, administrators must conduct thorough evaluations of how these changes will impact both current and future applications. That includes assessing dependencies and compatibility to avoid unintended disruptions. Tools such as `ADSchemaAnalyzer` provide a critical function by comparing proposed updates to the existing schema and flagging potential conflicts, giving administrators an opportunity to resolve these issues before they escalate. In multi-domain environments, the schema master domain controller plays a pivotal role in overseeing all schema changes. It is essential to ensure that the schema master is adequately configured and closely monitored and that only authorized changes are allowed to proceed. Mismanagement at this level can lead to unauthorized modifications that compromise the entire AD infrastructure.

Once schema changes are ready to be applied, **testing** in a non-production or isolated environment becomes a key safeguard. That allows administrators to identify and address any issues before changes are deployed across live environments. In the event that conflicts do arise, AD's schema versioning system offers flexibility by enabling rollbacks or modifications to resolve the problem without destabilizing the directory. Additionally, ongoing auditing of schema changes and reviewing version history are essential for maintaining a well-controlled and secure environment, as they provide insights into when and how changes were made, ensuring accountability and transparency.

By taking a disciplined, systematic approach to managing schema conflicts and versioning, organizations can protect their AD infrastructure while still allowing the integration of new applications, services, and technologies. This strategy not only prevents conflicts but also ensures smooth, scalable growth and seamless operations across diverse and dynamic IT environments.

> **Note**
> Schema changes are irreversible. Therefore, before making any updates, it is crucial to export and review the current schema version. Thoroughly test any extensions or changes in a lab environment to prevent conflicts. This careful approach ensures that potential issues are identified and resolved before they impact the live environment.

Having addressed the intricacies of managing schema conflicts and versioning, we now turn our attention to the best practices for schema design and maintenance. The upcoming subsection will delve into practical strategies for designing and maintaining a robust AD schema, ensuring it supports both current and future directory requirements while minimizing potential issues.

Best practices for schema design and maintenance

Adhering to best practices is crucial for ensuring a scalable, reliable, and efficient directory service environment when managing schema design and maintenance in AD for Windows Server 2025:

- **Thoughtful Schema Design:** A thoughtful approach to schema design starts with understanding both current and future organizational needs, ensuring that schema modifications align with these requirements while avoiding unnecessary complexity. Begin by defining clear objectives for schema changes and ensuring that any new attributes or classes added are essential for supporting business applications and services.

- **Assessing Schema Modifications:** To minimize disruptions and maintain schema integrity, it is imperative to thoroughly **assess the necessity and impact of each proposed schema** modification. Changes should be justified with a clear understanding of how they will affect existing directory structures and applications. Utilizing tools such as `ADSchemaAnalyzer` helps analyze proposed changes against the current schema, identify potential conflicts, and ensure that the updates will not adversely affect the directory environment.

- **Rigorous Change Management:** Implementing a **rigorous change management process** is a best practice for schema maintenance. This process includes conducting extensive testing of schema changes in a non-production environment to uncover any issues before they impact the live system. Additionally, administrators should establish and adhere to a change control policy that includes documentation and approval workflows to manage schema modifications systematically.

- **Regular Audits and Reviews:** Regular audits and reviews of the schema are also essential. That involves periodically evaluating schema attributes and classes to ensure they remain relevant and optimized. Removing obsolete or unused schema elements helps prevent clutter, reduces complexity, and improves overall performance. Maintaining comprehensive documentation and version history of schema changes facilitates better tracking, troubleshooting, and understanding of modifications over time.

- **Disaster Recovery Planning:** Another critical aspect of schema management is **disaster recovery planning**. It is important to develop and maintain a detailed recovery plan that includes procedures for rolling back schema changes if necessary. That ensures that any unforeseen issues can be addressed quickly, minimizing potential disruptions to the directory service.

- **Ongoing Monitoring and Performance Analysis:** Ongoing **monitoring and performance analysis** of the schema help ensure its continued effectiveness. Implementing monitoring tools that provide real-time insights into schema performance and integrity allows administrators to address any emerging issues proactively.

By following these best practices for schema design and maintenance, organizations can ensure a stable and efficient AD infrastructure that supports current operations and future growth while maintaining the reliability and integrity of the directory service.

> **Note**
>
> Minimize the frequency of schema changes to avoid unnecessary conflicts and increased complexity. Schema updates should only be made when necessary. Always adhere to best practices for designing schema updates and ensure proper versioning to maintain stability.

This section has thoroughly examined schema updates and the expansion of AD schema capabilities, emphasizing the management of schema conflicts and the adoption of best practices for design and maintenance. Building on these foundational elements, the next section will transition to utilizing AD object repair for enhanced object management. This forthcoming discussion will delve into effective strategies for identifying, diagnosing, and repairing AD object issues, ensuring the ongoing stability and efficiency of your directory environment.

Utilizing AD object repair for enhanced object management

The introduction of enhanced object repair functionality in Windows Server 2025 marks a significant advancement in AD management, providing administrators with greater efficiency in **restoring and repairing** corrupted or deleted AD objects. These improvements reduce downtime while maintaining the integrity of the directory environment by enabling granular recovery of individual objects, eliminating the need for full database restores, and streamlining the repair process. Key tools such as `LDP.exe` and the **AD Recycle Bin** are essential for facilitating robust and flexible object recovery. At the same time, the newly added granular restore features allow administrators to target specific attributes within an object for precise repair operations. In modern IT infrastructures, where the integrity and reliability of AD objects are critical for operational continuity and security, AD object repair is a vital tool for detecting, diagnosing, and addressing issues, such as corrupt or misconfigured objects. This functionality not only helps maintain compliance by restoring objects to a secure state but also ensures minimal disruption to the AD environment. By mastering these tools, administrators can significantly reduce downtime, enhance security, and maintain a resilient and well-functioning directory service, making AD object repair a key component in managing and optimizing directory performance.

Identifying and diagnosing AD Object issues

Efficient AD object management hinges on the proactive **identification and diagnosis** of potential issues. A proactive monitoring strategy is not just important. It is crucial for maintaining a reliable AD infrastructure. By leveraging built-in tools, such as Windows event logs and diagnostic utilities, administrators can closely monitor AD object activities and quickly detect any irregularities that could signal more profound problems. These tools provide a detailed view of the directory's health, enabling IT professionals to address minor issues before they escalate into severe disruptions.

Understanding common AD object issues is key to effective diagnosis. Problems such as replication conflicts, orphaned objects, and attribute corruption can severely compromise the integrity of the directory. **Replication conflicts** happen when updates to AD objects on one domain controller are not properly synchronized with others, leading to inconsistencies. **Orphaned objects** occur when deletions are incomplete, leaving directory entries without valid parent references. **Attribute corruption** involves errors in object properties, which can cause malfunctioning or misconfiguration of directory services.

To tackle these challenges, administrators use powerful diagnostic tools, such as `dcdiag` and `repadmin`. `dcdiag` (as shown in *Figure 9.8*) evaluates the health of domain controllers by checking for various indicators, while `repadmin` offers insights into replication processes and failures. These tools provide actionable information, enabling administrators to troubleshoot AD object issues efficiently. Automated consistency checkers can also enhance diagnostics by regularly scanning for replication errors and attribute mismatches, alerting administrators to potential issues early.

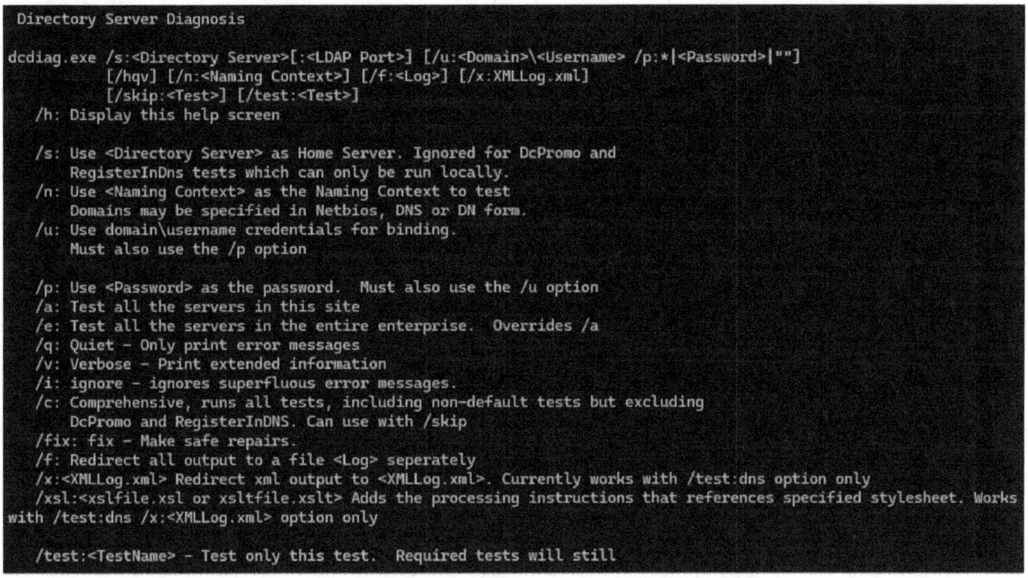

```
Directory Server Diagnosis

dcdiag.exe /s:<Directory Server>[:<LDAP Port>] [/u:<Domain>\<Username> /p:*|<Password>|""]
          [/hqv] [/n:<Naming Context>] [/f:<Log>] [/x:XMLLog.xml]
          [/skip:<Test>] [/test:<Test>]
  /h: Display this help screen

  /s: Use <Directory Server> as Home Server. Ignored for DcPromo and
      RegisterInDns tests which can only be run locally.
  /n: Use <Naming Context> as the Naming Context to test
      Domains may be specified in Netbios, DNS or DN form.
  /u: Use domain\username credentials for binding.
      Must also use the /p option

  /p: Use <Password> as the password.  Must also use the /u option
  /a: Test all the servers in this site
  /e: Test all the servers in the entire enterprise.  Overrides /a
  /q: Quiet - Only print error messages
  /v: Verbose - Print extended information
  /i: ignore - ignores superfluous error messages.
  /c: Comprehensive, runs all tests, including non-default tests but excluding
      DcPromo and RegisterInDNS. Can use with /skip
  /fix: fix - Make safe repairs.
  /f: Redirect all output to a file <Log> seperately
  /x:<XMLLog.xml> Redirect xml output to <XMLLog.xml>. Currently works with /test:dns option only
  /xsl:<xslfile.xsl or xsltfile.xslt> Adds the processing instructions that references specified stylesheet. Works
with /test:dns /x:<XMLLog.xml> option only

  /test:<TestName> - Test only this test.  Required tests will still
```

Figure 9.8 – The dcdiag.exe directory server diagnostic tool

The ability to identify and diagnose AD object issues is fundamental to maintaining a well-functioning AD environment. By implementing thorough monitoring strategies, understanding common AD challenges, and utilizing advanced diagnostic tools, IT professionals can proactively address potential problems. This approach helps ensure the directory's integrity, reduces downtime, and supports the continued stability and efficiency of the AD infrastructure.

> **Note**
>
> When diagnosing AD object issues, it is essential to enable auditing for object-level changes. This practice helps track the root cause of object corruption or deletion, providing valuable insights for resolving these issues effectively.

Having covered the crucial aspects of identifying and diagnosing AD object issues, we now turn our attention to the processes involved in repairing and restoring these objects. The following subsection will explore the methods and tools available for effectively addressing and recovering from AD object problems, ensuring minimal disruption to your directory services.

Repairing and restoring AD objects

Maintaining the integrity and functionality of AD objects is crucial for any organization's directory services. With the advancements in Windows Server 2025, administrators now have access to powerful tools that enhance their ability to repair and restore AD objects with increased accuracy and efficiency. A key utility is `LDP.exe`, a versatile tool that allows administrators to inspect and manipulate AD objects thoroughly. It is particularly useful for recovering deleted objects by examining their attributes and facilitating their restoration.

The **AD Recycle Bin**, as depicted in *Figure 9.9*, is another essential feature. It greatly simplifies the recovery process by preserving the attributes and relationships of deleted objects. This feature reduces the need for extensive database restores, thus minimizing downtime and administrative burdens. The Recycle Bin's ability to retain all object properties ensures that restored objects integrate seamlessly back into the directory, maintaining operational continuity.

Figure 9.9 – AD Recycle Bin in Windows Server 2025

Additionally, Windows Server 2025 introduces **granular restore capabilities** that represent a significant advancement in AD object management. These features enable administrators to restore specific attributes within an object, providing precise solutions for issues such as attribute corruption without requiring a full object recovery. This capability streamlines the repair process and enhances administrators' confidence in managing AD object issues effectively.

Proficiency in using these tools and understanding the associated restoration procedures are vital for IT professionals who aim to sustain a robust AD infrastructure. Ongoing training and hands-on practice with these utilities empower administrators to quickly address and resolve potential disruptions, ensuring a stable and reliable directory environment. By incorporating these advanced repair and restoration techniques into their regular maintenance practices, IT professionals can safeguard the health of AD objects and support the operational continuity of their organizations.

> **Note**
> When restoring AD objects, it is essential to utilize the Active Directory Recycle Bin whenever possible. This feature preserves object attributes and relationships, thereby minimizing potential data loss and ensuring a smoother recovery process.

With a solid understanding of the repair and restoration processes, it is essential to adopt best practices for AD object management and recovery. The upcoming subsection will guide on implementing effective strategies and procedures to maintain a resilient AD environment, emphasizing proactive measures and efficient recovery techniques.

Best practices for AD object management and recovery

Managing and recovering AD objects is crucial for maintaining a robust and secure IT infrastructure. Implementing best practices in this area ensures the health and continuity of your AD environment:

- **Comprehensive Training and Documentation:** Providing thorough education on AD object management procedures equips administrators with the knowledge to address issues confidently and effectively: continuous training sessions and up-to-date documentation support quick problem resolution and standardized processes within the organization.

- **Robust Backup and Recovery Plans:** Establishing **robust backup and recovery plans** is vital. These plans safeguard data integrity and enable rapid restoration in case of system failures or disruptions. Regularly scheduled backups and frequent testing ensure their effectiveness. Automated backup solutions can further streamline this process, providing critical data is consistently protected without manual intervention.

- **Proactive Audits and Continuous Monitoring:** Proactive audits and continuous monitoring are crucial for early detection of potential issues. Utilizing built-in Windows event logs and diagnostic tools allows administrators to track AD object activities and identify anomalies early. This approach not only reduces risks but also strengthens the overall security of the directory environment. Regular audits help verify compliance with policies and uncover unauthorized changes or discrepancies.

- **Automated Consistency Checkers:** Deploying automated consistency checkers can significantly enhance the diagnostic process. These tools periodically assess the directory, checking for attribute mismatches and replication errors. By alerting administrators to issues that need attention, consistency checkers facilitate timely resolution, maintaining the stability and reliability of AD objects.

- **PowerShell Scripts for Automation:** Using **PowerShell scripts** to automate routine repair tasks and streamline object management processes can reduce administrative overhead and minimize human error. Custom scripts designed for specific organizational needs enhance efficiency and effectiveness in AD object management.

Adopting these best practices as part of routine maintenance empowers IT professionals to maintain a secure, stable, and resilient AD infrastructure, supporting the organization's operational continuity.

> **Note**
> Consistently review and audit object-level permissions and configurations to prevent accidental deletion or corruption of critical objects. Implement an automated backup system to facilitate frequent object recovery in case of emergencies.

Practical applications of diagnostic tools in Active Directory

In the realm of AD management, understanding and effectively utilizing diagnostic tools is essential for maintaining a robust and efficient environment. By illustrating real-world scenarios where these tools are applied, you can gain valuable insights into your practical benefits:

- **Enhanced Troubleshooting Capabilities**: Diagnostic tools, such as dcdiag, repadmin, and DTrace, provide administrators with comprehensive diagnostic capabilities to identify and resolve issues within their AD environments. For example, dcdiag can assess the health of domain controllers, pinpointing potential failures before they impact user experience. This proactive approach reduces downtime and enhances overall system reliability.

- **Streamlined Performance Monitoring**: When an organization experiences slow logins or authentication issues, employing tools such as repadmin allows administrators to track replication status and identify bottlenecks in the replication process. Understanding these dynamics helps optimize performance and ensure users have quick access to resources.

- **Informed Decision-Making**: Illustrating how these tools can diagnose and solve specific problems equips you with the knowledge to make informed decisions when faced with similar challenges. This hands-on understanding empowers IT professionals to not only react to issues but also to implement preventative measures that enhance the overall health of their AD infrastructure.

- **Contextual Learning**: By embedding examples that depict the application of these diagnostic tools, you can connect theoretical knowledge with real-world situations. This contextual learning aids in retention and application, ensuring that the lessons learned extend beyond the pages of the book and into their daily operational practices.

Incorporating these practical applications will significantly enhance the relevance of the chapter, providing you with actionable insights they can apply within their environments. Next, in more detail, we will discuss key diagnostic tools, such as `dcdiag`, `repadmin`, and `DTrace`.

Key diagnostic tools for Active Directory management

To effectively manage and troubleshoot AD DS, administrators must familiarize themselves with a range of diagnostic tools that can aid in identifying and resolving issues within the environment. This section introduces three essential tools: `dcdiag`, `repadmin`, and `DTrace`, along with their practical applications.

dcdiag

`dcdiag` (Domain Controller Diagnostic) is a command-line tool that runs a series of tests on domain controllers to verify their health and functionality. It evaluates various aspects of AD, including replication status, connectivity, and service health. The tool provides detailed output for each test, enabling administrators to pinpoint issues quickly. Key uses of `dcdiag` include the following:

- **Identifying Replication Problems**: By running replication diagnostics, administrators can determine whether domain controllers are successfully communicating with each other
- **Checking Services**: It verifies that essential services, such as the Kerberos **Key Distribution Center (KDC)** and the Global Catalog, are functioning correctly
- **Analyzing Network Connectivity**: `dcdiag` assesses network connections and DNS configurations, which are critical for AD operations

repadmin

`repadmin` is another command-line utility designed for monitoring and troubleshooting AD replication. It provides a comprehensive view of replication topology, status, and latency across domain controllers. Its key functionalities include the following:

- **Monitoring Replication Status**: Administrators can use `repadmin` to check the health of replication between domain controllers and view replication metadata
- **Force Replication**: The tool allows administrators to initiate replication manually, which can be crucial for ensuring timely updates across the network
- **Viewing Replication Delays**: By analyzing replication latency, administrators can identify potential bottlenecks that may affect directory updates

DTrace

DTrace is a robust dynamic tracing framework that provides real-time observability of system behavior. In the context of AD, it can be utilized to monitor and troubleshoot performance issues, particularly within Windows Server environments. Its notable features include the following:

- **Real-Time Data Collection**: DTrace can collect data on AD operations, allowing administrators to see what processes are executing and where potential delays occur

- **Customized Tracing**: Administrators can create custom scripts to trace specific operations or events, making it easier to focus on problem areas within the AD environment

- **Performance Analysis**: By analyzing the collected data, administrators can gain insights into performance bottlenecks and optimize AD operations accordingly

Incorporating these diagnostic tools into your AD management practices will significantly enhance your ability to maintain a healthy and efficient AD environment. By familiarizing yourself with their functionalities and practical applications, you will be better equipped to troubleshoot issues and ensure optimal performance of your AD DS.

This section has provided an in-depth look at utilizing AD object repair for enhanced object management, covering the identification, diagnosis, repair, and restoration of AD objects. As we progress, the next section will focus on a practical chapter exercise centered on implementing the 32k database page size. This exercise will consolidate the concepts discussed, offering hands-on experience with scalability improvements and performance optimization for large-scale AD environments.

Chapter exercise – implementing 32k database page size in Windows Server 2025

For this chapter's exercise, you will be guided through the steps to implement the 32 K database page size in Windows Server 2025. This feature is designed to optimize AD performance, especially in large-scale environments, by increasing database scalability and improving replication efficiency.

The exercise begins by modifying the Windows Registry to adjust the database page size, followed by configuring AD DS to enable the 32k pages feature. Through detailed instructions, you will perform the necessary configurations and restart the server to apply these changes. Afterward, you will verify the implementation using PowerShell commands and Event Viewer to confirm that the new page size is active.

This hands-on exercise is essential for administrators who manage AD in large or complex environments. It ensures that the directory can handle extensive data loads while maintaining high performance and reliability. By completing this exercise, you will develop practical skills that enhance your understanding of AD's scalability features, equipping you to manage and optimize directory services in enterprise-level infrastructures.

To start the process of implementing the database 32k page size in Windows Server 2025, follow these steps:

1. Right-click the Start button and select **Run**.

2. In the **Run** dialog box, type `regedit` and press *Enter* to open the Registry Editor.

3. In the Registry Editor, navigate to `HKEY_LOCAL_MACHINE\SYSTEM\CurrentControlSet\Services\NTDS\Parameters`.

4. Look for the **Database Page Size** entry. If it does not exist, proceed to the next step to create it.

5. Right-click on an empty area in the right pane, select **New | DWORD (32-bit) value**, and name the new key `Database Page Size`.

6. Right-click the newly created **Database Page Size** key and choose **Modify....** In the **Value** data field, enter `32768` (32 K bytes). Under the **Base** section, select **Decimal**, then click **OK** (see *Figure 9.10*).

Figure 9.10 – Entering the decimal value for Database Page Size

7. Close the Registry Editor and restart the server for the changes to take effect.

8. After the server restarts, right-click the Start button and select **Terminal (Admin)** to open PowerShell with administrative privileges.

9. In the PowerShell window, execute the following command to enable the 32k page size feature:

```
$params = @{
Identity = 'Database 32k pages feature'
Scope = 'ForestOrConfigurationSet'
Server = 'DAUTTI'  # Replace 'DAUTTI' with your server name
Target = 'dautti.local'  # Replace 'dautti.local' with your domain
}
Enable-ADOptionalFeature @params.
```

10. If prompted, type Yes or Yes to All to proceed with the execution of the command, as shown in *Figure 9.11*.

```
PS C:\Users\Administrator>
PS C:\Users\Administrator> $params = @{
>>      Identity = 'Database 32k pages feature'
>>      Scope = 'ForestOrConfigurationSet'
>>      Server = 'DAUTTI'
>>      Target = 'dautti.local'
>> }
PS C:\Users\Administrator> Enable-ADOptionalFeature @params
WARNING: Enabling 'Database 32k Pages Feature' on 'CN=Partitions,CN=Configuration,DC=dautti,DC=local' is an
irreversible action! You will not be able to disable 'Database 32k Pages Feature' on
'CN=Partitions,CN=Configuration,DC=dautti,DC=local' if you proceed.

Confirm
Are you sure you want to perform this action?
Performing the operation "Enable" on target "Database 32k Pages Feature".
[Y] Yes  [A] Yes to All  [N] No  [L] No to All  [S] Suspend  [?] Help (default is "Y"): A
```

Figure 9.11 – Enabling Database 32k page size in Windows Server 2025

11. Open Event Viewer by typing Event Viewer in the Start menu search bar.

12. Navigate to **Applications and Services Logs | Directory Service**.

13. Check the logs for events related to the AD database startup and confirm that the new 32k page size is being used, as illustrated in *Figure 9.12*.

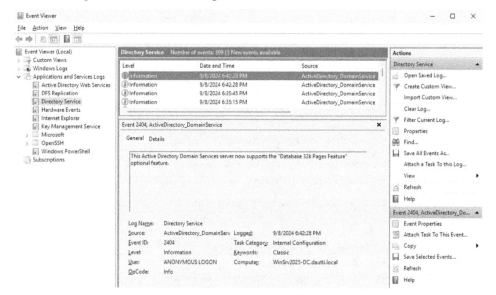

Figure 9.12 – Confirming that the database 32k page size is being used

These steps will help you successfully implement the 32k database page size in Windows Server 2025, ensuring optimal performance and scalability.

Summary

In this chapter, you gained a comprehensive understanding of the key advancements in AD DS for Windows Server 2025, with a focus on scalability, security, and cloud integration. We explored enhanced authentication mechanisms, security features, and AD DS integration with cloud services for seamless collaboration between on-premises and hybrid environments. You also learned about the 32k database page size update, which improves scalability for large environments by optimizing replication, backup, and recovery processes, with step-by-step guidance on configuring this using the `ntdsutil` tool. We covered important schema updates, best practices for managing conflicts, and versioning and extending schema capabilities to support modern applications. Additionally, we examined AD object repair features for diagnosing, repairing, and restoring damaged or deleted AD objects, alongside best practices for object management. The chapter concluded with a hands-on exercise on implementing the 32 K database page size, reinforcing your knowledge and practical skills. Moving forward, the next chapter will focus on configuring SMB over QUIC in Windows Server 2025 to optimize network security and communication further.

Questions

1. **True or False**: AD DS in Windows Server 2025 improves integration with cloud services for hybrid environments.

2. **Fill in the Blank**: _____ is the tool used to configure the 32k database page size in Windows Server 2025.

3. **Multiple Choice**: Which of the following enhancements are introduced in Windows Server 2025 for security and authentication? (*Choose all that apply.*)

    A. Improved authentication mechanisms

    B. SSO enhancements

    C. Biometric authentication

    D. All of the above

4. **True or False**: The 32k database page size optimizes replication for large environments in AD DS.

5. **Fill in the Blank**: _____ is the mechanism that helps resolve AD DS schema conflicts in a hybrid cloud setup.

6. **Multiple Choice**: Which of the following backup mechanisms are enhanced in AD DS for Windows Server 2025? (*Choose all that apply.*)

    A. Full backup

    B. Incremental backup

    C. Cloud backup

    D. Enhanced differential backup

7. **True or False**: Managing schema conflicts and versioning helps ensure the long-term stability of the AD DS infrastructure.

8. **Fill in the Blank**: _____ is the process used to diagnose and repair AD objects in Windows Server 2025.

9. **Multiple Choice**: Which of the following is a best practice for schema design and maintenance? (*Choose all that apply.*)

    A. Regular updates to schema attributes

    B. Avoid unnecessary schema extensions

    C. Frequent schema versioning

    D. All of the above

10. **True or False**: AD object repair features help identify, diagnose, and _____ damaged or deleted AD objects.

11. **Multiple Choice**: Which of the following are key enhancements in AD DS for Windows Server 2025? (*Choose all that apply.*)

    A. Increased scalability

    B. Integration with on-premises and cloud environments

    C. Enhanced security protocols

    D. All of the above

12. **Short Answer**: Discuss the benefits of implementing the 32k database page size in large-scale AD DS environments.

13. **Short Answer**: Discuss the significance of AD object repair features in improving directory services management.

Further reading

- *What's new in Windows Server 2025*: https://learn.microsoft.com/en-us/windows-server/get-started/whats-new-windows-server-2025

- *Database 32k pages for AD*: https://learn.microsoft.com/en-us/windows-server/identity/ad-ds/32k-pages-optional-feature

- *About schema extensions for Configuration Manager*: https://learn.microsoft.com/en-us/mem/configmgr/core/plan-design/network/schema-extensions

- *Restoring AD objects using granular recovery*: https://docs.rubrik.com/en-us/saas/adds/restoring_ad_objects_using_granular_recovery.html

- *Enable Database 32k pages optional feature in AD DS*: https://learn.microsoft.com/en-us/windows-server/identity/ad-ds/enable-32k-pages-optional-feature

- *OSConfig overview*: https://learn.microsoft.com/en-us/windows-server/security/osconfig/osconfig-overview

---

Unlock this book's exclusive benefits now

This book comes with additional benefits designed to elevate your learning experience.

Note: Have your purchase invoice ready before you begin.

https://www.packtpub.com/unlock/9781836205012

10

Configuring SMB over QUIC in Windows Server 2025

This chapter offers a comprehensive understanding of **Server Message Block (SMB) over Quick UDP Internet Connections (QUIC)**, its evolution, and the benefits of implementing this protocol in modern Windows Server environments. It covers the basics of SMB and how QUIC enhances network communication with improved security, lower latency, and optimized data transfer. The chapter begins with a look at the historical context and technological advancements behind SMB over QUIC, followed by an analysis of its key advantages for enterprises. You'll explore essential security considerations, including encryption protocols and best practices, along with detailed steps to configure security settings. Next, the focus shifts to performance optimization, covering network and hardware configurations, performance tuning, and monitoring strategies to ensure a reliable infrastructure. Common troubleshooting techniques are addressed, along with preventative measures for long-term stability. The chapter concludes with a step-by-step exercise on configuring and enabling SMB over QUIC in Windows Server 2025 to reinforce practical knowledge.

In this chapter, we're going to cover the following main topics:

- Introduction to SMB over QUIC in Windows Server 2025
- Understanding security considerations and encryption protocols
- Optimizing SMB over QUIC performance
- Troubleshooting SMB over QUIC implementations
- Configuring and enabling SMB over QUIC in Windows Server 2025

Technical requirements

To complete the exercises in this chapter, you will require the following hardware:

- A **Windows 11 Pro** PC equipped with a minimum of 16 GB of RAM, a 1 TB **hard disk drive (HDD)**, and a stable internet connection

- A **Windows Server 2025 Standard** (Desktop Experience) virtual machine, designated as Virtual Machine 1, configured with an AD DS, featuring at least 8 GB of RAM, 100 GB of HDD space, and internet access

This setup ensures that you have the necessary resources and configurations to perform all tasks effectively.

Introduction to SMB over QUIC in Windows Server 2025

The introduction of **SMB over QUIC** in Windows Server 2025 represents a transformative advancement in network communication. By combining the well-established, feature-rich SMB protocol with the cutting-edge, high-performance QUIC, this integration delivers a powerful solution for enterprises seeking to optimize their digital infrastructures. With SMB's capabilities in file sharing and security, paired with QUIC's ability to enhance speed and reduce latency, IT professionals can harness these technologies to significantly boost data transfer efficiency, strengthen network reliability, and improve security measures. This section explores the evolution of SMB over QUIC, offering a detailed analysis of its functionality and highlighting the key advantages that make it an essential component of modern network ecosystems.

Overview of SMB and QUIC

SMB and **QUIC** are critical components of modern network communication, each playing a distinct but complementary role. For IT professionals working with Windows Server 2025, understanding how these two technologies intersect is key to optimizing network performance, security, and efficiency:

- **SMB**: This is a longstanding protocol utilized by Microsoft in both client and server **operating systems (OSs)**, enabling file, printer, and device sharing across networks. Over the years, it has evolved with enhancements in functionality, security, and performance. Operating primarily over **TCP/IP**, SMB provides critical features such as encryption, signing, and versioning, which ensure the secure and reliable exchange of data across different platforms and devices. SMB has become a cornerstone for enterprises seeking robust, cross-platform data-sharing capabilities.

- **QUIC**: This in contrast, is a relatively new protocol developed by Google. Operating at the transport layer, QUIC uses **User Datagram Protocol** (**UDP**) a fast, connectionless protocol used for transmitting data without error correction or delivery guarantees) rather than TCP to establish faster connections with reduced latency. Its innovative features, including multiplexing without head-of-line blocking, forward error correction, and improved congestion control, make QUIC particularly well-suited for high-performance, low-latency applications. These attributes are essential for web-based and real-time services where speed and resilience are paramount.

The integration of SMB over QUIC in Windows Server 2025 combines SMB's feature-rich environment with QUIC's high-speed, low-latency connection capabilities, enabling faster and more resilient data transfers, even in less reliable network conditions. That is particularly beneficial for remote or mobile users who often face fluctuating network quality. From a security standpoint, SMB over QUIC enhances data protection by leveraging QUIC's built-in encryption, ensuring secure data transmission by default. This robust security framework strengthens SMB's security measures, safeguarding sensitive data from unauthorized access.

The **secure file-sharing** process over the Internet without the need for a VPN starts with the TCP handshake, establishing a reliable connection between the client and server. That is followed by the **TLS handshake** to negotiate encryption protocols. Once the encrypted channel is established, data transfer occurs using SMB over QUIC, providing efficient and secure file sharing. This process benefits from QUIC's low latency, faster connection establishment, and enhanced error recovery. Figure 10.1 compares the round-trip times (RTTs) required for establishing connections and transferring data between clients and servers using different protocols: TCP+TLS1.2, TCP+TLS1.3, and QUIC. It highlights that QUIC significantly reduces latency by requiring fewer RTTs compared to the other protocols, making it more efficient for faster and more reliable data transfers.

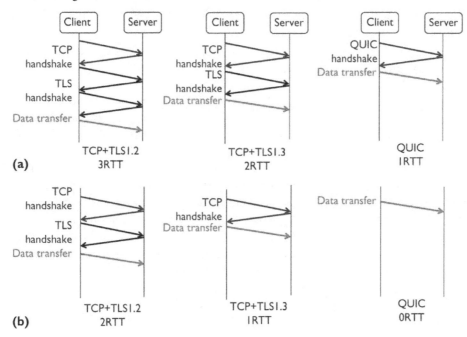

Figure 10.1 – File sharing over the internet without VPN using SMB
over QUIC (source – Microsoft Tech Community)

Administrators will also find the deployment of SMB over QUIC in Windows Server 2025 to be **user-friendly**. The integration process has been streamlined, minimizing downtime and disruption. With familiar management tools and interfaces, IT teams can easily configure and maintain SMB over QUIC, ensuring a seamless transition without requiring extensive retraining.

Overall, the integration of SMB and QUIC within Windows Server 2025 offers a dynamic solution that boosts data transfer speeds, enhances network reliability, and strengthens security. This powerful combination equips IT professionals with the advanced tools required to address the challenges of today's evolving digital landscape, driving greater efficiency and protecting enterprise networks.

> **Note**
>
> When implementing SMB over QUIC, ensure that both client and server environments support the QUIC protocol. Additionally, ensure that the necessary firewall ports are correctly configured to permit QUIC traffic, as this can significantly impact connectivity and performance.

Having explored the essential features and purposes of both SMB and QUIC, it is important to delve deeper into the historical development of these protocols. Understanding their evolution highlights the key advancements that led to the current integration in Windows Server 2025 and explains how they have adapted to meet the demands of modern enterprise networks.

Historical context and evolution

The integration of SMB over QUIC in Windows Server 2025 has its foundation in the rich histories of both protocols, each evolving to address the changing demands of digital communication and enterprise networking. IBM first introduced SMB in the mid-1980s as a protocol designed to facilitate file and printer sharing across **local area networks** (**LANs**). Over time, SMB has been continually refined, incorporating significant improvements such as Unicode support, the ability to handle larger file sizes, and advanced access control mechanisms. These enhancements have made SMB a reliable, secure, and essential tool for network resource access and data sharing in enterprise environments. *Table 10.1* shows the significant versions of SMBs along with their key features and advancements across the timeline.

Year	Version	Key Features and Developments
1983	SMB 1.0	Developed by Barry Feigenbaum at IBM; supported by Microsoft for LAN Manager; operated over NetBIOS frames.
1990	SMB 1.0	Microsoft integrates SMB into LAN Manager for OS/2.
1992	SMB 1.0	SMB continued to evolve with Windows for Workgroups, which initially used flawed DES-based authentication.
1996	CIFS	Renamed **Common Internet File System** (**CIFS**); added features such as symbolic/hard links, large file support, and experimental TCP.
2006	SMB 2.0	Introduced with Windows Vista and Windows Server 2008, reduced chattiness, support for pipelining, and durable file handles.
2009	SMB 2.1	Introduced with Windows 7 and Server 2008 R2; added opportunistic locking improvements.

Year	Version	Key Features and Developments
2012	SMB 3.0	Released with Windows 8 and Server 2012; added SMB Direct, SMB Multichannel, Transparent Failover, and AES-based encryption.
2013	SMB 1.0 Deprecated	Microsoft deprecated SMB 1.0 due to security and performance issues.
2013	SMB 3.0.2	Introduced with Windows 8.1 and Server 2012 R2; improved security; allowed optional disabling of SMB 1.0.
2016	SMB 3.1.1	Introduced with Windows 10 and Server 2016; added AES-128 GCM encryption and pre-authentication integrity with SHA-512.

Table 10.1 – SMBs timeline (source – Wikipedia)

Simultaneously, QUIC emerged as a groundbreaking protocol developed by Google in 2013. Created to overcome the limitations of traditional TCP, QUIC leverages UDP to reduce latency and accelerate connection times, making it ideal for the high-performance demands of modern web applications. QUIC was designed to minimize buffering, improve data flow efficiency, and enhance security with built-in encryption. Its formal standardization by the **Internet Engineering Task Force (IETF)** in 2021 further cemented its role as a key innovation in the realm of network protocols. *Table 10.2* shows the QUIC timeline based on the adoption details provided:

Year	Event	Details
2012	Google Chrome development	QUIC code experimentally developed in Google Chrome.
August 2013	Chromium version 29	QUIC was announced as part of the Chromium 29 release.
July 2016	Akamai support	Akamai Technologies has started supporting QUIC.
July 2017	LiteSpeed support	LiteSpeed Technologies officially supports QUIC in its load balancer and web server products.
September 2019	cURL 7.66 release	cURL 7.66 adds support for HTTP/3 and QUIC.
October 2019	QUIC usage statistics	88.6% of QUIC websites use LiteSpeed, and 10.8% use Nginx.
April 2020	Safari Technology Preview 104	Apple adds experimental QUIC support in WebKit through Safari Technology Preview 104.
October 2020	Facebook migration	Facebook migrates 75% of its internet traffic, including apps such as Instagram, to QUIC.
March 2021	QUIC web adoption	5% of all websites use QUIC.
May 2021	Firefox support	Firefox adds QUIC support.

Year	Event	Details
March 2022	HAProxy support	HAProxy load balancer adds experimental QUIC support.
2022	Windows Server 2022 support	Microsoft Windows Server 2022 supports HTTP/3 and SMB over QUIC via MsQuic.
March 2023	HAProxy production support	HAProxy declares QUIC support as production-ready.
April 2023	QUIC web adoption	8.9% of all websites use QUIC.

Table 10.2 – QUIC timeline (source – Wikipedia)

The convergence of SMB and QUIC in Windows Server 2025 represents a strategic alignment of their strengths, addressing the ever-increasing need for speed, security, and network resilience. This integration not only enhances performance but also responds to the shifting landscape of enterprise IT, where seamless and secure communication is paramount. The historical progression of both SMB and QUIC highlights their continuous adaptation to emerging challenges and opportunities, ultimately paving the way for this powerful combination in Windows Server 2025.

By integrating SMB's robust file-sharing capabilities with QUIC's high-performance, low-latency networking, Windows Server 2025 offers IT professionals an advanced solution for optimizing network operations and enhancing system resilience. This evolution underscores the relentless innovation in network communication, providing a cutting-edge solution that meets the dynamic requirements of modern digital infrastructures.

> **Note**
> Understanding the historical evolution of SMB and QUIC is crucial for ensuring backward compatibility. Before upgrading to SMB over QUIC, ensure that legacy systems are appropriately handled to prevent compatibility issues that could disrupt file-sharing services.

With a solid grasp of the historical context, we can now shift our focus to the tangible advantages that arise from the fusion of these two protocols. By analyzing the key benefits of implementing SMB over QUIC, we uncover the significant improvements in performance, security, and reliability that IT professionals can leverage in their network infrastructures.

Key benefits of implementing SMB over QUIC

Implementing SMB over QUIC in Windows Server 2025 offers a unique set of advantages that cater to the dynamic needs of today's enterprises:

- **Significant Boost in Data Transfer Speeds:** The most compelling benefit is the significant boost in **data transfer speeds,** made possible by QUIC's use of UDP for faster connection setups and lower latency. This results in swift and efficient file transfers, which are particularly beneficial for scenarios involving large data volumes or real-time access where speed is crucial.

- **Enhanced Security:** The built-in encryption of QUIC, combined with SMB's established security features, forms a robust defense against unauthorized access and breaches. All data transferred via SMB over QUIC is automatically encrypted, providing a strong safeguard for sensitive enterprise information and instilling confidence in the network's security.

- **Improved Network Reliability:** Thanks to features such as multiplexing and advanced congestion control, QUIC performs well over unstable or unreliable networks and ensures smooth and consistent data transfers even under challenging network conditions. That is particularly valuable for remote or mobile users who frequently encounter variable network quality. IT professionals can guarantee uninterrupted access to resources, regardless of the user's location or connection stability.

- **Enhanced User Experience:** Features such as forward error correction and reduced head-of-line blocking help minimize buffering and optimize data flow, ensuring smoother and more responsive interactions. This efficiency boosts productivity by reducing data wait times, allowing users to focus more on their primary tasks.

- **Simplicity in Deployment:** The streamlined integration process minimizes downtime, enabling IT administrators to configure and manage the setup using familiar tools quickly. This ease of implementation reduces the learning curve, allowing organizations to take advantage of the protocol's features with minimal disruption to daily operations.

> **Note**
>
> Maximizing the benefits of SMB over QUIC requires proper network and hardware support. Ensure that your infrastructure is optimized to leverage reduced latency and improved security features inherent to the QUIC protocol.

This section has provided a comprehensive understanding of SMB over QUIC, from its foundational concepts to its evolutionary background and the key benefits it offers. As IT professionals navigate the challenges of modern networking, the adoption of SMB over QUIC emerges as a crucial tool to optimize operations, enhance security, and maintain reliable connectivity. Next, we will explore *Understanding security considerations and encryption protocols*, where the focus will shift to examining how SMB over QUIC strengthens data protection and ensures compliance with stringent security standards through advanced encryption protocols. That is essential in safeguarding sensitive information within enterprise environments.

Understanding security considerations and encryption protocols

In today's rapidly evolving digital security landscape, IT professionals must have a deep understanding of encryption protocols and security strategies to protect their organizations' data effectively. The introduction of SMB over QUIC in Windows Server 2025 adds an advanced layer of security specifically designed to address the modern challenges of safeguarding sensitive information during transmission. This section provides a detailed exploration of the critical security considerations and encryption protocols that underpin the use of SMB over QUIC, offering IT administrators a comprehensive view of the security mechanisms involved. At the core of this discussion is the robust encryption framework embedded within SMB over QUIC, which ensures that all transmitted data is both confidential and protected from tampering. By employing cutting-edge cryptographic techniques, these protocols offer a strong defense against cyber threats and unauthorized access, elevating the reliability and security of the network infrastructure. These encryption measures ensure that data remains secure even in environments with varying levels of network reliability.

Beyond the encryption capabilities, this section also focuses on the practical aspect of configuring security settings. It offers guidance for administrators on how to fine-tune their systems to adhere to stringent data protection standards. Through an in-depth analysis of best practices, IT professionals will gain the necessary knowledge to implement, maintain, and optimize secure networking environments. This proactive approach to network security is vital in preventing data breaches and ensuring long-term resilience. As businesses undergo digital transformation and expand their networks, robust security protocols are more critical than ever. A thorough understanding of the security features embedded in SMB over QUIC will enable IT professionals to maintain the confidentiality, integrity, and availability of their organizational data. That, in turn, helps secure a competitive advantage in a world that is increasingly driven by digital connectivity and data exchange.

Public key infrastructure (PKI)

Public key infrastructure (**PKI**) is a critical framework that supports secure communication across digital networks by using a combination of cryptography, authentication, and digital certificates. In Windows Server environments, PKI forms the backbone of secure data exchange, ensuring that transmitted data remains confidential and unaltered. This subsection explores the essential components of PKI, its functions, and the role it plays in protecting network transactions. The key elements of PKI are as follows:

Certificates and digital identities

A **digital certificate** serves as an online credential, proving the identity of the entity (user, device, or server) involved in a communication. A trusted authority issues certificates that are essential for secure connections, enabling users to verify the legitimacy of entities within a network.

Certificate authority (CA)

The **certificate authority** (**CA**) is a trusted organization or server that validates and issues digital certificates. As the backbone of PKI, the CA performs rigorous checks to ensure that the requester is genuine. In Windows Server 2025, **Active Directory Certificate Services** (**AD CS**) is commonly used to establish an internal CA, providing the organization with more control over certificate issuance and management.

Registration authority (RA)

Working closely with the CA, the **registration authority** (**RA**) acts as a gateway, verifying user or device credentials before a certificate is issued. It provides an additional layer of identity validation, which is especially useful in more extensive, distributed environments. The RA forwards verified requests to the CA, reducing risk by separating the validation and issuance functions.

Public and private keys

PKI utilizes asymmetric encryption, which involves a pair of keys—public and private, as shown in *Figure 10.2*. The public key is accessible to anyone, while the owner securely holds the private key. Only the other key can decrypt data when it is encrypted with one key. This ensures that only the intended recipient, possessing the corresponding private key, can decrypt data encrypted with the public key.

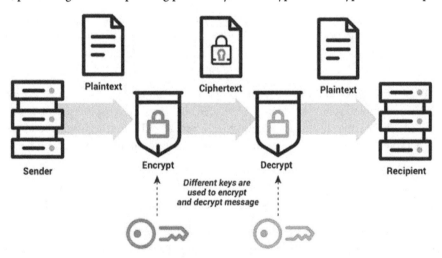

Figure 10.2 – Public and Private keys in PKI (source – Sectigo)

Certificate revocation list (CRL) and Online Certificate Status Protocol (OCSP)

Certificates can be revoked if compromised, expired, or no longer needed. The **certificate revocation list** (**CRL**) is a list of such certificates, allowing entities to check certificate validity before establishing secure communications. The **Online Certificate Status Protocol** (**OCSP**), an alternative to the CRL, is a protocol that provides real-time certificate status, ensuring that revoked or expired certificates are promptly detected.

With a foundational understanding of PKI in place, let us now explore the mechanics of how PKI operates in practice, from authentication to non-repudiation to secure data encryption and authentication processes.

How PKI secures network communications

As network security demands evolve, PKI has become essential for establishing trust and securing digital interactions. By leveraging cryptographic keys and digital certificates, PKI ensures that network communications within Windows Server environments are authenticated, confidential, and tamper-resistant. This foundational technology underpins many security protocols, including SMB over QUIC, by enabling secure, reliable data exchanges across distributed networks.

PKI enhances security across Windows Server networks in the following ways:

- **Authentication**: PKI authenticates users and devices by issuing certificates, ensuring that only authorized entities can access network resources. Certificates serve as secure identifiers, verified through the CA. In SMB over QUIC setups, PKI confirms the legitimacy of clients and servers, providing an added layer of defense against spoofing and unauthorized access.

- **Data Integrity**: Digital signatures within PKI help ensure that transmitted data remains unaltered. When data is signed with a private key, any tampering in transit invalidates the signature, alerting the receiver to possible alterations. This integrity check is essential in enterprise environments, where maintaining the consistency of sensitive data is crucial.

- **Encryption and Confidentiality**: PKI encrypts data, protecting it from unauthorized access. By using public and private key pairs, PKI secures information during transit, making it unreadable to external parties. Protocols such as QUIC leverage PKI-based certificates to establish secure, encrypted connections, safeguarding data from eavesdropping and interception.

- **Non-Repudiation**: Digital signatures provided by PKI offer non-repudiation, ensuring that the sender cannot deny their involvement in sending the data. This feature is critical for secure transactions and compliance with regulatory standards, as it creates a reliable audit trail.

Imagine a user sitting at their computer, looking to visit a secure website. As they initiate a new connection, their computer acts as the client, reaching out to the web server. The web server, in turn, sends over its SSL/TLS certificate, a kind of digital ID that proves its identity. Upon receiving this certificate, the client doesn't just accept it unquestioningly—instead, it verifies the web server's identity to ensure an imposter is not tricking it. Once the verification is complete, both the client and the server exchange critical information, using this trust to establish a secure, encrypted connection. From that moment on, all data exchanged between the client and the web server is transmitted securely over HTTPS, safeguarding it from interception or alteration of data. This seamless process of verifying and securing the connection, as illustrated in *Figure 10.3*, is made possible through PKI, which helps ensure the authenticity and confidentiality of the data transmitted between both parties.

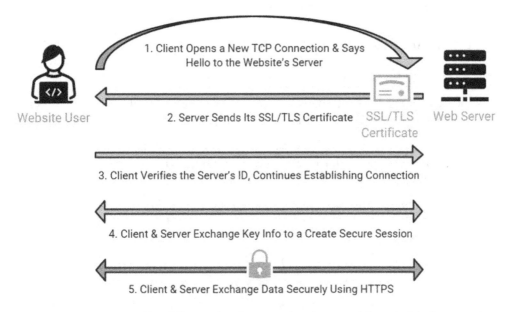

1. Client Opens a New TCP Connection & Says Hello to the Website's Server

Website User

2. Server Sends Its SSL/TLS Certificate   SSL/TLS Certificate   Web Server

3. Client Verifies the Server's ID, Continues Establishing Connection

4. Client & Server Exchange Key Info to a Create Secure Session

5. Client & Server Exchange Data Securely Using HTTPS

Figure 10.3 – How PKI secures web connections (source – Infosec Insights)

Having established a foundational understanding of PKI's role in securing network communications, we will now move forward to explore the practical aspects of Implementing PKI in Windows Server 2025.

Implementing PKI in Windows Server 2025

Establishing a robust PKI within Windows Server 2025 is a key step toward securing network communications and ensuring identity management for devices, users, and services. To deploy PKI, administrators typically utilize AD CS, which enables the organization to run its own internal CA for issuing and managing certificates. With AD CS, organizations can create a scalable PKI solution tailored to their network security requirements.

The key steps in implementing PKI in Windows Server 2025 include the following:

- **Configuring the CA and RA**: Administrators set up the CA and RA to handle certificate requests, verify identities, and manage digital certificates for clients, devices, and servers within the network.

- **Issuing Certificates:** Certificates are issued to clients, servers, and devices based on specific organizational policies. These certificates ensure that only authenticated entities can access network resources and establish secure communications.

- **Setting up the CRL and OCSP**: The CRL and OCSP are essential components in ensuring certificate validity. These mechanisms allow administrators to track expired or compromised certificates and maintain up-to-date status checks.

Best practices for PKI management

Once PKI is deployed, following best practices is essential to ensure ongoing security and efficiency:

- **Regularly Update Certificates**: Certificates should be periodically updated or replaced before expiration to avoid lapses in security.

- **Secure Private Keys**: To prevent unauthorized access, private keys should be stored in secure environments, such as **hardware security modules** (**HSMs**), which provide high levels of protection.

- **Monitor for Compromise**: Routine monitoring for potential compromise of certificates is essential. Any exposed or compromised certificates should be revoked immediately to maintain the integrity of the PKI.

Successfully implementing PKI in Windows Server 2025 helps bolster the security of network communications, including SMB over QUIC, by providing a reliable and scalable identity management framework. The next step in securing SMB over QUIC is to explore the encryption mechanisms in SMB over QUIC, which utilize the PKI infrastructure for enhanced security in data transmission.

Encryption mechanisms in SMB over QUIC

The encryption mechanisms in SMB over QUIC are not just designed. They are engineered to deliver a robust level of security. This robustness ensures both the confidentiality and integrity of data as it traverses the network. Central to these mechanisms is the application of advanced **cryptographic protocols** that provide end-to-end encryption for data packets, effectively preventing unauthorized access and manipulation. This level of security should instill confidence in the integrity of your network.

One of the key components of this security framework is QUIC's built-in **TLS 1.3 protocol**, illustrated in *Figure 10.4*, which offers cutting-edge cryptographic protection. This protocol ensures that all data transmitted over the network is encrypted, utilizing forward secrecy and authenticated encryption. Forward secrecy protects past communications, even if a session key is compromised, while authenticated encryption guarantees that the data is both encrypted and verified, preventing tampering or forgery during transmission.

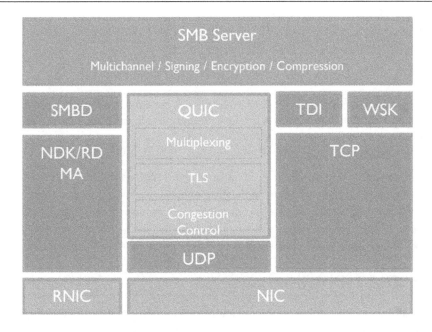

Figure 10.4 – Transport methods for SMB (source – 4SySOps)

In addition to the security features offered by QUIC, SMB adds a further layer of encryption tailored for secure file sharing. Utilizing the **Advanced Encryption Standard** (**AES**) with **128-bit or 256-bit encryption keys**, SMB safeguards data both in transit and at rest. These encryption keys are dynamically managed, minimizing the risk of exposure and further enhancing data security. The combination of QUIC's encryption with SMB's file-sharing encryption forms a robust double-layer security structure, significantly reducing the risk of breaches.

As an IT professional, your role in configuring SMB over QUIC is not just important; it's crucial. You have the power to implement mutual authentication, which requires both the client and server to validate each other's identities before a connection is established. That is typically achieved through certificates issued by trusted CAs, ensuring that only legitimate entities are involved in the communication process and strengthening the network's trustworthiness. Your actions in this process are key to the network's security.

Moreover, Windows Server 2025 simplifies the process of configuring these encryption mechanisms by integrating them seamlessly into its architecture. Administrators can leverage **group policies** and **PowerShell cmdlets** to automate the deployment of security configurations, ensuring that encryption is consistently enforced across the network. That not only bolsters security but also eases the administrative burden, allowing IT professionals to streamline network management while focusing on other critical tasks.

For IT professionals, a solid grasp of these encryption protocols is essential for defending organizational data against evolving cyber threats. By implementing the encryption capabilities offered by SMB over

QUIC, enterprises can ensure a secure and resilient network infrastructure that is aligned with the highest standards of data protection and compliance.

> **Note**
>
> When configuring encryption for SMB over QUIC, ensure that **TLS 1.3** is enabled to utilize end-to-end encryption fully. Failure to use the recommended encryption standards may expose your environment to security vulnerabilities.

While understanding the encryption mechanisms behind SMB over QUIC is fundamental, securing your network goes beyond just knowing the protocols. The next step involves correctly configuring security settings to maximize the effectiveness of these encryption mechanisms. Proper configuration ensures that the theoretical advantages of encryption are fully realized in practical scenarios, providing a fortified defense against cyber threats.

Configuring security settings

Adequate digital security relies on the meticulous configuration of security settings to protect an organization's data. In the context of configuring SMB over QUIC in Windows Server 2025, IT professionals must follow a systematic approach to ensure optimal protection. Central to this process is a robust certificate management system; trusted CAs issue certificates that are essential for mutual authentication. Administrators must ensure their certificate infrastructure is secure, regularly updated, and compliant with industry standards. That includes periodic certificate renewals and the prompt revocation of any compromised certificates to preserve network integrity and trustworthiness.

In addition, careful configuration of encryption protocols is crucial. SMB over QUIC employs AES (as shown in *Figure 10.5*) with 128-bit or 256-bit keys. IT professionals should mandate the use of these strong encryption algorithms to safeguard data both at rest and during transit. Routine audits and reviews of encryption settings help to ensure that all communications remain securely encrypted, thereby closing any potential vulnerabilities within the network.

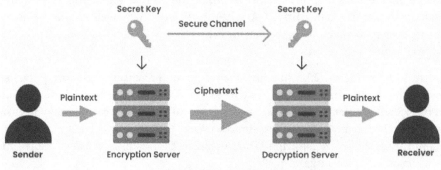

Figure 10.5 – How AES works (source – Cheap SSL Web)

Implementing stringent access controls is another key component in bolstering network security. **Role-based access control** (**RBAC**) should be employed to restrict user and device permissions, thereby minimizing the risk of unauthorized access. IT administrators should periodically review and update access control policies to keep pace with evolving security threats. Automated tools, such as group policies and PowerShell scripts, play a crucial role in applying security settings consistently and efficiently across the network. These tools help reduce human error, enforce compliance, and allow IT professionals to concentrate on more strategic tasks.

Continuous monitoring and logging are essential for maintaining a secure network environment. Comprehensive logging mechanisms enable administrators to track and analyze SMB over QUIC traffic, providing vital visibility for detecting anomalies and potential security incidents. Secure storage and regular review of logs ensure that network security is continually assessed and updated.

Keeping abreast of the latest security threats and best practices is also critical. The cybersecurity landscape is ever-evolving, with new vulnerabilities and attack vectors emerging regularly. IT professionals should engage in ongoing education, attend industry conferences, and subscribe to security advisories to stay informed and enhance their organization's security posture.

By meticulously configuring security settings, utilizing automation tools, and maintaining vigilant monitoring practices, IT professionals can ensure that their deployment of SMB over QUIC in Windows Server 2025 is robust against current cyber threats. This proactive strategy not only secures organizational data but also builds confidence in the network's resilience against sophisticated challenges.

> **Note**
> After configuring SMB over QUIC, always validate your security settings by conducting regular audits. Improperly configured settings may lead to data breaches or unauthorized access, potentially compromising sensitive information.

Following the exploration of encryption mechanisms, we moved on to configuring security settings. This subsection provided a comprehensive overview of how to implement and manage security settings to enhance the protection of SMBs over QUIC. Emphasis was placed on the importance of certificate management, enforcing strong encryption protocols, and maintaining strict access controls. Through meticulous configuration and regular monitoring, IT professionals can fortify their network's defenses against evolving threats.

Best practices for security

To achieve optimal security when configuring SMB over QUIC in Windows Server 2025, IT professionals should follow a comprehensive set of best practices, combining strategic foresight with meticulous implementation:

- **Establish a Strong Certificate Management System:** Mutual authentication depends on certificates issued by trusted CAs. It is essential to maintain a secure and up-to-date certificate infrastructure, regularly renew certificates, and revoke any that may be compromised. That ensures that the integrity and trust of the network remain intact and compliant with industry standards.

- **Careful Configuration of Encryption Protocols:** SMB over QUIC uses robust encryption standards, such as AES with 128-bit or 256-bit keys, to secure data during transmission and while at rest. IT administrators should enforce these encryption algorithms across the network and conduct routine audits to ensure there are no vulnerabilities or unencrypted communications that could expose sensitive information.

- **Implement Strict Access Controls:** Role-based Access Control should be used to manage user and device permissions, minimizing the risk of unauthorized access. That ensures that only authenticated and authorized entities can engage in SMB over QUIC operations. Administrators should regularly review and adjust these access control policies to meet evolving security requirements.

- **Utilize Automation Tools:** The use of automation tools such as group policies and PowerShell scripts is another best practice. These tools streamline the deployment of security configurations across the network, reducing manual errors and ensuring consistent application of security policies. By automating these processes, IT professionals can enhance operational efficiency and focus on broader security initiatives.

- **Monitoring and Logging:** Comprehensive logging mechanisms provide visibility into all SMBs over QUIC activity, enabling administrators to detect unusual patterns, identify potential security incidents, and conduct post-event analysis. To maintain effective oversight, logs should be securely stored, regularly reviewed, and monitored for real-time insights into network behavior.

- **Stay Informed About Emerging Cyber Threats:** As the threat landscape evolves, IT professionals must keep pace by engaging in continuous learning, attending industry events, and monitoring security advisories. This proactive approach helps organizations remain resilient against new vulnerabilities and reinforces their security frameworks.

By rigorously applying these best practices, IT professionals can significantly strengthen the security of their networks and ensure that SMB over QUIC operates in a safe, resilient, and compliant manner. These measures not only protect critical data but also enhance trust in the network's ability to withstand the sophisticated security challenges of the digital age.

> **Note**
>
> Implementing **multi-factor authentication** (**MFA**) and strict access controls is essential to securing SMBs over QUIC. Review and update your security practices regularly to stay compliant with industry standards and reduce the risk of unauthorized access.

In this subsection, we discussed best practices for ensuring robust security in SMB over QUIC deployments. These included strategies for maintaining up-to-date security measures, leveraging automation tools for consistency, and engaging in continuous monitoring and education. Adhering to these best practices helps sustain a secure network environment and adapt to new security challenges. As we transition to the following section, we shift our focus from securing SMB over QUIC to enhancing its performance. In the forthcoming section, we will explore various strategies and techniques for optimizing SMB over QUIC performance. We will examine how to fine-tune configurations, monitor performance metrics, and address any potential bottlenecks to ensure that your SMB over QUIC deployment operates efficiently and effectively.

Optimizing SMB over QUIC performance

Enhancing the performance of SMB over QUIC is crucial for IT professionals aiming to maximize the efficiency and dependability of their network systems. With organizations increasingly adopting this advanced communication protocol, it is essential to fine-tune various deployment aspects to achieve peak performance. This section provides a comprehensive examination of key considerations and strategies required for optimizing SMB over QUIC in Windows Server 2025. By carefully configuring network settings, choosing suitable hardware, and engaging in ongoing performance tuning and monitoring, IT teams can significantly improve the throughput, responsiveness, and overall resilience of their SMB over QUIC setups. This proactive approach not only enhances user experience but also strengthens the network's ability to manage large data transfers, minimize latency, and ensure smooth operations within dynamic IT environments. Through an in-depth analysis of network configuration, hardware selection, and performance management, this section aims to provide IT professionals with the necessary insights and tools to optimize their SMB over QUIC deployments effectively.

Network configuration for optimal performance

To attain optimal performance for SMB over QUIC in Windows Server 2025, IT professionals must employ a thorough and multifaceted approach to network configuration. The process begins with ensuring that the network infrastructure is robust enough to support high-speed data transfers. That involves upgrading network hardware, such as routers and switches, to the latest standards and verifying that network interfaces can handle gigabit or higher speeds. Additionally, proper configuration of **quality of service (QoS)** settings is crucial. QoS allows for the prioritization of SMB over QUIC traffic over other types of network traffic, thereby reducing latency and improving responsiveness. For large enterprises, while upgrading to the latest version may not always be feasible, the minimum requirement for implementing QUIC is ensuring that the network infrastructure supports UDP-based protocols and that the OSs and applications are compatible with QUIC. This includes using Windows Server 2022 or the latest one, Windows Server 2025, and ensuring appropriate networking configurations are in place to handle QUIC's low-latency, secure connections.

Optimizing **TCP settings** is another critical component. Adjusting TCP window sizes and enabling TCP offloading can significantly enhance data throughput and alleviate congestion, leading to more efficient data transmission. Moreover, advanced techniques such as network segmentation should be employed. By segmenting the network, SMB over QUIC traffic can be isolated from other types of traffic, as depicted in *Figure 10.6*, which helps protect it from potential interference and security threats.

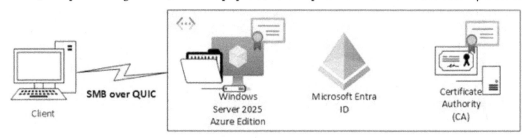

Figure 10.6 – Exposing all data in Azure files via SMB over QUIC (source – Visuality Systems)

Explicit congestion notification (**ECN**) should also be enabled and configured. ECN helps reduce packet loss by allowing the network to signal congestion without dropping packets, ensuring smoother data flow during peak usage times. In addition, leveraging modern load balancing solutions can distribute the network load more evenly across multiple servers or paths, preventing any single point from becoming a bottleneck and thus improving overall network efficiency.

Incorporating redundancy and failover strategies is also advisable. Implementing multiple network paths and backup systems can provide resilience and ensure continuous availability even in the event of hardware failures or unexpected disruptions. Regular performance monitoring and tuning are essential to adapt to changing network conditions and evolving usage patterns.

By addressing these critical aspects—upgrading hardware, configuring QoS, optimizing TCP settings, segmenting the network, enabling ECN, and employing load balancing and redundancy—IT professionals can establish a high-performance network environment. This comprehensive approach maximizes the potential of SMB over QUIC, ensuring seamless, efficient, and reliable data transfer throughout the organization.

> **Note**
> Ensure that your network is configured with proper QoS settings to prioritize SMB over QUIC traffic. Failure to optimize network configurations may result in latency and degraded performance during peak usage.

After establishing a solid foundation in network configuration, the next critical step is to consider the hardware components that underpin SMB over QUIC performance. In the following subsection, we will examine how the right hardware choices and configurations can further enhance network efficiency and reliability.

Hardware considerations

Optimizing the performance of SMB over QUIC in Windows Server 2025 requires a careful evaluation and strategic enhancement of the network's hardware components. A critical first step is upgrading network interfaces to support gigabit or higher speeds. **Network Interface Cards** (**NICs**) with advanced offloading capabilities, such as **TCP Offload Engine** (**TOE**), can offload specific tasks from the CPU, reducing processor load and improving overall data throughput. Additionally, deploying high-performance routers and switches that adhere to the latest standards, such as 100 GbE or higher, ensures that the network infrastructure can efficiently manage increased data flow.

Storage subsystems are another key consideration. Replacing traditional HDDs with **solid-state drives** (**SSDs**) can yield significant improvements in both data access speed and reliability. **NVMe SSDs** offer superior performance with their **low latency** and high **input/output operations per second** (**IOPS**), which is crucial for handling large volumes of data. Equipping servers that host SMB services with sufficient CPU power and memory is equally important. Multi-core processors and ample RAM ensure that the computational demands of the encryption and decryption processes associated with QUIC are met without compromising performance.

Power redundancy and cooling systems are vital to ensuring continuous availability and preventing performance bottlenecks. **Uninterruptible power supplies** (**UPS**) and redundant power supplies safeguard hardware from power fluctuations, reducing the risk of downtime. Effective cooling solutions, such as advanced air conditioning or liquid cooling systems, are necessary to prevent overheating, which can lead to hardware throttling and degraded performance under heavy loads.

Regular hardware maintenance and timely upgrades are essential to maintain optimal performance levels. Keeping firmware and driver software updated resolves compatibility issues and ensures the hardware operates at peak capacity. By meticulously addressing these hardware considerations, IT professionals can establish a robust and reliable infrastructure that fully leverages the capabilities of SMB over QUIC, ensuring seamless, efficient, and resilient data transfer across the network.

In this subsection, we delve into the essential hardware considerations for optimizing SMB over QUIC. The selection and configuration of network hardware, including interface cards, routers, and switches, play a crucial role in ensuring that the network can handle high-speed data transfers and low-latency operations effectively. Upgrading to advanced hardware, such as gigabit or higher-speed interfaces and SSDs, can significantly impact overall performance. Ensuring that servers are equipped with adequate CPU resources and memory and maintaining power redundancy and cooling solutions are also vital for sustaining high performance.

> **Note**
>
> When optimizing hardware for SMB over QUIC, make sure that NICs, routers, and switches are updated with the latest firmware. Outdated hardware may limit performance and fail to support QUIC's high-speed data transfer capabilities fully.

With the hardware considerations addressed, the focus shifts to performance tuning and monitoring. In the following subsection, we will explore the techniques and tools necessary for fine-tuning performance and maintaining optimal operations. Regular performance tuning, combined with real-time monitoring and automated alerting systems, enables IT professionals to proactively manage and optimize SMB over QUIC deployments, ensuring that the system remains efficient and responsive.

Performance tuning and monitoring

In the rapidly evolving landscape of network infrastructure, performance tuning and monitoring are critical for ensuring that SMB over QUIC in Windows Server 2025 achieves optimal efficiency and reliability.

IT professionals must take a proactive, systematic approach to maintain peak performance. That begins with a comprehensive analysis of network performance metrics to identify potential bottlenecks. Utilizing advanced monitoring tools such as **Microsoft's Performance Monitor**, **Wireshark**, and **SolarWinds Network Performance Monitor** provides real-time insights into traffic patterns, latency, and data throughput (see *Figure 10.7*). These tools offer granular visibility, enabling administrators to detect and address performance issues before they escalate swiftly.

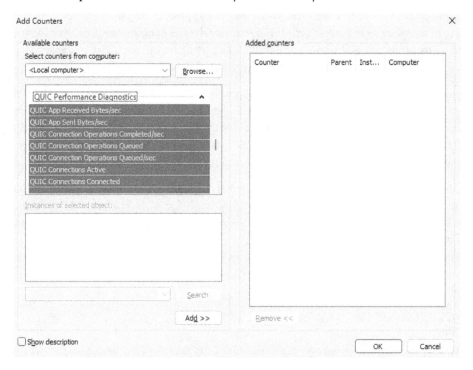

Figure 10.7 – QUIC counters in Performance Monitor

Equally essential is the ongoing process of **performance tuning**. IT teams should frequently assess and adjust **TCP settings**, including window sizes and congestion control mechanisms, such as ECN, to improve data flow and reduce latency. The TCP window sizes, in particular, determine the amount of data that can be sent before receiving an acknowledgment, helping to manage flow control. When an application is installed on a server, it may adjust the window size based on its specific network requirements, impacting data transmission efficiency. These adjustments significantly enhance the user experience by ensuring smoother and more efficient data transfers. Additionally, optimizing QoS settings prioritizes SMB over QUIC traffic over other network activities, ensuring maximum responsiveness and minimizing delays during critical operations.

Regular performance audits are crucial in maintaining network health and resilience. These audits should include stress testing under peak load conditions to assess the scalability and robustness of the infrastructure. By simulating high-traffic scenarios, IT professionals can identify and resolve potential performance issues before they impact users. Monitoring hardware performance, including CPU, memory, and storage, ensures that resources are not overburdened, which is essential for maintaining sustained high performance across the network.

Automated alerting systems also play a vital role in effective performance monitoring. Configuring real-time alerts for predefined performance thresholds enables IT teams to react promptly to deviations, reducing response time and minimizing the impact of performance degradation. Automation improves the efficiency of monitoring efforts while reducing the risk of human error, ensuring more consistent and accurate oversight of network operations.

Furthermore, continuous education and skill development are essential for IT teams to stay ahead in managing and optimizing SMB over QUIC deployments. Given the rapidly changing nature of network technologies, ongoing training, participation in industry conferences, and pursuing relevant certifications ensure that IT staff are well-equipped to handle the latest challenges and innovations in performance optimization.

A well-executed approach to performance tuning and monitoring is essential for maintaining the efficiency and stability of SMB over QUIC in Windows Server 2025. When IT professionals combine real-time performance analysis, ongoing tuning, regular system evaluations, and automated monitoring tools, they enable the network to operate at peak levels. Moreover, investing in continuous training ensures that teams are well prepared to adapt to the evolving demands of network infrastructure, resulting in a more robust, agile, and reliable environment capable of handling modern workloads with ease.

> **Note**
>
> Monitor network performance regularly and fine-tune TCP settings, such as adjusting buffer sizes and enabling ECN. Neglecting to monitor performance metrics may result in undetected bottlenecks and suboptimal performance.

By thoroughly addressing network configuration, hardware considerations, and performance tuning, IT professionals can optimize SMB over QUIC to achieve exceptional performance and reliability. Each of these areas contributes to creating a robust and efficient network environment capable of handling high data volumes and minimizing latency. Nevertheless, challenges can still arise even in well-optimized systems. In the next section, *Troubleshooting SMB over QUIC implementations*, we will cover common issues, diagnostic methods, and practical solutions to address problems that may occur during deployment and operation.

Troubleshooting SMB over QUIC implementations

Implementing SMB over QUIC in Windows Server 2025 involves navigating a range of complex technical challenges. Even with careful planning and deployment, issues are bound to arise, making effective troubleshooting crucial for sustaining peak performance and reliability. This section focuses on key practices and strategies IT professionals should adopt to diagnose and resolve common problems encountered by SMBs over QUIC. By recognizing frequent issues, applying specific solutions, and instituting preventative measures, IT teams can ensure the smooth functioning of their network infrastructure. This thorough approach helps minimize downtime, enhances the user experience, and strengthens the deployment against potential disruptions. Through systematic troubleshooting and ongoing refinement, organizations can fully leverage SMB over QUIC's capabilities, achieving robust data transfer and reliable network performance.

Identifying common issues

When deploying SMB over QUIC in Windows Server 2025, IT professionals often face a range of challenges that can disrupt network performance. Some common issues are as follows:

- **Connection instability**: This issue may present sporadic connectivity losses or frequent disconnections. This problem frequently arises from network misconfigurations or hardware incompatibilities. To alleviate these issues, it is crucial to verify that network devices are compatible with the latest QUIC protocol standards and that all configurations are thoroughly checked.

- **Performance degradation**: This is another frequent concern, often caused by inadequate network settings, insufficient bandwidth allocation, or overburdened hardware. IT teams should actively monitor network traffic and adjust QoS settings to prioritize SMB over QUIC traffic. Additionally, updating hardware components, such as NICs and routers, with the latest firmware can help prevent performance bottlenecks and improve throughput.

- **Security issues**: These also present significant challenges, particularly in environments with strict data protection requirements. Risks such as unauthorized access, data breaches, and encryption failures can jeopardize the integrity of SMB over QUIC implementations. To mitigate these risks, it is essential to implement robust encryption protocols, conduct regular security audits, and enforce stringent access controls to protect sensitive data and comply with industry standards.

- **Latency and high packet loss**: These are further complications that can hinder data transfer efficiency. These problems may result from network congestion, improper TCP parameter settings, or inadequate load balancing. Using advanced network monitoring tools to pinpoint congestion areas and fine-tuning TCP settings—such as adjusting window sizes and enabling ECN—can enhance data flow and reduce delays.

- **Compatibility issues** These occur between different software versions or network devices and can obstruct the successful deployment of SMB over QUIC. Ensuring that all network infrastructure components, including OSs, applications, and hardware, are compatible and updated regularly is vital for maintaining smooth operations. Continuous education and certification can also provide IT professionals with the latest skills and knowledge to address these challenges effectively.

By proactively identifying and resolving these common issues, IT teams can ensure a stable and high-performing SMB over QUIC deployment in Windows Server 2025, facilitating efficient and reliable data transfer across their network.

> **Note**
> Common issues, such as connection instability or high latency, can often be traced back to network misconfigurations or outdated firmware. Always begin troubleshooting by verifying network settings and ensuring compatibility with the latest QUIC standards.

In this subsection, we explored various common issues, such as connection instability, performance degradation, and security challenges, that IT professionals may face when implementing SMB over QUIC. Now, in the following subsection, we will shift our focus toward specific solutions and fixes. By leveraging tailored strategies, IT teams can address these challenges effectively, ensuring enhanced performance and network reliability.

Solutions and fixes

Addressing the challenges that arise during the implementation of SMB over QUIC in Windows Server 2025 demands a comprehensive and tailored approach:

- **Connection Instability:** Often caused by network misconfigurations or hardware incompatibilities, connection instability can be resolved by ensuring that all network devices are updated to support the latest QUIC protocol standards. That includes checking for firmware and driver updates on routers, switches, and Network Interface Cards (NICs). Conducting thorough configuration audits will help identify and correct any inconsistencies.

- **Latency and High Packet Loss:** These issues, which can significantly impair data transfer efficiency, require the deployment of advanced network monitoring tools. Tools such as SolarWinds Network Performance Monitor and Wireshark offer real-time insights into traffic patterns and congestion points. Fine-tuning TCP settings, such as adjusting window sizes and enabling ECN, can significantly improve data flow and reduce delays. Implementing QoS policies to prioritize SMB over QUIC traffic ensures that critical data transfers receive adequate bandwidth.

- **Security Concerns:** Especially in environments with stringent data protection requirements. IT professionals should implement robust encryption protocols, such as AES-256, illustrated in *Figure 10.8*, to protect data in transit. Regular security audits and compliance checks are essential to identify and address vulnerabilities. Employing strict access controls and multi-factor authentication can further safeguard against unauthorized access and enhance the security of the SMB over QUIC deployment.

Figure 10.8 – AES encryption ciphers

- **Performance Degradation:** Performance degradation, Often caused by suboptimal network settings or inadequate hardware resources, this issue managed through regular monitoring and optimization. IT teams should frequently review and adjust QoS settings to ensure sufficient bandwidth for SMB over QUIC traffic. Upgrading hardware components, including NICs, routers, and switches, to support higher speeds and advanced offloading capabilities can help alleviate bottlenecks. Additionally, ensuring servers are equipped with multi-core processors and ample memory will aid in handling the computational demands of encryption and decryption processes.

- **Compatibility Issues:** Compatibility issues between different software versions or network devices can hinder the deployment of SMB over QUIC. It is crucial to maintain an updated inventory of network infrastructure components and ensure compatibility with the latest software updates. Continuous education and certification programs for IT staff will provide them with the knowledge and skills needed to manage these challenges effectively.

- **Proactive Performance Tuning and Monitoring:** A proactive and systematic approach to performance tuning and monitoring is essential for optimizing SMB over QUIC. Advanced tools must be utilized to analyze network performance metrics, identify bottlenecks, and implement corrective measures. Regular performance audits, including stress testing under peak load conditions, will help assess the infrastructure's resilience and scalability. By simulating high-traffic scenarios, potential issues can be identified and addressed before they affect end-users.

By integrating detailed performance analysis, iterative tuning, regular audits, and ongoing professional development, IT professionals can effectively troubleshoot and optimize SMB over QUIC implementations. This comprehensive approach ensures a high-performance, resilient, and reliable network environment that meets the demands of modern digital infrastructure.

> **Note**
> When applying fixes to resolve SMB over QUIC issues, ensure that any changes made to network or security configurations are thoroughly tested in a controlled environment before applying them to the production network. That prevents unintended service disruptions.

In this subsection, we examined practical fixes and solutions to the issues identified earlier. However, to prevent these problems from recurring, proactive strategies are essential. In the upcoming subsection, we will explore a series of preventative measures designed to mitigate future risks, optimize performance, and fortify the security of SMB over QUIC deployments.

Preventative measures

Implementing preventative measures is crucial for maintaining the performance and reliability of SMB over QUIC in Windows Server 2025:

- **Regular Updates and Patches:** Ensuring that both software and firmware are up to date is vital for addressing security vulnerabilities and ensuring compatibility with the latest standards. Adhering to a structured update schedule aligned with the vendor's release cycle helps maintain a secure and efficient network environment.

- **Meticulous Network Configuration Management:**Utilizing configuration management tools to monitor and document changes across the network provides a clear view of network topology, facilitating the rapid identification and correction of misconfigurations. Routine configuration audits help enforce best practices and prevent configuration drift, which can lead to performance issues and security vulnerabilities.

- **Proactive Resource Allocation:** Allocating sufficient bandwidth to SMB over QUIC traffic through QoS policies, as depicted in *Figure 10.9*, helps prevent congestion and ensures that data flows are prioritized appropriately. Regularly reviewing and adjusting these policies based on actual network usage patterns allows for dynamic adaptation to changing demands, thus maintaining optimal performance.

Bandwith with no Quality of Service rules applied

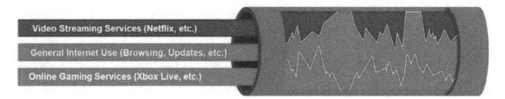

Bandwidth with Quality of Service rules applied

Figure 10.9 – Bandwidth with QOS versus bandwidth with no QoS (source – Cyber Hoot)

- **Robust Security Measures:** Employing strong encryption protocols such as AES-256, combined with MFA, strengthens defenses against unauthorized access and data breaches. Conducting regular security audits and vulnerability assessments helps identify and address potential threats. Additionally, implementing strict access controls and network segmentation further reduces the risk of security breaches by minimizing the attack surface.

- **Performance Monitoring and Automated Alerting Systems:** Advanced monitoring tools provide real-time insights into network performance, enabling IT professionals to detect anomalies and receive immediate alerts when predefined thresholds are exceeded. That allows for prompt intervention, preventing minor issues from escalating and ensuring continuous service delivery.

- **Ongoing Professional Development for IT Staff:** Participating in training programs, attending industry conferences, and obtaining certifications keeps the team updated on the latest advancements and best practices. This continuous learning equips IT professionals with the knowledge and skills to anticipate and address potential challenges, thereby enhancing the resilience and efficiency of SMB over QUIC deployments.

By incorporating these preventative measures, organizations can establish a robust framework that not only addresses potential issues proactively but also optimizes the performance and security of SMB over QUIC implementations in Windows Server 2025.

> **Note**
>
> To prevent future issues with SMB over QUIC, schedule regular updates for both hardware and software components. Additionally, perform frequent audits and stress tests to ensure that your network can handle increased traffic loads without compromising performance.

By systematically identifying issues, applying targeted solutions, and adopting preventative strategies, IT professionals can maintain a stable and efficient SMB in the QUIC environment. These steps not only improve current operations but also reduce the likelihood of future disruptions.

Understanding the relevance of SMB over QUIC in different network environments

SMB over QUIC offers significant advantages in improving network performance and security, especially in environments with remote work or hybrid cloud integration. However, its applicability can vary based on the size and complexity of your network. This subsection will help clarify when implementing SMB over QUIC is beneficial, explore its relevance to different network environments, and answer common questions regarding its implementation.

What is SMB over QUIC, and why is it important?

SMB over QUIC is an enhancement to the traditional SMB protocol, leveraging QUIC to improve network performance and security. By utilizing UDP, QUIC reduces latency and enhances security with end-to-end encryption, making it ideal for modern hybrid and remote network environments.

Is SMB over QUIC required for all network environments?

While SMB over QUIC provides significant benefits, it is not necessarily required for every network. It is particularly useful for organizations that rely on secure, high-performance file sharing over untrusted networks, such as remote offices, hybrid environments, or cloud-based systems. For smaller, internal-only networks or where security and performance concerns are minimal, traditional SMB (via TCP/IP) may suffice.

Does SMB over QUIC apply to small businesses or SMBs?

Small businesses or **small and medium-sized businesses (SMBs)** can benefit from SMB over QUIC, but its relevance largely depends on their network structure and future growth. If an SMB is growing and embracing remote work, hybrid cloud models, or accessing sensitive resources from outside the corporate network, SMB over QUIC can offer enhanced security and performance. However, for businesses with limited network complexity and a smaller user base, traditional SMBs may still meet their needs.

Do we need QoS to implement SMB over QUIC?

No, QoS is not a prerequisite for implementing SMB over QUIC. While QoS can enhance traffic prioritization on networks that support it, SMB over QUIC works independently of QoS configurations. If your network does not currently have QoS implemented, SMB over QUIC will still function, although the performance optimizations provided by QoS may not be leveraged.

When should I consider implementing SMB over QUIC?

Consider implementing SMB over QUIC when the following is the case:

- Your network operates across remote or hybrid environments with higher security needs
- You are dealing with sensitive data and need to ensure encrypted, secure file transfers over public or untrusted networks
- You need to optimize performance, reduce latency, and ensure more reliable file access over a VPN or similar remote setup
- Your organization is adopting cloud-based applications or services that require secure, efficient data access

Are there specific network conditions where SMB over QUIC becomes essential?

SMB over QUIC is particularly beneficial in the following scenarios:

- **Hybrid and Remote Work Environments**: When employees access company resources from various locations and need secure, fast connections
- **Cloud Integration**: For organizations integrating on-premises systems with cloud services, ensuring secure and optimized access to remote resources
- **Poor Network Conditions**: In situations with high-latency or unreliable networks, such as over VPNs, QUIC's UDP-based protocol can provide more reliable performance than traditional TCP-based SMBs

What size of organization benefits most from SMB over QUIC?

Larger enterprises and organizations with significant remote access requirements or multi-location offices tend to benefit most from SMB over QUIC due to its ability to enhance security and reduce latency. However, SMBs with increasing remote work needs or secure file-sharing requirements can also benefit from adopting this technology.

Can we implement SMB over QUIC if our network does not use QoS?

Yes, SMB over QUIC can still be implemented on networks without QoS. While QoS can help optimize traffic flow, it is not a requirement for SMB over QUIC. Organizations that do not have QoS implemented can still take advantage of SMB over QUIC's security and performance benefits without any issues.

How does SMB over QUIC compare to traditional SMB?

Traditional SMB relies on TCP, which can introduce higher latency and less efficient performance, particularly in remote and hybrid environments. SMB over QUIC, on the other hand, uses UDP for faster data transmission with lower latency, making it more suitable for modern networking scenarios, such as remote access, cloud services, and mobile workforces. It also provides built-in security with encryption and improved reliability across varied network conditions.

By addressing these common questions, readers can better understand when SMB over QUIC is relevant, how it benefits different organizational sizes, and the key considerations when implementing it within their network environment.

As we transition to the next section, we will engage in a practical exercise that demonstrates how to configure and enable SMB over QUIC in Windows Server 2025, solidifying your understanding of these core concepts through hands-on application.

Chapter exercise – configuring and enabling SMB over QUIC in Windows Server 2025

For this chapter's exercise, you will be guided through the steps to configure and enable SMB over QUIC in Windows Server 2025, a critical feature for secure and efficient file transfers in modern network environments. This exercise will begin with preparing your server by ensuring that all necessary updates are applied and that both SMB and QUIC protocols are available and properly configured. You will then proceed to install the required server roles and features, such as the SMB service and QUIC support, using Windows Admin Center or PowerShell. Detailed instructions will guide you through configuring the server firewall to allow QUIC traffic, as well as setting up certificates to secure the SMB over the QUIC connection.

Once the initial setup is complete, you will move on to configuring SMB share properties to utilize QUIC, adjusting network policies, and fine-tuning the settings to optimize performance and security. That includes defining encryption levels, access controls, and connection settings to ensure that the SMB over QUIC implementation meets your organization's specific security and operational requirements. After completing the configuration, you will validate the setup using PowerShell commands and network diagnostic tools to confirm that SMB over QUIC is operational and that file transfers are secure and efficient.

This hands-on exercise is vital for system administrators who seek to enhance their knowledge of secure file transfer protocols in hybrid or cloud environments. By following this step-by-step guide, you will gain practical skills in deploying and managing SMB over QUIC, enabling your infrastructure to leverage the full potential of this advanced protocol. You will also develop the ability to troubleshoot and optimize the system for maximum performance and security, ensuring that your network services remain robust and reliable in the face of evolving cybersecurity threats. Completing this exercise will not only solidify your understanding of SMB over QUIC but also prepare you to implement these best practices in real-world enterprise environments.

To start configuring and enabling SMB over QUIC in Windows Server 2025, follow these steps:

1. On a Windows 11 computer, download Windows Admin Center from `https://www.microsoft.com/en-us/evalcenter/download-windows-admin-center`. Then, run the installer and follow the on-screen instructions. Once installed, launch Windows Admin Center.

2. On **Windows Admin Center**, click **Settings** on the right side of the screen, and then, from the navigation on the left, click the **Register** option to register with Azure, as in *Figure 10.10*.

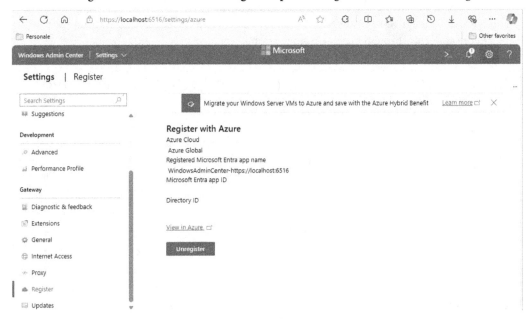

Figure 10.10 – Registering Windows Admin Center with Azure

3. On the horizontal navigation, click **Windows Admin Center** and then click **+ Add**. On **Add or Create resources**, click the **Add** button on the **Azure VMs** section. Make sure that you are running **Windows Server 2025 Data Center - Azure** on a server.

4. From within the Windows Admin Center, get connected to the **Windows Server 2025** instance and install a certificate to facilitate communication between the server and clients. This certificate can be from a public authority, or it can be created within your own CA.

5. On **Add an Azure VM**, click the **Sign in** button and then specify the entries for **Subscription**, **Resource Group**, **Virtual Machine**, and **IP address** accordingly, as illustrated in *Figure 10.11*. Next, click **Add**.

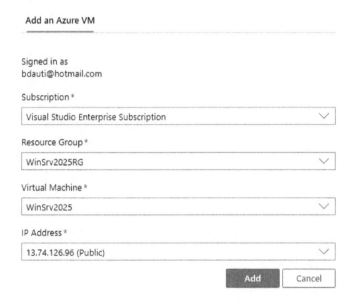

Figure 10.11 – Adding an Azure VM in Windows Admin Center

6. In **Windows Admin Center**, select the **Windows Server 2025** instance. On the vertical navigation, click **Settings** and then choose the **File shares (SMB server)** option in the **General** section.

7. On the right-hand side at the bottom, click **Configure** in the **SMB over QUIC is not configured** section, as depicted in *Figure 10.12*.

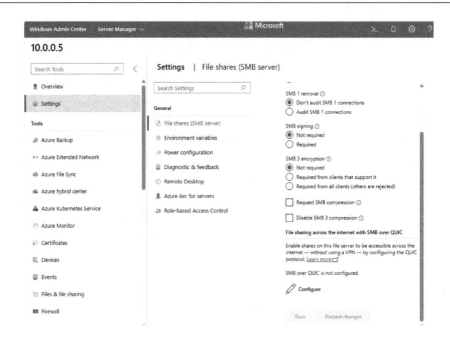

Figure 10.12 – Configuring SMB over QUIC

8. On **Configure file sharing across the Internet with SMB over QUIC**, select the TLS certificate to be used for secure communication and which port (default is UDP 443) to use for the **Kerberos service via Proxy** (**KDC Proxy**). Next, click **Enable**.

Once the configuration is complete, the service will be ready for use and marked as *available*. You may want to test the clients, but ensure that the file server is accessible over the internet through the DNS record specified in the digital certificate.

Summary

In this chapter, you gained an in-depth understanding of SMB over QUIC in Windows Server 2025, covering its evolution, key benefits, and how it enhances modern server environments. We explored the core principles of SMB and how QUIC improves network communication with enhanced security, reduced latency, and optimized data transfers. You also learned about essential security considerations, including encryption mechanisms, best practices for securing SMB over QUIC, and detailed steps for configuring security settings to ensure a robust and compliant network environment. The chapter further delved into optimizing SMB over QUIC performance, examining network configuration, hardware considerations, and strategies for performance tuning and ongoing monitoring to maintain reliability and efficiency. Troubleshooting techniques were addressed as well, highlighting common issues, their solutions, and preventative measures to ensure the long-term stability of your SMB over QUIC deployment. The chapter concluded with a hands-on exercise for configuring and enabling SMB over QUIC, reinforcing your practical understanding. Moving forward, the next chapter will focus on implementing new security enhancements in Windows Server 2025 to fortify your network infrastructure further.

Questions

1. **True or False**: SMB over QUIC in Windows Server 2025 enhances network security and performance.

2. **Fill in the Blank**: _____ is the protocol that improves data transfer security and reduces latency in Windows Server 2025.

3. **Multiple Choice**: Which of the following are the key benefits of implementing SMB over QUIC in a modern enterprise network? (*Choose all that apply.*)

   - Enhanced security

   - Lower latency

   - Optimized data transfers

   - All of the above

4. **Fill in the Blank**: QUIC is primarily used for enhancing _____ within network communication protocols.

5. **Multiple Choice**: Which of the following security configurations are recommended for securing SMB over QUIC? (*Choose all that apply.*)

   - Enabling TLS 1.3

   - Configuring firewall rules

   - Implementing MFA

   - All of the above

6. **True or False**: Properly configuring SMB over QUIC ensures compliance with modern cybersecurity standards.

7. **Fill in the Blank**: _____ is the hardware component most critical for ensuring optimal performance with SMB over QUIC.

8. **Multiple Choice**: Which of the following performance optimizations are vital for SMB over QUIC? (*Choose all that apply.*)

   - Network bandwidth tuning

   - Optimized CPU allocation

   - Data compression adjustments

   - All of the above

9. **Fill in the Blank**: Preventative maintenance for SMB over QUIC includes _____ to prevent issues before they occur.

10. **Multiple Choice**: Which of the following troubleshooting techniques helps resolve common issues in SMB over QUIC implementations? (*Choose all that apply.*)

    A. Verifying network configurations

    B. Checking encryption settings

    C. Monitoring server load

    D. All of the above

11. **Short Answer**: Discuss the importance of encryption mechanisms when implementing SMB over QUIC.

12. **Short Answer**: Explain the performance benefits of SMB over QUIC in high-traffic enterprise networks.

Further reading

- *SMB over QUIC*: https://learn.microsoft.com/en-us/windows-server/storage/file-server/smb-over-quic

- *Network Configuration for SMB over QUIC*: https://learn.microsoft.com/en-us/windows-server/networking/technologies/network-subsystem/net-sub-performance-top

- *Best Practices for Securing SMB*: https://learn.microsoft.com/en-us/windows/security/threat-protection/windows-firewall/best-practices-configuring

- *Troubleshooting SMB over QUIC*: https://learn.microsoft.com/en-us/windows-server/storage/file-server/troubleshoot-smb

- *Monitor Windows Server performance*: https://learn.microsoft.com/en-us/training/modules/monitor-windows-server-performance/

- *New-SelfSignedCertificate*: https://learn.microsoft.com/en-us/powershell/module/pki/new-selfsignedcertificate

11

Implementing New Security Enhancements in Windows Server 2025

This chapter covers the advanced security and authentication features in Windows Server 2025, focusing on improvements that enhance security, streamline authentication, and protect communication channels. It begins with an overview of new security enhancements, including better access controls, advanced threat detection, and automated response systems.

The chapter explores advancements in authentication and authorization, such as biometric authentication, Conditional Access policies, and OAuth 2.0. It also addresses securing communication channels with TLS, HTTPS, IPSec, and SSH and emphasizes best practices in patch management, audit logging, and regular security assessments. The chapter concludes with a hands-on exercise on configuring firewall rules, enabling TLS encryption, and setting up audit logs, reinforcing your practical skills and understanding of Windows Server 2025's security features. By the end of this chapter, you will be equipped to secure and manage your Windows Server 2025 environment effectively.

In this chapter, we're going to cover the following main topics:

- Overview of new security enhancements in Windows Server 2025
- Enhancing authentication and authorization mechanisms
- Securing communication channels with TLS and other protocols
- Implementing security best practices in Windows Server 2025
- Configuring firewall rules, enabling TLS encryption, and setting up audit logs

Technical requirements

To complete the exercises in this chapter, you will require the following hardware:

- A Windows 11 Pro PC equipped with a minimum of 16 GB of RAM, 1 TB of storage, and a stable internet connection

- A Windows Server 2025 Standard (Desktop Experience) virtual machine, designated as Virtual Machine 1, configured with an AD DS, featuring at least 8 GB of RAM, 100 GB of HDD space, and internet access

- An Azure account and subscription

This setup ensures that you have the necessary resources and configurations to perform all tasks effectively.

Overview of new security enhancements in Windows Server 2025

Windows Server 2025 introduces a robust suite of security enhancements to address the growing sophistication and frequency of cyber threats faced by modern IT infrastructures. These new features are designed to provide a multi-layered defense by enhancing access control mechanisms, utilizing advanced threat detection powered by machine learning and artificial intelligence, and incorporating highly efficient automated response systems. These tools work together to proactively identify, prevent, and mitigate potential security breaches before they can cause significant harm.

Additionally, the new security framework integrates seamlessly with existing security policies, making it easier for IT administrators to manage and enforce security best practices across their environments. By fortifying defenses against both internal and external threats, Windows Server 2025 ensures that businesses can maintain the integrity, confidentiality, and availability of critical systems and data, ultimately creating a more secure and resilient enterprise environment.

Understanding improved access controls

The **improved access controls** in Windows Server 2025 introduce a transformative approach to safeguarding IT environments. By providing administrators with highly granular control over user permissions, these advanced features enable precise management of who can access specific resources and what actions they can perform. Leveraging technologies such as **role-based access control** (**RBAC**) and **multi-factor authentication** (**MFA**), Windows Server 2025 creates a more secure and controlled framework for protecting sensitive data and critical systems:

- **RBAC** in Windows Server 2025, as illustrated in *Figure 11.1*, allows for the creation of finely tuned access policies that align closely with users' roles and responsibilities within the organization. This approach not only simplifies the often-complex task of permission management but also ensures that users are granted access to only the resources they need to perform their jobs, adhering to the principle of least privilege. Such granularity is critical in minimizing the attack surface, as it limits the number of individuals who can interact with high-value systems or sensitive information. A notable example of RBAC's effectiveness can be seen in a healthcare organization that implemented these controls to protect patient data. By assigning roles based on job functions, the organization ensured that only authorized personnel could access sensitive health records. When a phishing attack targeted several employees, the RBAC system limited access, preventing unauthorized users from reaching critical information, even when they attempted to use stolen credentials. This incident underscored the importance of implementing RBAC to mitigate potential breaches.

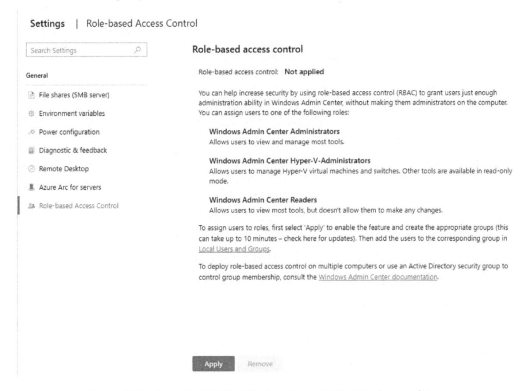

Figure 11.1 – Applying RBAC in Windows Server 2025 x64 – Azure edition

- **MFA**, illustrated in *Figure 11.2*, further strengthens the security landscape by requiring multiple layers of verification before granting access. By demanding a combination of something the user knows (such as a password), something they have (such as a mobile device), or something they are (biometrics), MFA adds a robust defense against unauthorized access. That drastically reduces the likelihood of credential-based attacks, ensuring that even if a password is compromised, additional security hurdles must be overcome. For instance, a financial institution that adopted MFA reported a significant decrease in fraud attempts. After implementing MFA, they thwarted an attack where an unauthorized user attempted to access client accounts using stolen login credentials. The added layer of security, requiring a one-time code sent to the user's mobile device, prevented access and protected sensitive financial information, illustrating how MFA can serve as a critical line of defense.

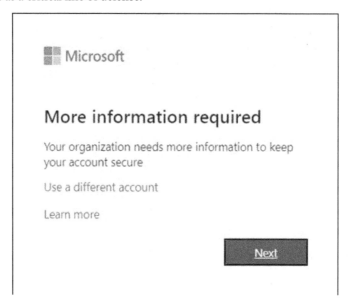

Figure 11.2 – MFA, an extra layer of security

In addition to these access controls, Windows Server 2025 introduces advanced auditing and monitoring tools that give administrators deeper visibility into user behavior. These capabilities allow the real-time tracking of access attempts and provide insights into potential security breaches or unusual activity patterns. With the ability to monitor access attempts across the environment, administrators can quickly detect and respond to suspicious activity, reducing the window of opportunity for an attacker to exploit vulnerabilities.

Moreover, the integration of automated threat detection within these controls ensures that any irregular or potentially dangerous behavior is flagged immediately, allowing for swift responses. This continuous surveillance enhances the overall security posture by enabling proactive mitigation of risks before they can cause significant damage. Administrators can set up alerts for unauthorized access attempts, identify recurring anomalies, and even adjust policies dynamically to respond to emerging threats.

The comprehensive nature of these access control enhancements in Windows Server 2025 not only increases the security of IT infrastructure but also streamlines the day-to-day administration of permissions and user management. These improvements empower organizations to defend against increasingly sophisticated cyberattacks while maintaining operational efficiency. By adopting this advanced access management framework, IT professionals can ensure that their systems remain resilient, secure, and adaptable in an ever-evolving threat landscape.

Configuring RBAC

RBAC allows administrators to define roles with specific permissions and assign these roles to users based on their job functions. This approach simplifies the management of user access rights and ensures that employees only have access to the resources necessary for their roles. Effective RBAC implementation reduces the risk of unauthorized access and enhances overall security. To effectively configure RBAC, follow these essential steps:

1. **Define roles**: Identify key roles in your organization, such as *HR Manager* or *IT Administrator*. Document these roles and their responsibilities to understand each role's access needs.

2. **Create role definitions**: Using the Windows Server management console, create and customize role definitions. For example, set permissions for *HR Manager* to access payroll data while restricting *IT Administrator* to system configurations and maintenance tasks.

3. **Assign users**: Allocate these roles to users based on their job functions. Ensure that each user has access only to the resources necessary for their role, enhancing both security and operational efficiency.

Practical exercise

To solidify your understanding of RBAC, you will perform a practical exercise that involves defining roles, setting permissions, and testing access controls. This exercise will help you apply the concepts learned and verify that RBAC is configured correctly in a test environment:

1. **Create roles**: Define roles for a fictional department in the Windows Server management console.

2. **Set permissions**: Assign specific permissions to each role, such as granting access to sensitive payroll information for *HR Manager* and system control for *IT Administrator*.

3. **Test access**: Assign these roles to users and verify that they can access only the designated resources. Ensure that unauthorized users cannot access restricted areas.

> **Note**
>
> When setting up RBAC, start with predefined roles to avoid common misconfigurations. You can always customize them as your system grows. For a detailed guide on configuring RBAC in Windows Server 2025, refer to the Microsoft documentation titled *Manage Role Based Access Control with Server Manager* available at `https://learn.microsoft.com/en-us/windows-server/networking/technologies/ipam/manage-role-based-access-control-with-server-manager`.

Setting up MFA

MFA enhances security by requiring users to provide multiple forms of verification before gaining access to systems. By setting up MFA, you add a layer of protection that significantly reduces the risk of unauthorized access, even if passwords are compromised. Configuring MFA involves enabling the feature, selecting verification methods, and testing the setup to ensure proper functionality. To effectively configure MFA, follow these essential steps:

1. **Access MFA settings**: Navigate to the security settings in the Windows Admin Center.

2. **Enable MFA**: Select the **Multi-Factor Authentication** option. Configure MFA to use multiple verification methods, such as SMS, email, or biometrics, to enhance security.

3. **Test configuration**: Have users log in and complete the multi-factor verification process to ensure MFA is functioning correctly.

> **Note**
>
> **Windows Admin Center (WAC)** does not directly manage MFA settings. To enable MFA within WAC, ensure the Windows Server is connected to Microsoft Entra ID. If not, join the server to Microsoft Entra ID to gain access to MFA features.

Practical exercise

This practical exercise will help you configure and test MFA, ensuring that it works as expected and provides the necessary level of security. By simulating logins and verification processes, you can verify that MFA is correctly implemented and functioning in your environment:

1. **Configure MFA**: Set up MFA for a test user account using various verification methods.

2. **Simulate login**: Perform a test login and complete the MFA process. Verify that the system requires and validates multiple authentication factors before granting access.

With access controls now solidified through RBAC and MFA, the focus shifts to protecting your infrastructure from emerging threats. In the following subsection, we will explore how Windows Server 2025's advanced threat detection mechanisms leverage artificial intelligence and machine learning to identify potential security risks proactively.

Overview of advanced threat detection

As cyber threats grow increasingly complex and persistent, effective threat detection mechanisms are vital to safeguarding IT environments. Windows Server 2025 takes significant steps to meet these challenges by integrating cutting-edge threat detection technologies that leverage **machine learning (ML)** and **artificial intelligence (AI)**. These advanced systems are designed to monitor network activity continuously, analyzing vast datasets to recognize patterns, anomalies, and subtle indicators that may signal malicious intent. This real-time analysis allows for early identification of potential threats, enabling IT teams to respond swiftly and prevent damage before it escalates.

In addition to real-time threat detection, Windows Server 2025 enhances investigative capabilities through **deep forensic analysis**. This feature allows IT professionals to thoroughly examine incidents post-breach, identifying root causes and improving the ability to prevent similar future attacks.

The platform also incorporates behavioral analytics, which monitors user and system behaviors for deviations from established norms. This technology is instrumental in detecting insider threats or compromised accounts that might otherwise go unnoticed. Additionally, the platform can integrate with external threat intelligence feeds, constantly updating its defenses with the latest knowledge of emerging vulnerabilities and attack vectors.

Windows Server 2025 doesn't stop at detection—it also introduces automated response mechanisms that are designed to neutralize threats as soon as they are detected. These preconfigured actions can automatically isolate affected systems, shut down unauthorized access, or deploy countermeasures, reducing the time between detection and response. This automation minimizes human intervention in critical moments, ensuring that threats are managed efficiently and with minimal impact on business operations.

To further enhance protection, Windows Server 2025's threat detection integrates seamlessly with existing security tools and frameworks, allowing IT teams to build a more cohesive security ecosystem. That means that organizations can layer Windows Server's capabilities with other security systems, creating a multi-faceted defense strategy that adapts to both known and unknown threats. By combining AI-driven analytics, real-time monitoring, and automated mitigation, the platform delivers an adaptive and resilient security solution that is capable of evolving with the rapidly shifting cyber threat landscape.

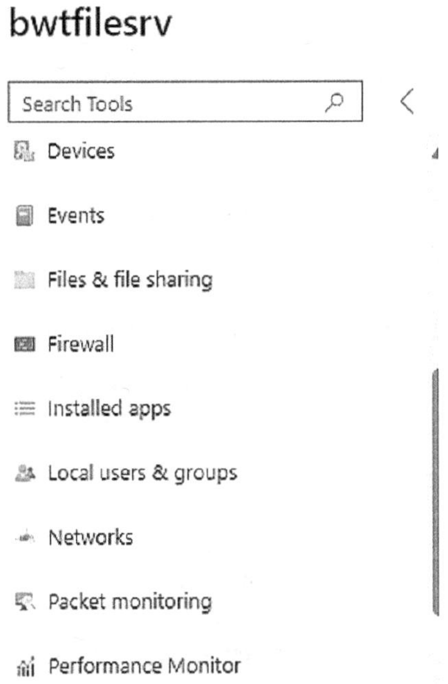

bwtfilesrv

Search Tools

- Devices
- Events
- Files & file sharing
- Firewall
- Installed apps
- Local users & groups
- Networks
- Packet monitoring
- Performance Monitor

Figure 11.3 Securing Windows Server 2025 x64 Azure edition with MDC

This comprehensive suite of advanced detection and response features not only strengthens the overall security architecture but also empowers IT teams to take a proactive role in safeguarding critical infrastructure. As the cyber threat landscape continues to evolve, these enhancements enable organizations to stay ahead of adversaries, ensuring that their IT environments remain secure, resilient, and protected against the most sophisticated attacks.

Configuring threat detection

Configuring threat detection involves setting up systems to monitor network activity and identify potential security threats. By defining monitoring parameters and integrating with threat intelligence feeds, you can ensure that your threat detection system remains up to date and responsive to new and emerging threats. To effectively configure threat detection, follow these essential steps:

1. **Activate threat detection**: Access the **Security Dashboard** in the WAC. Enable threat detection and specify the types of threats to monitor, such as unusual login patterns or unexpected data access.

2. **Set up monitoring parameters**: Define what constitutes unusual activity, such as login attempts from unfamiliar IP addresses or unexpected data access patterns.

3. **Integrate with threat intelligence**: Connect your threat detection system with external threat intelligence feeds to keep it updated with the latest threat information.

Practical exercise

To gain hands-on experience with threat detection, you will configure monitoring settings, simulate threats, and analyze alerts. This exercise will help you understand how to set up and utilize threat detection systems effectively:

1. **Enable detection**: Configure threat detection settings in the WAC to monitor for specific anomalies, such as unusual login attempts.

2. **Simulate threats**: Generate test alerts by simulating abnormal activities. Verify that the system detects these anomalies and generates appropriate alerts.

3. **Analyze alerts**: Review the alerts and use forensic tools to analyze the simulated threats. Determine the cause and impact, and take corrective actions as necessary.

Investigating detected threats

Investigating detected threats involves analyzing alerts to identify patterns or anomalies, conducting forensic analysis to understand the impact, and taking remedial actions to mitigate risks. This process ensures that threats are effectively managed and resolved, minimizing potential damage to the organization. To effectively investigate detected threats, follow these essential steps:

1. **Review alerts**: Examine the alerts generated by the threat detection system to identify patterns or anomalies.

2. **Conduct forensic analysis**: Utilize forensic tools to analyze logs and data, investigating the cause and impact of the detected threats.

3. **Take remedial actions**: Based on your findings, take appropriate actions such as isolating affected systems or changing access controls to mitigate risks.

Practical exercise

Engaging in this practical exercise will help you effectively investigate and respond to detected threats. By reviewing alerts, conducting forensic analysis, and taking remedial actions, you can develop the skills needed to manage security incidents efficiently:

- **Review and analyze:** Examine and analyze alerts from simulated threats to understand their nature and impact.

- **Forensic investigation:** Use forensic tools to conduct a detailed investigation of the simulated incidents, documenting your findings and corrective actions.

> **Note**
>
> Update your threat intelligence feeds regularly and integrate them with the WAC for proactive threat detection. To fully leverage AI and ML technologies for enhanced security, check out *Securing the Future of Artificial Intelligence and Machine Learning at Microsoft*: `https://learn.microsoft.com/en-us/security/engineering/securing-artificial-intelligence-machine-learning`.

Microsoft Defender Antivirus for Windows Server 2025

Microsoft Defender Antivirus is a key security feature within Windows Server 2025, designed to provide comprehensive protection against a wide array of cyber threats. Offering real-time defense, advanced threat detection, and automated response capabilities, it ensures the security and integrity of your server environment.

Key features

Microsoft Defender Antivirus for Windows Server 2025 offers a suite of powerful features designed to provide comprehensive, real-time protection against modern cyber threats.

- **Real-time protection**: Continuously monitors the server to detect and mitigate malicious activities, such as malware and ransomware, in real time. This proactive defense reduces the risk of system compromise.

- **Advanced threat detection**: Utilizing ML and behavioral analytics, Defender Antivirus identifies and neutralizes advanced threats. It leverages cloud intelligence to stay current with emerging threats and updated signatures.

- **Automated response**: Upon threat detection, Defender Antivirus automatically quarantines or removes malicious software, minimizing the need for manual intervention and ensuring seamless server operation.

- **Comprehensive reporting**: Detailed reports and alerts provide valuable insights into server security, helping IT administrators track threat patterns and refine their security strategies.

- **Integration with WAC**: Defender Antivirus integrates smoothly with the WAC, allowing administrators to manage security settings, monitor threats, and run scans from a unified interface. This integration streamlines security management and enhances efficiency.

Implementation steps

1. To effectively deploy Microsoft Defender Antivirus on your Windows Server 2025, follow these essential steps to configure and manage its security capabilities:

2. **Enable Microsoft Defender Antivirus**: Activate Microsoft Defender Antivirus on your Windows Server 2025 using either Windows Admin Center or PowerShell commands.

3. **Update security intelligence**: Regularly update security definitions to ensure Defender Antivirus can protect against the latest threats. Automatic updates can be configured for convenience.

4. **Configure exclusions**: Create exclusions for trusted applications and files to prevent unnecessary disruptions and reduce false positives, ensuring smooth server operation.

5. **Monitor and respond**: Use the reporting tools to continuously monitor security status and respond swiftly to any detected threats.

6. By integrating Microsoft Defender Antivirus into your Windows Server 2025 setup, you significantly boost your server's security, providing robust protection against a wide range of evolving cyber threats. This proactive approach is critical for maintaining the security and stability of your IT infrastructure.

By integrating Microsoft Defender Antivirus into your Windows Server 2025 setup, you significantly boost your server's security, providing robust protection against a wide range of evolving cyber threats. This proactive approach is critical for maintaining the security and stability of your IT infrastructure.

Having introduced Windows Defender Antivirus, we will now turn our attention to automated response systems. These systems are designed to swiftly and effectively address risks, minimizing the need for manual intervention. In the following subsection, we will dive into how these automated response systems work to safeguard your environment.

What are automated response systems?

In today's rapidly changing cybersecurity landscape, the ability to respond swiftly and effectively to emerging threats is critical. Windows Server 2025 addresses this challenge with its advanced automated response systems, which are designed to mitigate risks proactively in real time. These systems utilize cutting-edge technologies to detect anomalies and automatically initiate preconfigured actions that neutralize threats before they cause significant harm. Whether isolating compromised systems, terminating suspicious processes, or deploying patches, the automated responses are fine-tuned to maximize security while minimizing operational disruption.

Leveraging ML and AI, these systems continually evolve, learning from new threat data to stay ahead of emerging attack vectors. This adaptability allows the defense mechanisms to respond dynamically to the latest cyber threats, ensuring a robust and resilient security posture. Additionally, the automation of these processes reduces the workload on IT teams, freeing them from routine incident responses so they can focus on more strategic initiatives that drive business value.

The integration of automated response mechanisms also eliminates human error, which is a common factor in manual security responses. The predefined actions are executed with precision and speed, ensuring that security incidents are addressed consistently and accurately. Moreover, the flexibility of these systems allows organizations to tailor their automated responses to align with specific security policies and regulatory compliance standards. This customized approach ensures that the protective measures are comprehensive yet adaptable to each organization's unique requirements.

Windows Server 2025 empowers IT administrators by offering granular control over the automated response protocols. Administrators can define specific triggers and corresponding actions, ensuring that responses are appropriate to the severity of the threat. This approach ensures operational continuity while addressing security concerns in a precise and efficient manner. The seamless integration of these automated systems into the broader security infrastructure of Windows Server 2025 reflects the platform's commitment to providing a holistic, advanced approach to safeguarding critical IT assets.

The automated response systems in Windows Server 2025 represent a significant leap forward in cybersecurity. By combining real-time threat detection with automated, intelligent mitigation strategies, these systems enhance the overall security framework while empowering IT professionals to manage risks more efficiently. As cyber threats grow increasingly sophisticated, these automated systems play a pivotal role in maintaining the integrity and security of digital environments.

Implementing automated responses

Implementing automated responses involves configuring the system to react to specific triggers by taking predefined actions. This automation helps ensure that threats are addressed promptly and consistently, reducing the burden on IT staff and minimizing potential damage. To effectively implement automated threats, follow these essential steps:

1. **Configure response actions**: Access the **Automated Response** settings in the WAC. Define actions to be taken upon detecting specific triggers, such as isolating a system or terminating suspicious processes.

2. **Define triggers**: Set up conditions that will activate automated responses, such as detecting unauthorized access attempts or high CPU usage.

3. **Test automated responses**: Conduct tests to ensure that automated responses work as intended. Simulate various scenarios to verify that the system reacts appropriately.

Practical exercise

This practical exercise will help you configure and test automated response systems, allowing you to see how they function in real-world scenarios. By setting up responses, simulating threats, and evaluating effectiveness, you can ensure that your automated systems are reliable and aligned with organizational policies.

1. **Set up responses**: Configure automated responses for a test environment, such as quarantining a server when malware is detected.

2. **Simulate threats**: Trigger automated responses by simulating threats, such as unauthorized access attempts or malware infections.

3. **Evaluate effectiveness**: Assess the system's response to these simulations. Ensure that responses are effective, do not disrupt normal operations, and are aligned with organizational policies.

> **Note**
>
> Test automated responses in a sandbox environment to ensure they do not disrupt normal operations before applying them to live servers. For a step-by-step guide on configuring automated responses in Windows Server 2025, check out *Onboard Windows servers to the Microsoft Defender for Endpoint service*: `https://learn.microsoft.com/en-us/defender-endpoint/configure-server-endpoints`.

Customizing automated responses

Customizing automated responses involves regularly reviewing and adjusting response protocols to address new threats and changes in your IT environment. Monitoring system performance and updating response protocols help ensure that automated responses remain effective and do not negatively impact user experience. To effectively customize automated threats, follow these essential steps:

1. **Review and adjust**: Regularly evaluate the effectiveness of automated responses and adjust triggers and actions based on new threat information or changes in your IT environment.

2. **Monitor system performance**: Ensure that automated responses do not negatively impact system performance or user experience. Balance security with operational efficiency.

3. **Update response protocols**: Stay informed about emerging threats and update automated response protocols to address new risks effectively.

Practical exercise

Engaging in this practical exercise to customize automated responses will help you adapt to evolving security needs and ensure that your response systems remain effective. By reviewing protocols and monitoring impact, you can maintain a balanced and responsive security posture.

- **Review protocols**: Regularly review and update automated response settings to adapt to new threats and changes in your IT environment.

- **Monitor impact**: Assess the impact of automated responses on system performance and user experience, making adjustments as needed to maintain balance.

Having explored the advanced tools for detecting and responding to threats, we now move forward to understanding how to enhance authentication and authorization mechanisms. The following section will focus on strengthening identity management, including password policies and authentication strategies that further protect your server environment.

Enhancing authentication and authorization mechanisms

In today's fast-paced digital environment, the demand for advanced authentication and authorization systems has become more critical than ever. As organizations increasingly depend on digital platforms to handle sensitive data and manage operations, safeguarding access to these resources is essential. Implementing sophisticated authentication and authorization mechanisms not only strengthens security but also improves user access efficiency and overall experience. This section examines the modern solutions integrated into Windows Server 2025, including biometric authentication, the deployment of Conditional Access policies, and the use of OAuth 2.0. These technologies are key components in establishing a resilient security framework that evolves in response to new threats and organizational needs. Through the strategic use of these tools, IT administrators can elevate security measures, reduce vulnerabilities, and ensure the integrity of their digital environments.

Biometric authentication explained

Biometric authentication, an innovative cornerstone of modern security strategies, offers a robust and dependable method for verifying user identities, far surpassing traditional systems. Unlike passwords or PINs (which are prone to being forgotten, stolen, or compromised), biometric authentication harnesses unique physiological or behavioral traits (as in *Figure 11.4*) such as fingerprints, facial recognition, iris scans, and voice patterns. These traits are inherently difficult to replicate, making biometric systems exceptionally effective in preventing unauthorized access and significantly reducing the risk of identity theft.

Figure 11.4 – Setting up fingerprint and face sign-in in Windows Server 2025

The integration of biometric authentication into Windows Server 2025 represents a significant leap forward in bolstering IT security. By utilizing biometric modalities, administrators can ensure that access to sensitive data and systems is limited to authorized individuals, providing both enhanced security and a user experience that is not just seamless and intuitive but also user-friendly. That eliminates the need for users to remember complex passwords or rely on physical security tokens, streamlining the authentication process while maintaining stringent security protocols.

One of the standout features of biometric authentication is its ability to offer continuous, real-time verification. Unlike static credentials, which can be misused once obtained, biometric data remains tied to the individual, allowing for ongoing validation during active sessions. This unique capability is instrumental in mitigating insider threats, where malicious actions may be carried out by individuals who initially had legitimate access.

Windows Server 2025 also addresses **privacy** and **security** concerns associated with biometric data through advanced encryption techniques. Safeguarding biometric templates is critical, as any compromise could have far-reaching consequences. By utilizing secure storage and transmission protocols, the platform ensures that biometric information remains protected from interception or tampering.

Additionally, biometric authentication integrates seamlessly with MFA, further enhancing security by adding another layer of protection. When combined with other authentication methods such as smart cards or one-time passwords, biometrics fortify an organization's defenses against even the most sophisticated attacks. This layered approach ensures that if one factor is compromised, other security measures remain intact.

From an operational standpoint, biometric authentication simplifies access management for IT administrators. The centralized consoles in Windows Server 2025 allow for easy enrollment and management of biometric data, ensuring consistent adherence to security policies. Administrators can swiftly revoke or update biometric credentials, enhancing responsiveness to potential security threats while ensuring that security operations remain agile.

The adoption of biometric authentication in Windows Server 2025 reflects a forward-thinking approach to IT security, combining cutting-edge technology with ease of use. As cyber threats grow increasingly complex, deploying biometric authentication provides organizations with a powerful tool to safeguard digital assets while enhancing user convenience and operational efficiency. This strategic integration reinforces the overall resilience of IT environments, making it a crucial component of modern cybersecurity frameworks.

Implementing biometric authentication

To ensure robust security and user-friendly access control, implementing biometric authentication involves several key steps. These steps help configure the necessary hardware, enroll users, and integrate biometric authentication with other security measures such as MFA. Following this process ensures that your organization's sensitive data is protected while providing a seamless user experience. To effectively implement biometric authentication, follow these essential steps:

1. **Configure biometric devices**: Begin by setting up biometric hardware compatible with Windows Server 2025. That includes installing and configuring devices such as fingerprint scanners or facial recognition cameras.

2. **Enroll users**: Use the Windows Server management console to enroll users by capturing their biometric data. This step involves registering the unique traits of each user to enable authentication.

3. **Integrate with MFA**: Combine biometric authentication with MFA to add an extra layer of security. This integration ensures that users must verify their identity through multiple methods, enhancing overall protection.

Practical exercise

This practical exercise is essential for understanding and mastering the implementation of biometric authentication. This hands-on approach allows you to set up devices, enroll test users, and verify that the authentication system functions as intended. Completing this exercise will solidify your understanding and ensure that the biometric system integrates effectively with existing security measures:

1. **Set up biometric devices**: Install and configure a biometric device on a test server, ensuring it operates correctly with Windows Server 2025.

2. **Enroll test users**: Register several test users by capturing their biometric data. Confirm that the enrollment process is completed accurately and securely.

3. **Test authentication**: Have test users log in using their biometric data and MFA. Verify that the authentication system works as expected and integrates seamlessly with other security measures.

> **Note**
>
> Ensure that biometric devices are properly calibrated and tested in a non-production environment to avoid enrollment or authentication issues during initial setup. Visit *How Windows Hello for Business Works* to learn how to set up and integrate biometric devices in Windows Server 2025: `https://learn.microsoft.com/en-us/windows/security/identity-protection/hello-for-business/how-it-works`.

Overview of Conditional Access policies

Conditional Access policies in Windows Server 2025 offer a dynamic and highly secure method for managing access to organizational resources. These policies allow IT administrators to enforce granular control based on a variety of real-time factors, including user identity, device compliance, geographical location, and risk levels. By evaluating these conditions, the system ensures that only properly authenticated and authorized users are granted access to sensitive systems and data, significantly reducing the likelihood of unauthorized entry and potential security breaches.

A key advantage of Conditional Access policies is their ability to apply MFA selectively, depicted in *Figure 11.5*, based on contextual factors. For example, if a user attempts to access resources from a compliant device within a trusted network, the system may not require additional authentication steps. However, if access is attempted from an unknown device or location, MFA can be enforced to add an extra layer of security. This adaptive model enhances overall security while maintaining a seamless user experience by adjusting authentication requirements according to the level of risk associated with each access attempt.

Figure 11.5 – MFA in Azure

These policies are further bolstered by their integration with other advanced security features within Windows Server 2025, including threat intelligence and automated response systems. This real-time integration enables access decisions to be informed by the latest threat data, allowing the system to adjust access controls in response to emerging risks automatically. In high-risk scenarios, Conditional Access policies can tighten security measures, such as requiring stricter authentication or even blocking access, to defend against potential threats proactively.

Administrators can easily configure and manage these policies through a centralized console, which streamlines deployment and enforcement across the organization. This unified management approach ensures consistent application of security standards. At the same time, the ability to generate detailed reports on access activities and policy enforcement provides valuable insights for security assessments and compliance audits.

By utilizing Conditional Access policies, organizations can implement an intelligent and highly adaptable access control framework that integrates contextual information with advanced security features. This approach not only strengthens the protection of critical digital assets but also improves operational efficiency and user convenience, making it a vital component of any modern cybersecurity strategy.

Configuring Conditional Access policies

Configuring Conditional Access policies involves creating rules that enforce access control based on real-time data. By defining conditions and setting up policies, administrators can ensure that access to sensitive systems is granted only under secure and compliant circumstances. This approach helps maintain a balance between security and user convenience. To effectively configure conditional access policies, follow these essential steps:

1. **Define conditions**: Identify the conditions under which access should be granted or restricted. These conditions might include user roles, device compliance, and geographic location.

2. **Create policies**: Use the WAC to create and configure policies that enforce access rules based on the defined conditions. This step ensures that only authorized users can access sensitive systems and data.

3. **Monitor and adjust**: Regularly review the effectiveness of these policies and make adjustments based on new threat intelligence or changes in organizational needs.

Practical exercise

Engaging in this practical exercise helps you apply Conditional Access policies in real-world scenarios. By creating and testing policies, you gain hands-on experience in managing access control based on varying conditions, ensuring that your security measures are both effective and adaptable:

1. **Create access policies**: Implement Conditional Access policies for various user groups within the WAC. For instance, enforce MFA for access from outside the corporate network.

2. **Simulate access scenarios**: Test the policies by accessing resources from different devices and locations. Confirm that the system enforces the correct authentication requirements based on the set conditions.

3. **Review policy reports**: Generate and analyze reports on access attempts and policy enforcement. Use these insights to refine policies and enhance security measures.

> **Note**
>
> Use Conditional Access policies to enforce location-based security, restricting access from specific geographical regions to minimize risk. Explore *Plan a Conditional Access deployment* to achieve your organization's access strategy for apps and resources: `https://learn.microsoft.com/en-us/entra/identity/conditional-access/plan-conditional-access`.

Understanding OAuth 2.0 integration in Windows Server 2025

OAuth, also known as **Open Authorization**, is an open standard designed for access delegation. It is frequently utilized to grant websites or applications restricted access to a user's resources without revealing their credentials. The integration of OAuth 2.0 within Windows Server 2025, as illustrated in *Figure 11.6*, introduces a significant leap in modern authentication standards, providing a highly secure and flexible framework for managing authorization. By leveraging OAuth 2.0, applications can request limited access to user accounts via the HTTP service, ensuring strong access control without unnecessary complexity. This setup allows IT administrators to secure organizational resources more effectively, reducing risks while simplifying user interactions.

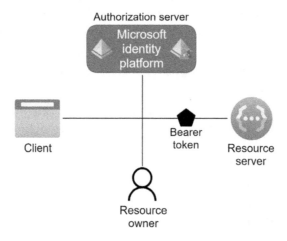

Figure 11.6 – The OAuth architecture (source – Microsoft)

With OAuth 2.0, security is enhanced through a token-based system that eliminates the need for applications to handle sensitive credentials directly. This approach helps mitigate the risk of credential exposure or misuse. Additionally, the protocol supports various authorization methods—such as authorization code, implicit, and client credentials—giving administrators the flexibility to adapt the authentication process to their specific needs. The ability to issue temporary tokens rather than storing static credentials provides an added layer of protection against cyberattacks.

In this context, the diagram illustrates the flow of authentication and authorization using the Microsoft identity platform. The client (application or user) is authenticated by the authorization server (Microsoft identity platform), which then issues a bearer token. This token is presented to the resource server to gain access to the resource, proving that the client has been authorized. This token-based approach ensures that only authenticated and authorized clients can access protected resources, enhancing overall security.

The framework's versatility also promotes interoperability between different services and platforms, a key benefit in today's interconnected IT environments. By enabling **single sign-on (SSO)**, OAuth 2.0 allows users to authenticate once and gain secure access to multiple applications without the need to re-enter their credentials for each session. This capability not only boosts efficiency but also enhances overall security by reducing the number of authentication points where vulnerabilities could arise. OAuth 2.0's support for federated identity management further allows secure collaboration with external partners while maintaining tight access controls.

Windows Server 2025's adoption of OAuth 2.0 illustrates a forward-thinking approach to defending against modern cyber threats. The protocol's use of secure tokens rather than traditional, persistent credentials strengthens defenses against attacks such as phishing or credential stuffing. Additionally, administrators gain the ability to revoke tokens and adjust access permissions dynamically in response to shifting security needs or evolving risks, ensuring a more agile security environment.

By embedding OAuth 2.0 within the Windows Server infrastructure, IT administrators are empowered to create a more cohesive and secure ecosystem. This integration not only enhances security through advanced authorization mechanisms but also fosters a smoother and more integrated user experience, reflecting the growing demand for secure yet user-friendly IT environments. The ability to implement OAuth 2.0's powerful features while maintaining robust control over resource access exemplifies the platform's capability to meet the challenges of increasingly sophisticated digital threats.

Implementing OAuth 2.0

Implementing OAuth 2.0 involves configuring the framework to handle authorization securely and efficiently. By setting up OAuth 2.0 and integrating it with applications, you can ensure that access to resources is controlled via secure tokens. This process also involves managing tokens and adjusting permissions to meet evolving security needs. To effectively implement OAuth 2.0, follow these essential steps:

1. **Set up OAuth 2.0**: Configure OAuth 2.0 settings in Windows Server 2025 to allow applications to request limited access to user accounts. Define the necessary authorization methods, such as authorization codes or client credentials.

2. **Integrate with applications**: Update applications to use OAuth 2.0 for authentication and authorization. Ensure proper token handling to maintain security.

3. **Manage tokens**: Monitor and manage issued tokens, implementing mechanisms for revoking and adjusting permissions in response to evolving security needs.

Practical exercise

This practical exercise helps solidify your understanding of OAuth 2.0 integration by providing hands-on experience with configuration and application updates. Testing OAuth 2.0 in a controlled environment allows you to validate the setup and ensure that tokens are managed effectively:

1. **Configure OAuth 2.0**: Set up OAuth 2.0 in a test environment, defining the authorization methods and token settings required for your applications.

2. **Integrate with applications**: Modify a sample application to utilize OAuth 2.0 for authentication. Test the integration by logging in with OAuth tokens and accessing secured resources.

3. **Monitor and adjust**: Track token usage and adjust settings as needed to ensure secure and effective authorization—test token revocation and permission adjustments in response to simulated security events.

> **Note**
>
> Combine OAuth 2.0 with MFA for an added layer of security when integrating external applications with your server. For modern authorization methods, check *OAuth 2.0 authorization with Microsoft Entra ID*: `https://learn.microsoft.com/en-us/entra/architecture/auth-oauth2`.

Securing communication channels with TLS and other protocols

In today's digital landscape, where data breaches and cyber threats are growing more sophisticated, securing communication channels has become paramount. This section explores the critical need for strengthening these channels by focusing on the implementation of **Transport Layer Security (TLS)** and other advanced security protocols. It offers an in-depth guide on deploying TLS effectively while also examining secure alternatives such as HTTPS, IPSec, and SSH. Additionally, it highlights the importance of continuous monitoring to maintain the integrity and confidentiality of data in transit. By implementing these security measures, organizations can protect sensitive information and cultivate a trust-based environment for their stakeholders. Leveraging your expertise in this area is essential for ensuring the resilience of these communication systems and navigating evolving security challenges.

TLS explained

TLS in Windows Server 2025, as illustrated in *Figure 11.7*, introduces several advanced features tailored to address the evolving needs of cybersecurity and data integrity. A key enhancement is the full integration of TLS 1.3, which brings faster performance and stronger security by streamlining the handshake process and removing outdated cryptographic algorithms. That significantly reduces handshake latency, improves overall efficiency, and minimizes the system's attack surface, providing robust protection against modern threats.

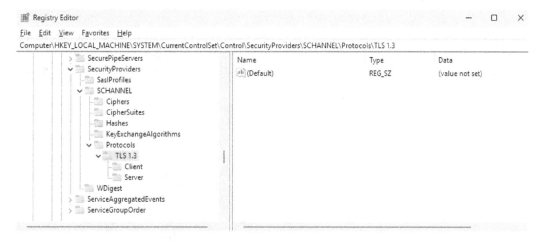

Figure 11.7 – Enabling TLS 1.3 in Windows Server 2025

Administrators benefit from the user-friendly interface of the upgraded WAC, which simplifies the configuration and management of TLS across various server roles, services, and applications. Through this interface, managing TLS policies is more accessible, and server environments can be monitored efficiently. In addition, Windows Server 2025 enhances certificate management by automating certificate issuance, renewal, and revocation through integration with **Active Directory Certificate Services** (**AD CS**). This automation reduces the administrative overhead, ensures continuous security, and eliminates risks associated with expired or mismanaged certificates.

The server also adopts the latest cryptographic suites, offering organizations the flexibility to implement cutting-edge encryption standards. That ensures compliance with strict industry regulations such as GDPR, HIPAA, and PCI DSS, giving enterprises peace of mind when handling sensitive data. Further strengthening security, the inclusion of comprehensive auditing tools enables detailed logging and real-time alerts, empowering IT administrators to identify and address potential vulnerabilities or suspicious activities quickly.

By deploying TLS within Windows Server 2025, organizations secure data in transit and bolster the resilience of their IT infrastructure. Your expertise in optimizing these security protocols is essential to ensuring that communications remain secure and resistant to current and emerging cyber threats.

> **Note**
>
> To ensure compliance with the latest security standards, it's critical to disable older versions of TLS (e.g., TLS 1.0 and 1.1) to prevent potential vulnerabilities. Windows Server 2025 supports TLS 1.3 by default, which should be the preferred protocol for secure communications. According to Microsoft, Azure support for TLS 1.0 and TLS 1.1 ended on 31 October 2024: `https://azure.microsoft.com/en-us/updates/azure-support-tls-will-end-by-31-october-2024-2/`.

Having established the fundamentals of TLS and its pivotal role in securing communication, it's important to explore other essential secure protocols. Understanding how protocols such as HTTPS, IPSec, and SSH contribute to overall security will provide a more comprehensive view of protecting a server's communication channels.

Overview of other secure protocols (HTTPS, IPSec, and SSH)

Implementing robust security protocols is a cornerstone of safeguarding modern IT infrastructure, and Windows Server 2025 provides unparalleled support in this regard. Beyond the enhancements brought by TLS, the server also offers extensive capabilities with other secure protocols such as HTTPS, IPSec, and SSH:

- **HTTPS**, or **HyperText Transfer Protocol Secure**, ensures that web communications are encrypted, protecting sensitive data from man-in-the-middle attacks and eavesdropping. In Windows Server 2025, administrators can effortlessly configure HTTPS to secure web applications and services through the WAC, leveraging features such as automatic HTTPS certificate binding and integration with AD CS for streamlined certificate management.

- **Internet Protocol Security** (**IPSec**) is another critical protocol provided by Windows Server 2025. IPSec operates at the network layer, securing data packets exchanged between devices over an IP network. This protocol is essential for creating **virtual private networks** (**VPNs**) and securing internal network traffic. The advanced cryptographic algorithms included in IPSec for Windows Server 2025 enhance data integrity and authentication, ensuring that data is not tampered with during transit. Administrators can deploy IPSec policies using Group Policy, providing a centralized way to enforce security across the entire network.

- **Secure Shell** (**SSH**) also plays a vital role in safeguarding server communications. SSH is widely used for secure remote administration, allowing administrators to manage servers, transfer files, and execute commands over an encrypted channel. Windows Server 2025 supports SSH natively (see *Figure 11.8*), enabling seamless and secure remote management. The integration of SSH into Windows Server 2025 ensures compatibility with various automation tools and scripts, enhancing operational efficiency while maintaining security.

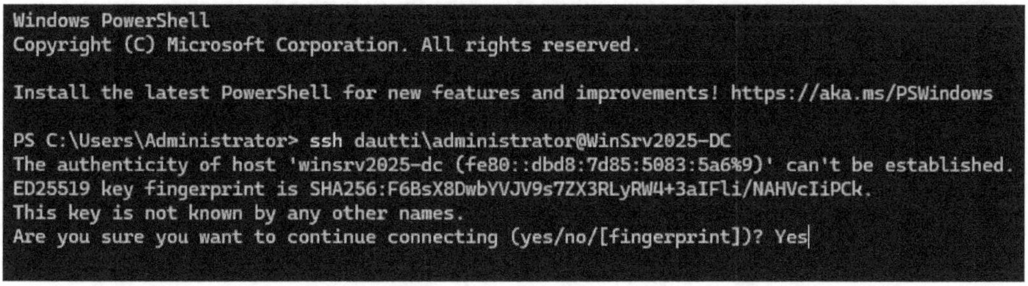

```
Windows PowerShell
Copyright (C) Microsoft Corporation. All rights reserved.

Install the latest PowerShell for new features and improvements! https://aka.ms/PSWindows

PS C:\Users\Administrator> ssh dautti\administrator@WinSrv2025-DC
The authenticity of host 'winsrv2025-dc (fe80::dbd8:7d85:5083:5a6%9)' can't be established.
ED25519 key fingerprint is SHA256:F6BsX8DwbYVJV9s7ZX3RLyRW4+3aIFli/NAHVcIiPCk.
This key is not known by any other names.
Are you sure you want to continue connecting (yes/no/[fingerprint])? Yes
```

Figure 11.8 – Enabling SSH in Windows Server 2025

Your expertise is crucial in optimizing the deployment and management of these secure protocols. By leveraging HTTPS, IPSec, and SSH, organizations can establish a multi-layered security framework that addresses different aspects of data protection. Ensuring the correct implementation and continuous monitoring of these protocols can significantly reduce vulnerabilities and foster a secure operational environment. Your role in this process is indispensable, as your deep understanding of these systems will help maintain the integrity and confidentiality of our communications and data transmissions.

> **Note**
>
> Always configure IPSec policies with both integrity and encryption settings to ensure data is protected in transit. Combining IPSec with Group Policy can automate policy deployment across large environments, increasing security without manual intervention. Here's how you could implement IPSec in the Windows domain: `https://michaelfirsov.wordpress.com/implemeting-ipsec-in-windows-domain-part-1/`.

With a detailed grasp of HTTPS, IPSec, and SSH, the next step is to monitor these secure channels to ensure they are functioning as intended. Effective monitoring is crucial for maintaining the integrity and security of communications in Windows Server 2025.

How to monitor secure channels

Monitoring secure communication channels is vital to ensuring a resilient and secure IT infrastructure, and Windows Server 2025 is equipped with advanced tools to support this crucial task. The platform offers a range of features designed to streamline the monitoring and management of secure communication protocols, allowing administrators to detect and mitigate risks before they escalate into threats. Continuous monitoring is key to identifying vulnerabilities or suspicious activities, enabling swift intervention and reinforcing the security of data transmissions.

A standout feature of Windows Server 2025 is its *enhanced auditing capabilities*, which provide detailed logging and alert mechanisms. These tools allow administrators to track the security status of their networks closely, making it easier to identify the source of any anomalies and respond quickly. Advanced analytics further strengthen this defense, as they can recognize patterns indicative of emerging cyber threats, helping security teams adopt proactive strategies.

The WAC simplifies the monitoring process by offering a centralized platform where administrators can configure and oversee secure protocols such as TLS, HTTPS, IPSec, and SSH. This unified interface enhances operational efficiency and ensures that security measures are consistently applied across the organization. With real-time dashboards providing up-to-the-minute insights into the health and security of communication channels, administrators can make informed decisions and stay ahead of potential issues.

Automation also plays a critical role in maintaining secure channels. Windows Server 2025 supports automated tools, such as those for certificate management through AD CS, which handles the issuance and renewal of security certificates. This automation reduces manual intervention and minimizes the risk of human error, ensuring that encrypted communications remain secure and compliant with best practices.

Your expertise in managing these monitoring systems is essential to optimizing their performance. By applying your deep knowledge of secure protocols and their implementation, you can help safeguard communication channels from evolving cyber threats. Your role in continuously refining monitoring strategies and adapting them to new challenges is key to maintaining the highest levels of data security and trust. Through these efforts, we can create a robust and secure IT environment that protects sensitive information and strengthens stakeholder confidence.

> **Note**
>
> Monitor failed TLS/SSL handshakes using event ID `36874`. These logs are helpful for quickly detecting misconfigurations or expired certificates that could jeopardize secure communication channels. For more details, review the *Schannel Events* documentation at `https://learn.microsoft.com/en-us/previous-versions/windows/it-pro/windows-server-2012-r2-and-2012/dn786445(v=ws.11)`.

After exploring the mechanisms for securing and monitoring communication channels, we now turn our attention to utilizing the advanced security features in Windows Server 2025 and beyond through Azure integration.

Leveraging security features in Windows Server 2025 and beyond with Azure integration

As organizations work to strengthen their security posture, Windows Server 2025 offers a rich set of security features that protect data, control access, and defend against threats. For those looking to take security even further, integrating with Azure unlocks advanced tools and capabilities that deepen protection and offer proactive security insights. Whether securing a standalone server or enhancing it with Azure, these tools provide IT professionals with flexible options to meet a range of security needs.

Key security features in Windows Server 2025

In standalone mode, Windows Server 2025 delivers powerful security features, offering robust protection for many organizations' core needs:

- **Access controls and authentication**: With built-in RBAC and Conditional Access policies, administrators can precisely manage permissions and reduce unauthorized access risks. MFA, biometric options, and OAuth 2.0 support add layers of security for sensitive data and applications.

- **Threat detection and real-time protection**: Windows Defender's advanced threat detection tools protect against malware, ransomware, and other security threats. Regular updates and real-time monitoring capabilities ensure timely response to known risks.

- **Secure communication channels**: Windows Server 2025 supports industry-standard encryption protocols such as TLS 1.3, HTTPS, IPSec, and SSH to secure data in transit. These protocols ensure that critical communication channels remain protected against interception and tampering.

- **Patch management and audit logging**: Automated patch management keeps systems up to date with the latest security fixes, while audit logs offer visibility into server activity, helping to identify and respond to potential vulnerabilities.

Enhanced security features with Azure integration

Integrating Windows Server 2025 with Azure and Azure Security Center unlocks advanced security features, creating a more layered defense. These enhancements are designed for environments where additional insights and scalable protections are needed, particularly in hybrid or cloud-dependent infrastructures:

- **Advanced threat intelligence and response**: Azure Security Center and Azure Sentinel extend threat detection capabilities with ML, real-time intelligence, and **security information and event management (SIEM)** to help IT teams detect and respond to complex threats

- **Centralized policy and compliance management**: Azure integration allows for streamlined management of security policies and compliance across multiple servers, using tools such as Azure Policy to audit configurations and ensure regulatory compliance

- **Data protection with Azure Key Vault**: Azure Key Vault enables secure management of encryption keys and sensitive data, adding a critical layer of data security for organizations with high regulatory requirements

- **Advanced identity protection with Microsoft Entra ID**: Integrating AAD brings enhanced identity protection, including Conditional Access policies that adjust based on user risk, location, and device. Azure MFA and SSO capabilities further enhance identity security

- **Automatic updates and compliance**: With Azure, organizations benefit from seamless access to Microsoft's latest security updates, ensuring that environments remain secure without manual patching

For organizations that require basic but solid security on an on-premises basis, the standalone features of Windows Server 2025 will provide robust and foundational protection. However, Azure integration offers valuable additions for enterprises needing enhanced visibility, proactive threat response, and streamlined compliance across hybrid environments. By understanding the strengths of both standalone and Azure-enhanced configurations, IT professionals can select the best combination of tools to protect and manage their Windows Server 2025 environments with confidence, adapting security to fit their unique needs and operational goals.

With an understanding of leveraging security features in Windows Server 2025 and beyond through Azure integration, we now shift focus to the licensing and cost considerations involved in deploying these advanced security features.

Licensing and cost considerations for deploying advanced security features

Understanding the licensing and cost implications is essential when deploying security features in Windows Server 2025, especially when integrating with Azure and Azure Security Center. For standalone servers, the primary costs include Windows Server licensing, which varies by edition (Standard or Datacenter) and depends on factors such as the number of cores and users. These editions offer many default security features, including local RBAC and enhanced auditing. Still, licensing costs increase with the addition of more advanced features or multiple instances in a data center environment:

- **Azure Integration Considerations:** When extending Windows Server 2025 to include Azure integration, there are additional considerations. For example, leveraging AAD for Conditional Access and extended RBAC capabilities requires an AAD Premium license, typically included in Microsoft 365 E5 subscriptions or available as a standalone license. For organizations needing to implement multi-layered security with Conditional Access, the AAD Premium P1 or P2 tiers offer this functionality, with P2 providing more advanced features, such as identity protection, for an additional cost.

- **Azure Security Center Deployment:** Deploying Azure Security Center—an essential service for organizations needing real-time threat intelligence, vulnerability assessments, and compliance tracking—also involves costs that vary depending on the chosen tier. Azure Security Center is available in both Free and Standard tiers, with the Standard tier providing enhanced capabilities such as continuous threat detection, **just-in-time** (**JIT**) VM access, and adaptive application control. Costs for the Standard tier are usage-based, depending on the number of virtual machines and data processed.

- **Azure Hybrid Benefit:** The Azure Hybrid Benefit allows organizations to leverage their on-premises Windows Server licenses in Azure to reduce costs on virtual machines, making it a valuable option for those moving workloads to the cloud. This benefit enables significant savings on Azure VM licensing, allowing Windows Server Datacenter or Standard edition licenses with Software Assurance to be used in the cloud.

While the core Windows Server 2025 license provides foundational security features, extending these capabilities with AAD, Conditional Access, Azure Security Center, and Hybrid Benefit requires additional licensing and monthly costs. These investments, however, provide robust security, scalability, and management features that enhance an organization's ability to secure and control its infrastructure effectively.

After addressing the licensing and cost considerations for deploying advanced security features, we now turn our attention to Microsoft Defender for Servers Plan 1 and Plan 2.

Microsoft Defender for Servers Plan 1 and Plan 2

Microsoft Defender for Servers provides robust security solutions for both on-premises and cloud-based servers, offering a comprehensive layer of protection. With two distinct plans—Plan 1 and Plan 2—this service enables businesses to scale their security efforts based on their needs, especially when integrating with Azure.

Microsoft Defender for Servers Plan 1 focuses on foundational protection, offering real-time monitoring and threat detection for vulnerabilities in your server environment. It provides security alerts for potential threats, enabling security teams to take proactive steps in mitigating risks. Key capabilities include the following:

- **Threat detection**: Identifies and responds to real-time threats, helping detect malicious activity on servers
- **Security posture assessment**: Provides insights into security gaps, allowing for targeted security improvements
- **Advanced vulnerability management**: Scans for vulnerabilities in both operating systems and applications, ensuring that critical patches and updates are applied

Microsoft Defender for Servers Plan 2 builds upon Plan 1 with added features for more advanced protection. This plan is particularly useful for organizations requiring enhanced security measures as they onboard their servers to Azure. It integrates deeper with Azure Security Center to provide an even more comprehensive security framework, which includes the following:

- **Endpoint detection and response** (EDR): Tracks and responds to advanced threats across server endpoints, offering more profound analysis and more granular control over server activities
- **JIT VM access**: Limits access to virtual machines by providing time-bound access based on need, reducing exposure to potential vulnerabilities

- **Adaptive application controls**: Helps ensure that only approved applications are allowed to run on the server, mitigating the risk of unauthorized software or malware

- **Advanced threat protection** (**ATP**): Continuously monitors for sophisticated attacks and applies ML and behavioral analysis to detect anomalies that might otherwise go unnoticed

When a server is onboarded to Azure, these advanced capabilities are seamlessly integrated with Azure's native security tools, enhancing protection across hybrid environments. Whether the server resides on-premises or in the cloud, these plans enable organizations to adopt a unified, dynamic security strategy that evolves with emerging threats.

By choosing the appropriate plan, organizations can tailor their security measures to their specific needs, ensuring a scalable and adaptive defense strategy for their server environments.

After reviewing the Microsoft Defender for Servers Plan 1 and Plan 2, we now turn to implementing security best practices within Windows Server 2025. The upcoming section delves deeper into these practices, providing insights to strengthen the security and resilience of your IT infrastructure.

Implementing security best practices in Windows Server 2025

In today's constantly shifting cybersecurity landscape, adhering to security best practices is crucial for safeguarding an organization's IT infrastructure. Windows Server 2025 serves as a robust platform, integrating cutting-edge security features that mitigate risks and bolster overall system resilience. This section explores the critical components of securing Windows Server 2025, emphasizing the key practices administrators must implement to protect their environments effectively.

These practices include thorough patch management, detailed audit logging, and the consistent performance of security assessments. Each of these elements is vital in reinforcing server defenses against vulnerabilities, ensuring alignment with industry standards, and maintaining compliance. By adopting these practices, organizations can proactively shield themselves from breaches, safeguard operational integrity, and preserve the trust of their stakeholders in a digital landscape increasingly defined by sophisticated cyber threats.

Overview of patch management

Patch management in Windows Server 2025 plays a vital role in ensuring a secure, resilient IT environment by systematically applying updates and patches that address security vulnerabilities, enhance performance, and ensure compliance with industry standards. Windows Server 2025 introduces several enhancements to make the patch management process more efficient, reliable, and streamlined.

One of the core improvements is its integration with **Windows Update for Business**, allowing administrators to manage updates across multiple servers from a centralized dashboard. This feature provides granular control over update policies, such as deferral periods and maintenance windows, enabling seamless patch deployment with minimal disruption to business operations. Additionally, the platform's advanced reporting capabilities give administrators detailed insights into the status of patch deployments, including applied, pending, or problematic updates. These reporting tools are essential for maintaining compliance with regulatory standards and conducting post-deployment analyses.

Windows Server 2025 also offers *automated patch management tools*, reducing the need for manual intervention. Automation ensures that critical patches (see *Figure 11.9*) are deployed in a timely manner, minimizes human error, and allows IT teams to focus on more strategic initiatives. The platform includes rollback options, providing the ability to revert to previous configurations if an update causes unforeseen issues and adding a layer of safety during the patching process.

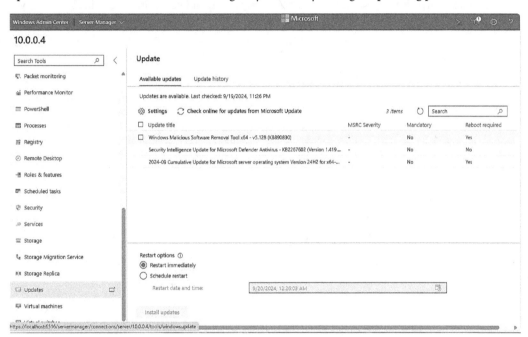

Figure 11.9 – Managing and applying updates in the WAC

Your expertise is essential in optimizing these patch management procedures. With your deep understanding of system vulnerabilities and update protocols, you can ensure that patch deployment is both practical and efficient while addressing any issues that arise. By actively monitoring the patching process, you help maintain the integrity and security of the IT infrastructure.

Patch management in Windows Server 2025's enhanced capabilities directly addresses the challenges posed by modern cybersecurity threats. By implementing a robust patch management strategy, organizations can effectively safeguard their systems, ensure operational continuity, and maintain compliance with industry standards. These tools and features are critical for proactively defending against vulnerabilities and maintaining the trust and reliability essential in today's digital infrastructure.

> **Note**
>
> Activating automatic updates for critical security patches is vital to maintaining a secure server environment. In environments where uptime is critical, **Windows Server Update Services (WSUS)** provides more control over the timing of patch deployment. Learn how to configure Group Policy settings for automatic updates by visiting `https://learn.microsoft.com/en-us/windows-server/administration/windows-server-update-services/deploy/4-configure-group-policy-settings-for-automatic-updates`.

With a comprehensive understanding of patch management and its significance in maintaining system security, the next crucial aspect is audit logging. Exploring how audit logs function within Windows Server 2025 will further enhance your ability to monitor and respond to potential security incidents.

Understanding audit logging

Audit logging is a fundamental element of Windows Server 2025, essential for maintaining a secure and compliant IT environment. This feature allows administrators to monitor and record a wide range of server activities, including user logins, access attempts, system changes, and application usage. By capturing these events in detail, audit logs create a thorough record that supports the detection of anomalies, investigation of security incidents, and adherence to regulatory standards.

Windows Server 2025 enhances audit logging, as depicted in *Figure 11.10*, with advanced capabilities, providing administrators with granular control over which activities are logged. Detailed policies can be configured to ensure that the audit process aligns with the specific security requirements of the organization. This customization is particularly valuable in environments with varied data sensitivity and compliance needs across different departments and systems.

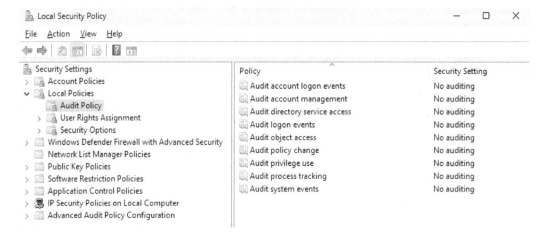

Figure 11.10 – Audit Policy in Windows Server 2025

The integration of sophisticated analytics with audit logging in Windows Server 2025 further improves threat detection. ML algorithms and pattern recognition techniques enable the real-time identification of anomalies and potential security breaches. This proactive approach not only aids in quickly mitigating risks but also strengthens the organization's overall security posture. Additionally, the ability to generate detailed reports from audit logs supports thorough post-incident analysis, offering insights into the nature and scope of security events.

IT professionals' role in optimizing audit logging is crucial. Your expertise in configuring and managing audit logs ensures that they provide actionable intelligence while avoiding system overload. Achieving a balance between comprehensive data capture and system efficiency is key, and your understanding of system operations and security protocols is essential in this regard.

Moreover, audit logs play a vital role in meeting industry standards and legal requirements. By maintaining accurate and complete records of system activities, organizations can demonstrate their commitment to accountability and transparency, which is critical for regulatory compliance and certifications. Your efforts in ensuring the integrity and reliability of audit logs directly support the organization's compliance obligations.

Overall, mastering audit logging in Windows Server 2025 is essential for protecting an organization's IT infrastructure. Your role in effectively configuring, monitoring, and analyzing these logs is integral to ensuring high standards of security and compliance. Through diligent management, you contribute to building a resilient and secure IT environment capable of withstanding the evolving landscape of cyber threats.

> **Note**
>
> Set up audit policies that record both successful and failed login attempts. Monitoring these events is key to detecting potential security breaches or abnormal user behavior. For detailed steps on configuring audit policies for Windows event logs, visit `https://learn.microsoft.com/en-us/defender-for-identity/deploy/configure-windows-event-collection`.

Having delved into the details of audit logging, which plays a critical role in tracking and analyzing system activities, the next step is to focus on regular security assessments. These assessments will help you evaluate the effectiveness of your security measures and ensure your system remains resilient against emerging threats.

Why regular security assessments?

Regular security assessments are vital for protecting an organization's IT infrastructure. In Windows Server 2025, these assessments are designed to uncover vulnerabilities, evaluate existing security measures, and ensure adherence to industry standards and regulations. By conducting these evaluations periodically, IT professionals can gain a thorough understanding of their system's security status, allowing them to address weaknesses before malicious actors can exploit them proactively.

The assessment process in Windows Server 2025 typically employs a combination of **automated** and **manual** techniques. Automated vulnerability scanners efficiently detect known security gaps, while manual penetration testing provides a more detailed examination of the server's defenses against sophisticated threats. These integrated tools enable IT professionals to perform comprehensive and effective assessments, ensuring all aspects of security are thoroughly reviewed.

Beyond identifying vulnerabilities, security assessments are crucial for validating the effectiveness of existing security policies and controls. Regular reviews and tests confirm that these measures are functioning as intended and are capable of addressing the latest threats. Your expertise is essential in analyzing assessment results and crafting actionable recommendations to enhance security based on these findings.

The insights gained from security assessments guide strategic decisions regarding resource allocation, risk management, and the prioritization of security initiatives. By continuously updating security strategies in response to assessment outcomes, IT professionals can maintain a proactive defense posture that adapts to emerging cyber threats. Additionally, these assessments provide essential documentation for demonstrating compliance during audits, reinforcing the organization's commitment to maintaining high-security standards.

In essence, regular security assessments in Windows Server 2025 are crucial for maintaining a secure and resilient IT environment. Your role in conducting these assessments and implementing improvements based on their findings is critical for ensuring that the organization's infrastructure remains robust and capable of withstanding the evolving threat landscape.

> **Note**
>
> Frequently perform Windows Defender ATP assessments to detect vulnerabilities early and receive actionable security recommendations, helping your systems remain compliant with security standards. For more details, check out Microsoft's 2016 announcement about Windows Defender ATP: `https://blogs.windows.com/windowsexperience/2016/03/01/announcing-windows-defender-advanced-threat-protection/`.

Integration and requirements for Microsoft Defender for Endpoint on Windows Server 2025

Microsoft Defender for Endpoint (**MDE**) offers advanced security capabilities for Windows Server 2025, providing robust protection against complex cyber threats. Here's an in-depth look at the integration process and system requirements.

Integration with Azure

To fully leverage MDE's security capabilities, integration with Azure is essential. This connection provides centralized management and powerful threat analytics:

- **Azure tenant requirement**: To utilize MDE effectively, an Azure tenant is necessary. This enables centralized management and access to advanced analytics through the Azure portal.

- **Microsoft Entra ID**: Integration with Microsoft Entra ID is crucial for managing user identities and access controls, enabling advanced security features such as Conditional Access and Identity Protection.

Licensing options

MDE is available in two primary plans—Plan 1 and Plan 2—with varying capabilities:

- **Plan 1 (Standard)**: Includes essential features such as next-gen protection, attack surface reduction, and EDR

- **Plan 2 (Advanced)**: Adds advanced features such as automated investigation, remediation, vulnerability management, and advanced hunting capabilities

Selecting the right plan

Organizations should assess their security needs to choose between Plan 1 or Plan 2. Plan 2 is recommended for those requiring more comprehensive security measures and advanced features.

Additional system requirements are listed as follows:

- **Log Analytics**: For advanced threat analytics and detailed reporting, integrating with Azure Log Analytics is highly recommended. This service gathers and analyzes data to provide critical security insights.

- **Microsoft Defender Security Center**: This centralized platform allows administrators to monitor and manage endpoint security, providing real-time alerts and detailed threat reports.

- **System updates**: Ensure that Windows Server 2025 is fully updated with the latest patches to maintain security and compatibility with MDE.

Implementation steps

To enable MDE on your Windows Server 2025, follow these key steps:

1. **Set up Azure tenant**: Ensure you have an Azure tenant and link your server with AAD.

2. **Choose licensing plan**: Select the appropriate plan (Plan 1 or Plan 2) based on your security requirements.

3. **Enable MDE**: Configure MDE on your server via the Azure portal.

4. **Integrate Log Analytics**: Set up Azure Log Analytics to collect and analyze security-related data.

5. **Monitor and manage**: Use the Microsoft Defender Security Center to monitor threats, manage security settings, and generate comprehensive reports.

By incorporating MDE into Windows Server 2025, organizations can achieve a robust security framework capable of defending against modern, sophisticated threats while simplifying management with integrated tools and detailed analytics.

Having covered integration and requirements of Windows Defender Antivirus in Windows Server 2025, the focus now shifts to a note on security baselines and monitoring drift.

Note on security baselines and monitoring drift

Setting security baselines is a crucial practice for maintaining a secure and compliant IT environment. A security baseline is a set of minimum security configurations that align with organizational policies and industry best practices. Establishing these baselines ensures that all systems meet fundamental security requirements, reducing vulnerabilities and simplifying the process of maintaining consistency across your network.

Monitoring drift refers to tracking changes from the defined baseline settings, whether intentional or accidental. This is vital for detecting unauthorized modifications or misconfigurations that could introduce security risks. Regularly checking for drift ensures that your systems remain aligned with the organization's security standards.

PowerShell example – checking security baseline drift

Here is a basic example of using PowerShell to check whether specific security settings match your baseline configuration:

```
# Example to check the status of Windows Defender Antivirus
$baselineStatus = $false
$currentStatus = (Get-MpPreference).DisableRealtimeMonitoring
if ($currentStatus -eq $baselineStatus) {
    Write-Host "Security baseline is intact."
} else {
    Write-Host "Security baseline drift detected. Review settings."
}
```

This simple script checks whether Windows Defender real-time monitoring is enabled and compares it to the desired baseline setting. If there's a mismatch, the administrator is notified to review the system's configuration.

By regularly running such checks, you can maintain security standards and detect drift early, preventing potential vulnerabilities from going unnoticed.

After covering security baselines and monitoring drift, the following section provides practical exercises. These exercises will guide you through configuring firewall rules, enabling TLS encryption, and setting up audit logs, allowing you to apply the best practices discussed in a hands-on manner.

Chapter exercise – configuring firewall rules, enabling TLS encryption, and setting up audit logs

For this chapter's exercises, you will be guided through the steps to configure firewall rules, enable TLS encryption, and set up audit logs in Windows Server 2025. These essential security measures are designed to enhance the protection of your server environment by controlling network traffic, securing data in transit, and monitoring user activities.

The exercises begin with configuring Windows Defender Firewall rules to specify which traffic is allowed or blocked, ensuring that only authorized connections are permitted. Next, you will enable TLS encryption to secure communications between your server and clients, protecting sensitive data from interception. Finally, you will set up audit logs to monitor and record significant activities within the server, helping you identify potential security breaches or unusual user behavior.

Through detailed, step-by-step instructions, you will perform these crucial configurations, verify their effectiveness, and develop practical skills that enhance your ability to manage and secure your server environment. These hands-on exercises are vital for administrators seeking to maintain a robust security posture in their organizations, ensuring compliance with best practices and regulatory standards. By completing these exercises, you will gain a deeper understanding of essential security features in Windows Server 2025, equipping you to safeguard your infrastructure effectively.

Exercise 11.1 – Configuring firewall rules

To configure an inbound firewall rule using Windows Defender Firewall in Windows Server 2025, follow these steps:

1. Open the **Start** menu and search for Windows Defender Firewall. Select it from the search results.

2. In the left pane, click **Advanced Settings** to access the **Windows Defender Firewall with Advanced Security** console.

3. In the console, select **Inbound Rules** from the left pane.

4. In the right pane, click **New Rule...** to launch **New Inbound Rule Wizard**.

5. On the wizard's first screen, choose **Port** and click **Next**.

6. On the **Protocols and Ports** page, select **TCP** and input 3389 as the port number, as illustrated in *Figure 11.11*. Click **Next**.

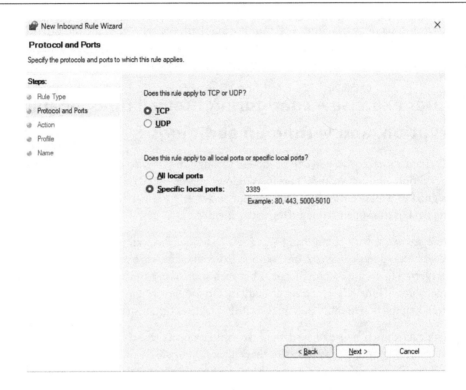

Figure 11.11 – Specifying the protocol and the port of the rule

7. On the **Action** page, choose **Allow the connection**, then click **Next**.

8. On the **Profile** page, select the profiles to which the rule should apply (**Domain**, **Private**, or **Public**), and click **Next**.

9. On the **Name** page, provide a name and description for the rule, and click **Finish**.

To set up an outbound firewall rule, follow the same steps but select **Outbound Rules** in the left pane.

Exercise 11.2 – Enabling TLS encryption

To enable TLS encryption using Group Policy Management in Windows Server 2025 (domain controller), follow these steps:

1. Open the **Start** menu and type `Group Policy Management`. Select the application from the results.

2. In the **Group Policy Management** console, navigate to your domain.

3. Right-click on **Default Domain Policy** and choose **Edit**.

4. Go to **Computer Configuration** > **Policies** > **Administrative Templates** > **Network** > **SSL Configuration Settings**.

5. Modify **SSL Cipher Suite Order** to prioritize TLS 1.3 and other secure cipher suites, as shown in *Figure 11.12*. You can refer to Microsoft's documentation (*Cipher Suites in TLS/SSL (Schannel SSP)*: `https://learn.microsoft.com/en-us/windows/win32/secauthn/cipher-suites-in-schannel`) or follow security best practices for the recommended cipher suite order.

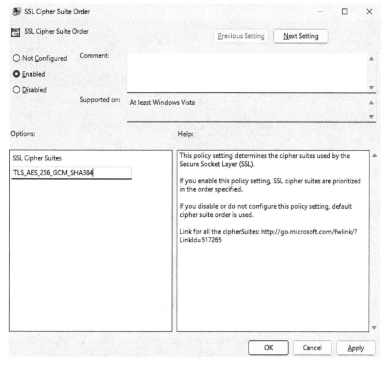

Figure 11.12 – Specifying the TLS 1.3 and other secure cipher suites

6. Click **Apply**, then click **OK**.

7. To immediately apply the updated policy settings, run `gpupdate /force` in the Command Prompt.

Exercise 11.3 – Setting up audit logs

To set up audit logs using the Local Security Policy in Windows Server 2025, follow these steps:

1. Open the **Start** menu and search for `Local Security Policy`, then select the application.

2. In the **Local Security Policy** console, go to **Local Policies** > **Audit Policy**.

3. Double-click on **Audit logon events**.

4. Select **Success** and **Failure**, as depicted in *Figure 11.13*, to record both successful and failed login attempts, then click **Apply** and **OK**.

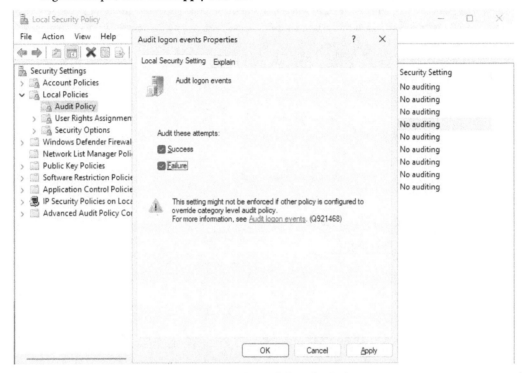

Figure 11.13 – Setting up the audit logs for the logon events

5. Depending on your security requirements, repeat this process for other policies such as **Audit account logon events**, **Audit policy changes**, and **Audit system events**.

These steps will guide you through successfully configuring firewall rules, enabling TLS encryption, and setting up audit logs in Windows Server 2025, ensuring enhanced security and compliance for your server environment. By completing these exercises, you will strengthen your system's defenses and improve overall visibility into network and user activities.

Summary

In this chapter, you gained a comprehensive understanding of the new security enhancements in Windows Server 2025, with a focus on improving access controls, threat detection, and automated response systems. We explored advanced authentication mechanisms such as biometric authentication, Conditional Access policies, and OAuth 2.0 integration to ensure stronger user verification and secure access to resources. You also learned about securing communication channels using TLS, HTTPS,

IPSec, and SSH, as well as the importance of monitoring secure channels to maintain data integrity and prevent potential breaches. Additionally, we discussed implementing security best practices, including effective patch management, detailed audit logging, and conducting regular security assessments, to fortify server environments against emerging threats. The chapter concluded with hands-on exercises where you configured firewall rules, enabled TLS encryption, and set up audit logs, reinforcing your practical understanding of these crucial security measures. Moving forward, the next chapter will focus on utilizing Hotpatch with Azure Arc to enhance system updates and patch management in hybrid cloud environments.

Questions

1. **True or false:** Windows Server 2025 introduces improved access controls as part of its new security enhancements.

2. **Fill in the blank:** _____ is the key feature in Windows Server 2025 for detecting and responding to advanced threats automatically.

3. **Multiple choice:** Which of the following secure authentication mechanisms are enhanced in Windows Server 2025? (Choose all that apply.)

    A. Biometric authentication

    B. Conditional Access policies

    C. OAuth 2.0 integration

    D. All of the above

4. **True or false:** TLS is used to secure communication channels in Windows Server 2025.

5. **Fill in the blank:** _____ is a widely used protocol alongside TLS for securing communication channels in Windows Server 2025.

6. **Multiple choice:** Which of the following protocols can be used to monitor and secure data communication channels in Windows Server 2025? (Choose all that apply.)

    A. HTTPS

    B. IPSec

    C. SSH

    D. All of the above

7. **True or false:** Patch management in Windows Server 2025 helps ensure that servers remain secure and up to date.

8. **Fill in the blank:** _____ is the audit log setting that can help administrators track security breaches and system anomalies in Windows Server 2025.

9. **Multiple choice:** Which of the following are considered security best practices for Windows Server 2025? (Choose all that apply.)

    A. Regular security assessments

    B. Detailed audit logging

    C. Consistent patch management

    D. All of the above

10. **Fill in the blank:** The regular execution of _____ is crucial to maintaining system security and identifying vulnerabilities in Windows Server 2025.

11. **Multiple choice:** Which of the following features enhance security in Windows Server 2025? (Choose all that apply.)

    A. Advanced threat detection

    B. Biometric authentication

    C. Automated response systems

    D. All of the above

12. **Short answer:** Discuss the importance of securing communication channels in Windows Server 2025 through TLS and other protocols.

13. **Short answer:** Explain how implementing audit logging in Windows Server 2025 improves system security and helps in incident management.

Further reading

- *Gain enhanced security and performance with Windows Server 2025*: `https://www.microsoft.com/en-us/windows-server/blog/2024/05/29/gain-enhanced-security-and-performance-with-windows-server-2025/`

- *Configuring Azure Active Directory Conditional Access*: `https://learn.microsoft.com/fi-fi/appcenter/general/configuring-aad-conditional-access`

- *Hotpatching is now available on Windows Server 2025 Evaluation VMs in Azure*: `https://techcommunity.microsoft.com/t5/windows-server-news-and-best/hotpatching-is-now-available-in-preview-on-windows-server-2025/ba-p/4203451`

- *OAuth 2.0 and OpenID Connect (OIDC) are on the Microsoft identity platform*: `https://learn.microsoft.com/en-us/entra/identity-platform/v2-protocols`

- *One simple action you can take to prevent 99.9 percent of attacks on your accounts*: `https://www.microsoft.com/en-us/security/blog/2019/08/20/one-simple-action-you-can-take-to-prevent-99-9-percent-of-account-attacks`

- *Announcing Windows Server 2025 Security Baseline Preview*: `https://techcommunity.microsoft.com/discussions/windowsserverinsiders/announcing-windows-server-2025-security-baseline-preview/4257686`

- *Microsoft Defender Antivirus on Windows Server*: `https://learn.microsoft.com/en-us/defender-endpoint/microsoft-defender-antivirus-on-windows-server`

- *Deploy OSConfig security baselines locally*: `https://learn.microsoft.com/en-us/windows-server/security/osconfig/osconfig-how-to-configure-security-baselines`

Unlock this book's exclusive benefits now

This book comes with additional benefits designed to elevate your learning experience.

Note: Have your purchase invoice ready before you begin.

`https://www.packtpub.com/unlock/9781836205012`

12

Managing Updates with Hotpatching, Azure Arc, and More in Windows Server 2025

This chapter provides a comprehensive guide on utilizing **hotpatching** with **Azure Arc** in Windows Server 2025, ensuring seamless server updates with minimal disruption. We begin by introducing the concept of server hotpatching and how Azure Arc can be leveraged to manage on-premises servers efficiently, highlighting the key benefits of this integration, such as minimizing downtime and maintaining continuous server availability. The chapter also outlines the specific compatibility features of Windows Server 2025, setting the stage for hotpatching implementation. Next, you'll be guided through the process of preparing servers for hotpatching, applying updates in real time without reboots, and validating patches to confirm the successful deployment.

Additionally, the chapter emphasizes strategies for managing the server lifecycle, with a focus on automating update management tasks to reduce administrative overhead. At the same time, monitoring and reporting tools are explored to ensure long-term server health. Troubleshooting techniques are discussed in the final section, covering common issues, diagnostic tools, and best practices to address potential challenges during hotpatching. The chapter concludes with a hands-on exercise in which you will configure Azure Arc on an on-premises Windows Server 2025 instance, allowing you to apply and monitor your first hotpatch in a practical setting.

In this chapter, we're going to cover the following main topics:

- Introduction to server hotpatching with Azure Arc in Windows Server 2025
- Applying hotfixes and updates using hotpatching
- Managing the server lifecycle and updates efficiently
- Troubleshooting hotpatching implementations
- Setting up Azure Arc in Windows Server 2025

Technical requirements

To complete the exercises in this chapter, you will require the following hardware:

- A Windows 11 Pro PC equipped with a minimum of 16 GB of RAM, a 1 TB hard disk drive (HDD), and a stable internet connection

- A Windows Server 2025 Standard (Desktop Experience) virtual machine, designated as Virtual Machine 1, configured with an AD DS, featuring at least 8 GB of RAM, 100 GB of HDD space, and internet access

- An Azure account and subscription

This setup ensures that you have the necessary resources and configurations to perform all tasks effectively.

Introduction to server hotpatching with Azure Arc in Windows Server 2025

In modern IT environments, *maintaining server availability* while *minimizing downtime* during updates is critical for uninterrupted operations. **Hotpatching**, a feature that allows system updates to be applied without the need for a reboot, is key to addressing this challenge. This section explores the implementation of server hotpatching in Windows Server 2025, explaining how it streamlines the update process for improved efficiency. With the integration of **Azure Arc**, Microsoft's hybrid cloud management solution, administrators can extend these hotpatching capabilities to manage both cloud and on-premises Windows Server environments efficiently. This section covers the fundamental concepts of hotpatching, emphasizes the benefits of Azure Arc in hybrid infrastructures, and outlines the specific compatibility and prerequisites for Windows Server 2025. By the end of this section, you will have a thorough grasp of how hotpatching supports modern server management and the critical role Azure Arc plays in expanding these capabilities across diverse IT infrastructures.

Overview of hotpatching

Hotpatching marks a major leap forward in server management, particularly when it comes to ensuring continuous operation without interruptions. This advanced feature allows system updates to be applied without the need for a reboot, significantly minimizing downtime and boosting server availability. In today's IT landscape, where operational efficiency and reliability are critical, hotpatching addresses a longstanding challenge in infrastructure management by offering a seamless solution for applying updates. Windows Server 2025 incorporates hotpatching to optimize the update process, allowing administrators to deploy essential patches and updates with minimal disruption. This capability is particularly valuable in environments where high availability is crucial—such as data centers and enterprise networks—where even brief outages can cause substantial operational issues and financial repercussions.

To utilize hotpatching in Windows Server 2025, specific requirements must be met:

- **Windows Server 2025 Datacenter or Standard Edition**: Ensure you are using the appropriate edition of Windows Server 2025

- **Azure Arc connectivity**: The server must be connected to Azure Arc, which facilitates the management and deployment of hotpatches

- **Software Assurance**: A valid Software Assurance subscription is required to access hotpatching features

- **Virtualization-Based Security (VBS)**: VBS must be enabled and operational on the server

- **Specific Security Updates**: Ensure that particular updates are installed

The integration of hotpatching with Azure Arc further extends its capabilities, enabling a unified management experience across various infrastructures. Azure Arc, depicted in *Figure 12.1*, Microsoft's hybrid cloud management platform, empowers IT professionals to govern on-premises, multi-cloud, and edge environments from a single control plane. By using Azure Arc, administrators can implement hotpatching across both cloud-based and on-premises Windows Server instances, ensuring that updates are applied consistently and securely without the need for reboots. This not only simplifies the update management process but also enhances system security by ensuring that servers are always running the latest patches.

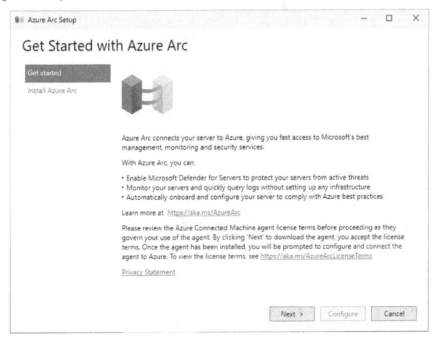

Figure 12.1 – Azure Arc setup in Windows Server 2025

Hotpatching in Windows Server 2025 is designed to work seamlessly with modern hardware and software configurations, allowing organizations to leverage their existing IT investments fully. By following the compatibility guidelines and utilizing Microsoft's extensive documentation, IT professionals can effectively implement and manage hotpatching within their environments. This feature represents a vital innovation in server management, offering a reliable and efficient way to apply updates. Specific requirements must be met to utilize hotpatching, including the use of **Virtualization-Based Security** (**VBS**) enclaves. VBS enclaves provide an isolated environment that enhances security by protecting critical processes from potential threats. This requirement ensures that hotpatching can be performed securely and effectively.

The integration of hotpatching with Azure Arc amplifies its effectiveness, providing a robust solution (as illustrated in *Figure 12.2*) for managing updates across a wide range of infrastructures. Patches are created and deployed efficiently, while update management tools help track and schedule them. Azure Arc integration allows consistent updates across diverse infrastructures—on-premises, cloud, and hybrid—while hotpatching minimizes downtime by applying updates without rebooting systems. Verification and reporting ensure the patches are successfully applied, increasing security and stability across the organization. As IT environments continue to evolve, hot patching becomes an indispensable tool in modern server management strategies. It plays an increasingly essential role in maintaining continuous operations and ensuring update efficiency.

Figure 12.2 – Hotpatching workflow

> **Note:**
> When implementing hotpatching, ensure that all server roles and applications are compatible with this feature. To avoid disruptions in service, regularly review Microsoft's documentation for updates regarding supported configurations.

After exploring the initial overview of hotpatching and its importance in maintaining operational continuity, it is crucial to understand the benefits of integrating Azure Arc. This integration not only improves server management but also simplifies operations across diverse environments.

Benefits of using Azure Arc

The integration of Azure Arc with Windows Server 2025 offers a wide array of benefits for IT professionals managing hybrid and multi-cloud environments. Primarily, Azure Arc extends Azure's management capabilities to on-premises, cloud-based, and edge resources, creating a unified control plane that simplifies administration. By utilizing familiar Azure tools, administrators can efficiently manage Windows Server instances regardless of their location, reducing complexity and operational costs.

A major advantage lies in the *improved security and compliance* Azure Arc brings. IT teams can enforce consistent security policies and standards across all servers, whether they reside on-premises or in the cloud. This unified approach strengthens an organization's overall security posture while enabling advanced threat protection and real-time monitoring to address potential risks swiftly. Azure Arc also provides significant *flexibility and scalability*, which is crucial for growing businesses. It allows organizations to seamlessly integrate new resources into their existing environments, dynamically managing resources without the need for extensive reconfiguration. That ensures that, as operational demands increase, businesses can scale their infrastructure efficiently without sacrificing performance or security.

Additionally, the combination of Azure Arc and hotpatching in Windows Server 2025 ensures continuous system availability by *reducing downtime* during updates. With the ability to apply critical patches without rebooting, businesses can keep services running smoothly, maintaining productivity while minimizing disruption. That is particularly beneficial for high-availability environments, where even short downtime can be costly. Azure Arc's support for hybrid and multi-cloud environments further enhances its value. By breaking down silos between different platforms, it provides a cohesive management framework that improves resource utilization, streamlines cost management, and enforces consistent policies across diverse infrastructure landscapes.

In essence, the integration of Azure Arc with Windows Server 2025 equips IT professionals with enhanced control, security, scalability, and operational efficiency. It ensures minimal downtime while empowering organizations to achieve greater agility, resilience, and optimization of their IT operations, aligning with the evolving needs of modern enterprises.

> **Note:**
> While Azure Arc offers significant advantages in managing hybrid environments, it's crucial to regularly audit your security policies and compliance measures across both on-premises and cloud resources. This proactive approach helps mitigate risks associated with diverse infrastructures.

Having established the benefits of Azure Arc, it is crucial to examine the compatibility features of Windows Server 2025. Understanding how this operating system seamlessly integrates with existing infrastructures ensures that organizations can effectively leverage the advantages of hotpatching while preserving their current investments.

Windows Server 2025 compatibility

Windows Server 2025 is engineered to *integrate seamlessly* with existing IT infrastructures, ensuring broad compatibility across diverse environments. This design allows organizations to upgrade without the need for a full-scale overhaul, conserving resources and minimizing disruptions. With backward compatibility, legacy applications and services continue to function efficiently, ensuring smooth transitions and uninterrupted operations.

Windows Server 2025 further leverages *advanced compatibility layers and virtualization technologies* to accommodate complex IT environments. This feature is particularly advantageous for enterprises with a blend of modern and legacy systems, allowing various technologies to coexist within a unified management framework. IT professionals can confidently deploy new features and updates, knowing that compatibility challenges will not disrupt their operations. The operating system's compatibility also extends to a wide range of hardware configurations, from traditional on-premises servers to modern cloud-based infrastructures. This adaptability ensures that organizations can maintain high performance and reliability regardless of their chosen hardware platform. Microsoft's rigorous testing and certification processes, in collaboration with hardware vendors and software developers, further bolster compatibility by ensuring that products meet stringent performance and security standards.

Additionally, Windows Server 2025 supports a broad array of *security protocols and compliance standards*, enabling organizations to meet industry regulations and maintain robust security practices. That is particularly important for highly regulated industries that require strict adherence to security guidelines. Seamless integration with existing security frameworks helps protect infrastructure and data from evolving threats. The compatibility also extends to management tools such as **System Center** and **Azure Arc**, depicted in *Figure 12.3*, offering IT professionals a centralized platform to manage, monitor, and optimize their server environments. The inclusion of containerization technologies such as **Docker** and **Kubernetes** is another highlight, facilitating the deployment and scaling of containerized applications essential for modern DevOps workflows and microservices architectures.

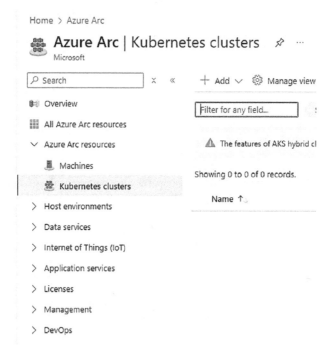

Figure 12.3 – Kubernetes clusters within Azure Arc resources

Windows Server 2025's hybrid cloud support further enhances its flexibility, allowing businesses to extend their on-premises infrastructure into cloud platforms such as Microsoft Azure. This hybrid capability enables organizations to take advantage of cloud scalability while maintaining control over on-premises resources, meeting dynamic business demands with greater operational agility.

This compatibility makes Windows Server 2025 an essential upgrade, empowering IT teams to maintain performance, security, and continuity while benefiting from the latest innovations. Microsoft's focus on compatibility ensures that enterprises can innovate without compromising their existing investments, reinforcing the platform's role in modern IT environments.

> **Note:**
> Always verify the compatibility of your existing hardware and software with Windows Server 2025 before upgrading. Utilize Microsoft's compatibility testing tools to ensure a smooth transition and avoid potential operational disruptions. Keeping a detailed inventory of your current systems will facilitate better planning and execution of upgrades.

With a thorough grasp of hotpatching, its benefits through Azure Arc, and the compatibility of Windows Server 2025, we are well-positioned to explore practical applications in the next section. The upcoming discussion will focus on applying hotfixes and updates using hotpatching, providing insights into how these features can be effectively utilized to enhance server management and operational efficiency.

Applying hotfixes and updates using hotpatching

Maintaining the security, stability, and performance of IT infrastructures is paramount, especially in enterprise environments that demand continuous availability and high operational efficiency. In this landscape, hotpatching stands out as a vital technique that enables IT professionals to apply updates and patches without requiring system reboots or causing significant downtime. This capability is particularly crucial for organizations running mission-critical applications or services, as even minor interruptions can lead to considerable operational and financial impacts.

The upcoming subsections will explore the detailed process of implementing *hotfixes* and *updates* through hotpatching, starting with the necessary preparatory steps to facilitate the seamless integration of patches. Hotfixes and updates are essential in maintaining system stability and security. A hotfix is a small, targeted software patch that addresses specific issues, often applied to resolve critical bugs or security vulnerabilities quickly without rebooting. In contrast, updates are broader, scheduled releases that can include new features, performance improvements, and cumulative fixes. These updates often require a system reboot and are essential for maintaining the overall health and functionality of servers and systems. Following this, we will examine the execution of hotpatches, offering comprehensive insights into the methodologies and best practices for applying updates in a live environment. Finally, we will address post-patching validation procedures, which are essential for confirming the successful application of patches and ensuring that the system continues to meet optimal performance and security standards. This structured approach will equip IT professionals with the knowledge and strategies needed to effectively utilize hotpatching, ultimately enhancing their system management practices and fostering greater operational resilience and efficiency.

Preparing for hotpatching

Before embarking on the hotpatching journey, thorough preparation is essential to ensure seamless integration with minimal disruption to business operations. The complexities of modern IT environments necessitate a proactive approach to patch management, where meticulous planning can significantly enhance the likelihood of successful deployments. In this section, we will outline the crucial preparatory steps that IT professionals should undertake to lay the groundwork for effective hotpatching. From conducting a comprehensive evaluation of the existing system to formulating a detailed patch management plan, each step plays a pivotal role in mitigating risks and ensuring operational continuity. Here are the key steps involved in preparing for hotpatching:

- **Conduct a Comprehensive Evaluation:** Effective hotpatching necessitates *thorough preparation* to ensure smooth integration and minimal disruption to business operations. The initial step in this process is to conduct a comprehensive evaluation of the existing system environment. IT professionals should carry out a detailed audit of all systems slated for hotpatching, documenting *hardware configurations*, *software versions*, and *network dependencies*. This baseline assessment is vital for identifying any potential conflicts or compatibility issues that may emerge during the patching process.

- **Formulate a Detailed Patch Management Plan:** Once the assessment is complete, the next critical task is to formulate a detailed **patch management plan**. This plan should specify the *patches to be applied*, the *order of application*, and the *designated maintenance windows*. Additionally, it must outline *rollback procedures* to revert the system to its prior state in case of any unforeseen complications. Effective communication with all stakeholders is essential at this stage to ensure that everyone is aware of the scheduled maintenance and its potential impact on system availability.

- **Confirm Backups and Test Patches:** Before implementing the hotpatches, it is crucial to confirm that all backups are current and complete. A *solid backup strategy* guarantees that critical data and system configurations can be restored swiftly if needed. Furthermore, IT professionals should test the patches in a controlled environment that simulates the production setup. This *testing phase* is vital for identifying unexpected issues and refining the patching process. *Establishing* a *fallback environment* that can be activated quickly in case of significant problems during deployment is also advisable.

- **Ensure Security Compliance:** Security considerations are paramount throughout the preparation phase. IT professionals must ensure compliance with all *security protocols* and verify that patches originate from *trusted vendors*. Reviewing the release notes and documentation of the patches is important to understand the specific vulnerabilities they address and any prerequisites for their successful application. Additionally, conducting a *security risk assessment* before patching aids in identifying potential threats and implementing necessary countermeasures.

- **Prepare Tools and Resources:** Lastly, preparing for hotpatching involves ensuring that all required tools and resources are *readily accessible*. That includes utilizing the latest patch management software, ensuring team members are well-trained, and establishing monitoring systems to track the progress and success of the hotpatching process in real time. Having a *dedicated response team* on standby to address any issues that may arise during the patching process is also beneficial. By adhering to these preparatory steps, IT professionals can embark on hotpatching with confidence, knowing they have effectively mitigated risks and established a solid foundation for a smooth and efficient update process.

Table 12.1 lists the crucial elements required for IT professionals to facilitate a smooth and efficient hotpatching process. It serves as an invaluable resource to enhance operational readiness and minimize disruptions during system updates.

Step	Description
1. **System Environment Audit**	Conduct a thorough audit of all systems scheduled for hotpatching, documenting hardware configurations, software versions, and network dependencies.
2. **Develop a Patch Management Plan**	Outline the specific patches to be applied, the sequence of their application, and designated maintenance windows. Include rollback procedures and communicate with stakeholders.
3. **Verify Backups**	Ensure all backups are current and complete. A robust backup strategy allows for quick restoration of critical data and system configurations if necessary.
4. **Test Patches in a Controlled Environment**	Test patches in a controlled environment that mirrors the production setup to identify any unforeseen issues and refine the patching process.
5. **Establish a Fallback Environment**	Set up a fallback environment that can be quickly activated if the patch deployment encounters significant problems.
6. **Security Considerations**	Ensure all security protocols are adhered to, verify patches from trusted vendors, and review release notes and documentation. Conduct a security risk assessment prior to patching.
7. **Prepare Tools and Resources**	Ensure access to the latest patch management software, train team members adequately, and set up monitoring systems to track the hotpatching process in real time.
8. **Have a Response Team Ready**	Have a dedicated response team on standby to address any issues that may arise during the patching process.

Table 12.1 – Hotpatching preparation list

> **Note:**
> Always ensure that you maintain an *updated inventory* of your system configurations and installed software versions before beginning the hotpatching process. This inventory serves as a crucial reference point for troubleshooting and can expedite the rollback process if issues arise post-patching. Having an accurate record allows you to quickly identify potential conflicts and compatibility issues, significantly enhancing the effectiveness of your patch management strategy.

With a comprehensive understanding of the preparation process established, we can now transition to the next phase: executing hotpatches. This stage is critical for ensuring the successful application of updates in a live environment while maintaining operational continuity.

Executing Hotpatches

The execution phase, as illustrated in *Figure 12.4*, of hotpatching is a crucial responsibility for IT professionals, requiring *precision*, *expertise*, and a *systematic approach* to ensure a seamless and successful deployment. The following steps outline the essential tasks that need to be completed during this phase:

1. **Initiate Hotpatch Application:** Once all preparatory steps have been thoroughly completed, you can initiate the application of hotpatches in the live environment. The first step is to verify the *integrity and authenticity* of the hotpatch files. For instance, cryptographic hash functions, such as **SHA-256**, are utilized, which is an algorithm that transforms input data into a **fixed-size string** called a hash. It's primarily used for verifying data integrity, as even minor changes in input generate a significantly different hash. Hash functions are key to encryption, ensuring secure password storage and data verification. Therefore, verifying the integrity and authenticity of the hotpatch involves comparing the hash values of the files against those provided by the vendor. This process helps prevent the application of unauthorized or corrupted patches, which could compromise system stability and security.

2. **Apply Hotpatches:** After verification, proceed to apply the hotpatches in the *order* outlined in the **patch management plan**. Automated patch management tools such as Microsoft **System Center Configuration Manager** (**SCCM**) or **Red Hat Satellite** can streamline and enhance the deployment process's accuracy. These tools often offer real-time monitoring and logging features, allowing the IT team to track the status of each patch and address any arising issues promptly.

3. **Maintain Communication:** Throughout the patching process, maintaining *clear and effective communication* with all relevant stakeholders is essential. That ensures that any unexpected disruptions or performance impacts can be communicated swiftly and managed efficiently. Your proactive updates will help stakeholders feel engaged and informed, contributing to a smoother patching experience. Additionally, actively monitoring system performance metrics using tools such as **Nagios** or **Zabbix** during the patching process is critical. This real-time oversight aids in identifying any adverse effects from the patches, enabling rapid remediation to preserve system integrity.

4. **Schedule Maintenance Windows:** To mitigate potential disruptions, apply hotpatches during *predefined* maintenance windows, ideally during periods of low activity, such as late night or early morning. However, thanks to the nature of hotpatching, which eliminates the need for system reboots, these windows can be more flexible as long as adequate monitoring and contingency plans are in place. For instance, an e-commerce platform might choose to apply patches at 2 A.M. when user activity is at its lowest.

5. **Validate Patched Systems:** Following the successful application of hotpatches, it is essential to conduct a comprehensive *validation* of the patched systems. This validation involves running tests to ensure that all applications and services are operating correctly. Your role during this phase is vital, as you should review *system logs* and *performance reports* for any anomalies introduced during the patching process. For example, executing a suite of automated regression tests can help validate the functionality and performance of an internal ERP system.

6. **Execute Rollback Procedures:** Should any issues arise, promptly executing the *predefined rollback procedures* is crucial to restoring the system to its prior state. This contingency plan ensures that business operations can continue with minimal disruption while the IT team investigates and resolves the underlying problems. For instance, if a hotpatch leads to a critical application crash, the IT team should have a rollback script ready to revert the patch and restore the application to its previous operational state.

7. **Document the Process:** Finally, *thorough documentation* of the hotpatching process is essential. This documentation should encompass the patches applied, any issues encountered, and the steps taken to resolve them. Such records are invaluable for future reference and the continuous improvement of patch management practices. By following these best practices, IT professionals can effectively execute hotpatches, ultimately enhancing the security, stability, and performance of their enterprise IT environments.

Figure 12.4 – Hotpatching flowchart

> **Note:**
> Implement a comprehensive logging mechanism during the execution of hotpatches. Detailed logs of the deployment process not only aid in monitoring the success of each patch but also provide invaluable insight for post-patching validation and troubleshooting. In the event of unexpected behavior or failures, these logs can be instrumental in diagnosing problems and refining future patching efforts.

Having executed the hotpatches with precision, it is now essential to focus on post-patching validation. This step will confirm that the patches have been effectively integrated, ensuring that all systems are functioning as intended and that security standards are upheld.

Post-patching validation

After the application of hotpatches, the next critical phase is post-patching validation, depicted in *Figure 12.5*, which serves as a safeguard to confirm that the updates have been successfully integrated into the system without compromising its overall integrity and functionality. IT professionals should prioritize their validation efforts, focusing first on critical applications that impact business operations, as these require immediate attention. This phase is essential for mitigating risks associated with patching, as it ensures that any issues arising from the new patches are identified and addressed promptly. By conducting a thorough assessment of the patched environment, IT professionals can validate both the functional and non-functional aspects of the system. In the following sections, we will explore the key components of post-patching validation, highlighting the importance of analyzing system performance, conducting security assessments, and maintaining clear communication throughout the process. Here are the critical steps involved in post-patching validation.

1. **Analyze System Logs and Performance Metrics:** IT professionals must carefully *analyze system logs*, *performance metrics*, and *application behavior* to identify any discrepancies or anomalies that may have emerged following the patching. Attention to detail is vital; for example, after applying a patch to a database management system, IT staff should evaluate database query performance and error rates to confirm that no new issues have surfaced. It is also essential to conduct a combination of *automated and manual tests* to validate the functionality of key applications and services. *Regression testing* can help verify that existing features within a web application operate without interruption, while load testing ensures the system can accommodate anticipated user traffic without performance degradation.

2. **Conduct Security Assessments:** Another critical component of post-patching validation involves *conducting security assessments* to confirm that the patches have successfully addressed the targeted vulnerabilities. This process includes performing *vulnerability scans* and *penetration tests* to identify any remaining security gaps. For instance, after patching a known vulnerability in a web server, IT professionals should conduct a security scan to ensure that the vulnerability has been effectively mitigated and that no new vulnerabilities have been introduced. Reviewing the patch vendor's release notes and documentation is also essential to understand the specific vulnerabilities addressed and to confirm that all security measures have been properly implemented.

3. **Maintain Effective Communication and Documentation:** *Effective communication* and *meticulous documentation* are paramount during this phase. Relevant stakeholders must be updated on the validation results and any issues encountered. Thoroughly maintained detailed records of the patches applied, validation steps undertaken, and outcomes achieved should be maintained. This documentation not only serves as a future reference for subsequent patching activities but also aids in meeting compliance and auditing requirements. For example, keeping a log of all applied patches and their validation outcomes helps track the system's security posture over time.

4. **Initiate Remediation or Rollback Procedures:** If issues are identified during this phase, IT professionals must promptly initiate *predefined remediation* or *rollback procedures* to restore system stability. That ensures that business operations can continue with minimal disruption while the root causes of the problems are investigated and resolved. For instance, if a patch leads to an application crash, the rollback procedure should restore the application to its previous stable state. Continuous monitoring should also be maintained to detect any delayed issues that might arise after the initial validation phase. IT teams may utilize application performance monitoring tools to oversee the ongoing performance of the system following the patching.

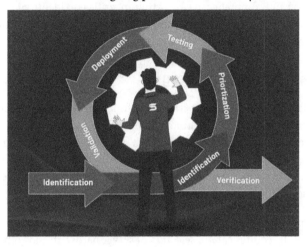

Figure 12.5 – Post-patching validation process (source – SecPod)

By following these best practices, IT professionals can ensure that post-patching validation is comprehensive and practical, thereby enhancing the overall security, stability, and resilience of the IT infrastructure. This structured approach to validation emphasizes the importance of meticulous planning and execution in maintaining robust and reliable enterprise systems.

> **Note:**
> Regularly schedule *follow-up audits* after completing post-patching validation. This proactive measure ensures that any latent issues that may not have been immediately apparent are identified and addressed promptly. Continuous monitoring and periodic assessments of system performance and security can help safeguard against vulnerabilities that might emerge after patch deployment, ensuring sustained operational integrity.

After completing the validation process to ensure that all patches have been integrated successfully, we can now shift our focus to the next section. We will explore strategies and best practices for overseeing the entire lifecycle of servers, including how to effectively manage updates and maintenance tasks to enhance overall system performance and reliability.

Managing the server lifecycle and updates efficiently

As IT infrastructure continues to evolve, managing the lifecycle and updates of servers efficiently is vital for maintaining optimal *system performance*, *security*, and *stability*. This section focuses on key practices for server lifecycle management, covering every phase from deployment to decommissioning. Effective management ensures that servers are configured and maintained to meet business objectives and keep pace with technological advancements. Automation of update processes further reduces manual tasks, minimizes downtime, and guarantees uniformity across the server environment. Additionally, proactive monitoring and comprehensive reporting are critical to identifying issues early, maintaining compliance, and driving informed decision-making. Together, these strategies provide a structured framework for ensuring the reliability and efficiency of IT operations.

Lifecycle management strategies

A well-executed lifecycle management strategy is fundamental to maintaining a secure, efficient, and adaptable IT infrastructure. These strategies provide a structured approach that spans the entire server lifecycle, from initial deployment through to decommissioning, ensuring systems are aligned with both current and future business demands. By adopting a comprehensive, forward-looking perspective, organizations can effectively mitigate challenges, enhancing the stability and resilience of their IT operations:

- **Deployment Phase:** The **deployment phase** marks the foundation of effective lifecycle management. It requires careful selection of server hardware and software configurations that address present workloads while allowing for future scalability. Standardizing installation and configuration processes ensures consistency across the infrastructure, reducing variability and promoting operational efficiency.

- **Maintenance and Updates:** Once operational, the focus shifts to **maintaining** server health through regular updates and patch management. Automating these tasks is critical to minimizing human error and ensuring uniform application across all systems. Automated tools also simplify the process of identifying, scheduling, and applying updates during low-usage periods, which reduces downtime and potential service interruptions.

- **Monitoring and Reporting: Monitoring and reporting** play pivotal roles in preemptively addressing issues before they impact system performance. Advanced monitoring tools provide real-time insights, enabling IT teams to detect anomalies and address them before they escalate. Detailed reporting further enhances this process by offering an in-depth analysis of system health, compliance, and efficiency, which informs strategic decision-making.

- **Decommissioning:** As servers near the end of their lifecycle, **decommissioning** must be executed with minimal disruption. That involves safely deactivating legacy hardware and transferring data and services to newer platforms. Comprehensive documentation, maintained throughout the server's life is critical for ensuring seamless decommissioning and serves as a valuable resource for future projects.

The **Lifecycle Management Flowchart**, presented in *Table 12.2*, represents the stages of server lifecycle management, providing a comprehensive overview of the processes involved from the deployment phase to decommissioning. This flowchart serves as a crucial reference for IT professionals and administrators, enabling them to understand the interconnected activities and best practices essential for maintaining a robust server environment.

Stage	Key Activities and Considerations
Deployment	• Select appropriate hardware and software configurations. • Establish standardized installation and configuration procedures. • Ensure scalability for future expansion.
Maintenance	• Automate regular updates and patch management. • Implement routine checks to safeguard against vulnerabilities. • Utilize tools to streamline the update process and minimize downtime.
Monitoring	• Implement advanced monitoring tools to track system performance. • Detect anomalies and preemptively address potential problems. • Generate comprehensive reports for system health and compliance.
Decommissioning	• Deactivate and remove outdated hardware securely. • Migrate data and services to newer platforms. • Maintain proper documentation throughout the lifecycle.

Table 12.2 – Lifecycle management flowchart

Ultimately, the success of lifecycle management depends on an integrated approach that encompasses deployment, maintenance, monitoring, and decommissioning. By leveraging automation and advanced tools, organizations can ensure a resilient, secure, and scalable IT environment that evolves alongside business needs and technological advancements.

> **Note:**
> Always maintain an updated inventory of your server assets, including their roles, configurations, and lifecycle stages. This practice not only aids in effective lifecycle management but also facilitates quicker decision-making regarding upgrades, decommissioning, and compliance audits. Leveraging tools that automate asset tracking can further enhance this process, ensuring accuracy and reducing manual oversight.

Implementing robust lifecycle management strategies is essential for maximizing the efficiency and longevity of server environments. This subsection outlines best practices for planning, deploying, and decommissioning servers, ensuring that each phase of the lifecycle is managed effectively to reduce downtime and enhance resource utilization. Transitioning from lifecycle management, the focus shifts to how automating update processes can further streamline server management.

Automating update management

In modern IT infrastructure, automating update management is an essential strategy for maintaining secure, stable, and efficient server environments. This process not only ensures timely patching and updates but also minimizes the risk of human error, which is critical to maintaining system integrity. By leveraging automation tools, IT teams can streamline update management, creating a consistent approach across the entire server ecosystem, a key factor in enhancing overall system reliability.

Updates are automated by deploying specialized software designed to identify, download, and apply necessary patches. Tools such as **Azure Update Manager**, as shown in *Figure 12.6*, which illustrates how SCCM enables centralized management of software deployment, updates, and security across Microsoft's IT infrastructure, and **Red Hat Satellite** are commonly used to execute these updates during off-peak hours, minimizing disruptions to daily operations. Automation also allows for systematic scheduling of updates, which is crucial for environments with stringent uptime requirements, ensuring patches are applied in a controlled manner without risking service continuity. One of the core benefits of automating update management is achieving uniformity across servers, regardless of their location or function.

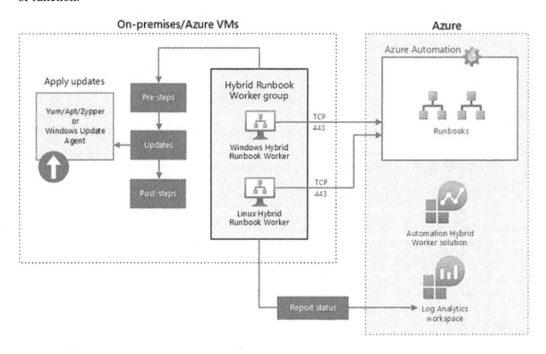

Figure 12.6 – Automating Updates with Azure Update Manager (source – Microsoft)

The **Azure Update Automation** solution demonstrates the deployment and management of updates for both on-premises and cloud-based virtual machines and resources. Automating the scheduling, monitoring, and reporting of update processes ensures that every server, whether local or remote (Azure VMs), consistently receives the same updates, thereby maintaining security and compliance. For instance, **Microsoft System Center Configuration Manager (SCCM)** can efficiently apply security patches across many servers, reducing potential vulnerabilities. These tools and solutions also generate detailed logs and reports, providing insights into deployment success and assisting with compliance and audit reporting.

Additionally, automated update management facilitates proactive monitoring and rapid issue resolution. It can identify anomalies during the update process and trigger immediate corrective actions, ensuring problems are resolved before they impact system performance. Integrating intelligent analytics within these solutions enables IT professionals to predict potential risks and focus on more strategic initiatives, leaving routine maintenance tasks to automation. Automation also enables continuous improvement through feedback loops. IT teams can analyze the performance of automated updates and refine processes for enhanced efficiency. This adaptability ensures that update management evolves with emerging technologies and business needs. For example, using **Azure DevOps** for **continuous integration and continuous delivery (CI/CD)** allows automated testing and deployment of updates, ensuring seamless system evolution in response to new challenges and opportunities.

Automating update management is a critical aspect of IT infrastructure, enhancing operational efficiency, security, and scalability. Organizations can maintain resilient server environments by utilizing tools like **SCCM and Intune** while freeing up IT resources for more strategic, high-value tasks.

> **Note:**
> Implement a *rollback strategy* before applying any automated updates, particularly in production environments. That ensures that if an update leads to unforeseen issues, you can quickly revert to the previous stable state. Additionally, scheduling updates during off-peak hours should be considered to minimize disruption to users and services, thus maintaining business continuity.

Implementing robust lifecycle management strategies is essential for maximizing the efficiency and longevity of server environments. This subsection outlines best practices for planning, deploying, and decommissioning servers, ensuring that each phase of the lifecycle is managed effectively to reduce downtime and enhance resource utilization. Transitioning from lifecycle management, the focus shifts to how automating update processes can further streamline server management.

Monitoring and reporting

In the realm of IT infrastructure management, the significance of *monitoring and reporting* cannot be overstated, as they are crucial for ensuring the optimal health and performance of server environments. Effective monitoring encompasses real-time tracking of various system metrics, including resource utilization, application performance, and network throughput. By utilizing advanced monitoring solutions such as **Nagios**, **Zabbix**, and **SolarWinds**, IT professionals can swiftly identify anomalies and irregularities before they develop into critical issues. For instance, Nagios can trigger an alert if a server's CPU usage remains above 90% for an extended period, enabling the IT team to investigate and address the issue proactively.

Additionally, robust reporting mechanisms play a vital role in transforming raw data into actionable insights. Comprehensive reports on *system performance*, *security compliance*, and *operational efficiency* are essential for informed strategic planning and decision-making. Such reports help IT teams recognize trends, evaluate the effects of recent changes, and anticipate future needs. For example, regular performance reports may reveal recurring bottlenecks, prompting proactive measures to optimize resource allocation and enhance overall system performance. This could involve identifying peak network traffic times during the week and subsequently deciding to increase bandwidth during those periods. The integration of automated monitoring and reporting significantly improves the accuracy and consistency of data collection. Automation ensures continuous oversight while reducing the likelihood of human error, thereby establishing a reliable foundation for decision-making. Advanced analytics within these monitoring tools can also predict potential failures and suggest preventative actions, further reinforcing system integrity. For instance, predictive analytics in SolarWinds may indicate an impending hard drive failure by analyzing temperature trends and usage patterns, facilitating preemptive replacement to avert data loss.

Moreover, real-time monitoring and reporting, depicted in *Figure 12.7*, are essential for maintaining *regulatory compliance* and *audit readiness*. Many industries face strict regulatory mandates requiring thorough documentation and reporting of IT activities. Automated tools aid in compliance by keeping detailed and up-to-date records of *system changes*, *security incidents*, and *patch applications*. That streamlines the audit process and ensures organizations adhere to best practices and regulatory standards. For instance, in healthcare, automated reporting can support adherence to the **Health Insurance Portability and Accountability Act** (**HIPAA**) regulations—standards designed to safeguard the privacy and security of personal medical information and provide guidelines for the electronic sharing of health data—by consistently monitoring and recording access to patient information. The scope of monitoring and reporting transcends immediate issue resolution, encompassing the long-term optimization of systems. Continuous feedback loops, supported by detailed performance data, empower IT teams to refine their strategies and enhance overall infrastructure management. This iterative approach ensures that the server environment remains adaptable to changing technological landscapes and business requirements, thereby sustaining its relevance and effectiveness. For example, performance analytics might reveal that a specific application underperforms due to inadequate memory allocation, prompting a strategic decision to upgrade the server's RAM.

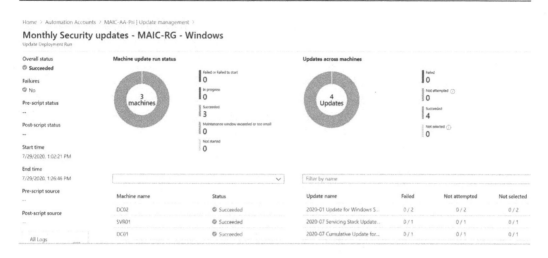

Figure 12.7 – Monitoring update deployments (source – Microsoft)

🔍 Quick tip: Need to see a high-resolution version of this image? Open this book in the next-gen Packt Reader or view it in the PDF/ePub copy.

🔒 **The next-gen Packt Reader** and a **free PDF/ePub copy** of this book are included with your purchase. Unlock them by scanning the QR code below or visiting `https://www.packtpub.com/unlock/9781836205012`.

Robust monitoring and reporting frameworks are essential for maintaining a secure, efficient, and resilient IT infrastructure. By leveraging sophisticated tools and automation, organizations can achieve heightened operational excellence, ensuring their IT environments are equipped to support dynamic business operations and foster future growth.

Note:

Regularly review and refine your monitoring thresholds and reporting parameters to align with evolving business needs and system performance. What works well today may not be sufficient tomorrow. Utilizing adaptive monitoring tools that learn from historical data can help you anticipate future issues and improve the overall effectiveness of your monitoring strategy.

Monitoring and reporting are integral components of effective server management. They allow IT professionals to track performance metrics and identify potential issues before they escalate. This subsection elaborates on the significance of real-time monitoring tools and comprehensive reporting mechanisms, highlighting their impact on strategic planning and operational efficiency. As we conclude this section on managing server lifecycles and updates, the focus will shift to troubleshooting hotpatching implementations. This next section will address common challenges and solutions associated with applying hotpatching techniques, providing valuable insights for maintaining server stability during updates.

Troubleshooting hotpatching implementations

In managing IT infrastructure, **troubleshooting** hotpatching implementations is a vital responsibility to ensure smooth server operations. Hotpatching provides significant benefits by reducing downtime and ensuring continuous service availability. However, its complexity can introduce several challenges that IT professionals must be prepared to handle. Successful troubleshooting is crucial in mitigating these challenges, preserving both system stability and performance while fully capitalizing on the advantages of hotpatching. This section explores the common issues that arise during hotpatching, along with the diagnostic tools and techniques necessary for identifying and addressing these problems. It also outlines best practices to streamline the troubleshooting process. By mastering these aspects, IT teams can safeguard their infrastructure's reliability, maximizing the potential of hotpatching as a key operational strategy.

Common issues and solutions

Hotpatching, though highly beneficial for maintaining system uptime, often presents several challenges that require careful troubleshooting.

- One frequent issue involves compatibility conflicts between hotpatches and existing software or hardware configurations. For instance, a hotpatch aimed at updating security protocols might cause older applications to malfunction, leading to system instability or application failures. To prevent these risks, conducting thorough **pre-deployment testing** in a controlled environment is critical to identify and resolve potential incompatibilities.

- Another common issue stems from insufficient logging and monitoring practices. Without detailed logs and real-time monitoring, diagnosing hotpatching problems can be complex and time-consuming. For example, a network outage coinciding with a hotpatch deployment may be challenging to link to the patch without proper logging. Implementing comprehensive logging systems and utilizing advanced monitoring tools allows IT teams to detect and address issues more effectively before they escalate.

- Network-related problems also recur during hotpatching. Large-scale hotpatch deployments can overwhelm network resources, leading to latency issues, packet loss, or incomplete updates. To avoid these disruptions, network performance should be assessed in advance, and configurations should be optimized. Establishing **fallback mechanisms**, such as **rollback procedures** and **redundant pathways**, ensures system stability if network issues arise.

- *Security concerns* are a critical aspect of hotpatching, particularly the risk of introducing vulnerabilities through unverified or malicious patches. For example, downloading a patch from an untrusted source could expose the system to malware. To mitigate this, strict **patch validation protocols** must be enforced, and patches should only be sourced from trusted providers. Regular security audits and vulnerability assessments also help ensure that hotpatching does not compromise system security.

- User resistance and lack of training can hinder effective hotpatching implementation. Users may be wary of live updates or may lack the knowledge to manage hotpatching processes correctly. For example, an inexperienced IT technician might unintentionally cause service disruptions during patch deployment. Providing comprehensive training and clear communication about the benefits and safeguards of hotpatching can alleviate user concerns and support smooth adoption.

By proactively addressing these common challenges with best practices and strategic solutions, IT professionals can fully leverage hotpatching to maintain high availability and performance in their server environments.

> **Note:**
> It is crucial to always maintain a reliable backup before applying any hotpatch, no matter how small the update seems. Even with extensive testing, unforeseen issues can occur, making it essential to have a rollback plan ready. A proactive backup strategy helps to avoid potential downtime and ensures business continuity in case the patch introduces unexpected problems.

As we conclude the discussion on common issues and their solutions in hotpatching implementations, it is equally important to understand the tools that can help diagnose and resolve these challenges. The following subsection will focus on diagnostic tools and techniques that provide the necessary insights for effective troubleshooting.

Diagnostic tools and techniques

Utilizing robust *diagnostic tools and techniques* is essential to ensuring the successful implementation of hot patching and effectively addressing related challenges. These tools equip IT professionals with the insights necessary to efficiently *identify*, *analyze*, and *resolve* issues, thereby safeguarding system stability and performance. A crucial diagnostic tool is the **system log analyzer**, which examines logs generated during hotpatch deployments. Solutions such as **Azure Performance Diagnostics** (illustrated in *Figure 12.8*) involve :

1. Signing in to the Azure Portal,
2. Selecting your VM,
3. Going to the Extensions section,
4. Clicking Add,

5. Selecting Performance Diagnostics and

6. Following the prompts to complete the installation.

Additionally, tools such as **Splunk** and the ELK Stack, which includes **Elasticsearch, Logstash, and Kibana**, enable IT teams to aggregate and analyze large volumes of log data from computers, servers, and VMs, both on-premises and in the cloud, assisting in identifying anomalies and uncovering root causes such as software conflicts or performance issues. Advanced log analyzers often include real-time alerting and automated anomaly detection features, enabling proactive issue management before they impact system operations.

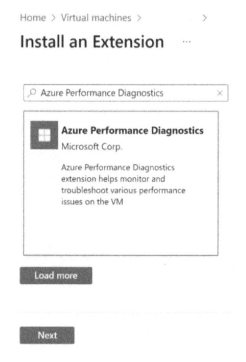

Figure 12.8 – Azure Performance Diagnostics solution (source – Microsoft)

Network monitoring tools are equally critical for diagnosing connectivity problems that may arise during hotpatching. Solutions such as **Nagios** and **SolarWinds** provide real-time insights into network traffic, latency, and packet loss, helping identify network congestion or disruptions that could obstruct patch deployments. These tools also frequently offer network simulation capabilities, allowing IT teams to evaluate the network's ability to handle hotpatching activities without disruption. Performance monitoring tools, such as New Relic and Dynatrace, are invaluable for tracking the impact of hotpatches on system resources. By continuously monitoring metrics such as CPU usage, memory consumption, and application response times, IT professionals can quickly detect performance degradation linked to recent patch installations and take corrective action to optimize system performance.

In terms of security, *vulnerability scanners* and *integrity checkers* are vital diagnostic tools. Solutions such as **Nessus** and **OpenVAS** help identify security vulnerabilities that could be exploited during or after hotpatch deployments. Integrity checkers such as **Tripwire** ensure the authenticity and integrity of patches, protecting systems from malicious code or unauthorized changes. Diagnostic techniques such as sandbox testing and rollback procedures also enhance the troubleshooting process. Tools such as **VMware** and **Docker** enable IT teams to deploy hotpatches in a controlled, isolated environment that mirrors production systems, allowing them to evaluate patch behavior and compatibility without risking production stability. *Rollback mechanisms*, facilitated by tools such as **Ansible** and **Git**, ensure that in the event of a failed deployment, the system can quickly revert to its pre-patch state, minimizing downtime. Collaboration platforms such as **Confluence** and **Slack** further aid in diagnosing and resolving hot patch-related issues by fostering effective communication and knowledge sharing. These platforms allow teams to document findings, share insights, and collaboratively develop solutions, promoting continuous improvement and operational excellence.

By integrating these diagnostic tools and techniques into the hotpatching process, IT professionals can establish a streamlined approach to managing live system updates. This proactive strategy boosts system resilience and performance and ensures uninterrupted service availability in dynamic IT environments.

> **Note:**
> While using diagnostic tools such as log analyzers and network monitors, ensure that they are correctly configured and maintained. Misconfigured diagnostic tools can lead to false positives or missed errors, delaying troubleshooting efforts. Regularly audit your monitoring solutions to verify that they are accurately capturing system events and performance metrics.

Having reviewed the essential diagnostic tools and techniques, we now turn to best practices for troubleshooting hotpatching implementations. These best practices serve as guiding principles to enhance the overall success and reliability of your hotpatching efforts.

Best practices for troubleshooting

Effectively managing hotpatching implementations requires a structured approach guided by best practices that ensure system reliability and the successful introduction of live updates. For IT professionals tasked with maintaining high availability, these practices help mitigate risks and enhance the overall efficiency of hotpatching procedures:

- **Conduct Rigorous Pre-Deployment Testing:** Before applying a hotpatch in a live production environment, it is essential to first test it in a *controlled, isolated environment* that closely mimics the live system. For example, an organization deploying a hotpatch to a critical application should simulate identical workloads and conditions to assess any potential performance impacts. Utilizing *sandbox environments* or *virtual machines* from platforms such as **VMware** and **Docker** allows teams to thoroughly evaluate patches without disrupting system operations.

- **Implement Comprehensive Logging and Monitoring Mechanisms:** Detailed logs capture important events during hotpatch deployments and are vital for identifying and diagnosing potential issues. IT teams can use tools such as **Splunk** or the **ELK Stack** to analyze logs, track deployment steps, and pinpoint errors. Paired with real-time monitoring solutions such as Nagios or SolarWinds, these tools provide continuous visibility into system performance, enabling proactive detection and resolution of any issues.

- **Ensure Network Readiness:** Ensuring *network readiness* is equally important, as hotpatching can place significant demands on network resources. Inadequate network capacity may result in latency, packet loss, or even failed deployments. Tools such as **iPerf** can simulate network traffic to evaluate how well the network handles the added load. IT professionals should perform network assessments and optimize configurations to prevent disruptions. They should also establish fallback mechanisms, such as *redundant pathways* and *rollback procedures*, to ensure smooth operations in case of failure.

- **Maintain Security:** *Security* is paramount in hotpatching, and *strict validation procedures* are required to prevent vulnerabilities from being introduced. Hotpatches should only be sourced from trusted vendors and must undergo thorough scanning with tools such as **Nessus** or **OpenVAS** to detect potential security flaws. Tools such as Tripwire can verify patch integrity to prevent malicious code from being introduced during the update process. Regular security audits help reinforce these efforts, ensuring a secure patching process.

- **Foster Collaboration and Knowledge Sharing:** *Collaboration and knowledge sharing* also play a vital role in troubleshooting and continuous improvement. Platforms such as **Confluence** and **Slack** facilitate team communication, allowing IT professionals to document findings, share best practices, and troubleshoot collectively. Maintaining a shared knowledge base helps streamline processes and enhance problem-solving capabilities across the organization.

- **Provide User Training and Clear Communication:** Lastly, *user training and clear communication* are critical to gaining support for hotpatching initiatives. IT staff and end users alike must understand the benefits and safety measures of live updates. Comprehensive training programs, workshops, and detailed documentation help ensure that everyone involved is familiar with the procedures and potential impacts, reducing resistance and fostering smooth deployments.

Adhering to these best practices enables IT professionals to confidently navigate the complexities of hotpatching, ensuring system resilience, optimal performance, and continuous service availability. These guidelines form the foundation of a successful hotpatching strategy, enabling organizations to leverage live updates efficiently in their IT operations.

> **Note:**
> Document every step of your troubleshooting process. Having a clear record of actions taken, tests conducted, and solutions implemented can be invaluable for future reference. That also promotes faster resolution times when similar issues arise and contributes to a shared knowledge base within the IT team.

With a comprehensive understanding of the common issues, diagnostic tools, and troubleshooting best practices for hotpatching implementations, you are better equipped to ensure system stability and performance. In the next section, we will move on to the hands-on chapter exercise, focusing on setting up Azure Arc in Windows Server 2025, an essential step in managing hybrid environments effectively.

Chapter exercise – setting up Azure Arc in Windows Server 2025

For this chapter's exercise, you will be guided through the steps to set up **Azure Arc** in Windows Server 2025. That will empower you to extend Azure management capabilities to your on-premises servers. This exercise will enable you to unify your resources and seamlessly integrate them with Azure services, enhancing your operational efficiency and security.

The exercise begins with the initial configuration of Azure Arc, where you will register your Windows Server with Azure, allowing it to be managed through the Azure portal. Next, you will configure Azure Policy to enforce compliance across your hybrid environment, ensuring that your servers meet organizational standards and best practices. Additionally, you will set up Azure Monitor to gain insights into your server's performance and health, enabling proactive management and issue resolution.

Through detailed, step-by-step instructions, you will implement these essential configurations, verify their successful integration, and develop practical skills that enhance your ability to manage a hybrid infrastructure effectively. This hands-on exercise is vital for IT administrators looking to leverage cloud technologies while maintaining control over their on-premises resources. By completing this exercise, you will gain a deeper understanding of Azure Arc's functionalities, equipping you to optimize your server environment and harness the full potential of Azure services.

Here is a list of steps for setting up Azure Arc on Windows Server 2025:

1. Ensure you have an active Azure subscription.
2. Verify that the Windows Server 2025 machine meets the requirements.
3. Ensure you have administrative access to the server.
4. Locate the **Azure Arc** system tray icon on your Windows Server 2025 machine. Alternatively, access the setup through **Server Manager** or the **Start** menu.

5. Click on the **Azure Arc** system tray icon and select **Launch Azure Arc Setup** to initiate the **Azure Arc Configuration wizard**, as shown in *Figure 12.9*.

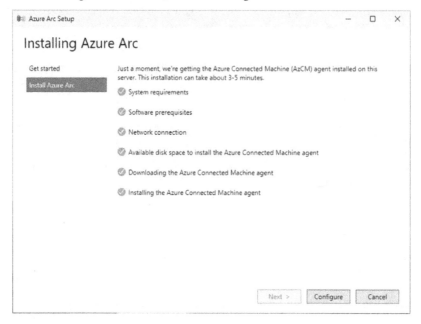

Figure 12.9 – Installing Azure Arc in Windows Server 2025

6. Follow the setup wizard, which will check for prerequisites and install the **Azure Connected Machine** agent.

7. Click **Configure**, then **Next**.

8. On the *Sign in to Azure page*, select an **Azure cloud**, sign in, and **generate code**. Click **Next**.

9. On the *Resource details* page, select the **tenant, subscription, resource group**, and **Azure Region**. If required, configure any **proxy settings**. Click Next.

10. On the **Claim Software Assurance benefits** page, check the box I attest that I have a license covered by Software Assurance if your organization has a license that Software Assurance covers. Click Next..

11. On the *Connecting your server* page, the wizard will prompt you to connect your server to **Azure Arc**. Click **Next** to **Connect the server with Azure Arc**.

12. Once the connection is completed, you will receive the **Connection and configuration successful**, as shown in Figure 12.10.

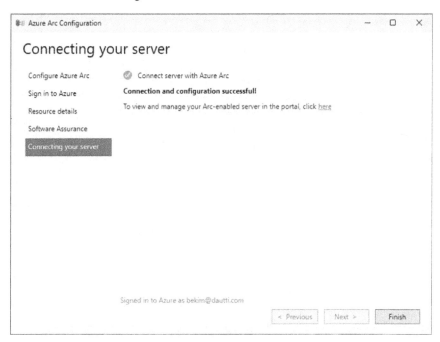

Figure 12.10 Succesful configuration of Azure Arc and connection to Azure Portal

13. After completing the setup, verify the connection in the **Azure portal**.

14. Navigate to the **Azure Arc** section and ensure your **server is listed** as an *Azure Arc-enabled resource*.

15. Optionally, enable *additional features* such as **Hotpatch, Updates, Logs**, etc., as depicted in Figure 12.11.

Figure 12.11- Verifying that the server is listed in Azure Arc and enabling features

Upon completing these steps, you will have successfully set up Azure Arc on your Windows Server 2025 environment, allowing for centralized management and enhanced visibility across your server infrastructure. This exercise not only equips you with the practical skills necessary for integrating Azure services but also reinforces your understanding of cloud management principles. By following these procedures, you will streamline your server operations and ensure that your systems are effectively connected and managed within the Azure ecosystem.

Summary

In this chapter, you gained a comprehensive understanding of utilizing hotpatching with Azure Arc in Windows Server 2025 to streamline server updates and maintain system stability. We explored the fundamentals of hotpatching, including its benefits and how Azure Arc enhances compatibility and management capabilities. You learned how to prepare for, execute, and validate hotpatches, ensuring a smooth and effective update process. Additionally, we covered lifecycle management strategies, automating updates, and leveraging monitoring and reporting tools to manage server updates efficiently. The chapter also delved into troubleshooting hotpatching implementations, discussing common issues, diagnostic tools, and best practices for resolving problems. The chapter concluded with a hands-on exercise where you set up Azure Arc in Windows Server 2025, reinforcing your practical understanding of hotpatching techniques. Moving forward, the next chapter will focus on tuning and maintaining Windows Server 2025.

Questions

1. **True or False**: Hotpatching in Windows Server 2025 allows updates to be installed without restarting the server.

2. **Fill in the Blank**: _____ is the platform used in conjunction with Windows Server 2025 to streamline hotpatching and extend management across hybrid environments.

3. **Multiple Choice**: Which of the following are the key benefits of using Azure Arc with hotpatching in Windows Server 2025? (*Choose all that apply*)

   - Centralized management

   - Improved update automation

   - Enhanced compatibility

   - All of the above

4. **True or False**: Hotpatching eliminates the need for post-patching validation in Windows Server 2025.

5. **Fill in the Blank**: _____ is the process of verifying that hotpatches have been successfully applied and have not introduced new issues into the system.

6. **Multiple Choice**: Which of the following tools can be used to monitor server lifecycle and updates in Windows Server 2025? (*Choose all that apply*)

   - Microsoft System Center

   - Azure Monitor

   - Windows Admin Center

   - All of the above

7. **True or False**: Automating update management in Windows Server 2025 helps ensure that servers remain up to date with minimal manual intervention.

8. **Fill in the Blank**: _____ is a critical feature used to diagnose and resolve issues that arise during hotpatching implementations in Windows Server 2025.

9. **Multiple Choice**: Which of the following tools can assist in troubleshooting hotpatching issues in Windows Server 2025? (*Choose all that apply*)

   - System Log Analyzer

   - Network monitoring tools

   - Performance monitoring tools

   - All of the above

10. **True or False**: Performance monitoring tools such as New Relic and Dynatrace are essential for tracking system resources after applying hotpatches in Windows Server 2025.

11. **Fill in the Blank**: _____ is a process that ensures servers can quickly revert to a previous state in case of a failed hotpatch deployment.

12. **Short Answer**: Explain the benefits of using Azure Arc in managing Windows Server 2025 hotpatches, especially in hybrid cloud environments.

13. **Short Answer**: Discuss the importance of diagnostic tools in troubleshooting hotpatching implementations and ensuring system stability.

Further reading

- *Azure Arc overview:* https://learn.microsoft.com/en-us/azure/azure-arc/overview

- *Hotpatch for Windows Server 2025:* https://techcommunity.microsoft.com/t5/windows-server-news-and-best/now-in-preview-hotpatch-for-windows-server-2025/ba-p/4248296

- *Hotpatch for virtual machines:* https://learn.microsoft.com/en-us/windows-server/get-started/hotpatch

- *How to preview: Azure Arc-connected Hotpatching for Windows Server 2025:* https://techcommunity.microsoft.com/blog/windowsservernewsandbestpractices/how-to-preview-azure-arc-connected-hotpatching-for-windows-server-2025/424689

Part 5: Managing and Maintaining Windows Server 2025

This part discusses essential tasks for optimizing performance, ensuring reliable and effective troubleshooting in Windows Server 2025. You will gain practical skills in server tuning, routine maintenance, update management, and troubleshooting methodologies to ensure seamless server operations.

This part contains the following chapters:

- *Chapter 13, Tuning and Maintaining Windows Server 2025*
- *Chapter 14, Updating and Troubleshooting Windows Server 2025*

13

Tuning and Maintaining Windows Server 2025

This chapter aims to equip you with knowledge about the factors influencing *server hardware selection* and the best practices for *evaluating server performance*. Understanding the server's role within a network, as well as its hardware components, will enable you to choose the most suitable server hardware for your requirements and troubleshoot hardware-related issues effectively. Moreover, the chapter will cover the techniques and strategies for monitoring server performance. Effective performance monitoring involves not only identifying and mitigating potential performance issues before they escalate but also actively engaging in prompt responses to prevent further performance degradation. Establishing a performance baseline—documenting the server's performance under typical workloads—is crucial for generating comprehensive reports on overall performance and playing a vital role in the monitoring process. The chapter concludes with a practical exercise focused on analyzing performance logs and setting up alerts.

In this chapter, we're going to cover the following main topics:

- Understanding server hardware components and their roles in Windows Server 2025
- Performance monitoring tools and methodologies in Windows Server 2025
- Utilizing Performance Monitor, Resource Monitor, and Task Manager for performance tuning
- Interpreting performance counters for optimizing server performance
- Performance logs and alerts service

Technical requirements

Before you start the lab for this chapter, you will need the following equipment:

- A PC with **Windows 11 Pro**, at least 16 GB of **Random Access Memory (RAM)**, 1 TB of **Hard Disk Drive (HDD)** space, and internet connectivity

- A virtual machine with **Windows Server 2025 Standard**, at least 4 GB of RAM, 100 GB of HDD, and internet connectivity

These specifications are necessary to complete the exercise and achieve the desired outcomes successfully.

Understanding server hardware components and their roles in Windows Server 2025

A server functions as a specialized computer designed to deliver network services and handle user requests through its dedicated hardware components. These server hardware components are fundamental to the server's operational efficiency and performance. Understanding these components, their specific roles, and their impact on overall server capabilities is crucial when selecting or configuring server hardware. This chapter delves into the various server hardware components, examining their functions and the effects they have on server performance and reliability. The goal is to emphasize the importance of carefully managing and configuring server hardware to optimize functionality and ensure reliable operation.

Processor overview

The processor, or **CPU**, depicted in *Figure 13.1*, is the central unit responsible for executing instructions and processing data within a computer system. Its performance is often gauged by its speed, typically measured in **Hertz (Hz)**, with most modern processors operating in the **Gigahertz (GHz)** range. However, speed alone does not determine a processor's overall effectiveness. Several additional factors contribute to its performance:

- **Cache memory**: This is a type of high-speed memory used by the processor to store frequently accessed data, enhancing processing efficiency. Modern processors feature multiple levels of cache—**L1, L2, and L3**. L1 and L2 caches are built directly into the processor, offering the fastest access speeds, while the L3 cache, which resides outside the processor, provides additional storage but with slightly slower access. Examples of server-grade processors with optimized cache architectures include Intel Xeon with Smart Cache and AMD EPYC with their Infinity Cache, both designed to boost server performance in demanding workloads.

- **Cores**: These are individual processing units within the CPU. Early processors had a single core, but contemporary models may have two, four, eight, or more. Each core can handle separate tasks simultaneously, thus improving the processor's ability to perform parallel processing.

- **Word size**: This refers to the processor's internal architecture, determining the size of data buses, instruction sets, and addressable memory. Processors are commonly 32- or 64-bit, with the bit number indicating the volume of data the processor can handle at once and its interaction with system memory.

- **Registers**: These are small, ultra-fast storage locations within the processor used to hold data and instructions temporarily. Registers are crucial for quick access to the data required for ongoing computations, making them the fastest component within the processor.

- **Virtualization technology**: This capability determines how well the processor can support virtualization, allowing multiple operating systems to share resources efficiently and simultaneously.

Figure 13.1 – Intel's Xeon quad-core processors

In summary, while the processor is a pivotal component in server performance, it relies on memory to function effectively. Understanding these aspects of processors can help you select the proper hardware for optimal performance and efficiency.

A processor is undeniably crucial for a server's operation, but its functionality is heavily reliant on memory. Without adequate memory, the processor would struggle to perform efficiently. Therefore, it's essential to understand the role and characteristics of memory to appreciate how it supports and enhances server performance fully. Let us explore this fundamental component in more detail in the following subsection.

Understanding memory

Memory plays a pivotal role in computer systems, serving as a temporary storage area that allows the processor to access and process data swiftly. This component also acts as a *bridge* between applications and peripheral devices, ensuring smooth and efficient operation. The two primary types of memory in computers are RAM and **Read-Only Memory** (**ROM**):

- RAM is *volatile memory*, meaning that it loses all stored data when the power is turned off. It provides high-speed data access and is used to store data that the processor is actively working with. RAM is essential for the smooth execution of applications and operating systems, as it allows for rapid data retrieval and manipulation. In servers, RAM modules are typically designed with additional features to support high performance and reliability. For instance, **Error-Correcting Code (ECC) RAM**, as shown in *Figure 13.2*, can detect and correct data errors, which is critical for maintaining data integrity in server environments. Servers may also use **Single Device Data Correction (SDDC)** or **Double Device Data Correction (DDDC) RAM**, which enhances error correction capabilities by addressing multiple errors simultaneously. These advanced features make server RAM more expensive, but they are crucial for ensuring reliable server operation.

Figure 13.2 – ECC RAM modules placed in memory banks

- ROM, on the other hand, is *non-volatile memory*, meaning it retains data even when the power is off. ROM is used to store firmware and essential system instructions that do not change frequently, such as the BIOS or system firmware. It provides a stable and reliable way to store critical code necessary for booting the computer and initiating hardware functionality.

While RAM offers high-speed access and is crucial for temporary data storage during active processing, disc storage serves as non-volatile secondary storage. Discs (HDDs or **Solid State Drives (SSDs)**) retain data persistently and are used for long-term data storage, such as operating system files, applications, and user data. Understanding the differences between RAM and disc storage, along with their respective roles, is vital for optimizing server performance and ensuring efficient data management.

In contrast to RAM, which is temporary storage that requires power to keep its data, the disc is permanent storage that can preserve data even without power. The disc is a crucial component of a computer system, as it stores the operating system, applications, and user files. Therefore, it is important to learn about the disc's structure, function, and types. In the following subsection, we will discuss how discs work and what role they play in a computer system.

Understanding the disc

The disc serves as the primary long-term storage device in a computer system, maintaining data integrity even when power is lost. Unlike volatile memory such as RAM, which only stores data temporarily, the disc retains the operating system, applications, and user files persistently. That makes the disc a critical component for ensuring data durability and system functionality.

In server environments, where continuous operation and accessibility are paramount, the disc's role becomes even more crucial. Servers typically utilize **Direct-Attached Storage** (**DAS**), which consists of discs directly connected to the server. This setup facilitates high-speed data access and supports the server's demanding workload. To further enhance reliability, many servers are equipped with hot-swappable discs. This feature allows administrators to replace or add discs without shutting down the server, minimizing downtime and maintaining service availability.

Modern servers frequently utilize advanced storage technologies such as **Serial Attached Small Computer System Interfaces** (**SCSIs**), commonly referred to as **SAS**, which is depicted in *Figure 13.3*. SAS is a widely adopted standard that enables high-speed data transfer between servers and peripheral devices. In addition to SAS, SSDs are increasingly used, delivering superior performance and reliability compared to traditional HDDs. Having a solid grasp of these technologies and their functions is vital for effective server storage management and ensuring the availability of critical data and services.

Figure 13.3 – SAS HDDs

In the following subsection, we will explore the network interface, another crucial component of server hardware that facilitates connectivity and data exchange.

Understanding the network interface

The network interface is a fundamental component that facilitates the connection between a computer and a network, enabling communication and data exchange. This interface can be either physical, such as a **Network Interface Card** (**NIC**), or logical, as seen in virtual environments where network connections are simulated through software. Servers often feature multiple network interfaces (see

Figure 13.4), which enhance their ability to handle network traffic and improve overall performance. If your server does not currently have multiple NICs, it is highly recommended that you consider adding them to optimize network operations.

Figure 13.4 – Server network interfaces

The advantages of incorporating *multiple NICs* are substantial and can significantly enhance network performance. For instance, NIC teaming aggregates multiple network connections to increase the overall bandwidth available to and from the server. This setup not only enhances data transfer speeds but also provides redundancy in case one NIC fails. **Network Load Balancing** (**NLB**) further optimizes performance by distributing network traffic evenly across several servers, preventing any single server from becoming overwhelmed and ensuring a more reliable and efficient network experience.

Moreover, network separation allows for the isolation of different types of network traffic. By segregating intranet traffic and internet traffic, you can enhance security and ensure that critical internal communications are not compromised by external network activity. This separation also helps manage network resources more effectively and maintain performance levels.

Understanding the broader network architecture, which encompasses the design and layout of the entire network infrastructure, is crucial. This understanding is key to designing a robust and scalable network that can meet the demands of modern IT environments. In the following section, we will explore the differences between 32- and 64-bit architectures, which are essential for understanding server and software compatibility.

Understanding 32- and 64-bit architectures

The distinction between *32-bit* and *64-bit architectures* extends beyond a mere numerical difference, encompassing significant variations in processing power, memory management, and overall system performance. At a fundamental level, the architecture of a processor—32- or 64-bit—determines the amount of memory it can access and how efficiently it can process data.

A 32-bit processor can address up to 2^{32} memory locations, which translates to a maximum of approximately 4 GB of RAM. This limitation restricts the amount of memory available for applications and system processes, often leading to performance bottlenecks in memory-intensive tasks. Conversely, a 64-bit processor can address up to 2^{64} memory locations, providing access to a theoretical maximum of 16 exabytes of RAM. This vast addressable memory space allows for significantly greater memory capacity and enables the efficient handling of more extensive datasets and more demanding applications.

In addition to *enhanced memory capabilities*, 64-bit processors offer improved computational performance and multitasking efficiency. They support both 32- and 64-bit applications, providing greater flexibility in software usage and allowing for a smoother transition from older 32-bit applications to modern 64-bit software. On the other hand, 32-bit processors are limited to running only 32-bit applications, which may restrict software options and performance capabilities.

Security is another crucial advantage of 64-bit architectures. They enforce *driver signing*, a security feature that ensures the authenticity and integrity of device drivers. This requirement helps prevent the installation of malicious or unreliable drivers, contributing to a more secure and stable system environment. For these reasons, it is strongly recommended to utilize 64-bit hardware and software for servers and critical applications. That ensures compatibility with modern operating systems, applications, and device drivers, ultimately enhancing system performance and reliability.

While secondary memory in computers is typically fixed and non-removable, offering stability and permanence, removable storage technologies provide flexibility and convenience for data transfer and backup. In the following subsection, we will delve into the various types of removable drives, their characteristics, and their practical applications.

Understanding external drives

Removable drives are external, portable storage devices designed for easy connection and disconnection from a computer system without needing to power down the machine. These drives utilize *hot-swappable technology*, which allows them to be attached or removed. At the same time, the system is operational, as discussed earlier in the *Understanding the disc* section of this chapter. They connect to servers and computers through interfaces such as USB and IEEE 1394 ports, providing a convenient means for expanding storage capacity and facilitating data transfer.

The various types of removable drives include **CDs** and **DVDs** for optical storage, HDDs for large-capacity storage solutions, floppy drives (an older technology replaced mainly by newer methods), **USB flash drives** for quick and portable data access, and specialized backup drives designed for comprehensive data backup and recovery. These drives offer flexibility and portability, making them useful for a range of tasks, from data transport to system backups. Examples of these drives are illustrated in *Figure 13.5*, highlighting devices such as USB flash drives, which are widely used for their convenience and ease of use.

Figure 13.5 – Removable drive and USB flash drives

In addition to removable drives, servers may also need a dedicated graphics card to manage video data efficiently, especially when dealing with high-resolution graphics or complex visual applications. The following subsection will explore the role of graphics cards in server systems and how they contribute to handling graphical tasks effectively.

Impact of external USB drives on server performance

External USB drives are commonly used for expanding storage or facilitating data transfers, but their impact on server performance, particularly in a Windows Server 2025 environment, cannot be overlooked. While these drives can offer valuable benefits, it is essential to manage and optimize them correctly to avoid potential performance degradation.

Positive impacts on performance

On the positive side, external USB drives can provide much-needed additional storage space for applications or services that demand large volumes of data, thus reducing the load on internal storage. They also offer a convenient solution for backing up critical data and transferring large files. When properly configured, external drives can offload backup tasks from the internal server, ensuring that server performance remains optimal during peak usage times.

Negative impacts on performance

However, the use of external USB drives can introduce several performance challenges:

- One notable concern is slower data access speeds. Although USB 3.0 and USB-C drives offer faster transfer rates than their predecessors, they are still generally slower than internal SSDs or RAID arrays, especially when handling I/O-intensive tasks. That can lead to delays in data access, mainly when large volumes of read and write operations are processed.

- Additionally, connecting multiple external devices to the server can overwhelm the USB bus, creating bottlenecks that disrupt overall server performance, mainly when dealing with large datasets or running demanding applications.

- Furthermore, unreliable connections, especially with low-quality or aging drives, can cause intermittent disconnections, leading to data corruption, crashes, or system slowdowns.

- Lastly, external drives may consume additional power, potentially putting stress on the server's power supply and reducing energy efficiency.

Best practices for optimizing external USB drives

To mitigate these issues and optimize the performance of external USB drives, it is important to follow best practices:

- First, invest in high-performance USB 3.0 or USB-C drives that offer quick read and write speeds to minimize potential slowdowns.

- Limit the number of devices connected to the server to prevent overloading the USB bus and prioritize critical peripherals while disconnecting non-essential devices.

- External USB drives should be reserved primarily for backups or non-critical applications, as using them for high-frequency data processing can adversely affect performance.

- Additionally, Windows Server 2025's built-in Resource Monitor and Performance Monitor tools should be used to track the impact of external drives on system performance. Set up alerts to identify any significant changes in disc usage or performance drops.

- Finally, ensure that all USB connections are stable and secure, and consider using powered USB hubs to maintain optimal connectivity and avoid power strain on the server.

By understanding the potential benefits and drawbacks of external USB drives and implementing these best practices, you can ensure that their use contributes to, rather than detracts from, the performance of your Windows Server 2025 environment.

Understanding graphics cards

Typically, servers operate as backend systems and do not require high-end graphics cards due to their primary role in client/server architecture, where they handle data processing and storage rather than graphical tasks. However, the need for a *sophisticated graphics card* can arise depending on the specific functions of the server. For instance, if a server is tasked with processing complex graphics or video data, it may necessitate an advanced graphics card, as illustrated in *Figure 13.6*. A graphics card, also known as a **video card** or **graphics adapter**, is an internal component responsible for rendering images and video on the screen. These cards are essential in fields such as gaming, 3D animation, AutoCAD, and other graphically intensive applications.

Figure 13.6 – AMD's Radeon video graphic adapter

Modern graphics cards are equipped with their dedicated processors, known as **Graphics Processing Units (GPUs)**, and possess their video memory, distinct from the system's RAM. This specialized hardware enables efficient handling of high-resolution graphics and complex visual tasks. The preceding figure showcases an AMD Radeon video graphics adapter, demonstrating these features.

Given that servers can become overheated under heavy workloads, effective cooling solutions are essential to maintain optimal operating temperatures. The following section will delve into cooling mechanisms and their importance in preventing overheating in server systems.

Cooling essentials

Processors and HDDs are significant sources of heat within a server, necessitating *effective cooling solutions* to prevent overheating and maintain optimal performance. To address this, servers are equipped with specialized cooling mechanisms. Processor coolers, such as heatsinks and fans, are designed to dissipate the heat generated by the CPU. Additionally, servers incorporate multiple case fans that circulate air to expel hot air from the computer case, as illustrated in *Figure 13.7*.

Figure 13.7 – Cooling system in a server's case

In rack-mounted servers, which often experience higher heat loads due to their dense configuration, additional cooling solutions such as rack-mounted fans or air distribution units are employed to ensure that each server unit remains within its recommended temperature range. Beyond internal cooling solutions, *air conditioning systems* are essential for maintaining the overall climate of server rooms and data centers. These systems regulate the ambient temperature and humidity levels, providing a controlled environment that enhances the reliability and longevity of the server hardware.

Next, we will examine the role of the power supply in server operations.

Power supply basics

The **Power Supply Unit (PSU)** is a critical component in server architecture, responsible for converting **alternating current (AC)** from the power outlet into **direct current (DC)** and distributing it to various internal components. This conversion is achieved using an input power transformer, which adjusts the voltage to meet the specific requirements of the server's hardware. The internal components relying on this DC power include processors, hard drives, network interfaces, motherboards, graphics cards, RAID controllers, optical drives, and backup tapes, among others.

In addition to its primary function of power conversion, the PSU also plays a key role in managing the server's *thermal environment*. It aids in cooling by facilitating airflow within the server case, which is essential for preventing overheating and ensuring the stability of the server's operations. Most power supplies incorporate built-in cooling mechanisms, such as fans, to support this function.

To enhance reliability and ensure uninterrupted operations, most servers are equipped with redundant power supplies. This setup typically involves two or more PSUs that operate in tandem. If one PSU fails, the remaining units continue to provide power, thereby minimizing potential downtime. These redundant PSUs are often hot-swappable, allowing faulty units to be replaced without shutting down the server, which is crucial for maintaining high availability in enterprise environments (see *Figure 13.8*).

Figure 13.8 – Server PSUs

Understanding the power supply's role is essential for ensuring the consistent operation of server hardware, making its selection and maintenance critical aspects of effective server management.

Next, we will explore the importance of physical ports and their relevance to server connectivity and functionality.

Exploring physical ports

Servers are equipped with a diverse array of *physical ports*, each tailored to facilitate specific connections between the server and external devices or components. A physical port is a crucial interface that enables communication and data transfer between the server and other hardware. The variety of ports found on a server support different functions and connectivity needs.

At the rear of most servers, you'll find several key types of ports. *AC power connectors* are used to supply electricity to the server. *Ethernet ports* enable network connectivity, allowing the server to communicate with other devices and systems over a network. **Peripheral Component Interconnect**

Express (PCIe) ports are used for installing expansion cards, which can add additional capabilities to the server, such as enhanced graphics or additional storage controllers. *USB ports* provide connections for various peripherals like keyboards, mice, and external drives. *HD-15 video connectors* are used to connect displays for video output. *Management ports* are dedicated to remote server management and diagnostics, enabling administrators to monitor and control the server even when the operating system is not running.

While many may already be familiar with legacy ports, it's worth briefly noting their functions. *Serial ports* were traditionally used for connecting devices such as modems, *parallel ports* were common for printers, and *PS/2* ports connected keyboards and mice. Though largely outdated in modern server setups, these ports may still appear in older systems or specialized use cases (see *Figure 13.9*). Understanding their presence in legacy environments can be helpful when dealing with older hardware configurations.

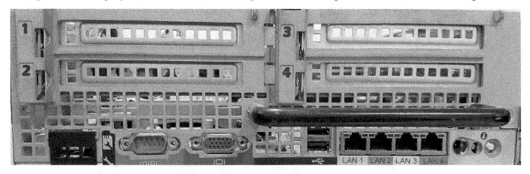

Figure 13.9 – Various ports to connect a variety of devices

The presence and configuration of these physical ports are essential for the server's functionality, influencing how it connects to power sources, networks, and external devices. Understanding the purpose and capabilities of each port type ensures that the server can be effectively integrated into its operational environment and that all necessary connections can be made efficiently.

This section has provided an overview of various server components, including processors, memory, discs, and network interfaces, as well as elaborating on the distinctions between 32- and 64-bit architectures. We have also discussed removable drives, graphics cards, cooling systems, and power supply considerations, as well as the role of physical ports. The subsequent section will focus on monitoring server performance to ensure that the server operates optimally and reliably.

Performance monitoring tools and methodologies in Windows Server 2025

Server maintenance is greatly enhanced by adhering to the principle of *prevention is better than cure*. Effective monitoring of server performance allows for the early detection of potential issues, enabling resolution before they develop into costly problems that could disrupt operations and impact business performance. To achieve effective performance monitoring, it is crucial to implement a *well-defined plan* and utilize *appropriate tools*. This process includes establishing *performance metrics*, which involve collecting baseline data. Baseline data serves as a reference point to compare current performance levels, determine when hardware or software upgrades are necessary, and evaluate whether a new system configuration offers improvements over previous setups.

> **Note**
>
> Microsoft's TechNet website, available at `https://learn.microsoft.com/en-us/previous-versions/windows/desktop/bb226833(v=vs.85)`, offers a wealth of valuable information regarding Microsoft products, including comprehensive resources on monitoring techniques and best practices.

In the following subsection, we will delve into the methodologies for performance monitoring, providing insights into how to assess and optimize server performance systematically.

Implementing a systematic approach to performance monitoring

The *performance monitoring methodology* involves a comprehensive, systematic approach that goes beyond simple data collection. It is crucial not to only gather data but also to interpret it effectively to ensure sound decision-making. Without a structured plan, the risk of obtaining inaccurate or misleading information increases, which can result in detrimental business decisions. This methodology is designed to provide a clear framework for assessing performance by focusing on several key components. These include the following:

- **Defining a research question**: This serves as a guide for the performance monitoring process, aligning with the overall objectives. This question should address the issue of understanding the specific role and function of the server within the broader network infrastructure. This ensures that the monitoring is aligned with the server's intended use and responsibilities.

- **Understanding the specific role and function of the server within the broader network infrastructure:** This ensures that the monitoring is aligned with the server's intended use and responsibilities.

- **Identifying the critical services and components of the server that need to be monitored**: This helps focus on areas vital for maintaining server health and performance.

- **Establishing the criteria and metrics for measuring the performance of each component**: Clear measurement parameters ensure that performance evaluations are accurate and relevant.

- **Selecting appropriate tools for system analysis and data collection**: Choosing the right tools is essential for effectively capturing and analyzing performance data, enabling actionable insights.

> **Note**
>
> For detailed information on monitoring and optimizing server performance, you can visit MSDN's comprehensive guide at `https://learn.microsoft.com/en-us/previous-versions/windows/it-pro/windows-2000-server/bb742410(v=technet.10)?redirectedfrom=MSDN`.

By adhering to this structured methodology, organizations can systematically monitor server performance, anticipate potential issues, and make informed decisions to enhance system reliability and efficiency. The following subsection will delve into the specific steps involved in implementing an effective performance monitoring strategy.

Applying performance monitoring procedures

The performance monitoring methodology provides a structured framework for systematically evaluating and improving server performance. This framework is implemented through specific *performance monitoring procedures*, which are essential for optimizing server efficiency. To effectively apply these procedures, follow these comprehensive steps:

- **Document system details**: Begin by recording detailed information about the server's hardware, software, and configuration. That includes specifications of processors, memory, storage, network interfaces, and installed software. Creating a comprehensive inventory helps establish a baseline, which serves as a reference point for measuring performance changes over time.

- **Establish a baseline**: Develop a baseline by capturing performance metrics under normal operating conditions. That involves monitoring **key performance indicators** (**KPIs**) such as CPU utilization, memory usage, disc I/O, and network throughput. The baseline provides a benchmark for future comparisons and helps identify deviations from expected performance.

- **Update and maintain components**: Regularly update the server's hardware and software to ensure that it is running the latest and most stable versions. That includes applying patches, updating drivers, and replacing outdated hardware. Keeping the system current helps mitigate performance issues and vulnerabilities.

- **Reassess and compare**: After updates and maintenance, rerun the performance monitoring tools to capture new data. Compare these new metrics with the baseline to assess any changes in performance. This comparison helps identify areas where performance has improved or declined.

- **Identify and address issues**: Analyze the performance data to pinpoint any issues or bottlenecks. That could involve high CPU usage, memory leaks, slow disc access, or network latency. Use the insights gained to implement corrective measures, such as optimizing configurations, upgrading hardware, or adjusting software settings.

- **Implement and review adjustments**: Apply the necessary adjustments based on the identified issues. After implementing changes, continue to monitor the server's performance to ensure that the adjustments have had the desired effect. Regular reviews and fine-tuning are essential for maintaining optimal performance.

Establishing a baseline is a critical first step in these procedures. It provides a reference point against which future performance can be measured, allowing for effective monitoring and optimization. Let us delve into the process of creating an accurate and useful baseline for your server.

Establishing server baselines

Effective server performance monitoring hinges on having a reliable reference point to gauge normal operational conditions. This reference point, known as a *baseline*, is a snapshot of the server's performance metrics captured under typical workloads. Establishing a baseline is crucial for several reasons: it enables system administrators to compare current performance against expected standards, identify deviations, and diagnose potential performance issues or bottlenecks before they escalate into significant problems. To create a comprehensive baseline, focus on key performance metrics such as the following:

- **Processor usage**: This metric tracks the percentage of CPU capacity being utilized, providing insight into how effectively the server's processing power is being used and whether it is reaching capacity limits

- **Memory usage**: Monitoring RAM usage helps assess how much memory is consumed by applications and system processes, revealing potential memory leaks or inefficiencies

- **Disc I/O operations**: Evaluating read and write operations on storage devices helps identify issues related to data access speeds and storage performance, which can impact overall server efficiency

- **Network connection usage**: Measuring bandwidth consumption and network traffic helps determine whether the server's network interface is operating within expected parameters and can highlight potential connectivity issues or bottlenecks

Beyond these core metrics, it's important to customize the baseline according to the server's specific role and configuration within your network. Different servers, whether handling web applications, databases, or file storage, have unique performance characteristics and requirements. Therefore, tailor your baseline to reflect the server's intended functions and expected workload. This approach ensures that the baseline serves as a meaningful reference point for ongoing performance monitoring and optimization. Regularly revisiting and updating the baseline in response to changes in server usage, upgrades, or configuration adjustments will help maintain its relevance and effectiveness in managing server performance.

> **Note**
>
> You can obtain the security baselines from Microsoft at `https://www.microsoft.com/en-us/download/details.aspx?id=55319`. These baselines offer a comprehensive set of security configurations and recommendations designed to enhance the protection and integrity of your systems.

Utilizing Performance Monitor, Resource Monitor, and Task Manager for performance tuning

Practical performance tuning of a server involves a thorough understanding and analysis of various *system metrics* and *resource usage*. To achieve this, system administrators can leverage built-in tools such as Performance Monitor, Resource Monitor, and Task Manager. These utilities provide detailed insights into server performance, enabling administrators to identify and address potential issues before they impact the system's stability and efficiency. Performance Monitor offers a comprehensive view of system metrics through customizable counters and data collection sets, allowing for long-term trend analysis. Resource Monitor provides real-time information about CPU, memory, disc, and network usage, helping to pinpoint resource-intensive processes. Task Manager, on the other hand, offers an accessible overview of running applications and system performance, facilitating quick diagnosis of immediate performance concerns. By effectively utilizing these tools, administrators can optimize server performance, ensuring smooth operation and minimal downtime.

What Does Performance Monitor do?

Performance Monitor is a powerful utility included with the **Microsoft Management Console** (**MMC**) in Windows Server environments, designed to track and analyze server performance. It provides a comprehensive view of various performance metrics, enabling system administrators to observe real-time data or review historical information from saved log files. Performance Monitor supports various data visualization methods, including line graphs, histogram bars, and detailed reports, offering flexibility in how performance data is presented. That allows administrators to monitor key indicators such as CPU usage, memory consumption, disc activity, and network performance. By leveraging these visualizations, users can gain insights into system behavior, identify performance bottlenecks, and make informed decisions to optimize server efficiency.

How to launch Performance Monitor

To access Performance Monitor in Windows Server 2025, follow these steps:

1. Press *Windows + R* to open the **Run** dialog box.
2. Type perfmon.exe and press *Enter* to launch the **Performance Monitor** application.
3. The **Performance Monitor** window will appear, displaying a variety of performance metrics and visualization options, as shown in *Figure 13.10*.

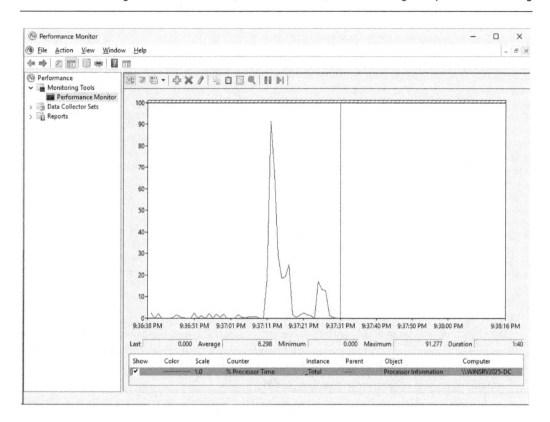

Figure 13.10 – Performance Monitor in Windows Server 2025

To provide a clearer connection to the figure, let's briefly explain a couple of key metrics commonly displayed in the **Performance Monitor** window. For instance, CPU usage measures the percentage of the processor's capacity being used by running tasks, helping administrators identify overutilization or potential bottlenecks in processing power. Similarly, memory consumption tracks the amount of RAM in use, which can indicate whether a server is running efficiently or whether additional memory resources are needed. By understanding these metrics, administrators can better relate the visual data to real-world server performance issues.

Once **Performance Monitor** is open, you can begin configuring it to track specific performance counters and analyze data in real time. This tool will be instrumental in your performance-tuning efforts. Next, we will explore Resource Monitor, another valuable tool for monitoring and optimizing server performance.

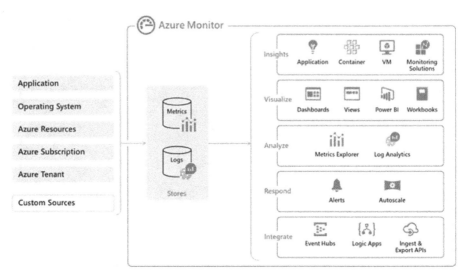

Figure 13.11 – Insights in Azure Monitor(source – Microsoft)

Azure Monitor also integrates seamlessly with other Microsoft and third-party tools, enhancing its capabilities for comprehensive monitoring and management. By leveraging Azure Monitor, organizations can ensure the smooth operation of their IT infrastructure, proactively address potential issues, and maintain high levels of performance and reliability.

Next, we will explore Resource Monitor, another valuable tool for monitoring and optimizing server performance.

What does Resource Monitor do?

A frequent challenge for Windows users is the gradual decline in system performance, which can affect both personal computers and servers. Fortunately, Windows provides a powerful tool called Resource Monitor, which aids in diagnosing and addressing performance issues. Resource Monitor allows users to monitor the utilization of hardware and software resources in real time, offering insights into CPU, memory, disc, and network activity. That enables users to pinpoint resource bottlenecks, identify processes consuming excessive resources, and take corrective actions to restore optimal performance.

> **Note**
>
> You can access Resource Monitor directly from within Performance Monitor. This integration allows you to seamlessly transition between the two tools, enhancing your ability to monitor and analyze server performance comprehensively. By opening Resource Monitor through Performance Monitor, you gain access to detailed insights into system resource usage, including CPU, memory, disk, and network activity. This unified approach streamlines performance diagnostics and helps efficiently address any issues that may arise.

How to launch Resource Monitor

To access Resource Monitor in Windows Server 2025, follow these steps:

1. Press *Windows + R* to open the **Run** dialog box.

2. Type resmon.exe and press **Enter**.

3. The **Resource Monitor** window will launch, displaying various tabs that provide detailed information about system resource usage, as depicted in *Figure 13.12*.

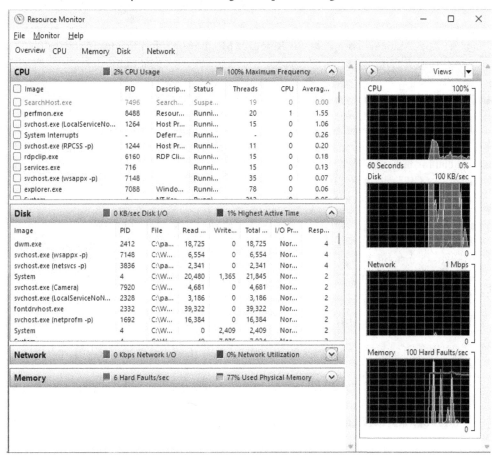

Figure 13.12 – Resource Monitor in Windows Server 2025

To enhance the connection with the figure, let's highlight a few key metrics displayed in **Resource Monitor**. For instance, CPU usage shows the percentage of processor resources consumed by active processes, helping administrators identify tasks that may be overloading the system. The memory usage metric indicates how much RAM is being utilized by applications, enabling users to spot memory-intensive processes that could hinder performance. Additionally, disc activity tracks the read/write operations happening on the disc, revealing if specific applications are causing high disc utilization. Lastly, network activity monitors data sent and received over the network, allowing administrators to assess bandwidth consumption and identify any applications that may be monopolizing network resources. By understanding these metrics, administrators can easily relate the visual data to performance bottlenecks and take the necessary steps to resolve them.

Resource Monitor offers a comprehensive view of how system resources are allocated and used, helping users diagnose issues that might be affecting system performance. It provides detailed graphs and tables for real-time monitoring, making it easier to identify and resolve performance-related problems.

In addition to Resource Monitor, another crucial tool for managing system performance is Task Manager. Task Manager complements Resource Monitor by offering a more streamlined view of running processes and system performance, which will be discussed in the next section.

What does Task Manager do?

Task Manager is an essential tool for monitoring and managing system performance on Windows Server 2025. It provides an in-depth view of the processes, services, and performance metrics that are crucial for maintaining optimal server operations. Through Task Manager, you can track the utilization of CPU, memory, disc, and network resources, offering valuable insights into how various components of your server are performing.

In addition to performance monitoring, Task Manager allows you to *manage running applications and background processes*, which can help identify and resolve issues that might be causing system slowdowns or instability. It provides a graphical representation of the server's performance, which can be switched between a summary view for a high-level overview and a detailed graph view for more specific data.

How to launch Task Manager

To access Task Manager in Windows Server 2025, follow these steps:

1. Right-click on the taskbar and select **Task Manager** from the context menu.
2. The **Task Manager** interface will open, as shown in *Figure 13.13*, displaying various tabs such as **Processes**, **Performance**, and **Services**.

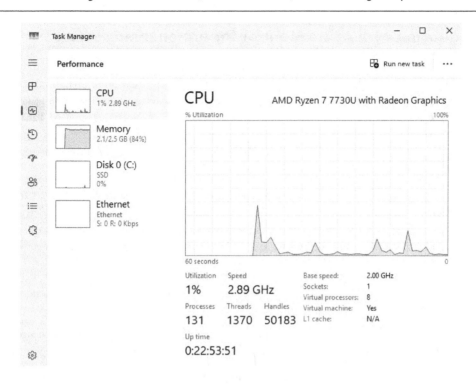

Figure 13.13 – Task Manager in Windows Server 2025

The **Performance** tab of **Task Manager** prominently displays key metrics, including **CPU** usage, which reflects the percentage of processing power being utilized by all active processes; **Memory** usage, which shows the total amount of RAM currently in use and available; **Disc** activity, indicating the read and write operations being performed on your storage drives; and **Ethernet** usage, which monitors the data being transmitted over the network. Each of these metrics provides essential insights that enable system administrators to identify performance bottlenecks and optimize server functionality effectively.

Note

Task Manager in Windows Server 2025 offers in-depth insights into system performance, enabling administrators to monitor real-time resource usage, manage processes, and address performance issues efficiently. Its detailed metrics and intuitive interface are crucial for maintaining server efficiency and stability.

With Task Manager, administrators can quickly end unresponsive tasks, manage system resources, and diagnose performance bottlenecks.

Monitoring with Azure Monitor for Arc-enabled servers

As hybrid cloud environments become more prevalent, organizations need reliable monitoring tools to ensure the health and performance of their infrastructure. Azure Monitor, when integrated with Azure Arc, offers a unified solution for tracking the performance and health of on-premises servers, bridging the gap between cloud and on-premises resources. Moreover, Azure Monitor is a robust platform designed to collect, analyze, and respond to telemetry data from both cloud and on-premises systems. It provides actionable insights into the operation of your infrastructure, enabling IT teams to identify potential issues and optimize server performance proactively.

By enabling Azure Arc on on-premises servers, organizations extend the capabilities of Azure Monitor to their on-premise infrastructure. This integration allows for real-time insights and metrics that are essential for ensuring the successful deployment of hot patches, which can be applied without causing system downtime or compromising performance. The key features of Azure Monitoring are as follows:

- **Unified monitoring**: Azure Monitor consolidates monitoring for both cloud-based and on-premises resources in one dashboard, simplifying the management process and improving visibility across diverse environments

- **Performance metrics**: It collects key performance data such as CPU usage, memory load, and disc I/O, which helps administrators detect system bottlenecks before they become significant issues

- **Log analytics**: Azure Monitor aggregates logs from multiple sources, enabling deep analysis and correlation of events; this is essential for troubleshooting problems and maintaining system health

- **Alerts and notifications**: Customizable alerts notify system administrators of potential problems, helping them address issues quickly and minimize downtime

When Azure Arc is used to manage on-premises servers, especially those involved in hot patching, Azure Monitor provides a range of benefits:

- **Real-time monitoring**: Azure Monitor continuously tracks the system's performance during the hot patching process, ensuring that updates are applied without causing disruptions

- **Historical data analysis**: Administrators can review past performance metrics to assess the impact of hot patching, allowing them to make data-driven decisions for future updates

- **Automated responses**: Through integration with Azure Automation, specific responses can be automatically triggered based on predefined conditions, streamlining operations and reducing manual intervention

To set up Azure Monitor for an Azure Arc-enabled server, follow these steps:

- **Deploy the Azure Monitor agent**: Install the Azure Monitor agent on the server. That can be accomplished through the Azure portal, PowerShell, or ARM templates.

- **Configure data collection**: Configure data collection rules to define which performance metrics and logs should be collected. This ensures that only the necessary data is gathered, optimizing both storage and analysis.

- **Enable insights:** In the Azure portal, select the Arc-enabled server and activate **VM insights** under the **Monitoring** section to receive a detailed view of the server's health and performance metrics.

By leveraging Azure Monitor alongside Azure Arc, organizations can effectively manage their on-premises servers, ensuring that critical updates such as hot patches are deployed efficiently without affecting system availability or performance.

In the next section, we will delve into performance counters, another vital tool for detailed performance analysis and system tuning.

Interpreting performance counters for optimizing server performance

Optimizing server performance often involves leveraging Performance Monitor to gather and analyze data from various performance counters associated with different objects. These objects represent categories of server resources or components, such as memory, processors, discs, and network interfaces, which impact overall system efficiency. Each object is monitored through specific counters that track various performance metrics, including data transfer rates, usage percentages, and error rates. Additionally, instances refer to individual occurrences of these objects, such as separate disc drives or processor cores. By thoroughly examining the data provided by these counters and instances, you can pinpoint performance issues and implement targeted solutions to address them.

The following subsection will give a detailed guide on how to utilize performance counters effectively for performance optimization.

Creating Data Collector Sets

A Data Collector Set in Windows Server 2025 is a powerful tool designed to help you monitor and capture the performance metrics of your server efficiently. By grouping various performance counters, you can obtain a comprehensive view of your server's operational health.

Follow these steps to create a Data Collector Set.

How to create a Data Collector Set

Here's a practical guide to help you create a Data Collector Set:

1. Press the *Windows* key + *R* to open the **Run** dialog box.

2. Type `perfmon.exe` and press *Enter* to launch the **Performance Monitor** application.

3. Right-click on **Performance Monitor** and choose **New | Data Collector Set** to start the creation process.

4. Provide a descriptive name for your Data Collector Set to identify it more easily later, then click **Next**.

5. Click **Browse** to specify the directory where you want to store the collected data files. Choose an appropriate location that offers sufficient space, and then click **Next**.

6. Determine the user account under which the Data Collector Set will run. You can select **Start this data collector set now** to begin monitoring immediately or choose **Save and close** if you wish to configure it later.

7. Click **Finish** to create the Data Collector Set.

8. To customize the data collection, right-click on the graph area and select **Add Counters...**. That will allow you to specify which performance metrics to monitor.

9. In the **Add Counters** dialog, select the performance counters you wish to track from the **Available counters** list. Click **Add** to move these counters to the **Added counters** section. This step can be repeated to include additional counters as necessary.

10. Once you have added all required counters, click **OK** to close the dialog and apply your configuration, as demonstrated in *Figure 13.14*.

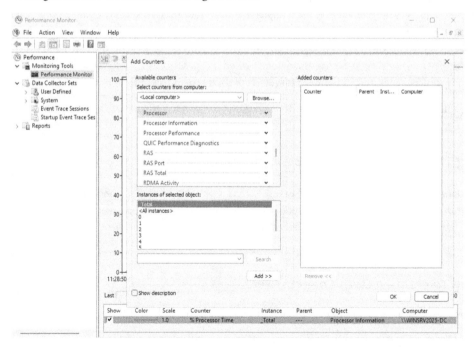

Figure 13.14 – Performance Monitor counters in Windows Server 2025

11. The Data Collector Set will now start collecting data according to the specified parameters, providing valuable insights into server performance.

This comprehensive approach to setting up Data Collector Sets ensures that you can gather detailed performance data, which is crucial for monitoring server health and diagnosing potential issues.

> **Note**
>
> For detailed information on performance monitoring thresholds and other valuable insights into monitoring various technologies, visit the **ManageEngine Network Performance Monitoring** resource at `https://www.manageengine.com/network-monitoring/network-performance-monitoring.html`. This site provides comprehensive guidance on setting performance thresholds and optimizing monitoring practices across different network environments.

In the following subsection, we will examine how to interpret performance logs and configure alerts to further enhance your server management capabilities.

The purpose of performance logs and alerts

Effective performance monitoring is a crucial, ongoing responsibility for system administrators, requiring both diligence and a deep understanding of monitoring methodologies. To ensure server stability and efficiency, administrators must use specialized tools that provide timely insights into system health. Performance logs and alerts are essential components of this toolkit. *Logs* capture and store detailed performance data over time, facilitating comprehensive analysis and reporting. This historical data can help identify trends, diagnose persistent issues, and guide long-term improvements. *Alerts* offer immediate notifications about performance anomalies or potential problems, allowing administrators to address issues before they impact server operations. Together, these tools help maintain optimal server performance and prevent downtime.

The following section will provide detailed instructions on setting up performance logs and alerts in Windows Server 2025, enhancing your ability to monitor and manage server health effectively.

Chapter exercise – the performance logs and alerts service

In this exercise, you will engage in essential activities for effective performance monitoring:

- Initially, you will start the **performance logs and alerts service**, which is crucial for enabling the system to capture and track performance data continuously.

- Following this, you will access the **Performance Monitor logs folder**, which houses the detailed logs and provides a centralized location for data review and management.

- You will then create **performance data logs** to systematically record metrics and trends over time, facilitating in-depth analysis and reporting.

- Lastly, you will set up **performance counter alerts** to configure notifications for specific performance thresholds, ensuring that you receive timely warnings about potential issues and enabling prompt corrective actions to maintain optimal system performance.

This exercise will provide a practical understanding of managing and optimizing performance through the effective use of logs and alerts.

Activating the service for performance logs and alerts

To activate the Performance Logs and Alerts service in Windows Server 2025, follow these detailed steps to ensure proper setup for monitoring and recording system performance:

1. Press the *Windows* key + *R* to open the **Run** dialog box, then type `services.msc` and press *Enter*. That will open the **Services** management console.

2. In the **Services** window, scroll through the list to locate the **Performance Logs & Alerts** service (shown in *Figure 13.15*). This service is critical for tracking and managing performance metrics.

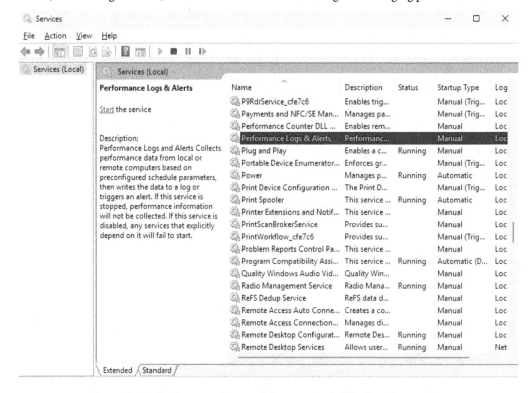

Figure 13.15 – Performance logs and alerts service in Windows Server 2025

Once the **Performance Logs & Alerts** service is active, you can proceed to the next steps of monitoring and managing performance data by accessing the Performance Monitor's `logs` folder. This setup is crucial for maintaining a comprehensive view of your server's performance and ensuring timely intervention when issues arise.

Navigating to the PerfLogs folder

To access the `PerfLogs` folder, which is crucial for storing performance data logs used in diagnosing and analyzing your server's performance, follow these steps on Windows Server 2025:

1. Press the *Windows* key + *R* to open the **Run** dialog box.

2. Type C: and press *Enter* to navigate to the root directory of the C: drive. That is where system folders are located.

3. Locate and open the `PerfLogs` folder, which contains subdirectories with performance logs. *Figure 13.16* shows this folder.

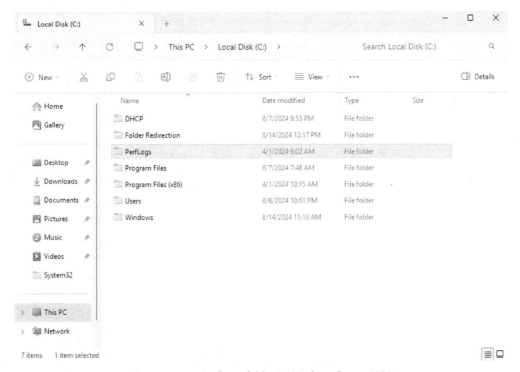

Figure 13.16 – PerfLogs folder in Windows Server 2025

The `PerfLogs` folder holds detailed logs of performance metrics, including system resource usage and performance counters. By reviewing these logs, administrators can gain insights into server behavior, identify potential issues, and make informed decisions about performance optimizations. After accessing the `PerfLogs` folder, our next point of focus will be on creating and configuring performance data logs to tailor monitoring to specific needs and ensure comprehensive performance management.

Generating performance data logs

To generate performance data logs in Windows Server 2025, follow these detailed steps:

1. Open Performance Monitor and expand the **Data Collector Sets** section. Navigate to **User Defined**.

2. Right-click on **User Defined** and select **New | Data Collector Set** from the context menu to initiate the creation process.

3. Provide a meaningful name for your new Data Collector Set to help identify its purpose and click **Next**.

4. Choose the **Create manually (Advanced)** option to access advanced configuration settings and click **Next** to continue.

5. Opt for the **Create data logs** option and select **Performance counter** as the log type. That will allow you to monitor specific metrics related to system performance. Click **Next** to proceed.

6. Click the **Add** button to open a list of available performance counters. From this list, select the counters you want to monitor, as shown in *Figure 13.17*. Set the appropriate time interval for data collection based on your monitoring needs and click **Next**.

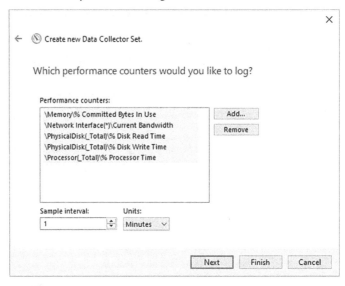

Figure 13.17 – Changing the default logs location in Windows Server 2025

7. Ensure that the data logs are set to be stored in the default `PerfLogs` folder, which is crucial for organizing and accessing log files later. Confirm the location and click **Next**.

8. Configure the data collector set to start immediately by choosing the **Start this data collector set now** option under the **User in Run** settings. Click **Finish** to complete the setup.

By following these steps, you will have successfully created and initiated a Data Collector Set that captures performance data based on your selected counters. This setup is essential for ongoing performance analysis and troubleshooting. In the next section, we will focus on configuring performance counter alerts to enhance proactive monitoring and response to performance issues.

Creating performance counter alerts

Configuring performance counter alerts in Windows Server 2025 is crucial for proactive system management and early detection of potential issues. These alerts allow you to receive notifications when performance metrics exceed or fall below predefined thresholds, ensuring that you can take timely corrective actions. Here is a detailed guide for setting up performance counter alerts:

1. Start by opening Performance Monitor and following the same initial steps as in the section on creating performance data logs, including expanding **Data Collector Sets** and selecting **User Defined**.

2. Choose the **Performance Counter Alert** option and click **Next** to move to the configuration settings.

3. Click the **Add** button to select the relevant performance counters that you wish to monitor. As shown in *Figure 13.18*, you will need to define the alert limits for each counter, which triggers notifications when the performance metrics breach these limits. Click **Next** once you've configured these settings.

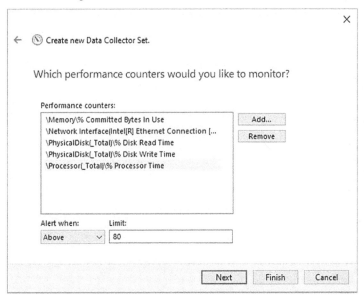

Figure 13.18 – Setting up the performance counter alert

4. Set the **User in Run** options according to your preferences and select **Start this data collector set now** to activate the alert immediately.

5. Click **Finish** to finalize the setup and activate the performance counter alerts.

By completing these steps, you will have established a robust monitoring system that helps ensure optimal server performance by alerting you to critical issues before they impact operations. This proactive approach is essential for maintaining the health and efficiency of Windows Server 2025.

Summary

This chapter provided an overview of essential server hardware components, as well as the utilization of Windows Server 2025 tools and utilities for managing and enhancing server performance. It covered the roles and functions of critical hardware elements, such as processors, memory, discs, network interfaces, removable drives, graphics cards, cooling systems, power supplies, and physical ports. You also explored the implications of 32-bit versus 64-bit architectures on server performance. The chapter delved into performance monitoring tools and techniques within Windows Server 2025, including methodologies, procedures, server baselines, and various snap-ins such as Performance Monitor, Resource Monitor, Task Manager, and performance counters. Additionally, you learned how to interpret performance counters and set up performance logs and alerts. The chapter concluded with a hands-on exercise on managing the performance logs and alerts service. The next chapter will focus on updating and troubleshooting Windows Server 2025.

Questions

1. **True or false**: Servers provide network services and handle user requests to access services.

2. **Fill in the blank**: _____ represents a snapshot of your server's performance under a normal workload.

3. **Multiple choice**: Which of the following is related to processors? (*Choose two*)

   A. Cache

   B. Cores

   C. NIC teaming

   D. Hot-swap

4. **True or false**: Task Manager enables you to monitor the processes, performance, and services currently running on your server.

5. **Fill in the blank**: _____ is the hardware that generates the most thermal heat.

6. **Multiple choice**: Which of the following benefits from having multiple NICs on the server? (*Choose two*)

   A. NLB

   B. Network separation

   C. Word size

   D. Virtualization technology

7. **True or false**: Since power supplies are not considered a single point of failure, servers are not equipped with a redundant power supply.

8. **Fill in the blank**: _____ concerns the processor's internal architecture, which defines the size of the data bus, instructions, and address.

9. **Multiple choice**: Which of the following Windows MMCs are used for performance and resource monitoring? (*Choose two*)

   A. Performance Monitor

   B. Resource Monitor

   C. Server Manager

   D. Device Manager

10. **True or false**: Counters provide performance information on how well an operating system, application, service, or driver works.

11. **Fill in the blank**: _____ helps identify server problems at an early stage of development and takes the necessary steps to prevent them from becoming costly issues in terms of time and business.

12. **Multiple choice**: Which of the following are considered to be a server's primary storage? (*Choose two*)

    A. RAM

    B. ROM

    C. HDD

    D. USB flash drive

13. **Short answer**: Discuss Performance Monitor and Resource Monitor.

14. **Short answer**: Discuss performance logs and alerts.

Further reading

- *Key Considerations in Server Hardware Selection*: `https://www.hostmines.com/blog/server-hardware-selection/`

- *Server hardware performance considerations*: `https://learn.microsoft.com/en-us/windows-server/administration/performance-tuning/hardware/`

- *How to use Performance Monitor to collect event trace data*: `https://docs.microsoft.com/en-us/dynamics365/business-central/dev-itpro/administration/monitor-use-performance-monitor-collect-event-trace-data`

14

Updating and Troubleshooting Windows Server 2025

In this chapter, you will explore how to update and troubleshoot Windows Server 2025, tackling some of the more challenging aspects of server management. With a well-defined plan and strategy, even the most complex tasks can be managed effectively. The chapter emphasizes the importance of troubleshooting, updating, monitoring, and maintaining servers to ensure business continuity, which, in turn, provides a competitive advantage in the market. That underscores the critical role IT professionals play within an organization.

Building on the previous chapter, you will learn how to implement the **Windows Server backup and restore disaster recovery plan** and perform updates to Windows Server 2025, server hardware, and third-party software. Additionally, you will be introduced to the **Event Viewer**, a valuable tool for examining various logs on Windows Server 2025, which aids in troubleshooting and problem-solving. Gaining these skills will help minimize downtime and reduce financial losses for the business.

The chapter concludes with a practical exercise on using the Event Viewer to monitor and manage Windows Server 2025 logs.

In this chapter, we're going to cover the following main topics:

- Managing updates for the OS, drivers, and applications in Windows Server 2025
- Troubleshooting methodologies and best practices
- Implementing business continuity strategies in Windows Server 2025 environments
- Maintaining business continuity through backup, restore, and disaster recovery planning
- Utilizing Event Viewer to monitor system logs and perform troubleshooting
- Using Event Viewer to monitor and manage logs

Technical requirements

For the exercise outlined in this chapter, ensure you have the following equipment:

- A PC running **Windows 11 Pro** with a minimum of 16 GB of RAM, 1 TB of HDD storage, and a stable internet connection
- A virtual machine configured with **Windows Server 2025 Standard**, equipped with at least 4 GB of RAM, 100 GB of HDD storage, and an internet connection

These specifications are necessary to complete the exercise and achieve the desired outcomes successfully.

Managing updates for the OS, drivers, and applications in Windows Server 2025

After installing a Windows OS, one of the best practices is to use the Windows Update service to check for and install any available updates. This process is crucial for enhancing the security of your Windows OS by protecting it from potential threats, ensuring that drivers for hardware devices are correctly installed, and improving or adding new features. Additionally, updates often address and resolve existing problems and errors within the system. Thus, updating Windows Server 2025 is a key step to perform after setting it up on either a new or existing server.

Keeping Windows Server up to date

Maintaining an up-to-date Windows Server 2025 is a critical responsibility for IT professionals, ensuring that the operating system and its applications benefit from the latest features, security enhancements, and bug fixes provided by Microsoft. Updates are released monthly on the second Tuesday, known as *Patch Tuesday*, and can be accessed via the **Windows Update** service or the dedicated website. Additionally, reminders may appear in the system tray and Notification Center indicating that you need some updates, as illustrated in *Figure 14.1*.

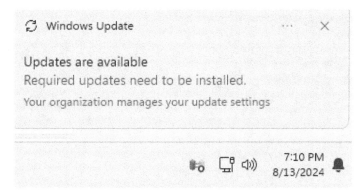

Figure 14.1 – Windows Update notifications

The **Windows Update** settings in Windows Server 2025, although like those in Windows Server 2022, have been updated with new appearance and options. Key settings include:

- **Get the latest updates as soon as they're available:** This feature allows you to receive updates as soon as they are released, ensuring your system is always up-to-date with the latest features and security enhancements.

- **Pause Updates:** This option enables you to postpone updates for a week. The Windows Update page will confirm the pause, and you can extend it by selecting "Pause for 1 week."

- **Update History:** This feature lets you review the list of installed updates and their statuses, uninstall updates if necessary, and access recovery options.

- **Advanced Options:** This setting allows you to choose how updates are installed, including options to receive updates for other Microsoft products when updating Windows or to defer feature updates.

Refer to *Figure 14.2* and follow the subsequent instructions for a detailed exploration of how to update Windows Server 2025 specifically.

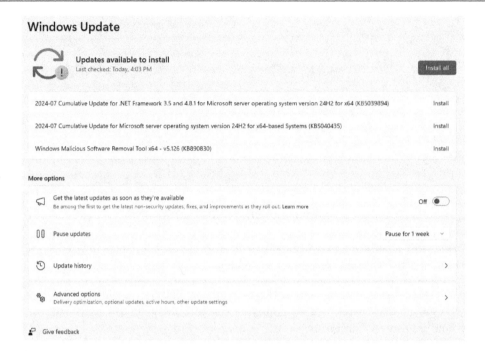

Figure 14.2 – Updating Windows Server 2025

With an understanding of the general Windows Update process established, let us delve into the specific steps required to update Windows Server 2025.

Installing updates on Windows Server 2025

Regular updates are crucial for maintaining the security and functionality of Windows Server 2025. Keeping the operating system and applications up to date ensures that your server benefits from the latest security patches, bug fixes, and enhancements. To update Windows Server 2025 using Windows Update, follow these steps:

1. Open the Windows Settings app by pressing the *Windows* key + *I*.

2. Navigate to **Update & Security** in the Windows Settings app.

3. Click the **Check for updates** button under **Update status**. Windows Update will then scan your system for any available updates.

4. If updates are detected, you will be prompted to install them. The installation progress can be monitored within the Windows Settings app (see *Figure 14.3*).

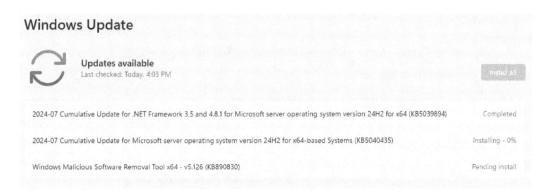

Windows Update

Updates available
Last checked: Today, 4:03 PM

[install all]

2024-07 Cumulative Update for .NET Framework 3.5 and 4.8.1 for Microsoft server operating system version 24H2 for x64 (KB5039894) — Completed

2024-07 Cumulative Update for Microsoft server operating system version 24H2 for x64-based Systems (KB5040435) — Installing - 0%

Windows Malicious Software Removal Tool x64 - v5.126 (KB890830) — Pending install

Figure 14.3 – Installing updates on Windows Server 2025

5. Once the updates are installed, a server restart may be required for the changes to take effect.

Having covered how to update Windows Server 2025 using Windows Update, the next section will guide you on updating both Microsoft and third-party applications on your server.

> **Note**
>
> Windows 10 and 11 include a feature known as Windows as a Service, which ensures that the operating system continuously receives updates and new releases through Windows Update. Despite this, some users might choose to remain on their current version and delay receiving these updates. To accommodate this preference, Microsoft offers an option called *defer feature updates*. This feature allows users to postpone the installation of new releases for a specified duration. For more information about how this feature works, you can visit this link: `https://www.onmsft.com/news/mean-defer-feature-updates-windows-10`.

The previous subsections showed you how to use Windows Update to keep your Windows Server 2025 operating system up to date. However, updating the operating system is not enough; you also need to update the software applications that run on a server, whether they are from Microsoft or other vendors. In the following subsection, we will explain how to do that.

Updating Microsoft programs

In addition to keeping your operating system current, it's essential to update the applications running on your Windows Server 2025, such as **Exchange**, **SQL Server**, and **SharePoint**. These Microsoft programs provide critical server functionalities such as email, database management, and collaboration tools. Regular updates are crucial for maintaining optimal performance and security. To ensure that these Microsoft programs are updated, you need to configure Windows Update to include updates for other Microsoft products.

Follow these steps:

1. Press the *Windows* key + *I* to open the Windows Settings app.

2. Select **Update & Security**.

3. Click on **Advanced options** under **Update settings**.

4. Check the box labeled **Receive updates for other Microsoft products** when you update Windows (refer to *Figure 14.4*).

Figure 14.4 – Updating Microsoft programs

After completing these steps, you will receive updates for Microsoft programs through Windows Update. Note that this process does not extend to third-party applications, which will be covered in the following section.

Microsoft programs typically receive updates via the Windows Update service. However, this service does not extend to applications developed by third-party vendors. Consequently, it is necessary to update these external programs manually. In the following section, we will guide you through the process of updating non-Microsoft applications to ensure they are up to date and functioning optimally.

Updating third-party programs

In addition to Microsoft programs, Windows Server 2025 may also host third-party applications, such as Oracle databases, Apache web servers, and VMware virtualization platforms. For a system administrator, understanding how to update these third-party programs is crucial, as their update procedures differ from those of Microsoft products. While Windows Update typically handles updates for Microsoft operating systems and applications, third-party software requires a distinct update process. For example, to update Adobe Acrobat Reader DC on Windows Server 2025, follow these steps:

1. Open Adobe Acrobat Reader DC from the **Start** menu.

2. Navigate to the **Help** menu and select **Check for Updates**.

3. The Adobe Acrobat Reader DC Updater will scan for available updates and notify you if any are found.

4. Click the **Download** button to initiate the update process.

5. The *System Tray* icon will display the download progress.

6. Once the download is complete, the updater will prompt you to install the update.

7. Click **Install**, as illustrated in *Figure 14.5*.

Figure 14.5 – Updating a non-Microsoft program

8. Confirm the UAC dialog by clicking **Yes**.

9. After the installation is finished, close Adobe Acrobat Reader DC by clicking **Close**.

Updating applications with Winget

Keeping applications up to date is essential for system security, performance, and compatibility, and Windows Package Manager, or Winget, offers a powerful tool for this purpose. Winget simplifies application management on Windows by enabling administrators to install, update, and configure software through command-line operations. One of its most valuable commands, `winget upgrade --all`, allows administrators to update all installed applications in a single step, making it easier to maintain up-to-date, secure software across systems.

Using Winget

The `winget upgrade --all` command, as shown in Figure 14.6, is one of the most effective ways to keep all applications on a Windows system updated with minimal effort. By running this single command, system administrators can automate the update process, ensuring that each application is running the latest version available. This approach not only streamlines software maintenance but also reinforces system security by addressing potential vulnerabilities across applications. The `winget` `upgrade --all` command is remarkably efficient, as it scans, downloads, and installs updates for all installed applications. Here is an overview of how it works:

1. **Scanning for updates**: Winget first checks each application against its repository to identify any available updates.

2. **Downloading updates**: Once updates are found, Winget automatically downloads the latest versions.

3. **Installing updates**: Finally, Winget installs the updates to bring all applications to their current versions.

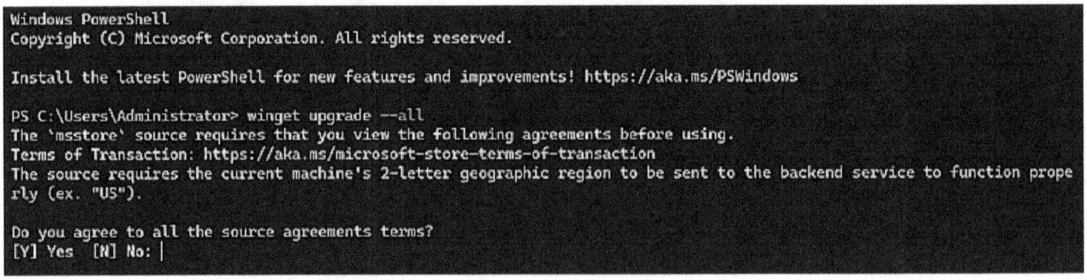

```
Windows PowerShell
Copyright (C) Microsoft Corporation. All rights reserved.

Install the latest PowerShell for new features and improvements! https://aka.ms/PSWindows

PS C:\Users\Administrator> winget upgrade --all
The 'msstore' source requires that you view the following agreements before using.
Terms of Transaction: https://aka.ms/microsoft-store-terms-of-transaction
The source requires the current machine's 2-letter geographic region to be sent to the backend service to function prope
rly (ex. "US").

Do you agree to all the source agreements terms?
[Y] Yes  [N] No: |
```

Figure 14.6 – Updating Windows Server applications using Winget

Benefits of Winget

Utilizing the `winget upgrade --all` command provides several key advantages that make it an essential tool in application management. This command allows for efficient, consistent, and secure updating, saving administrators time while helping to maintain system stability and security. The following are some of the main benefits that make `winget upgrade --all` a valuable addition to any routine maintenance strategy:

- **Efficiency**: This command automates the update process, saving time and reducing the need for manual intervention

- **Consistency**: By updating all applications at once, administrators can ensure uniform versions across systems, reducing compatibility issues

- **Enhanced security**: Regular updates help patch security vulnerabilities, which is critical for safeguarding systems from potential threats

By leveraging Winget's `winget upgrade --all` commands and scheduling periodic updates, administrators can maintain a secure and stable application environment with minimal manual effort. This approach not only saves time but also ensures that all software remains up to date, enhancing overall system resilience.

With the process of updating both Microsoft and third-party programs covered and using Winget, the next step is to address updating device drivers.

Configuring Windows Update to check for device drivers

As covered in *Chapter 3*, *What to Do After Installing Windows Server 2025*, updating device drivers can traditionally be done using the Device Manager tool. This method requires manual searching and installation of the latest drivers for each device. Alternatively, Windows Update offers an automated solution to detect and download the most current drivers and updates for your devices. To configure Windows Update for this purpose, follow these steps:

1. Press the *Windows* key + *R*, type `Control Panel`, and press *Enter*.

2. Select **Hardware**.

3. Clicking on **Devices and Printers** opens **Printers & scanners**.

4. In the **Printers & scanners** window, select the device by clicking on its right.

5. On the device's page, click **Hardware Properties** to open its properties window.

6. On the device's properties window, click the **Settings** tab and then click the **Devices and Printers** folder button.

7. In the **Devices and Printers** window, right-click on the server and choose **Device installation settings** from the context menu, as depicted in *Figure 14.7*.

Figure 14.7 – Device installation settings

8. To enable automatic updates for device drivers, select the **Yes (recommended)** option, as shown in *Figure 14.8*.

Figure 14.8 – Setting up a device driver update

9. Click **Save Changes** to close the **Device installation settings** window.

Enabling this setting ensures that your server's devices are continuously updated with the latest drivers from Microsoft. Additionally, Microsoft offers a tool called Windows Server Update Services (WSUS) for managing and organizing product updates. The details of WSUS will be discussed in the following subsection.

WSUS overview

Windows Server Update Services (**WSUS**) is a vital tool for system administrators, designed to streamline the management of Microsoft's product updates across an organization's network. WSUS functions by downloading *updates*, *patches*, and *fixes* from Microsoft Update to a centralized server within the organization. This server then distributes the updates to other computers on the network. With WSUS, administrators gain control over which updates are installed or declined, can schedule update installations, and generate reports to track the update status of each computer. This setup eliminates the need for individual computers to connect directly to Microsoft Update, as WSUS handles the update distribution.

In Windows Server 2025, WSUS is available as a *role* that can be installed via **Server Manager**. To install the WSUS role, follow these steps:

Press the *Windows* key + *R*, type `servermanager.exe`, and press *Enter*.

1. In the **Server Manager** console, click on **Add Roles and Features**.

2. On the **Before You Begin** page, click **Next**.

3. On the **Installation Type** page, select **Role-based or Feature-based Installation**, and click **Next**.

4. On the **Server Selection** page, ensure that **Select a server from the server pool** is chosen, then click **Next**.

5. On the **Server Roles** page, check the box for **Windows Server Update Services** (as shown in *Figure 14.9*), and click **Next**.

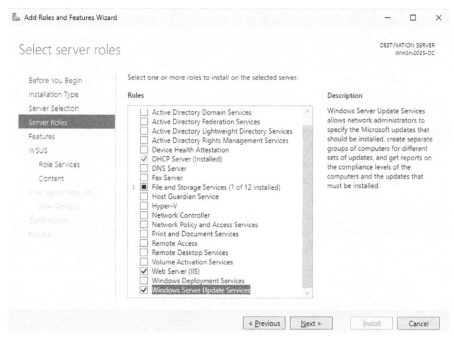

Figure 14.9 – Installing Windows Server Update Services

6. On the **Features** page, no additional features need to be added, so click **Next**.

7. On the **WSUS** page, review the description and installation notes, then click **Next**.

8. On the **Role Services** page, **WID Connectivity** and **WSUS Services** are selected by default. Click **Next**.

9. On the **Content** page, specify the local or network location for storing the updates, and click **Next**.

10. On the **Confirmation** page, click **Install**.

11. After the installation is complete, click **Close** to exit **Add Roles and Features Wizard**.

This section has provided an overview of the Microsoft Windows Updates feature, the process for updating Windows Server 2025, and how to manage updates for Microsoft and non-Microsoft programs, as well as device drivers and WSUS. The following section will focus on troubleshooting methodologies.

Troubleshooting methodologies and best practices

Troubleshooting is an essential skill in IT that can be significantly enhanced through practice and experience. Each issue you resolve boosts your confidence, expands your knowledge, and improves your proficiency. This continuous learning and hands-on approach are crucial for developing practical problem-solving abilities. By investing time in mastering troubleshooting techniques, you increase your capability to address and resolve issues efficiently.

Before diving into troubleshooting, it's important to familiarize yourself with the best practices, guidelines, and methodologies that underpin effective problem resolution. Understanding these foundational elements will better prepare you to tackle and resolve technical challenges effectively.

Best practices, guidelines, and procedures

Best practices represent *established and proven methods* for addressing IT challenges effectively. They are designed to ensure that organizational policies and procedures are managed both efficiently and effectively. These practices are integral to recognized management standards such as *ISO 9000* and *ISO 14001*, and adhering to them can lead to improved server performance, more reliable network services, enhanced security for client/server applications, and more adaptable network infrastructures. In addition to best practices, guidelines provide valuable suggestions or recommendations that help meet policy standards. Procedures, on the other hand, offer detailed instructions on how to implement various policy components.

> **Note**
>
> For further information on the ISO 9000 standard, you can visit the overview page at `http://asq.org/learn-about-quality/iso-9000/overview/overview.html`. To learn more about the ISO 14001 standard, refer to the details provided at `http://asq.org/learn-about-quality/learn-about-standards/iso-14001`.

With this understanding of best practices, guidelines, and procedures, we can now begin troubleshooting.

How do you troubleshoot effectively?

Effective troubleshooting involves a systematic approach to diagnosing and resolving specific server issues. One of the most widely accepted methodologies is the *six-step model* outlined by **CompTIA** and utilized by Microsoft support engineers. The process involves the following steps:

1. **Identify the problem**: Gather detailed technical data to understand the issue entirely.

2. **Review system configuration**: Investigate recent changes to hardware, software, or network settings by asking pertinent questions.

3. **Generate potential solutions**: Develop a list of possible fixes by systematically removing or turning off relevant hardware or software components.

4. **Implement the plan**: Test the proposed solutions, ensuring you have a backup plan if needed.

5. **Verify results**: Assess whether the issue is resolved; if not, revisit the potential solutions.

6. **Document changes**: Keep a record of all modifications made during the troubleshooting process for future reference.

> **Note**
>
> For more detailed information on the general troubleshooting process and specific detection methods, you can visit the TechNet website at `https://technet.microsoft.com/en-ca`.

Following these steps will help ensure a thorough and systematic approach to problem resolution. Additionally, troubleshooting involves employing two key approaches, which will be explored in the following subsection.

Comparing systematic and specific approaches in troubleshooting

When addressing server issues, the method we choose can significantly impact both the effectiveness and efficiency of the troubleshooting process. Typically, there are two predominant approaches to problem-solving:

- **Systematic approach**: This method is characterized by a structured and sequential process designed to address problems methodically, regardless of their nature. It follows a predefined set of steps, ensuring a thorough examination and resolution of issues through a logical, step-by-step approach. This method is ideal for complex or unfamiliar problems, providing a clear path to identify and resolve issues systematically.

- **Specific approach**: In contrast, this strategy relies on deep expertise and prior experience with similar problems. It emphasizes intuition and educated guesses, drawing on familiarity with the issue at hand. This approach is often faster for well-known problems but may involve a degree of trial and error.

Understanding these approaches will help refine your troubleshooting skills and apply the most effective strategy for different scenarios. In the following sections, we will explore these procedures in greater detail, offering insights into how to implement each approach effectively.

Understanding troubleshooting procedures

Troubleshooting is a critical skill for any server technician, honed through experience, expertise, and effective communication. It involves adhering to specific guidelines that ensure a structured and logical approach to resolving issues with computers and servers. Essential steps in the troubleshooting process include the following:

- **Reviewing documentation** to check whether the problem has been previously encountered
- **Examining logs** such as those in the **Event Viewer**
- **Consulting** relevant **Microsoft Knowledge Base** (**KB**) articles
- **Using diagnostic utility programs** to identify and resolve problems
- **Running a backup** before implementing any solutions

Various utility programs can aid in troubleshooting server issues, including the following:

- **Advanced Boot Options**: To access **Safe Mode** and **Windows Repair** options
- **Memory Diagnostics**: To check for memory-related problems
- **System Information**: To gather comprehensive system details
- **Device Manager**: To manage and troubleshoot hardware devices
- **Task Manager**: To monitor and manage running processes
- **Performance Monitor**: To analyze system performance metrics
- **Resource Monitor**: To track resource usage and system performance
- **Event Viewer**: To review system logs for errors and warnings

In the following subsection, we will explore the **Information Technology Infrastructure Library** (**ITIL**), which provides a framework for tailoring IT services to meet business requirements.

Understanding ITIL

The ITIL framework was developed in response to businesses' increasing reliance on computer and network technologies in the 1980s. Recognizing IT as a key driver for enhancing efficiency and productivity, ITIL was created to offer standardized practices for managing IT services throughout their lifecycle. This structured framework includes best practices for planning, implementing, operating, and maintaining IT services, which are documented in a series of publications known as the *ITIL core books*. The latest iteration, **ITIL v4**, was released between 2019 and 2020 and covers several core concepts, including the following:

- **Service strategy**: Establishes objectives and goals for both businesses and their customers
- **Service design**: Addresses IT components such as policies, architectures, and documentation

- **Service transition**: Emphasizes the management of changes within IT services

- **Service operation**: Focuses on the effective management of IT operations

- **Continual service improvement**: Involves ongoing enhancements and updates to policies and practices

ITIL provides organizations with a framework to tailor IT services according to their specific business needs, reinforcing IT's role as a crucial element in today's economy.

> **Note**
>
> For more information on ITIL and its comprehensive framework for IT service management, you can visit the official **Axelos** website at `https://www.axelos.com/best-practice-solutions/itil`. This resource provides detailed insights and guidance on implementing ITIL best practices to enhance IT service delivery and organizational efficiency.

In the upcoming section, we will explore the implementation of business continuity strategies within Windows Server 2025 environments. This discussion will focus on methods and best practices for ensuring that your server infrastructure remains resilient and operational, even in the face of potential disruptions.

Implementing business continuity strategies in Windows Server 2025 environments

In the modern digital landscape, system administrators play a crucial role in maintaining the continuous availability and functionality of IT services within an organization. Any disruption or malfunction in these services can lead to substantial business losses. Therefore, you need to anticipate potential failure points and implement appropriate preventive measures to safeguard against them.

Before we move forward, it is essential to introduce the concept of a **disaster recovery plan** (**DRP**).

What is a DRP?

A DRP is an essential, detailed document designed to guide an organization in resuming or maintaining its operations following a significant disruption or crisis. The primary goal of a DRP is to mitigate the impact of unexpected events—such as natural disasters, cyber-attacks, or system failures—by providing structured procedures to restore critical services and minimize downtime. As a core element of business continuity planning, a well-constructed DRP encompasses several crucial components:

- **Inventory of assets**: Catalog all hardware and software components critical to the organization's operations. This inventory ensures that every essential element is accounted for and prioritized during recovery efforts.

- **Risk assessment**: Identify and evaluate potential risks and vulnerabilities that could impact the organization. Understanding these risks helps in developing targeted strategies to address and mitigate them.

- **Objectives and goals**: Define clear recovery objectives and goals, including acceptable **recovery time objectives (RTOs)** and **recovery point objectives (RPOs)**. These metrics determine the maximum acceptable downtime and data loss.

- **Disruption tolerance**: Establish the level of acceptable disruption or downtime that the organization can endure. That helps in setting realistic recovery targets and expectations.

- **Review of past strategies**: Analyze previous disaster response strategies to understand their effectiveness and identify areas for improvement.

- **Staff safety**: Prioritize the safety and well-being of employees above data and service recovery. Ensure that emergency procedures include measures for staff evacuation and welfare.

- **Testing and drills**: Conduct regular simulations and drills to test the DRP's effectiveness. These exercises help identify gaps in the plan and improve response procedures.

- **Management approval**: Secure formal approval from management to ensure that the DRP is endorsed at the highest level and that resources are allocated for its implementation.

- **Plan maintenance**: Regularly update the DRP to reflect changes in technology, organizational structure, and business processes. An outdated plan may fail to address current risks and recovery needs.

By addressing these elements, organizations can enhance their resilience to disruptions and ensure a swift and organized recovery process. Next, we will explore data redundancy, a critical technique for ensuring service continuity and data integrity in the face of disasters.

Business continuity and disaster recovery differences

In today's IT environment, where cloud technology and resilient infrastructures are increasingly central, distinguishing between **business continuity (BC)** and **disaster recovery (DR)** is crucial for comprehensive planning. Although these concepts are related, each addresses different aspects of safeguarding an organization's operations in the face of disruptions:

- BC emphasizes keeping critical business functions running smoothly, even amid interruptions. BC planning involves implementing strategies and tools that minimize downtime and ensure ongoing productivity. That often includes building redundancies and establishing failover systems that allow business processes to continue without significant impact. For instance, utilizing cloud services with multi-region availability can help maintain operations, even if a specific region faces technical issues.

- DR, however, focuses specifically on the swift restoration of IT systems and data after a disruption. DR strategies typically involve setting up robust backup, replication, and recovery solutions to restore systems to their operational state as quickly as possible after an incident. Organizations might, for example, deploy automated data replication to cloud storage or maintain offsite backup locations to accelerate recovery times when an outage occurs.

Modern cloud capabilities have made it easier for organizations to integrate both BC and DR into their IT strategies, allowing for a more resilient approach to disruptions. By combining proactive continuity planning with adequate disaster recovery protocols, businesses can not only maintain essential operations during interruptions but also restore full functionality with minimal data loss, thus ensuring operational resilience and data protection.

Next, we will learn about data redundancy, which is a valuable technique for restoring services after a natural disaster.

How does data redundancy work?

Data redundancy involves creating multiple copies of data and storing them in different locations to safeguard against data loss and ensure high availability. This process allows for automatic synchronization and backup, which is crucial for protecting critical business information. By having redundant copies, organizations can recover data more quickly in the event of hardware failures, data corruption, or other disasters.

However, data redundancy introduces potential risks, particularly concerning *data consistency*. When data is updated, all copies must be synchronized accurately to prevent discrepancies. If updates are not uniformly applied, inconsistent data can result, compromising its quality and integrity. To mitigate these risks, organizations must implement robust data management practices and monitoring systems. That includes setting up effective synchronization protocols, regular integrity checks, and automated tools to handle large volumes of data across multiple storage locations.

Properly managed data redundancy ensures that businesses can maintain continuity and recover swiftly from disruptions. It is essential for maintaining operational efficiency and safeguarding against data loss.

In the following subsection, we will examine clustering, a technique that enhances system performance by combining the computational power of multiple servers.

What is clustering?

Clustering is an advanced technique designed to enhance the availability and performance of IT services by grouping multiple servers into a cohesive system that shares resources such as CPU, memory, disk space, and network connections. This approach ensures that services remain operational even if one or more servers fail, and it optimizes performance by distributing workloads effectively. There are two primary clustering methods:

- **Failover clustering**: This method involves a minimum of two servers configured in an active-passive model. In this setup, one server is actively running and handling requests while the other remains on standby. Should the active server encounter a failure, the passive server automatically takes over, minimizing downtime and maintaining service availability. Failover clustering is particularly effective for applications requiring high availability, such as databases and email servers, where uninterrupted service is crucial.

- **Load-balancing clustering**: This method uses at least two servers that work together as a single virtual server. Each server in the cluster shares the workload, distributing user requests and processing tasks evenly among them. From the user's perspective, they interact with a single server, but in reality, the load is balanced across multiple servers. This approach is ideal for web servers and other applications that handle large volumes of concurrent requests, enhancing performance and scalability.

Effective clustering not only improves service reliability and performance but also facilitates more manageable maintenance and scalability of IT infrastructure. By using clustering techniques, organizations can ensure high availability, efficient load distribution, and minimal service disruption.

Next, we will explore redirection, a technique that allows users to access files and resources within a network environment more efficiently.

Maintaining BC through backup, restore, and DR planning

Ensuring the continuous operation of IT services is crucial for any organization, making a well-structured business continuity plan essential. This section explores the key elements of maintaining BC through effective backup, restore, and DR strategies. Proper data backup and restoration are fundamental practices to safeguard against data loss and minimize system downtime. Additionally, understanding the nuances of **Active Directory** (**AD**) restoration is vital for recovering important user and system information. Folder redirection enhances data accessibility and recovery by directing user files to secure locations, ensuring critical data remains available even in the event of a system failure. Power redundancy plays a crucial role in DR, providing an uninterrupted power supply to prevent outages that could disrupt system operations. We will delve into each of these components in detail, equipping you with the knowledge and skills necessary to protect and maintain your organization's IT infrastructure effectively.

Implementing *robust backup solutions* is essential to prevent data loss and ensure continuity. Let's explore the fundamentals of backup and restore processes next.

Backup and restore basics

One of the primary responsibilities in server administration is safeguarding server data from loss or damage. Backups are crucial for this purpose, as they enable the duplication of data to alternative locations or devices. However, the efficacy of backups hinges on the ability to restore data when necessary, which is where the restore process comes into play—retrieving data from backups and reinstating it to the server. Several backup types cater to different needs based on frequency and scope:

- **Full backup**: This method creates a complete copy of all server data. Only the latest full backup is required to restore, ensuring a straightforward restoration process.

- **Incremental backup**: This approach saves only the data altered since the last backup of any type. Typically performed daily, excluding the day of the full backup (often on Friday), incremental backups speed up the backup process but require the most recent full backup along with all subsequent incremental backups for restoration, which can make the restoration process more time-consuming.

- **Differential backup**: This backs up only the data modified since the last full backup. Like incremental backups, differential backups are generally done daily, except on the day of the full backup. To restore, the latest full backup and the most recent differential backup are needed, which accelerates the restore process but may slow down the backup operation.

Backup media choices depend on the importance and volume of data. Options include CDs, DVDs, removable hard drives, backup tapes, **network-attached storage (NAS)**, and **storage area networks (SANs)**. Increasingly, organizations are adopting online backup services due to their convenience, security, and cost-effectiveness. Additionally, the **grandfather-father-son (GFS)** backup rotation scheme is commonly used, where daily backups are referred to as *son* backups, weekly backups are *father* backups, and monthly backups are *grandfather* backups, ensuring a structured and reliable backup strategy.

Installing and using Windows Server Backup in Windows Server 2025

Windows Server Backup is a crucial feature for data protection in Windows Server 2025, and it can be activated through the Server Manager. To set up Windows Server Backup, follow these steps:

1. Press the *Windows* key + *R*, type `servermanager.exe`, and hit *Enter*.

2. In the **Server Manager** console, choose **Add Roles and Features**.

3. On the **Before You Begin** page, click **Next**.

4. On the **Installation Type** page, select **Role-based or Feature-based Installation**, then click **Next**.

5. On the **Server Selection** page, pick a server from the server pool and click **Next**.

6. No additional roles need to be added, so proceed by clicking **Next**.

7. On the **Features** page, scroll through the list and check **Windows Server Backup** (refer to *Figure 14.10*). Click **Next**.

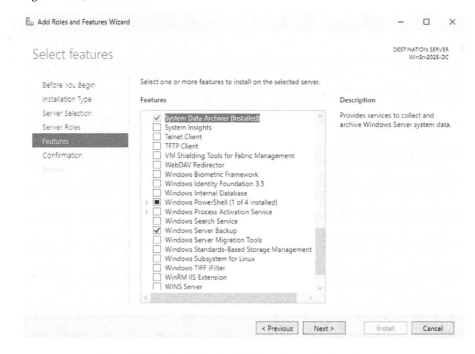

Figure 14.10 – Installing the Windows Server Backup feature

8. On the **Confirmation** page, click **Install**.

9. After the installation is complete, click **Close** to exit **Add Roles and Features Wizard**.

The landscape of backup technologies has evolved significantly over the years. Traditional methods such as **write once, read many** (**WORM**) storage, **digital audio tape** (**DAT**), and **Travan data line tape** (**TDLT**) are becoming less common due to their limitations in scalability, speed, and offsite accessibility. In contrast, modern solutions such as **disaster recovery as a service** (**DRaaS**) and **backup as a service** (**BaaS**) are increasingly being adopted for their secure, scalable, and efficient offsite data protection capabilities. These services enable organizations to store backups in remote, cloud-based locations, ensuring that critical data remains safe and accessible even in the event of a disaster. By utilizing DRaaS and BaaS, businesses can enhance their backup strategies, improving both disaster recovery capabilities and overall business continuity. Additionally, these cloud-based solutions offer greater flexibility, allowing companies to scale their backup resources according to growing data needs while reducing the complexity of managing on-premises storage infrastructure.

With Windows Server Backup installed, you're now ready to proceed with the following essential tasks, such as performing an AD restore.

Restoring AD

As discussed in *Chapter 4, Directory Services in Windows Server 2025*, during the installation of the **Active Directory Domain Services (AD DS)** role, you were required to set a **Directory Services Restore Mode (DSRM)** password, as shown in *Figure 14.11*. This password is vital for the restoration process, and it is crucial to remember it. DSRM is a specialized mode that facilitates the *repair or recovery* of AD in cases of corruption or damage.

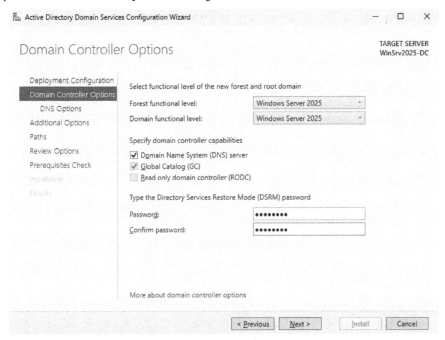

Figure 14.11 – Setting up the DSRM password

There are typically two methods for restoring data on a **domain controller (DC)**. The first involves reinstalling the operating system, reconfiguring the DC, and allowing it to synchronize with another DC on the network through standard replication. The second method uses a backup to restore the data on the DC, which can be performed in one of two ways:

- **Non-authoritative restore**: This approach is used when a DC fails due to hardware or software issues. You restore the AD structure from a backup, and then the DC updates itself from another DC on the network via regular replication.

- **Authoritative restore**: This method follows a non-authoritative restore and is used to revert the system to a state before particular AD objects are deleted. It involves using the Ntdsutil command to authoritatively restore the entire AD, ensuring that the restored data is recognized as the current version.

Once AD has been successfully restored, it is essential to implement folder redirection. This process ensures that users can access their documents and data seamlessly within a network environment. Folder redirection helps centralize data storage, making it more accessible and secure, and enhances the efficiency of data management across the network. By redirecting user folders to a specified network location, organizations can maintain consistent access to important files, even if individual workstations or servers experience issues.

Volume Shadow Copy Service explained

Volume Shadow Copy Service (**VSS**) is an essential feature within the Windows Server environment, designed to create stable, point-in-time snapshots of data—referred to as "shadow copies"—without disrupting ongoing applications. Initially introduced in Windows Server 2003, VSS has become a cornerstone of consistent, reliable backups, thus continuing to be available in Windows Server 2025. By managing data consistency even while files are in use, VSS allows for dependable backups critical to BC and data protection.

The process behind VSS relies on three core components working together to generate these snapshots seamlessly:

- **VSS service**: This foundational component within the Windows OS manages the entire snapshot process, facilitating coordination between requesters and writers.

- **VSS requester**: Generally, in a backup application, the requester initiates the creation of shadow copies. Examples of VSS requesters include tools such as Windows Server Backup and System Center Data Protection Manager.

- **VSS writer**: Integrated into various applications such as SQL Server or Exchange Server, the writer ensures that each application's data is consistent and ready for backup. This component is crucial for preserving the integrity of complex applications during snapshot creation.

VSS offers several key advantages that enhance data protection and reliability in Windows Server environments. By creating consistent, point-in-time snapshots, VSS enables seamless backups even when applications are in use, minimizing downtime and disruption. Its versatility allows it to support various backup and recovery scenarios, making it an invaluable tool for maintaining data integrity and ensuring business continuity. The following are some of the main benefits VSS brings to a robust backup strategy:

- **Data consistency**: By capturing data in a consistent state, VSS ensures that backups are dependable, even if files are actively in use

- **Minimal disruption**: Because VSS snapshots do not require applications to pause or stop, organizations can perform backups with minimal downtime, preserving productivity

- **Flexibility**: VSS is versatile, supporting a range of backup scenarios from disk-to-disk and disk-to-tape backups to quick data recovery processes

VSS is widely used across Windows Server to support essential backup and recovery functions, making it a critical component in data management. From ensuring reliable backups to allowing users to restore previous file versions, VSS enhances data resilience across various applications. The following are some common uses of VSS within Windows Server, each contributing to a comprehensive data protection strategy:

- **Windows Server Backup**: This built-in solution utilizes VSS to provide robust backup and recovery options for server environments

- **Shadow Copies for Shared Folders**: This feature allows users to restore previous versions of files on network shares, reducing the need for administrative recovery tasks

- **System Center Data Protection Manager**: An enterprise-grade tool, this leverages VSS to deliver comprehensive data protection and quick recovery capabilities for a wide array of workloads

Incorporating VSS into your data protection strategy enhances the reliability and flexibility of backups, allowing organizations to safeguard essential data without interrupting daily operations.

Understanding folder redirection

Folder redirection is a vital task for system administrators that involves changing the location of user folders from a local computer or network share to a different, centralized location. This feature allows users to access their files as though they were stored on their machines while actually being managed on a server. To configure folder redirection in Windows Server 2025, you will need to set up a **Group Policy Object (GPO)** that dictates the redirection settings. Here is how to set it up:

1. Launch the **Group Policy Management (GPM)** console by pressing the *Windows* key + *R*, typing gpmc.msc, and hitting *Enter*.
2. On the left pane of the GPM console, right-click **Default Domain Policy** and select **Edit**.
3. In the GPM Editor, navigate to **User Configuration**, expand **Policies**, then **Windows Settings**, and select **Folder Redirection**.
4. Right-click on **Documents** and choose **Properties**.
5. Opt for the **Basic - Redirect everyone's folder to the same location** setting.
6. Under **Target folder location**, select **Redirect to the following location**.
7. Specify the root path to the desired destination for the redirected folders, as depicted in *Figure 14.12*.

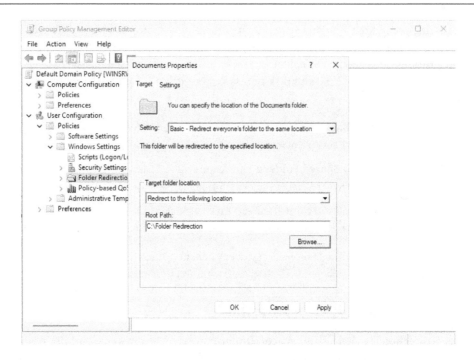

Figure 14.12 – Creating a GPO for folder redirection

8.   Click **OK** to save the settings and close the **Documents Properties** window.

By implementing these steps, you ensure that users' documents are consistently available and centrally managed.

Next, we will address how to handle power supply issues, which are critical for maintaining server performance and reliability.

Power redundancy explained

Maintaining a consistent power supply is fundamental for the reliable operation of a server, which depends on its processor, memory, storage, and network resources. To address the risk of power interruptions, servers often employ an **uninterruptible power supply** (**UPS**), as shown in *Figure 14.13*. A UPS provides a temporary battery-powered backup that ensures the server remains operational for a short period during a power outage. This temporary power allows for graceful shutdowns or continuity of critical operations until the main power is restored. However, given that a UPS can only support power for a limited duration, it is insufficient for extended outages. For prolonged power interruptions, a **generator** is typically used as a supplementary power source to ensure continuous operation and avoid any disruption to business functions.

Figure 14.13 - Rack-mountable UPS

Power redundancy is a crucial component of a comprehensive disaster recovery plan, helping to mitigate the risk of data loss and system downtime. By integrating both UPS and generator solutions, organizations can safeguard against various scenarios of power failure, thereby enhancing their overall resilience and reliability.

Implementing a DRP for Windows Server 2025

In today's rapidly evolving IT landscape, having a robust DRP is essential to ensure that your organization can swiftly recover from unforeseen disruptions. Implementing an effective DRP for Windows Server 2025 involves several critical steps. These steps are designed to assess potential risks, establish clear recovery objectives, and develop comprehensive recovery strategies to safeguard your IT infrastructure. To implement a DRP in Windows Server 2025, you need to consider the following steps:

1. **Assess the risks and potential threats** that could affect your IT infrastructure and identify the key assets and resources that need to be protected.

2. **Define the recovery objectives and priorities** for each system and service, such as the RPO, which is the maximum amount of data loss that is acceptable, and the RTO, which is the maximum amount of time that is acceptable to restore the system or service.

3. **Design and document the recovery strategies and procedures** for each scenario, such as backup and restore, failover and failback, replication and synchronization, or cloud-based solutions. Specify the roles and responsibilities of the staff who will execute the plan and the communication channels that will be used.

4. **Test and validate the plan regularly** to ensure that it works as expected and meets the recovery objectives and requirements. Update the plan as needed to reflect any changes in the IT environment or the business needs.

5. **Review and audit the plan periodically** to evaluate its effectiveness and compliance with the best practices and standards. Incorporate feedback and lessons learned from the testing and validation process.

Types of recovery sites for effective DRP

In the context of a DRP, evaluating and selecting the appropriate types of recovery sites is crucial for ensuring that your organization can quickly and effectively resume operations after a disaster. **Recovery sites** are categorized based on their level of readiness and the speed at which they can be operationalized. Each type of recovery site has distinct characteristics, advantages, and trade-offs, which can significantly impact your organization's recovery strategy and overall business continuity. Understanding these types of recovery sites—cold sites, warm sites, and hot sites—will help you tailor your DRP to align with your organization's needs, budget, and recovery objectives. By carefully choosing and implementing the correct type of recovery site, you can enhance your ability to minimize downtime and mitigate the impact of potential disruptions on your IT infrastructure and services:

- **Cold site**: This is a backup facility that has the necessary infrastructure, such as power and networking, but no pre-installed hardware or software. In the event of a disaster, you must transport and set up the required equipment and restore data from backups. Cold sites are cost-effective but involve longer recovery times.

- **Warm site**: A warm site is partially equipped with hardware and networking capabilities, but it requires configuration and data restoration before becoming fully operational. This type of site offers a balance between cost and recovery speed, providing quicker recovery times than cold sites but at a higher cost.

- **Hot site**: A hot site is a fully equipped and operational backup facility that mirrors the primary site's systems and data. It offers the fastest recovery times since it is ready to take over operations almost immediately after a disaster. Hot sites are the most expensive option but provide the highest level of business continuity.

By incorporating these site options into your DRP, you can tailor your recovery strategy to meet your organization's specific needs and ensure minimal disruption to your IT services.

In this section, we have covered a range of topics, including backup and restore processes, AD restoration, folder redirection, power redundancy, and implementing DRP. The following section will guide you through the aspects of monitoring and managing logs using Event Viewer, a vital tool for effective server management and troubleshooting.

Utilizing Event Viewer to monitor system logs and perform troubleshooting

Event Viewer is a crucial tool for system administrators, designed to assist in troubleshooting issues within Windows operating systems by providing a comprehensive view of events occurring on servers. This utility logs and displays records of critical activities and modifications that impact the server's software, hardware, or network components. Through Event Viewer, administrators can effectively monitor server performance and security, as well as pinpoint the root causes of various problems. By analyzing the events recorded, administrators can gain valuable insights into system operations and address issues promptly, ensuring optimal server functionality and stability.

Overview of Event Viewer

Event Viewer, as shown in *Figure 14.14*, is a vital tool for system administrators, designed to facilitate the diagnosis of various issues within Windows operating systems by providing a detailed account of events occurring on servers. It functions by logging significant activities or changes impacting the server's software, hardware, or network components. With Event Viewer, administrators can effectively monitor server performance and security, as well as identify the root causes of any encountered problems. Event Viewer offers five distinct types of logs to monitor, each serving a specific purpose:

- **Application logs**: These logs capture events generated by applications or programs running on the server

- **Security logs**: These logs track security-related events, such as failed login attempts or access to restricted folders, and require auditing to be enabled

- **Setup logs**: These logs record events related to the installation and configuration of applications

- **System logs**: These logs document events related to the functioning of Windows system components

- **Forwarded events logs**: These logs contain events collected from remote computers, necessitating the creation of an event subscription

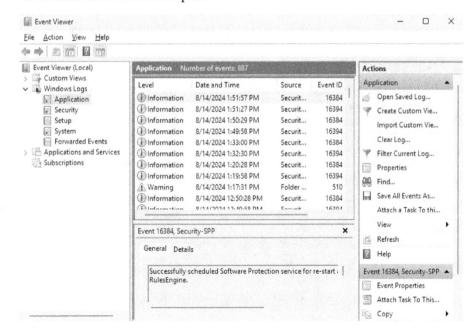

Figure 14.14 – The Event Viewer

> **Note**
>
> It is essential to configure the minimum retention time for logs correctly. If not properly set, logs may be overwritten, resulting in the loss of crucial information needed for troubleshooting. By default, Windows Server logs are retained based on the maximum log size. Once the log reaches its maximum size, the oldest entries are overwritten by new ones. You can adjust the retention settings through Group Policy or the Registry Editor to specify a different retention method or log size.

This section introduced the Event Viewer tool. In the following section, we will explore practical exercises for monitoring and managing logs using Event Viewer to enhance system oversight and troubleshooting capabilities.

Chapter exercise - using Event Viewer to monitor and manage logs

In this exercise, you will gain hands-on experience with key tasks related to managing Event Viewer and setting up centralized monitoring. The tasks include configuring centralized monitoring, filtering Event Viewer logs, and modifying the default logs location:

- **Centralized monitoring** involves gathering and reviewing events from multiple servers at a single location, enhancing your ability to oversee and analyze server activities. You can accomplish this by using Windows PowerShell or the **Event Viewer** console to set up an event subscription, which specifies the types of events to be forwarded from source computers to a designated collector computer.

- **Filtering Event Viewer logs** is essential for focusing on specific events relevant to troubleshooting or analysis. By applying filters based on criteria such as log name, event level, date and time, source, event ID, task category, user, computer, or keywords, you can narrow down the event list. Additionally, you have the option to save these filters as custom views for efficient future reference.

- **Modifying the default logs location** allows you to change where logs are stored on your disk. This adjustment can help free up space on the system drive, enhance log performance, or facilitate backing up logs to an alternate location. You can achieve this by using the Registry Editor or the `wevtutil` command to update the default logs storage path.

This exercise will provide practical experience with these essential management tasks, crucial for effective server monitoring and maintenance.

Configuring centralized monitoring in Windows Server 2025

Centralized monitoring in Windows Server 2025 enables you to gather and review events from multiple servers at a single location, streamlining event management and analysis. To set up centralized monitoring, follow these steps:

1. Launch **Command Prompt** as an administrator, enter `winrm quickconfig`, and press *Enter* to configure **Windows Remote Management**.

2. Right-click the **Start** button, select **Computer Management**, expand **Local Users and Groups**, click **Groups**, open the **Administrators** group, and add the **Central Server**.

3. Open **Command Prompt** as an administrator, enter `wecutil qc`, and press *Enter*. Confirm the action by pressing *Y* (for yes) when prompted.

4. From **Command Prompt**, type `eventvwr.exe`, and press *Enter* to access **Event Viewer**.

5. In **Event Viewer**, right-click on **Subscriptions** and choose **Create Subscription**. Enter a name and description for the subscription.

6. Set **Forwarded Events** as the destination log.

7. Click on **Select Computer**, as shown in *Figure 14.15* select the remote servers from which you want to collect events, and click **OK**.

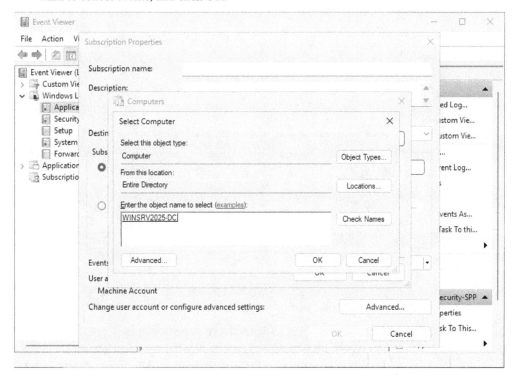

Figure 14.15 - Adding Remote Server to collect events

8. In the **Subscription Properties** window, click **Select Events**, choose **Edit**, and define the filtering criteria in the **Query Filter** window before clicking **OK**.

9. Click the **Advanced** button, ensure the machine account is selected, and then click **OK**.

10. Click **OK** to close the **Subscription Properties** window.

After completing these steps, you will have successfully configured centralized monitoring. The next step is to learn how to filter Event Viewer logs effectively.

How do you apply filters to Event Viewer logs?

To refine the events displayed in Event Viewer logs on Windows Server 2022, you can use the filtering options to customize the criteria for viewing specific events. Here is how to apply filters:

1. Press the *Windows* key + *R*, type `eventvwr.msc`, and press *Enter* to launch Event Viewer.

2. In the **Event Viewer** console, navigate to **Windows Logs**, and choose the log category you wish to filter, such as **Application**, **Security**, or **System**.

3. In the **Actions** pane on the right, click on **Filter Current Log**, as illustrated in *Figure 14.16*.

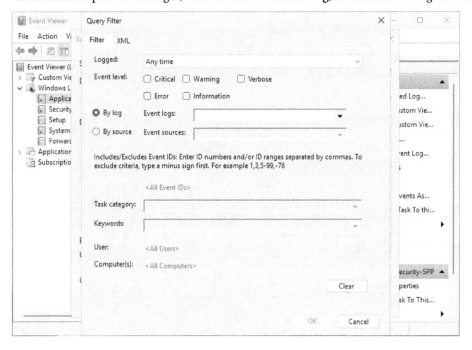

Figure 14.16 – Filtering Event Viewer logs

4. In the **Filter Current Log** window, specify the parameters for filtering, including **Event Level**, **Event Source**, or **Keywords**, to tailor the events displayed according to your needs.

5. Click **OK** to apply the filter settings and view the refined list of events.

With these steps, you can effectively narrow down the events shown in Event Viewer. Next, we will explore how to change the default location where logs are stored.

How do you modify the default location for logs?

In Windows Server 2025, you can change the default location where logs are stored by adjusting the registry settings. Follow these steps to update the log storage path:

1. Press the *Windows* key + *R*, type `regedit`, and press *Enter* to launch the **Registry Editor**.

2. Go to the following path: `HKEY_LOCAL_MACHINE\System\CurrentControlSet\ Services\EventLog\System`.

3. In the `System` folder, double-click the **File** value, enter the new path for the log files in the **Value data** box, as shown in *Figure 14.17*, and click **OK**.

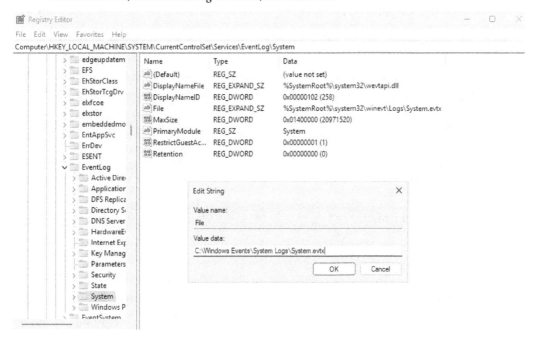

Figure 14.17 – Changing the default logs location in Windows Server 2025

4. Navigate to `HKEY_LOCAL_MACHINE\System\CurrentControlSet\Services\ EventLog\Application` to update the location for application logs.

5. Go to `HKEY_LOCAL_MACHINE\System\CurrentControlSet\Services\ EventLog\Security` to modify the default location for security logs.

6. Exit the **Registry Editor** window.

By completing these steps, you have successfully reconfigured the default storage locations for various types of logs in Windows Server 2025. This exercise demonstrates the effective management and monitoring of logs using Event Viewer.

Summary

In this chapter, we explored the procedures for updating and troubleshooting Windows Server 2025. We began by examining Windows Update, detailing how to apply updates to Windows Server 2025, along with Microsoft and third-party applications and device drivers, and how to utilize WSUS. We then delved into troubleshooting methodologies, covering best practices, guidelines, systematic and specific troubleshooting approaches, and ITIL principles. The chapter further addressed business continuity, including detailed discussions on DRP, data redundancy, clustering, folder redirection, backup and restore processes, AD restoration, and power redundancy. We also introduced Event Viewer, outlining its capabilities and concluding with an exercise on managing and monitoring logs.

In the upcoming chapter, we will shift focus to Microsoft certifications, specifically preparing for the AZ-800 certification exam.

Questions

1. **Fill in the blank:** _____ is an MMC snap-in that enables system administrators to monitor events in servers.

2. **Multiple choice:** Which of the following are troubleshooting methods? (Choose all that apply.)

   • Rational approach

   • Pragmatic approach

   • Systematic approach

   • Specific approach

3. **True or false?** Engineers use a six-step troubleshooting model known as the detection method.

4. **Fill in the blank:** _____ is a device with a battery that continues to supply the server with power when a power outage occurs.

5. **Multiple choice:** Which of the following are Event Viewer types of logs? (Choose all that apply.)

   • Application

   • Security

   • Software

   • Driver

6. **True or false?** The DRP is a well-structured plan that ensures the organization will continue to provide services or recover from situations when a disaster occurs as soon as possible.

7. **Fill in the blank**: _____ is a diagnostic test that verifies whether or not the server hardware is working correctly.

8. **Fill in the blank**: _____ refers to a group of servers that combine processor power, RAM, storage capacity, and network interfaces to achieve high service availability.

9. **Multiple choice**: Which of the following are backup types? (Choose all that apply.)

   - Incremental

   - Differential

   - Arithmetic

   - Geometric

10. **Short answer**: Discuss the troubleshooting process and the key steps involved in diagnosing and resolving server issues.

11. **Short answer**: Explain how Event Viewer filtering works and the importance of central logging in maintaining server health.

Further reading

- *How Windows Update works*: https://learn.microsoft.com/en-us/windows/deployment/update/how-windows-update-works

- *Troubleshooting Windows Server components*: https://learn.microsoft.com/en-us/windows-server/troubleshoot/windows-server-troubleshooting

- *Advanced troubleshooting for Windows boot problems*: https://learn.microsoft.com/en-us/windows/client-management/advanced-troubleshooting-boot-problems

---

Unlock this book's exclusive benefits now

This book comes with additional benefits designed to elevate your learning experience.

Note: Have your purchase invoice ready before you begin.

https://www.packtpub.com/unlock/9781836205012

Part 6:
Studying and Preparing for the AZ-800 Certification Exam

This part is designed to help you effectively prepare for the AZ-800 certification exam, which evaluates proficiency in Windows Server 2025 administration. It provides a comprehensive guide to the exam objectives, aiding candidates in identifying and improving areas of weakness. By mastering the topics covered, you will gain the confidence and skills required to successfully pass the AZ-800 certification exam and demonstrate your expertise in administering Windows Server 2025.

This part contains the following chapter:

- *Chapter 15, Understanding Microsoft Certifications and Preparing for the AZ-800 Exam*

15

Understanding Microsoft Certifications and Preparing for the AZ-800 Exam

This chapter offers a thorough guide for candidates aiming to achieve Microsoft certifications for **Windows Server 2025,** the latest version of Microsoft's server operating system. It is designed to prepare individuals for deploying, managing, and optimizing Windows Server environments in both on-premises and hybrid cloud settings. The chapter delves into the essentials of Microsoft certifications, detailing the skills assessed in exams and emphasizing the significance of role-specific certifications in the IT industry. It provides practical advice for passing certification exams, including effective study strategies, and outlines the exam registration process to simplify enrollment for candidates. Additionally, it offers a range of valuable resources, such as **study materials**, **practice exams**, and **community forums**, to support and connect candidates. By ensuring candidates are well informed about Microsoft certifications and the necessary steps for exam success, this chapter aims to equip individuals with the skills needed to become **Microsoft-Certified Professionals** (**MCPs**). It also provides a detailed overview of the **AZ-800 certification exam** objectives, including recent updates as of April 25, 2024, for Windows Server 2025 administration. That includes insights into the exam's purpose, structure, and any recent changes, helping candidates navigate their path to certification and leverage the latest advancements in Windows Server 2025.

In this chapter, we're going to cover the following main topics:

- The value of Microsoft certifications
- The impact of Microsoft role-based certifications
- Identifying the target audience for Microsoft certifications
- Skills measured in Microsoft certification exams
- Success strategies and preparation tips for Microsoft certifications

- Essential resources for Microsoft certification preparation

- Navigating the Microsoft certification exam registration process

- Exam day guidelines for Microsoft certification

- New validity and renewal requirements for Microsoft certifications

The value of Microsoft certifications

Microsoft certifications, as illustrated in *Figure 15.1*, are highly esteemed within the IT sector. These certifications are internationally acknowledged for confirming an individual's proficiency and expertise in specific Microsoft technologies. They validate that the certificate holder possesses the essential skills, knowledge, and experience in the relevant technology. According to Todd Thibodeaux, president and CEO of CompTIA, certifications are strong indicators of both current and advanced expertise.

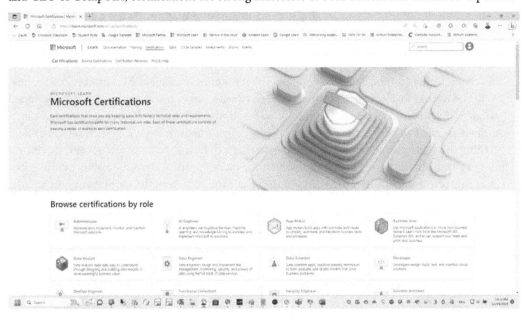

Figure 15.1 – Microsoft Certifications portal

It is crucial to differentiate between various types of Microsoft-related documentation, as not all certificates represent formal Microsoft certifications. For instance, a certificate of attendance from a Microsoft Learning Partner training does not equate to a Microsoft certification unless it is linked to a specific certification exam.

Microsoft certification involves a thorough process where individuals undergo training to develop technical skills and prepare for a certification exam. Successfully passing this exam and obtaining the associated credential signifies the completion of the Microsoft certification process.

In summary, completing the training and passing the certification exam is pivotal to earning a Microsoft certificate and achieving the designation of MCP. This certification process not only ensures that individuals meet industry standards but also enhances career prospects by providing access to various opportunities within the IT industry.

> **Note**
>
> For more detailed information on Microsoft certifications, visit the Microsoft Learn Certifications page at `https://docs.microsoft.com/en-us/learn/certifications`. This resource offers extensive information on certification paths, role-based and specialty certifications, skills assessed, exam requirements, preparation materials, study groups, and renewal information.

The impact of Microsoft role-based certifications

In early 2019, Microsoft updated its certification program to better align with the evolving technology landscape. The revised certifications are designed around specific job roles, as illustrated in *Figure 15.2*, reflecting the skills and knowledge pertinent to these positions. These **role-based certifications** enable professionals to demonstrate their expertise to potential employers and peers, thereby enhancing their career prospects and opportunities for advancement.

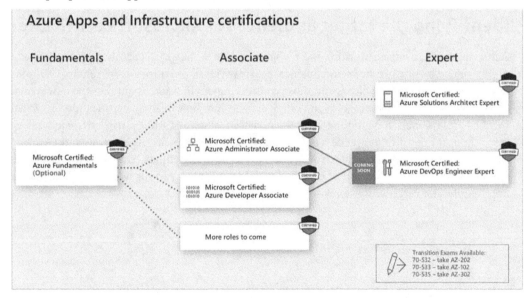

Figure 15.2 – Role-based certifications for Azure apps and infrastructure

The increasing specialization and variety within IT roles drove the move toward role-based certifications. Traditional roles, such as system administrator and system engineer, are becoming less common.

Today's job titles are more specific, including roles such as Azure administrator and Azure security engineer, with some positions even more narrowly defined. Microsoft has developed certifications tailored to these particular career paths, providing focused and relevant training that surpasses a broad industry overview.

In summary, Microsoft's role-based certifications are designed to equip individuals with the expertise needed for specific job roles and to help them stay aligned with the industry's evolving demands. By concentrating on the skills required for particular positions, these certifications enable professionals to distinguish themselves and maintain a competitive advantage in a rapidly changing technological environment.

> **Note**
>
> The Microsoft certification program has also been updated to provide greater flexibility and accessibility, including options for online proctoring, shorter exams, and more frequent updates. Microsoft offers a diverse range of role-based certifications across domains such as **Azure**, **Microsoft 365**, **Dynamics 365**, and **Power Platform**. For a comprehensive list of these certifications and the certification roadmap, visit the Microsoft Learn Certifications page: `https://learn.microsoft.com/en-us/certifications/posts/new-role-based-certification-and-training-is-here`.

Identifying the target audience for Microsoft certifications

Achieving a Microsoft certification is a recognized way to showcase technical proficiency and is highly valued by organizations and businesses. This section provides a comprehensive guide for both current certification holders and those considering certification. It outlines the new structure of Microsoft's certification program and offers insights into how to attain certification. For existing certified professionals, this guide explains the updated framework, while prospective candidates can learn about the certification process and its potential career benefits. As illustrated in *Figure 15.3*, Microsoft certification offers numerous advantages, including enhanced employability, validated expertise, practical application of knowledge, adaptability to various work environments, and opportunities for career advancement.

Source: Pearson VUE, *2018 Value of IT Certification*, 2019

Figure 15.3 – Pearson VUE survey on the value of IT certification (source – Microsoft)

Microsoft certification distinguishes individuals by offering globally recognized, industry-approved validation of their skills, indicating their capability to handle emerging technologies. To support diverse learning preferences, Microsoft provides various training and certification options:

- **Microsoft Learn**: This offers accessible, self-paced learning paths with comprehensive training materials and hands-on product experience

- **Microsoft Learning Partners**: This provides instructor-led training sessions

- **MeasureUp**: This supplies official practice tests to aid in exam preparation

After successfully passing a certification exam, candidates receive an email notification about their certification status and instructions on how to claim their certification badge. For those who have previously achieved certifications, **badge claiming** is managed through the **Microsoft Learn portal** (`https://info.credly.com`), which stores all Microsoft-issued badges earned from past certifications. This streamlined process ensures that professionals can easily access and showcase their credentials.

> **Note**
>
> The link `https://query.prod.cms.rt.microsoft.com/cms/api/am/binary/RE2PjDI` directs you to a detailed PDF document on the Microsoft website, which offers an in-depth overview of Microsoft's certification program. This document outlines the benefits of obtaining certification, describes the various certification paths and types available, and details the certification process candidates must follow. Additionally, it provides information on the exams required for each certification and lists resources to assist candidates in their preparation.

Skills measured in Microsoft certification exams

A fundamental aspect of Microsoft's certification program is its **suite of certification exams**, designed to assess candidates' technical expertise across various domains. Microsoft regularly updates these exams to reflect advancements in technology, ensuring their continued relevance and accuracy. For instance, the **AZ-800 exam** tests candidates' skills in managing core Windows Server workloads across diverse environments, including on-premises, hybrid, and cloud setups.

Candidates preparing for the AZ-800 exam must demonstrate proficiency in implementing and managing a range of solutions related to identity, management, computing, networking, and storage. Familiarity with administrative tools such as **Windows Admin Center**, **PowerShell**, **Azure Arc**, and **IaaS Virtual Machine (VM) management** is also essential.

Candidates should be aware that certification exams may be frequently updated or retired to align with industry trends and technological advancements. For example, the **MTA 98-365** exam, which covered Windows Server administration fundamentals, was retired on June 30, 2022. Staying informed about these changes allows candidates to adapt their study strategies and ensure they acquire the relevant knowledge and skills for their career goals.

By keeping up-to-date with the latest exam content and understanding the skills measured, candidates can better prepare for their certification journey and enhance their career prospects in the ever-evolving IT landscape.

> **Note**
>
> The link `https://query.prod.cms.rt.microsoft.com/cms/api/am/binary/RWKI0r` leads to a PDF study guide specifically designed for candidates preparing for the AZ-800 exam. This guide is an essential resource for those aiming to demonstrate their skills in managing core Windows Server workloads across various environments, including on-premises, hybrid, and cloud settings. It outlines the key competencies assessed in the exam, details the exam format, and explains the scoring methodology. Additionally, the guide includes sample questions, case studies, and valuable preparation tips to enhance candidates' understanding of the exam's content and structure.

AZ-800 Exam Study Guide

The AZ-800 exam study guide is an essential resource for candidates aiming to showcase their proficiency in managing core Windows Server workloads across diverse scenarios, including on-premises, hybrid, and cloud environments. This guide details the skills assessed in the exam, outlines the exam format, and explains the scoring system. It also provides sample questions, case studies, and strategic tips for adequate exam preparation, helping candidates gain a clear understanding of the exam's content and structure.

A crucial aspect of preparing for the AZ-800 certification is developing a thorough understanding of the skills tested. As illustrated in *Figure 15.4*, this clarity helps candidates focus their study efforts effectively. The AZ-800 exam evaluates skills in designing and implementing solutions that utilize various Azure services while integrating with on-premises technologies. Candidates must also weigh trade-offs and plan for public and hybrid cloud environments.

Skills measured

- The English language version of this exam was updated on July 26, 2024. Review the study guide linked in the preceding "Tip" box for details about the skills measured and latest changes.
- Deploy and manage Active Directory Domain Services (AD DS) in on-premises and cloud environments (30–35%)
- Manage Windows Servers and workloads in a hybrid environment (10–15%)
- Manage virtual machines and containers (15–20%)
- Implement and manage an on-premises and hybrid networking infrastructure (15–20%)
- Manage storage and file services (15–20%)

Figure 15.4 – Skills measured for AZ-800 exam

In addition to technical competencies, the exam assesses project management and governance abilities, including knowledge of **project delivery methodologies**, **budgeting**, **timeline management**, and **risk assessment**. By understanding the scope of the skills required, candidates can tailor their study plans to ensure comprehensive preparation and readiness for the certification.

As cloud technology advances and becomes increasingly embedded in business operations, the demand for skilled professionals who can design and implement cloud solutions is rising. Achieving certifications such as AZ-800 not only validates expertise in modern cloud technologies but also provides a competitive advantage in the IT job market. Utilize the skills outlined in the *Deploy and manage AD DS in on-premises and cloud environments* domain objective of the AZ-800 exam to streamline your exam preparation.

Deploy and manage AD DS in on-premises and cloud environments (30–35%)

To meet this exam objective, a thorough grasp of several key components is essential. Initially, you must be proficient in deploying and managing domain controllers and configuring multi-site, domain, and forest environments. Additionally, it is crucial to apply **Active Directory Domain Services (AD DS) security principles** and manage hybrid identities effectively. Another important skill is the ability to utilize **group policies** for **Windows Server management**. Mastering these fundamental concepts will not only prepare you to meet the exam requirements but also equip you with practical skills for effective server management in real-world scenarios.

To deploy and manage **AD DS domain controllers**, you should know how to do the following:

- Deploy and manage domain controllers on-premises
- Deploy and manage domain controllers in Azure
- Deploy **Read-Only Domain Controllers (RODCs)**
- Troubleshoot **Flexible Single Master Operations (FSMO) roles**

To configure and manage **multi-site, multi-domain, and multi-forest environments**, you should know how to do the following:

- Configure and manage forest and domain trusts
- Configure and manage AD DS sites
- Configure and manage AD DS replication

To create and manage **AD DS security principles**, you must know how to do the following:

- Create and manage AD DS users and groups
- Manage users and groups in multi-domain and multi-forest scenarios

- Implement **Group Managed Service Accounts (gMSA)**
- Join Windows Servers to AD DS, Azure AD DS, and Microsoft Entra ID (formerly **Azure Active Directory (Azure AD)**)

To implement and manage **hybrid identities**, you must know how to do the following:

- Integrate Microsoft Azure AD, part of Microsoft Entra and AD DS
- Implement Azure AD Connect
- Manage Azure AD Connect synchronization
- Implement Azure AD Connect cloud sync
- Manage Azure AD DS
- Manage Azure AD Connect Health
- Manage authentication in on-premises and hybrid environments
- Configure and manage AD DS passwords

To manage Windows Server by using domain-based **group policies**, you must know how to do the following:

- Implement Group Policy in AD DS
- Implement Group Policy Preferences in AD DS
- Implement Group Policy in Azure AD DS

In this section, you gained an understanding of the essential components of deploying and managing AD DS in both on-premises and cloud environments. That included mastering the deployment of domain controllers, configuring multi-site and multi-domain setups, implementing security principles, and managing hybrid identities through group policies.

> **Note**
>
> The percentages indicated next to each measured skill, such as *Deploy and manage AD DS in on-premises and cloud environments (30–35%)*, reflect the significance of that topic in the AZ-800 exam. It signifies that a specific portion of the exam questions will focus on that particular skill, helping to direct your study efforts. For example, if a skill is designated as 30–35%, you can anticipate that roughly 30 to 35 percent of the exam questions will relate to that topic. Utilize these percentages to prioritize your study plan and ensure you dedicate adequate time to the most critical areas.

Manage Windows Servers and workloads in a hybrid environment (10–15%)

To meet this exam objective, it is crucial to have expertise in managing Windows Servers both on-premises and within the cloud. That includes a comprehensive understanding of workload management in the Azure environment, which is vital for contemporary IT professionals. Effective management of Windows Servers encompasses skills in server deployment, configuration, and maintenance, as well as the ability to monitor and troubleshoot server performance and efficiently handle server storage and networking resources. In the Azure environment, you need to master key concepts such as deploying and managing VMs, utilizing Azure services such as **Azure AD** and **Azure Storage**, and optimizing Azure workloads for performance and efficiency. Demonstrating proficiency in these areas will prepare you for the exam and equip you to address real-world scenarios. As cloud technology continues to grow and integrate into business operations, having a solid foundation in cloud-based management will be an indispensable asset in the IT field.

To manage Windows Servers in a **hybrid environment**, you should know how to do the following:

- Deploy a WAC gateway server
- Configure a target machine for WAC
- Configure PowerShell remoting
- Configure CredSSP or Kerberos delegation for second-hop remoting
- Configure **Just Enough Administration (JEA)** for PowerShell remoting

To manage Windows Servers and workloads by using **Azure services**, you should know how to do the following:

- Manage Windows Servers using Azure Arc
- Assign Azure Policy guest configuration
- Deploy Azure services using Azure VM extensions on non-Azure machines
- Manage updates for Windows machines
- Integrate Windows Servers with Log Analytics
- Integrate Windows Servers with Microsoft Defender for Cloud
- Manage IaaS VMs in Azure that run Windows Server
- Implement Azure Automation for hybrid workloads
- Create runbooks to automate tasks on target VMs
- Implement **Azure Automation State Configuration** to prevent configuration drift in IaaS machines

In this section, you had the opportunity to learn about effectively managing Windows Servers and workloads in both on-premises and cloud environments. That included mastering key concepts related to Azure services and hybrid management strategies that are essential for contemporary IT professionals.

Manage virtual machines and containers (15–20%)

To successfully meet this exam objective, you need a comprehensive understanding of managing VMs using **Hyper-V Manager**. That involves not only creating, configuring, and maintaining VMs but also effectively managing their associated resources, including storage and networking. Additionally, expertise in setting up and managing containers is vital, given their integral role in modern IT environments. That requires knowledge of container architecture, environment configuration, and management of container images and repositories. Experience with Windows Server VMs in Azure is also necessary, covering the deployment and configuration of these VMs and the management of their resources. Proficiency in using Azure tools, such as **Azure PowerShell**, to manage Azure resources, including VMs, is important. Mastering these areas will prepare you for the exam and enable you to tackle real-world IT scenarios effectively. As virtualization and cloud technologies become more central to IT operations, a deep understanding of VM and container management will be essential for success in the field.

To manage **Hyper-V** and **guest VMs**, you should know how to do the following:

- Enable VM enhanced session mode
- Manage a VM using **PowerShell remoting**, **PowerShell Direct**, and **SSH Direct** (for Linux VMs)
- Configure nested virtualization
- Configure VM memory
- Configure integration services
- Configure **Discrete Device Assignment**
- Configure VM resource groups
- Configure VM CPU groups
- Configure hypervisor scheduling types
- Manage VM checkpoints
- Implementing high availability for VMs
- Manage **Virtual Hard Disk (VHD)** and **Virtual Hard Disk Extended (VHDX)** files
- Configure a Hyper-V network adapter
- Configure NIC teaming
- Configure Hyper-V Switch

To create and manage **containers**, you must know how to do the following:

- Create Windows Server container images

- Manage Windows Server container images

- Configure container networking

- Manage container instances

To manage **Azure VMs** that run Windows Server, you must know how to do the following:

- Manage data disks

- Resize an Azure VM

- Configure continuous delivery for an Azure VM

- Configure connections to VMs

- Manage Azure VM network configuration

In this section, you explored the critical aspects of managing VMs and containers in hybrid environments, including the use of Hyper-V Manager and Azure tools. You gained insights into essential practices for configuring, maintaining, and optimizing VMs, as well as the importance of container management in modern IT infrastructures. Understanding these concepts has equipped you with valuable skills for effective management and deployment in real-world scenarios.

Implement and manage an on-premises and hybrid networking infrastructure (15–20%)

To meet this exam objective, it is crucial to master the deployment of **name resolution** and the management of **IP addressing** and **network connectivity** across various environments, including both on-premises and cloud settings. Name resolution involves assigning identifiers to network resources such as computers, printers, and servers to simplify access and management. This process utilizes technologies such as **Domain Name System (DNS)** and **Windows Internet Naming Service (WINS)**. Proficiency in deploying name resolution solutions and troubleshooting related issues is essential. Additionally, managing IP addressing and network connectivity involves configuring and maintaining IP addresses, subnets, and network gateways on devices such as routers, switches, and firewalls. Familiarity with IP address types, subnet masks, and default gateways, along with the ability to address configuration and connectivity issues, is important. For cloud environments, you need to be adept at managing network connectivity, which includes setting up virtual networks, network security groups, and load balancers in platforms such as Azure and AWS. Mastery of these skills will not only prepare you for the exam but also equip you to handle practical networking challenges. As network connectivity becomes increasingly vital for business operations, a strong understanding of network management is essential for success in IT.

To implement on-premises and hybrid **name resolution**, you must know how to do the following:

- Integrate DNS with AD DS
- Create and manage DNS zones and records
- Configure DNS forwarding/conditional forwarding
- Integrate Windows Server DNS with Azure DNS private zones
- Implement **Domain Name System Security Extensions (DNSSEC)**

To manage **IP addressing** in on-premises and hybrid scenarios, you must know how to do the following:

- Implement and manage **IP Address Management (IPAM)**
- Implement and configure the **Dynamic Host Configuration Protocol (DHCP) server role** (on-premises only)
- Resolve IP address issues in hybrid environments
- Create and manage scopes
- Create and manage IP reservations
- Implement DHCP high availability

To implement on-premises and hybrid **network connectivity**, you should know how to do the following:

- Implement and manage the Remote Access role
- Implement and manage Azure Network Adapter
- Implement and manage an Azure extended network
- Implement and manage the Network Policy Server role
- Implement Web Application Proxy
- Implement Azure Relay
- Implement a site-to-site VPN
- Implement Azure Virtual WAN
- Implement Azure AD Application Proxy

In this section, you gained an understanding of how to implement and manage an on-premises and hybrid networking infrastructure, focusing on name resolution, IP addressing, and network connectivity. Mastery of these concepts is crucial for both the exam and practical IT networking tasks.

Manage storage and file services (15–20%)

A key skill evaluated in this exam objective is the ability to configure and manage **file synchronization** in Azure and handle **file shares and storage** within Windows Server. Mastery of **Azure File Sync** is essential, as it allows organizations to maintain files in Azure while accessing them locally. That includes setting up synchronization policies, managing conflicts, and monitoring sync activities. On the other hand, managing file shares and storage in Windows Server involves tasks such as creating and overseeing file shares, assigning permissions to users and groups, and configuring storage features such as quotas and replication. Proficiency in handling storage resources, including disks and volumes, and utilizing tools such as Storage Spaces to enhance storage efficiency is also required.

Furthermore, understanding how to manage file shares and storage in cloud environments is crucial. That involves using **Azure Files** for cloud-based file shares and **Azure Blob Storage** for handling unstructured data such as images and videos. Gaining expertise in these areas will prepare you to meet the exam objectives and address real-world challenges effectively. As data and file storage become increasingly critical for business operations, a solid grasp of file synchronization and storage management is essential for success in IT.

To configure and manage **Azure File Sync**, you should know how to do the following:

- Create an Azure File Sync service
- Create sync groups
- Create cloud endpoints
- Register servers
- Create server endpoints
- Configure cloud tiering
- Monitor File Sync
- Migrate **Distributed File System (DFS)** to Azure File Sync

To configure and manage **Windows Server file shares**, you must know how to do the following:

- Configure Windows Server file share access
- Configuring file screens
- Configure **File Server Resource Manager (FSRM)** quotas
- Configure BranchCache
- Implement and configure DFS

To configure **Windows Server storage**, you should know how to do the following:

- Configure disks and volumes

- Configure and manage Storage Spaces

- Configure and manage Storage Replica

- Configure Data Deduplication

- Configure SMB Direct

- Configure Storage QoS

- Configure filesystems

In this section, you learned how to configure and manage file synchronization in Azure, as well as handling file shares and storage within Windows Server. You gained insights into utilizing Azure File Sync and managing various storage resources effectively.

Success strategies and preparation tips for Microsoft certifications

Microsoft certification exams typically feature between 40 and 60 questions, with the duration of the exam varying depending on its type. Additional time is allocated for preliminary instructions and surveys. To pass the exam, candidates must achieve a minimum score of 700. During the exam, you have the option to flag questions for later review, provided you manage your time effectively. The exam interface includes user-friendly features such as the **Previous** and **Next** buttons, which enable you to navigate through questions, review, and modify your answers before final submission. Utilizing these tools, especially the flagging feature, is essential for optimizing your performance and ensuring you complete the exam efficiently. For more information on what to expect during your Microsoft exam, check out the *What to expect on your Microsoft exam* guide, shown in *Figure 15.5*, featuring Liberty Munson, director of psychometrics at Microsoft. She discusses the importance of psychometrics in ensuring the validity, reliability, and fairness of the assessment tools used in Microsoft certifications. Liberty focuses on role-based and specialty exams, providing insights that can help you prepare for your Microsoft certification journey. You can view the video at `https://learn.microsoft.com/en-us/shows/exam-readiness-zone/what-to-expect-on-your-microsoft-exam`.

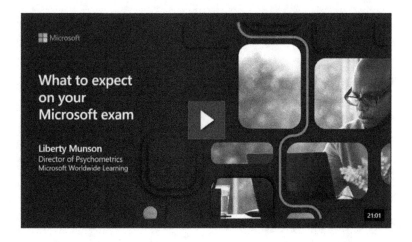

EPISODE

What to expect on your Microsoft exam

with Liberty Munson

Exam Readiness Zone

Jul 2, 2023

Figure 15.5 – What to expect on your Microsoft exam by Liberty Munson

> **Note**
>
> The resource `https://docs.microsoft.com/en-us/learn/certifications/exam-duration-question-types`, available at Microsoft Certification Exam Details, provides comprehensive information about the duration, scoring requirements, and question types for Microsoft certification exams. It details how long exams typically take, the minimum score required to pass, and the various question formats you might encounter. Additionally, it outlines valuable features within the exam interface, such as the ability to flag questions for later review and navigate between questions. Leveraging these features effectively can enhance your exam performance and ensure successful completion.

Essential resources for Microsoft certification preparation

To effectively prepare for Microsoft certification exams, candidates should employ strategies tailored to their learning preferences and the specific requirements of the exams. While there is no one-size-fits-all approach, several best practices can enhance preparation:

- **Industry experience:** Gaining practical experience in the IT sector for 6-12 months can deepen candidates' understanding of Microsoft technologies and concepts, enhancing their skills

- **Training with Microsoft Learning Partners**: Participating in structured training sessions provided by Microsoft Learning Partners offers candidates expert guidance and insights from seasoned instructors

- **Utilizing learning resources**: Leveraging study materials such as Microsoft technology books and the Microsoft Learn portal provides candidates with comprehensive and interactive learning experiences

- **Hands-on practice**: Engaging in practical exercises through labs, simulations, and real-world scenarios helps candidates build proficiency and confidence with Microsoft technologies

- **Exploring additional certifications**: Earning certifications from other vendors, such as CompTIA, can broaden candidates' knowledge and skills, contributing to a more robust expertise

- **Practice tests**: Completing practice exams allows candidates to become familiar with the test format, question types, and time constraints, aiding in better exam preparedness

- **Seeking guidance**: Connecting with peers who have successfully passed Microsoft certification exams can provide valuable insights, tips, and advice based on their personal experiences

Incorporating these strategies, as illustrated in *Figure 15.6*, into study routines can significantly improve candidates' readiness for Microsoft certification exams and boost their chances of success. It is crucial to recognize that each exam evaluates specific skills, necessitating customized preparation approaches to meet the distinct objectives and requirements of each certification.

Figure 15.6 – Microsoft's strategy for getting certified

> **Note**
>
> One valuable resource for preparing for Microsoft certification exams is the exam demo, accessible via this link: `https://aka.ms/examdemo`. The exam demo provides candidates with an opportunity to experience the exam format, interface, and sample questions firsthand. This exposure helps familiarize candidates with the structure and expectations of the actual exam, enabling them to assess their readiness and pinpoint areas that may need further improvement. Additionally, interacting with the exam demo can alleviate exam-related anxiety and bolster confidence by familiarizing candidates with the exam environment and its features. Consequently, incorporating the exam demo into your preparation strategy can be highly beneficial for successfully navigating Microsoft certification exams.

Navigating the Microsoft certification exam registration process

Candidates wishing to register for a Microsoft certification exam have two primary options:

- **Online registration**: Candidates can create an account and register through the Pearson VUE website, which serves as the official provider for Microsoft exams

- **In-person or phone registration**: Alternatively, candidates can contact a Pearson VUE-authorized testing center to register either by phone or in person

Microsoft certification exams are delivered through **Certiport** and **Pearson VUE**, as illustrated in *Figure 15.7*, and are available in two formats:

- **Proctored exams**: Conducted at authorized testing centers, where candidates are monitored in secure environments to ensure exam integrity.

- **Online exams**: Available for completion at home or work without a proctor. This option requires candidates to meet specific technical and environmental criteria.

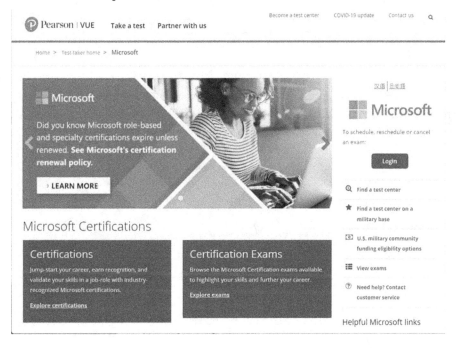

Figure 15.7 – Pearson VUE website for Microsoft exam registration

The trend of offering online exams grew significantly during the COVID-19 pandemic, with many organizations adopting remote testing solutions. However, Microsoft had already been providing online exam options through Pearson VUE prior to the pandemic, reflecting its proactive approach to embracing digital advancements in the certification process:

> **Note**
>
> If you are considering earning a Microsoft certification, you can access comprehensive information through the Microsoft certification page on the Pearson VUE website at `https://home.pearsonvue.com/microsoft`. This resource provides detailed insights into various certification paths, exam formats, and the registration process. You can use the site to schedule your exam, find nearby testing centers, and explore valuable resources to aid in your exam preparation.

Exam day guidelines for Microsoft certification

Preparing for a certification exam extends beyond studying and practicing; it also requires mental and physical readiness on the exam day. Ensure you get a good night's sleep and manage stress effectively to perform at your best. Arrive at the test center or begin the online check-in process at least 30 minutes before your scheduled exam time. Bring the necessary identification and adhere to the *Pearson VUE Candidate Rules Agreement*.

Once at the workstation, stay calm, take deep breaths, and carefully review the exam instructions, as illustrated in *Figure 15.8*. Focus on each question and avoid rushing. If uncertain about a question, use the flagging feature to mark it for later review or navigate back using the **Previous** button. Effective time management is crucial, so strive to address all questions within the allotted time.

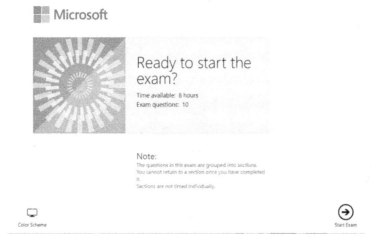

Figure 15.8 – Microsoft demo exam

Upon completing the exam, you'll receive your results, which may elicit various emotions. If you pass, take time to celebrate your success. If not, use the experience to identify areas for improvement and prepare for a retake. Remember, each exam attempt provides valuable expertise, enhancing your chances of success in future endeavors.

> **Note**
>
> The *Pearson VUE Candidate Rules Agreement*, available on the Pearson VUE administration website (`https://home.pearsonvue.com/candidate-rules-agreement`), provides a comprehensive outline of the regulations and procedures candidates must adhere to during their exam, whether taken at a test center or online. It is crucial to thoroughly review this document prior to exam day to prevent any potential issues or disqualifications. The agreement addresses various aspects, including identification requirements, conduct expectations, security protocols, and privacy measures. Ensuring familiarity with these guidelines helps candidates navigate the exam process smoothly and comply with all necessary protocols.

New validity and renewal requirements for Microsoft certifications

Microsoft maintains the relevance of its certifications by frequently updating its formats to align with the latest industry trends and required skills. For example, in the spring of 2021, Microsoft revised the validity period and renewal process for its certifications, with the exception of those in the Fundamentals track (exam series such as AI-900, AZ-900, DP-900, MS-900, PL-900, and SC-900). The Fundamentals track is designed for individuals new to the technology field or those looking to validate their foundational knowledge. Unlike other certifications, which now require renewal every year, as illustrated in *Figure 15.9*, certifications in this track remain valid indefinitely, allowing candidates to maintain their credentials without the need for frequent updates.

Under the new policy, Microsoft certifications outside the Fundamentals track are valid for one year and can be renewed at no additional cost through the Microsoft Learn portal. Additionally, Microsoft sends email notifications to candidates six months before their certifications expire, guiding them through the renewal process. This approach ensures that professionals can keep their skills current and stay competitive in the rapidly evolving technology landscape.

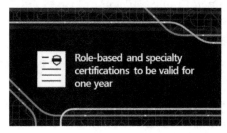

Figure 15.9 – New Microsoft certification validity and renewal requirements

> **Note**
>
> Microsoft has implemented a **revised validity period** and **renewal process** for its certifications to ensure that professionals keep their skills up to date and stay competitive in the IT industry. Professionals can renew their certifications at no cost through the Microsoft Learn portal, which provides access to the latest learning resources and assessments. To assist with planning, Microsoft will send email reminders six months prior to the expiration of certifications. This proactive approach allows individuals to stay informed and manage their certification status effectively. Renewing Microsoft certifications is crucial for keeping credentials current and showcasing proficiency in the most recent technologies. For more details, visit the Microsoft certification renewal page: `https://docs.microsoft.com/en-us/learn/certifications/renew-your-microsoft-certification`.

This chapter exercise has taught you how to perform the initial configuration of Windows Server 2025 using Server Manager and Server Configuration.

Summary

This chapter has delved into the realm of Microsoft certification, providing you with relevant information on the process for obtaining these credentials. You now have a comprehensive understanding of the various Microsoft certifications available and the steps required to achieve them, helping you to stay engaged and interested in your professional goals. Through the example of the AZ-800 exam, you have learned about the skills assessed and the types of questions featured on these exams. Additionally, the chapter has offered expert recommendations for exam preparation, ensuring you are fully prepared for what to expect on the day of the test. Lastly, you have been informed about recent updates to certification validity periods and renewal processes, ensuring your credentials remain current and relevant.

Further reading

- *New to Microsoft Certification exams? We have something you need to try*: `https://techcommunity.microsoft.com/t5/microsoft-learn-blog/new-to-microsoft-certification-exams-we-have-something-you-need/bc-p/3057356#M1599`.

- *Welcoming the Microsoft Exam Simulator*: `https://thecloudmarathoner.com/index.php/2022/01/11/welcoming-the-microsoft-exam-simulator-%e2%9c%94%ef%b8%8f/`

- *Microsoft Certifications*: `https://docs.microsoft.com/en-us/learn/certifications/`

- *Request exam accommodations*: `https://docs.microsoft.com/en-us/learn/certifications/request-accommodations`

- *Exam duration and question types*: `https://docs.microsoft.com/en-us/learn/certifications/exam-duration-question-types`

Appendix

Assessments

This appendix provides comprehensive answers to the questions from all chapters.

Chapter 1: Network Fundamentals and Introduction to Windows Server 2025

1. True
2. Clients and servers
3. All of the above
4. True
5. Windows Server
6. True
7. Peer-to-peer (P2P) and Client/Server
8. True
9. Hardware and software
10. IPv4 and IPv6
11. True
12. Containerization
13. Windows Admin Center
14. A well-designed network architecture is crucial for supporting modern business operations as it ensures efficient communication, resource sharing, and data management. It enhances scalability, security, and reliability, enabling businesses to adapt to changing demands and maintain seamless operations.
15. The CPU processes instructions and performs calculations, memory stores data for quick access, the disk provides long-term storage, and the network facilitates data transfer between systems. Together, these components optimize server performance by ensuring efficient processing, storage, and communication.

Chapter 2: Installing Windows Server 2025

1. GPT (GUID Partition Table)

2. False

3. Nano Server

4. Windows ADK and MDT

5. False

6. Migration

7. Desktop Experience, Server Core, and Nano Server

8.

A. Installation Media (DVD): Pros include reliability and ease of use; cons include slower installation speed and the need for physical media.

B. USB Flash Drive: Pros include faster installation speed and portability; cons include the need for a compatible USB port and the potential for data corruption.

C. Network Boot: Pros include centralized management and no need for physical media; cons include dependency on network stability and configuration complexity.

9.

A. Clean Installation: This involves installing the OS from scratch and ensuring a fresh start but requiring data backup and reinstallation of applications.

B. Network Installation: Allows automated installation over a network. It is ideal for multiple installations but requires network setup and configuration.

C. Unattended or Automated Installation: Answer files are used to automate the installation process, reducing manual intervention but requiring careful preparation of answer files.

D. In-Place Upgrade: Upgrades the existing OS to a new version, preserving data and applications but potentially carrying over existing issues.

E. Migration: Moves roles, features, apps, and settings to a new machine, ensuring continuity but requiring thorough planning and execution.

Chapter 3: What to Do After Installing Windows Server 2025

1. True

2. Plug and Play (PnP)

3. IRQ and DMA

4. True

5. Windows Registry

6. Device Manager and Registry Editor

7. Service Control Manager and Registry Editor

8. Local System Account

9. Windows Registry keys are hierarchical database structures that store configuration settings and options for the operating system, applications, and hardware devices. They are organized into five main root keys: HKEY_CLASSES_ROOT, HKEY_CURRENT_USER, HKEY_LOCAL_MACHINE, HKEY_USERS, and HKEY_CURRENT_CONFIG. Each key contains subkeys and values that define specific settings and parameters.

10. Windows service startup types determine how and when a service starts. There are four main types: Automatic (starts the service at system boot), Automatic (Delayed Start) (starts the service after a short delay following system boot), Manual (requires a user or application to start the service), and Disabled (prevents the service from starting).

Chapter 4: Directory Services in Windows Server 2025

1. True

2. Role-based access control (RBAC)

3. Roaming user profile and Mandatory user profile

4. False

5. Replication topology

6. Global Group and Universal Group

7. True

8. Domain Controller (DC)

9. Active Directory Administrative Center and Active Directory Users and Computers

10. True

11. Primary DNS Server

12. Master schema and Domain naming master

13.

A. AD DS (Active Directory Domain Services): AD DS is a directory service that provides a centralized location for network administration and security. It stores information about users, computers, and other resources on the network, and it helps administrators manage this information securely and efficiently. AD DS is implemented through domain controllers, which authenticate and authorize users and computers in a Windows domain network.

B. DNS (Domain Name System): DNS is a hierarchical system that translates human-readable domain names (like www.example.com) into IP addresses that computers use to identify each other on the network. DNS roles include the DNS server, which hosts the DNS database and responds to queries, and the DNS client, which sends queries to the DNS server. Implementing DNS ensures that users can access resources using easy-to-remember domain names instead of numerical IP addresses.

14.

A. AGDLP (Accounts, Global, Domain Local, Permissions): This model recommends placing user accounts into global groups, placing global groups into domain local groups, and assigning permissions to domain local groups. This approach simplifies permission management and enhances security by ensuring that permissions are assigned to groups rather than individual users.

B. AGUDLP (Accounts, Global, Universal, Domain Local, Permissions): Similar to AGDLP, this model adds a layer by using universal groups. User accounts are placed into global groups, global groups into universal groups, universal groups into domain local groups, and permissions are assigned to domain local groups. This model is beneficial in multi-domain environments, as universal groups can span multiple domains, providing greater flexibility and scalability.

Chapter 5: Adding Roles to Windows Server 2025

1. True

2. File Transfer Protocol (FTP)

3. Modify, Write, and Read

4. False

5. Port

6. Simple Mail Transfer Protocol (SMTP) and Post Office Protocol (POP)

7. True

8. SSL/TLS (Secure Sockets Layer/Transport Layer Security)

9. 3389

10. False

11. Share permissions

12. Read and Change

13.

    A.   Remote Access: This role allows users to connect to the network remotely, providing secure access to internal resources from external locations. It includes technologies like VPN (Virtual Private Network) and DirectAccess, which enable remote users to access the network as if they were physically present in the office.

    B.   Remote Desktop Services (RDS): RDS enables users to access applications and desktops hosted on a remote server. It provides a virtual desktop infrastructure (VDI) and session-based desktops, allowing users to work from anywhere while maintaining centralized control and security. RDS supports features like RemoteApp, which allows specific applications to run on a remote server but appear as if they are running on the user's local device.

14.

    A.   User Rights: These define the actions that users can perform on a system, such as logging on locally or accessing the system remotely. User rights are assigned through the Group Policy and apply to user accounts or groups.

    B.   NTFS Permissions: These control access to files and folders on NTFS-formatted drives. NTFS permissions include Full Control, Modify, Read & Execute, List Folder Contents, Read, and Write. They provide granular control over who can access and modify files and folders.

    C.   Share Permissions: These control access to shared folders over the network. Share permissions include Read, Change, and Full Control. They apply to users accessing the shared folder over the network and can be combined with NTFS permissions to provide layered security.

Chapter 6: Group Policy in Windows Server 2025

1. True

2. Group Policy Objects (GPOs)

3. Enabled and Disabled

4. True

5. Group Policy Management Console (GPMC); Group Policy Object Editor

6. gpupdate /force

7. True

8. Local Group Policy Editor

9. Turned on

Chapter 7: Virtualization with Windows Server 2025

1. True

2. Hyper-V architecture

3. Fully virtualized mode and Paravirtualized mode

4. True

5. VMBus and Integration Services

6. Production checkpoints and Standard checkpoints

7. True

8. Hyper-V Manager

9. Hypervisor and Root

10. Nested Virtualization: Nested virtualization allows you to run a virtual machine (VM) inside another VM. This feature is handy for testing and development environments where you need to simulate a multi-layered virtual infrastructure. It enables scenarios such as running Hyper-V within a Hyper-V VM, allowing for more complex and flexible testing setups without requiring additional physical hardware.

11. P2V Conversion (Physical to Virtual): P2V conversion involves migrating a physical server to a virtual machine. This process helps organizations reduce hardware costs, improve resource utilization, and simplify management. Tools like Microsoft Virtual Machine Converter (MVMC) or System Center Virtual Machine Manager (SCVMM) can be used to perform P2V conversions, ensuring that the physical server's data, applications, and configurations are accurately transferred to the virtual environment.

12. V2P Conversion (Virtual to Physical): V2P conversion involves migrating a virtual machine back to a physical server. This process may be necessary for performance reasons, compliance requirements, or specific application needs that are better suited to physical hardware. V2P conversions can be more complex than P2V conversions, as they require careful planning to ensure compatibility with the physical hardware and minimal disruption to services.

Chapter 8: Storing Data in Windows Server 2025

1. True

2. Network Attached Storage (NAS)

3. DAS and NAS

4. False

5. Disk Controller

6. SCSI and FC

7. True

8. High Availability

9. RAID 1 and RAID 5

10. True

11. Parallel ATA (PATA)

12. CD-ROM and DVD-RAM

13. Deduplication (dedup) in Windows Server 2025: Deduplication is a data compression technique that reduces storage space by eliminating duplicate copies of repeating data. In Windows Server 2025, deduplication is used to optimize storage efficiency, particularly in environments with large volumes of redundant data, such as virtualized environments and backup storage. It works by identifying and storing unique chunks of data once while maintaining references to these chunks for duplicate data. This process significantly reduces the amount of storage required, improves storage utilization, and can lead to cost savings.

14. Storage Spaces Direct (S2D) in Windows Server 2025: S2D is a feature in Windows Server 2025 that enables the creation of highly available and scalable storage systems using local storage. It leverages industry-standard servers with local-attached drives to create a software-defined storage solution. S2D pools together the storage resources of multiple servers, providing a unified storage infrastructure that supports features like deduplication, compression, and erasure coding. It enhances performance, simplifies management, and provides resilience against hardware failures, making it ideal for hyper-converged infrastructure deployments.

Chapter 9: Active Directory Domain Services (AD DS) Enhancements

1. True

2. NTDSUtil

3. All of the above

4. True

5. Schema Versioning

6. Full Backup, Incremental Backup, Cloud Backup, and Enhanced Differential Backup

7. True

8. AD Object Repair

9. All of the above

10. True

11. All of the above

12. Benefits of Implementing the 32k Database Page Size in Large-Scale AD DS Environments: The 32k database page size in AD DS optimizes replication and performance in large-scale environments. It allows for more efficient data storage and retrieval, reducing the number of I/O operations required. This enhancement improves the overall scalability and responsiveness of the directory service, making it better suited for handling large volumes of data and high transaction rates.

13. Significance of AD Object Repair Features in Improving Directory Services Management: AD Object Repair features are crucial for maintaining the integrity and availability of directory services. They help identify, diagnose, and repair damaged or deleted AD objects, ensuring that the directory remains consistent and functional. These features reduce downtime and administrative overhead by automating the repair process and providing tools for quick recovery from issues. That enhances the reliability and stability of the AD DS infrastructure, supporting continuous business operations.

Chapter 10: Configuring SMB over QUIC in Windows Server 2025

1. True

2. QUIC (Quick UDP Internet Connections)

3. All of the above

4. Data transfer security and performance

5. All of the above

6. True

7. Network Interface Card (NIC)

8. All of the above

9. Regular updates and monitoring

10. All of the above

11. Importance of Encryption Mechanisms when Implementing SMB over QUIC: Encryption mechanisms are crucial when implementing SMB over QUIC to ensure data security and privacy. By encrypting data in transit, these mechanisms protect sensitive information from unauthorized access and interception. TLS 1.3, for example, provides robust encryption and improved performance, making it an essential component of a secure SMB over QUIC implementation. Additionally, encryption helps organizations comply with regulatory requirements and industry standards, further safeguarding their data.

12. Performance Benefits of SMB over QUIC in High-Traffic Enterprise Networks: SMB over QUIC offers significant performance benefits in high-traffic enterprise networks. It reduces latency and improves data transfer speeds by leveraging the QUIC protocol, which is designed for low-latency communication. This results in faster file access and smoother user experiences, even in congested network environments. Additionally, SMB over QUIC enhances network efficiency by optimizing data transfers and reducing the overhead associated with traditional TCP-based protocols, leading to better overall network performance.

Chapter 11: Implementing New Security Enhancements in Windows Server 2025

1. True

2. Advanced Threat Detection

3. All of the above

4. True

5. IPSec

6. All of the above

7. True

8. Security Audit Policy

9. All of the above

10. Security assessments

11. All of the above

12. Importance of Securing Communication Channels in Windows Server 2025 through TLS and Other Protocols: Securing communication channels is crucial to protect data integrity and confidentiality. TLS (Transport Layer Security) ensures that data transmitted between clients and servers is encrypted, preventing unauthorized access and eavesdropping. Alongside TLS, protocols like IPSec (Internet Protocol Security) provide additional layers of security by authenticating and encrypting IP packets. These measures help safeguard sensitive information, comply with regulatory requirements, and maintain trust in the network infrastructure.

13. Implementing Audit Logging in Windows Server 2025: Audit logging is essential for improving system security and managing incidents. By maintaining detailed logs of system activities, administrators can track security breaches, detect anomalies, and investigate suspicious behavior. Audit logs provide a historical record of events, aiding in forensic analysis and compliance reporting. They also enable proactive monitoring, allowing administrators to identify and address potential security threats before they escalate, thereby enhancing the overall security posture of the organization.

Chapter 12: Utilizing Hotpatching with Azure Arc in Windows Server 2025

1. True

2. Azure Arc

3. All of the above

4. False

5. Post-patching validation

6. All of the above

7. True

8. Diagnostic tools

9. All of the above

10. True

11. Rollback mechanism

12. Benefits of Using Azure Arc in Managing Windows Server 2025 Hotpatches: Azure Arc extends Azure management capabilities to Windows Server 2025, enabling centralized management across hybrid environments. It simplifies hotpatching by automating updates, ensuring compatibility, and providing a unified management interface. This integration enhances operational efficiency, reduces downtime, and improves security by ensuring that all servers, whether on-premises or in the cloud, are consistently updated and managed.

13. Importance of Diagnostic Tools in Troubleshooting Hotpatching Implementations: Diagnostic tools are essential for identifying, analyzing, and resolving issues that arise during hotpatching. They provide detailed logs, real-time monitoring, and automated alerts, enabling IT professionals to detect and address problems before they escalate. Tools like System Log Analyzer, Network Monitoring Tools, and Performance Monitoring Tools help ensure system stability by providing insights into system performance, network health, and potential conflicts, thereby maintaining the reliability and availability of the server environment.

Chapter 13: Tuning and Maintaining Windows Server 2025

1. True

2. Baseline

3. Cache and Cores

4. True

5. CPU (Central Processing Unit)

6. Network Load Balancing (NLB) and Network Separation

7. False

8. Word Size

9. Performance Monitor and Resource Monitor

10. True

11. Preventative Maintenance

12. RAM and HDD

13.

   A. Performance Monitor: Performance Monitor is a Windows MMC snap-in tool that provides detailed information about the performance of your server. It allows you to track various performance metrics, such as CPU usage, memory usage, disk activity, and network activity. By using performance counters, you can monitor the health and performance of your server in real time and identify potential bottlenecks or issues that may affect system performance.

   B. Resource Monitor: Resource Monitor is another Windows tool that provides a more detailed view of the system's resource usage. It allows you to monitor CPU, memory, disk, and network usage in real time. Resource Monitor provides a graphical representation of resource usage, making it easier to identify which processes or services are consuming the most resources. This tool is helpful for diagnosing performance issues and optimizing resource allocation.

14. Performance Logs and Alerts: Performance logs and alerts are essential for proactive server management. Performance logs allow you to record performance data over time, which can be used for trend analysis and capacity planning. By setting up performance alerts, you can receive notifications when specific performance thresholds are exceeded. That enables you to take corrective actions before performance issues impact users. Performance logs and alerts help ensure that your server operates efficiently and remains responsive to user demands.

Chapter 14: Updating and Troubleshooting Windows Server 2025

1. Event Viewer

2. Rational approach and Systematic approach

3. False

4. Uninterruptible Power Supply (UPS)

5. Application and Security

6. True

7. POST (Power-On Self-Test)

8. Server Cluster

9. Incremental and Differential

10. Troubleshooting Process: The troubleshooting process involves several key steps to diagnose and resolve server issues. First, identify the problem by gathering information and understanding the symptoms. Next, establish a theory of probable cause and test it to determine the root cause. Once identified, develop and implement a solution to resolve the issue. Finally, verify that the solution has resolved the problem and document the findings for future reference. This systematic approach ensures that issues are addressed efficiently and effectively.

11. Event Viewer Filtering and Central Logging: Event Viewer filtering allows administrators to focus on specific types of events by applying filters based on criteria such as event level, source, and ID. That helps quickly identify relevant events and diagnose issues. Central logging involves aggregating logs from multiple servers into a single location, making it easier to monitor and analyze system activities. Central logging enhances server health by providing a comprehensive view of the environment, enabling proactive identification and resolution of potential issues.

Unlock this book's exclusive benefits now

This book comes with additional benefits designed to elevate your learning experience.

Note: Have your purchase invoice ready before you begin.

https://www.packtpub.com/
unlock/9781836205012

Index

Symbols

A

packtpub.com

Subscribe to our online digital library for full access to over 7,000 books and videos, as well as industry leading tools to help you plan your personal development and advance your career. For more information, please visit our website.

Why subscribe?

- Spend less time learning and more time coding with practical eBooks and Videos from over 4,000 industry professionals

- Improve your learning with Skill Plans built especially for you

- Get a free eBook or video every month

- Fully searchable for easy access to vital information

- Copy and paste, print, and bookmark content

Did you know that Packt offers eBook versions of every book published, with PDF and ePub files available? You can upgrade to the eBook version at packtpub.com and as a print book customer, you are entitled to a discount on the eBook copy. Get in touch with us at customercare@packtpub.com for more details.

At www.packtpub.com, you can also read a collection of free technical articles, sign up for a range of free newsletters, and receive exclusive discounts and offers on Packt books and eBooks.

Other Books You May Enjoy

If you enjoyed this book, you may be interested in these other books by Packt:

Microsoft 365 Security, Compliance, and Identity Administration

Peter Rising

ISBN: 978-1-80461-192-0

- Get up to speed with implementing and managing identity and access
- Understand how to employ and manage threat protection
- Manage Microsoft 365's governance and compliance features
- Implement and manage information protection techniques
- Explore best practices for effective configuration and deployment
- Ensure security and compliance at all levels of Microsoft 365

Oracle Linux Cookbook

Erik Benner, Erik B. Thomsen, Jonathan Spindel

ISBN: 978-1-80324-928-5

- Master the use of DNF for package management and stream-specific installations
- Implement high availability services through Podman and Oracle Linux Automation Manager
- Secure your system with Secure Boot and at-rest disk encryption techniques
- Achieve rebootless system updates using the Ksplice technology
- Optimize large-scale deployments with Oracle Linux Automation Manager and Ansible
- Gain practical insights into storage management using Btrfs and LVM

Packt is searching for authors like you

If you're interested in becoming an author for Packt, please visit `authors.packtpub.com` and apply today. We have worked with thousands of developers and tech professionals, just like you, to help them share their insight with the global tech community. You can make a general application, apply for a specific hot topic that we are recruiting an author for, or submit your own idea.

Share Your Thoughts

Now you've finished *Windows Server 2025 Administration Fundamentals*, we'd love to hear your thoughts! Scan the QR code below to go straight to the Amazon review page for this book and share your feedback or leave a review on the site that you purchased it from.

https://packt.link/r/1-836-20501-5

Your review is important to us and the tech community and will help us make sure we're delivering excellent quality content.

www.ingramcontent.com/pod-product-compliance
Lightning Source LLC
LaVergne TN
LVHW082125070326
832902LV00041B/2486